LIFE
OF
IBSEN

*Translated and Edited
by Einar Haugen and
A. E. Santaniello*

LIFE OF IBSEN

HALVDAN KOHT

lom, Inc., Publishers, New York 1971

Translated from the new revised Norwegian language edition
(H. Aschehaug & Co.: 1954) by arrangement with the copyright
holder, Sigmund Skard, American Institute, Oslo, Norway
© 1971 by Benjamin Blom, Inc., New York, N.Y. 10025

Library of Congress Catalog Card Number 69-16322

Printed in the United States of America

CONTENTS

This edition of Halvdan Koht's *Life of Ibsen* is based on the completely revised version of the original edition (1928-29) which was published in 1954. The 1954 revised edition, which has never been translated into English before, is distinguished not only by the addition of a considerable body of new biographical material discovered in the intervening years, but also by a new point of view adopted by the author. The 1928-29 version of the book, issued as it was to commemorate the centennial of Ibsen's birth, emphasized the dramatist's contribution to history, particularly the history of the struggle to win intellectual freedom for the drama. In the 1954 edition, Koht shifted the focus of the book to bear on Ibsen's psychological insight and his skill as master craftsman of the drama. Ibsen the poet, rather than Ibsen the thinker, became the center of attention. This changing view accords well with the general critical reorientation to Ibsen, a new evaluation of the poet which had already been greatly influenced by Koht's writing.

The present translation has been made in complete independence of the English version of the first edition, published in 1931. The translators followed closely the original Norwegian text (Koht's book is written in the type of Norwegian called *nynorsk*, "New Norwegian," or *landsmål*, "National Language"). Until his death in 1965, Koht read sample chapters of the work in progress; the editing, correcting, and reorganizing that the translators did were with the author's approval and encouragement. Upon Koht's death the manuscript was read and approved by his son-in-law and literary executor, Professor Sigmund Skard, of the American Institute, Oslo. At their discretion, and with the approval indicated above, the translators abridged allusions to relatively obscure persons or events; information necessary to clarify either factual or critical matters was interpolated into the text or added in footnotes. No attempt was made to give poetic translations for the many extracts from Ibsen's poetry or that of others quoted throughout the text. To avoid distortions of either form or content, English prose translations have been given, with the texts in the original language.

The footnotes and other references, except those marked Translators' Note, are based on Koht's own notes. The bibliography gives complete data on all books, authors, and articles consulted. These are referred to elsewhere only by author's name and date. For later Ibsen scholarship and criticism the reader is referred to the bibliographies in the annual *Ibsen-årbok* and the volume *Contemporary Approaches to Ibsen* (Oslo, 1966), which was, most fittingly, dedicated to the memory of Halvdan Koht.

EINAR HAUGEN
Harvard University

A. E. SANTANIELLO
Fordham University
1970

Many have written about Ibsen, wisely as well as foolishly. Brilliant commentators have exploited him, as George Bernard Shaw did when he foisted the quintessence of Shavianism off as Ibsenism. Moralists have confirmed his satirical pictures of them by roundly denying him a place among the saved. Marxists have read him out of the party for failing to explode the torpedo he placed under the ark of society. Few have, like Halvdan Koht, patiently and skillfully tried to explore the drama of Ibsen's inner stage. Koht was not a literary critic in the sense either of a man absorbed with style and nuance or of one given to sybaritic lip-smacking. Nor was he an *explicateur de texte,* trying to formalize the literary structure or the means of its realization in the drama. This current mood of criticism has only recently begun to find the way through Ibsen's intricate web of allusion, poetry, and symbol (see the proceedings of the International Ibsen Seminar of 1965, published as *Contemporary Approaches to Ibsen,* Universitetsforlaget, Oslo, 1966). Koht lived to take part in that seminar and in his ninety-second year to greet the scholars assembled in an enthusiastic welcome hailing the hope of youth as Ibsen himself might have done.

Koht's achievement was to combine into one great work all the available facts of Ibsen's life and impose upon them an imaginative interpretation which drew its illumination from the plays and in return cast its light back upon them. His was the historian's approach, patiently checking every source and running down every fact, but then (in contrast with a mere chronicler) seeing these facts as part of a larger scheme. Few historians recorded more different historical facts than Koht, who was internationally known for his work in political and cultural history, but his goal was the great synthesis in the tradition of Gibbon and Hume, of Spengler and Toynbee. One of his many books bears the challenging title, *Driving Forces in History* (Harvard Press, 1964); the noted American historian Peter Gay has written that "every

9

historian (especially every young historian) might do well to read it."
In this book Koht attributes to William McDougall, founder of social
psychology, the inspiration for his own work in trying "to write history
from the point of view of psychology." He defines McDougall's contribution in words that could fittingly be applied to himself: "McDougall
made his contribution by penetrating to the deepest urges of all human
beings and pointing out how these urges constantly lived and had power
in human society through all changes in external conditions."

In his classic Ibsen biography Koht has been able to fit all the bits of
information about the man together into a convincing and consecutive
narrative of the unfolding of his inner drama. He rejects the shallow
notion that Ibsen was trying to impose an ideology, but emphasizes the
ethical drive on behalf of human creativity, which even went beyond
the ethical to a potentially religious conviction.

Koht had singular opportunities not only for gathering the data but
also for finding their proper interpretation. He was young when Ibsen
was old, and he was brilliant enough in his youth to be entrusted with
important assignments. He was rebellious enough himself (as a young
socialist) to appreciate the rebel in Ibsen. Twenty-nine years old, he
was asked in 1902 to prepare bibliographical notes for the last volume
of Ibsen's collected works, and a year later to help edit Ibsen's letters
(published in 1904). He met Ibsen only once, but his work with the
letters gave him an insight into Ibsen's self-expression outside the plays
that became the basis of a lifelong concern with the dramatist's personality. As he wrote in his autobiography: "I learned how to read between the lines of his dry letters." (*Education of an Historian*, Robert
Speller and Sons, New York, 1957, p. 151). When the time come to publish Ibsen's posthumous writings three years after his death, Koht was
the obvious choice as editor.

Finally, after more than two decades of historical research and university teaching, Koht gathered his materials into a first version of the
Ibsen biography (which Edmund Gosse had advised him to write years
earlier). It appeared in time for the Ibsen centennial in 1928, celebrated with pomp and circumstance in Oslo. In that year a great
national edition of Ibsen's *Collected Works* began appearing, with Koht
as one of its three editors. But Koht's *Henrik Ibsen, eit diktarliv* was the
climax of the occasion. In the words of his colleague Francis Bull, himself a noted Ibsen scholar: "The biography is well composed, clear and
confident in every detail, straightforward and sound in its presentation,
an admirable achievement." Three years later it was translated into

English as *The Life of Ibsen* (New York, W. W. Norton, 1931) and has since remained the chief source of information on Ibsen's life in the English-speaking world.

Koht was not through with Ibsen, however. It might have seemed so, for in 1935 his career drew him away from teaching into a position as foreign minister of Norway. He was in this post when the Nazis invaded Norway in 1940; he fled with his government and eventually went into exile with it in London. After a time he resigned his post and came to the United States, where he lived until the end of the war. On his return to Norway he initiated a new career of research and writing, this time as a retired professor and statesman. His amazing productivity bore witness to unflagging powers far into his later years. One of the fruits of these years was his complete revision of the Ibsen biography, in which he subjected it to close scrutiny, not only in the light of new data about Ibsen, but also of the new world coming into being after the war. The book appeared in 1954 in a greatly enlarged and extensively rewritten version, a new book in every sense and the author's last word on Ibsen.

This new version brings to the English-speaking world, which has taken Ibsen to its heart, an insight into Ibsen that has never been surpassed. Koht's Ibsen is probably as close as we can get to Ibsen the Man, whose share in Ibsen the Poet is inestimable.

E. H.

IBSEN'S LIFE AND WRITINGS

Age	Year	
	1828	March 20, Henrik Johan Ibsen born in Skien, Norway, son of Knud and Marichen Ibsen.
15	1843	Confirmed in Gjerpen church, leaves for Grimstad.
19	1867	Earliest known poem, "Resignation," probably written this year.
20	1848-49	Writes first play, *Catiline*, while studying for university entrance examinations.
21	1849	First poem in print, "In Autumn." Writes a verse play, *The Normans* (*Normannerne*), and starts a novel, *The Prisoner of Agershuus* (*Fangen på Agershuus*).
22	1850	April 12, *Catiline* (*Catilina*) published; leaves Grimstad for Oslo [Christiania], visiting his family in Skien, for the last time. In Oslo rewrites *The Normans* as *The Warrior's Barrow* (*Kjæmpehøjen*) and part of *The Ptarmigan in Justedal* (*Rypen i Justedal*); the former is staged at the Christiania Theatre.
23	1851	Journalistic activities, especially the paper *Andhrimmer*; writes *Norma, or a Politician's Love* (*Norma, eller en Politikers Kjærlighed*). Engaged as playwright at the National Theatre in Bergen.
24	1852	Studies the theatre in Copenhagen and Dresden (April-July); is made stage manager at National Theatre.
25	1853	*Saint John's Night* (*Sancthansnatten*) performed in Bergen.
26	1854	*The Warrior's Barrow* performed in Bergen in a rewritten version.
27	1855	*Lady Inger of Østråt* (*Fru Inger til Østerraad*) first performed in Bergen.
28	1856	*The Feast at Solhaug* (*Gildet på Solhaug*) first performed in Bergen.
29	1857	*Olaf Liljekrans*, rewritten from *The Ptarmigan in Justedal*, performed in Bergen; Ibsen becomes artistic director of the Norwegian Theatre in Oslo.
30	1858	June 18, marries Suzannah Thoresen; produces *The Vikings at Helgeland* (*Hærmændene på Helgeland*) at the Norwegian Theatre.
31	1859	Writes poems "On the Heights" ("Paa Vidderne") and "In the Picture Gallery" ("I Billedgalleriet"); son Sigurd born; founds The Norwegian Society.
32	1860	Starts writing *Svanhild*, later revised as *Love's Comedy*.
33	1861	Writes poem "Terje Vigen."
34	1862	Field trip to collect folklore in Norwegian countryside; Norwegian Theatre forced to close; *Love's Comedy* (*Kjærlighedens Komedie*) published.
35	1863	*The Pretenders* (*Kongsemnerne*) published.
36	1864	April 5, leaves Norway for Italy, settling in Rome.

38	1866	*Brand* published in Copenhagen by Gyldendal, as are all his later plays; Ibsen's first popular success.
39	1867	*Peer Gynt* published.
40	1868	Ibsen moves to Dresden; first summer in Berchtesgaden.
41	1869	*The League of Youth (De unges Forbund)* published; Ibsen visits Sweden (July-September); attends opening of Suez Canal as delegate from Norway (October-December).
42	1870	Visit to Copenhagen (July-September).
43	1871	*Poems (Digte)* published.
45	1873	*Emperor and Galilean (Kejser og Galilæer)* published.
46	1874	Visits Norway for first time since his departure (July-September).
47	1875	Moves to Munich, where his son Sigurd enters *gymnasium*.
48	1876	*Peer Gynt* performed at Christiania Theatre with music by Edvard Grieg.
49	1877	*The Pillars of Society (Samfundets Støtter)* published; honorary doctor's degree from Uppsala University.
50	1878	Moves to Rome, where Sigurd enters university.
51	1879	*A Doll's House (Et Dukkehjem)* published; returns to Munich for the winter.
52	1880	Summer at Berchtesgaden, winter in Rome; starts writing his memoirs.
53	1881	*Ghosts (Gengangere)* published; summer in Sorrento.
54	1882	*An Enemy of the People (En Folkefiende)* published; summer in Gossensass, as in 1883 and 1884.
56	1884	*The Wild Duck (Vildanden)* published.
57	1885	Leaves Rome for a visit to Norway (June-September); settles in Munich (October).
58	1886	*Rosmersholm* published.
59	1887	Visits Denmark and Sweden (July-October).
60	1888	*The Lady from the Sea (Fruen fra Havet)* published.
61	1889	Summer in Gossensass; meets Emilie Bardach and Helene Raff.
62	1890	*Hedda Gabler* published.
63	1891	Leaves Munich to settle in Norway (July), finds apartment in Oslo; meets Hildur Andersen.
64	1892	*The Master Builder (Bygmester Solness)* published.
66	1894	*Little Eyolf (Lille Eyolf)* published.
68	1896	*John Gabriel Borkman* published.
70	1898	*Collected Works (Samlede Værker)* begins appearing in Denmark and Germany; Ibsen's seventieth birthday celebrated.
71	1899	*When We Dead Awaken (Når vi døde vågner)* published.
73	1901	Suffers first stroke.
78	1906	May 23, dies in Oslo.

LIFE OF IBSEN

CHAPTER ONE

THE DRAMATIC POET

IN ALL THE YEARS since his death in 1906, Henrik Ibsen has never lost his hold on the readers of his books or the audiences who see his plays. He has remained a source of intellectual stimulation, and as man continues to probe his innermost self, Ibsen's profound understanding of human psychology becomes more and more evident. It was man's secret self that Ibsen was most conscious of, and with this knowledge he was able to create dramatic characters who, although inextricably a part of nineteenth-century Norwegian provincial life, have proved to be symbols of the conflicts that beset all men. Relevance to his own day has not limited his relevance to us; he epitomizes his age and transcends it. This is the root of Ibsen's greatness as a dramatic poet.

It is the poet who still lives. Many have tried to make of him something else—philosopher, social critic, revolutionary, reformer. At times he believed he was or ought to be one of these, or all. But he was, always and inescapably, a poet, driven on by a conviction and a need to speak out that few writers can equal. To a young man who wanted to be a poet, Ibsen defined what the calling meant: "To be a poet is to *see*." The phrase, almost an admonition, summed up his life goal. He meant more than the usual advice to go to school to nature and recreate her honestly. The truly creative man has to see more than what is offered to his eyes; he must break through the visible to the essence of things beyond. And this is how his own dramatic poetry took shape, as from the real world he seized images that grew in his own consciousness. The independent life they assumed could not be denied.

Receptive and sensitive to the world around him, he could say of every experience that it became a part of his inner world. Of people, things, literature, art, of all of his daily life he said: "I look into myself; there is my battleground." The world lived on his inner stage and took the shape of his own personality; out of it came the poetry that he called, with perfect justice, "self-anatomizing." He had himself "lived through" everything of value he had ever created; his greatest works are those

17

wherein he gives himself fully, with least restraint, becoming the thing he creates, making it the truest reflector of its creator. In one epigrammatic verse he wrote:

At *leve* er—krig med trolde i hjertets og hjernens hvælv. At *digte*—det er at holde dommedag over sig selv.	*Life*—a war with demons waged in the caverns of our hearts and minds. *Poetry*—that is to hold doomsday judgment over ourselves.

His inner struggle forged drama out of poetic insights. The conflicts and contradictions he felt took shape as the characters he sent into battle, actually on his own behalf. And the contradictions he would never resolve became the dynamic impulse behind his existence as a poet. All his characters, no matter how different they seem — Brånd and Peêr Gynt, King Haakon and Duke Skule, Bishop Nikolas himself—are creatures of his personality, and they live in drama, where, as Ibsen knew, the fullest life could be lived. Ibsen once wrote to his friend Bjørnson: "I think that to realize oneself in one's life is the highest goal man can attain." The outer events of his life would not realize this ideal; it would come only through his work. There he would pass judgment on himself and on the world in which he lived.

For those who failed to "realize themselves" he felt a special contempt. The dishonesty, apathy, indifference of so many lives and so many ideas were pitiful; but anger drove out pity and he said with Juvenal: *Indignatio facit versus*, "Indignation makes the verse." He said of himself, borrowing the phrase from Ludvig Holberg, that he had accepted the position of royal Norwegian "state satirist." He thoroughly enjoyed the position, and when he gave full vent to his anger the most full-blooded, dynamic of his characters came forth. The series of dramas from *Love's Comedy* to *Rosmersholm* are the most intensely angry; they are also the most accurate expressions of his own personality.

But there wàs more than just anger prompting his response to the weakness of man; there were his own severe ethical demands. Man had first to be freed from the cowardice that kept him from satisfying his most human needs. He had to be free—but Ibsen did not put his trust in the mere political freedom that parties and organizations used on their banners. He asked only if one had inner freedom, the kind that makes a man refuse to be chained by social conventions or anything that is not of his own choosing. This was the only "program" that Ibsen had, and it was all he needed to become a revolutionary, an emancipator of man's mind:

The ethical demands for self-fulfillment that Ibsen made were deeply rooted in a religious idea. To be true to oneself was to follow the call that each man has from God. Ibsen was no more interested in advocating any particular moral code than he was in crusading for any particular political cause. All he wanted was to awaken man to his responsibilities and the need to think for himself. For those who sought platforms or answers in his plays, he answered:

Jeg spørger helst; mit kald er ej   I do but ask; my call is not
        at svare.   to answer.

He believed in his calling and struggled to fulfill it in his work. The tremendous difficulties he met at every stage did not make him lessen the demand on himself; but the difficulties did give him the understanding necessary to portray those who were unequal to the task. At times he seems to side with those who insist that the struggle is indeed impossible, and shrink from it; at times he is with those who insist that the challenge be accepted. He knew both emotions, and when he portrayed the impulse each man has to become fully himself and the instinct to flee from life's most painful task, he was drawing on his own "self-anatomizing" experiences. The questions he asked were those that forced men to come to terms with themselves and to face at last the most crucial decision in their lives. This was the kind of drama that Ibsen experienced in his own soul, the drama out of which he created his poetry; it is the drama of every man's life.

CHAPTER TWO

FAMILY HERITAGE

WHENEVER IBSEN was out of humor with his countrymen, which was not infrequently, he took a sardonic delight in assuring them that he had not one drop of Norwegian blood; every one of his ancestors had come from abroad. There was truth as well as sarcasm in his boast, for the names of his ancestors had all been non-Norwegian for some three or four generations back. The name Ibsen itself was Danish, originally a patronymic from the name Ib, a shortened form of Jacob. There were many Ibsens who migrated from Denmark in the eighteenth century; the dramatist's ancestor was Peter Ibsen, a sea skipper, who had arrived in Bergen in the 1720's (see the genealogical chart on page 22.) Peter's father Rasmus had also been a skipper, in the town of Stege on the island of Møn. Since he was also called "Holst," he may have immigrated from Holstein.

Peter Ibsen was the youngest in the family; he came to Bergen with one of his brothers because a third had already settled there. All three married daughters of Heinrich Holtermann, a merchant who had immigrated from Hannover; thus the name Henrik (as it was written in Denmark and Norway) was brought into the family. There is no information about the personalities of this first Norwegian Ibsen and his wife, but it should be noted that he was a skipper and this profession was passed on to his son and his grandson. Henrik Ibsen, the playwright, came to look more and more like a skipper as he grew older.

One of Peter Ibsen's sons was named Henrik, and like his father became a skipper in Bergen. He no sooner married than died (at the age of 39) leaving a posthumous son, also called Henrik, born in 1765. The mother of this second Henrik Ibsen bore a Scottish name, Wenche Dishington, although her family had been in Norway for at least four generations and had intermarried with the local bourgeoisie of Bergen. (Her father's family had come to Bergen from Scotland, but on her mother's side she was said to be Frisian, from South Jutland.) Wenche Dishington was not a woman to remain unwed long, and after a respectable period of widowhood she married a Bergen pastor, Jacob von der Lippe. In 1771, when her son Henrik was six years old, she moved with the pastor to a parish in Solum near Skien, in the eastern part of Norway. In this way the Ibsen family divided, with one branch remaining in Bergen and the other settling in Skien.

The second Henrik carried on the family profession for eight or nine years, when his vessel is said to have vanished with all aboard off the town of Grimstad. A few years before this he had married Johanne Cathrine Plesner, a merchant's daughter in Skien. On her father's side Johanne Cathrine was Danish, with some German blood, and her grand-parents were from Kærteminde, a town on the Danish island of Fyen, near Odense. Within a year of her first husband's death she remarried, again to a skipper. This union with Ole Paus was long and fruitful, last-ing almost fifty years. She lived until 1847, reaching the age of 77, and her grandson, the future playwright, became well-acquainted with her. The Paus family was an eminent one; the playwright's oldest uncle, his namesake, became a judge, as did a younger uncle, Christian. Two of Johanne Cathrine's sisters married leading merchants in Skien, Diderik Cappelen of "The Cloister" (on Gjemsøy) and Johan Blom. Thus the Ibsen family gained entrance into the upper level of Skien society. Johanne Cathrine's son by her first marriage, Knud Ibsen, would be the father of the playwright.

All this serves to confirm the judgment that Henrik Ibsen's ancestry was overwhelmingly foreign. But in view of the fact that we know so little about the personal character of these remote Danish, German, and Scottish ancestors, it seems unwarranted to correlate this mixed ances-try with specific traits of the playwright's personality and writing, as some of his biographers have attempted to do.

The percentage of Norwegian blood is higher on his mother's side. Her name, Marichen Altenburg, clearly suggests German ancestry, but her family had been in Norway for at least five generations. The earliest known Altenburg was a judge in Norway in the late seventeenth cen-tury. His son, who was Danish on his mother's side, settled in Bergen and married a woman with a German name. This son's grandson was Johan Altenburg, Marichen's father, who was at first a skipper and then a merchant in Skien. Johan's mother, Marichen Barth from Kragerø, belonged on her father's side to a family that had immigrated from Saxony in the early seventeenth century. But her mother's family was Norwegian, the oldest known member being a municipal judge in Kragerø named Roland Knudsen, a versifier of the mid-seventeenth cen-tury. If his verses had not been dry as dust, one might be tempted to trace Ibsen's talents back to him.

HENRIK IBSEN'S GENEALOGY

(according to Johan K. Bergwitz, 1916, p. 62)

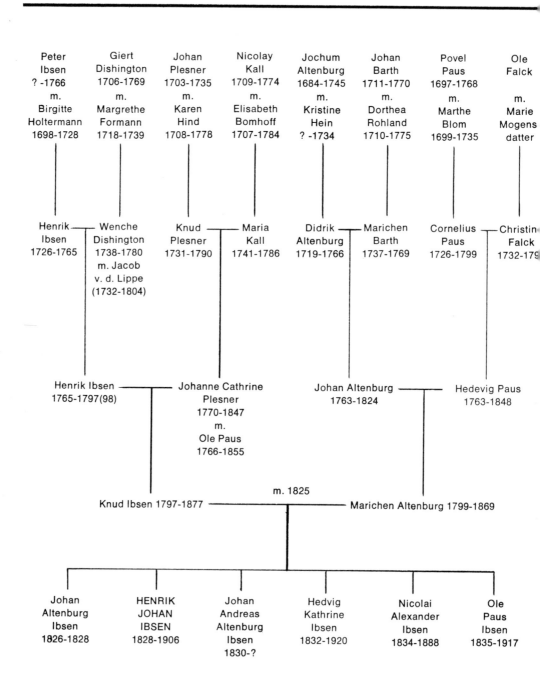

Marichen Altenburg's mother was Hedevig Paus, a sister of that Ole Paus who was the second husband of Henrik's grandmother. Henrik knew his grandmother on his mother's side as well, for she lived to be more than 84 years old, dying in 1848. Through her, Henrik was related to the Paus's, and from them he derived an almost wholly Norwegian line of ancestors. Hedevig's mother descended from a family of workers at Kongsberg, while the Paus name had originally been Paulson — a humbler version that stemmed from the Telemark region. Among its members there was even a poet who wrote occasional verse in the Telemark dialect, some of which was good enough to be included in M. B. Landstad's famous ballad collection of 1853. Henrik Ibsen had no reason to be ashamed of his Norwegian ancestry. As for the proportion of true Norwegian blood in him, his French biographer, P. G. la Chesnais, once calculated that two-thirds of his heritage was Norwegian, with the remaining third evenly divided between Danish and German.

What this genealogical record tells us is only that Ibsen's ancestry was typically that of the older Norwegian bourgeoisie. Although part of the line reaches back to Denmark and even to Scotland, most of his ancestors had settled in Norway by 1700. Only three of his sixteen great-grandparents — Peter Ibsen and the Plesners — were born outside Norway. The Norwegian middle class was in many ways culturally dependent on Denmark, but it identified with its homeland and made important contributions to the developing Norwegian traditions. The small-town bourgeois society which his ancestors helped to create left deeper traces on Ibsen's thinking than all his foreign ancestry.

These remote ancestors of the playwright are little more than names to us today. How, out of this stock, did a genius arise? How did their personalities contribute to that genius? These are questions no biographer can presume to answer. About the influence of his parents we can speak with more certainty, yet even here, while we recognize certain traits of mother and father in the son, we must move cautiously when trying to determine what was actually "inherited" by the playwright.

Ibsen's mother had been interested in the theatre and in poetry in her younger years. She had some artistic talent, as her still-preserved drawings indicate. In this she was like her sister, Christine Altenburg, Ibsen's only maternal aunt. Christine drew and painted and her watercolor landscapes seem fresher and more individual than Marichen's. Perhaps the young Ibsen's interest in color and form was stimulated by watching the two women at work. On the whole, however, his mother's influence on him was of a nature other than artistic. After her marriage she devoted herself entirely to her children and home, caring for them with a tenderness that all who knew her have commented on. Ibsen realized the love that motivated her; he also knew of her unexpressed dreams, her longing to flee the harsher realities of life, her need for a world of poetry and make-believe. Above all he understood her patience and resignation. When Inga, the King's mother in *The Pretenders,* goes into exile without anger or bitterness, she calls to mind the qualities of this long-suffering woman. Again, in Mother Åse in *Peer Gynt,* Ibsen draws on memories of his own mother. Over her children Marichen exercised so strong an influence that none dared disobey, not from fear but from a desire never to offend her. In her later years she withdrew into a private world of religious brooding. "We belong to a silent tribe," would be the poignant comment of Ibsen's sister Hedvig.

The father, Knud Ibsen, was more out of the ordinary. He seems not to have inspired much affection in his children, but he may have been the more decisive influence on Henrik. Hedvig said her brother did not resemble anyone in the family, yet there was an unmistakable physical resemblance between father and son; both were short and sturdy, with strong noses.

Knud Ibsen had grown up with his stepfather, Ole Paus, on the Rising farm in Gjerpen, a little north of Skien. He learned the merchant trade from his uncle, Nicolai Plesner, in Skien, and was granted trading privileges in 1825. He married soon after, when he was 28 and Marichen 26. They were an ill-matched couple—she was reticent and introverted, he boisterous and gregarious — and with the years they grew even further apart. Knud started his business career with great élan, speculating and making money. He was a man of the world and enjoyed having guests around. People liked his company, not only for his good table, and generosity with wine, but for his jovial personality and quick wit. "A gay dog and a witty man," was the way one old resident of Skien described him. Perhaps his tongue was too quick on occasion and made him enemies, but the jests that have been remembered are innocuous enough, with the keen edge taken off by self-satire. There is only one example of maliciousness, and that is in his only known letter to the playwright, written when he was almost 78 years old. He comments on a young friend of Henrik's from Gjerpen who had social pretensions and wanted to "marry a duke's daughter," but in the end had to settle for "one of his serving girls."

Knud Ibsen's prosperity did not continue long. In 1834 he overextended himself and within the year, despite frantic efforts to salvage what he could, lost everything. In 1835 he was forced to give up both house and business in Skien and move out to the farm he had acquired in Gjerpen, called Venstøp. He soon had to give up ownership of this too, but he continued to live there for some years. For a time he tried to make a living as a ship broker, but without success. In these years of decline, with little income and a damaged reputation, forced to borrow from friends and turning more and more to drink, he managed to keep up a jovial front, garrulous and as full of jests as ever. And he still kept the saving grace of self-satire: "Everyone who has been elected a captain of the guard in this town has gone bankrupt. I got two votes for the office, and that was enough to finish me!" Actually he had not been legally declared a bankrupt, and he was even elected to some positions of trust. Around 1840 he was an alternate on the town council of Gjerpen and met several times with the council; the Gjerpen Welfare Association held its annual meetings at his house, and the Sharpshooters' Association had their yearly parties there (he was an ardent huntsman and kept both trotting and riding horses).

In the first years of his financial difficulties, Knud Ibsen was still considered socially acceptable. His moral and social decline did not start until well after Henrik left home. But the young boy took with him the image of his father and from it created Daniel Hejre, the "ex-capitalist" in *The League of Youth*, who is forever prattling of his unfinished lawsuits.

Henrik Ibsen's talent for shaping pointed, biting epigrams might have been an art he learned early in life, listening to his father regale his guests. Ibsen's urge for success, and his determination to steel his will so that he would succeed, may also have been inspired by the spectacle of his father's failure and disgrace.

CHAPTER THREE

BOYHOOD IN SKIEN (1828-43)

Henrik Johan Ibsen was born in Skien on March 20, 1828, the second child in the family. His parents were married on December 1, 1825, and had their first son, christened Johan Altenburg after his grandfather, on October 3, 1826. Henrik Johan, whose two given names were in honor of his paternal and maternal grandfathers, was baptized at home a mere eight days after birth, although he was not churched until June 10. This early baptism was probably decided on through fear that the child would not survive; on April 14, just three and a half weeks after Henrik's birth, the first born son died. The tragedy made Henrik doubly precious, especially to his mother, and the ties that would bind him closer to her than to his father can be traced back to this unhappy time.

Four more children were to follow: Johan Andreas Altenburg (March 17, 1830); Hedvig Kathrine (November 20, 1832); Nicolai Alexander (September 18, 1834); and Ole Paus (December 19, 1835). The daughter was named after her two grandmothers; the last son after the paternal grandmother's second husband. Nicolai Alexander seems to have been the result of Knud Ibsen's admiration for the Russian Czar, who was reported to be negotiating an alliance with King Carl Johan of Norway and Sweden in 1834. Among these first companions of his youth Henrik felt a natural superiority; not only was he the oldest, he was also the favorite, especially of the mother.

At the time of his birth his parents lived in a building known as Stockmann House, opposite the old church on the main square in the center of town. The house had its name from the owner, who has gone down in literary history because of Ibsen's use of the name in *An Enemy of the People*. In the play Ibsen uses the word, with its suggestion of *stokk*, a stick, log, or cane, for the overtones of rigidity and stiffness it conveys, although the name is actually derived from the town of Stokke in the Vestfold district of Eastern Norway. A pastor who had come to Skien from Stokke was a great-grandfather of Hedevig Paus and thus a distant ancestor of Ibsen; the playwright could in fact have claimed more than just figurative kinship with his creation. There is one other literary connection between the names Ibsen and Stockmann: Christian Leth, a Danish ne'er-do-well of the Ulrik Brendel type, in 1832 thanked the citizens of Skien in doggerel verse for gifts he had received: a handsome frock coat from "Ipsen," and a vest from Stock-mann. Stockmann bestowed the vest with a rather weak pun: "There it is, I have no cane for you."

From the three or four years he lived in Stockmann house come Ibsen's first remembered experiences. One day the maid took him to the tower of the church across the square and let him look down on the town and its people. He never forgot the vivid impression this sight made on him. The biographer's impulse to see deep psychological implications in this should be checked; what Ibsen remembered most was the thrill of look-ing down into the crowns of people's hats. If the church tower remained a vivid memory, it was probably because of his wonder at seeing a world and its people from a totally different point of view. While the boy was enjoying the view, his mother happened to glance up. She screamed and fainted; when the boy was brought down to earth she smothered him with tearful kisses. But here also it is difficult to gauge the psy-chological impact of the event on him; Ibsen did not himself remember this part of the story, but recounted it as he had heard others tell it. If his mother again felt the terror of losing a precious boy, she no doubt must have drawn him even closer to her.

His only other recollection from this period was of a silver coin that rolled out of his hand and disappeared down a crack in the floor. He felt like a thief, and when a policeman happened to approach the house he fled to his room and hid under the bed. Such guilt feelings are com-mon enough in childhood, and were perhaps more so in those days when discipline was so rigid. Ibsen may have felt both the guilt and the in-justice more keenly than other children, and from such events may have developed the defensiveness he showed, particularly in relations with adults.

When he was three or four years old the family moved to the Alten-burg house, which Knud Ibsen had bought from his mother-in-law. This house was less hemmed in than the first one, and was surrounded by a garden, as were many of the homes on the street that followed the town brook. Farther from the center of town the world had a different look and sound, as he later wrote: "The air was filled the whole day long with the low, rumbling roar from the falls of Langefoss, of Kloster-fossen, and many other rushing waters. Through the noise of the falls there was a sharp, snarling sound from morning to night, sometimes

like the shrieks and sometimes like the moans of women. Hundreds of
buzz saws were working in the falls." Later he would add to this description: "Skien is the city of the storming, snarling waters. That is how
I remember it." And in this recollection (written in 1895) he indicates
how closely akin he felt himself to the roaring music of the waters:
"Not for nothing was I born in the city of the raging waterfalls."

Equally vivid were the memories of the impressive buildings in the
town, particularly the old church across the way from where he was
born. His mother brought him frequently to church, and so carefully
had she schooled him in the Bible that he must have approached the
holy place with the same sense of awe that was to remain with him for
years to come; he understood the power of faith in human life at an
early age. But he no doubt responded with as much awe to the great
angel carved of white stone that was placed up at the church ceiling, and
brought down to earth for every baptism. If anything could be more
exciting than floating stone angels, it must have been the great black
dog with fiery eyes that skulked in the church tower and appeared only
on New Year's Eve to terrify the night watchman. This terror was
matched by the town jail with its stocks and the awful stories that were
told about them, fit images with which to frighten a child into obedience.

These recollections suggest he had a keen and impressionable mind,
even if one that dwelt on somber and fear-ridden thoughts. As he grew
older there were happier things to think about and he recalled these as
well. Skien was a lively town and despite its scant 2,000 inhabitants
was active in industry and trade, particularly the cutting and exporting
of lumber. (Edmund Gosse, Ibsen's English biographer, rightly compares Skien to the English city of Dartmouth.) In addition to the lumber
industry, the town's merchant fleet of thirty-odd vessels traded with
Denmark, Sweden, England, and France. The traffic was as brisk in
news as in goods, and Ibsen's family, with its traditional profession of
sea skipper, must have shared in it.

The Ibsens had a socially advantageous situation in Skien. Although the
city had its wealthy merchant elite, a circle of inter-related families who
lived either in town or on surrounding estates, class distinctions within
his circle were not so rigid as to prevent mingling; the Ibsens knew both
the highest of the elite, and the not-so-high. Social life was active, with
dinners, balls, and musicales. Like many families in town, the Ibsens'
home was constantly invaded by guests from the country. At market
time and during the Christmas holidays, the house was full and the
table spread from morning to evening. Ibsen would record the impression these days made on him, not only in his memoirs, but (with the

inevitable exaggerations) in the lavish feasts of "rich Jon Gynt" in *Peer Gynt*.

Then suddenly the rich life ended. In 1835, when Henrik was seven, Knud Ibsen had to give up the house in Skien and move the family to Venstøp farm. The distance from the farm to town took three quarters of an hour to cover, no difficulty for Knud, who could ride; for the children and mother it meant isolation. The estrangement between husband and wife may have begun at this time; the last child, Ole, was born at Venstøp in 1835. A perceptive child like Henrik would no doubt be conscious of the developing coolness between his parents and the necessity to maneuver carefully between them. This feeling of uncertainty, which would produce a rather pessimistic view of marriage, is expressed in those draft sketches where Ibsen developed the character of Gregers Werle, the lonely brooder who bears so much resemblance to Ibsen himself. Ibsen was fifty-five when he wrote them, but in these notes one can still sense the bewildering pain the child must have felt: "Gregers' experiences of the child's first and deepest sorrows. These are not sorrows of love; no, they are family sorrows—the everyday anguish of family life."

From Venstøp farm the road to the church at Gjerpen, a road no doubt frequently travelled by Henrik and his mother, led past the Rising farm, where old Madame Paus, Marichen Ibsen's mother, lived. Madame Paus was a strict and sober Christian who thought deeply about the beliefs on which she had built her life. Henrik must have profited from close association with this devout woman; his deep respect for the sacred, already implanted by his mother, was thus reinforced. Knud, on the other hand, had little interest in such matters. Carefree and self-centered, he let the mother train the boy in religious as well as in all other values. He demanded merely the results of such training, and Henrik had ample opportunity to feel his father's heavy-handed insistence on obedience.

The boy's first schooling has not been recorded; he may have begun in kindergarten in Skien, or he may have been sent to proprietor Løvenskiold's workers' school at Fossum, across the river from Venstøp. Whichever school came first, it was not pleasant for the boy; in 1850 he wrote a poem, "The Tear," in which he describes how bitterly he wept when "as a lad I was brought to school for the first time." But if the time of his first formal schooling is uncertain, his first enthrallment with books is not. The magic of books seized him in his earliest youth. He built a reading nook in a hall closet; secreted there he plowed through huge tomes that, as his sister later conjectured, must have included the

Bible and the sages of old Norway. These volumes he may have dragged down from the attic, a mysterious place which held other books left by a sailor. Dead the year of Henrik's birth, he was a young lad from Risør whom they called the "Flying Dutchman," and who had endured slavery in the Barbary states and imprisonment in England. In the attic were also English books which he couldn't read, although he did pore over the pictures. One of these English volumes, a huge folio, printed in 1775, called *Harrison's History of London* is the very book Hedvig, in *The Wild Duck*, speaks of: "There are so terribly many pictures in it. In the front there is a picture of Death, with an hourglass, and a maiden. I think that's frightening. But then there are all kinds of pictures of churches and palaces and streets and great ships that sail the seas."

With these pictures as inspiration he began to draw and paint. He got hold of a paintbox and worked industriously at pictures of people in elegantly colorful costumes. These he would cut out and paste on wooden blocks; when he had a sizeable group assembled, he would arrange them so that they seemed to be conversing together, some jokingly, some seriously. No one dared touch his little puppet show, on pain of his wrath. Alone, he would play with these figures, sometimes creating such comic exchanges between characters that he shook with silent delight.

When he was a little older, he was given some instruction by Mikkel Mandt, a Telemark artist who had done a portrait of Ole Paus at the Rising estate. Henrik then began painting landscapes of the Fossum estate and other places around Skien, or romantic landscapes like those found in his books. But with his keen eye for the absurdities of people, he quickly discovered the pleasures of caricature, pleasures that could also become a weapon of defense. His brothers and sisters were usually annoyed by his solitary habits, and they tried to get him to join their games by throwing rocks or snowballs against the wall of his retreat. Henrik would tear after them like a demon and drive them off, then he would take out his anger by transforming them into monkeys or other animals in his caricatures.

Although he had a strong temper and would frequently scold and beat his brothers and sisters, a word from his mother would suffice to check him. He could be considerate and helpful, provided it involved something he was interested in. Once, as his sister Hedvig recalled, he offered to paint a face on a doll their mother had made for her. But this gracious offer immediately became suspect when Hedvig heard him laughing slyly to himself. Hedvig protested to the mother, and she, knowing how wicked the boy's brush could be, warned him: "I'll be very angry if you do anything but a nice face." Henrik replied: "Yes, mother, you can see that I'm doing it as nicely as possible." He had only been laughing because he thought of what a frightful face he *could* have drawn.

What impresses one most about these early years at Venstøp is how much they were lived *internally* by the young Henrik. He shut himself in and mounted guard against any intruder. The general attitude toward children in those days discouraged any intimate confiding in parents or other adults, and children of keen sensibilities had no choice but to build, in St. Catherine of Siena's image, "the interior castle." This is what he did, and he guarded his castle of spiritual freedom with a vigilance that would never slacken his whole life long.

"Aloof," "peculiar," were the words used to describe him in his youth; and there is no doubt that he felt superior to his contemporaries and showed it. He would gather his brother Johan's playmates together and harangue them from the top of a barrel. Johan ended the annoying experience by kicking over the barrel. A more pleasant outcome to this youthful display of hubris took place on those Sunday nights when he was allowed to entertain the neighbors with the magic tricks he was so clever at. Although the audience went away muttering that there was "something queer about that Henrik," the simple truth was that he was assisted by his brother Nicolai, hidden in the big wooden box from which seemed to emanate all the magic. And yet, pride had its fall; the children who knew of the ruse used their knowledge as a hold over the boy, who even at this early age felt that horror of the slightest taint of scandal that would be such a controlling impulse in his later life.

A part of this concern with appearance can be noted in his early attention to matters of dress. He was the "meticulous" Henrik to his friends, and his father was so proud of this trait that he always bought him fine clothes; too fine, according to some of the family friends. His interest in clothes can be explained simply—color and variety fascinated him. On the neighboring farm, Årthus, there was an old man who used to dress for festive occasions in an elegant, old-fashioned costume—brown frock coat, starched neckcloth, silk vest with brown and yellow stripes, velvet trousers, and buckled shoes. Henrik's favorite moments were when he was allowed to watch the old man get into this regalia. With such an image of elegance in his mind, Henrik naturally was overly concerned with his own clothes; he seldom took part in games that might dirty them, and although he was strong enough, he engaged in no sports except swimming.

As he grew older he found companions beyond his home. There is a record of two boys he knew from neighboring farms in Gjerpen. Neither of these boys was a farm lad, one being the son of Sexton Lund of Århus,

whose grandfather dressed so elegantly in brown frock coat; the other
was the son of Sheriff Pedersen of Limi. They too found Henrik snob-
bish and aloof, and the sheriff's boy beat him for showing such disdain.
Around the age of twelve he began to meet girls at the dances held at
Venstøp, Århus, and Limi. Because he was handsome and sported such
fine clothes he was popular as a dancing partner, even though his skill
at dancing was so limited that he preferred to break in one partner and
keep her all evening, rather than risk exposing his clumsiness to another.
The reports that have come down from this period are mixed: some who
met him recalled that he could be "unpleasant" and rough with girls;
those who danced with him felt it an honor to be asked.

But such diversions were not frequent in his youth. Beyond an occasional ball there were the Christmas "capers" (*julebukk*), somewhat akin
to American Hallowe'en escapades, which he liked because he could
deck himself out impressively. The St. John's Eve bonfires drew him
only once as a participant; henceforth, he was only an observer. And as
an observer he attended the Skien market fair, where, as he said, he
was most interested in "seeing the jugglers and the tightrope walkers
and the bareback riders." Time and again in his own recollections and in
those of his friends the same comment is made: he was the outsider.
He was, he wrote, "mostly present only as an observer." It is an accurate
summary of his personality at this time.

To what extent the young Ibsen was affected by the drastic change
in his family's social position is a topic often treated in studies of the
playwright's psychological development. But perhaps too much emphasis has been placed on the material deprivations the boy might have
been exposed to. It was inevitable that he noticed the scarcity of money
in the house — some of his childhood friends have said that he spoke
bitterly of it — and he certainly saw the struggle his father made to salvage his career. Perhaps his father's self-assertion bred in him the same
trait, so strong later in life, along with his insistence on being regarded
as first in society, no matter what his financial situation. But no external
circumstance can account for the inward-turning of the young boy. That
was part of his nature; he knew he would have to draw his greatest
riches from within.

When the question of his further education came up, the state of the
family's finances became a paramount issue. His intention to go to the
University was apparently formed at an early age—his friend Paul Botten
Hansen says he planned on a career in medicine from his youth. He
would have to pass the Artium examination for entrance to the University, and the Latin School at Skien would be the first step in that direc-

tion. But he was not able to go to the Latin School. The school had actually declined from its former prestige; only fifteen students registered between 1838 and 1841, and the majority of these left before taking the Artium. Örn, the old principal, retired in 1841 and the post was left vacant until 1844. In 1840 there only twenty boys in all six forms. Yet the thought that he was not among them surely rankled Ibsen, especially when he saw some of his young companions enrolled.

School cost money; the matriculation fee was four dollars specie, tuition was thirty-two dollars specie a year, plus four dollars and ninety-six shillings for light and firewood — nearly forty-one dollars in all, no petty sum in those days. Nevertheless, it is hard to believe that money alone stood in his way; Knud Ibsen could easily have obtained a tuition scholarship for his talented son. Rather he seems to have decided that the boy should earn a living as soon as he was confirmed, thus a lengthy schooling leading to the Artium examination was out of the question. Poor people could not afford such luxuries. No one bothered to ask Henrik what his wishes were, and since he lacked the courage to speak about his dreams for the future, he swallowed his disappointment and obeyed. As he finished his thirteenth year, he was enrolled in a private two-year school that had opened in Skien in March, 1841, under the direction of two theological candidates, Johan Hansen and W. F. Stockfleth. Despite the inauspicious circumstances surrounding his enrollment, Ibsen's years at the school were pleasant ones; the instruction was methodical, much broader than he had received on the elementary level (he was now learning German), and he had private lessons in Latin from Hansen—thus keeping alive the possibility of ultimately trying for the University examination. Henrik's favorite subjects were the humanities, particularly history and theology. Ancient history fired his imagination, and the study of the Bible brought out that characteristic need to probe to the source of things which made him track down each biblical quotation in his textbook.

Here he was meeting new companions, boys who shared his interests and with whom he could discuss the problems of life. One of his friends from this period later described him as "the schoolboy with the good head, deep understanding, somewhat quick and irritable temperament, and satiric bent. But all the same friendly and comradely." He later spoke of these days himself, and the recollection is curiously like his youthful repression of the urge to draw something frightening on his sister's doll. He would sit in class and contemplate some perfect outrage against the teacher. What if he rapped the man on the snout with his own ruler? What an uproar! These impulses never got beyond the contemplative stage, yet from their persistence he learned that within himself, within that inner world he preferred, there were forces he would have to struggle to control.

School must also have opened his eyes to new kinds of literature. There was a lending library at a bookdealer in town, and from here he probably obtained copies of stories by the Norwegian, Mauritz Hansen, the most popular writer of the day. Hansen specialized in depicting eccentrics, whose puzzling contradictions were offered to the reader for psychological investigation. Not only did these stories stimulate Ibsen's interest in human psychology; the technique Hansen used — suspense achieved through disclosure of an old secret—must also have struck a responsive chord. Some stories perhaps touched more deeply. In "The Mother" a poor boy is sent to sea, even though he longs to become an artist, and yet he eventually does succeed in becoming what he wishes. In "The Miner" the main character lives shut off from mankind, deep in the earth. There was certainly something of himself here.

Of more importance is the suggestion of rebellion that occasionally troubles the usually placid surface of Hansen's stories. He could at times portray with sympathy the passions leading to revolt against the "conventions" (his own word) that frustrate the free expression of one's nature. This was a welcome message to a restless youth. Hansen's colloquial style, just beginning to appear in his stories, was an indication of the trend to freer expression in matters literary, cultural, and political that was spreading through Norway in the 1840's. A glance at even the local Skien paper would have shown the same spirit of restlessness to the young Ibsen.

Literature reached him in other ways. In the years between 1838 and 1843, Danish theatrical companies frequently visited Skien. The plays they performed were usually popular comedies and operettas of French or Danish vintage, particularly those of Johan Ludvig Heiberg (1791-1860) and Eugène Scribe (1791-1861). We know that Ibsen was an eager theatre-goer, and he probably saw performances of the two most demanding works in the repertory of these companies: Scribe's comedy Le Verre d'eau (1840), and the Danish romantic writer Adam Oehlenschläger's Axel og Valborg (1810). In addition, he may have seen Andreas Munch's Donna Clara (1840), the only Norwegian play to gain popularity at the time. He must also have read plays, among them probably Schiller's Wilhelm Tell (1804), which was among the books at home.

He would naturally have begun to try his hand at "practicing poetry," as he said some of his companions had begun to do. Some of the girls in his circle of friends have reported that he used to read them totally incomprehensible poems. One schoolmate has described an exercise Henrik read in class, probably at the age of fourteen. The assigned theme, a vision in a graveyard, was a very fashionable one; young Norwegian writers like Johan S. C. Welhaven, Henrik Wergeland, and Mauritz Hansen all wrote graveyard poetry. In Henrik's composition an entire city of the dead was described, with a concluding moral: "Thus you see, all is vanity." The composition has been lost, but Ibsen has substantiated this description, adding that it gave rise to an argument between him and Stockfleth, his teacher, who said the essay was too good not to have been plagiarized. Ibsen protested vigorously, and for a long time was on bad terms with the teacher, despite the fondness he felt for him.

Although his interests were turning to literature, and he dreamed of becoming a writer, he continued to draw and paint. Either poet or painter, then; or better yet, why not both poet and painter? This was the career he dreamed of as he finished his fifteenth year and prepared to leave his parents' home.

CHAPTER FOUR

GRIMSTAD (1844-50)

WHEN IBSEN FINISHED school in the spring of 1843, he began preparation for confirmation, the ceremony that meant the end of childhood and the beginning of adult responsibilities. He was confirmed in the Gjerpen church on October 1, 1843. His father was indignant that the boy was not given the place of honor in the church, although he merited it because of his outstanding performance in the catechization. He had to yield place to the sons of a skipper and a sheriff, who had, at least in Knud Ibsen's opinion, bought the honor by making the pastor a fat offering of "an elegant veal roast." If Henrik himself felt insulted, he never mentioned it.

Shortly after this the family moved back to Skien and rented a house at Snipetorp, on the Bratsberg road, on an estate that one of Knud Ibsen's half-brothers had recently bought. Ibsen spent only a few months in this, his last home in Skien. The decision was soon made that he was to go out and earn his own living as quickly as possible.

It is not known why Ibsen decided to look for a job in a pharmacy, but his plans to study medicine probably had something to do with the choice. A friend of his father's who traveled as a salesman along the south coast of Norway told him of a position open in a pharmacy at Grimstad. Ibsen left Skien on a small boat with the auspicious name "Lucky Chance." The boat probably sailed on December 27 (it had been cleared on December 23, however), and arrived in Grimstad on January 3, 1844. Grimstad would be his home for the next six years.

One can imagine his mixed feelings during these days: anger at being sent away empty-handed and with an incomplete education to fend for himself even before his sixteenth birthday; but also joy at being released from those burdensome family restrictions. Now he was free. And in this first freedom he may have begun to think about the problem that would later occupy his brooding spirit—the conflict between freedom and responsibility:

Nar begynder ansvarsvægten af   When does the burden of responsibility
    ens arvelod fra slægten?   for one's heritage begin?

He was still emotionally tied to home and felt these ties both a comfort and a torment. The more he yearned to break them, the more he learned how tightly they held him. He looked forward to returning during his vacation, and he wrote letters to the family, all unfortunately lost.

The six years in Grimstad were a crucial period in Ibsen's development, for it was then he discovered his vocation as poet. It was a time of great trial for the young man and he never wished to think back on it as it really was. He did describe these days, a quarter century later, when he was preparing a new edition of *Catiline*, the play he wrote in Grimstad. In the gently ironic tone the reminiscences take, his life is seen as a constant series of skirmishes with the petty society into which fate had thrown him. This picture of the impoverished but happy warrior is true of only the last two or three years of his stay in Grimstad. In actuality his early years there were among the most depressing in his whole life. This small shipping community with its 800 inhabitants —fewer even than Skien—had an elite of merchants and officials that was at least as inaccessible and aloof as that of his birthplace. With no friends to bring him into this closed society, he soon learned what it was to be an outsider, a pale, thin, insignificant-looking stranger whom no one bothered to notice.

The pharmacy where Ibsen worked had only recently been opened and the owner, Jens Arup Reimann, was heavily in debt. He could not provide decent wages or even adequate food for his help; one of the girls who worked as a maid later recalled how she and Ibsen would taken turns buying bread to help fill out particularly skimpy dinners. And they were cold too; on one occasion they had to sneak out and steal firewood from a lot near the shore to keep from freezing to death. The "Pharmacist's Boy" was in truth a very poor boy, and his clothes proclaimed it loudly. Although he was naturally neat and tidy, he could not escape the telltale signs of his profession; as one of the maids said many years later, his clothes were stained by boiling drugs and making plasters. The same girl recalled that he wore his suits "until they were as shiny as the stove." He had no money to buy the kind of clothing that would be suitable for a young man of good family, and had to make each suit last as long as possible. Ibsen was so concerned with his appearance that he refused to sit at table when the pharmacist had dinner guests. Another humiliation was to have to share a bedroom with the little boys of the family, rather than have a place of his own. Even worse, to get to this little boys' room he had to pass through the

girls' bedroom. He was quickly made to realize that he was not his
own master and that even his free time — what little there was of it —
was not his own. Only on Sundays, and not always then either, could
he escape. Sometimes he rowed out to Maløya to pick herbs for the
pharmacist, or else walked up to Varden, the lookout behind the town,
to gaze out to sea or to work at his painting.

In these years between his sixteenth and nineteenth birthdays he
kept to himself and made no friends. His only companion was Svein,
"the Mountaineer" from Telemark, a serious-minded workman in his
fifties who assisted in the pharmacy. Svein had a little cottage in the
neighboring parish of Fjære, and on Sundays he and Ibsen made excursions to the churchyard where they passed the time with the folktales
and anecdotes of Svein's home valley. Ibsen no doubt enjoyed hearing
these tales told in the Telemark dialect, just as he enjoyed listening to
the old tars on the waterfront talking about their adventures. But he
made no acquaintances other than Svein, and at times in his loneliness
had only the pharmacist's maids to confide in. One of them recalled
his complaint that his father never sent him any money. More than
once she heard him sigh, "I'll never find my place in this life."

These years brought many humiliations to the young man, but worst
of all was the shame he felt when a servant girl, fully ten years older
than he, bore him a child. Ibsen was just eighteen then, and for the next
fourteen or fifteen years had to pay for the support of his son. Unquestionably he draws on this painful experience when he describes how the
greenclad troll woman brings Peer Gynt their bastard child. Peer feels
too "foul and coarse" to return to Solveig: "Filthy thoughts will follow
me in." Out of this experience too comes that distaste for the physical
aspect of the relationship between man and woman that can be noted
in his work. Ideally, love should be a purely spiritual bond, he said,
husbands and wives ought to be merely friends, use the formal pronoun
to each other, and live on separate floors.

The only thing that could have given him the strength to survive in
this grim period was his determination to succeed, and his conviction
that the future would be his. He read intensely, particularly from the
boxful of books that was his most important baggage when he left home.
His health was excellent and he knew how to apply himself. He planned
to get at least to the preliminary examination. If he could pass this he
would try for a "Norwegian" medical degree, that is, one without the
Latin requirement he knew would be so difficult to fulfill.

He was reading more than the assigned books for his examination,
borrowing from the same Grimstad reading society, founded in 1835,
that pharmacist Reimann belonged to. The society's collection was

strong in history and fiction, both in Danish and in translation. Among the authors represented were Dickens, Sir Walter Scott, B. S. Ingemann (Scott's Danish imitator), Fredrika Bremer, the Swedish novelist, Madame Gyllembourg, the Danish writer, and the Dano-Norwegian playwright and historian Ludvig Holberg. Ibsen is known to have borrowed books from an elderly English woman, Miss Crawford, although probably not until his last years in Grimstad. Among these books were probably the works of Kierkegaard, the Danish romantic poet Oehlenschläger, and the Norwegian Henrik Wergeland. He is also said to have studied Voltaire "with zeal." Through all these works he became aware of the intellectual currents of the time and found stimulus for his own imagination.

This kind of reading was much more attractive than the dry texts assigned for his professional studies. He already knew that his true vocation was not medicine; he felt himself drawn more and more to literature, even though he had not yet entirely discounted painting as a possible career. His earliest dated poem, "Resignation" (1847), questions whether he has a genuine gift for poetry and indicates that he must have been trying to write for some time:

Var forgjæves al min Higen,	Was my longing all in vain,
Var min Drøm kuns et Fantom,	Was my dream just a phantom,
Er mig nægtet Sjælens Stigen,	Am I denied the soul's ascent,
Var min Digten kold og tom?	Were my poems cold and empty?

Within, he feels some power stirring:

— Glimt fra Sjælens Dunkle,	Glimpses from my spirit's depths
Der ig jennem Mulmet brød,	Break through the dead of night,
Om som Lynblink monne funkle.	Flash like a streak of lightning.

Unable to satisfy the longing to give life to the poetic impulses he felt, he destroyed all his early poems. Doubtful that he could create anything new, he wondered if it might not be better to keep his dreams to himself, "to live forgotten and forgotten die." The next preserved poem, "By the Sea," written early in 1848, strikes the same note; he is like the ocean wave that breaks defiantly and joyously against the cliff, only to sink back and die amid other waves.

The way might have seemed hopeless, but his gifts of humor and anger saved him from despair. His mood is reflected in the only two letters that survive from the Grimstad period: the first, dated May 20, 1844, is to a friend in Skien; the second, October 6, to a cousin in Porsgrunn. Both are spirited and full of salty humor. To his friend he reports that he is "very well satisfied" with his decision to come to Grimstad, and boasts that he has won the favor of the ladies—although he admits that the favors are rather easily won. He was unquestionably stretching a point here, for his major triumph in Grimstad was with the boys in the poor section of town where the pharmacy was located. They formed a very appreciative audience when he lampooned the honored citizens of the town, and they clamored for the rhymes he tossed off. Although the satire was rather tame — the only one that has been preserved is a harmless ditty about a merchant and his servants—the victims did not like their names and likenesses (for this "Pharmacist's Boy" even presumed to sketch them) bandied about town.

Beginning in 1847 things began to improve. The previous year saw the end of poor Reimann's pharmacy, foreclosed at auction in August, 1846. Reimann was not a bad sort, but the pressure of his activities outside the pharmacy did not give his apprentice the chance to see much of his kind heart. (Madame Reimann was something else altogether, and Ibsen remarks in one of his letters that she was as adept at boxing ears as a cat is at catching mice.) The pharmacy was again sold (in March, 1847), this time to a former assistant of Reimann's, Lars Nielsen. Ibsen had already passed his examination and rose to the new dignity of "Pharmacist's Assistant." The new owner was unmarried and only four years older than the new assistant, and they were more like equals. The business was moved to a better part of town into a larger building (Østre Gate 13), that offered much improved lodgings. He was paid better, although still he had little to spare. Now he began to prepare for the University under the tutorship of S. C. Monrad and then Emil Bie, a young theology student living in Grimstad. Since the Storting had voted in 1845 to eliminate the "preliminary" examination after 1849, Ibsen had to take the regular Artium examination, in Latin, Greek, and mathematics, the last of which he had to prepare on his own, since Bie was weak in the subject. He also wrote essays in Norwegian for a private tutor in Oslo. A few of these have survived, and the one called "On the Importance of Self-Knowledge" seems very typical of the young man in its insistence on the need for self-analysis.

He began to make friends, among them Christopher Due, a clerk at the customs house. Due had come to Grimstad in 1845 and soon heard that the "Pharmacist's Boy" was an unusual character. Although his curiosity prompted him to visit the pharmacy, it was not until Reimann introduced them that the two young men became friends. Due, in turn, introduced Ibsen to Ole Schulerud, son of the new customs officer, who had come to Grimstad in 1847, and the three became fast friends. The experience was totally new for Ibsen and he always remembered it. Twenty-odd years later, long after Schulerud's death, he wrote to his widow: "He was a friend in truth, completely faithful. When I look back I can see no one who was so intimately a part of my youth....He

was a friend in those days when I had to renounce everything and prepare for my future." He could have written the same of Due, although
it was always difficult for him to express such feelings directly. Due
noted that no matter how close they became, Ibsen kept his deepest
feelings hidden; his friends could share in his intellectual and imaginative life, but he never told them of his suffering or his ambition to
achieve the extraordinary. It was a long time before Due even learned
how poor his friend was—Ibsen kept his emotions as neat and orderly
as his clothes, and outwardly he was respectable, no matter what storm
raged within.

Evening after evening the three friends sat in the pharmacy and
talked. Due, whose gentle temperament was shocked by Ibsen's hereti-
cal opinions on love, marriage, religion, and morality, describes how the
young rebel threw over his childhood faith in a personal God. But
Due's reports do not comment on what it may have cost his friend to
reject the teaching of his childhood, and we were not told if the break
with religion had already begun before Grimstad. It is tempting to
interpret a speech of the Emperor Julian as a reference to Ibsen's own
feelings at this time. Julian laments that whenever he thirsted for life
and beauty, whenever he felt "the sweet lust of the body," "then the
Christian call struck me down with its demand: 'Die here so that you
may live hereafter.'" Always the "inexorable demand" Thou shalt! made
every human desire unlawful; and the healthy human soul revolted.
Ibsen said that there was much "self-anatomy" in the portrait of Julian,
but how much his rebellion at this time was motivated by the excessive
demands religion might have made on him is not clear; we know too
little about the importance he placed on Christianity as a youth. Other
references to religion in the plays may also be based on memories from
the Grimstad days. In A Doll's House Nora describes how she began
to wonder if everything the minister told her was true; and in Ghosts
Mrs. Alving breaks with traditional beliefs after reading anti-clerical
works.

The seriousness of the search for truth and the need to break with all
authoritarian doctrine are inescapable elements in the formation of that
spirit of relentless and often angry criticism that is Ibsen's. And the
age itself nourished the development of that spirit: "Those were stirring times," he wrote in 1875. "The February Revolution, the uprisings
in Hungary and elsewhere, the fighting in Schleswig — all this had a
powerful and maturing influence on my development." The young man
cheered anything that looked like an upheaval, a break with the past,
even though he had not yet formulated a position for himself. He
swung back and forth in the welter of new ideas that he had discovered

—deism from Voltaire, pantheism from Goethe, philosophical speculations based on the idea of natural evolution. In a poem of 1848 he
describes in rather exaggerated language how he hung between "Doubt
and Hope":

O, som Orkaners vilde Jagt	O like the wild chase of hurricanes
Det stormer i min Sjæl, —	Are the storms within my soul, —
Og inger Leder, ingen Vei	And no guide, no path
I dette Tvivlens Hav! — —	On this sea of doubt! — —

He envies his childhood years:

Men ak, jeg er ei Barn meer,	But alas, I am no more a child,
Og har ei Barnets Sind! — —	Have no more a child's heart! — —

Now he feels only "black night in his heart" and longs to believe again.

There was no turning back. The turmoil of the age drew him on as
new life and courage began to urge him to speak out. The wild paradoxes and unorthodox ideas he tossed out in conversation with his
friends turned the conventional world upside down. He railed against
the government for not aiding Denmark in its struggle with Prussia in
the Schleswig war. He spoke with scorn of the brutal forces that were
crushing the struggle for freedom in Europe and yearned to take part
in the great war that was remaking the world. This insistence on freedom in everything was probably derived from the works of Kierkegaard
that Ibsen and his friends were poring over. The emphasis on individualism in Kierkegaard finds an echo in Ibsen's radicalism, which from
the beginning is a cry for personal liberation from all the forces that
hold man in bondage.

Soon the good citizens of Grimstad were shaking their heads over the
"demagoguery" of the young firebrand at the pharmacy. Ibsen later
said that they considered it "astonishing in the highest degree that a
young person in my subordinate position should undertake to discuss
matters on which they themselves never dared to have an opinion."
Although the elders shuddered at this self-styled "atheist" and "repub-
lican," the young people found his mockery entertaining, and on Sunday evenings a whole little company gathered at the pharmacy, including members of the influential Holst family. Ibsen propounded his
radical theories and lampooned people and events in town, sometimes
setting them to tunes borrowed from Christian Hostrup's popular Danish operetta *Gjenboerne* (The Neighbors, 1844), then being performed
in Norway by various Danish theatrical companies. The company got
the greatest enjoyment when one of Ibsen's victims could be persuaded
to sing the verses that mocked him. The verses were often accompanied by satiric drawings. The only one of these that has survived,
"Sigurd von Finkelbeck's Grave," has four "inscriptions" that describe

the life of this regular purchaser of bitters as an alcoholic spree from start to finish:

Da sidstegang Brændeviins-
    flasken var tom,
Man bar ham til Graven hen;
De Blomster som findes at
    voxe derom
Dufte af Finkelen end!
	When the last whiskey bottle
	    was drained,
	They carried him off to the grave;
	The flowers that sprout there
	Still waft the perfume of booze!

These verses are not, as has been claimed, the earliest we have from Ibsen, but they are the only ones of their kind. Another set of verses, probably more characteristic, was intended to accompany a series of drawings wherein one of his friends, racing his horse, comes to look like the animal at the same time as the animal begins to resemble the master.

At other times Ibsen and his friends sat up late drinking punch, when they could afford it, and playing cards, or went out to play billiards at a place where they could also get a toddy. Sometimes they worked off their excess energy in noisy but harmless escapades in the streets. Ibsen was enjoying his freedom, and as he later wrote: "I was quite unable to find an outlet for all that was seething within me except through madcap pranks that won me the aversion of all respectable citizens, who knew nothing of the inner world I was struggling with all by myself." Ibsen perhaps exaggerated his role in these pranks, and it has been said that while he had more ingenuity than the others in inventing annoying tricks to play on people, he usually stayed in the background when they were being carried out. He probably enjoyed the role of observer in Grimstad as much as he had in Skien.

All his new friends belonged to the middle-class society from which he had been excluded and had therefore treated as an enemy. He did not always think much of them and at times ridiculed them openly, as he had done in Gjerpen when he stood on the barrel and harangued his playmates. He and his two friends from the customs office must have felt bitter at the contrast between their poverty and the affluence of the others. But despite this antagonism Ibsen gradually won some acceptance. In the summer of 1849 he went on boat trips and excursions, and in the winter he was invited to dances, particularly at the Holsts', where he promptly became infatuated with one of the daughters. He had challenged this society to battle, and now seemed to be giving in to it peacefully.

His poetry reflects both the challenge and the reconciliation. He began to write in earnest as faith in his talents stifled his earlier doubts. In the notebook called "Miscellaneous Writings" there are only three poems from 1848; there is a whole flood from 1849. And at the same time as the poems there is the poetic drama, inspired at once by the struggle in his own soul and by the great conflicts of the day, on the rebel Catiline. In 1848, in preparation for the Artium examination, he read through Cicero's orations against Catiline and Sallust's account of the conspiracy. He was fascinated by these accounts and although both authors condemned Catiline, he felt they also revealed the talents, fierce ambition, and paradoxical spirit of idealism of the great revolutionary. The inner contradiction in this demonic man gave Ibsen the germ of the idea for his first play.

Ibsen was unaware of the many other plays inspired by Catiline in the past, and had not even heard of the drama by Dumas *père*, performed in Paris in October, 1848. The Dumas play is a vapid *pièce à intrigue* that could not have had much influence on Ibsen, since his interest in Catiline was so personal; he had only to look within to find the irresistible urge to rebel against conventions and the fierce desire to break the bonds that life forces on a man's will and genius. He knew what it was to long for something and not attain it, and always to fear that one would never be equal to the goal. Catiline would be the first of the Ibsen rebels who carried in himself the seeds of his own destruction.

Ibsen's first intention was to dramatize Catiline's ambition as something actually prompted by an idealistic desire for social revolution — the same kind of idealism he saw in the rebellions of 1848. But this intention was forgotten as the writing of the play continued. The social reformer is changed into the firebrand who wants to blow up the entire social order, and the drama focuses on the moral and psychological conflicts within the man himself, who as he rises to fight for his noblest ideals is confronted by the unexpiated sins of his past that will drive him to destruction.

The plan for *Catiline* appears to have been formed during Christmas, 1848, and the play was written in the next three months. The original manuscript, which was the only complete draft written, has been preserved. Ibsen obviously did not take time, or perhaps had not yet learned how, to reshape and polish the lines that came with such urgency that he had to rush forward without a backward glance. (He could work on the play only at night and he later remarked that "this is the deep, unconscious reason that almost the entire action takes place at night.")

Many years later when he was asked what he knew of dramatic literature when he wrote *Catiline*, he said that he had read only Holberg and Oehlenschläger. This seems as exaggerated as his claim that at the time Shakespeare was only a name to him, and that he had never read Schiller. (He had certainly read *Wilhelm Tell* in Skien.) Ibsen did not like to admit that he was influenced by other writers, and perhaps the intensity with which he felt his dramatic themes as personal experiences made him discount the influence of other plays. Despite the personal quality of the Catiline theme, literature also helped shape the play, and it bears the marks of the great number of books he devoured, as well as the plays he saw in Skien and Grimstad. There are obvious suggestions of classical drama of the seventeenth and eighteenth centuries in his note: "Struggle between love and duty, — the former wins." The dominant mood of the play recalls the revolutionary romanticism of Schiller, Goethe, Hugo, Byron, and Wergeland. More specific influences can be seen in the use of iambic pentameter, as in Shakespeare, Wergeland, and Oehlenschläger. He imitates Oehlenschläger's use of long trochees as substitutes for iambs, as well as the use of rapidly shifting scenes. Not only is the style of the dialogue reminiscent of Oehlenschläger, but an important scene, the final encounter of Catiline and Aurelia, suggests the encounter between Earl Hakon and Thora in *Hakon Jarl* (1807). Other echoes in the play and their origins can be pointed out: the ghostly appearance of Sulla in the last act reminds one of *Julius Caesar;* Catiline murders his love just as Karl Moor does in Schiller's *Die Räuber;* Catiline's position between two contrasted women recalls Wergeland's *Sinclars Død;* and Furia seems to have been borrowed in part from the Danish poem "The Vestal Virgin" by Paludan-Müller.

The basic plot of the secret that comes to light may have been suggested by Mauritz Hansen's story "Two Sisters," where a sister avenges the seduction of her sister by destroying the hero. Guilt is the essential theme of both plots; for Ibsen, guilt is the agent of man's defeat and only death can bring expiation. In some of his later writings Ibsen would dramatize the old romantic concept that the power of a woman's love can be stronger than guilt, but in this play nemesis cannot be averted by love. The hero is driven on, and the words that open the play, "I must, I must," echo from act to act until the end. (In the following year Ibsen wrote in the prose section of the poem "Memories of the Ball": "Remember these words, you without feelings who condemn the passions in a human heart—remember them and never forget that in them you read the justification for so many lives, maddening — and destructive!") From *Catiline* to the end of his career, this sense of the force of compulsion in man would be the basis for Ibsen's dramatic art. Although this play is imperfect, with careless structure, sketchy characterizations, and ranting language, it is more than an amateur's exercise; it sweeps from beginning to end with an inexorable logic that reveals the hand of a genuine dramatist.

Twenty-five years later when he reviewed the play Ibsen wrote: "A great deal of what has been the theme of my writing—the contrast between talent and ambition, and between will and possibility, at once the tragedy and comedy of mankind and man—is intimated here." But in preparing a new edition of the play, he treated it as though he no longer appreciated its essential quality. Important lines in the final scene of reckoning were eliminated in favor of others that introduced new ideas, and he omitted some of the lines that clarified the major theme, particularly in Catiline's farewell to life:

Er ikke Livet da en stadig Kamp	Is not life a constant struggle between
imellem Sjælens fiendtlige Kræfter,—	the hostile forces of the soul,—
og denne Kamp er Sjælens eget Liv.	and this struggle is the very life
	of the soul.

Ibsen felt tremendous satisfaction in writing the play, not because he believed he had recreated the historical Catiline, since history is treated rather casually throughout, but he had succeeded, as he noted in a post-script, in using the historical elements to embody his own ideas and convictions. When he read the play aloud to his friends, they were enthusiastic. Due made a clean copy and Schulerud agreed to take it when he left for the capital in the fall and have it both printed and performed. But despite this encouragement and his satisfaction with the play, Ibsen was reluctant to put his name to it, using instead the pseudonym "Brynjolf Bjarme." (Why he picked this name is not clear, although he could have derived it from Oehlenschläger's *Ørvarodds Saga*, which describes trading expeditions to Bjarmeland, the Old Norse name for northern Russia. "Brynjolf" may have been chosen for the sake of alliteration.)

Now he began to dream of becoming a great national poet, one who would goad the Norwegian people to action. The spirit of nationalism was in the air, and when the German army marched into Denmark in the spring of 1849, many Norwegians and Swedes, particularly the young and the very deeply pan-Scandinavian academic community, felt that all Scandinavia was menaced. Under the title "Manifesto to the Norwegian and Swedish Brothers" he wrote a dozen sonnets urging action in defense of Denmark. "Awake, Scandinavians," he cried, for one day history would demand to know how they had answered this challenge to faith and honor.

Hun kræver Daad for hvad dit Indre nærte og ikke klingende Tirader kun.	She asks for deeds to match your thoughts, and not resounding tirades only.

Unfortunately the verses themselves are more "tirades" than compelling poetry; there is not much more creative force in the lines written when Hungary too was subjugated a few months later. The fallen Magyars are comforted with the hope that in the future their name would be a battle cry for the new generation that was to "overthrow the pillars of tyranny." The more he spoke of the "tempest" in his breast the less convincing the verses became: the struggle that had raged within him seemed to be growing faint. He had traded the waterfalls of Skien for the raging seas of Grimstad, which would live in his memory as an image of freedom. But for the present his images were drawn rather from the hushed and tranquil woods beyond the town, where he walked in the evening and listened, like Catiline, to the mournful sound of the owl, and dreamt. He returned to the graveyard theme and the "music of the dead" which echoes in the night like the "last sigh from a breaking heart."

Soon he discovered a livelier theme; he was smitten by first one lady and then another, until he met his "Stella," Clara Ebbell, who reigned as the bright star in his heaven. She was musical and poetic, admired Beethoven and Wergeland, and could talk about religion. But she became engaged to another and Ibsen was forced to agree with Kierkegaard, who had just explained that the loss of one's beloved was an excellent stimulus for poetry. In the fall of 1849 and the spring of 1850 Ibsen wrote many love lyrics, most of them rather dreamy and limp:

O, med Mindernes Skat Gjennem Fremtidens Nat Vil jeg sværme paa Drommenes Hav.	O, with my hoard of memories I will romance on the sea of dreams Through the night of the future.

In place of the poet of the battle cry, we have the gentle dreamer who wants to gather "sacred blossoms of memory" and "keep them as his heart's best treasure." If the verses were sincerely felt, they were also sincerely imitative of the literary vogue for romantic dreaming and sweet memories. Echoes of Oehlenschläger and his many Norwegian imitators are heard on every page. On the whole the value of these verses lies in the way they illustrate Ibsen's growing mastery of the techniques of romantic poetry. One of the few poems that does seem marked with a more personal feeling is "Memories of the Ball," written in 1850. Here he creates a little drama about a life so blissful it can culminate only in death. Other aspects of his poetry at this time that are noteworthy are the appearance of the familiar theme of conflict between the roles of observer and doer, and the predominance of sound impressions over visual images.

Finally a poem appeared in the public press. Christopher Due, who had become correspondent for the *Christiania-Posten* in Grimstad, placed the poem "In Autumn" signed Brynjolf Bjarme — a complaint about the autumn winds that swept away all the summer hopes, leaving only memory—in the issue for September 28, 1849. Due later described how Ibsen turned pale when he first heard the news, and then blushed with joy. Three or four years later Ibsen himself described his excitement in a poem called "Building Plans":

Jeg husker saa grant, som om idag
  det var hændt,
Dengang jeg saa i Bladet mit første
  Digt paa Prent;
Der sad jeg i mit Kammer og med
  dampende Drag
Jer røgede min Pibe i saligt
  Selvbehag.

Jeg nynned og jeg læste vist for
  tyvende Gang
Avisen, som jeg den Dag fandt
  Særdeles interessant;
Og Phantasien drev sit ubændige
  Spil; —
Ak Herregud! lidt Sværmen hører
  Livet dog til!

Et Drømmeslot jeg byggede; det gik
  lystigt og fort,
Jeg satte mig to Formaal, et lidet
  og et stort,
Det Store var at blive en udødelig
  Mand,
Det Lille var at eie en deilig
  Liljevand.

I recall it as though it just
  happened today,
the time I saw my first poem in print;
there I sat in my room and with
  great puffs
smoked my pipe in blissful self-delight.

I hummed and read for the
  twentieth time
the paper that I found unusually
  interesting that day;
and my imagination played
  wild tricks; —
Ah heavens! a little day-dreaming
  is a part of life!

I built myself a dream palace,
  quickly and merrily,
I set myself two goals, one small
  one great,
the great—to become one of
  the immortals,
the small—to own one lovely maid.

Both goals were equally real for him—a new love and new writing. In mid October, 1849, he wrote to Schulerud in Oslo that he had completed almost the entire first act of a play about King Olaf Trygvason (died A.D. 1000), one of Norway's national heroes, and its first Christian missionary. (The play was undoubtedly suggested by Oehlenschläger's *Hakon Jarl.*) Before completing this he wrote a short one-act play, *The Normans*, which attempts to describe the conflict between paganism and Christianity among the Norwegian Vikings. This too is derived from Oehlenschläger. Before the end of 1849 he tried his hand at a prose narrative, a "national-historical tale" to be called "The Prisoner at

Agershuus." This he envisioned as his first major work since *Catiline*, and it was to deal with Christian Lofthuus, the Norwegian leader of the peasant rebellions in the 1780's. To judge from the start he made, it is clear that the plan was derived entirely from Mauritz Hansen. Ibsen was obviously responding with heart and soul to the romantic notions of nationalism so much in the air at the time.

He also began to versify folktales and stories from Telemark and to set them to well-known folk tunes, and he wrote a poem about Møllar-guten ("The Miller's Boy"), a fiddler whom the Norwegian violinist Ole Bull had taken from his home in the mountain valleys to perform before the educated public. Ibsen's poem was set to the tune of a folksong from Romerike ("Kjøre vatn og kjøre ved") that had appeared in Jørgen Moe's collection of 1840. Early in 1850 he wrote a poem "To the Poets of Norway" which attempts to set up a program for creating a whole new national literature, much as Wergeland had advocated in a pro-grammatic poem written twenty years earlier.

Hvi sværme I, Skjalde! for Fortidens Fjerne,	Why, poets, do you go in for the distant past,
For skrinlagte Old med de smuldrende Minder?	For a sepulchred antiquity with crumbling memorials?
O, fagre Gestalter i Nuet jo vinke,— Fra Dalen, fra Fjeldet, fra Vinter og Sommer.	Oh, fair shapes do beckon us in the present, — From the vale, from the mountain, from winter and summer.
Ha, see I ei Skatten saa glimrende blinke,	Ah, see you not the treasure twinkle and gleam,
— En Folkelivsdigtning med deilige Bloomer!	—A poetry of folk life with beautiful blossoms!

Neither the verses nor the program was very original, since everywhere writers were trying to recover the poetry and lore of the people. But he was deeply committed to the movement and even tried to express his feelings in painting. (He later dated as 1849 a painting of a pilot who sits gazing out to sea.)

No matter what his convictions were about the nationalistic move-ment, it could not be his future course; he had to try many paths before he could come to realize that only in *Catiline*, in the dramatic form, had he been truly himself. Thus, much of his poetry of this period is stereotyped and impersonal, full of "hollow booming" (to use one of his favorite phrases from the verses). He felt that he had not found himself in poetry, and in lines written in the spring of 1850 he asked, "Is not the poet coming?"—the poet who could part the veil of darkness and bring forth a poetry that "revealed the force of clear vision."

On April 12, 1850, he gave away the last poem he was to write in

Grimstad, "Moonlight Promenade after a Ball," the usual refrain about the soul "gliding on a sea of dreams with a treasure of memories," which he had written for Sophie Holst, one of his dancing partners. The next day, early on Saturday morning, he left Grimstad. He was now past twenty-two, and if people had remarked how old he looked when he arrived six years earlier, the great black beard he now wore must have added many more years. His first goal was to take the Artium examination for the University. Then he would take his destiny in hand and make the assault on the world of literature.

CHAPTER FIVE

LEAVING HOME (APRIL 1850)

URING HIS ENTIRE STAY in Grimstad, Ibsen wrote to his family, particularly to his mother and his young sister Hedvig. He always disliked writing long letters and at times let long periods lapse between letters, but he always kept in touch with home and spoke frequently of returning for the summer vacations, although as far as can be discovered he came back only once, in 1848. When he left the pharmacy he intended to go directly to Oslo to prepare for his examination, but a letter from home urged him to stop first at Skien. He wrote saying that he had not mentioned returning, although he wanted to, because he was not sure his father would "approve." Why Ibsen felt this way is not certain, but he seems to have been somewhat intimidated by his father. If his father had given him money for his studies, perhaps Ibsen did not want to appear thriftless in spending it on a pleasure trip to Skien.

He returned to Skien a bit more grandly than he left, coming by the steamer which had only begun its run in early April that year, since the fjord had been closed by heavy ice till then. On April 13 the young poet boarded the *Prince Carl*, got off at Brevik, and reached Skien, where he remained a fortnight until the same vessel carried him off to Oslo. We know nothing of his stay at the family house at Snipetorp, unless this was the time of a conversation his sister Hedvig later described. On a walk up to the heights of Bratsberg, Ibsen held forth on his dreams for the future and his desire to give perfect clarity to all that his imagination could conceive. Hedvig asked, "What will you do then?" He replied, "Then I will die." During these two weeks the sight of the cloister at Gjemsøy, across the fjord from Bratsberg, called up images of Norway's Middle Ages that he shaped into a poem. Later he would rework this material into the larger historical perspective of the poem "At Akershus." He seems to have been in good spirits during the vacation, with faith in his talents and hope for the future.

51

When he left Skien he made his farewell not only to the town, but to his family as well; he never returned to see either again, and he stopped writing. What happened on this short visit to cause such a sudden and complete break is not clear. Perhaps he asked his wealthy relatives, the Paus family, for financial support and became bitter at their refusal. The Paus's would have had good reason for rejecting a plea from Knud Ibsen's son—Knud was at odds with merchants in the town because of his activity as a broker, and he was not always on good terms with his half-brothers. Evidence to explain the break with his immediate family can be gathered from a number of sources. In 1867 Ibsen wrote to Björnson: "Do you know that I have broken with my own parents, my whole family, because I could not stand only half-understanding and being only half-understood?" In the 1870's his biographer John Paulsen asked him if he corresponded with his sister. "He smiled strangely," wrote Paulsen, "and said that it would be a hard task, because of her peculiar outlook." When his sister wrote to tell him that their mother had died on June 3, 1869, it was not until September 26, almost four months later, that he answered her. He realized that he had to make excuses for such indifference: "There is so much that stands between us, between me and home; understand, and don't think that I have been silent these long years, and this summer, because I am not concerned about you. I cannot write letters; I must be near to give myself fully."

The same letter goes on to make clear that religion was the cause of the barrier between them: "I look inside myself; there is my battlefield where I win and lose. I can't write this in a letter. Don't try to convert me. I want to be true; what will happen, will happen." What he is saying is that he would not allow anyone to interfere with his inner life or to try to sway him in this or that direction. If they tried, he withdrew. He is even more explicit in a letter to Judge Christian Paus after his father's death in 1877: "To outsiders it looks as if I have willingly and deliberately made myself a stranger to my family and have cut myself off from them once and for all. But I think I can say that circumstances beyond my control were the real cause." He then mentions several reasons for the break: "The main reason I scarcely ever wrote my parents during these years of struggle was that I could not aid or comfort them. I felt it would be useless to write when I was unable to act. I kept hoping that things would improve, but they did not do so until just recently." He cites another reason: "I felt a deep desire to avoid contact with certain attitudes which prevailed there and with which I was out of sympathy. I wanted to avoid the unpleasantness or at least bad feelings that might have resulted."

It is certain that the "attitudes" he refers to were associated with the religious revival, at its height during his visit, which had been sparked by the well-known Rev. Gustav Lammers. Since his installation as pastor in 1849, Lammers was busy stirring up his congregation with fiery revivalist sermons. A few days before Ibsen's return in April, Lammers issued an appeal for funds to build a meeting house on the very grounds of the parsonage—an obvious challenge to the Lutheran State Church, of which Lammers was supposedly a servant, and an indication that he planned on using the prayer meetings and revival enthusiasm to build a private following of believers. Marichen Ibsen and two of her children—Hedvig and the youngest son, Ole Paus—were among the first to join the flock. Close friends of the Ibsen's, among them the Ording and Lieungh families, also turned into zealots.

Ibsen's development during the six years at Grimstad had made this kind of religious fervor even more alien to him than before. As far as the true believers were concerned, the more they saw of the young poet and his works, the more they counted him among the godless lost. Hedvig alone tried to maintain some contact with the prodigal, but he ignored her letters appealing for his conversion. Knud Ibsen told her she was foolish to keep it up, and on one occasion laughed outright when she told him Henrik had sent a letter, "full of barbs." Ibsen was concerned about his father's attitude toward all this, and the letter he wrote Hedvig after their mother's death asks her to greet his father, "lovingly," and "explain to him what you so well understand about me—he may not understand." But Knud Ibsen was the only one in the family who did understand; from *Brand* on he read all his son's works. The father answered with pride when the family scorned the son: "When the Paus's die, they'll be dead; *my* name will live!"

Ibsen's family were more strangers to him than he to them, and one by one they drifted away. They had no contact with his life, and hardly any interest in his work. Hedvig was almost an old woman before she began reading her brother's books, and only then did she understand him fully. Ole Paus admitted at the age of eighty, ten years after Ibsen's death, that all he had read was a bit of *Brand* and *Pillars of Society.* The oldest brother, Johan, emigrated to America in 1849. There is one extant letter to his father, dated May 1850, and mention of several others, mostly to his mother, but the correspondence soon ended and the family knew nothing more than rumors that he had been seen in

California or at sea. The two younger brothers tried shopkeeping, but failed. Nicolai, the next to youngest, left for America in 1870 and he too was lost to the family, although they advertised for him in the papers when the father died in 1877. He died poor and alone in 1888, "By Strangers honored and by Strangers mourned," as the legend on his tombstone in Estherville, Iowa, reads. When Ibsen learned of his brother's death he asked his son Sigurd, then in the Norwegian diplomatic corps in Washington, to see that the grave was tended. About the same time, the youngest brother, Ole, asked Ibsen to use his influence when he applied for a job as lighthouse keeper. On October 3, 1887, Ibsen sent Ole's application papers to Johan Sverdrup, then Prime Minister of Norway, only asking that he read them—"I have nothing further to add," he concluded. (This was not much of a recommendation, but it did get Ole the job.)

In spite of this alienation Ibsen still felt bound to his home—"the old place where I still have so many roots after all," as he wrote to Hedvig in 1869. This strange state of being uprooted and still rooted, of being alienated yet attached, had an effect on his work for a long time. Memories of Skien are real enough in 1865 to help shape the action of *Brand; The League of Youth*, in 1869, actually uses Skien as its setting. In 1875, when he was revising *Catiline* and remembering Grimstad, he also thought of Skien, and on February 25, wrote to his old father from Germany. It was the first letter in twenty-five years and he mentions that he is thinking of visiting Norway, perhaps even Skien. The letter is lost, but Knud Ibsen's reply expresses his delight at hearing from his son after so long. But Ibsen never returned to Skien after he left in 1850, and as the months and years went by filled with the struggle of creation, it became impossible to write his family about his feelings. After all, as Hedvig said, they all did belong "to a silent tribe." Home and his childhood would always return in memory, and he would never be free of them. He may even at times have felt the same guilt that oppresses King Haakon in *The Pretenders,* who thinks God's punishment comes because he closed his heart to his mother.

CHAPTER SIX

APPRENTICE YEARS IN OSLO (1850-51)

WHEN IBSEN ARRIVED in Oslo, then called Christiania, his pseudonym "Brynjolf Bjarme" was probably already known by most people with a serious interest in literature. Not that anyone paid particular attention to the few poems that had appeared in *Christiania-Posten* (the first on September 28, 1849, and another on February 16, 1850). This latter was a threnody for Oehlenschläger. It was written in "melancholy ardor," in a meter that had been a favorite of the Danish poet's, that of the old Norse poem *Eiriksmál*. The publication of *Catiline* on April 12, 1850, finally focused attention on "Brynjolf Bjarme."

Ole Schulerud did not have much success when he tried to place the play after his arrival in the capital in September, 1849. Christiania Theatre was not interested in producing it, although they admitted the play was well written. When Schulerud wrote to Ibsen that this rejection was no defeat, Ibsen was quick to agree: the play was certainly the "forerunner" of great drama. Schulerud had no better luck with the booksellers who usually acted as publishers; the only one who would take it demanded a subsidy and refused to give any royalties. Schulerud did not lose heart but wrote that he would use a small inheritance of his own to print the book. The two would divide the profits on this first venture; from then on Ibsen would write two or three plays a year, Schulerud would publish them, and both would soon be rich enough to make the grand tour. As things turned out, *Catiline* was the only Ibsen play that Schulerud published; but to this courageous friend goes the honor of being the first to publish a play by Ibsen.

Nothing like this play had ever appeared in Norway, a country still so culturally unformed that it had not yet produced a living dramatic literature. The capital had had a regular theatre since 1827, which offered almost nothing but plays in translation. There were no more than a baker's dozen of Norwegian plays, and the only dramatist of any significance was Henrik Wergeland, whose *The Venetians* was printed in 1843. There would not be another new play printed in Norway until *Catiline*. The first reviewer of Ibsen's play, writing not for the general public but for the more interested audience of university students, pointed out this sad fact in *Samfundsbladet*, a handwritten newspaper of the Student Society *(Studentersamfundet)*. The article was read aloud to the society at its meeting on April 13. The author of the review was certainly one of the paper's editors, Paul Botten Hansen. This young man, soon to play an important part in Ibsen's life, was eagerly looking for new talent and was ecstatic to at last meet a writer who cared nothing for popular taste, but sought to conquer by "genuine, sound poetry." The new playwright showed promise of "an almost Shakespearean vigor and seriousness." Hansen was aware of the weaknesses in both verse form and dramatic structure, but he saluted the playwright on his debut because his theme, Catiline's destruction by an inner conflict, was a genuinely tragic one.

The first and only review in the public press was printed in *Christiania-Posten* on May 16. The article was not signed but it was undoubtedly written by the classical scholar and headmaster F. L. Vibe. Naturally, the classicist regretted the playwright's casual treatment of historical facts; a more serious objection was the one raised, quite justly, to the "occasionally exaggerated pathetic effects," that reminded one of the excesses satirized in Wessel's *Love Without Stockings* (1772). He also found cause to praise the play: "The author has an unusual skill in creating high tragic tension, as well as remarkable skill in depicting the passions in all their force. His language is of a purity seldom met." His conclusion was that despite its faults, one puts the tragedy down with a feeling of satisfaction—"it reveals an unmistakable talent."

In October, 1850, the play was reviewed in the most important Norwegian journal, *Norsk Tidsskrift for Videnskab og Litteratur*. Carl Müller, also a classicist, was the reviewer, and he was much more severe than Vibe. With satiric talent he laid bare the thin bones of Ibsen's plot, and neatly caught the inconsistencies in the development of character. Only the form of the play revealed the qualities that led him to believe that one day "Brynjolf Bjarme" would "give us something better." The editor of the journal, Professor M. J. Monrad, added some dissenting opinions of his own to the review. He did not believe the playwright showed any great mastery of form; what he found deeply significant was that the play was informed by an idea, a theme that was both "clear and beautiful," — the conflict between the individual's obscure longing for freedom and his awareness that his soul is not pure. He was certain that a writer who had such a vigorous life of ideas within him would one day find the form he needed.

"Brynjolf Bjarme" had won recognition from the literary critics, even if the praise was cautious. But sales were miserable and neither publisher nor playwright made money. Of the 250 copies that were put on sale, 205 remained a year later.

Ibsen arrived in Oslo on April 28 and immediately registered at a school recently established by Henrik Heltberg for students who were cramming for the Artium examination—the place was known familiarly as the "Student Factory." He was not really interested in his studies, nor were the friends he had made the kind who would inspire him in that direction. There was A. O. Vinje, who would one day be a venerated poet, but was now a bearded farm youth ten years older than Ibsen. Vinje had been a constant contributor to the newspapers and had started writing poetry for the radical newspaper *Folkets Røst*, (Voice of the People) in May, 1850. A satirist and a rebel, he was the one who meant most to Ibsen and with whom Ibsen felt the closest kinship. Another of his fellow-students was Frithiof Foss, likewise an aspiring poet. (Bjørnstjerne Bjørnson, Ibsen's sometime friend and future rival, had arrived in town that spring, but he did not enter the school until the fall term, by which time Ibsen had left.)

During his first months in Oslo, Ibsen lived with Ole Schulerud in the garret of a house owned by a famous "healing woman" known as Mother Sæter. It was situated in the Vika district of the town, the rather run-down harbor area where the City Hall is now located. The house stood in a passage known as Filosofgangen (Philosopher's Lane), on the corner of Vinkelgata. Ibsen paid for his rooms, at least in part, by giving lessons to Mother Sæter's son (he seems to have given her a painting for rent money as well). One of his fellow lodgers was the law student Theodor Abildgaard, a radical who was about to join the new and revolutionary labor movement. Abildgaard may have introduced Ibsen to Paul Botten Hansen, a rebel of the type who preferred to mock society with a derisive smile. Abildgaard and Vinje were certainly the ones who got Ibsen to attend the demonstration at Klingenberg on May 29, 1850, protesting the deportation of the Danish revolutionary Harro Harring, editor of *Folkets Røst*. Ibsen would naturally sympathize with the demand for freedom this meeting voiced.

His real interest was literature, however, and he used the first chance he got, the Whitsun vacation after May 17, to revise the one-act play *The Normans*. Renamed *The Warrior's Barrow*, it was sent to Christiania Theatre, again under the pseudonym of "Brynjolf Bjarme." More adapted to contemporary taste than *Catiline*, the play was quickly accepted and put on early in the fall season, on September 26, 1850. There were three performances, the last on October 24, and that was all; not quite a triumph, yet thrilling enough for the playwright watching his work for the first time on a stage. "It was terrible," he said later, "I hid in the darkest corner of the theatre."

The Warrior's Barrow has none of the tragic intensity of *Catiline;* in fact it is hardly even a play, but rather a poem in dramatic form. The plot is a wildly romantic tale about a troop of Vikings in the tenth century who land on an island near Sicily. Because their king fell on this same soil, they are determined to kill an old hermit and a young girl they discover. At first the hermit meekly acquiesces, then declares himself the killer of the king, then reveals that he is the king. The theme of the play, derived from Oehlenschläger, is the conflict between paganism and Christianity; the Ibsen touch is apparent only in that the conflict rages in the mind of one man, Gandalf, the son who is determined to avenge his father. Unfortunately, the rage is so low-keyed it scarcely sets up a ripple on the surface of the play.

Ibsen excluded *The Warrior's Barrow* from the collected edition of his works he prepared at the end of his life. (He allowed it to remain in the German translation, however, saying that "the old text is surely adequate as the basis of a translation.") The collected edition was based on his conception that all his works were part of a "coherent, continuous whole"; he always denied writing a play just because he had chanced on the idea: "Everything I have written has its source in a life situation and a mood; I have never composed anything because I had, as they say, happened on a good subject." He excluded *The Warrior's Barrow* primarily because he believed the form of the play was inadequate, and the entire work extraneous to the "coherent, continuous whole" his writings created. And yet, in spite of its formal weakness, there is something of felt life in the play. Blanka, the young girl who speaks to Gandalf of Christianity and love, is most probably based on Clara Ebbell, the girl Ibsen loved in Grimstad. The name suggests a star, and it was to her he dedicated the poem "To the Star," when he describes how she tried to dispel the "black cloud of doubt" which hung over his soul and in its place bring "a dawn of blessed trust." Blanka is the only character in the play who is a living person; in addition, the struggle between Christianity and doubt was written out of his own experience.

The reviewers in *Christiania-Posten* and in *Krydseren* praised the play for its beautiful, resonant verse; although many of the lines have a genuine lyric beauty, there is still much of the chime and tinkling of the Oehlenschläger style — the "music of memory" that "trembled through harp strings of the heart"—all the bad habits he brought with him from Grimstad but was slowly shaking off. In one direction, greater control over the excesses of pathos that marred *Catiline,* he was already making much headway.

Ibsen was admitted to the university examination in August, 1850, duly certified in Latin (testimonial by Th. J. Lie) that he had qualified himself for the examination "by outstanding diligence and firm purpose, assisted by auspicious abilities." But the examination turned out badly. On a scale running from a high of 1 to a low of 6 the best he scored was 2 (very good) in German; most subjects, including written Norwegian, were rated only 3 (good). He received three grades in Latin: a 3, 4 (fairly good), and 5 (passable). In Greek and arithmetic he failed with a 6. His average for all subjects was the lowest passing grade, 3.67 "non contemnendus," and the Greek and arithmetic would have to be taken over again. He never bothered, and he was not able to formally matriculate at the university.

He received a testimonial (signed by the poet Welhaven, Dean of Faculty) that entitled him to call himself "Student Ibsen" and to take part in the activity of the Student Society. This was really all that interested him now, and medicine was abandoned for aesthetics and literature, which he studied intensely. He attended lectures in philosophy and literature, including those Welhaven gave on Holberg in the spring of 1851. He became an active member of the Literary Society formed the previous year by the Student Society. New members had to deliver a lecture upon admission to the Literary Society, and in the six sonnets Ibsen used to introduce his lecture the emphasis is placed, as it had been in the past, on the importance of a serious theme in literature, a theme that served a "spiritual ideal."

But he was not making a living this way. *Catiline* had been a total financial loss, and the royalties from *The Warrior's Barrow* must have been small. The only money he made from literature was a ten dollar advance from the bookseller Steensballe (who had sold copies of *Catiline*); Schulerud had sold him the rights to *The Warrior's Barrow* and a poem "The Golden Harp." The rest of the money never appeared and neither did the book.

Ibsen and Schulerud left Mother Sæter's for a small room with kitchen and alcove in a house at the foot of the Hammersborg hill, rented by a Miss Holt in Møllergata. This was more elegant than Vika and at first they lived comfortably, chiefly on the monthly allowance that Schulerud was happy to share with his friend. They could eat dinner at Miss Holt's and for a time even kept a servant—who was liable to go off on an occasional spree, but was cheerful and resourceful. But prosperity ended, dinners at Miss Holt's ended, and they squeezed to pay the rent, even with the added resources of Schulerud's younger brother who came to live with them. They had to disguise the fact that they were too poor to dine out lest their credit suffer, so they dressed each evening and walked out on the town, then crept back to their bread and cheese and coffee. One day there was no bread and no coffee—the grocer cut off their credit—and Ibsen had to visit the pawnbroker, from whom he returned with two dollars. On another occasion he resurrected an armful of *Catiline* from the attic and sold them to the grocer, for wrapping paper. Whenever they did manage to pick up some money, they lived high on stoltser cheese instead of the usual *nøkkelostt* (clove cheese), smoked herring, and eggs. In addition there were hot toddy and card playing sessions with friends, especially Abildgaard and Botten Hansen.

Twenty-five years later Ibsen would talk about this time of poverty and smile, but he suffered greatly in these years, in silence—he was too proud and too diffident to let anyone know. Hansen, who saw Ibsen almost every day, said that he never realized how poor his friend was until a long time afterwards.

But in spite of the suffering, this first year in Oslo was a fruitful time. He was free and the world was opening up. Around him were pulsating those social and cultural movements he had once only read about at a distance. Here was a "Democratic Society" and a "Workingmen's Society," and also the entrenched bureaucracy that fought agrarian reform and all other radical ideas; here were the leaders of science and scholarship, and here was the center of artistic and literary life. It was more than just a town of 30,000; it was already a microcosm of all Norway, and even, in part, of Europe.

Reaction against the revolutions of 1848 was in full swing, but in Norway the forces of progress were still active. The Storting election of 1850 brought in a majority of representatives who favored agrarian and democratic reforms. Workers were joining forces to press their interests as never before; there was a nationwide congress at Bygdøy in August, 1850, and another in Oslo in June, 1851. New classes were challenging the control of the bourgeoisie and the bureaucracy over the country.

Farmers and laborers were organizing their demands for power, significantly expressed in terms of *freedom;* the Agrarian Party called for freedom of apprenticeship, freedom of trade, and freedom to start new sawmills; the labor program of 1850 gave priority to a demand for freedom of external and internal trade. Although the leader of the movement, Marcus Thrane, called himsef a socialist there was little socialism in the movement; behind his demands for a more democratic government and for curbs on capitalism lay an ideal of freedom for the people and the individual, and not an ideology of socialism. The same insistence on freedom can be found in other countries in the 1850's, even in those nations where capitalism was already in full force. According to the spirit of liberalism the salvation for man and society lay in the free and responsible individual.

The demand for freedom struck a responsive chord in Ibsen, who understood his society and its deepest needs. His own rebellious nature drove him to explore the problem of freedom, not in its economic or political aspect but as a spiritual and moral dilemma. That he would do so was clear already in Grimstad when he first read about Kierke-gaard's struggle for personal honesty and freedom of soul. He was annoyed later when he was made out to be a mere follower of Kierke-gaard, and on several occasions he even said he had "read only a little and understood even less" of the Danish philosopher. The reference here is most probably to the purely philosophical writings; he cer-tainly knew Kierkegaard's more psychological-literary works, such as the studies of love in *Repetition,* or *The Seducer's Diary* in *Either-Or.* What is most important is that he understood Kierkegaard's intellectual struggle.

The philosophy of Hegel, with its primary tenet of the supremacy of the human intellect, was sweeping through Europe and was now winning advocates in Norway, among them the new Professor of Phi-losophy, M. J. Monrad. The cultural leader of the 1850's, particularly in the field of aesthetics, was the Danish poet and critic Johan Ludvig Heiberg, whose book *On Human Liberty,* published in 1824, had first brought Hegelian ideas to Scandinavia. Ibsen would later call the Norwegian literary critics of the same period mere imitators of Heiberg, but he too studied and idolized Heiberg in those years. Heiberg in-sisted that the poet should master his inspiration by his intellect, rather than be swept away by it. Through self-reflection and soul-searching (an essential aspect of Romanticism that can be seen in almost psycho-pathic intensity in Kierkegaard), a man could rise above his bonds and become inwardly, if not outwardly, free. Ibsen was attracted by these ideas even though he does not refer to them in his poem to Heiberg's memory after his death in 1860; here he speaks only of the critic's struggle: "Sharply he fought against the monsters of the age . . . may he teach you to use your sword!"

On Human Liberty considers the problem of freedom in Hegelian and very dramatic terms. The demand for freedom, an inner necessity that recreates the humanity of man, inevitably leads to rebellion; born of strife, it can live only in strife. Hegel said that everything in life provokes its own opposite and in reality lives only in this opposition.

Oppression thus becomes a prerequisite of freedom, and life and thought turn into continuous struggle and drama. In this idea of opposition Ibsen found a philosophical basis for his own tendency to shape his ideas into dramatic conflicts. Hegel and Heiberg helped him to choose the drama as his form, a drama that would derive its driving force from the necessity for inner freedom and truth. Ibsen did not become a philosopher. He never mastered the abstract language of philosophy and never constructed a philosophical system of his beliefs; he probably never resolved for himself the disagreement between Hegel's objectivity and Kierkegaard's impassioned subjectivity. He simply took what he needed from each and thus parted company with both. The break was inevitable: once they had created the systems to contain their thoughts, the systems became immutable truth to them; they could then settle down as good conservative citizens. But in Ibsen there lived an eternal rebel, and his concerns were for the inner necessity, free will, the course of spiritual development, the struggle itself. In *The Warrior's Barrow* as in *Catiline* the same conclusion is drawn:

Ja vel, den indre Strid og Aandens Kamp	Yes, inner strife and struggle of spirit
Og Lysets skjønne Seier over Mørket,	Splendid victory of light over darkness,
Viid, denne *Strid,* er Livets Formaal, Hedning.	Know, pagan, this strife is life's purpose.

The inner struggle found its first expression in poetry, but not such poetry as he wrote in Grimstad. In these first Oslo years Ibsen began to gather poems together for publication, but as he worked on them he rejected one after the other until all the Grimstad poetry was eliminated, and there was nothing left to publish. His life in Oslo had led him away from the "mood poems" which had never born the stamp of a personal form. Now he turned to what he called "idea poems" and was at last able to draw on his most deeply felt experiences; not immediately, for the poems were often derivative, but in a small group of them the new man becomes evident.

The poems were printed throughout 1851, although the most important were written in the fall of 1850. In the sonnets to The Literary Society he had contrasted poetry with the prosaic demands of life and called on poets (including himself) to "fight boldly, energetically" for an ideal that bore "the noble stamp of the spirit." But he could promise little more than "a treasury of memories," a flower "with withered leaves, but fresh remembrances!" In the poem "Dreams of Youth" the dreamy reminiscences of the Grimstad style give way somewhat to a more energetic image: the flower is happiest when the bud struggles to break its bonds:

Og denne Sjælens Higen efter	And this passion of the soul for
Frihed	freedom
Er just til Livets sande Liv indviet!	Is dedicated to the living truth of life!

But even here the poet is resigned to enjoying the "sad memories" of youth's struggle. The flower ought to die the moment the bud breaks forth, as he had written to Clara Ebbell; he expressed the same idea to his sister in Skien when he told her he wanted to die after he had achieved perfect clarity. The struggle was a torture that seemed to go on endlessly, and he no longer had the comforts of memory. In depressed moments he sees defeat ahead: "Bird and Bird Catcher" describes the terror of soaring upwards to light and freedom, and then:

| Segner jeg med knækket Vinge | I topple with broken wing |
| Ned ifra min drømte Bane! | Down from my imagined course! |

"The Eider Duck" ends with the bird robbed of hope, strength, courage; only the "bleeding breast" is left.

These two poems were among the first he thought good enough to be included in the volume he published twenty years later, but then he was able to give "The Eider Duck" a more hopeful and defiant ending. At that time he also rewrote the one poem from 1850 which bares his true feelings more than any other, "The Miner."

The symbol in the poem is a familiar one in Romantic poetry, and since he certainly never set foot inside a mine, he must have found it in his reading, probably in a story by Mauritz Hansen he had read as a boy. But one need only compare his treatment of the theme with those of major Romantic poets in Denmark and Sweden to see the tremendous power and freshness he infuses into the trite image. Oehlenschläger's translation (1803) of a Novalis poem on the subject, and the poem by the Swedish Geijer (1812) are false and pallid by comparison. In the former we are given a miner who praises the "darkness of the mine" because it permits him to extract nature's secrets; the miner in the second poem is equally delighted to live in darkness since he can be in peace far from the struggles of mankind. Ibsen, on the other hand, shows the miner's life as harsh, endless struggle; his miner yearns and toils to break through "life's dim riddle," but finds neither sun nor light. The poem creates the effect of eternal, weary hammer blows by the use of heavy trochees and spondees, as opposed to the light iambics of Oehlenschläger and Geijer:

| Ban mig Veien, Tunge Hammer! | Clear my path, mighty hammer, |
| Til Naturens Hjertekammer! | To Nature's secret room! |

The miner "falls weary and weakened," unsuccessful. The poem's reflection of both determination and weakness suggests the state of Ibsen that fall in Oslo. Seeking, he thought he glimpsed light, but so much darkness lay ahead that more than once he despaired of reaching the goal.

He was still deeply committed to the romantic type of nationalism then fashionable, and the narrative poem "The Golden Harp," which he planned to publish in the fall of 1850, must have had a nationalistic theme, although nothing else is known of this projected work. In the later months of the year he worked on "The Grouse of Justedal," a "national play in four acts," based on Norwegian folktales. All that survives of this is a manuscript copy that ends in the middle of Act II, and we do not know if he ever finished it, although from the dry and dull lines that remain one can readily understand why the play was laid aside. It was perhaps early in 1851 that he wrote a narrative poem called "Helge Hundingsbane," another Oehlenschläger-inspired pastiche drawn from Old Norse heroic lays, totally lacking in personal conviction. In "At Akershus," a short poem about the fortress that dominates the Oslo fjord, there is a deeper note, but the work is still disfigured by the familiar "mighty dreams" and "vanished figures from distant times" that haunt the midnight hour. Ten years later he would make of this poem an omen for the times.

In "A Saturday Night in Hardanger," most likely written in the fall of 1850, there is a strange duality despite the derivative nature of the theme. He had never been to Hardanger, but this celebrated fjord region was used frequently as a theme in romantic poetry. Ibsen cuts across the romanticism with the ironic hint that he would be happy to escape from its romantic witchery. The same tone can be seen in "The Boy in the Blueberry Patch" where he drily contrasts the poet's vision of the simple life with the prosaic reality; the boy is picking berries to sell in town so he can buy his ailing sister a cooky.

As Ibsen began to move away from Romanticism, he was aided by his two closest friends, Botten Hansen and A. O. Vinje. Hansen was three years older than Ibsen and a devotee of Henrich Heine, whose critical irony matched his own preference for taking a satirical, outsider's view of parties, rather than engaging in the struggle itself. Vinje modeled himself on the Danish critic and journalist Aaron Meïr Goldschmidt, an activist, but one who flailed out in all directions. Vinje too was above political parties and believed that partisanship made the free spirit a draught-horse for power politics. He held that truth was constant growth and change, and "true liberalism" the ability to see the right and wrong on both sides. Freedom came from this duality of vision. But he was also a born fighter and his independence of party, rather than making him passive, brought him to the forefront of every ideal-

istic conflict. At the same time his tenderness of heart made him deeply
romantic. Ibsen at last had found friends who were not only his intellectual equals but at times more mature. His rebelliousness was strengthened and he was drawn into their struggles.

At New Year's, 1851, he was chosen to succeed Hansen obviously on
the latter's suggestion as editor of *Samfundsbladet,* the student newspaper. He did not dispatch his duties very energetically; in nine months
he put out only four issues: three the first quarter, one the second, and
none at all in the last. He worked much harder, however, on the periodical he and his two friends had started themselves. Vinje, who had co-
edited a couple of political papers in 1850 (both of which had failed
within the year) probably originated the idea of a new literary-political
journal modeled on Goldschmidt's *The Corsair,* published in Denmark.
Subscribers were promised poems by "Brynjolf Bjarme," and in addition to these got theatrical reviews. Ibsen had a pass to the theatre now
and by April began to review plays as well as write political articles
when Vinje was away from May to August. The editors remained anonymous, as was the custom, and the journal itself was without a name;
instead of a masthead it carried a drawing of a man wearing a very
satiric expression, and thus it was called simply *The Man.* After six
months it was christened *Andhrimner,* for the cook who served the old
Norse gods. Within a quarter of a year, however, the journal expired,
twenty-nine issues old. It had fewer than a hundred subscribers, and
Axelson, the printer, was not willing to throw away money on a journal
that alienated everybody. (Ibsen is recalling Axelson when he created
the printer Aslaksen in *The League of Youth;* he says he "can't make
a living on a good newspaper.")

The Man hardly had time enough to make much of an impression on
its contemporaries, and yet it brought a remarkable new spirit to Norwegian journalism. It claimed the right to stand outside parties and
satirize them all, whether they were literary or political cliques. Botten
Hansen parodied national romanticism, first in "Norwegian Mysteries,"
a Heinesque story with illustrations by Ibsen, and in a three-act play,
"The Fairy Wedding." (This amusing piece influenced Ibsen's writing
from *The Comedy of Love* to *Peer Gynt.*) Even more belligerent were
the political satires on the Storting; neither the Left nor the Right was
spared, but the lash cut deepest on the "Democrats" who had been
elected on a program of freedom and had then "betrayed" it under their
leader, A. B. Stabell. *The Man's* radicalism was directed against all
who spoke honorable words, but failed to put them into action.

Ibsen was probably not much interested in the particular causes that
the journal took up: the problems of the navy, the mint, the cotters,

etc. The general moral issue engaged him, and his anger rose when he saw the Storting majority too cowardly to carry out its own declared policy. His first political essays were gibes at A. B. Stabell, whom he lampooned in prose and in caricature. He even wrote a little play about him, O. G. Ueland, and other members of the opposition who had yielded to reactionism. Some of the epigrammatic lines of this playlet foreshadow *Peer Gynt,* particularly in the conclusion of a speech on freedom delivered by Ueland:

Det var desuden mit Princip alt fra jeg var liden, At holde mig en Hestelængde bagud for Tiden.	It has been my principle since I was very small, To keep a horse's length behind the times.

Because he sympathized with the yearning of the poor to be free, he jeered at the politicians who only wanted people free—so they could be skinned by money lenders. And he mocked the bravery of soldiers who suppressed the demonstrating laborers. When Swedish journalists flayed the Norwegian movement for independence, he took delight in demonstrating that they were nothing but lackeys of the "mouldy Swedish aristocracy," that ludicrous anachronism from the "murky Middle Ages," which was still clinging to life "in a new age of enlightenment and liberalism." Obviously, from a small town scoffer, Ibsen had become the "state satirist" on the model of Holberg; he never liked men in authority and he enjoyed cracking the whip over them. *The Man* gave him a perfect opportunity to express this strong impulse.

He gave less of himself in the theatre criticism he wrote. A generation later he described how a man came to be a drama critic in Oslo in the 1850's: "It's like this: after trying his hand in *Samfundsbladet* for a while and after listening to after-theatre talk at Treschow's cafe or at Ingebret's, the budding critic clumps over to Johan Dahl's bookstore and orders from Copenhagen a copy of J. L. Heiberg's *Prose Writings* because he heard they contain a disquisition on 'Musical Comedy.' He reads this, mulls it over, maybe even understands a bit." Ibsen could have been describing himself in this passage, except that he probably read Heiberg more carefully, as is evident when one reads his theatre essays. He echoes Heiberg's ideas about the ideal purpose of student theatre and about the necessity for harmony between words and music in opera. The characteristics he shows are a youthful arrogance and a pugnacity in attacking the "theatrical bonbons of Scribe & Co.," and the clumsy coincidences in German historical drama. He seems little concerned with the actual production of plays at Christiania Theatre, and has nothing but generalities to offer on performance. What he was looking for was the *idea* that would raise the play above the trivial or the sensual. When he is repelled by the "Frenchness of moral idea" in a light Parisian comedy, it is not simply the petty bourgeois prude speaking; although he has not yet found the way to express his feelings, he is instinctively associating art and morality — such a performance must "offend the ethical and therefore also the aesthetic sensibilities of many."

He also attacks such plays because they "weaken our sense of nationality." But at the same time he delivers the harshest criticism given to P. A. Jensen's operetta *The Fairy's Home,* the play Christiania Theatre presented as its contribution to nationalism. The play, he wrote, had only nationalistic tinsel, but no spirit of true nationalism: "The national author is one who can give his work the authentic voice that calls out to us from vale and mountain, from shore and hillside, above all *from our own hearts.*" He expressed the same idea in a poem written at this time, "The Voice of Nature." A real poet must not repeat another's words, but find his own expression of the true and the genuine. He was struggling to find his own genuine voice, and he used the journal to defend others who he thought were doing the same, even daring to take on the poet and critic Welhaven, whose lectures on Holberg he had attended. Welhaven had attacked the "mythological poetry" of the day, particularly the writings of the Dane Paludan-Müller, whose satirical poem *Adam Homo* (1841-48) would be one of the sources for *Peer Gynt.* Ibsen wrote that Welhaven was condemning "many of his own poems" in condemning Paludan-Müller. The warmth of his defense indicates that he felt a kinship with the Danish poet's "philosophical poetry," a poetry in keeping with the "cultural spirit of the age," and one to which he would devote himself once he had become free of the phrases and ideas of others.

The same spirit of social protest that informed *The Man* can be seen in Ibsen's involvement in the labor movement. At New Year's, 1851, his friend Theodor Abildgaard was made editor of *Arbeider-Foreningernes Blad* (The Journal of the Workingman's Societies), established by Marcus Thrane. Although the journal's purpose was to shift the aim of the labor movement from a revolutionary to a parliamentary one, it was nonetheless on the extreme left of the political spectrum. Ibsen agreed to write for the paper and to join Abildgaard as instructor in a Sunday School conducted by the Christiania Workers' Society.

Inevitably the movement came under the surveillance of the police, and on July 7, 1851, Thrane, Abildgaard, and several others were thrown into jail. Ibsen had no taste for this kind of scandal, and was thoroughly frightened because some of his manuscripts were in the editors' hands. He was relieved to find that the foreman in the printing shop had been quick enough to throw the manuscripts on the floor, thus deluding the police into believing they were waste paper. The Sunday School closed, "since student Ibsen did not feel able to take over the entire instruction," and when it opened again in October, Ibsen was about to leave Oslo, and Vinje took his place. Ibsen's involvement with the movement was a brief one, yet it was as much as he would ever be involved in any political activity.

The July imprisonments did not put an end to Ibsen's connection with *Arbeider-Foreningernes Blad*. Bernhard Hansen, a mason's apprentice who edited the paper until he too was jailed at the end of September, reported in later years that Ibsen had helped him with verses he tried to write. Ibsen's hand can be detected in at least two poems: "The Usurer's Complaint" (July 12) and "They Hang the Little Thieves and Let the Great Ones Go" (August 16). He may have contributed other things, but he said that what he wrote was unimportant stuff. In this extreme secretiveness there can be detected the characteristic trait of the observer, the man who prefers to avoid the uproar of participation. He would become a participator only through the characters in his works.

There are only two or three poems from the period when he served as editor of *The Man*, and there is no indication that he began a new play. *Olaf Trygvason* was abandoned and *The Grouse of Justedal* left unfinished. Insignificant pieces like *Norma*, a political satire in quasi-dramatic form, and humorous passages in three chapters of "The Hatmakers' Feud in Ringerike" can hardly be considered exceptions. His articles written for *The Man* fill no more than 65 pages of the collected works; and there are 13 additional pages of material written for *Samfundsbladet*. The reasons for this paucity of original composition during these months are not clear. Perhaps an answer lies in the effect of Heiberg's aesthetic theories on him. He had planned to write historical plays, but he read that Heiberg considered them undramatic—not even Goethe could be rated a true dramatist, and Schiller was out completely. The tyro playwright might well have paused, even though he had discovered that the drama was his favorite form of composition.

The opportunity to see regular repertory theatre and not just visiting troupes was crucial in this discovery, even though Christiania Theatre was little more than a Danish provincial showhouse, where performances were limited to two or three a week and where the repertory consisted of French and Danish comedies and operettas, the efforts of Scribe and Heiberg and their followers. Ibsen felt that most of this old-fashioned material should have been put to rest long ago. The only moving experiences the theatre offered were the operas of Rossini, Bellini, and Auber, but a playwright could learn little from these. One play by Holberg, *The Political Tinker*, was given, but the performance was a disappointment; some tragedies by Oehlenschläger—*Axel and Valborg*, and *Queen Margaret*—were produced, but these too offered nothing new. If he saw the lyrical pieces of the Danish writer Henrik Hertz, he does not mention it at this time, although he later (1883) attacked them. Christiania Theatre offered little he could profit by and served mainly as a goad; in his critical reviews his dissatisfaction with the theatre and with himself is evident.

His editorial work with *Andhrimner* ended on September 28, 1851; his last piece appeared on August 31. Although the experience would ultimately prove to be a valuable one, he would never again be connected with a journal. Now the road lay in a different direction; the theatre was his passion.

CHAPTER SEVEN

AT THE THEATRE IN BERGEN (1851-57)

Ibsen used the pseudonym "Brynjolf Bjarne" for the last time in July, 1851, on the poem "Helge Hundingsbane" that appeared in *Andhrimner*. His own name had already appeared in June, on the program of the Scandinavian Student Congress; the two beautiful and technically perfect songs he wrote drew the audience's attention to the young poet whose authentic Norwegian voice could be heard even in a program that included such celebrated older poets as Welhaven, Andreas Munch, and Jørgen Moe.

The public first became aware of him as a nationalistic poet, and the events of the next few months would make him a major figure in the national literature. In September, 1851, the renowned violinist and patriot, Ole Bull, pleaded before the Storting for support of the Norwegian theatre he had established in Bergen the year before. But the Storting was deaf to his exhortation that a truly native theatre was in the country's best interest, and refused any financial aid. Bull, however, had supporters; *Andhrimner* devoted its last issue to satires on the Storting's purblind views, and Vinje wrote verses in honor of the patriot in *Morgenbladet*. But more important than the consolation of verse was the chance Bull had to meet Ibsen. Bull knew immediately that he had found the man to serve as playwright in his new theatre.

As a poet, Ibsen had drawn on Norwegian history and folklore, but he was a severe critic of those who expected a Norwegian national theatre to come into being immediately after hiring actors who happened to speak Norwegian—in plays that had no artistic value at all. If the theatre-goers of Oslo had such poor taste that they praised the worthless *The Fairy's Home,* their demands for a "national theatre" could not be taken seriously. Good plays written by poets of integrity were the first requisite. He also pointed out that it was nonsensical for dilettantes to rhapsodize about the romance of Norwegian nationalism while they

supported a theatre whose official stage language was still pure Danish.*
(This irrationality was confirmed when the Dane Carl Borgaard was
appointed manager of the theatre.) Ole Bull's daring plan for the Bergen
theatre seemed to Ibsen to promise hope for achieving the ideals he had
set: valid art, and authentic Norwegian art. Bull's enthusiasm easily convinced Ibsen that together they could create a new theatre.

The national theatre quickly became a topic of controversy. The
issue was debated at a meeting of the students' Literary Society, where
the song writer Andreas Borchgrevink (who used the pen name "Per
Studiosus") gave a ludicrous account of a visit to Bull's theatre; poor
stagecraft and worse dramaturgy were thinly disguised under a heavy
layer of patriotic sentiment. Ibsen leapt up to make a rebuttal, his face
(as a spectator reported) speaking "the unmistakable language of
anger." In the Student Society a proposal was made by the composer
Johannes D. Behrens, and seconded by many others, that a musical evening be held to raise money for Bull's theatre and to protest the obstinacy
of the Storting. After sharp debate an overwhelming majority approved
the motion, and the musical evening arranged for October 15, 1851, in
the Masonic Temple (Frimurerlogen) turned into a notable occasion.
Ole Bull performed on the violin, Emma Dahl sang operatic selections,
and three local choruses were heard — the Student Chorus, the Merchants' Chorus, and the Craftsmen's Chorus. The house, which could
accommodate a thousand, was sold out and many had to be turned
away. Three hundred dollars was raised for the theatre, and Ibsen
scored his first poetic triumph.

The verse prologue he wrote was read "with great feeling and spontaneity" by Laura Svendsen, the young actress who had played Blanka
in The Warrior's Barrow the year before. He also contributed a song,
set to "grand and impressive music by Ole Bull," that was sung by the
three-chorus ensemble. Never before had the young poet been given
such prominence and his "handsome poems" were praised in the newspapers. Even his home town was proud of him; the Skien Correspondenten ran a notice of his triumph and carefully noted that "Mr. Ibsen
is a son of Merchant Knud Ibsen of Skien."

He had already agreed to accept Bull's offer before the musical evening; the prospect of a salary was an added incentive, since most of the
writing he had done in Oslo was without payment. Before the end of
October he was in Bergen. On November 6 a contract was signed; he
was to "assist the theatre as a dramatic author" and was to be paid
twenty dollars a month during the six month season.

---

*See Translators' Note: "Norwegians and Danish Speech," in References, Chapter
Seven.

He began his work for the theatre by writing a prologue for the performance of November 17, a benefit for the Student Society's building fund, and another for the anniversary of the theatre on January 2, 1852. Even if he had no plays ready for the theatre, he could serve it as poet—and as defender against hostile critics. Paul Stub, at one time Ibsen's tutor in Norwegian, attacked the theatre in the Bergen newspapers and treated Ibsen's first essays as though they were classroom exercises. Ibsen retorted with as much arrogance and lectured his former teacher on the art of writing theatre criticism. Ibsen's articles in *The Man* left something to be desired, but he had read much since then and now displayed his knowledge to advantage; he also had many valid things to say about the duties of a drama critic. Thus he first appeared before the Bergen public as a very self-assured young student. He would learn before he left Bergen that his schooling was not over.

The directors of the theatre quickly discovered that keeping a writer who had no steady task was an expensive business. They decided to grant him 200 dollars so that he could go to Denmark and Germany at the end of the season to study stage techniques. He would then have to work as a stage manager and director, under a five-year contract at 300 dollars a year. This trip, his first abroad, lasted for three and a half months and had important results as far as his understanding of the practical aspects of theatre was concerned. His ideas on playwriting were also affected by what he learned on the trip.

He left Bergen on April 15, in the company of two of the theatre's most promising actors, Johannes Brun and his wife Louise, who were to be his informal students on the trip. They went by way of Hamburg to Copenhagen and Ibsen's first report to the directors of the theatre, dated April 25, describes their cordial reception: "The Danes are remarkably polite and helpful, and far from feeling any ill will because we are trying to free ourselves of their influence, they are actually surprised that we didn't do so long ago." He had a letter of introduction to the director of the Royal Danish Theatre, J. L. Heiberg, from an old acquaintance in Bergen, the City Judge Chr. R. Hansson, who had literary interests. Heiberg invited him to dinner once shortly before his departure, but Ibsen had little opportunity to converse with his host. The dinner was an elegant affair, and he thought it a great honor to be asked by an author he had so long admired, but he was disappointed that the "Etatsråd" (Councillor of State) did not speak about literature or politics, but devoted himself to "problems of culinary interest."

Heiberg turned him over to the stage manager Th. Overskou, and he was able to study the stage machinery and layout of the theatre. When

Overskou described the young man as "a tight-lipped little Norwegian with watchful eyes" he hit him off perfectly. Ibsen was keeping his eyes open to see how things were done. At the same time he hired a dancing teacher so that his actors could learn "how to look graceful on stage"; and he bought paintings, plays, and music for use in the theatre—all on a very small budget. He also spoke to playwrights in the city in hope of getting them to write for the theatre in Bergen. He met Chr. Hostrup, who later recalled him as "a rather obscure young man with a quiet, retiring manner"; he spoke with Hans Christian Andersen who, as he noted later, advised him to go on to Vienna where he himself had recently gotten the inspiration for a short series of folk-tale comedies.

Life in Copenhagen was stimulating, particularly the theatre, and although he seems to have led a rather solitary life during his stay, he did use the pass to the Royal Theatre that Heiberg had given him. Ibsen wrote home that he and the Bruns had been "lucky as far as the repertory went," seeing four comedies by Holberg, Oehlenschläger's *Hakon Jarl* and *Dronning Margareta,* and for the first time a series of plays by Shakespeare, including *Hamlet* and *King Lear.* The acting was particularly good, since this was a great era in the history of Danish acting. Ibsen saw Johanne Luise Heiberg, then at her best, in both tragic and comic roles—in Hamlet, in Holberg's *The Inconstant One,* in Oehlenschläger's *The Varangians in Miklagard,* in Hertz's *King René's Daughter.* He also saw the great tragedian Michael Wiehe, who appeared opposite Madame Heiberg in *King René's Daughter,* and the young Fredrik Høedt, who had broken with the old, stylized acting and was trying to create a new, realistic method.

He stayed in Copenhagen for a while after the season ended in order to study stage machinery more conveniently, and on June 6 set out for Dresden alone. He was virtually unknown in Dresden, although a month earlier a German theatrical journal had printed a notice that "Student H. Ibsen" of Bergen had received a stipend to study theatre art. He was befriended by a countryman, the well-known painter Professor Johan Christian Dahl, who arranged for him to study the staging and machinery at the Court Opera, but Ibsen could not take much advantage of this opportunity, since he had to pay for his tickets, and his money was too low to permit him to go often. He did see *Hamlet* and was able to compare the free acting style of the German who played the title role with the performance he had seen in Copenhagen. Perhaps more important than the theatre was the impression made on him by the Royal Picture Gallery, where a new world of beauty opened up to him.

The most significant experience in Dresden was his reading of *Das Moderne Drama,* a recently published book by the young German critic

Hermann Hettner. Here Ibsen found an answer to all the doubts that Heiberg had aroused in him. Hettner called his book "aesthetische Undersuchungen," although it was actually an exhortation to young German actors to take their profession seriously. It was also a manifesto and a program for reform in the theatre. Various types of drama—historical tragedy, middle-class drama, and comedy—are analyzed and the same goal is set for each: the pursuit of a high ideal. Hettner detested the usual historical drama of his day. He accepted it as valid tragedy only insofar as it was capable of becoming a psychological drama of character that showed the kind of conflict of opposing forces a contemporary audience could respond to. Thus the only difference between historical and modern drama was that they took their themes from different ages and societies. Their goals were the same; their methods must therefore be the same. In each case he called for the elimination of coincidence, of intrigue, or anything else that obscured or weakened the central issue—the struggle of conflicting forces in the soul. In comedy, chance and intrigue were valid, but even in comedy the emphasis must be on character and dramatic conflict.

Ibsen felt that Hettner had clarified his own ideas for a new drama. In *Catiline* he had tried to create a historical tragedy on these very principles, and now he felt justified—in following the instinctive urge that made him build the catastrophe as an inevitable consequence of the hero's will and guilt. He wanted *Catiline* to be a genuine psychological drama. If he did not totally succeed, it was because he was not yet strong enough to free himself of literary influences, nor had he learned enough through bitter experience. Both would eventually happen, and then his work would be born of inner strife and need. For now, Hettner kept his determination alive and taught him to set standards he would have to struggle to fulfill.

After Dresden his funds were too low to permit him to go on to Berlin and Hamburg (Vienna was out of the question) as he had planned, and he returned to Bergen at the end of July. In evaluating his subsequent work at the theatre, one must remember that he was never the director or manager of the theatre, and therefore his artistic taste or judgment cannot be measured by the kind of plays that were put on. He was allowed to make suggestions, but no one was obliged to follow them. Final decisions were made by the directing board of the theatre, in conference with the inspector, or the artistic director. The man who held this position was a university graduate, Herman Laading, who had been appointed in October, 1851, shortly before Ibsen came to Bergen, and was now Ibsen's superior.

In the actual direction of plays, Laading's function was that of "role instructor" *(rolleinstruktør);* he was to read through the play with the actors and direct them in the creation of the various parts. Ibsen was the "scene instructor" *(sceneinstruktør);* his task was to block the roles on stage, to mark entries and exits and actors' places, and to supervise dialogue. This is what Ibsen had learned from Overskou in Copenhagen. He would remain essentially a stage manager in the theatre.

It was not easy to keep the functions of the two instructors separate, and the two men were not always on friendly terms. Laading was well-educated and fifteen years older than Ibsen; he naturally insisted on exercising control. In addition, he had a quick temper. Ibsen was sensitive and easily wounded, and he too could fly off the handle. He is said to have challenged Laading to a duel, but the directing board arbitrated and the duel was given up—fortunately for Ibsen since Laading was a competent fencer and an outstanding pistol shot. The two men continued to work together and in time Laading came to like his young assistant. The question of reorganizing the directorial branch of the theatre was posed many times, but the only change made was to define more carefully the areas of responsibilities for each instructor.

As stage manager Ibsen also had supervision of costumes, properties, and decor. It took some time before he learned to master these details, but he was as conscientious and as anxious to fulfill his duty as he had been in Grimstad. He had trouble with estimates and budgets in the first years, but he managed to keep his books in order. One of these, from the season of 1852-53, is still extant, and its neat handwriting and scores of sketches of sets and properties are an indication of his painstaking care. He was learning the art of the theatre from the bottom up; he wrote to Laading in 1875, "Yes, those years in Bergen were indeed my apprentice years!"

At the theatre Ibsen went about his work in his usual quiet, withdrawn manner. Wrapped usually in a wide, rather worn cape, he padded about behind the scenes, pale and tight-lipped, rarely speaking and rarely spoken to. Even the bold and flippant Lucie Johannesen (later Lucie Wolf) did not dare approach him. Her remarks about him are characteristically disrespectful, but they also indicate that she held him in some awe: "Look how he shrinks into his cape, and look how it swells out all over. Those are the great ideas he is hatching; they're all there, ready to burst out; they want to fly out into the world."

He was also shy, especially when he had to correct or discipline the actresses. He did not like liberties taken with an author's work and kept close watch that every word and direction was followed precisely.

Although he said little at rehearsals, his taste was sound. Shortly after he began working, he met a young actress who had married and left the theatre. She greeted him on the street and said in her snippiest Bergenese: "So, Student Ibsen, you're the one who's going to teach Johannes and Luise and the others to play theatre! Well, God help you, and good luck." Ibsen answered with his sad smile: "Yes, good lady, I'll need God's help. I'm just learning myself—but if you don't tell the others maybe they won't notice." But he knew that they had noticed. During a rehearsal he whispered to a young actress: "Did you hear how false that line sounded?" The actress answered: "Why don't you tell her, Mr. Ibsen?" All he could reply was: "Who can say, Miss Jensen?" The fact was that this was not part of his job; Laading, the "role instructor," was supposed to take care of such problems.

For the first three or four years in Bergen he kept very much to himself. He lived first at Mrs. Helene Sontum's hotel in Tollbualmenningen, and even when he moved into two rooms in the theatre annex in May, 1853, he continued to have dinner there. He was treated like a son by the Sontums and remained a life-long friend of the family. He was invited out even by the best families, but he did not like to visit and was a rather cold and aloof guest, although proper and quite presentable. He had not a single friend to share his interests, and when he openly complained, it was of this; he would always be alone, no one cared for him, no one believed in him. In 1875 he gave this interpretation to his lonely period: "I was then in a state of ferment that did not allow me to be close or open with anyone." He was in some degree struggling with himself, and he did at times lash out against the restraints that duty and social conventions placed on him; for the most part he accepted in silence the values of his environment, the upper bourgeoisie of Bergen. He actually feared he would not meet their standards of elegance. Magdalene Thoresen, his future mother-in-law, said in her forthright manner that when he first came to Bergen he looked like a "shy little marmot," comically anxious about his appearance. He overdressed, wore a frilled shirt front and lace cuffs, and was even seen on the streets sporting yellow kid gloves. He could hardly make ends meet on the 25 dollars he made each month and his "fine clothes" were necessarily old-fashioned. He was pathetically defenseless and worried about looking ridiculous.

New debts began to augment the ones he already had. But he had no choice but to try to live up to society's expectations. At work too he began to feel the same pressure to conform. He lacked the strength of

will to break with this society, and so at times he could even imagine
he was serving his own purposes when he knew in his heart that he
was simply being used.

The program on which the theatre had been founded called for the
creation of a Norwegian theatre. However unclear Ole Bull, the founder,
had been about details, he understood the main point; merely substituting Norwegian actors for Danish would not produce the total change
he envisioned. But there were many obstacles to Bull's plan, including
lack of comprehension of those he had put in charge. There was no
systematic encouragement of the Norwegian elements in spoken dialogue; nearly everything except the actual sounds and intonation was
Danish. Herman Laading was a director of the old school and taught
the actors to declaim rather than to speak naturally, and it is easy to
believe that some of the strife between him and Ibsen was caused by
difference of opinion on this subject. By making the actors enounce
according to spelling Laading encouraged a stiff and un-colloquial diction that had nothing in common with everyday speech. Only rarely
would Norwegian dialect be used on stage, as when Johannnes Brun
played the peasant in Holberg's *Jeppe of the Hill* in the Sogn dialect.
A further problem was the complete lack of Norwegian plays in the
repertoire. Holberg, an eighteenth century Dano-Norwegian writer, was
the most Norwegian playwright available. In Bergen as in Oslo the stage
was dominated by the operettas of the Dane Heiberg and Danish versions of Scribe's intrigues. Ibsen had to mount these, together with such
trash as *The Fairy's Home*, no matter how distasteful he found it.

This was the situation he had been appointed to remedy. *Bergens
Stifstidende* for November 20, 1851, added this note of welcome to a
drama criticism: "Mr. Ibsen has been appointed theatre poet, and now
that he knows our theatre, we hope we may have from his hand some
national plays, suitable to our resources that will give our stage its
national identity." He knew what his obligation was, and had already
announced his own program in the prologue written for the fund-raising
concert held in October, 1851. He would help restore the era of the court
poets, the *skalds*, who interpreted the lives of the heroes to the people,
the old heroic past when poetry and action were one. He envisioned a
poetry that would steel the people and give them the will to achieve
great new things:

> Thi Kunsten er en Harpes Sangbund lig,   For Art is the sounding board of the harp
> Der Lægger Kraft i Folkesjælens Strenge,   That reinforces the strings of the nation's soul

For at dens Tone, svulmende og rig,	And makes its melody, rich and
Kan Klinge Kraftig og vibrere længe!	swelling,
	Ring out with strength and long
	resound.

He wanted to summon up the "rich images of the distant past," the "melodies of woods and meadows," "the beautiful visions of vale and mountain," the whole world seen in "the life and labor of our people."

This program for a truly national romantic drama was restated year after year in the prologues he wrote for the National Theatre in Bergen. Time after time, perhaps too often in too similar language, he spoke of the intimate connection between art and the people, and of the obligation literature had to present the life of the nation. He wanted to make live on stage the very spirit of the nation, whatever it was that made the people one with their homeland.

CHAPTER EIGHT

FROM *SAINT JOHN'S NIGHT* TO *LADY INGER* (1852-54)

ONE PLAY A YEAR, to be performed on the theatre's anniversary day, January 2; this was the obligation Ibsen had assumed. He was not expected to have anything ready for the anniversary in 1852, but for the next year and every one after that, there had to be a play.

In the enthusiasm and confidence of his youth he had no doubt imagined that it would be easy to fulfill this obligation, and thought that dramatic themes would come crowding in on him. But years were to pass before he found the right form for the ideas that struggled within him. All he had lived through since he wrote *Catiline* was fermenting within, but there was not yet a proper outlet. In the poem "In the Picture Gallery" (published in 1859) he recalls the summer of 1852 when he walked in the Dresden gallery and "drank enthusiasm from the well of its riches." The great art there had moved him so deeply that he felt his own soul grow strong and courageous, ready to "crush the demon Doubt within my heart." The black spirit of Doubt had whispered to him that his inspiration was nothing but the autumn wind rustling in the dry leaves, his writing nothing but imitation. He might comfort himself with Heiberg's teaching that in art one need not ask "what," but rather "how." He knew this was no answer; a personal content, an idea, and a will had to infuse the outer form if the work were to come alive. So far the idea and the will were not personal to him, but borrowed and external.

On his return from abroad he finished the play he intended for January 2, 1853, *Saint John's Night*. It is difficult to evaluate its place in his intellectual and artistic development, and Ibsen's later statements about it further obscure the issue. In 1897, when Julius Elias, the editor of the collected works in German, was urging Ibsen to include the play, he received an angry protest against reprinting "that trash." Ibsen wrote: "The play is a wretched thing, not really from *my* hand. It is built on a poor, dilettantish draft sent to me by a fellow student, which I revised and put my name to, but which I cannot now possibly claim.... Far from explaining my later work, it is quite without connection; I have thus regarded it for many years as unwritten and non-existent."

What he did not mention in the letter is how the fellow student came to send him the draft. He did, however, reveal to Henrik Jæger that he himself had asked a friend to collaborate on a comedy. This friend was a fellow examinee for the Artium in 1850, Theodor Bernhoft, son of a writer. He was only 19 in 1852, and deeply interested in the theatre. Jæger apparently thought the collaboration was refused, but the two young men evidently discussed the idea of the play and Bernhoft then prepared a first draft. Ibsen is therefore more responsible for the draft than his letter to Elias suggests, and in an 1863 application for a subsidy, he lists the play without reservation as one of his works.

Since the basic idea was his, he was able to appropriate the draft without protest from Bernhoft and finish the play as his own. But his evaluation of it is accurate; the action is confused, the dialogue is tedious, and the inserted poems have little vitality. On the whole it is an uninspired, "made-to-order" piece. The play, described as a "fairy-tale comedy," has a mixed cast of brownies (nisser) and elves and human beings, and has many literary ancestors: Oehlenschläger's *St. John's Eve Play;* romantic fairy comedies by Heiberg and Hans Christian Andersen; and the popular *Master and Apprentice* by Chr. Hostrup, which Ibsen probably saw in Copenhagen. The theme of the contrast between genuine and false romanticism was probably derived from *The Fairy Wedding* which Botten Hansen had written for *Andhrimner,* at the same time as Ibsen was developing the idea for the comedy. The major influence on the work, however, is Shakespeare's *Midsummer Night's Dream;* the Norwegian *nisse* here take over Puck's role of opening men's eyes to the unseen powers of life.

The theme of the play is that only the innocent and the naive can make contact with the deepest truth in life, the truth that is revealed only in folklore. (Ibsen expressed the same idea in his sonnets of 1850 where he emphasized the superiority of poetry and spirit to dry bourgeois prose.) In stressing the need for an innocent naturalness, Ibsen ridicules all who pretend to be "poetic" by tricking themselves out in stilted "nationalistic" phrases, but who are ignorant of both the life and poetry of the people. He also attacks those who wish to revive the "ancient Norse tongue" and claim to speak "new Norse," but in such a way that they are unintelligible. Here Ibsen was alluding to the language controversy that had just broken out in Norway.* But although he advocated an authentically Norwegian culture, the elements that make

---

* See Translators' Note: "Language Reform," in References, Chapter Eleven.

up *Saint John's Night* are not particularly Norwegian. The ballads, for example, are based on Danish and Swedish models. (Landstad's collection of Norwegian ballads was not to appear until 1853.) What is significant about the play is that it stressed the need for a genuine cultural ideal, as opposed to literary or political artifice.

In spite of its limitations as a work of art, *Saint John's Night* is important because it foreshadows many later developments. Specific instances can be pointed out; for example, the short poem in ballad style that suggests "Solveig's Song," but more important is the unmistakably Ibsen style of satire. Julian Paulsen, the poet who mouths cliches from Heiberg and Kierkegaard—"To love is to long for love"—is a caricature who will be fully developed in Peer Gynt and Hjalmar Ekdal. Paulsen's "demonic" temperament and his romantically schizoid personality will be more adequately caricatured in Molvig in *The Wild Duck*. Julian's last words about the differences between being in love and being engaged and married will be used as a theme of *Love's Comedy*. Although he rejected *Saint John's Night*, Ibsen would return to many of its ideas and use them later in a more perfect form.

For the opening performance Ibsen wrote a prologue in which he praised the theme of homeland and asked for "leniency" for the poetry being presented:

> Husk, at ikkun Fod for Fod   Remember, only foot by foot
> Kan en Kunstnerbane brydes!   Can an artist make his way.

But the audience was not lenient. They had come with great expectations, eager to see what the student from Oslo had to offer. The theatre had gone to the expense of making new sets. The debut of the new Norwegian drama was to be a festive occasion and the house was sold out. But instead of festivity there was fiasco, with whistling and shushing where there should have been applause. When the play was again performed three days later, the benches were empty; it was never put on again.

His first attempt to create a national drama was a failure, and though Ibsen had not given much of himself in the play, he must have felt the disappointment keenly. Worse—he had nothing new to offer for the 1854 anniversary. The best he could do was return to *The Warrior's Barrow*, the one-act play performed in 1850 at Christiania Theatre.

In reworking the play, he left the plot just as romantic and irrational as before, but verse and dialogue underwent radical change, dictated now by his desire to probe into the psychological conflict between paganism and Christianity. He removed much of the sentimentality and the Oehlenschläger influence. Instead of using words for their "poetic" resoundings, he searched for words that would give an honest interpretation of the characters' feelings. The work was more nearly a drama now, and its romanticism of a different sort.

Nevertheless, it too failed. In Oslo there had been three performances; in Bergen there was one, with a single repeat two years later. One of the newspapers, *Bergenske Blade,* then printed it as a serial, and thus it became Ibsen's second play to be published. But no one was interested.

Ibsen's reasons for rewriting *The Warrior's Barrow* may have been personal. It has been noted that Blanka was probably modeled on a girl he loved during his last year in Grimstad; now he was in the midst of a new love, one that was born in the spring and blossomed in the summer:

—hun er et Markens Friluftsbarn,	—she is a girl of the open air,
Og sexten Skjærsommere gammel!	And only sixteen summers old!

Her name was Rikke (Henrikke) Holst, and she was not quite sixteen. When he met her at Madame Sontum's, Ibsen was immediately interested, since she was a cousin of one of the Grimstad girls he had flirted with. She was pert and vivacious and he was captivated by her sparkling brown eyes. He bought her pastries, sent flowers, and walked with her; here at last he found someone with whom he could talk about his hopes and his disappointments. The effect on his poetry was immediate. In "Wild Flowers and Potted Plants" he explains why he could not act rationally and pick "one of the average ladies" for his love. The "great plan" he had in Grimstad—"to become one of the immortals" —has given way to the "little plan"—"to own a lovely maid."

Det Store blev saa lidet, det Lille blev mig Alt.	The great plan turned to nothing; the little to everything.

He was happy in love and relaxed for the first time since he came to Bergen. On Whitsunday, May 15, 1853, he made an excursion with a group of young people to the top of Ulrikken, one of the surrounding mountains—and surprised everyone by suddenly leaping to his feet and entoning a poem he had just composed, a humorous verse in the style of the old "Ballad of Sinclair" that included a delightful "prospect" of Old Bergen as seen from the air. Two days later in the Constitution Day celebration, he led the men of the theatre (women were excluded from such events) in the parade. They wore tasseled Hungarian caps of grayish-green in honor of Kossuth and the Hungarian revolution, which had been exciting hopes again. At the end of the season, he and some of the actors went hiking in Voss and Hardanger (or did he perhaps just imagine this happened?). Out of this real or imagined experience came the happiest poem of his life, "Wanderer's Song," which although excluded from the collected works, got into all Norwegian song-books and is still his most popular poem. There is not one original image in the poem, and one can understand why Ibsen dropped it. Yet it does reflect a moment when his heart was full and he felt that the world was before him and that he had the courage to take it.

Rikke Holst was the happiest event to befall him in Bergen; he felt she loved him in return, and he proposed early in June, 1853, describing in a versified letter the hopes he was too shy to speak directly. Rikke went to her father for advice and he, a skipper and solid citizen, would not hear of an engagement for his young daughter—after all, she was not yet confirmed. He forbade her to keep company with the penniless poet, a man ten years her senior who should have had more sense. But the two saw each other anyway and went walking in the Nygård Allé and out to the headland at Nordnes, where they sealed their engagement in true romantic fashion by tying their rings together and tossing them out into the fjord, where they would never be parted.

Ibsen was happy, though not a little afraid. Although they persuaded a girl friend of Rikke's to keep watch for them and frequently took Rikke's five-year-old brother with them as proof that all was proper, the father found them out. Her brother, Lars (later a well-known journalist), once told the author of this book how he remembered his father rushing after the couple with raised arms and clenched fists. "His face was livid with anger," Rikke later said. Ibsen ran, and her love died. Thirty years later, after each had been married many years, Ibsen met her on one of his visits to Bergen. Some of the old feeling came back to him and he asked, wonderingly: "But how was it nothing came of our affair?" Rikke laughed in her old, vivacious way: "But my dear Ibsen, did you forget that you ran away?" "Yes, yes," he answered, apologetically, "I was never a brave man face to face."

He put it a little less bluntly in the poem "A Birdsong," written when the affair was over. Perhaps the most charming of all his lyrics, it recalls the beautiful day in the allé, when—

Jeg malte Tankebilleder	I painted images
Med broget Farvespil,	In many colors
Hun stirred stille for sig hen	She gazed quietly into the
Og lyttede dertil.	Sky and listened.
Men vi—vi tog et smukt Farvel	But we—we said a fond goodbye
Og mødtes aldrig mer.	And never met again.

It was hard to have lost her, and even worse to have shown such little courage. Now he went from intense joy to awful dejection. When he walked the same paths alone in the next spring, he imagined the birds whispering of what he had lost. Two or three years later, in the poem "My Young Wine," he tries to jest about his first love's engagement to another (Rikke was married on June 12, 1856), but the bitter tone shows that he had not forgotten even then.

It was shortly after the break with Rikke that he most probably wrote the poem cycle "In the Picture Gallery," the most dejected of all his poetry. When he collected his poetry in 1871, he included from this cycle such poems as "Afraid of the Light," "The Gorge," and "A Swan," all permeated with:

...de ængstelige Tanker,	...the anxious thoughts
Der vugge Sindet mellem Frygt og Haab,	That toss the soul between fear and hope,
Og vække Tvivl og Tro paa Kaldets Daab.	Arousing doubt and faith in one's calling.

Slowly he bore through this pain and out of the struggle came a new drama, the first genuinely personal expression since *Catiline;* he said in a letter in 1870 that the origin of *Lady Inger of Østråt* (1854) was "the quickly formed and quickly ended love affair," with Rikke. The statement has been a source of trouble for Ibsen scholars and some have felt that Ibsen was actually referring to a later play, *The Feast at Solhaug.* However, this latter play is mentioned in the same letter as also having "a personal background." We shall have to take his word for it and try to determine what he meant.

Most students of Ibsen have assumed that the personal note in *Lady Inger of Østråt* lies in the love affair, running through all five acts, between Lady Inger's daughter Eline and Nils Lykke. Eline dreams of an irresistible knight, but also speaks proudly of avenging her dishonored sister and restoring the honor of her country. She meets her knight and gives herself to him totally and blindly, even though he is the one who has betrayed her sister and kept Norway under Danish rule. The notion of an irresistible love may have reference to Ibsen's affair with Rikke, but there is little of that gay young girl in the proud Eline, "now pensive and pale, now wild and passionate." If Ibsen felt that the relation between Eline and Nils Lykke, the knight, was the basis for the whole play, he probably would have given it more central importance in the drama; as it stands the love theme appears in each act, yet is peripheral to the main action.

On the other hand, a Dutch scholar, Clara Stuyver, has maintained that Lucie, Lady Inger's elder daughter, who committed suicide after her betrayal by Nils Lykke, represents Rikke. Lucie's temperament is more like Rikke's than Eline's, but obviously their stories have nothing in common. It seems more probable that Ibsen's love is reflected in Lady Inger's youthful affair with Sten Sture. Although brief and chaotic, the

affair had consequences for her entire life, not only in the son she bore
Sture, but in the sense of guilt that forever sapped her strength and her
will. She wanted to avenge her nation's dishonor, but, weak as any
woman, she fell in love, with a man from the enemy's side. The inner
conflict she suffers was Ibsen's too, and thus he dramatizes it in his central character, using as he often does for special effect, a female to portray himself. (He makes her a particularly forthright and "masculine"
person, however.) Lady Inger is therefore not only a spokesman in the
debate over Norway's cultural independence; she dramatizes the problem of love and the mortifying sense of defeat Ibsen felt over his cowardice. In addition to presenting this conflict, he was also able to
recapture the tenderness of his love affair in the relation between Eline
and Nils Lykke.

The answer to the further question of why he chose Lady Inger for
protagonist can be found in the historical situation at the time he wrote
the play. He called the work a "historical drama," one that tried to
epitomize the Norwegian struggle against Danish hegemony which was
such a burning issue of his day. There was a growing concern in the
1850's with the question of why Norway had lost her independence in
the late Middle Ages. In every field scholars sought bridges between
medieval and modern Norway; history, ballads, folktales, music, and
language made clear that a nation had survived the intervening times
of darkness. But why had the nation bowed to foreign domination? To
discover the nation that had existed in the past and to make it live again
in the future became the quest of historians, scholars, and men of letters.
They felt their work was a matter of life and death for the whole people,
a question of its very will to exist.

Two figures had been singled out by historians as the major leaders in
the Norwegian struggle for independence in the late Middle Ages. One,
Sir Knut Alvsson, had been treacherously murdered by Henrik Krum-
medige in 1502; the other, Herlog Hudfat, was executed by King Christiern II in 1508. Ibsen had already evoked their memories in the poem
he wrote at Akershus in 1850, basing his work on Andreas Munch's
story of Alvsson's murder ("En Aften paa Akershus Slot," in *Billeder
fra Nord og Syd,* Christiania, 1849). His thoughts now returned to these
old memories, "gripped by a quiet shudder." The old royal hall in Bergen, Haakonshallen, a counterpart to Akershus in Oslo, impressed its
"golden harvest of memories" on him and turned his thoughts to that
past golden age and the contrasting decline. In the spring of 1854 he
went with the actors to Trondheim, the third of the three medieval capital cities, where the company gave a month-long guest appearance.

Near that city had been the manor of Lady Inger (or Ingerd, as she spelled it) Ottesdatter of Østråt; thus the theme of his play could have come to him.

In 1838, P. A. Munch, the great Norwegian historian, had indicated that Lady Inger could have led the uprising for independence. If Ibsen took this hint from Munch, it would not be the last time he felt the historian's influence. Other historical works emphasized the importance of Lady Inger and her era. In the spring of 1854, the Danish historian C. Paludan-Müller published the second volume of *Grevens Feide,* in which he recounted the efforts of the Danish nobleman Vincents Lunge and the last Norwegian archbishop, Olav Engelbriktsson, to sustain Norwegian independence within the Scandinavian union. As a prologue to his account, Paludan-Müller described the attempts of the archbishop and Lady Inger to aid the rebellion Peder Chancellor had raised in Sweden in the name of the "Dal-Junker," who claimed to be a son of Sten Sture. Three other Danish books on the same historical matter appeared in 1854: C. F. Allen's collection of documents; J. N. Høst's somewhat romanticized account of King Christiern II; and Fr. Hemmerich's vivid picture of Norway's national stagnation in the years immediately after 1523. These works all helped to bring to life the period when Norwegian independence was finally lost, the last years before the Reformation. For Ibsen the last battle became drama.

In later years he wrote: "I was driven to steep myself in the literature and history of the Norwegian Middle Ages, especially their ending. I tried my best to enter into the spirit of the time, its customs and habits, its thinking and feeling and modes of expression." For source material he had the books mentioned above, as well as the two volumes of official documents, *Diplomatarium Norvegicum,* which had appeared by this time. Most important of all, however, were the documents relating to the "Dal-Junker" which G. F. Lundh had printed in the first volume of *Samlinger til det Norske Folks Sprog og Historie (Materials in the Language and History of the Norwegian People)* the first Norwegian historical journal (1833).

All those who have studied the relation between Ibsen's play and historical fact have based their conclusions on later research which has made it clear that Lady Inger was in no wise a national leader. But the documents Ibsen read described her as much more of a revolutionary. He colored the portrait with reminiscences from Andreas Munch's study of the widow of Sir Knut Alvsson; both she and Lady Inger dream of becoming "mother of a great dynasty." The hard fact which a modern historian must recognize is that there was virtually no nationalistic sentiment in sixteenth-century Norway, and almost no resistance to Danish rule. (The only effective opponent was the archbishop Olav Engelbriktsson.) When Ibsen wrote his play, an intensely felt nationalism was simply being projected back to the period of Norway's decline, and Denmark was being made the major villain in the national tragedy. This thinking is apparent in the notice about the play Ibsen sent to the newspapers. It concerns, he wrote, "that period of our national history when the Danes completed their suppression of Norwegian freedom...."

Twenty years later, when the problem became the center of a heated debate, the historian Ludvig Daae called the play a breviary for chauvinists. When Ibsen was preparing a new edition of his works in 1873, Daae wrote to him saying that a Norwegian writer ought to think twice before again presenting the public with a distorted picture of the late medieval era, especially since one's attitude toward many problems of the present was conditioned by one's attitude toward that period. To have bowed to such a request would have been to throw away the play entirely; Ibsen knew instinctively that the struggle for national identity was more than just a matter of accurate history. Moreover, it was not the historical but the psychological conflict that occupied him here: the human dilemma of Lady Inger. In the second edition he simply eliminated the subtitle, "historical drama."

The borrowings from *Catiline* are so extensive that one might conjecture he had dismissed the play entirely and was rescuing whatever of value there was in it. Parallels are numerous: the relationship between Nils Lykke and the sisters Eline and Lucie is a variation on that between Catiline and the vestal virgins, Furia and her sister; the action of the entire five acts again takes place in a single night; and most importantly, the same contradiction between will and action, the basic theme of *Catiline*, is repeated. The conflict in Catiline's two women has been incorporated into the portrait of one character, Lady Inger.

Shakespeare's influence is quite apparent in the play. As far as is known, Ibsen was first exposed to the playwright on his trip abroad in 1852. By 1855 he was familiar enough with him to select the theme "Shakespeare and His Influence on Scandinavian Art" for his first lecture to a Bergen literary society. (The lecture is not extant, but one can imagine that it dealt mostly with the influence Shakespeare *ought* to have on Norwegian or Nordic dramatic art.) He had also just been working on a Shakespearian production at the theatre. Although the influence is a rather diffuse one in the play, certain specific echoes can be detected: the opening exchange between two servants suggests the

grave-digger scene in *Hamlet;* the psychological analysis owes something to *Macbeth* and more particularly to *Hamlet,* for the study of one
whose will is made sickly with the "pale cast of thought." Hamlet particularly intrigued Ibsen, for here he found himself mirrored—the man
who hears the call to perform great deeds and still doubts his ability to
achieve them.

This is Lady Inger's dilemma. Over the corpse of Knut Alvsson she
has sworn to devote her life to vengeance and the struggle for her
country's freedom. "I felt the strength of the Lord in my breast and
from that day I believed and all believed that Heaven had marked me
as leader of the sacred cause." But self-doubt prevents her from following the call: "Woe, woe to one who has a great calling in life, and no
strength to follow it. It is said: the woman shall leave father and mother
and cling to her husband. But the one who is marked as Heaven's in-
strument dares to hold nothing dear—neither husband nor child, kins-
men nor home. This, you see, is the curse of the chosen one." Not able
to dedicate her life exclusively to her mission, she loved and bore children. The standard of revolt was raised by Herlog Hudfat, and a springtide of hope rose in the land. But she kept apart: "I...I waited in doubt,
far from the conflict, on my lonely manor. At moments God himself
seemed to call me to arms for my people; but I hesitated, and again
mortal terror fell on me. 'Whose victory?' The question was asked and
asked in my ear, and my will froze."

We recognize the conflict as Ibsen's, but there is more than autobiography here. He was answering Hermann Hettner's call for a psychological tragedy of character, now set in the perspective of a great historical conflict that would determine the fate of the people for centuries
to come. This was genuine tragedy; unfortunately it was weakened by
the very kind of theatrical intrigue Hettner had warned against. Ibsen's
model here is probably Scribe's *Les Contes de la Reine de Navarre*
(1850), a historical drama performed at the Bergen theatre in October,
1854.

Les Contes has more of an authentic historical mood than most of
Scribe's plays, and Ibsen was no doubt attracted by the patriotic theme
developed in relation to King Francis I. Curiously enough, the events
of the play are almost exactly contemporaneous with those of *Lady
Inger.* Nevertheless, the intrigue was what interested Scribe, who regarded drama as a type of chess game. In the play the conflict between
Emperor Charles V and Marguerite, the King's sister, is symbolized by
a game of chess. Lady Inger repeats the idea: "The game of Norway's
fate is played out this night." Nils Lykke also uses the simile of a game,

this time cards. Many other details are reminiscent of Scribe—letters are confused and misdelivered, deception is added to deception, particularly in two scenes where Nils Lykke tries to trick a stranger into revealing a secret by pretending he knows it already—the same trick Lord Bolingbroke uses to outwit the Duchess of Marlborough in Scribe's *Le Verre d'Eau* (1840), which Ibsen saw more than once. The result of the intrigue is to obscure the psychological conflict, as Hettner explained, and to make moral decisions a matter of performing clever tricks, rather than of inner crisis.

But there is a great difference between Ibsen's play and Scribe. First of all, Ibsen does have a serious psychological theme, and he finally succeeds in creating live characters, men and women in conflict, who can bare their souls to us. In an effort to create a convincing historical picture he gave up verse for a vigorous, terse prose. He had moved away from Oehlenschläger and was beginning to find a new, essentially Norwegian style.

He was justifiably proud of the play. "My best play," he called it in 1857. He seems to have been proud even of the intrigue, which has worn least well. In any case, once he had mastered it in this play he never relied on intrigue again. From now on he would create his own dramatic form, one with stronger and clearer lines.

After his first two failures, he naturally felt uncertain about his new play. Peter Blytt, chairman of the board of directors, recalls that one day in the fall of 1854 Ibsen came to his home with a thick copybook under his arm. He seemed more embarrassed and uncomfortable than usual, but managed to explain that he had nothing for the anniversary except a copy of a play an anonymous friend had sent him from Oslo. He would not venture an opinion on the work himself, but wondered if the chairman would read it through and see if it was worth submitting to the board. The play was, of course, *Fru Inger til Østerraad* (as Ibsen called it then). Blytt was delighted with it, and it was accepted at once. The mystery of the authorship persisted until one day during rehearsal when Ibsen rushed from the wings in great anger, snatched away the prompt book and read one of the speeches to the actor as it should have been read. Then he apologized and "padded" out, his anger gone. Blytt noticed that he had given the speech from memory. But even when Ibsen acknowledged the play, it was announced and performed without his name.

Lady Inger was performed at the anniversary celebration on January 2, 1855, with the company's best players in the leading roles: Louise Brun as Lady Inger and Jakob Prom as Nils Lykke. Again there was failure. The audience was not impressed and it was dropped after two performances. The press ignored it until half a year later when there was a comprehensive critique in two issues of *Bergensposten*. The reviewer was mainly concerned with demonstrating that the author had not succeeded with the portrait of Lady Inger: "Neither she nor her fate attracts and moves us." He found Eline the "most interesting" character and felt some of her scenes were unquestionably beautiful. He concluded, "Several scenes have a tone, and a purity and vigor of language, that promise well for the author's literary future." He hoped the playwright would profit from his critique.

It was a well-intentioned criticism, and the writer evidently knew who the author was, although he never mentions him by name. But Ibsen was not inclined to accept advice, particularly since the reviewer had totally misunderstood his intention, especially in the case of Lady Inger. Naturally, he was disappointed, but this time he did not despair. He knew he had done a good job; his soul was in the work and the work revealed his soul. He was on firm ground now—his own.

CHAPTER NINE

BALLAD DRAMA (1855-56)

The road ahead seemed to open of itself. But the material out of which he would make his plays would not come from the late medieval era, the setting of *Lady Inger*. He had suddenly become aware of the history of Norway, and in the future would try to dramatize that. Sometime later he wrote of the historical period in which *Lady Inger* is set: "The era is rather forbidding and does not offer much material for dramatic treatment." There were actually very few sources for him to draw on for this period, and so he dug further back in time to the era of the old sagas, reading the heroic tales of the kings of Norway. He probably consulted P. A. Munch's *History of the Norwegian People,* the third volume of which, continuing the story to the reign of King Magnus Erlingson (1163-1184), had appeared in 1855. Nothing quickened into drama in his mind, but in the related group of Icelandic sagas he found what he was searching for. As he later said, "In the Icelandic sagas I found in rich measure the flesh and blood embodiment of the moods and ideas that were taking shape, more or less clearly, in my mind."

It is a curious indication of the almost total absence of national consciousness in nineteenth-century Norwegian education and cultural life that a man of Ibsen's intelligence and interests could have reached his twenty-seventh year knowing nothing of the great heritage of Icelandic sagas; he admitted that he had hardly even heard of them, and the best evidence of this ignorance is that the inspiration for his Viking play, *The Warrior's Barrow,* is drawn entirely from secondary sources, through Oehlenschläger. Now he began to read the sagas, in N. M. Petersen's four-volume Danish translation of *Historical Tales of the Exploits of Icelanders Abroad and at Home* (1839-44), which remained to the end of the century the standard edition.

So it was in Danish that Ibsen first read of the glorious deeds of Egill Skallagrimsson and Burnt Njáll, of the Eredwellers, the Laxdalers, and the Vatsdalers, of Gísli Súrsson, Gunnlaugr Ormstunga, and Grettir the Strong. Since his only previous knowledge of the saga style was from Oehlenschläger, and since his literary tastes were still largely Danish, he found Petersen's translations "excellent," at least "as far as style is concerned." It must be granted that Petersen was an improvement over Oehlenschläger; he kept the terse, pithy style of the original, drawing heavily on strong Danish folk idiom. Ibsen was particularly struck by the sagas' vivid dramatic content, their incisive characterization and mighty conflicts between man and man, woman and woman. The women especially captivated his sense of the dramatic: Hallgerd of the *Njála*, or Gudrun of the *Laxdœla Saga*, the hard Valkyrie with the wounded heart who incites others to mortal conflict with the man she loves. In contrast to her he would create the image of the peace-loving woman, tender and loyal. He began to imagine a great feasting scene where sharp-edged, taunting words were hurled and conflicts ended in life and death battles. He wanted to sum up that whole ancient world in this feast.

But not yet, not in the next play. There were distractions, most of them, as he admitted, "of a personal nature; the strongest, most decisive distractions." He never explained further, but perhaps his love for Rikke Holst was moving him toward lyric, rather than epic expression. In *Lady Inger* he had worked out the pain of their separation; the memories he he would use now were happy ones. The saga framework would, however, be useless to express these. Or perhaps he had found someone in Rikke's place. The answer is not given, but he did write love poetry again, not in simple lyrics but in dramatic form: *The Feast at Solhaug.*

Georg Brandes once said that Ibsen had had his lyrical Pegasus shot out from under him; it is conspicuous that after that summer of 1853 with Rikke he wrote amazingly few poems. Instead, his next plays were suffused with an intense lyric quality, none more so than *The Feast at Solhaug*. His first inspiration was from the ballads. "I feel sure," he wrote, "that it is significant that I was then poring over Landstad's collection of *Norwegian Ballads*, issued a couple of years before." Long before he wrote the play he had felt this hunger for a genuine Norwegian folk poetry to replace the superficially "nationalistic" trivia his contemporaries were then applauding. In *Saint John's Night*, amid all the Danish-Swedish material, he had inserted a ballad from Landstad, "Little Kersti." In *Lady Inger* he had written verses in imitation of another Landstad poem, not a ballad but a century-old poem in the Telemark dialect. Thus the theme of *The Feast* was taking shape before it assumed dramatic form in his imagination; it was not until *Lady Inger* had been completed that his fascination with the ballad momentarily swept aside both history and saga.

He gave a "literary" interpretation of the reason for his preference for ballad over history or saga in an essay written right after the play was completed, "On the Ballad and Its Significance for Art Poetry" (printed in *Illustreret Nyhedsblad* in early 1857). Comparing the dramatic potential of ballad and saga, he finds that at the present time "the ballad is far better suited for dramatic treatment than the saga." The old Icelandic saga is "a great, cold, complete, and self-contained epic, in its essence objective and foreign to the lyric spirit." He seemed to believe that he would not be able to use the sagas without infusing them with an emotional, lyric quality, a quality alien to their very nature. In the ballad, on the other hand, the lyric quality was interwoven with the epic, and "the playwright who draws his theme from the ballads does not have to transform his materials as the one who draws on the sagas must."

While the basic idea of this theory could have been derived from a noteworthy discussion of *Njála* which the Dane Carsten Hauch published in 1855, Ibsen felt there was a personal reason why he was drawn to the ballads. In 1883 he wrote, "The mood I was then in was more in harmony with the literary romanticism of the Middle Ages than with the facts of the sagas, with verse rather than prose, with musical language rather than descriptive style." It must be granted that he wrote this to defend himself from critics who considered *The Feast at Solhaug* imitative. He was determined to "establish and maintain that the present play is, to the same extent as all my dramatic writing, an inevitable expression of my life at a particular time. It arose from within, without external pressure or influence." A few years earlier, however, in 1870, when the break with his previous writing had just been made, he wrote that the play was "a study I no longer recognize as my own." This is an admission that purely literary influences were stronger in the play than personal conviction. What the "mood" he speaks of in 1883 actually was, and what personal influences shaped the play are uncertain. It does seem clear that the conflict in *The Feast at Solhaug* was not "lived through" in the way Ibsen insisted that the basic theme of his plays must be.

The play was written in the summer of 1855; Ibsen calls attention to the "light summery air that plays over the rhythms of the work." This summer lightness hovers most delicately over the figure of Signe, one of the two sisters who are the central characters in the play. In her we recognize the image of Rikke Holst—but this seems to be the only thing in the play derived from Ibsen's personal life. The rest is purely literary, convincing in its own right perhaps, but without the note of inner necessity. Ibsen has described how he took from the sagas the idea of two opposing images of woman; as he read the ballads, he found them again in individual poems. His imagination reunited them, and he sharpened the dramatic contrast by making them sisters. The Viking chieftain who would have stood between them in a saga tale is here transformed into a wandering singer. The feast that was to have merely sparked the great clash is now made the focal point of the play; the wild tragedy of the heroic age is softened to a melancholy lyricism.

John Paulsen has said that Ibsen used Magdalene Thoresen, his future mother-in-law, as the model for Margit, the older sister. Ibsen must have been acquainted with her by this time, although he never visited in her home before writing *The Feast*. While he was working at the theatre, she wrote a whole series of plays for it. If Margit is actually based on her, it is only one more proof that the play was more external than personal; he imagines her dominating her household (which Magdalene did not) and subjected to great passions, of which he could have had little direct knowledge at this time.

The criticism of the play that particularly rankled was that he had imitated Henrik Hertz's *Svend Dyrings Huus (Svend Dyring's House*, 1837). "This critical assertion is baseless and false," he protested. "Hertz never appealed to me as a dramatist. I for one can not understand how he is supposed to have influenced my plays without my being aware of it." Nevertheless, it is difficult to deny that *The Feast* probably would never had existed if *Svend Dyring's House* had not been written. As Ibsen read the Norwegian ballads, the idea must have occurred to him that one could do the same with this material as Hertz had done with Danish ballads. Whether Ibsen intended to rival Hertz's play or not, there were enough similarities—the use of the same meter and echoes of ballads throughout—to make people think Hertz was the model.

But Ibsen's theme is entirely different. It is true that both portray a young woman desperately in love with a man who is indifferent to her. In Ibsen's play the woman persists in loving the boy from her youth even though she marries another, who then falls in love with her sister. Her love thus becomes an uncontrollable force that drives her to crime, as well as an inner conflict that creates the psychological drama in the play. This conflict is no doubt patterned on the one in Scribe's comedy *Une chaîne* (1841), which Ibsen is sure to have known since it played at the Bergen theatre in his last year there. In the Scribe play a young musician shifts his love from a married woman to another, younger woman just as suddenly as in Ibsen's drama. But the Scribe influence did not lead to artificial plot intrigue; the dramatic crisis is prepared for simply and powerfully.

Further comparison of the play with *Svend Dyring's House* reveals Ibsen's advance in the direction of dramatic realism. Everything is honestly motivated; every action has its roots in personality, no witch-craft, no ghosts, no chorus of angels. There is unquestionably more vigor in Hertz's portrayal of the brute force of a wild and uncontrollable passion, but this passion is aroused by magic runes that have been intended for another:

O, I veed ikke hvad hemmelig Magt	O, you know not what hidden power
I denne Leeg med Runer blev lagt!	Was locked in this game of runes!

Ibsen's more profound handling of the theme seems almost a conscious denial of Hertz:

Hvad for en fristende, koglende Magt	What a tempting, enchanting power
Er der dog ikke i *Synden* lagt!	Is there not embedded in *sin!*

Impulses hidden within the soul are laid bare without artifice, solely through the dramatized conflict. The difference between the plays de-rives from the different way each playwright uses the ballads. Hertz took his theme from two Danish ballads, one about the use of magic runes as love charms; the other about a mother who returns to protect her children from an evil stepmother. Aside from the use of the themes, the ballad influence in Hertz is minimal. The opposite is the case with Ibsen; he invented the theme himself, rather than utilizing one from the bal-lads. But the ballad style informs the entire drama. True there are themes in ballads similar to Ibsen's; Margit herself speaks of the ballad of "Little Kersti," and there is the tale of Margit Hjukse, who was carried off by the little people in the mountains. Signe and her lover are named after the ballad of Gudmund and little Signe. On the whole, how-ever, the ballads supply a symbolic rather than a thematic background for the play.

An interesting point about Ibsen's treatment of the ballads in the play is the inspired hunch which made him place his dramatic version of them about the year 1300—the very period which later research showed to be the golden age of ballad making. Although in his essay on ballads he stated that they dated back to pagan times, he must have sensed the kinship between balladry and the Christian Middle Ages, a period previously known only through the folktales.

Almost every line of the play echoes the ballads. He had so saturated himself with them, had read them so intently, that his own personality was in danger of disappearing as it took on so intimately the style of one after another of these old songs. But this perfect recreation of the lost world of balladry is finally just a pastiche, another artifice.

The audience, however, was swept away by the poetry. When the play was performed at the annual festival in 1856, with Louise Brun as Margit, Jakob Prom as Gudmond, and the young Fredrikke Nielsen as Signe, Ibsen secured his first triumph in the theatre. He later described the night: "A splendid performance, an unusually poetic production. It was played with enthusiasm and devotion and received with the same feeling. In the packed house the spirit of 'Bergen lyricism' bloomed. Many curtain calls for actors and for author, and later that night the orchestra and many from the audience serenaded me at my lodgings. I think I was so carried away that I made a kind of speech to them all. I only know that I was enormously happy." Once he said that this was his only happy day in Bergen. After one of the next performances the actors honored him in a speech that Prom delivered. Ibsen, with his self-confidence strengthened, thanked them for "the recognition that would strengthen him in his struggle toward the goal he was trying to reach and," he added, "*would* reach."

The play was given six performances in the next few months, quite often for so small a city as Bergen; only the simple little nationalistic operetta *Til Sæters (To the Chalet)* by Claus Pavels Riis had been more popular. Ibsen would have been indignant by this kind of coupling, but it is well to remember the tastes of his audience and what they usually responded to.

The triumph was not limited to Bergen. He sent the play immediately to Christiania Theatre and it was performed on March 13. Here, too, it charmed the audience, and six performances were given that spring. He also persuaded the Oslo publisher Chr. Tønsberg to print it and it appeared on March 19, his first book to appear since *Catiline*. The play even went abroad. It was translated into Swedish by the poet F. A. Dahlgren (author of the popular folk play *Wermländningarne,* 1846), and was performed as such at the Dramatic Theatre in Stockholm on November 4, 1857, the commemoration day of the union of Sweden and Norway. (As far as can be ascertained, the only other Norwegian play previously performed there was Dahlgren's transplantation of *Til Sæters,* on November 4, 1856.) The success of *The Feast* carried *Lady Inger* in its wake, and that play was acted by traveling Swedish companies in the early 1860's. *The Feast* was performed at the

Casino in Copenhagen in 1861, with the Danish actor Vilhelm Wiehe; he had played Gudmund at Christiania Theatre and brought the play home with him. But many years were to pass before Ibsen was performed again in Copenhagen; even though the audiences were pleased, the critics saw no need for Ibsen's play when they had just had *Svend Dyring's House.*

Critics in Oslo were not too impressed either. Hartvig Lassen severely condemned it in *Aftenposten* as an imitation of Hertz. The young Bjørnstjerne Bjørnson defended it in *Morgenbladet*, however, as did Botten Hansen in *Illustreret Nyhedsblad.* But in spite of this praise, Ibsen kept for a long time his aversion to "fashionable criticism, composed by fashionable critics."

The printed play did not sell well (it took about fifteen years for the first edition to sell out), and consequently the publisher did not dare risk printing *Lady Inger.* When Ibsen got up enough courage to send it to Christiania Theatre, it was rejected. Borgaard, the Danish director of the theatre, found it "poetic, full of good characterization and strong dramatic themes." But Ibsen refused to make changes Borgaard asked for and so the play remained in his desk drawer.

He had thus tasted success and disappointment in one year after writing *The Feast at Solhaug,* but he could probably still call himself, as he had done on the night of his triumph, "enormously happy." For one thing, his social life was brightening. In the fall of 1855, Peter Blytt, chairman of the board, invited him to become a member of "The Society of December 22," a small literary and social group. On November 27 he gave his first talk, on Shakespeare, and on February 2, 1857, he spoke on the ballads. He wrote verses for the anniversary celebrations and thoroughly enjoyed the chance to meet with men who were sympathetic to his work and had faith in his ability. Now the happiness that his work needed in order to thrive had come; as he expressed it in lines written in a copy of *The Feast* sent to a lady:

> Min lille Bog er for mig en Blomst   My little book is to me a bloom
> Som jeg ret af Hjertet har kjær   That I am deeply fond of.

Part of this joy must have come from feeling that at last he had found the right field for his talents. And so it must have been at this time that he tried to write a long epic poem about the knight Audun Hugleiksson, a character in *The Feast.* The legends about the mysterious fate of Audun would have been a logical source of inspiration after working on the ballads. But the poem was too derivative and he abandoned it unfinished. He was drawn to try another ballad play, but as Bjørnson had noted, *The Feast* had translated the ballad into drama so perfectly that it could not be done twice with such success; there was no further traveling on that road.

He tried, however, experimenting with a different technique, but the effort inevitably failed. *Olaf Liljekrans* must have been conceived when he was still full of the success of *The Feast*. In early March, 1856, he left with the actors for nearly three months of guest appearances in Trondheim, but on March 31 he asked for permission to return to Bergen because the "daily tasks" prevented him from "engaging in undisturbed quiet on a work which it is of crucial importance to finish as quickly as possible." He left Trondheim three weeks later, too soon to share in the triumph of *The Feast* when it was performed at the end of May. While he was in Bergen, hard at work on *Olaf Liljekrans* he heard that the actors had "met on stage and drunk Ibsen's health at the expense of the box office."

A curious thing about this play is that while its theme is quite remote from that of *Svend Dyring's House,* it follows the ballad material much closer than *The Feast* did. The theme is taken directly from the ballad of "Olaf Liljekrans," but the ballad style and mood is not infused into the entire play. Olaf Liljekrans is a knight who is bewitched by elves into forgetting his fiancée and then dies in madness. As he had done before, he "humanizes" the story by changing the elf-maiden, who seduces Olaf, into the girl Alfhild, the same "Grouse of Justedal" he had tried to write about in 1850. This combination of folktale and ballad did not fuse and the peculiar vacillation between dream world and reality is more upsetting than in *Saint John's Night* because the theme of the play has nothing to do with this contrast. He provides a setting of saga-like family feuds and adds an intrigue of deception and misunderstanding; the result is the least stylistically consistent play he ever wrote. Alternating between saga, ballad, and "modern" realism, the play culminates in a last act which is almost a parody of stylistic confusion.

Six lines of the play still live, however, thanks to the musical setting Thorvald Lammers gave them half a century later. In the song "Sølvet det er sig saa ædelt Malm" (Silver is so noble an ore) some of the most profound notes in Ibsen's writing are sounded:

Livets Lyst er som Høstens Halm,   Life's joy is autumn straw,
Sorgen er Sølvet, det ædle Malm!   Sorrow is silver, the noble ore!

People fought to get tickets for the performance on January 2, 1857, and the house was sold out by morning. Once again Jakob Prom and

Louise Brun played the leads, and they both performed with lyric intensity. But the few brilliant lines it held could not save the play from being a helpless disaster. It was withdrawn after two performances.

The Bergen correspondent to Oslo's *Aftenbladet* wrote that he had seen the play just once, and this was "not enough to grasp all the confusion it contained." His judgment, he continued, could not be "particularly favorable to the author, who in contrast to the rich, poetic vein he seems to possess, has a shallow understanding of people and the world." In anger Ibsen wrote to the newspaper asking the reason for such a "careless and irresponsible" attack. No one answered him, and when his annoyance cooled he had to admit that the play was not worthy of his talents. He put it aside and never attempted to have it published.

That fall all ballad imitators, from Hertz to Ibsen, were silenced by Olaf Skavlan's witty parody *The Feast at Mærrahaug* ("Mare's Hill"). Romantic nationalism was strangled by caricature.

CHAPTER TEN

SUZANNAH THORESEN.
THE VIKINGS (1857)

WITH *The Feast at Solhaug* Ibsen had brought to fruition all the labor of romantic nationalism since 1840. The play heralded a new generation of Norwegian writers, whose standard bearer would be Henrik Ibsen. The play also marked a changing point in his personal life; through it he would find the strong-spirited woman who would be his companion to the end of his days.

On the night when *The Feast at Solhaug* scored such a happy success, Fru Magdalene Thoresen and her husband, the pastor of Bergen's Cross Church, were present at the theatre. As both playwright and translator of plays for the theatre, Fru Thoresen had frequently spoken with Ibsen about theatrical matters, but she had never invited him to the parsonage, where the most intelligent of the Bergen "nationalists" met. However, this evening, as she and the pastor walked home from the theatre, they decided to have the young man pay them a call.

Five days later, January 7, 1856, Ibsen visited the Thoresens for the first time. After tea he began to speak with Suzannah, the pastor's young daughter by an earlier marriage. (Her mother had been a Daae.) Just past nineteen, bright and bold and very much interested in the theatre, she captivated Ibsen at once by telling him how moved she had been by *Lady Inger of Østråt*—something nobody else had ever said. And as she spoke Ibsen interrupted her: "You are Eline now, Miss Thoresen, but you could be a Lady Inger." Neither of them forgot; more than twenty years later, when the play appeared for the first time in German, he gave her the book as a Christmas present, inscribed:

Til denne bog har Du
  ejendomsretten,
Du, some åndeligt stammer fra
  Østråt-ætten.

You, yes, you surely own this book,
You, whose spirit comes from Østråt
  stock.

What struck him most about this young girl was the breadth of spirit and will she showed. Her playmates knew the strong stuff she was made of; as children they played at theatre, often writing their own sketches, and in them Suzannah took the male roles. In one of them, a hyper-romantic thing called "The Robbers," she played the robber chieftain so realistically she drew blood—and tears—from one of the young males in the cast. "When I have the privilege of wearing a beard, I don't cry," she declared, and bore her own wound without a whimper. She loved grand and noble deeds and wished that she could take part in heroic exploits. In a letter to her brother Herman, written in 1873, she summed up her true nature: "I couldn't endure these men of jelly who lack both will and ability. The first prerequisite of manliness is energy and an unwavering will."

Ibsen was in love from the start. He invited her to a ball, but did not dare to dance with her. Before January was out he had proposed, in a poem called "To the Only One." She was the only woman he had ever met who took life seriously; in her eyes he read "dreamlike thoughts" and:

> Et Hjerte, som higer og banker   A heart that yearns and beats
> Og har ikke Livsens Fred.   And finds in life no peace.

And so he cries out to her:

> Du unge, drømmende Gaade,   Riddle of youth, of dreams,
> Turde jeg grunde Dig ud,   Dared I riddle thee out,
> Turde jeg kjækt Dig kaare   Dared I take thee straight
> Til mine Tankers Brud,   For soul-mate of my thoughts;
> Turde jeg dukke mig net i   Dared I sink deep deep into
> Dit rige, aandige Væld,   Thy soul's full treasure,
> Turde jeg skue tilbunds i   Dared I gauge full measure
> Din blomstrende Barnesjæl.   Thy blossoming, untouched soul.
>
> Da skulde fagre Digte   Then would lovely poems
> Svinge sig fra mit Bryst,   Spring up from my heart,
> Da skulde frit jeg seile   Then would I soar free,
> Som Fuglen mod Skyens Kyst.   A bird to heaven's rim.
> Og alle de spredte Syner   And every broken image
> Blev til en Enhedens Klang;   Would be one in harmony;
> Thi Livets fagreste Syner   For life's loveliest visions
> Spejled sig i min Sang.   Would be reflected in my song.

He sent the poem, and came in his finest for his answer. Solemnly he was ushered into the parlor to wait for her, but time went and Suzannah never came. He paced up and down, sat and stood, feverish, perplexed. At last, in black despair, he made for the door, only to hear a girl's ringing laughter and see a head of curls start up from behind the sofa. Ibsen got the answer he longed for.

"Only after I was married," he wrote in 1870, "did my life take on serious meaning." It happened before this, for as soon as he became engaged, he felt her influence. "Her personality is just the kind I need," he later wrote, "illogical, but naturally poetic, a great-souled way of thinking, with an almost violent hatred of all pettiness." Marriage would bring her influence to the fore, but Suzannah was so strong that he felt it even when they were just engaged.

Her influence on his thinking about Norwegian literature was deep and pervasive. Many years later, in 1894, when Ibsen spoke in honor of his mother-in-law's 75th birthday, Fru Thoresen replied to him, "It is easy for you, Ibsen. The rest of us had to toil over the sagas for years to make them say what we wanted. You had Suzannah, the living source from which you could get all you wanted of them." Ibsen had to answer, "You are right." Suzannah's spiritual home was the Norse saga and the age of heroes. As a child she was certain that she would one day be Queen of Iceland, and she read sagas and fairy-tales to her younger brothers and sisters. It was she who most probably guided Ibsen back to the old sagas, causing him to give up the ballads and infuse a bit of saga style into *Olaf Liljekrans.* The Ingeborg of this play, the girl who keeps her lover guessing while she herself arranges the abduction and marriage, may be a portrait of her. In any case, Ibsen himself has said that she was the model for those proud women with names from the old sagas, Hjørdis in *The Vikings at Helgeland,* and Svanhild in *Love's Comedy.* She was a Valkyrie, the shield-maiden who fought at his side throughout his life.

Teasingly he called her "my cat," and she gradually gathered together the small verses he addressed to her and called them her "cat poems." When he published his collected poems in 1871, she asked if he had included any of her cat poems, and he told her that if she would read one of the titles backwards she would find a "cat poem." And thus she read for the first time the new poem that summed up all she had given him: "Thanks" or *Tak,* "kat" backwards.

Hendes slægt er de skiftende skikkelsers rad, som skrider med viftende flag i mit kvad.	Her race is the motley pageant of figures Who stream through my song with banners triumphant.

It was not her philosophical spirit or her impeccable literary taste that made her his great helpmate, rather her temperament, her strength of will, her spontaneous poetry. These both spurred and steadied him; she was in fact "Storråde," or "great-minded," like Queen Sigrid of the old sagas. In daily contact with her, his spirit quickened; as she made demands on him, his own demands on himself grew more urgent and his emotional life took on a richer tone. Thus he tried to break free of the environment that had shackled him for so long; he sought a new foundation for his work and his life.

At the end of 1856 he wrote his essay on the ballads, intended as a theoretical projection of his future work. As we have seen, the essay rejects sagas as material for drama because they lacked lyricism; to introduce it as Oehlenschläger had done would be to "distort the original relationship between the material and the spectator." The essay had been delivered on February 2, 1857; on April 17 he sent it to Botten Hansen for publication. And in a letter of April 28 he announced: "I already have another dramatic work in hand; it will be rather different in tone and content from my earlier plays." This work would become *The Vikings at Helgeland*—despite all his theories, a saga drama.

What had happened was that he began to discover in the sagas more than enough lyricism, vitality, and strength to form the basis of drama. The saga meant not just "abstract, plastic beauty of form"; it was also "painting with colors, with light and shadow." Suzannah, a living embodiment of the warmth and strength of the saga woman, must have opened his eyes to this. Now he could write the play whose theme had dimly crossed his mind when he first read the sagas—the drama of the proud woman who goads men on to battle, even to the destruction of the one she loves. Thus Hjørdis, a more profound, a wilder image than the haughty Margit of *The Feast at Solhaug*, was conceived.

His theories about the saga continued to influence him. He had maintained that the poetry of the saga was "chiefly pagan"; when Christianity introduced romance and lyricism, the dramatic ballad was created. Thus saga themes should be treated in the "pagan" style of ancient Greek tragedy, as Oehlenschläger had done by adopting an antique style for his *Baldur the Good* (1807). Ibsen began to write *The Vikings* in this severe, "antique" iambic trimeter, rather than the lyric iambic pentameter of *The Warrior's Barrow*. Oehlenschläger had used iambic trimeter not only in *Baldur,* but also in *Kjartan and Gudrun* (1847); the latter play is of particular interest here since it is based on the *Laxdale Saga* and is reminiscent of the theme in Ibsen's play. But it was not long before he discovered that there was no important relationship between Greek and Norse "paganism," and he abandoned verse for prose.

It has been suggested that Bjørnson's one-act play on a saga theme, *Between the Battles,* influenced this decision. Although not printed until the end of 1857, Ibsen might have had an opportunity to see it when it was submitted to the theatre in 1856. But this is not likely. The play was read and rejected by the directors of the theatre, and Ibsen's position as a mere instructor hardly entitled him to share in their deliberations. In a letter of 1863 he categorically denies having read the play while working on *The Vikings,* and there is no reason to doubt him.

There are, moreover, important fundamental differences between the two plays. Bjørnson never intended to imitate the saga style, but was rather writing in a contemporary idiom whose only relation to the saga was that it stemmed from Old Norse. Later he even voiced regret that he had not written the play in Landsmål, the Norwegian folk language fashioned by Ivar Aasen. When he read *The Vikings,* he commented on the language: "You simply can't use the saga idiom today. Language has to be rooted in the now and make its advance from that point, if possible. It can't settle down outside its own country: outside the country there's a great ocean with as many islands as there are different language styles—here the ballad idiom, there the saga, there something that's both or neither." Ibsen, he continued, didn't recognize this principle: "In *The Feast at Solhaug* he drew so heavily on the ballads I felt he had become one great ballad himself. He swallowed it all, down to the very language. Now he plunges into the sagas, and bobs up with their turns of phrases, their language, their style, all of it prefabricated poetry." It was skillfully done, he admitted, but it all got an "angry snort" from him because it was an imitative art, a virtuoso stunt. Others may have been charmed, like the German poet Paul Heyse, who cried out after seeing the play, "So must the gods in Valhall have spoken." But the speech of the gods seemed rather out of place in a play about ordinary humans.

As modern Norwegian has grown less dependent on Danish and has taken on more of its own identity, Ibsen's saga style has lost much of its effectiveness. He was, after all, borrowing his "saga" words from the Danish translations he had read, and they betray their origin. The fashionable saga idiom he used had no more authentic Norwegian in it than, for example, the Danish Carsten Hauch's *Saga of Thorvald Vidførle* (1849), from whom Ibsen may actually have learned to imitate the saga. As a result the play seems excessively declamatory in modern productions. Perhaps a great tragic actress like Laura Gundersen brought the character of Hjørdis to life when she performed the role in her prime in the 1880's, but as she declined, even her performance became tedious. When Johanne Dybwad played the part in 1927 she infused the spirit of the heroic saga woman into the play, but even that performance became sheer rant at times; for example, in the great meeting between Hjørdis and Sigurd, the effect was unintentionally comic.

One major reason for the dwindling effectiveness of the play is that it was inspired more by literature than life. Once again Ibsen had not written out of his own spiritual struggle but had simply picked up a current topic. The times demanded that one be nationalistic, so he reached for a national theme. Both he and the times were content with a mere reflection of the past; they ignored Hettner's imperative that a historical drama must be vitalized by a psychological conflict that should have meaning for the present as well as the past. Ibsen was perhaps so concerned with creating a sense of the old national idiom that he buried the essential psychological drama under the historical superstructure.

The main theme of the play came from the Volsung Saga, as translated into Danish by C. C. Rafn in 1829.* In selecting the historical setting Ibsen showed the same intuitive sense as in *The Feast;* he placed the Volsung saga in the Viking period, where scholars now agree it belongs, although scholars of his day considered the legends prehistoric. He sensed their kinship with the later stories and was quite correct in saying that the basic source for his play was the Icelandic family sagas. He could thus logically transform legendary heroes and Valkyries into historical persons. (He was much more successful here than was Friedrich Hebbel, who tried to do the same thing a few years later with his *Nibelungen.)* He was also able to work in the theme of *The Warrior's Barrow,* the conflict between paganism and Christianity, in a particularly subtle manner; Sigurd does not reveal that he is a Christian until the hour of his death.

By coincidence Bjørnson was also working on a saga drama at this time, eventually called *Hulda the Lame,* and had also selected as his basic theme the words of Gudrun in the *Laxdale Saga:* "I was most savage toward him I most loved." Moreover, Bjørnson's play has much in common with *The Feast at Solhaug,* on which Ibsen was also drawing for the new drama.

Not only does Bjørnson use the same historical era, he adopts the same conflict that Ibsen had in *The Feast*—a man gripped by a new passion while still bound to the old. Bjørnson may have been trying to show how a psychological drama, rather than lyric balladry, could be made from the material. The differences between *Hulda the Lame* and *The Vikings* are all the more instructive because of these similarities. That one used poetry and the other prose is of minor importance; Bjørnson's intention was always, whether he wrote in poetry or prose, to build on living speech rather than to imitate an archaic idiom. The essential difference is in the psychology of each play. Bjørnson attempts to analyze universal human problems; Ibsen's psychological investigation is constricted by the historical setting. Although Bjørnson's play is clumsy and lacklustre, its characters are living people and it does try to show the consequences of divided emotional allegiance in a man and repressed love in a woman. Bjørnson's Hulda and Ibsen's Hjørdis both kill their lovers and themselves; but Hjørdis is driven by a more than human temperament and emotional life, she is a demon, akin to the evil spirits of the Wild Hunt,

---

*See translation by Margaret Schlauch (New York: American Scandinavian Foundation, 1930).

the Åsgårdsreien. The irrational acts of many others in the play can only
be explained by reference to the sagas; literature has clouded the poet's
insight into human psychology.

Despite the imitative elements there is still something genuinely
Ibsenian in the basic motivation of the play that gives it a definite
place in his personal and dramatic development. The portrait of Hjørdis
is a composite of Brynhild, of Gudrun Osvifsdóttir of the *Laxdæla Saga*,
and of Hallgerd Hoskuldsdóttir in the *Njáll's Saga*. Of Gudrun he could
use only certain idiosyncrasies and a few striking phrases. Her portrait
in the saga offered little to the playwright. As Hans E. Kinck's states,
she is hardly more than "the beautiful female . . . to whom Eros is all,
whose nature has no trace of Valkyrie in it." Hallgerd presented more
of a psychological dilemma; Kinck names her first among those characters "the sagas did not comprehend," the great example of "their
inability to grasp female psychology." Such characters, he felt, "lend
themselves to contemporary recreators of the saga."

Like Kinck, Ibsen must have puzzled over this enigmatic woman, so
strangely made up of grandeur and pettiness, whom the saga told bore
within herself the memory of Sigurd Dragon-Slayer and Brynhild. Kinck
maintained that she was not motivated, as the saga has it, by low con-
nivance, nor by simple eroticism, as in the case of Gudrun. Hallgerd's
soul burned for companionship with a great-souled man, and she longed
for this great adventure: "The miracle," in Ibsen's words. Hjørdis' longing to join Sigurd "not in love but sword play," to "fire him to battle
and manly deeds," reflects the Hallgerd of the saga. But Ibsen's emphasis is on the ethical question, of whether a man has the right to place
other considerations above love. The question was to return again and
again in his work. Here in *The Vikings* love is in opposition to the Old
Norse ethic of friendship; in his later plays the demands of love are in
conflict with a man's life calling. The formulation now is mainly historical, but the problem of the betrayal of love was for him not dependent on one place or time.

His answer is always no; nothing justifies betrayal. Hjørdis speaks in
his voice: "When you took another for your wife, Sigurd, I became
homeless in this world. A man can be gift-giver of all good things to his
faithful friend, but if he gives the woman he loves, the secret web of
Fate is rent. Two lives waste away." Hjørdis would defy the destiny that
Sigurd's youthful sin has made for them both, but Sigurd neither can
nor will. Ibsen believes such a sin brings nemesis, a mistake once made
is inexorable, the "bitter agony" lasts to the end of life. In *The Vikings*
he uses the formula "the secret web of the Norn," but the ethic here is

his personal one and it drives the tragedy to its end. There is at last
something of Ibsen himself in the saga play.

There are other personal notes, even in an apparently unmotivated
echo from the saga where the old chieftain, Ørnulf, composes a poem
to assuage his grief over the death of his sons. The scene dramatizes a
famous episode from the saga of the life of the poet-chieftain Egill. One
of Ibsen's deepest convictions was that poetic creation freed one's soul
from sorrow and returned it to life. He also realized that life had not
yet shaken his soul nor stirred the depths of his being. In a letter to a
friend written a few months after *The Vikings* he said: "I have longed,
almost prayed for a great suffering that would fill my life and give it
meaning." And in the previous year he had written in *Olaf Liljekans*
"Sorrow is silver, the noble ore." He knew his writing lacked power,
was still just "literature," because the "gift of sorrow" had not come to
spur him on to battle. He would have to feel that his life was at stake
before he could marshal his power to defend himself—then would the
act of creation become the very struggle for existence out of which
poetry is born. The character of old Ørnulf reveals that Ibsen suffered
with the knowledge that his writing and his life were not one. He wrote
chiefly for others, was happy when others were moved, but he had not
yet given himself fully.

The Vikings was a success as a play; Bjørnson called it the best drama
yet written in Norway. But no more than *The Feast* did it lead anywhere. It was, as Bjørnson said, perfect of its kind; nothing more need
be attempted in that style. Compared to *Catiline* and *Lady Inger* it was
a perfect literary exercise; all that was missing was life. Neither satisfied to do again what was perfectly executed nor content with an art that
was merely artful, Ibsen had to continue to seek the right foundation
for his life's work.

CHAPTER ELEVEN

THE NATIONAL MOVEMENT (1857-59)

A FEW DAYS after beginning *The Vikings at Helgeland,* Ibsen signed a new agreement with the Bergen theatre. The five-year term of his contract was over on April 1, 1857; on April 11 he agreed to remain another year at the same salary. His position was still that of a subordinate, although in the last few years he had been able to work a bit more on his own, at least with the instruction of the actors.

Then everything suddenly changed. Late that spring one of the actors got a letter from a trustee of the Christiania Norwegian Theatre inquiring about a suitable "artistic director" for the theatre. When asked, Ibsen promptly answered that he would be willing if the terms were suitable and if he could be released from his Bergen contract. He was so delighted with the idea of escaping from Bergen that he decided to go to Oslo to find out more about the theatre, but in mid-July on the very day he was to start out, he received a formal offer from Oslo, offering him the position of director at 600 dollars a year — twice his Bergen salary — with the prospect of a raise if the theatre was successful. With strengthened determination he went to Oslo; on July 23 he wrote back to the trustees of the Bergen theatre asking to be released: "The advantages to me of living in the capital I need not emphasize, and sorry as I am to leave Bergen and the theatre, I fear it would be indefensible of me to reject this opportunity to secure a fairly remunerative position. Though I speak of salary and advantage I am neither selfish nor ungrateful: I shall never forget what I owe the Bergen Theatre. But I have a responsibility to myself, and things at the theatre have long oppressed me. My way was blocked at every turn; I was never given a free hand, and every day I was depressed by the thought of working, while having no influence at all."

The letter clearly shows what freedom it was to get away from the tedious labor of five years. He "awaited with eagerness" the trustees' reply. They, in turn, understood his situation and granted his release at once. On August 11 he made a final agreement with the Christiania

Norwegian Theatre and hurried to Bergen to make arrangements for the move to Oslo. On September 3, 1857 he assumed the position of director.

He was now approaching thirty, and life probably never seemed so promising. He had never set out with such courage and hope as he now approached his new labors in Oslo. He felt confident in victory, especially since he had finally been able to publish the play he thought his best. Botten Hansen ran *Lady Inger of Østråt* first in *Illustreret Nyhesblad* and then had it reprinted in the fall. *The Vikings*, for which he had even more hopes, was almost complete.

To match his high spirits there was an invigorating, youthful spirit of nationalism in the air, not the rather faint-hearted nationalism of Welhaven or Andreas Munch or the superficial flag-waving of Rolf Olsen and P. A. Jensen. Writers like P. C. Asbjørsen, Jørgen Moe, N. R. Østgaard, M. B. Landstad, and Ivar Aasen had created a taste for a much more serious nationalism; now Bjørnson came forth with his first novel of folk life, *Synnøve Solbakken* (1857), which spoke more directly to the heart of the Norwegian people than had anything before.

Bjørnson was one of the first people Ibsen met in Oslo that summer, and they recognized at once that they were soldiers in the same battle. In a letter written in August Bjørnson mentioned that "the Bergen poet" was in town; he could already add: "I love him!" When Ibsen traveled overland to Bergen by way of Valdres, he had *Synnøve Solbakken* with him; the book sealed his devotion to Bjørnson. Two months later they watched together the first performance of Bjørnson's *Between the Battles* at Christiania Theatre; soon after they both submitted their saga plays to the trustees. Two weeks later, when Bjørnson took up the director's post at the theatre that Ibsen had just left, each had his own Norwegian theatre. They both found comfort and support in the knowledge that theirs was a true working fellowship.

Ibsen was director of the Christiania Norwegian Theatre for five years, and although he began his work with enthusiasm and was undoubtedly happy in Oslo, his energy was gradually overcome by a sense of defeat and disappointment. He would finally be more unhappy than he had ever been, even in the most trying years at Grimstad.

The theatre had just gone through a serious crisis when Ibsen took over its management. Applications for a subsidy and for a building loan had been rejected by the Storting, although by a narrow vote of 57 to 49. The theatre was forced to reorganize, which it did on July 21, the very day Ibsen came to Oslo to make arrangements for his new position. The reorganization involved putting the entire management in the hands of the new director. Ibsen was supposed to salvage the theatre.

When the theatre was founded in the fall of 1852, it had modestly

called itself simply a "dramatic school." Its program, however, was a
boldly national one; although it claimed to be inspired by the Norwegian
Theatre in Bergen, it really aimed at something more than that brand
of timid nationalism. According to its program, the literary language
was to be given a full native pronunciation and eventually even the
folk language was to be admitted to the stage. But in spite of these
noble intentions the theatre had inevitably to take second place to
Christiania Theatre. The facilities in Møllergata were small and incon-
venient, the actors were second rate, and the audiences so indifferent
that the only things they attended were Danish operettas and French
farces. The theatre was heavily in debt, and Ibsen was hired to solve
all its problems.

He began with determination and a program, which he announced
in a prologue written for *The Mountain Adventure (Fjeldeventyret)* in
September, 1857. In it he honored the author, A. M. Bjerregaard, and
the composer, Waldemar Thrane, as the first to release the "native voice"
that speaks in "our folk life," "our peasant lays," and in "the sound of
our mountain horn (the *lur*)." The program was the same as he had
outlined time and again in Bergen; now in Oslo he had the chance to
put it into effect. In November the theatre offered a prize for the best
play, preferably a musical, with a "subject taken from the folk life or
history of our people."

Ibsen's program for the theatre is also apparent in the drama reviews
he wrote that fall for *Illustreret Nyhedsblad*. It was peculiar for the
director of one theatre to review performances at another, and in a few
months the situation would become impossible, but Ibsen's articles during 1857 give us a clear indication of the standards he set for plays and
performances. He was better informed and more mature than when he
wrote for *The Man* in 1851 and could give more exact expression to the
ideals which he had always had. His condemnation of the whole French
dramatic school was stronger than ever—those plays were simply acting
parts and dialogue, without any intellectual content. Now he insisted
that the inner life of the drama, and not just its outward action, should
reflect the spirit of the nation — an idea in keeping with his constantly
reiterated plea that a work of art should strive to do more than simply
imitate nature or life. Art must search out spiritual truth, "that higher
symbolic representation of life [that would] clarify the quickening
thoughts of the people." He scorned a public that wanted only photographic art or failed to see that authentic art possessed an "elevating
power." He wanted to build the theatre's repertoire on these principles,
and for that the actors must share his ideals. Thus, one of his critiques
deals at length with the question of stage directing; the director must

try to express the author's real intention, so that even lines that seem on the surface insignificant can be made to assume dramatic and psychological meaning.

In the first year he had little chance to put these high ideals into practice; the theatre season was in full swing and he was unfamiliar with the actors. Things went on as before and the only new plays he tried were ones he knew from Bergen. He devoted much care to staging problems and ensemble playing, but otherwise there were few indications that the management had changed. He probably did not think he would have to devote all his time to directing, since he applied in November, 1857, for a fellowship in Nordic literature at the university, for which an annual grant of 250 dollars had recently been appropriated. His application was based on his newly printed treatise on the ballad. Two months later he withdrew the application, either because he learned his chances were poor, or because he felt he could not take part in the competition.

Another indication that he put his theatre in second place is that he offered *The Vikings at Helgeland* to Christiania Theatre early in November. The conflict that resulted with the rival theatre led to an even sharper struggle for nationalistic principles, both within the theatre and outside it. The play was accepted for performance in the spring of 1858, but when Ibsen inquired about its staging, he was informed that the trustees had postponed it because they could not afford the royalty that year. Ibsen was furious, and the next day, March 10, printed a sharp attack against Christiania Theatre in the national-liberal newspaper, *Aftenbladet*. The postponement of his play was for him a sign that the theatre was "unable to support, encourage, or in general bother itself about a Norwegian dramatic literature." It had in fact "broken the bridge" between itself and this literature. Now he proclaimed there would be open warfare between those who wanted a Norwegian theatre and those who preferred the Danish. The directors of Christiania Theatre had shown their true colors and had proved that they were no more interested in a national theatre now than they had been twenty years earlier.

Ibsen's polemic may seem in excess of the cause, and he was soon told that his own "unbridled vanity" made him carry on in this fashion; after all, he was not synonymous with all "Norwegian dramatic literature." But his sensitivity had nothing to do with his interpretation of the attitude of the theatre management; he saw clearly enough their contemptuous superiority to an insignificant *Norwegian* author, and his opinion was confirmed by the tone of the defense given by a representative of the theatre in *Christiania-Posten*. Ibsen, he wrote, is a "minor author" and cannot speak on behalf of a national literature. "Mr. Ibsen is a major nonentity, around whom the nation cannot with any conviction plant a protective hedge. *The Feast at Solhaug* is altogether too lacking in freshness of originality to inspire any confidence in his future, and his next dramatic work, *Lady Inger of Østråt*, is astonishingly bereft of idealism and poetry. Every character is marked with baseness.... Under these circumstances Mr. Ibsen surely realizes that the public is not anxiously looking forward to his Vikings; nor is the present time particularly auspicious for staging mediocrity." The writer, one Richard Petersen, at the time a prison warden, further stated that Ibsen's plays could not be considered national literature solely because they were written by a Norwegian: "A national sentiment which allows itself to batten on native weeds is not worth much attention." He, fortunately, knew where the nation could find proper food: "In Andreas Munch lies the interest of our nation. Mr. Ibsen cannot compare with him." He went on to add: "H. Ø. Blom's *Tordenskjold* is unquestionably the best play in Norwegian."

Such senseless carping was salt on the wound, and others besides Ibsen smarted. Bjørnson wrote in *Bergensposten* that *The Vikings* was the best play yet written in Norway and "would prove more effective on stage than any previous play of ours." When the play was published toward the end of April, J. Lieblein hailed it in *Morgenbladet* as "truly a national drama." Not everyone shared this enthusiasm, and opinion was divided, but on the whole, people thought that the play showed the days of the ancient sagas in a more authentically Norwegian manner than any play had ever done. Norwegian drama was rescued from Oehlenschläger.

Ibsen sent the play to the Royal Theatre in Copenhagen in February, but its unusual saga style caused it to be quickly rejected. J. L. Heiberg delivered his verdict in just five days, and ironically enough he based his rejection on the very argument Ibsen had used the past spring: "The Icelandic sagas have so marked an epic character that they can only be ruined by being transformed into drama. The epic style softens the barbarity and coarseness they portray; the moment they are dramatized all their crudity is exposed." Seven weeks earlier Heiberg had rejected Bjørnson's *Hulda the Lame* on the same grounds, and now he summed up his judgment: "A Norwegian theatre will hardly issue forth from these experimental laboratories; fortunately the Danish theatre is in no need of experiments."

Heiberg's prediction was right in Ibsen's case: *The Vikings* did not become the basis of a new kind of drama for him. But Heiberg's failure to respond to Ibsen's tremendous dramatic talent is another matter entirely. In any case, Ibsen thought he could still write in this manner. Just as he had gone on to repeat the material of *The Feast at Solhaug* in *Olaf Liljekrans,* so he began to plan a new saga play, taking his theme from the account of the civil wars of the twelth and thirteenth centuries in the latest volume of P. A. Munch's *History of the Norwegian People,* published in 1857. His imagination was fired by the picture of Skule Bårdsson, last of the pretenders to the Norwegian throne. In this rebel he thought he perceived the inner struggle that would make the dramatic conflict psychologically interesting. He also found here a contemporary theme; the civil wars underscored the need for national unity.

For the time being, while he searched for a proper dramatic form, the play remained only an idea; before he would create the right form, the entire concept was to undergo profound change. What happened now was that the argument over *The Vikings* expanded to include the entire issue of Norwegian versus Danish theatre in Norway. Ibsen made clear that he was promoting the idea of national culture in the interest of Scandinavian and European unity. "Culture is unthinkable apart from nationality," he wrote, "and the great ideal of Scandinavian unity," for which he had such enthusiasm, could never be realized unless Norway had her equality with other nations, "independent, in *all* things independent."

With this thought in mind he set himself to making his theatre the central arena for Norwegian dramatic art. He never worked harder in the theatre than in this year, 1858-59, producing twice as many new plays as in any other year, to general acclaim. It was on his own plays that he had to depend in order to make this theatre truly national and so, despite meager physical resources and unskilled performers, he produced *The Vikings* (in November, 1858) and *Lady Inger* (in April, 1859).

The Vikings was politely received. The theatre had gone to great expense to produce the play in proper style and the production was, as one reviewer put it, "free from virtually every positive fault." But expensive productions could not make up for the actors' inability to charge the drama with poetry. The play drew well at first and there were eight performances, but it was not a financial success. Bjørnson then produced it in Bergen, with even less success. The production of *Lady Inger* in the spring capped Ibsen's failure; the actors were totally inadequate and it was withdrawn after two performances.

Ibsen had lost the battle for a national theatre by losing his theatre's audience. True, more money had come in than before, but expenses leapt ahead and the season ended with a large deficit. That the theatre survived at all was due to the musicals and farces, now more frequently mounted than ever before. As he tried to balance accounts at the end of the year, he had to admit defeat: "At a theatre one learns to be practical, one gets used to accepting events and learns how to *put one's higher ideals aside* for a while when one can't do otherwise." It was a stinging humiliation to bow to the public's taste and replace Lady Inger with two "petite English dancing girls" who filled the house every night throughout the spring.

The new season, 1859-60, opened with *The Vikings,* now prefaced by a poetic prologue dedicated to the memory of King Oscar I. It too was a plea for a national literature such as had come into being during that monarch's reign:

Folkedigtet, Folkescenen	Native poetry, native drama
Under ham brød Banen kjæk.	Under him made bold advance.

Where does a people's strength come from, the poet asks:

Hvad gjør Folket stærkt og rigt	What more makes a people strong
Som dets Færd blandt Fjeldets	and rich
Rifter,	Than its living amid mountains,
Som dets Fædres Storbedrifter,	Than its ancestors' deeds of glory
Mal't i Kvad og Billeddigt?	Mirrored forth in song and drama?

Some day, "perhaps in the distant future," such a literature might flower.

The present, however, did not offer much promise. *The Vikings* was staged once and then gave way to the light entertainment the audience preferred—singing, slapstick, and pretty girls. The biggest hit of the season was a "dramatic diversion with singing and dancing" by Erik Bøgh, imported from Copenhagen. Especially written for the great Spanish dancer Pepita, though of course Oslo rated only a Danish dancer in the role, Erik Bøgh's *A Caprice* made a joke of Norwegian nationalism by poking fun at the "Norwegian Norseman," Herr Bjerkebæk from Drammen, the only one in the play to speak Norwegian. His Vika dialect, the speech of Oslo's working class, stood out comically amid the Danish or German of the rest of the play.

The newspapers complained about these "worthless bagatelles" and "empty trash" and wondered what had happened to the *Norwegian* theatre: "It is a mystery that the entire theatre, in undisturbed and genteel indolence, is allowed to amble along in the ruts of Danish inanity —all under the tutelage of a *Norwegian* dramatist." Ibsen was not in a very enviable position. He had thrown himself wholeheartedly into the nationalist cause, and he never felt more conviction about it than now. In his two years in Oslo he was the poet to be summoned for every national occasion: memorial celebrations, May 17th (Independence Day) anniversaries, meetings of the Turnvereins, the rifle corps gatherings, even for captions on nationalistic pictures. He had festive lyrics on call for every occasion, although we have some idea of how he valued them since they were almost all excluded from his later collected verse.

In the fall of 1858 he returned to the narrative poem about Audun Hugleiksson he had begun two years earlier and tried to "Norwegianize" it as much as possible. Under the new title of "King Haakon's Festival Hall" he began to print it in *Illustreret Nyhedsblad,* and again he was unable to finish. In spite of raven's cries and Old Norse poetic images —"stars of the eyebrows" for eyes, "planks of the billow" for ships—he could not give it an authentic national tone. He was more successful with his stirring "Gull's Cries," published on New Year's Day, 1859. In this reply to the Danish demand that Norwegians end their separatist activities, he wrote that although the cry of the Norwegian gull over the water was not a beautiful sound, it was the only noise its nature permitted it to make. Assuming an attitude as "hateful and indignant" as the Danes', he advised them to stand guard over their own language and nationality, rather than carp at the Norwegians:

Du danske Mand, selv er du arm	You, Dane! are poor yourself
Paa Magt og Marg i Maal.	In force and pith of language.

Danish poetry had too much of German spirit in it:

Du kvad om dine Sønners Daad,	You sang about your hero sons,
Men *tydsk* var Kvadets Gang,—	But *German* was the song —
Og *tydsk* var dine Døtres Graad,	And *German* flowed your daughters'
Som dine Skaldes Sang!	tears
Tydsk er din bedste Runestav	And so your bardic lays!
Om Sagafolkets Færd —;	German are your runic rimes
Bryd Bøilen, det er Tidens Krav!	About your saga deeds—;
Og tør Du ei—saa gaa i Grav —	The age insists: Shake off that yoke!
Du er ei bedre værd!	And if you dare not—find your grave—
	Of nothing better worthy!

The most intense controversy about language took place in the winter of 1858-59. Vinje threw down the gage in his own newspaper *Dølen* ("The Dalesman"), written in Ivar Aasen's newly devised Norwegian.[*] Both Ibsen and Bjørnson felt attracted by its new Norwegian tone, and Ibsen adopted forms and individual words in "Gull's Cries" and other poems. In verses written for a tableau staged at the theatre, he used so

---

[*]See Translators' Note: "Language Reform," in References, Chapter Eleven.

many Norwegian words that the Danish actor indignantly refused to read them; such words, he declared, were not fit for poetry. Ibsen went further: in 1859 he undertook to write the musical play on a national theme for which the theatre had been offering a prize, without success, for the last two years. He decided to rewrite *Olof Liljekrans* as an opera, calling it *The Mountain Bird,* and injecting into its Danish a greater proportion of peculiarly Norwegian words than he had ever used before. He never finished the work, and the fragment is somewhat labored since the language was not natural to him; but his patriotic intention was obvious.

He tried to champion the nationalist cause again in October, 1859, by preparing an application for an annual subsidy for the theatre. The amount he asked of the Storting was about two thousand dollars, twice as much as the entire deficit of the preceding season. In the application he spoke of the "importance of nationality, particularly national art, in the intellectual life and growth of a people." It would be disastrous if this art were "forced by adverse circumstances to take a false direction. A theatre is all too often forced to follow its public, instead of leading it, and thus allows itself to be carried away by the current, often corrupt taste, when it should dominate it." A large state subsidy was necessary if the Norwegian theatre was to be free to fulfill its national mission.

Ibsen had obviously not entirely given up hopes of rescuing himself and the theatre from its "false direction." When Bjørnson returned to Oslo in 1859 to become an editor of *Aftenbladet,* he found the ally he needed. Their friendship was renewed, and Bjørnson's faith and courage lent Ibsen much support. The following winter they lived in the same house (the new "Maltheby" in Akersgata), and they began to cooperate in the effort to forge a more national literature and art. Their friendship was so close that Bjørnson was sponsor at the baptism of Ibsen's son Sigurd, who was born at Christmastime 1859.

Now the Ibsen who would become a hater of all organizations and societies persuaded Bjørnson to help found The Norwegian Society in November, 1859, "to encourage nationalism in literature and art," especially dramatic art. Bjørnson was made president, and throughout the winter it was a gathering place for all sorts of people with national interests: members of the Storting, journalists, scholars, and artists. They met on Tuesday evenings to discuss and argue, or just to sing and amuse themselves. More "organization" work followed. In December both Ibsen and Bjørnson were members of a special committee which would attempt to gather all the Norwegian actors from the theatres in Oslo and Bergen for joint summer performances at Christiania Theatre. Ibsen had first proposed this idea in 1858, and now it became part of the program of The Norwegian Society to replace all the Danish actors in Oslo.

But his disenchantment with the work of the society was swift and lasting. It is rather sadly amusing to read his address, forty years later, to the Swedish Authors' Society: "It has been a strange experience for me to be here. I do not remember that I have ever belonged to any society before, and I think this is the first time I have ever been at a meeting like this." Although his memory for the great and small events of his life was prodigious, he seemed to want to forget all about his past involvement with organizations. But before he had created the image of the mighty solitary one, he had a brief moment as an organizer and a "joiner." He had been active in the Students' Association and its Literary Society for more than a year (1850-51); in his last two winters in Bergen (1855-57) he had been in "The Society of December 22"; he was a member of a Norwegian "Carl Johan Association" from its founding in 1858 until after 1880; he was a member of the Christiania Rifle-Corps from its organization in 1859; and then in 1859 came the founding of The Norwegian Society. His experience with the latter seems to have been distasteful to him, especially when its activities became too broad and too politically oriented. He did not enjoy large gatherings, particularly when heated by the controversy over the Reform Society and the Swedish Governor-General, which did not interest him to begin with. His dissatisfaction increased when the Storting again (on May 18, 1860) rejected his application for a theatre subsidy; only a tiny minority of 28 had voted for the subsidy, and there were many members of the society who were not among them. The final blow came when Christiania Theatre refused to allow the Norwegian performances the committee was trying to arrange for the summer. The society seemed to offer nothing but fine words and phrases.

Every road was blocked and in a mood as angry as the one he felt in the spring of 1858, he lashed out against his critics, particularly H. Ø. Blom, a poet of the old Wergeland school, who had published in *Morgenbladet* an anti-nationalistic farewell to the Danish actor Vilhelm Wiehe who was returning to Copenhagen. Blom had once been a nationalist himself, but now he lamented the departure of Danish actors as a catastrophe (a "Ragnarok") for the Norwegian stage. Decent theatre would be impossible in the country now, and as proof of this he pointed to Ibsen's theatre:

I Møllergaden vel et Sted man finder,	In Møllergaden there's a house where I found so-so entertainment.
Hvor jeg ofte har havt det saa som saa.	There's a bit of verve, and some actresses
Der er lidt verve, og der er Kunstnerinder,	one can listen to with pleasure,
Som med Fornøielse man hører paa,	But the language, the language! Blessed Lady,
Men Sproget, Sproget! himmelske Madame,	who proudly guards the gates of Thalia,
Som der saa kjækt staar paa Thalias Post!	if we are ever reduced to this
Hvis vi skal reduceres til de Samme,	I swear we'll be on slim rations.
Saa siger jeg, vi faae for skral en Kost.	

Blom went on to describe trumpeting voices and bleatings, along with other cacophonies, all of which made obvious the fact that Norwegians could not master the art of drama. Quite the contrary, he maintained:

—Nordens Mønster i Theatrets Sphære	—The pattern for the Nordic theatre Copenhagen will long remain.
Vil endnu længe være Kjøbenhavn.	

The attack was not only against all that Ibsen believed in, but against all the work he had dedicated his life to. His answer came three days later in a seventeen stanza "Letter to H. Ø. Blom" published in *Aften-bladet*. Unmercifully he belabored Blom for his poor verse and "currish thoughts"; he even compared him to an "embalmed corpse." But the anger is invigorating and beyond it there is the conviction that the "dawn of a new-born sun" waits beyond the hill top. The young poet is quite willing to believe that a final "Ragnarok" will descend on Blom's cherished "Valhall," the Danish Christiania Theatre. But as far as he is concerned there is a higher heaven, the "Gimle" which in Norse myth-ology superseded the Valhall of the old gods, obviously an allusion to a new Norwegian theatre.

He defends the native language against all abuse, and asks only that it become even more purely Norwegian:

Læs hvor Du vil, tag disse Strofer med;	Read where you will, even these very stanzas;
Dansk Ordlag raader jo i hver en Linje,	Danish idiom rules in every line, And shackles even a Vinje's thoughts.
Dansk Tænkesæt er Hemsko selv paa Vinje.	

Twenty years later when the poem was published in his collected verse, he eliminated this attack on the Danish language, but at the time he felt it deeply and honestly. Blom promptly retorted in *Morgenbladet* for December 13, in a poem as long and coarse as it was meager in content. Ten years older, he put the upstart in his place:

Men jeg er H. Ø. Blom, see det er Tingen!	But I am H. Ø. Blom, you'll notice!
Og du er Henrik Ibsen—ikke meer!	And you are Henrik Ibsen— nothing more.

The rest of the poem was gross abuse and hardly worth Ibsen's notice, but he was at least as indignant as before and rushed to *Aftenbladet* with a rhymed letter, "Lines in Haste to H. Ø. Blom," a mere fourteen stanzas long! Bjørnson pocketed the verses and never printed them— quite rightly since they were simply an anthology of rhymed invective. The rhymes are snappy and packed with ultra-Norwegian idioms, but they display more anger than art. Ibsen must have been touched on a sore spot to have cried out so loudly.

Anger was useless. He knew that his work was failing and he had been drawn into the nationalistic movement more deeply than his true convictions justified. He had to stop and ask himself if all this flag-waving was sincere.

CHAPTER TWELVE

A MIND DIVIDED (1858-62)

ALTHOUGH THE CAUSE of the Norwegian Theatre stirred his enthusiasm, and his friend Bjørnson urged him on to battle, still his mind was divided and forces within and without began to spread doubt and rouse his critical faculties.

In that very winter of 1859 when he persuaded Bjørnson to join in foundingThe Norwegian Society, he began to frequent another, quite different circle of friends who gathered under the name "The Erudite Holland." The phrase, a quote from Holberg's comedy *Jakob von Thyboe,* was first used in reference to Botten Hansen's book-lined study, because once when he had come upon a particularly rare book, his friend and fellow book collector Ludvig Daae had exclaimed, "Devil take the Dutchman—he has his spies everywhere!" The name of "aboriginal Dutchman" clung to Botten Hansen; his study became "the erudite Holland," and his associates were fellow "Dutchmen."

Botten Hansen was the most ardent and most important bibliophile in Norway, always on the lookout for rare, old, and odd-looking books, and even more interested in books that were rare because they were new and unknown. He had given up his youthful dreams of becoming a writer himself, but he kept a sharp eye out for new writers, whom he considered his foster-children. His weekly *Illustreret Nyhedsblad* grew into a veritable Baedeker to the literary life of his time and his "erudite Holland" in Rådstuegata was the Mecca for all lovers of books and letters. It was inevitable that Ibsen should become a frequent visitor to his friend's home when he returned to Oslo. Botten Hansen had kept their friendship alive by defending *The Feast at Solhaug* against attack and by publishing *Lady Inger of Østråt;* he would also publish *The Vikings at Helgeland.* Although he usually adopted a rather critically ironic tone even with his friends, Botten Hansen inspired Ibsen with confidence in their friendship. Ibsen felt safe in his "erudite Holland," and although he could not have created such a refuge himself, he relished the chance to meet new friends there, especially since they were among the most learned men in the country.

First among these intellectual "Dutchmen" was the future national archivist, M. Birkeland, the "grand vice-chairman" of the group and Botten Hansen's oldest friend. To history and politics rather than literature he applied his vast knowledge, unusually perceptive mind, and independent judgment. Another historian, Ludvig Daae, was of a totally different nature, although he idolized Birkeland. Birkeland was quiet and retiring; Daae was all fire, quite likely to express his joy or anger on any subject by solo dances among the bookcases. Unlike Botten Hansen he did not rely on the ironic smile, but vented his anger in a rich stream of invective, in either Norwegian or Latin. He did not have Birkeland's historical perspective, but was more of an antiquarian researcher who shared Botten Hansen's mania for collecting. Moreover, Daae had a special tie with Ibsen because he was Suzannah's second cousin. Although he was in Drammen between 1859 and 1863, he made regular trips to the capital. After 1859 the inner circle of the "erudite Holland" consisted of Botten Hansen, Birkeland, and Ibsen, and they met almost every day, either at a cafe or in the study. Their concern was always to try to discover the living man behind the book or the historical event. So they had themes aplenty for their talks, whether of new or old books of literature, or especially of current events.

Many others came to Botten Hansen's study. In 1860 the historian Oluf Rygh and the jurist O. A. Bachke became regulars, and in 1861 the linguist Jakob Løkke moved to the capital and renewed his friendship with Botten Hansen. A solid and reliable scholar, if more dogmatic than the rest (with the possible exception of Birkeland) he would eventually become, along with Birkeland, Daae, Bachke, and others, one of the leaders of the Conservative Party. But the sharp political differences which would separate these men from the liberal "Dutchmen"—A. O. Vinje, J. E. Sars, and in 1859-60 even Bjørnson—were not to appear until the end of the decade. For now all the "Dutchmen" had national, historical, and literary interests in common.

The spirit that animated this group was quite different from that of the Norwegian Society. The "Dutchmen" were distinguished by their sober sense of realism and a respect for facts which made them more interested in the past than the future and rather wary of idealistic talk about progress. They judged things by their observations of the here and now, and they suspected anything that wanted to reshape society according to ready-made plans. They opposed as unnatural all language reform, whether Bjørnson's attempts to force Norwegian words and idioms into the Danish literary language, or Vinje's efforts to develop

a new Norwegian literary language. They also tended to regard "democratic" politics as false and affected. They were in sum more interested
in a critical appraisal of life than in any crusade for reform.

It was natural then that Holberg should be their favorite author;
some knew his comedies by heart, and they all laced their conversation with his witticisms. Ibsen had loved Holberg since his days in Grimstad. In him he found that same sense of the ludicrous and that impulse
to mock that was so much a part of his own nature; after six lonely
years in Bergen it was a complete delight to feast on the satiric spirit
of Holberg. The "Dutchmen" even nicknamed him after a Holberg
character, Gert Westphaler, "the blabbering barber." The association of
the silent and unapproachable Ibsen and the non-stop talker Gert was
odd, but among good friends Ibsen did give vent to his feelings and
did talk a great deal. In anger he lashed out at current examples of hypocrisy and pettiness, hurling paradoxes from his corner of the sofa and
letting the epithets fall where they might. He began to experiment with
a peculiar form of dialectical argument: what would happen if an owl
grew afraid of the dark, or if a fish could not stand water, or if a man
were lowered to the center of the earth where there was neither up
nor down? Was the mathematical proposition two plus two equals four,
valid on the Dog star? Although all this was the blabbering of Gert
Westphaler to his friends, Ibsen felt he was testing his mind and formu-
lating those inner paradoxes and doubts that would soon burst forth
into an attack on accepted truth.

As long as he harbored this critical spirit, he never gave himself
fully to the influence of Bjørnson. The other "Dutchmen" had a great
dislike for Bjørnson and never accepted him as their leader. They admitted he was a great poet, perhaps Norway's greatest, but they were
basically indifferent to lyric poetry and made no effort to appreciate
him. Outside of poetry, especially in politics, they felt he had no ability
at all. An ardent admirer of Bjørnson has stated that immediately after
the poet's return to Oslo in 1859, Birkeland, Botten Hansen, and Ibsen
"made it their business to ignore Bjørnson." It is true that a number of
the group were delighted with Vinje's slashing of Bjørnson's new novel,
Arne. Their attitude is perhaps summed up by Vinje's comment to
Botten Hansen: "The man's a poor ignoramus." Some of Vinje's comments do sound as though Ibsen had thought them up. In an 1860 letter
Vinje writes, "Good Lord, if a person could only be as happy as Bjørnson
and believe he's a great man. Then one could sleep on one's laurels!"
And a few months later he wrote: "I do not have the happy disposition
of Bjørnson, who sails with the tide and never worries about the ebb."
This mixture of admiration and disdain must have filled Ibsen too.

On the whole Ibsen's early years in Oslo appear to have been happy ones. He found joy and much promise in his work, he had plans for his future writing, and his songs were full of courage and vigor. He planned a collection of his verse and began to test public opinion by publishing his 1853 love poems in *Illustreret Nyhedsblad* for March, 1858. In June he went to Bergen to marry his beloved Suzannah. Her father, Dean Thoresen, died a few days after Ibsen arrived, and so the wedding was celebrated quietly on June 18, 1858.

Now he was a married man with his own home in the capital. In this year he probably began the long poem "Life's Spring." Judging from its relation to other poems written in succeeding years, it was most likely begun after the wedding. The fragment that survives contains some of the most ebullient, perhaps "ecstatic" would be more apt, lines he ever wrote. The impersonal high spirits of the "Wanderer's Song" of 1853 are nothing compared to the personal exultation of this poem.

Jeg vil ud, jeg vil ud, i Guds Natur,
I Vaardagens skinnende Lyst;
Min Bringe bugner, jeg bryder
    mit Bur,
Jeg har Vinger og Mod til en Dyst!
Jeg har Mod til en Dyst mod
    Verdens Vee;
Den har lænket mig længe nok.
Nu vil jeg juble, nu vil jeg lee
Mellem Vaarens vingede Flok!
. . .
	I must away, away to God's world,
	The shining ecstasy of Spring;
	My breast swells, my bonds burst,
	I have courage, am winged for battle!
	I have courage for battle with the
	    world's ache;
	It has chained me long enough.
	Now will I exult, now laugh
	Amid spring's winged flock!
	. . .

Mit Sind er som Snekken med Seil i Top, Jeg er ungdomsvældig og fri; Nu gaar min Bane mod Høiden op, Jeg stævner jer alle forbi!	My heart a ship with all sails set, I am youth, and strength, and freedom; My path leads straight to the height, I'll pass you all on the way!

Overbord med Fornuftens Baglast
    kun!
Sæt saa til den sidste Klud!
Kanhænde jeg seiler min Skude
    paa Grund:
Men jeg seiler jer agterud!
	Toss over the ballast of common sense!
	Run up on high each sail!
	Perhaps my ship shall run aground;
	But I'll outstrip you every one!

Not only is this unrestrained, but its contempt for the elegiac mood is in sharp contradiction with his own earlier poetry:

Elegiske Rimblomster aanded jeg frem Paa Rudens isnende Glas; En hjertestraale fra Lysets Hjem Har nu dødet den klamme Stads.	Elegiac frost-flowers I did Breathe on my icy windowpanes; One ray of the heart-warmed sun Has dispelled the clammy stuff.

He felt new poetry break out as the springtide within gave birth to "jubilant songs of spring."

This is as far as the poem ever got; spring withered and he ended in mid-stanza on a strangely bitter note. As he looks out over the moor with its straight young spruces, he thinks:

Under dem gaar Veien fremad,	Under these the path pushes on,
Ligegodt hvorhen—	Never mind where —
Ligegodt naar kun ei hjemad—	Never mind, but never homeward —

Now it was not enough to escape to nature; he wanted to get far away from the homeland that had become a cage where his wings were clipped. Perhaps his joyous spring song is meant as a picture of a past now done and to be forgotten. He seems to confirm this speculation by a statement made in 1858 that he had already begun to think of the theme of *Love's Comedy*, the play that crowded out the saga drama on Earl Skule he had planned to write immediately after *The Vikings*. The image of running his ship aground appears in the new play, with an undertone of irony that suggests weariness and despair. "Life's Spring" ended in shipwreck.

More and more he grew obsessed with the contrast between life and poetry, particularly the kind of poetry he was called on to write. He was a facile versifier, his songs in demand for a hundred different occasions. Although he could respond with ringing appeals for action and struggle, he grew more and more disenchanted with this kind of work and often wound up with the poem unfinished and the printer's boy waiting on the doorstep. He felt his mind was being depleted at the same time that his soul was still without the great sorrow that would waken it. The daily round of life gradually tightened about him and he could not cry out.

His work at the theatre grew irksome. As he felt the growing insincerity of his involvement with the national cause and a general boredom with super-patriots, he began to object to the ultra-Norwegian pronunciation which Knud Knudsen had set down as the norm for the theatre. Ibsen advocated a freer, more natural form of cultivated speech for the actors, but he was ignored. His freedom of action and decision was greater than in Bergen, but the daily routine demanded so much attention that he had less free time than before. In Bergen he had been contracted to write plays; here there was no time. He frittered away his talent with indifferent verses and had not one play to show for the five years he was director at the theatre.

How deeply he resented this period in his life can be seen in a letter he wrote to Bjørnson in 1867, in which he advised him against accepting a similar position: "If it were just the loss of time involved, it might be all right; if all one's poetic inspiration and images could be pushed aside to be picked up later—but it *isn't* so! Other inspirations come, but the first die stillborn. For a dramatist to work in the theatre is for him *to perform an abortion every single day*. That crime is punished in civil law; I can't say if God is more liberal." And he added: "Talent is no privilege; it is a duty." He knew that he was betraying his greatest obligation in these years: he would write in *The Pretenders*, "Songs never sung remain ever the loveliest."

For consolation he could turn to his painting. In Bergen he had studied with J. L. Losting and benefitted greatly from the lessons, particularly in the costume drawings he had to make for stage productions. He also did landscape painting on his walking tours in the countryside. He had never given up the idea of perhaps making a career as painter. In the Grimstad days he had thought of combining painting with a literary career, and the same idea led him to study oil painting with Magnus Bagge in Oslo. At least as late as 1862 he always had some work in progress on his easel, but although he could express his creativity this way, he must have realized his talent here was never as great as in his writing. But would he have to settle for this second-best medium simply because self-doubt thwarted his writing?

While Ibsen fell silent, Bjørnson came forward as the great voice of young Norway. He had arrived later than Ibsen and had written much less, but his position was already much greater. And his books were much more the expression of a personal need than Ibsen's had been. He captivated his audience with *Synnøve Solbakken*. In 1859-60 first appeared *Arne*, and then *A Happy Boy*, plus other country tales, all fresh and personal in form and deeply heart-warming in content. Moreover, there was that aura of self-confidence and enthusiasm he always projected. He knew he was born to lead, and others knew it too from his erect, commanding figure. In Bergen he had made himself a political leader with a nationalistic platform, and although he was not as successful with the same program in Oslo, the songs that took the country by storm made him a national leader.

He threw Ibsen completely into the shade. A small man and timid in public, Ibsen did not have the resources to cause a stir around him. He was pushed aside as even Vinje, "the Dalesman," was given more attention than he. By 1858 Vinje, who was a shrewd newspaperman, had polished a highly personal idiom in verse, and had managed to get the city and even the entire country to notice him. Ibsen had a couple of nationalistic plays to his credit, plays that were appreciated but not considered particularly different from what had already been written. No one anticipated his rising to greater heights.

In the spring of 1860 Bjørnson, Ibsen, and Vinje applied to the government for travel grants: Bjørnson asked for support as a poet, which the other two did not dare do. Vinje said he wanted to study jurisprudence, folk life and folk-lore in England and Scotland; Ibsen said he wanted to take a six-month tour of theatres in London, Paris, Copen-hagen, Stockholm, and major cities in Germany. Bjørnson was bold enough to ask for 1000 dollars; Vinje asked for 500, and Ibsen for 400. The university gave its recommendation only to Vinje, but the cabinet awarded him a mere 250 dollars, while giving Bjørnson 500. No one thought it worth while to give Ibsen anything at all.

In torment and self-doubt, he returned to the pessimistic lines written in Bergen, "In the Picture Gallery," and readied them for publication. The self-castigation that fills the twenty-three sonnets of this cycle is in mocking contrast to "Life's Spring"; instead of happy voyaging he warned himself to haul in sail:

Seil med Forstand; thi   Sail with caution: your poetical bark
    Digtersnekken krænger   will overturn at the slightest puff of
Ved mindste Pust af Livets Ironi.   life's irony.

But from this impasse he was able to move on to the reckoning with himself he had planned in "Life's Spring." In 1870 he said that the first fruits of "the more serious meaning his life had taken on" were in the poem "On the Heights," composed in the last months of 1859 and printed shortly after New Year's, 1860. The relation of this poem to "Life's Spring" is clear from the question it asks:

Hjemad? Har da *der* jeg hjemme,   Homeward? Can I be at home *there*
    hvor min Hug ej længer færdes?   where my heart no longer dwells?

"On the Heights" presents an Ibsen in the midst of a crucial struggle between the two basic impulses of his nature, an aesthetic and an ethical view of life. This formulation of the struggle is easily identified as one of his legacies from Kierkegaard, where it is most clearly and fully expressed. For Ibsen it was not simply a philosophical problem but a conflict that filled his entire life until victory was won by the stronger, the ethical impulse. The question would return in his old age—had not the aesthetic defeated the ethical after all?

The poem shows a man mastered by aestheticism, a philosophy which makes life a drama to be enjoyed for its artistic value. One can stand outside life and observe like a spectator, or he may, like the "Seducer" in Kierkegaard's *Either-Or*, indulge his own dramatic instinct by egging on the response and conflicts of others. Aestheticism is the poison that saps the manly vigor of romanticism. It is what the Danish philosopher Sibbern called "the hollow eye" which sees only the reflections of life (*Huuløjet*) "as in a mirror darkly." When Heiberg called for "reflective-ness" rather than "inspiration," he was making it the basis of his poetic theory. But this endless self-analysis stifles a man's innate spontaneity.

The narrator of the poem tells how he has run away from mother and bride to live in the mountains with only his dreams and yearnings. The force that drives him away from life is embodied in the "Strange Hunter," who robs him of the "very power of will" and teaches him that the "freedom of the heights" will confirm his longing to live alone with his thoughts. And when his heart breaks as he watches his home and his mother perish in flames on Christmas Eve, the "Strange Hunter" coolly bids him notice the artistic effect of flames in moonlight. Then:

Han kikked gjennem den hule Haand	He peered down through his cupped hand
Til Vinding for Perspektivet —	To get the perspective right.

Now the man who at first thought only of his great loss had to admit that:

det *var* Effekt	it *was* effective,
I den dobbelte Natbelysning!	this coupled nocturnal lighting!

And when at Midsummer his young bride rides to her wedding with another, he watches the entire proceedings from his lofty pinnacle, "self-steeled," with his hand cupped "to get the perspective right." He actually enjoys seeing:

hvor smukt hendes røde Stak	how smartly her skirt gleams red
Mellem Bjerkestammerne lyser.	against birch-white.

He feels free, high above the people of the valley:

Mit Lavlandsliv har jeg levet ud;	My lowland-life is past and gone;
Heroppe paa Vidden er Frihed og Gud,	On the heights are freedom and God;
Dernede famler de Andre.	Down below the others grope.

No other poem bares Ibsen's inner conflict so totally, and few other poems examine so relentlessly the aesthetic view of life. Ten years later this would be the first poem to be included without change in his collected edition—unmistakable evidence of its importance to him and his evaluation of the success of its content and form.

He spoke of the poem as being born of "a need to free himself." But from what? If many students of Ibsen have come up with many answers to this question, it is perhaps a tribute to his great talent for posing rather than settling questions; that was his lifelong policy. The idea of liberation exists in several formulations in the poem. First there is the need to extricate himself from sorrow and pain and to arm himself against the world with an intellectual coat of steel-hard mail. Does this mean that he considers aestheticism as a possible way of life? More personally, does it mean he will look with dispassionate calm on his own mother from whom he has separated himself? Counterbalancing this, however, is the powerfully felt need to free himself of this very aestheticism. He struggled with all his power to avoid becoming that bloodless connoisseur of art, another "Strange Hunter." The thought of losing his will to act was torment, and he was in anguish to feel that:

Det flommer ei længer i Aarens Elv,	No longer do the rivers of my
Og jeg tror jeg mærker i Bringens	veins crest;
Hvælv	I think I feel at the roots of my heart
Alleslags Tegn til Forstening.	all the signs of stone.

The petrifaction of his heart was no ideal but death itself. He could never wish to become an aesthete, but was gathering his forces against the impulse he felt to go that way. He fought this battle for two years before he sighted victory — if it ever came. "My freedom did not find complete voice," he wrote in 1870, "until *Love's Comedy*." There is an intimate psychological connection between the poem and the play, reinforced by their proximity in time. The theme in both is the aesthetic view of life; the play was planned and partially written in 1860, immediately after the poem.

The play's first version, called *Svanhild*, is an uncompleted prose fragment, but it is clearly the same story and the same plot as the finished version. Ibsen was no doubt referring to his work on this first version when he wrote, three years later in 1860, apropos of *Love's Comedy:* "If there was ever a compulsion for an author to rid himself of a mood and a material, I felt it when I began this play." He noted that his wife was the model for Svanhild; he could probably have added that the play itself was born of their marriage. She had shown her hatred of conventional sentiment by making a statement that was immediately bruited about the whole apartment house where they were living. When she returned from the maternity clinic where their son Sigurd was born (of course, a Hjørdis had to give birth to a Sigurd), she bluntly and loudly announced that this was the end of child-bearing for her. Many a new mother has probably thought the same, but to say so was a scandal, almost the same as dissolving a marriage. Ibsen was caught in a dilemma. Here was the perfect application of those theoretical speculations he had indulged in in Grimstad, all about spouses living in separate apartments and using the formal mode of address to one another, but in practice . . .? Whatever sense of deprivation her decision may have caused him crashed head on with his intellectual convictions. The crisis led directly to the drama, where both sides are aired.

In *Svanhild* we meet the poet Falk, still in the aesthetic stage of development. Like the author, he longs to "beg a great pain from the Lord," in order to have something out of which to make poetry. He stones a starling so that he can make a poem about a dead bird; he urges Svanhild to sing for him until he is through with her and promises to repay her with his verses. Life exists for him merely as grist for his poetic mill. Svanhild, hardly more than a child, tells him that he is "really an evil man," and he must admit that this is not just childish prattle, but what he also feels to be true.

It is uncertain just how much of this version Ibsen had completed; he probably was having trouble with the ending. Falk was apparently ready to break out of the aesthetic shell, but the maiden Svanhild was hardly the type of strong-hearted woman he needed to spur him on. Ibsen may still have been drawing partly on the image of young Rikke Holst (Falk's speech about "flowers of the field and potted plants" recalls one of Ibsen's poems to Rikke), and the general impression the fragment gives is that the conflict of the play is not yet felt on a mature, personal level. He could not complete the play because he had not yet taken sides in the battle between the ethical and the aesthetic views of life.

As has been noted already, this was precisely the unresolved conflict that had been with him ever since he first dreamed of becoming a writer. Ten years before, while in his first love-disappointment, he wrote that happiness was not in the winning but in the yearning. He too wanted his young women to sing to him:

Hvad der bæver i din Sjæl,	All that pulses within your heart
Bærer jeg fra Fjeld til Fjeld,	I'll bear from peak to peak;
Fantaserer, naar du tier,	When you're still, I'll fantasize on all
Over dine Melodier!	your melodies!

But what had once been a consolation now became an inner conflict that had to be fought through before peace came. The same struggle appears in a poem written on the death of Heiberg in the summer of 1860. The author and critic had been the great Cham of Danish culture for many years, but in Ibsen's poem (later called "To the Survivors") he is transformed into a "thorn-crowned sower...borne down by traitor shields," and never appreciated in his lifetime! The reason for this peculiarly inept description is made clear in the lines that speak of others in Scandinavia "whose breasts are scorched by torches they themselves have fired." Ibsen, of course. He was so immersed in his own struggle that he transferred it unconsciously to the innocent Heiberg.

In this great depression, with the double refusal of funds for the theatre and for his own travel plans, he labored for three years without completing a play. Again doubts of his genius haunted him, and he must have felt, as Francis Bull has noted, "the loss of a guiding hand" when Bjørnson went abroad in the spring of 1860. He became rather slovenly and lost that old pride in his appearance; he wore a battered hat and let his beard and hair grow until it was all a tangled mass. And when he sat alone in cheap cafes, his chin propped up in one hand and marks of woe on his mouth, it seemed as if he had lost hope completely.

The most telling evidence of this is that he, who had always fulfilled his duties so conscientiously, now shirked them or did slipshod work. And this was the worst of all times for him to be derelict in his duties. The Norwegian Theatre had remodeled its building in the summer of 1860 and had collected money from all over the country to construct an efficient stage. The remodeling costs were higher than had been anticipated and the theatre entered the new season with an additional burden of debt. The director should have dug in now; instead he gave up the struggle.

It is pathetic to recall the plays he chose to open the new season — material that he despised from his soul: the operettas *Tordenskjold* by Blom and *The Fairy's Home* by Jensen, and finally *The Men of Gudbrandsdal* by Monsen, all examples of the worst kind of "national" play. Suzannah helped him with a new translation of a German historical play by Karl Gutzkow—a piece he had praised very modestly in his *Andhrimner* days. It was a bold effort, but a failure nonetheless; the public did not want it any more now than they had in 1851.

He entrusted *The Vikings at Helgeland* to the rival Christiania Theatre, where it was performed in 1861, with Laura Svendsen (later Laura Gundersen) in the lead role of Hjørdis. This was an important step forward for her, and she worked on the part more thoroughly than usual, trusting less to her moments of sudden inspiration than was her custom. If she did not totally succeed in achieving great art, it was in large measure the fault of a weak supporting cast. It has been reported that the first performance "managed to arouse quite unusual interest in the public," but *Morgenbladet* was the only newspaper that bothered to comment on the event. The other papers were silent, the public was indifferent, and the play was given up after five performances. It was hardly a triumph for Ibsen.

It was inevitable that the theatre should suffer from the discouragement he felt. Facile as he was at verse-making, he could not write a prologue for opening night; worse still, he became careless at rehearsals and was unable to discipline the actors and the orchestra. As the season wore on, he had fewer and fewer ideas to offer, while Christiania Theatre packed the house with the same Erik Bøgh musical Ibsen had staged the previous year. Audiences were not given much to choose from. The trustees were losing patience with him and behind his back said that his lack of enterprise was ruining the theatre. Soon they were saying it to his face. One stamped his foot at him in anger; another, an educator named Knud Knudsen, nicknamed "The Growler" by his pupils, dressed him down as if he were one of his schoolboys. Knudsen may have been especially annoyed by Ibsen's failure to support the nationalistic language program in the theatre. He later reported that he had "raked Ibsen

over the coals as he had probably never been raked before or since."
The chairman of the trustees felt that Knudsen had been too severe,
but Ibsen made no reply; occasionally he did try to defend himself,
but most of the time he just stayed away from board meetings. Sometimes the board had to track him down in a local cafe and hold meetings there.

The criticism was not limited to the theatre's staff and board; in the
fall of 1860 the newspapers began to complain about the lack of direction at the theatre. Ibsen was angry and defended himself, particularly
in a series of articles on "The Two Theatres of Christiania," in *Morgenbladet* in March and April of 1861. In these he asserted that the main
task was to create a truly national dramatic art, a problem which the
old Danish Christiania Theatre had never even thought of solving, but
one which the Norwegian Theatre with its improved stage facilities
could begin to attack. He even defended the previous year's repertory
on the grounds that it was not *what* was produced but *how* it was
produced.

However, he even lacked the interest to complete the articles in spite of
repeated requests to do so. Attack followed attack during May and June;
both *Christiania-Posten* and *Morgenbladet* contrasted his accomplish-
ments with his announced ideals and accused him of neglecting his
responsibility in selecting plays and supervising productions. He was
told flatly that he was unfit to be director and that Bjørnson ought to
replace him. He replied in *Aftenbladet,* but his defense, limited only to
his choice of plays, was more indignant than convincing. Botten Hansen
went to his defense in *Illustreret Nyhedsblad,* mainly to point out the
difficulties under which he labored. Even he had to grant that Ibsen
lacked interest in his work. The article indicated that "opinion was running against Ibsen," and this was confirmed at the annual meeting of
the theatre board in August when the chairman made public a statement
to the effect that "the artistic director has not shown as great a spirit of
enterprise as is considered desirable." And even one of Ibsen's own
actors gave a lecture at the Norwegian Society criticizing his slipshod
direction.

Finally he managed to break out of his depression and pull himself
together, and this victory is reflected in the great poem written toward
the end of 1861, "Terje Vigen." This is the only one of his narrative
poems he was willing to include in the collected edition and it remains
one of the most vital of his poetic works, still included in readers and
anthologies. The straightforward, terse, and vivid language echoes the
ballad style without imitating it; the ballad idiom lends strength and
variety to the lyric mood. In addition the story builds to such a tension-

filled climax that a great wave of pathos sweeps over the reader as he recognizes the national and the intensely personal implications of the verses. Ibsen's heart-blood was poured into the image of the strange and lonely islander Terje and his struggle with himself.

Why Ibsen should have returned to this Grimstad material is uncertain, unless the intensity of his suffering brought those days back to him. In the spring of 1861 he had also written the poem "Distress at Sea" (*I Havsnød*), about heroic seamanship off the Agder coast. The poem glances obliquely at the Schleswig-Holstein crisis that almost drove Denmark into war with Germany, and now as in 1848 Ibsen was wholeheartedly in favor of Swedish and Norwegian aid for Denmark. He remembered a story an old pilot had told him of three sailors who had fought the Danes, and then risked their lives to save a Danish ship simply because one could not let *Danes* perish without trying to save them. To Ibsen this was an image of how the most patriotic of Norwegians would be the first to stand up when Denmark was threatened. From the seascape and crisis of "Distress at Sea" to the old pilot Terje Vigen was a simple move.

Terje Vigen became a symbol of his own inner conflict; he too knew what it was to suffer:

De lange Aar i Prisonens Kvalm,	Endless years in the stifling dungeon
De gjorde mit Hjerte sygt.	That made me sick at heart.
Bagefter laa jeg, som Hejens Halm,	Beaten I lay, like wind-rolled grass,
Og saa i et Braadyb stygt.	And stared into the awful void.

But Terje's heart mends and he wins through the crisis:

Terjes Pande bar Klarhed og Fred,	On Terje's brow was light and peace,
Hans Bringe gik frit og stilt.	His heart beat free and soft.
. . .	. . .
Han aanded, som løst fra et Fængsels Hvælv,	He breathed as one from prison freed,
Hans Stemme lød rolig og jævn:	His voice grew steady and calm:
"Nu er Terje Vigen igjen sig selv.	"Now Terje Vigen's himself again.
. . .	. . .
Indtil nu gik mit Blod som en stenet Elv;	Till now my blood was a boiling torrent;
For jeg maatte—jeg maatte ha'e Hævn!"	I had to—had to have revenge!"
. . .	. . .
Drømmenes Uvejrskyer graa	One violent night had swept away
Fejed en Stormnat væk;	The gray, brooding clouds;
Og Terje bar atter saa rank, som Faa,	And Terje again held high the head
Den Nakke, der krøgtes hin Dag han laa	He had had to bow that day
Iknæ paa Korvettens Dæk.	He knelt on the war ship's plank.

During the months he was writing the poem, Ibsen is known to have been seriously ill with periods of depression and high fever that endangered his life. One time when he was left alone, he rushed wildly into the streets, driven by thoughts of suicide. Suzannah calmed him and watched over him patiently. She bore all this without complaint; their life was poor but she was proudly unbent as she went about her tasks with little Sigurd in her arms. Ibsen thought perhaps of her when he has Terje Vigen say:

Nei, den som frelste, da værst det kneb, Det var nok den Lille der!	The savior when things were worst, As surely the little one there!

He had snatched his life out of the abyss and now with courage took up the battle against the doubts and despair that had almost over-whelmed him. In the winter of 1861-62 he applied himself to his tasks at the theatre as never before. The quality of the new repertory was better than in any previous year, and he did not let his energies be sapped by trivial verse-making. The season opened with an original play, presented anonymously but actually by J. L. Sundt, titled *Niels Lykke*, a historical drama similar to his own *Lady Inger*. More important was the next play, Bjørnson's *King Sverre*. Ibsen invited the members of the Storting as well as the cabinet to the opening night. For the occasion he wrote an excellent prologue on the Norwegian flag, later called "The Storting House" (*Stortingsgården*), the only one of his many prologues he found good enough to be included in his collected poems. In the spring he staged Bjørnson's *Hulda the Lame*, which Christiania Theatre had held without producing for four years. He was also the first to produce Musset in Norway, putting on the lyrical drama *Un Caprice* (1847). He also put on one of two German historical dramas of Gustav Freytag, in the style of Karl Gutzkow, that Suzannah had translated. The rest of the repertory was equally rich and varied, and the theatre was praised for its outstanding ensemble playing. Ibsen was back on his feet hard at work and no longer adrift.

Then, after all this, the worst blow fell; the theatre had to close. When he became artistic director, the theatre had had a debt of 1800 dollars. After the theatre building was bought and extensive improvements made, the property was worth about 14,000 dollars, but the debt had by then risen to 28,000 dollars and creditors pressed harder and harder for payment. In the summer of 1862 the theatre was forced to give up its property in bankruptcy court. Salaries had already (at New Year's) been reduced by one sixth; now there were no salaries at all. Directors and actors were discharged as of June 1, 1862; the actors continued to play for whatever they could collect, but Ibsen was left without any source of income.

CHAPTER THIRTEEN

IN SEARCH OF FOLKLORE (1862)

THE LAST PERFORMANCE at the Norwegian Theatre took place on May 11, 1862. However painful it must have been to lose this regular employment, he must have felt great relief at being free. The last year had been a constant struggle to keep the theatre afloat; now he could rest. He was, in fact, free enough of burdens to let himself be hired again to produce occasional verse. These festive academic poems included one for Constitution Day, May 17, one for the inter-Scandinavian student festivities at Lund and Copenhagen (in which he did not participate), which was a salute to Sweden, sung at Lund on June 11, and a welcome to the returning students on June 22. The refrain of all these verses was the same, the old song about taking up the fight for freedom; the note of cheerful optimism suggests that he had taken heart himself.

There was one pleasant prospect: a summer of travel. When one considers how little people traveled in his day, Ibsen actually saw a great deal of his country. He had lived in two small towns and two of the largest cities, and he had twice visited Trondheim, the third largest city. He had traveled between Oslo and Bergen both by land and sea; he had gone by way of Valdres as well as Sogn; he had wandered in Voss and in Hardanger. Now he was to see new regions of the country, mountain valleys and fjords, and for a few weeks at any rate he would be free from financial worries. In March he hit upon the idea of applying to the university for one of the grants made for research trips within the country. His plan to use the summer months for collecting ballads and folk-tales in the western fjord districts from Hardanger north to Romsdalen fitted in neatly with his national-romantic writings. Moreover, he liked to think that his poetry had a scientific basis, and research on folk life and the folk imagination would demonstrate this. He applied for 120 dollars, which the university and the Ministry of Church and Education reduced to 110, according to the honored Norwegian bureaucratic tradition of never giving the requested amount. Nevertheless, this was a generous sum and more than enough to meet the modest travel and living expenses of the day. Ibsen was delighted when the grant was made on May 24.

A month later he set out, but not in the direction he had planned. Instead he went northwards to Lillehammer, and then up Gudbrandsdalen. There was a thunderstorm on the first day, which made him a bit nervous; at Hamar it rained and Lake Mjøsa was cold and forbidding. But the sun came out in Gudbrandsdalen and his mood so brightened that he thought an extraordinary adventure would happen at any moment; he might even run into Count Snoilsky, the young Swedish poet whose collected poems had just come out and whose name was on everyone's lips.

There were few of the legends and folk-tales he was looking for in Gudbrandsdalen, but he did speak with the people and learned much about their lives and adventures. He was curious about these people and many of the episodes he heard remained with him to reappear as the germ of later writings. On one of his last evenings he visited the parsonage at Lom; he was more than usually taciturn, but later events proved that he had listened keenly to stories the others were telling.

On Saturday, July 5, he crossed the mountains into Sogn, where the ice and snow-covered peaks, especially Fanaråken Mountain, made a tremendous impression on him. His companions here also impressed him. One was a young law graduate, L. M. B. Aubert, just engaged and filled with thoughts of his love; the other was a Catholic priest, Chr. Holfeldt-Houen, dark and severe and a fighter for his religion. When they arrived at Turtagrø and looked down on the Sogn Fjord, Ibsen was struck by the drama of nature and the equally dramatic contrast of his two companions.

In his travel diary he noted that he changed his itinerary the night he stayed at the parsonage in Lom. There he apparently decided to go to Sunnmøre as directly as possible, not stopping on the way any more than absolutely necessary. The first night in Sogn was spent at the Skjolden Inn in Lyster. That same evening he and his companions learned that they could leave on Sunday morning on the steamer Framnæs, which had ferried on the fjord since 1858. Ibsen left the steamer at Vadheim in outer Sogn and took the road north through Sunnfjord and Nordfjord. In the next few days he went by foot and by rowboat through Sanda and Førde, where he could see some of the most beautiful sights of the entire region, particularly on Lakes Jølster and Breim.

He found the countryside magnificent and wrote of the "splendid wilderness," where the road seemed to be blasting its way "through monstrous, undulating, riven mountain walls" and "fallen peaks and boulders so large that one could have carved an entire cathedral out of many of them." Although he was hurrying on his way, he still took time to make some sketches. Then he followed the old mountain road across from Breim, where the going was rough both up and down. At the summit of the mountain he saw an incomparable vista, with snow-clad peaks on all sides and the fjord far below. From Utvik he took a boat across the fjord to Faleide, climbed the steep hills to Hornindal, and then went on to Sunnylven in Sunnmøre. He traveled so quickly that he arrived by July 11; in this bare week he could hardly have gathered much folk-lore. But his interest was probably more taken by the natural beauty that surrounded him, a tonic for both body and spirit.

In Sunnylven he made the first long stop of the journey. The cloistered life of this out-of-the-way fjord community struck his imagination, and he could sense the overpowering pressure of the natural forces that hung over and cowed these villagers. From his youth he had known how the sea could annihilate man and his great works; now he heard how the mountains falling could sweep away both church and farm. The country people are said to have been suspicious of the "student" (for so he was still called) from the capital who went about writing down everything he was told. In addition to this suspicious practice he was reported to be a "freethinker" and was seeing much of a farmer, Steins-Knut, who was also suspect. Ibsen later said that Steins-Knut was "the most intelligent farmer I have ever met." Moreover, the minister was courteous, and this no doubt allayed suspicion in the village.

From here he took the steamer to Sjøholt in Ørskog, where he was probably the guest of his wife's cousin, attorney Ludvig Daae, at Solnær, who was a connoisseur of local history. Ibsen had met him a few years before in The Norwegian Society, and it was no doubt he who introduced Ibsen to Peder Fylling, the collector of folk-lore in Skodje. Here was finally a man who could help him. Peder was ten years older, and his historical work had been reported in an article in *Aftenbladet* in 1856. An injury in his youth made physical labor impossible, so he had devoted himself to gathering material for a history of his community and the neighboring region. Some twelve or fifteen years later he would begin to publish small collections of tales, but at this time he seemed content if he secured an audience for the stories he had gathered. Ibsen sat with him day after day, asking questions and taking it all down as fast as he could write. He amassed a sizeable volume, the most precious treasure of his travels.

From Skodje and Ørskog he next made his way to Vestnes in Romsdalen. There he called on the pastor, the notorious O. T. Krohg, whose articles in *Morgenbladet* had made him a favorite target for abuse. His three days in Vestnes were not profitable and he met no one who could be of service. The Vestnes episode would later be a cause of minor annoyance to him. In his article on the town in *Illustreret Nyhedsblad* he could not resist poking fun at the opinionated and self-satisfied pastor by paraphrasing sarcastically some of his articles, including a juicy bit about a widow whom the pastor had mentioned in one of his effusions. The pastor issued a severe reprimand in *Morgenbladet*, criticizing the "extraordinary irresponsibility" Ibsen had shown. It was a disgrace, he declared, that a man who has been given public funds to gather folk-tales should collect town "slander" instead. He also hinted that Ibsen was generally unreliable and full of "mischief." The editor of *Illustreret Nyhedsblad* was forced to "retract the rumor as without foundation and express regret that it had been allowed in our columns." But he did add that the pastor had used unnecessarily harsh words in condemning Ibsen's "inadvertent" remark. Even so, Ibsen must have smarted under this public trouncing.

From Vestnes he seems to have taken the shortest way home — up Romsdalen and down Gudbrandsdalen — arriving there in August. A drawing of a landscape in the latter region was shown in *Illustreret Nyhedsblad* on August 17; this and three drawings of the same trip published later was the only art work he ever made any money on. But now his steady income was gone and he had to try anything. He lived by his pen from week to week, and when that did not bring in enough, he had to borrow.

He printed four of Peder Fylling's tales in *Illustreret Nyhedsblad* in October and November. And in November he signed a contract with the bookseller Johan Dahl to publish a 250-page collection of tales. This was the first time since *The Feast at Solhaug* in 1856 that a publisher was willing to take on one of his books. The book was to include not only the tales collected on the trip, but other folk legends as well, so that it could serve as a replacement for Andreas Faye's collection of thirty years ago. He had planned to do the book during the winter, but when March, 1863, arrived, he was again applying to the university for another grant of 120 dollars for a tale-gathering trip to Trøndelag. He received only 100 dollars, the trip was never made, nor did the book ever appear. The manuscript itself disappeared until long after his death, when it was finally printed in a 1952 supplement to the centennial edition of his works. But material he had collected in 1862 was not included even in this definitive edition. According to his own report he had noted down many other folksongs and fairy tales, none of which has come to light.

The expedition was not in vain, however. He had seen and heard much that would become the material of his writing. He garnered a wealth of fresh impressions of nature and the folk life of his country, and they would come to life with deeper psychological implications when he had succeeded in freeing himself from the constrictions of the last three years. He was also learning to write in a more colloquial, popular style, as the tales he prepared for publication indicate. He would profit from what he had learned throughout his entire career as a writer.

CHAPTER FOURTEEN

THE ANGRY POET:
LOVE'S COMEDY (1862)

As soon as he returned from his summer field trip, Ibsen wrote two articles for *Illustreret Nyhedsblad* about a crisis which arose at Christiania Theatre when the actors had refused to work in the chorus. He stated that he wished to "defend an important aspect of dramatic art which might be ignored by the public," and appealed to the actors to show that kind of dedication to their art which would allow them to sacrifice personal considerations for the larger goal of the entire theatre. The highly personal note in this appeal stemmed from his own experiences and the problem he was now faced with. He pointed out that all artists had to endure deprivation and anxiety and were even forced into exile, but they remained faithful to their sacred mission. Actors were unfortunate in that they had "so far missed the blessing of self-denial, a fate which no man may enjoy without impunity. Any man of large vision who lacks the opportunity to starve or suffer has one less avenue to greatness open to him." He ended by recalling the Roman guard at Pompeii who did not flee the burning ash of Vesuvius because he was still on duty, and so died at his post: "Such a deed springs from the soul, and reveals that spirit which should rule not only in the army or the church, but in the field of art as well."

Since he was enjoying the "blessings of starvation" and suffering, as well as the strengthening of moral fiber that accompanied them, he imagined himself the soldier at that post. He wanted to stand in the rain of burning ash so that his life and his work would soar higher than if he fled to "more comfortable conditions." But his lofty idealism earned him nothing but scorn. He was addressed in a retort as the "sentimental, aesthetically overwrought writer," whose mind was "so benighted by half-baked aesthetic theories" that he could "hardly be brought back to a realistic view of the issue." *Morgenbladet* also used the occasion to insert a reminder that there were some not-to-be-mentioned theatre directors who had at one time been totally deficient in "enterprise and industry."

Ibsen clenched his teeth and threw himself into his work with even more determination. His mind was filled with a new play he was certain would show them all what he was capable of, and yet he had to earn a living. In these autumn months of 1862 he worked as theatre critic for *Morgenbladet* and revealed a sense of moderation and quiet authority that bore witness to his growing maturity and judgment from the days of those youthful critical bludgeonings administered in *Andhrimner*. His critical writing had improved since his work in *Illustreret Nyhedsblad* in 1857. Of course, the theatre now offered more for a critic to approve of than before, but it also seemed that his capacity to enjoy and admire had increased. He was especially kind to the actors, and was as willing to speak well of Danes, such as Chr. Jørgensen and Vilhelm Wiehe, as of Norwegians, such as Laura Svendsen and Johannes and Louise Brun. He rebuked the "carping attitude of our literary society," and showed his indignation at the public's habit of judging everything by preconceived notions that rejected the new or unusual.

When Bjørnson published his historical play *Sigurd Slembe* (1862), Ibsen wrote what amounted to a defense of the new dramatic type of which the play was an example. He spoke approvingly of Bjørnson's style, novel because the playwright was "the first to introduce it," yet traditional because "it already existed as our people's most completely satisfying means of expressing the spirit of nationalism in our day." This praise is unexpected because it amounts to a rejection of the saga style he had used himself in *The Vikings at Helgeland:* "The unusualness of the style lies in its use of the sagas only as an underlying idiom. An author cannot nor should he be original in any fashion but this." Ibsen recognizes his own essential problem when he points out that Bjørnson's intention was not to reflect any "historical event" or the overall "quality of the sagas"; rather, he had sought to embody the conflict in "the hero's inner struggle." Thus the protagonist is none other than the individual, single man, endowed with the capacity and the need for action, ever at war with "the mob," an uncomprehending society.

Worse than the resistance to any important innovation was the general indifference to the problems of art and artists. In both his first and his final reviews (September 11 and November 9) he vented his indignation at this "indifferentism — a worse portent than the most savage attack." He ended by pouring out his scorn on the whole Norwegian people for deluding itself with nationalistic boasting, while doing nothing at all to foster true nationalism: "The Norwegians are moreover a people of the future, that is, a people who are safely asleep in the present and can safely snooze through any possible future—for two reasons: first because we have historical proof that our ancestors did a good day's work; secondly, because we are quite sure that our descendants will on some day wake up to the great mission of the future."

He had declared war on romantic nationalism. And he had also indicated that he had no faith whatsoever in the "will of the people." The "people" was simply a construct of historians, but in actuality "the mob is never guided by a conscious thought or impulse, except one that is invented after the fact."

For all their moderation, the most remarkable thing about his articles at this time is the anger that keeps breaking out at the spiritual sloth of the Norwegian people. Even earlier when he was writing as a romantic nationalist his soul still smoldered with resentment at the indolence of the nation. He had revealed this anger in the sonnets of 1849, when he had tried without success to rouse the Norwegians and the Swedes to fight for South Jutland. His 1851 articles in *Andhrimner* are infused with his contempt for hypocrisy and betrayal of faith, and the same tone can be seen in the poems addressed to the nation throughout the 1850's. He demanded deeds for words. But all this indignation had not yet brought forth the works that would live in their own right; it had not become drama.

Now his locked-up anger overflowed like a volcano that had been gathering fire year after year. All his indignation at the wretchedness of existence in the world and especially in his country burst out in a drama that was at last truly from his own heart, a life he had himself lived, *Love's Comedy.*

The play had simply forced itself on him, he wrote the Danish critic Clemens Petersen shortly after it was produced. Ibsen naturally addressed himself to Petersen because it was he who had helped him make the final transition from a state of "wanting" to be a writer to the condition of "having" to be one. When Petersen insisted that true poetry is born only of burning inner necessity, Ibsen found the theoretical answer to his problem; here was the formulation of the psychological growth he had experienced over the years.

The theme of the play had been developing for many years and began to take shape in 1858, the year of his marriage, when he wrote "Life's Spring" (*En Livsvaar*), the word itself occurs again and again, and will be crucial to the play. The first draft, *Svanhild* (1860), was abandoned because it could not assume the shape of his inner necessity; when he returned to it in 1862 he had weathered the worst crisis of his life and was ready to come to terms with himself. Looking back over all he had done so far, he found nothing of his true self; now he would take up arms against himself and the age he had tried to serve. But he had enjoyed the battle, so it was to be a comedy, not a tragedy.

The first 1860 draft had been prose, but when he took the play up again in the spring of 1862 he began in verse, turning some passages, speech by speech into poetry, and making free verse paraphrases of others. On June 20 he signed a contract with Jonas Lie, the publisher of *Illustreret Nyhedsblad*, to have the play printed as a New Year's gift for the subscribers. He worked on it on his return from the summer field trip and just managed to complete it in time.

Except for the rather impersonally conceived *Saint John's Eve* of 1852, *Love's Comedy* was Ibsen's first drama of contemporary life. Now he did not seek out historical analogies in order to portray psychological conflicts. The play has almost no intrigue or surface plot; its entire substance is the inner life of the main characters. Ten years later Ibsen wrote to Edmund Gosse that the theme of the play was "the conflict between reality and ideal in every aspect of love and marriage in our society." He was perhaps closer to the truth of the play when in the second edition he wrote that it "lashed as best he could the notion of love and marriage" in his age.

These ideas have deep roots in his life, perhaps as far back as his childhood. They appeared as the paradoxes he tossed off in Grimstad; love and marriage are sharply distinguishable states. The affected poet-philosopher in *Saint John's Eve* expresses similar opinions. *Love's Comedy* was not to offer a program of practical reform for the situation; Ibsen wanted rather to hit out against all that angered him in the way society conventionally treated love and marriage. He wanted to show that convention was a stifling strait jacket on the individual's true feelings. Although the conclusion of the play, where the lovers decide to part, is a tragedy, at least for the woman, Ibsen's treatment of the theme is in the manner of the inveterate caricaturist he always was. This cheerful but cutting caricature could best show what society's rigid conventions were making of married and engaged people.

Contrary to the practice of many poets who preferred to use verse for the past and prose for the contemporary scene, Ibsen felt the material would be more natural in verse; prose seemed to make it all flat and tasteless. In 1866 he wrote to Clemens Petersen that he had correctly noted that "verse with symbolic reference is my most natural form of expression." It did actually appear that in certain periods of his life he could write verse much more easily than prose. Always when he was deeply moved, and moved to anger, he sought out verse to allow a bolder and freer sweep to his imagination; the rhythm and rhymes gave edge to the sword he brandished and the sparks flew when he struck. He had never exploited verse so richly or so humorously, or with such daring. He had always been an excellent hand at rhyming, but never before had he produced such comic extravagances as "dryssende —kyss hende," "faat hende—ottende," "rensdyr—imens flyr." He had tossed the rule book overboard.

The number of topical allusions remind one of Aristophanes, or the modern revue skit. He shot barbs at everything: Knud Knudsen's proposals for spelling reform in his 1856 grammar; "Dalesman" Vinje's private periodical, full of his poetry and propaganda; parliamentary discussions of wage hikes and bonuses; the 1862 civil service workers' petition for more pay; the Storting argument with Sweden; an 1860 revolt in Syria; plays by Scribe; well-known business-houses in the city, all called by name; the controversy over Munch's play *Lord William Russell;* the liberal newspaper *Morgenbladet;* and he even quotes from Wergeland and Holberg. He stopped at nothing in order to give the play the feeling of contemporary life.

He so sharpened his language that many of the epigrams have passed into common speech as proverbs of unknown origin. He took care that the merchant should speak in business language, the clerk in bureaucratic jargon, the pastor clerically, and the spinster spinsterly. Each character is etched with a fine ironic stroke that seems completely natural because of the poetic diction. Finally, each character is named after his occupation or main trait: Styver ("Farthing"), Straamand ("Strawman"), Halm ("Straw"), Falk ("Falcon"). The comic inventiveness throughout the play makes it easy to understand what he meant when he said he wrote the play "because he had to break loose."

But this world of caricature and comic exaggeration is only the background for the bitterly serious conflict of the play. Svanhild, a character from the same *Volsung Saga* that had given him the name Hjørdis for *The Vikings,* is the symbol for his theme. As he explained, "Svanhild is the daughter of the king, innocent, but nonetheless crushed under the horses' hoofs." He thought so much of Svanhild as a symbol that he originally intended to give her name to the play, as he would later do with "The Wild Duck" and other symbolic titles. In the play she stands for modern woman who would gladly move into the main arena of life, to struggle and achieve next to the man she loves, except that the "law of the times" and "the world" forbid it.

The issue Ibsen dramatizes was in many ways first examined by Camilla Collett in her novel *The Governor's Daughters* (1854-55), and he was undoubtedly deeply moved by this first, and for many years only, Norwegian work of imagination that could be compared with the best of Hawthorne or George Eliot. Here he learned of the tragedy that could befall a noble and generous spirit when it is hemmed in by a rigid society; here he read the bitter complaint that life and marriage conspire to destroy a woman's love. Its call for social and personal reform incited Ibsen and influenced him not only in his portrayal of all the misery that conventional marriage visited on women, but also in his study of the man who refuses marriage with the woman he loves because he would not "drag our love down into the spiritual bankruptcy of Norwegian middle-class domestic life."

Love's Comedy describes a revolt not only against the conventions of engagement and marriage, but against all social repression of personal freedom. Ironically, one could hardly imagine a man more fearful than Ibsen was of coming into conflict with or violating the laws and customs of his society. He tried to look and act as conventional as possible, thus the impulse to rebel began to work itself out in his writing, when he wrote that he was free to express himself and to declare war on all the "daily prophets of hypocrisy." In his battle-cry, social conventions were branded as "lies"; they could only be put to flight by truth.

A greater companion-in-arms than Camilla Collett appeared to Ibsen as he began this battle, Søren Kierkegaard. No work of Ibsen's is more strongly influenced by the philosopher than *Love's Comedy*. (Even P. G. la Chesnais, who has been most emphatic in denying Kierkegaard's influence on Ibsen, has had to admit that the play shows clear traces of the Dane's philosophy of revolt.) Although inspired by Collett's novel, Ibsen's central theme is quite different from hers. The novel is centered on the problem of the liberation of woman; Ibsen is dramatizing his personal awareness of the effect of modern marriage on a man, but particularly a man who is also a poet. Again, it was the dilemma of his own life and art—the conflict between what Kierkegaard called the aesthetic and the ethical views of life. Ibsen hardly ever escaped from this question, and it constantly led him back to the Kierkegaardian formulation. An additional explanation for the emphasis on this idea in the play is that in the 1860's the Kierkegaardian ideological problem was being discussed in Norwegian intellectual circles more eagerly than ever before.

It is possible that Ibsen was not himself aware of any direct influence from Kierkegaard, for it had been many years since he read anything by the philosopher. But the ideas must have sunk deep into his mind, and there are unmistakable similarities between *Love's Comedy* and at least two of Kierkegaard's writings, "The Seducer's Diary" in *Either-Or* (1843) and, more importantly, *Repetition* (also 1843), a short pamphlet which Kierkegaard called "An Essay in Experimental Psychology."

The psychological conflicts that the philosopher dramatized in these narratives must have remained in his memory.

In *Repetition* we are presented with a poet who is passionately in love but who feels that "his love cannot be realized in human terms": "The moment reality enters, all is lost, all is too late.... My love cannot be expressed in marriage." This is pretty much in the style of Julian in *Saint John's Night:* "Love is to long for love." As long as Kierkegaard's poet only longs for love, his poetic impulse is alive and he can create; as soon as the notion of marriage enters, he must "clip his own wings." It is vitally important that he persuade his loved one to give him up and marry someone else: "She made him a poet; and thus she signed her own death warrant." When he succeeds in making her leave him, he can say: "I am myself again.... It is over...my bark's afloat."

While the parallels are evident, the solution the play proposes is quite different from Kierkegaard's. Ibsen's Svanhild breaks free; she teaches the poet Falk that only by freeing himself from "yearning and wild desire" can he soar freely. She "fills his soul with brightness and poetry." Kierkegaard's poet also has a woman to thank for saving a "soul that was sunk in solitary despair." Now he can "experience the perils of life in the service of an ideal; experience the terrors of battle; experience the intoxication of victory." So too does Falk go off to perform "the work of the day ... answering the call to *struggle* and *renounce*." The play ends with the symbolic act of Falk's departure for the mountains with his companions. The act is the same as in "On the Heights," but the meaning is the opposite. In the poem the liberation on the mountain is an escape into a life of aesthetic self-indulgence; in the play, the experience on the mountain is a symbol of "living for a sacred duty," fully engaged. Falk is a poet still, but no longer a creator of paper flowers, or indoor verse; his poetry is now in the service of life. The aesthetic and the ethical demands are harmonized in a manner not anticipated in Kierkegaard's narrative.

Ibsen's own poetic nature led him to see the conflict from all sides. His characters are living entities and at times they turn against the implicit irony of his portrayal and address the reader persuasively and directly. Merchant Guldstad can speak with wisdom and profundity about the illusions of love, and he has ardent words about something as prosaic as marrying for money. Even the spiritually debased Pastor Strawman is allowed to speak with such pathos that he seems to be defying both the poet and the reader to pass hasty judgment on him. When he describes his ideal picture of a home, he rises to a lyric intensity that makes his words still live with power and conviction.

Ibsen took Suzannah for his model in creating Svanhild; he himself sat for the portrait of Falk. We recognize the self-satire when he has Falk beg for:

— om blot en Maanedstid paa Borg, En Kval, en knusende, en Kjæmpesorg.	—just a loan for a month or so Of a torment, flattening, horrendous pain.

When Falk is led to propose to Svanhild because she can make a poet of him, we can see a parody of his own proposal letter to Suzannah; Ibsen too had the "double-stringed sounding-board within his breast," which enabled him to create an authentic drama where the antagonists oppose one another sharply and convincingly. But each one is so alive in his own right that the reader is tempted to ask: which one is right? The serious and painful problem—how to reconcile the demands of life with the demands of the ideal—this is left without an answer, although one can hear the note of tragedy in the words he gives to Svanhild in conclusion:

Nu er jeg færdig med mit Friluftsliv; Nu falder Løvet—lad nu Verden faa mig!	Now is ended my life of freedom in the open air; Now the leaves are falling—now let the world have me!

He could also treat the same problem humorously, as in the poem "Complications" (Forviklinger), which Georg Brandes called the "wittiest and wisest" of his poems. It was intended for Love's Comedy, but he had it printed separately in the autumn of 1862. Using the image of a bee in a garden, he develops the idea of how love is transformed when one tries to seize it and hold it fast; reality is different from dream. Does it have to be so? "It all could have ended so charmingly" —if—but the situation never permits it to. Our thoughts always imagine another ending, and the eternal tension between dream and reality persists. Why it is so is a question the poem as well as the drama asks.

The play revealed a new Ibsen, one on fire with indignation at the way the world was arranged to stifle ideals and to incubate lies. Although he had tried to write from his heart before, he had not ever achieved this measure of success; the scorn he heaps on "indoor, paper" poetry must be read as self-accusation, a kind of expiation for the excessively "literary" quality of his earlier ballad and saga-derived works. Henceforth he would work from his own experience.

His contemporaries, those who called the tune in society, wanted none of the new poet. They did not understand what he was trying to say; they simply recognized it as satire, and therefore suspect. They thought he was being cynical, not idealistic, when he proclaimed that those who really love should never marry. The few reviews of the play, in February and March, 1863, indicate that the critics could not agree on anything except their revulsion. Ditmar Meidell, editor of *Aftenbladet*, regarded the play as just another "sorry product of the literary restlessness" that had reduced the world of letters to such confusion in recent years. Meidell looked over Ibsen's various flirtations with style after style and concluded that this latest infatuation had no more originality than any of the others. The times demanded novelty and Ibsen was supplying it, that was all. The playwright was "scrambling for effects, and in this wild chase does not hesitate to work the worst baroque and tasteless paradoxes to accomplish his ends." Then, in a rather surprising intellectual somersault, the editor concludes that Ibsen ought to return to his old, imitative style: "He doesn't have what we call genius; he has a talent for technical and literary feats. He could become a poet of taste, because he can easily imitate foreign styles and has a good ear for musical language." Unfortunately, the versification and the rhyming in this latest effort had gotten completely out of hand; "one can only regret the waste of a fine talent."

Professor Monrad, the philosopher who had once spoken well of *Catiline*, tried to analyze the play in *Morgenbladet*. He demonstrated that, philosophically speaking, *Love's Comedy* was no comedy at all, since it was properly speaking a satire. He could find no true drama in it, neither in plot nor catastrophe. By means of a Hegelian dialectic argument, he concluded that Ibsen ought to team up with Bjørnson—since they had exactly opposite poetic qualities: "Only by being taken together could they make up a completely satisfying whole."

Ibsen's new method was thus condemned from totally different points of view; but his ideas were even more upsetting to the critics. The mocking Meidell retold the plot as parody in order to contrast the poetic apparatus with the actual events. He misnamed the grandiloquent idealist Falk as "Mr. Falch," and made of him a complete petit bourgeois. Monrad was more serious than this. He suggested that perhaps Falk was intended to be a kind of Erasmus Montanus, the young student in Holberg's play who cannot adjust to his environment after receiving a smattering of learning. If Ibsen did not intend this, then Falk must be "what, poetically speaking, is almost the worst of all: a cross between a buffoon and a martyr."

For all their conventional morality, neither Meidell nor Monrad could remain insensitive to the searing anger of the play. Meidell admitted that "the ethical content and the aesthetic plan and purpose" of the play was a mystery to him, but he informed his readers that "the author

must have planned a frontal assault on one of the foundations of society."
The play "is finally an out-and-out barrage directed against family life
... it makes the most implacable attack on the one social institution
that philosophers have called the mother of the state — marriage." He
rejected the possibility that the author had only wanted to describe "the
seamy side of family life and its occasional deterioration.... He deliberately presents family life and marriage itself as the seamy side of
life, indeed as the source of all the misery in the world, because marriage
in his view extinguishes true love and forever closes one's eyes to the
ideal."

Monrad once had high hopes for Ibsen and now he was deeply
grieved that he had entered upon a "dangerous course, on which a not
inconsiderable poetic talent might easily founder. To make oneself a
spokesman for the distraught tendencies of the age and its spiritually
enfeebling atheism we regard as poetic ruin—for this Ibsen is surely
too good." But for all his concern, Monrad's judgment on the play was
severe; it was conducive to "a rupture with idealism revolting to human
feeling," and to a pessimism, which is in truth "morally and aesthetically
impossible." The play had to be condemned for both its content and its
form: "In general, the basic idea that dominates the play, namely that
love and marriage are irreconcilable opposites, is not only essentially
false but, in a profound sense, immoral because it debases both love
and marriage. It is also unpoetic, as is any view that presents ideals
and reality as irreconcilable."

Dr. Carl Rosenberg, the Danish critic who reviewed the play in
Dansk Maanedsskrift in February, 1864, had much the same to say.
Love's Comedy did not fit into his rigid definition of literary art either:
"Bitter indignation is the basic mood of this work, and that is not a
poetic mood." Ibsen would eventually demonstrate that great poetry
could be born of such indignation, but the critics would not accept this
from him now. Botten Hansen attempted a timid defense in *Illustreret
Nyhedsblad* by citing Heiberg's dictum that in a work of art it is not
a question of *what* but of *how*. But the public was not interested in such
subtleties; they had caught the words "improper" and "immoral" and
they turned their back on play and playwright.

In his preface to the new edition that appeared four years later in
Denmark, Ibsen wrote: "The play aroused a storm of opposition that
was more violent and extensive than most books could usually arouse
in a society where the majority of people looked on literary matters
with complete indifference."He believed it had been "a mistake to pub-

lish the book in Norway," and hoped that the Danish reviews would be
more favorable. They were, however, not much better. The best was
by Clemens Petersen, the distinguished reviewer of *Fædrelandet*, who
filled half the July, 1863, issue with the play. He had good things to
say about the skillful versification, but found too much artifice in the
rhymes and too little inevitability about the rhymed words; rhyme
seemed to dictate sense, rather than sense rhyme. He also objected to
the intellectual content as untrue and obscure. He had a more liberal
attitude toward poetry than the Norwegian reviewers, but he too had
fairly rigid notions of what poetry ought to be, and of how Ibsen ought
to have written it. He repeated the Norwegian rumor that Ibsen was
good only when working "in the shadow of a recognized model," and
concluded that all Ibsen's writing was "without individuality" because
it was full of contradiction. Ibsen had "a soft, delicate, entirely theoretical temperament," and quickly "vacillated and became unbalanced"
when working on his own. This was Ibsen's own fault, he believed,
because he had not yet "realized how to put his talents and his aims
in right relationship to"—Bjørnson! Petersen actually believed that
Ibsen had been struggling to compete with Bjørnson, sometimes by
imitating him and sometimes by refusing to imitate him. "With Ibsen's
sensitivity to models and his great capacity for pushing on where others
gave up," he should keep up with Bjørnson and help bring the old
order along into the new one that the really great poet-king was forging,
up there ahead.

This was hardly Ibsen's concept of his life's goal, and he protested
to Petersen that he had never imitated Bjørnson nor had he ever written
anything by looking to anyone but himself. But he was glad to have his
book so forcefully presented to the Danish reading public; unfortunately, they did not read it. It is doubtful if a single copy of the first
edition was sold in Denmark. When he wrote to Petersen to thank him
for the kind words about *Lady Inger of Østråt* in the same review, he
said that his comments were more valuable than those of one who did
not know "to what a dreadful extent I am psychologically isolated up
here" could imagine.

In 1867 he wrote that the play's reception did not surprise him; yet
it affected him profoundly. In a town as small as Christiania judgment
against the book quickly became judgment against the man. There was
the inevitable gossip about a married man who had such things to say
about marriage. In 1870 he wrote, "People tossed my personal life into
the discussion, and my reputation suffered greatly. My wife was the

only one who actually approved of the book at the time." Except for her, brave and strong at his side as always, he stood alone: "I was excommunicated; everyone was against me." He was recalling those days when he later wrote from abroad how he "walked through the sullen mob and knew their nasty smirks behind my back." It was a hard time for him. After the play was printed, it had been intimated that Christiania Theatre might produce it, but the general outcry made that impossible. The play was laid aside, and he was not allowed to try it on the stage. This was striking the very weapon out of his hand.

CHAPTER FIFTEEN

FAITH AND DOUBT:

THE PRETENDERS (1863)

IBSEN had played a part in at least one battle that ended happily for the theatre: the radical transformation of the art of acting. The new Norwegian style of acting threw over the rigid, traditional techniques for a more natural style, whose emphasis was on truthfulness to life. Bjørnson and a host of young Norwegian actors would be the ones to hammer out and finally secure the triumph of this style. Ibsen was much too hesitant in his work as stage director to dare such innovations on his own, yet it was his contributions to the discussion and above all his dramatic writings that were the intellectual sustenance upon which the reform movement fed.

After 1850, while the Norwegian theatres were being established in Bergen and Oslo, the old Danish Christiania Theatre began to use more and more Norwegian actors, particularly after the great "battle of the theatre" demonstration which Bjørnson had organized in 1856. Directors ceased to employ new Danish actors, and the old ones began to move out. When Christiania Norwegian Theatre folded in 1862, it was proposed that its actors be transferred to Christiania Theatre, and just as negotiations got under way the theatre discharged its Danish director, Carl Borgaard. As of New Year's, 1863, a five-man board of directors was put in charge, and Ibsen was made literary consultant. Six months later, when the actors trooped over from Møllergata to Bankpladsen, Christiania Theatre ceased to be Danish. Not only were there a mere six Danish actors in a total of forty but, more importantly, the leading performers were all Norwegian, among them the great tragedienne Laura Svendsen (Fru Gundersen after 1864), the versatile, comic-character Johannes Brun, the warmly lyrical Fru Louise Brun, the spirited Fru Lucie Wolf and Sofie Parelius, and such skillful character portrayers as Georg Krohn and Sigvard Gundersen. These formed the nucleus of the truly Norwegian theatre that would, when Bjørnson became director after New Year's, 1865, create a brilliant age of Norwegian dramatic art. In this golden age such as a nation rarely ex-

periences, the dramatic writings of both Ibsen and Bjørnson would urge
the actors on to richer and more convincing portrayals of human
personality.

For the better part of the first year Ibsen served merely as literary
consultant and had little direct influence on developments in acting
reform. He was not even earning his living in the theatre now, but
received a mere 25 dollars a month—and not always that amount in
full every month since he, as well as the actors, had to depend on box
office receipts for their salaries. It was a difficult time for him; on March
10, 1863, in a government application, he listed debts of 500 dollars,
a figure corresponding to a whole year's living expenses. Since he had
no property as collateral, he was probably paying high interest rates
to private lenders—the usurers or "professional Samaritans" he would
depict in *A Doll's House*. Months passed and he sank deeper and
deeper into debt.

As consultant to Christiania Theatre he could no longer write theatrical reviews for *Morgenbladet,* and in any case the paper was probably
not very eager to have him on its staff after the scandal of *Love's Comedy*.
His book reviews in *Illustreret Nyhedsblad* could hardly have been
very remunerative, and his other writing did not prosper. The 250-page
folk-tale collection he had planned was never carried through and it
had to be completed by his friend Ludvig Daae. He had some poems
from a new collection printed in *Illustreret Nyhedsblad* early in the
year, but that is as far as he went; he did not finish this collection either.
The picture suggests that he was again in a state of depression, an
ambivalent mood such as *Love's Comedy* clearly reflects.

It was most probably at this time that he finally gave up the poetic
cycle of 1859, "In the Picture Gallery," because he now made independent poems out of certain parts of it. He had written no poetry more
pessimistic and doubt-ridden than this since his first effort, the little
verse "Resignation." This spirit of nihilism was, however, no longer his
own, as is evident from his finally abandoning the cycle. In spite of it
all he would fight his way through.

Now he also reworked "The Miner," the most personal of his poems
from the *Andhrimner* period. The revisions were primarily to give the
language greater sonority, but he also made changes that gave an
entirely different tone to the central idea. At first the last lines had read:

Saadan gaar det Slag i Slag,	Thus blow by blow it goes,
Til han segner træt og svag.	Until weak and worn he falls.

But now he replaces the resignation of this image of a weary man giving
up the struggle with:

Hammerslag paa Hammerslag,	Hammer blow on hammer blow
Indtil Livets sidste Dag.	Until life's final day.

Weariness has yielded to an irrepressible will to endure, to fight on while life lasts, even if without hope of victory.

The poem still ends:

Ingen Morgenstraale skinner,	No ray of morning shines,
Ingen Haabets Sol oprinder.	No sun of hope dawns.

Ibsen's feeling that the struggle itself is life and that to yield is to lose self-respect was later echoed in the Swedish poet Gustaf Fröding's powerful "Hydra," where the poet is described receiving popular acclaim for the lines he creates out of his suffering, out of the very insanity that threatens him.

Nog är den tung, en kamp i ensamhet,	Hard enough the lonely struggle no man sees and no man knows,
some intet väsen ser och inger vet,	
men mera tung, när tusen ögon se mig	worse when a thousand eyes watch —me lying helpless before them,
—att ligga utsträckt med förlamad makt,	a thing for the horde's scorn;
ett mål för tusendens förakt,	but even alone—*I shall never yield.*
men ensam än—*dock skall jag aldrig eg mig.*	

This was also the time when he wrote the poem "With a Water Lily," which speaks of the dangers of excessive introspection:

Aa, jeg ved nok, at igrunden,	Ah, how well I know that in reality
Lurer der en Nøkk paa Bunden!	A goblin is lurking in the depths!

From the "Picture Gallery" cycle he also took the poem "Afraid of the Light," which tells of his fear of the "demons of daylight" and "the clatter of life," so that he is brave and himself only when hidden in the darkness of night. Now he adds a prophetic last stanza:

Ja, øver jeg engang et Storværk,	If ever I perform a deed,
Saa blir det en Mørkets Daad.	It will be a deed of darkness.

As he contended with the whole festering *Boyg* of society, he felt he was becoming a pariah; he feared for his sanity. Stronger men have been discouraged by less.

In the early months of 1863, he again began to accept commissions for festive poems of all kinds, particularly from the Student Society. In the six years from his return to Oslo in 1857 until the fall of 1863 he wrote a total of 38 such occasional poems: 23 of these were from the first three years—in 1859-60 he wrote no fewer than 13. There were only five in 1861, and just three in the summer of 1862. The reason for the decline at first was probably because his capacity for work had fallen, and then because of renewed concentration on his more important writing. Suddenly from New Year's, 1863 to the autumn of the year, he began to produce poetry to order again, undoubtedly because he was having trouble beginning a new work after the effort of *Love's Comedy;* and because the chance to take part in festivals and banquets helped relieve his growing sense of alienation.

But the festive poems of this period sounded a new note. No other writer of this kind of verse had been such an exponent of romantic nationalism; he had evoked memory after memory of the heroic past to stir his people's pride and urge them on. Now his face was set firmly against this glorification of the past. In the first poem of the year, written for the January 13 celebration in honor of the ancestors, he issued the same challenge to nationalism as in his last article for *Morgenbladet.* The poem became an indictment, not a hymn of joy:

> Vi sov i Nuet, sov os, smaa,—
> Og drømte os saa store;
> Men morgnens Vind skar Taagen graa,
> Og Dagen kom tilorde.

> We slept in the present, slept
>   and dwindled—
> And dreamt ourselves so great;
> But morning wind cut the gray fog,
> And the sunlight revealed the truth.

He wanted to put to flight "the vain dream of memory":

> Til Drøm er Natt, til Daad er Dag,
> Til Sejr i Kamp er hejst vort Flag.

> For dreams are nights, the days
>   for deeds,
> Our banner is raised for victory.

The banner is not to lie useless in "the casket of memory," and those who have come together to celebrate should not "feed off the ration of memories."

> Nej, *udad, fremad* vil vi see,
> Tilhavs i Dagens Bulder.

> No *outwards, forward* be our gaze,
> Our course set for the day's uproar.

> . . .
> Øg Sejl! Dit Minde, Nordens Mand,
> Er korset paa din Skulder!

> More sail! Your memories, Northman,
> Are the cross upon your shoulder.

In verse after verse the word "memory" becomes a term of abuse, like the lash of a whip with which he scourges himself. The style, the form, and the imagery of these poems were so similar to those chauvinistic ones he had served up for so many years that few of his contemporaries detected the changed attitude. The tune, "For Norway, Land of Heroes," to which the poem was set, was the same as ever, and the audience could easily assume that the words had the same import as of old. In fact a group of students even wrote a parody of the January 13 patriotic festival, and Olaf Skavlan, who had killed off ballad romanticism with his *The Feast of Mare's Hill,* signed the parody "Henr. Ibsen."

The young realists were more than willing to join in the flagellation Ibsen was inflicting on himself.

In February the government proposed to the Storting that Bjørnson be granted a permanent author's pension of 400 dollars a year. Riddervold, Minister of Church and Education, stated that the purpose of the grant was to help the author "develop more freely and make the execution of his works more perfect." He found it "desirable and worthy for the nation" to give such support to this "outstanding talent." Andreas Munch had been granted a similar pension three years earlier, and on April 10 the Storting approved the same annual sum for Bjørnson. Ibsen had applied for one of these grants on March 10, expressing the hope that it would enable him "to continue his literary activity." He recounted the struggles he faced in making a living, and the resulting debts and obligations that had been his only rewards. Since he could not expect to improve himself in his own country, his only hope was to emigrate to Denmark. For all its business-like tone, his letter of application sounds a poignant note: "To leave my native land and abandon an activity that I have so far regarded, and still regard, as my proper calling is a step that I find inexpressibly sad: to avoid this if at all possible I am now trying the last resort."

The Ministry of Church and Education was not moved. Riddervold was of the opinion that the state should not reward a writer who ridiculed the institution of holy matrimony. He was incensed at Ibsen's mockery of the sacred office of priesthood whose guardian he had been for fifteen years—Pastor Strawman in *Love's Comedy* was rumored to have been a caricature of the very kind of minister Riddervold favored. On March 18, therefore, the Ministry declared that while it might have been desirable to give Ibsen some support, there was not "the same grounds for taking action in this case as in the case of the author Bjørnstjerne Bjørnson." The cabinet resolved that "no action be taken" on Ibsen's request. But when the Storting began debate on the grant to Bjørnson, one of the leading Liberals, Judge Rolf Olsen, offered a bill to give the same support to Ibsen. The assembly tabled the recommendation by a vote of 49 to 40, thus taking the same negative position as the Ministry. Some hope was held out to him for the future, however. The Ministry pointed out that Ibsen's application for a foreign travel grant in 1860 had been turned down in favor of Bjørnson and Vinje. It now suggested that he should be first in line when grants were again made the coming autumn. At the same time that this application was being debated, Ibsen requested on March 6 a grant for another expedition to collect folk material. On May 23 he was given 100 dollars

for a trip to Nordmøre and the coastal districts of Trøndelag. As soon as
he received this, he applied again (May 27) for a foreign travel stipend.
He asked for 600 dollars "to study art, art history, and literature preferably in Rome or Paris." The purpose of the trip, he wrote, was to
gain an "all-round education" for his work as author.

The mere possibility of making such a journey so lifted his spirits
that ideas for poems and plays again filled his mind. He returned to a
theme that had occurred to him five years earlier, before *Love's Comedy*
began to engross him; he thought again about the rebellion of Earl
Skule, an episode of the thirteenth-century civil wars. It is easy to see
why he was fascinated by Skule, a man of great talents who had no opportunity to display them, consumed as he was by ambition and self-
doubt. That he found much of himself in Skule is confirmed in a letter
written to a friend in 1870: "That all were against me, that I had no one
outside my family who I could say believed in me, created a state of
mind, as you can readily imagine, that found an outlet in *The Pretenders.*" The struggle with the external and the internal world is reflected in the play.

Even so, it can hardly be chance that from this very month of May
we have a number of poems that proclaim a spirit of conciliation. One
of these is in honor of the poets Henrik Wergeland and J. S. C. Welhaven, bitter and irreconcilable enemies in life, but whose busts were
now simultaneously unveiled in the Student Society.

Synligt staar fra denne Dag   From this day forward stands manifest
Soningstankens Mærke.   The symbol of conciliation.

And in a farewell poem to the Danish actor Jørgensen he wrote:

Sænk dit Skjold, lægg Sværd   Lower thy shield, lay sword aside;
    og Bile;   Thou hast fought, now canst rest.
Du har stridt, kan roligt hvile.

Such words hinted at another kind of victory than the one the forces
within the symbolic figure of Earl Skule were struggling toward. Ibsen
was groping toward a new balance, and so for now his theme remained
unclear and the new drama unformed. Then came an event that suddenly cast light on his path and united his visions in one clear, forceful
image. The students had invited him to accompany them to a great songfest in Bergen, where a thousand singers from Oslo and other cities
in Norway were gathering. He accepted the invitation eagerly and
soon all three of Oslo's choruses were rehearsing his festival song:
"Hail to Melody!" (Hil Sangen!) The poem dealt with the dream of
unification — all Norwegians together, and perhaps even Norwegians
and Danes and Swedes—that was still such an ardent desire in his heart.

The idea of unity also harmonized with his dramatic theme of the civil wars.

The company sailed from Oslo on June 12 and arrived in Bergen on Sunday, June 14. The happy journey Ibsen would remember as itself a festival, out of which arose the poem "Sunday Cavalcade" (Søndag-stog). Here, a fisherman watches them sail by and feels much of the emotion Ibsen himself was experiencing:

Vi flyver med flagrende Faner,	We fly with flying banners,
Vi synger os fuglefri;	As free as birds' flight our song;
Han sidder igjen og aner:	*He* sits there and vaguely knows
Nu strøg noget Stort forbi.	Something of greatness passed by.

Ibsen knew that on this journey seeds were being sown that would "prosper in receptive soil." The three festival days in Bergen would fulfill this prophecy.

Since people in Bergen had heard rumors that Ibsen was blacklisted in Oslo, it was not easy to find anyone willing to receive him. Arrangements were finally made for him to board at shipowner Randolph Nilsen's, together with a friend who was a cousin of the hostess. The arrangements worked out for the best. As soon as he returned to Oslo, Ibsen wrote and thanked his host for "all the inexpressible kindness and friendliness" he had been shown. "Thank heavens," he continued, "I still feel the festive mood and hope I may keep it for a long time hence.... The festival and the many dear, unforgettable people I met, affect me like a salutary visit to church. With all my heart I hope this feeling will never be extinguished. All in Bergen were so kind to me — it is not so here, where many try to insult and wound me on every occasion." The friendship and good will he found there acted as a curative for his wounded feelings; this was "the most deeply beneficent effect of the festival," "this powerful, uplifting impression that makes one feel ennobled and improved in every thought."

The greatest revelation to him, the most important thing to happen during the festival, was seeing Bjørnson, just home from three years abroad and full of great plans which even his disappointment with the prosaic and material nature of his countrymen had not made him forget. The "unspeakable drowsiness" of Norwegian society toward all questions of the soul or of life did not stop him from trying to stir that society to creative life. He spoke at the songfest and naturally aroused controversy; everywhere he went there was a storm, and at the same time he charmed people and won them to his side.

He met Ibsen as a partisan and a friend. He had good reason to be grateful for the services Ibsen had rendered him during his absence. Ibsen had produced his plays *King Sverre* and *Hulda the Lame* at

Christiania Norwegian Theatre, and he was the first to tell the Norwegian reader what a new and exciting art was discovered in *Sigurd
Slembe*. Now Bjørnson returned thanks with a heartfelt friendliness
none could radiate more convincingly. He was well aware that he and
Ibsen were regarded as competitors, and he wanted to erase all feeling
of rivalry. Never in his life, before or after, did Ibsen respond so completely to an offer of friendship, and as he heard Bjørnson say all the
things he had dreamt possible for himself all his bitterness left him, his
faith in himself returned and he knew once and for all that he was capable of his dreams. He was no longer sick; he was strong, and courageous.

In the official report of the festival proceedings, we can trace clues
that tell us what transpired between the two men. When Bjørnson spoke
about the need for a national spirit to animate Bergen, he referred to
the unifying work of King Haakon Haakonsson, "Norway's best king."
Such unity had been a personal issue with the king, as it was with
Ibsen. He asked at the festival dinner on June 16—did not Norway need
song more than any other nation, song to charm away its stubborn-
ness and quarrelsomeness, but had it not also used its singers to serve
its rancorous spirit: "Have I not known my friend Ibsen pitted against
me, and I against him, to injure me, and to injure him?" Such strife
must give way before conciliation and harmony, and song would help
to bring about this harmony. After the speech when Ibsen's song of
conciliation, written especially for the festival, was sung, it was as
though the two men took each other by the hand before all the world.

On June 21 Ibsen was back in Oslo with his new play clearly and
solidly in his mind. Now, without any delay, it must be written. For
support he would use the 100 dollars the university had granted him.
Field trips to collect fairy-tales were out of the question now. He stole
a hundred dollars, and gave his people a masterpiece, *The Pretenders*.

In this drama about the struggle for Norwegian unification, the final
settlement is achieved when Haakon Haakonsson defeats the last rebel
king, Skule Baardsson, in 1240. But this political solution did not solve
the psychological problem. Would this union be more than an affair
of politics, a state organization? Would it be a force in the life of the
people, a truly national unification? Ibsen's genius succeeded in creating a sound vehicle for a modern psychological dilemma from a thirteenth century conflict. Thus out of the material of historical drama
he made a statement about a crucial issue of his own day. The play
gave Norway a battle-cry and a slogan, the cry of King Haakon: "Norway was a kingdom; it shall be a people. The men of Trøndelag have
fought the men of Viken, the men of Agder those of Hordaland, the

men of Haalogaland those of Sogn; after this all shall be one, and all shall know and understand that they are one!"

Ibsen put his heart and soul into the portrayal of the great conflict between King Haakon and Earl Skule, the believer and the doubter. Haakon's strength is in his belief that his call is from God. His belief in his calling is simple and uncomplicated by doubt; this certainty gives him a fully integrated personality. He is inevitably a leader. Yet from this very certitude comes his great sin against himself; he hardens himself and says "everyone too dear to the king must depart." His mother and his youthful love are rejected; his eyes are closed to the love his queen offers—until he begins to realize the flaw in his nature. Love must be a part of that nature if he is to be complete, if God is to be with him.

Ibsen had lived with this idea since his youth, the time of *Catiline*. He knew then that one who betrays love sins against his soul and will be avenged by his own will and his life's work. King Haakon learns of his mistake early enough to change; Earl Skule, guilty of the same sin, realizes too late and must pay with his life. The gift of this knowledge is to allow him to die with more readiness and purity. The first defect in Skule's character is the betrayal of love, although Ibsen does not spell this out in specific terms. Skule is ambitious for power and honor, and everything is sacrificed for these. Not evil at first, he grows corrupt when he is pushed aside by the young king. He believes his title to the throne is valid—he was brother and nearest heir to Inge Baardsson, the last king. He submits to the legal decision that gave the title to Haakon, but then begins to doubt if Haakon is in truth the late king's son. As this doubt festers within, he becomes sick at heart and confused; he is finally driven to crime, in thought some even worse than those he commits in deed. In the end he is guilty of the worst of crimes, he "doubted his own doubt."

Ibsen may perhaps have been indebted to Vinje for the enigmatic expression of this idea; Vinje had used it in *Andhrimner* to characterize their whole age, a generation that embraced conflicting points of view in a relativism that became "a suspension between Yea and Nay." But Ibsen was able to say that this precarious balance deprived one of the capacity to will or do: a "sickly doubt" is worse than death; it is a "twilight" that makes all gray in one's soul and leaves no path clear. When Skule comes to this state, all is lost.

In the last words of the play, King Haakon says that there was an enigma about Earl Skule, that he was "God's stepchild on earth." Removed from context, the line seems simply another terse riddle, and when the play was performed in Copenhagen, Fru Heiberg struck the line out: "God doesn't have stepchildren," she said. But in fact the whole play tells us that although Skule was at fault in not following God's call until the last moment, God's love had not been with him from the beginning. His life fulfilled the prophecy of his court poet, the skald who said: "A man can give his life for another's mission; but to live, he must live for his own." Skule could never become the great leader, nor could he be happy in life, for the secret of life is this: "The happiest man is the one who is greatest, who performs the greatest deeds, the one whom the needs of his time fill with a lust that begets thoughts he himself cannot grasp, thoughts that mark out a path whose direction is unknown to him, but still a path he walks and must walk until he hears men shout with joy. Then he opens his eyes wonderingly, and discovers that he has achieved a great work." Skule has "all the great gifts of soul, wisdom and courage," but he does not have genius. God's love has not marked him; he has not been called to greatness.

Is this riddle then the mystery of God's will? It is a mystery in all religions, and although for Ibsen it was not a mystery embedded in some dogma, nor even a philosophical tenet, it was a belief he felt with all the force of a living principle. He felt that his own talents and what they drove him to create were gifts from a supernatural power; with them came obligations and responsibilities that forced one to answer the call. To answer the call became for him a categorical imperative, a moral injunction so binding, it was his religion.

In the play Ibsen gave the sharpest delineation to the problem that had preoccupied him as far back as we can trace: the question of the "call" and of one's faith in it. It was present in his first preserved poem of 1847 when he asks himself: "Am I denied the soul's ascent?" It was Catiline's concern; one moment he believes:

> Jeg maa, jeg maa, saa byder mig   I must, I must, a voice
>   en Stemme   within my heart commands, and
> i Sjælens Dyb, og jeg vil følge den.   I will follow it.

But in a later hour he doubts and feels he must flee his fatal calling:

> Jeg maa, jeg maa! min Skjæbne   I must, I must! My fate forces me on!
>   driver mig!

In *Lady Inger* the same conflict appears and is waged.

What is unusual in *The Pretenders* is that here he confronts the doubter with a man who wholeheartedly believes in himself and his call. It can be said with certainty that Bjørnson was the one who gave him the conviction to create such a character; Bjørnson's faith is embodied in King Haakon. Ibsen had been aware of Bjørnson's self-confidence before this; he envied him and felt somewhat contemptuous of such simplicity and childish faith. But now that he had fallen under the man's strong spell, he recognized the greatness of such a child-like quality. This simple belief he would embody in Haakon. But if Haakon is an image of Bjørnson he is also a mirror of his creator's personality, for deep within Ibsen's soul there always lived faith, a faith that was achieved only through painful struggle. That he shared in this portrait of Haakon is indicated by the fact that he pictured his own mother as the king's. He did not wish to identify only with Skule, Haakon's opponent and opposite. A man who would steal another's idea and dress in borrowed greatness was certainly not Ibsen's idea of himself. He knew that he had within him the ambition to be a king of his calling; he did not need to borrow or steal another's life work since he had his own to live for. Despite all this a good deal of Ibsen went into the portrait of Skule; his self-doubt is Ibsen's own painful self-examination. This psychological conflict in Skule is the central theme of the play, and as Ibsen drew this portrait, he exorcized the demons of doubt by realizing them fully in a complete work of art.

Thus the play is much more than a drama about an important national problem; it is a drama about the struggle of deep-rooted impulses in the human psyche. The drama is embodied in the opposition of Haakon to Skule and in Skule's inner conflict as he both believes in Haakon's greatness and fights against it. Everything in the play sheds light on this great struggle, particularly in the description of Bishop Nikolas, the third major character in the play. He can be conceived as a fragment of Skule's nature, split off and given a life of its own, a living sign of all the doubts that plague him and urge him on to wild, black thoughts. The bishop is also the nation's nemesis, perpetually scheming to split the people and shatter their unity with petty bickering. He sets in motion the tragic course of action, and seems so much the realization of some malignant spirit that his spirit returns after his death to drive the action on to more ruinous paths as an inevitable conclusion. But he is convincingly human, nonetheless. With an unmistakable Ibsenian characteristic — he is *afraid*. From his youth he has yearned for greatness, but when the test finally comes he must run away. Although he tries time and again, he never masters his cowardice. These were Ibsen's own feelings; he too longed to be brave, but he had to hide from people, and his greatest battles were fought only in his imagination. He knew what such terror could lead to, and he portrayed it all in the bishop; ill-will, hatred of all who dared lift their heads higher than his: "There shall be no giants here, for I was never a giant!"

Another typically Ibsenian theme is the unslaked thirst for love, portrayed in the women who surround Haakon and Skule. The few strokes that etch each of their portraits are all dictated by one theme: "To love, to sacrifice all, and to be forgotten—that is a woman's story." The form of this love most strongly marked in the play is that of the mother, nowhere more beautifully illustrated than in the idyllic cradle song Ibsen wrote for Queen Margrete; but the love of children always called forth his warmest response, perhaps because he felt most secure and most himself with children rather than with adults. Like the men, the women of *The Pretenders* are born of Ibsen's own heart.

The characters of the play are all drawn from history and are all more or less accurately portrayed, being based on material he found in P. A. Munch's history of Norway; for example, a comment by the historian formed the basis for the character of the loving Queen Margrete. The historical characters are all highly controversial, even today, and open to many interpretations; of course, in writing the play Ibsen shaped them to his theme and gave them responses far beyond anything his sources justified. Although he exercised the poet's right to make history a part of his own conflict, he always made the historical fact the basis of his characters.

The dramatic conflict is straightforward and uncomplicated, despite traces of the Scribe apparatus in the mysterious letter that comes and goes. Ibsen is using this trite device to explore one of his most constant themes, the secret sin that bursts into the open and exposes the character for what he is. In his play the secret is never revealed but used simply to keep Skule's doubt alive and thus it is forced into a psychological function. There are traces of Shakespearean influence as well. Bishop Nikolas is a kinsman of Iago, and Skule can at times betray a jealousy almost as intense as Othello's. The contrast between Haakon and Skule is reminiscent of the relationship between Macbeth and Prince Malcolm, and there are echoes of *King Lear*. But all these influences do not make for imitation; the play is an original creation, even if in the Shakespearean tradition.

The play is in prose, as was the earlier saga play, *The Vikings at Helgeland,* but a prose that is as different as the contents and purpose of the new play are from the old. The flavor of the saga style is present, but there is no attempt to force everything into the saga idiom or to play up to a romantic audience by affecting an archaic diction. Here is a straightforward, living language, naturally colored by occasional references to the old sagas. Bjørnson no doubt helped Ibsen to find this new idiom, and Ibsen may have gotten his first notion that this was the right style for a Norwegian historical drama as long ago as that October evening in 1857, right after he had completed *The Vikings,* when he sat with Bjørnson in Christiania Theatre and watched the first performance of *Between the Battles.* When he directed *King Sverre* in 1861, he had another opportunity to observe Bjørnson's method, and he reviewed *Sigurd Slembe* the next year, he rejected his own saga style and openly acknowledged that Bjørnson's method was the right one. That review actually foretold what the style and form of *The Pretenders* would be.

While Ibsen was working on the play, Clemens Petersen's review of *Love's Comedy* appeared, with its uncompromising judgment: "Verse is Henrik Ibsen's nature; outside this medium he will hardly succeed in being natural." When Ibsen wrote three weeks later to thank him for the review, he stated that he had to write his new play in prose: "I *cannot* write it in verse." The play would not have the ring of truth in any other form, and now truth for him was a matter of life or death. Verse was natural in *Love's Comedy* since he wanted to give the satire greater freedom by using many terms and expressions not in ordinary, everyday usage. Prose was the natural medium for his new play, but even here there is the same urge to concentrate meaning in incisive epigrams and in aphoristic sayings that have in fact survived in the language as quotable axioms. This tendency to approach the economy and intensity of verse occasionally leads him to write lines that are there because they are well written, rather than psychologically inevitable; the characters speak beyond themselves.

When the author wants to speak in his own voice he does in fact turn to verse, in the scene where the shade of Bishop Nikolas returns to urge Skule to carry on the policies of the clerical party, the Baglers. The only excuse for the use of verse in this scene is that it represents a dream, a vision which expresses Skule's inner conflict, his temptation and his conquest of self. Still, this abrupt use of verse does violate the conventions of the play; and Ibsen seems well aware of it—he lets Skule tease the bishop for speaking in verse: "I notice you've learned the art of the skald!" But if Ibsen violated the formal integrity of his play, he secured an artistic triumph; few things he wrote have been more frequently quoted than these concluding lines:

Gaar til sin Gjerning de norske Mænd	Whenever Norsemen go to their work waveringly, without will, not knowing where,
Viljeløst vimrende, ved ej hvorhen,—	when hearts shrink and minds skulk,
Skrukker sig Hjerterne, smyger sig Sindene,	as willows weakly in the wind,
Veke, som vaggende Vidjer for Vindene,—	if then on one thing alone they unite, that every genius be stoned, be destroyed,
Kan kun om *en* Ting i Verden de enes,	if rags of wretchedness are unfurled as standards,
Den, at hver Storhed skal styrtes og stenes,	if honor is looked for in flight, in defeat,—
Hejses som Mærke Usseldoms Klude,	then Bishop Nikolas walks abroad, the Bagler Bishop, minding his flock!
Sætter de Aeren i Flugt og i Fald,—	
Da er det Bisp Nikolas som er ude,	
Bagler-Bispen, som røgter sit Kald!	

This passage immediately reveals the source of inspiration for the whole play—Ibsen's burning anger at his country's lack of will and lack of manhood. It is finally clear that this nationalistic, historical play has nothing to do with the ordinary brand of romanticized nationalism. This drama looks forward, not back, and it sets up a moral standard for the entire nation as well as for the individual.

While in the midst of work on the play, Ibsen was delighted to learn that Botten Hansen was going to write a biographical sketch of him for *Illustreret Nyhedsblad.* Two issues of the periodical in July, 1863, were devoted to A. O. Vinje; in the issue for July 19 the first published life of Ibsen appeared. For the first time the public was told of his struggle to support himself while he wrote, and was given a survey of his work to date. Hansen appraised his dramatic works as follows: "A keen eye for unusual psychological development, a talent for building a complicated plot, a quick perception of dramatic situations, the critical balance and intelligence necessary to hold his lyricism in check, and an experienced insight into the needs and requirements of the stage—these are the qualities out of which his works are created." Then, strangely enough for so good a friend, he continues: "If he only possessed the ability to believe and to hold conviction in the same degree, then he would be able to give us drama of the first rank." One might argue that there was a lack of "belief" in *Love's Comedy,* but anyone who knew Ibsen should have recognized that the slashing anger of the play was motivated by an idealistic belief that was, if anything, excessive, not deficient. *The Pretenders,* at any rate, would prove that he had more faith and power of conviction than most of his countrymen.

The play was written in a state of almost continual exaltation, and possessed him completely until it was done. It took less than two months; we have almost certain evidence that it was virtually all on paper on August 13, seven weeks after his return from Bergen. Only then could he tear himself away to see *Eystein Meila* by Kristian Elster, a new historical play about the same period of civil war. In his merciless review in *Illustreret Nyhedsblad,* Ibsen tells us something about his own requirements for a nationalist, historical drama, requirements he must have known he could fulfill himself: a strong intellectual content, organized by a single dramatic plot. *Eystein Meila,* he wrote, is not the kind of work that "will enrich our dramatic literature." He was certain that his play would.

In his letter of August 18 to Clemens Petersen, he mentions that he is working on a historical play in five acts; at this time it is certain he was busy with revisions, and the manuscript was transcribed in the first days of September. As he walked to the theatre he met the leading bookdealer of Oslo, old Johan Dahl, and told him of the new play whose fair copy he was carrying under his arm. He asked Dahl if he would be interested in publishing it. Dahl had given him the contract for the folk-tale collection the year before, but had given up all hope of ever getting the work. Now he accepted the play on the spot, and even promised a royalty of 150 dollars, which was generous for those days—*Love's Comedy* had netted only 100 dollars. The written contract was dated September 15; Dahl began printing the play immediately, and the book was on sale by the end October. This was Ibsen's second book to be published by a regular firm.

It could not be called an immediate success. The reading public was small and the sale was not large; it took six or seven years to sell a thousand copies. *Aftenbladet* published the first review on November 18, praising the play's dramatic structure but finding fault with its exaggerated effects. The reviewer apparently did not understand the play's psychological theme. But Professor Monrad did, as is evident in his review, which ran through three issues of *Morgenbladet* in January, 1864. He praised the play as a splendid tragedy of character and regretted only that it had not been written in verse. In February the Dane, C. Rosenberg had the same praise; he saw it as evidence of a new school of Norwegian dramatic writing, embodying a new psychology and a new style of dialogue. He compared it with Andreas Munch's *Earl Skule,* which had just appeared, and found that Munch's play was not only in the old tradition of Danish drama, but superficial as well. In this competition between old and new styles, he wrote, it seemed that, for the moment at least, Ibsen was obviously outstripping all the rest.

It was not equally obvious to everyone in Denmark, however.

Clemens Petersen wrote a testy review in *Fædrelandet* on April 2. He had expected something different and now tried to maintain that the play did not represent Ibsen's true talent, and was in fact essentially undramatic. The book had a minuscule sale in Denmark as a result, less than a score of copies.

Ibsen had not yet made his reputation in Denmark, although he had tried. After Petersen had praised *Lady Inger of Østråt* in his review of *Love's Comedy,* Ibsen had sent the play to the Royal Theatre in Copenhagen. In late October he also sent *The Pretenders* and requested that the play be performed. Unfortunately, the theatre's consultant at this time was Norwegian-born Carsten Hauch, himself busily writing historical plays (all failures). He did not consider Ibsen at all competent in the field. On October 4 he decided that *Lady Inger* was quite unsuitable, although "not without talent and invention." The intrigue was "full of abominations," and besides, the play was much too harsh on the Danish rulers of Norway. On December 19 he rejected *The Pretenders* even more flatly. Here, too, there were "traces of unusual talent," the play was still "impossible," the basic theme "senseless," and in addition was often "coupled with vulgarity and coarseness." On top of all this, the language was "even worse than that of the other super-Norwegian Norwegians," full of words from "assorted peasant dialects," that were supposed to "create on the spot a non-Danish language." Both plays reminded him of the dramatic works of the "more notorious than notable," now "late-departed" so-called "young Germany." He could in no way advise the Royal Theatre to perform such works. It would be another six or seven years, after he had established his name in all the other Scandinavian countries, before Ibsen would be allowed to appear on the foremost Danish stage.

But in Norway the play scored a victory; it was read and discussed and made a deep impression. It was accepted by Christiania Theatre in mid-September and was performed on Sunday, January 17, 1864. The performance was not entirely successful because the young actor Sigvard Gundersen did not possess the strength needed to create the impression of overwhelming force and genius in King Haakon. The Danish actor Wolf played Skule better than he had done any previous role, and captivated the audience by his brilliant acting in the scene of his encounter with his son. On the whole, however, he emphasized the heroic elements in Skule's nature, at the expense of the soul-weary doubter. The Dane Peter Nielsen played Bishop Nikolas with intelligence and consistency, but without the passion that was needed to bring the character to life. Only Laura Svendsen in the role of Queen Margrete was satisfactory among the supporting players. Although Ibsen himself directed, he did not seem able to give the actors much guidance.

But the play held the audience. Although it lasted nearly five hours (it was cut to four on the following evenings), it "was followed from beginning to end with intense attention." "After the curtain," this report continues, "there was a cry for the author, who was rewarded with thunderous applause when he appeared." The play was given eight times in less than two months, an extraordinary number considering the size of Oslo at the time and the limited audience for such a lengthy and weighty play. It was a greater and vastly more important victory than *The Feast at Solhaug*, since it made no concessions to popular tastes; on the contrary the demands on the audience were as severe as the ones the author had made on himself. He had reason enough to be proud of his success.

The Pretenders has become a regular repertory item in Norwegian theatre and the classic national saga play. It has not met with the same success abroad. It was performed in Copenhagen in 1871, after *Brand* had made Ibsen's name famous, and *The League of Youth* had shown the Danes that he could write good theatrical entertainment. It was successful the first year, but was never put into the repertory. The play was Ibsen's first to be produced outside Scandinavia. In 1875 the experimental court theatre of Meiningen performed it and brought it to Berlin the following year. Other German theatres followed suit, although the Meiningen company was the only one to score a definite success. This was not the play with which Ibsen would conquer Germany, and it never made much impression on German thinking: German critics declared it "ohne Bühnenwirkung." The play's fate varied with productions; it failed at the Schiller Theater in Berlin in 1901, but Max Reinhardt's production at Neues Theater in 1904 was a great success. The drama was too intimately bound up with Norwegian traditions to set down roots in other countries. The great nationalistic appeal of its "kingly thought" is directed specifically to Norwegian patriotic feelings; it is filled to overflowing with historical details that are vital to Norwegians but matters of indifference to others. Ibsen's victory was a Norwegian one; it brought him again to the forefront of his country's writers, on a par with Bjørnson.

The greatest victory was the one over himself; for the first time in his life he could breathe freely, fully confident in his calling and his ability to follow it. In *The Pretenders* Skule asks Jatgejr the Skald: "Do *you* always believe that you are really a poet?" Ibsen's own self-doubt is in the question, but now he knew, as Jatgejr did, that he had been called and would not sacrifice that for any price. With faith in himself he could speak with more courage and authority than ever before. He had been terrified at society's rejection of him after he exposed its lies in *Love's Comedy;* he had felt powerless against such odds. Now he felt his strength, and his fear subsided.

He was a man of thirty-six now. He had struggled many years to find himself and during that time had built up a hatred of the society that cowed him, or coaxed and threatened him to work for goals that were never wholly his own. Society appeared to him the monster that stifled man's will and made him a slave; it repressed all that was free and true, all that was natural, all personal calls for justice. Now he felt strong enough to raise a rebellion against this union of hypocrisy and repression. Within him was a moral will and an ethically motivated anger that would tear down conventions. It was his call to wake his people to honesty in thought, freedom in action.

One month after *The Pretenders,* he wrote a poem for the Student Society's gathering on October 2, 1863, whose refrain was:

Gaa foran! Det er Kravet.	*Lead on!* This the call.
Gaa foran al din Tid.	Lead on before your time.
Gaa foran, hvor det gjælder,	Lead on, wherever the need,
I Norges Ungdoms Strid!	In the struggle of Norway's youth!

Thus he cried to himself; before long the tocsin of his writing would ring throughout his country, throughout the world—stirring, rousing, waking.

CHAPTER SIXTEEN

THE GREAT DISILLUSIONMENT

(1863-64)

Ibsen had no sooner finished *The Pretenders* than he conceived the idea of another drama based on Norwegian history. Several times in the past he followed up a successfully completed work with one in a similar vein. He tried to repeat his achievement in *The Feast at Solhaug* with another ballad drama; after *The Vikings at Helgeland* he planned another saga play, the work that eventually became *The Pretenders*. He longed for continued success and also wanted to write something his countrymen would appreciate.

The theme for the new play was suggested by his friend Michael Birkeland, the recently appointed National Archivist, who drew his attention to Magnus Heineson, the Norwegian-Faroese Viking executed in 1589 and regarded as a kind of national martyr. The attraction this defeated rebel had for Ibsen is obvious from the many times he wrote about the type—Catiline, Lady Inger, Earl Skule. Heineson also fascinated Ibsen as another rebel, "a great scoundrel," as he jestingly told a small boy who asked who Heineson was. He began to gather material, making notes from the new volume of *Norske Rigs-Registranter*, and sketching out a long five-act drama. He would continue the work on his trip abroad which was at last to become a reality.

On September 12, 1863, the Cabinet granted him 400 dollars for travel. A number of Ibsen's friends had used their influence in obtaining the grant, among whom Emil Stang, son of the prime minister, was especially helpful. As usual, the stipend was less than had been asked for, less than what was needed for a year's journey through many countries. Ibsen's plans were to take the steamer to Hamburg in November, but since he hesitated to undertake the trip with so little money, he wound up spending half of it without ever leaving home. Finally Bjørnson managed to add enough to make the trip possible. Always the persuasive talker, Bjørnson succeeded in getting together 700 dollars from such influential friends as attorney Bernhard Dunker, Storting Member Johan Sverdrup, and other members of the Liberal opposition which Sverdrup would eventually head. The friendship between Ibsen and Bjørnson had deepened since the Bergen festival, and Bjørnson, always eager to help others, came loyally to his friend's aid.

On Saturday evening, April 2, Ibsen said farewell to his friends of the "Erudite Holland," at a party which also commemorated Botten Hansen's appointment as University Librarian. Early Tuesday morning, April 5, he took the first steamer to leave since the winter ice had broken. The next day he was in Copenhagen, although in a speech given there on April 1, 1898, he mistakenly said he had arrived on April 1. From Copenhagen he wrote Dunker about his plans for the new play, but his mind was too preoccupied to concentrate on writing. He was seeing the world and being deeply affected by it.

It was April, 1864—the date alone would summon up so much history when he recalled this journey years later. Denmark was at war. In December, 1863, German armies took up positions in Holstein; on February 1 Prussia and Austria sent their armies over the Eider River into Danish Schleswig. A few days later the Danes abandoned Danevirke, the old and honored fortifications built many centuries ago by Queen Tyra as a defense against the Germans. For ten weeks the Danes fought from the Dybbøl entrenchments, but on April 18 the Prussians broke the brave defense and drove them across to the island of Als.

Ibsen was in Copenhagen when news of the defeat reached the capital. He was deeply moved and it seemed to him that brute force had triumphed over right; his ideals had been trampled on and he felt a personal affront. He was not naive about war and brutality—in "Terje Vigen" he wrote vividly of a period when the English had spread terror over the seas; he knew how Russian forces had crushed the fight for freedom in Hungary. But one of these wars had been fought fifty years before the other took place in his childhood. He knew that sometimes the smaller nation wins, as the Danes had done in the Prusso-Danish War of 1848. Since then there had been only the Crimean War, and that had been sufficiently distant to fill him with a least a glimmer of idealism. This present war was simply a power play, where sheer force of numbers and steel would carry the day.

He was distressed and angry and he gave voice to his indignation most vividly in the poem "The Death of Abraham Lincoln," written in April, 1865. The European press had cried out in horror at the assassination, but Ibsen reacted in ironic surprise to this outburst. The world had seen worse things happen in cultured Europe: the English attack on Copenhagen in 1807, the subjugation of Poland, the German thrust against Denmark the previous year. Europe should congratulate itself for setting America an example:

Med glemte Løfter, med svegne Ord,
Med Tractaters forrevne Ark,
Med Brud fra iaar paa jer Ed
    fra ifjor
Har I gjødet Historiens mark.

With forgotten promises, treacherous
    words,
With solemn treaties torn,
With this year's lie given to last
    year's oath
You have manured history's soil.

But the last word had not yet been said; although events seemed at
their last extremity, a storm would break out and sweep away the
entire fabric:

En Villie vaager og holder Dom
Og knuser hvert Løgnens Bur;
Men Ormen maa først æde Skallen
    tom,
Og Tiden maa først faae krænget
    sig om
Til sin egen Karrikatur.

A waking eye holds judgment,
Will crush each citadel of lies;
But first the larva must break the
    chrysalis,
First the age must invert itself,
Become its own distorted mirror.

His hope was in revolution, and therefore the more corruption rampant, the sooner would revolution come:

—lad kun "Systemet" faa vrængt
    sig om—
Des før kommer Hævnen og holder
    Dom
Paa Tidsløgnens yderste Dag!

—let the "System" invert itself—
Vengeance and judgment are sooner
    come
To the final day of lies!

Philosophically speaking this is a romantic conception of political
change, but Ibsen was not interested in expressing a philosophy—he was
not a Hegelian Marxist—he was rather concerned with giving vent to
a moral indignation so strong that only the vision of a day of judgment
could contain it.

His fury and hurt at the defeat at Dybbøl came from more than the
injustice of the war; it was a reaction to the shameful refusal of Norwegians to come to the aid of Denmark. He, who had given his allegiance to a concept of Scandinavian unity and would keep this ideal most
tenaciously throughout his whole life, now became with his countrymen an accessory to the defeat of a Scandinavian nation.

The appeal of this ideal of "Scandinavianism" to intellectual youth,
in general, and to Ibsen, in particular, can readily be understood if one
considers the crass commercial and economic motivation behind most
political activity in the 1850's. The war of 1848 had come as a bitter
warning that the weak and small nations of Scandinavia were weakest
when isolated from one another. The Easter Sunday battle near Schleswig made Scandinavianism a burning issue in Norway, and the emphasis began to shift from an idealistic notion of a league of mutual assistance without selfish motivation to an insistence on cooperation as a
matter of honor and national survival. One of Ibsen's earliest poems,

"The Giant Oak" (Kjæmpeégen) heralded the unity of the North, and in 1849 he wrote "Awaken Scandinavians!" (Vaagner Skandinaver!), with its appeal to Norwegians and Swedes to aid their Danish brothers. The basis of his argument is still moral. It is moral perfidy to remain neutral; such a betrayal might never be remedied or atoned for:

Nei Brødre, mei, der er en hellig Lov	No, brothers, no! There is a law sacred
I Sjælens Dyb, den heder: Red din Broder!	In our soul that says: Save thy brother!
Den heder: Hjælp, hvad længst Naturen bandt	That says: What Nature has long ago bound
Med skjønne, faste Baand tæt til dit Hjerte.	With love, strong bonds to thy heart, save.
Vee, vee dig, svigter du i Farens Stund!	Woe, woe to thee if this test thou failest!

A people without honor is doomed, and so he continued to champion Scandinavianism year after year, "the best ideal of the North," as he called it in one of his poems for the student convention of 1851. It might appear that some of his nationalist activities in the 1850's implied a weakening of emphasis on Scandinavianism. Rather, he felt their connection to be inescapable. When he wrote a poem honoring King Carl Johan as "the first Scandinavian of the century" he was not only opening his campaign for a national theatre, he was also stating that national identity was a condition for Nordic unity. The Norwegians had to be equal to the Danes and Swedes in cultural and political affairs before they could enter into meaningful union and before such a union could gain any advantage from their participation.

He could answer angrily such Danish attacks on Norwegian demands for independence as in the Erik Bøgh operetta he directed in 1859, where the character Bjerkebæk is caricatured as a "Norse Norwegian." His answer to such slander is given in the poem "Distress at Sea" (I Havsnød) written when war was again threatening between Germany and Denmark in 1861:

Fortæl til de tydske Stormænd,	Tell the German warlords,
At maa I for Dannebrogsdugen slaa's,	If it's the Danish flag you fight for,
I faar vel en Haandsrækning oppe fra os,—	You'll have a helping hand from here,
Men *først* fra de *norske* Nordmænd!	From Norwegians who are *Norsemen first*.

The closer the danger of war appeared, the stronger he felt that Norway must help, if only for the sake of her own national honor. In his poem for Constitution Day, 1861, he said:

Fri er du først maar Nordens Hegn	You are only free while the North
I Syd staar rejst og fredet,—	Is safely bulwarked to the South,—
Mens mørskne Tiders Trældomstegn	While ancient bondage's symbols
I Øst er stængt bag Ledet.	Are barred and fenced off in the East.

Fri er du først med hele Nord!	You are only free when all the North
Thi ve den Mand, der kun har *Ord*	is free!
Til Hjælp i Nøden for sin Bro'r;—	But the one who has nought but words
Hans Glemselsgrav staar redet!	To feed his brother in distress—
	His unhonored grave is already dug!

For him the whole problem came down to one demand: keeping one's pledge—the pledge to Scandinavia which the Dane Orla Lehmann had demanded when he challenged an audience of 1,500 at the first student convention in 1845 to pledge their honor to the Nordic idea. The theme of Scandinavian unity was cheered at meeting after meeting, even at the convention of Lund and Copenhagen held in 1862. Ibsen knew that such pledges were not politically binding and had little effect on the government, especially the agrarian majority in the Storting who had no interest in the notion of Scandinavian unity. He and his fellow believers probably thought they had more support among the people than they really had. What the newspapers called "general opinion" was largely a reflection of the opinions of the professional and academic classes, both oriented toward Scandinavianism.

The issue gradually came down to a question of whether Norway and Sweden should support the Danish position on Schleswig. An aspect of the situation that seemed promising for the hopes of the Scandinavian unity party was that Carl XV, the young king of Norway and Sweden, and his Swedish foreign minister, Count Manderström, supported Denmark and had in fact encouraged the policies that ultimately provoked the Germans to war. King Carl even offered Denmark a military treaty, and Manderström wrote a series of notes whose meaning clearly suggests that Norway and Sweden would be firmly allied with Denmark. But Manderström's literary polish was intended to suffice in case action was needed as well. Ibsen was among those who believed that action would join words; he was obviously applying to international politics the private moral standards which dictated his writing. He had based his romantic nationalistic fervor on the hope that he could awaken the people to great deeds by reviving proud memories of the time of heroes. He believed this was possible; but he was never free of doubt if it was probable. In his *Andhrimner* period we find him doubting and mocking this hope; in later writing the call for action still quavers with a note of fear that the people's will would not respond to the call. *Love's Comedy* had proclaimed the hypocrisy of social attitudes and traditions and indicated that he expected little from a society so riddled with lies. When he broke with romantic nationalism in his poem of January 13, 1863, he based his last hope for the Norwegian people on its willingness to go to the aid of Denmark.

The crisis came within a few months. On March 30 the Danish king severed Schleswig from Holstein by proclamation. In November a new Danish constitution bound Schleswig more closely to Denmark; Christian IX then ascended the Danish throne, thereby reopening the question of succession in the Duchies. In December the German Confederation invaded Holstein and in mid-January, 1864, the Prussians and Austrians made an ultimatum to Denmark. Two weeks later war broke out. Although Danish policy was in line with her traditional stand, it was contrary to more recent shifts in position by the European powers, and in opposition to recent agreements. Open warfare became inevitable.

Count Manderström had made an open declaration that Norway and Sweden supported the new Danish policy. In May, 1863, a special committee of the Norwegian Storting supported this declaration, stating that the two countries would not tolerate a violation of Danish sovereignty. In July Manderström warned the Western powers that the two kingdoms would not remain neutral in a Dano-German war. A few days later Carl XV offered the Danes a military pact. At this point strong opposition began to form against this policy in Norway, and even more so in Sweden. The majority of the Swedish cabinet opposed the king and the prime minister. In September King Carl and Manderström were forced to alter their position and agree not to enter the war unless assured of support from the Western powers. In October the Danish government was informed that the military pact could not be ratified. Talks had not yet broken off, for the Danish government believed that the threat of Scandinavian military intervention might deter the Germans. The situation balanced precariously. Two weeks before Stockholm's message of military support, the Danes had presented the draft of their November constitution, and at the same time the German Federation warned that it would intervene in Holstein. Denmark clung to the hope of a Scandinavian deterrent as the only available straw in the situation.

In Sweden the desire to avoid a war with major European powers grew, and in the early part of December King Carl was forced to inform the Swedish Riksdag that no nation should count on their military support. Actually he continued to hope to bring his country into the war, and on December 15 the important Danish newspaper *Fædrelandet* wrote that he had promised to bring his army. The Danish people were not told that negotiations on the military pact had been dropped, and on the same day another major newspaper, *Dagbladet*, reported that Swedish-Norwegian aid was certain. Now would be the time to see, it added, "if Manderström is a true statesman or just a facile pen."

The description of the literary prime minister as a facile penman would remain attached to his name through Ibsen's use of it in his poetry.

On December 13, Ibsen issued his angry and powerful poem, "A Brother in Need!" (En Broder i Nød!):

Nu samler sig om Tyras Borg,—	On Tyra's ramparts gather now,—
Kan hænde, sidste Gang,—	The final time, perhaps—
Et Folk i nød, et Folk i Sorg,	A people in need, in suffering,
Med Flaget halvt paa Stang.	With flag at half-mast flown.
Forladt, forladt paa Farens Dag,	Betrayed, in the deadly hour betrayed,
Forladt i Stridens Stund!	Betrayed in the press of battle!
Var Saadan ment det Nævetag,	Was this the handclasp's meaning,
Der loved godt for Nordens Dag	The happy promise of Northmen days
i Axelstad og Lund?	In Axelstad* and Lund?
Det Ord, der fløD, some om det kom	The words that poured as though
Fra Hjertet lige hid,—	They sprung from our hearts direct—
Det var da kun en Fraseflom,—	Nothing but a spring of phrases:
Og nu er Tørkens Tid!	And now the drought!
Det Træ, som Blomstringsløfter gav	The tree that promised bloom
I Festens Solskinsvæld,	In gay sun and showers—
Det staar, af Stormen kvistet af,	Now stripped by storm is the
Som Kors paa Nordens Ungdoms Grav,	Grave-marker of Northmen young,
	On the vigil of their first trial!
Den første Alvorskveld!	

Angry and ashamed, the disillusioned poet was accusing his nation of a dishonorable betrayal, and damning it with words that stung:

Men Du, min frelste norske Broer,	You, my sheltered brother Norsemen,
Som staar paa fredlyst Grund	You stand on ground made sacred
I Kraft af Løftets fagre Ord,	By those brave promises you forgot
Forglemt i Stridens Stund,—	To keep in the fatal hour—
Stryg Du paa Flugt fra Fædrestavn,	Get out of your father's house!
Jag over Havets Hvælv;	Race the arching waves!
Gaa Glemselsgang fra Havn til Havn,	Lose your name from port to port
Og list Dig til et fremmed Navn,	Or slip behind a foreign tag—
Og gjem Dig for Dig selv!	Hide from yourself!

Few poets have so judged their people, but even in his fury he was reluctant to believe that honor and duty could be thus completely forgotten. There was still time:

Det var en Drøm. Vaagn stærk og kjæk	That was a dream. Wake strong and bold
Fra Folkesøvn til Daad!	from sleep and roused to action!
En Broer i Nød! Hver Mand paa Dæk!	A brother in need! Every man on deck!
Her Gjælder rappe Raad!	No second wasted!
End kan det staa i Saga slig:	We yet may read some saga's word:
Dansk, dansk er Tyras Vold!—	The Dane on Tyra's bastion stands!—
End Dannebrogs forrevne Flig	The Danish banner, tattered, still
Kan over Nordens Fremtid rig	waves red folds across the North,
slaa ud sin røde Fold!	a dawn of rich hope!

*Poetic term for Copenhagen.

The poem indicates that to Ibsen the issue was the spiritual life or death of his people and himself. In a fever pitch he waited. First to respond was the Student Society, which passed a resolution the very next day after the poem appeared (December 12), uring their fellow students in Sweden to consider the Danish cause theirs—to let Denmark stand alone would be shameful. Professor Aschehoug's address to the meeting described the difficulty a small nation had in thinking great thoughts. And in Norway a citizens' rally of 3,000 pledged their support to the king in a war to aid Denmark.

King Carl hoped that Norway might support him even though Sweden balked. In January, 1864, he issued a call for a March consultation with the Storting. But in the meantime the war had broken out and the Danish forces were in retreat. Now Denmark (and its king) looked to Norway as its last hope. The disillusionment with Scandinavian solidarity was confirmed. Only a minority of the Storting was willing to give the king a free hand; the majority as well as the cabinet were opposed. On March 29 they voted war appropriations, making it conditional on support from either England or France. Some even wanted it conditional on the participation of both powers. The Storting finally dealt a death blow to all ideals of Scandinavian cooperation by passing a resolution (although by a narrow majority) stating that the Norwegian people did not desire more intimate political ties with Denmark.

If there had been a great number of young men to volunteer for military service now, the Scandinavianists might have taken heart despite all the disappointments of the last months. A good many from both countries came forward, but hardly enough to make it seem that the Northmen were responding to the threat. One volunteer, a young theological candidate named Christopher Bruun, stood on the rostrum of the Student Society on April 2, 1864, and castigated his fellow students for lacking the virility or the courage to carry out the promises given freely at the student conventions. He got a cool reception. Ibsen was not present at this address, but in these days his ears were filled with similar omens. Official Norway had spoken in the Storting's refusal to aid Denmark; the young academic people were lukewarm in their feeling for their Danish brothers. Big words faded when time for action came. Ibsen felt cheapened and guilty; he was the one condemned to "lose himself from port to port" and "hide from himself." In this mood he left his country:

Jeg slynged på rim et klokkeklemt over landet ud; der blev ingen skræmt.	I flung my gauntlet in verse down on the land; no one moved.

Min gerning var gjort; jeg steg
   ombord
og stævned for damp fra det kære
   Nord.
	My labor ended, I went aboard
	and came away from my beloved
	   North.

Another incisive poem from the same time is "From Dybbøl Days," (later given the ironic title "Serenely Believing" *Troens Grund*). It too reflects the same bitter scorn for a people complacently unaware of its baseness. So filled was he with the national disgrace that he seems to have been unaware of Clemens Petersen's harsh review of *The Pretenders* in *Fædrelandet* for April 2. It took a national catastrophe to cause the unusually sensitive Ibsen to ignore a hostile review.

He stayed in Copenhagen for two weeks, vainly trying to work on the play about Magnus Heineson, but his thoughts were in Dybbøl, where the Prussian cannon leveled the Danish bulwarks. On April 20, two days after the fall of Dybbøl, he took the steamer to Lübeck, and on the way south he stopped in Berlin. All we know of this part of his journey is the suffering he felt when Danish cannon from Dybbøl were driven in triumph in the city's victory celebration: "I don't know how much of my sanity I could have retained, if I had stayed longer in Berlin," he wrote to a friend nine months later, "for there I saw the triumph in April, the screaming mob wallowing among trophies of Dybbøl, saw them riding gun carriages, spitting in the cannon — the same cannon that had gotten no help and yet had kept up fire until they burst." He wrote of Berlin almost a year later: "I saw the mob spit into the mouth of the cannon of Dybbøl, and it was a sign to me that one day history would spit on Norway and Sweden for this thing." He was right in saying that this was "no journey for pleasure"; unable to put away his "somber thoughts about things at home," he was in anguish on the whole journey.

CHAPTER SEVENTEEN

THE FIRST YEAR IN ROME (1864-65)

Ibsen never forgot the first, overwhelming impression of the south of Europe and Italy. He had hurried from Berlin to Vienna, where he took the Semmering railroad, the only line then leading through the Alps. The image of those mountains remained vividly with him, even thirty years later, when he described them on his seventieth birthday: "The clouds hung before the high mountain tops like heavy, dark curtains; under these we rode, through tunnels that suddenly burst out at Miramare, where the gorgeous South, a unique, shimmering light, gleaming white marble, suddenly revealed itself to me; and although it is not all beautiful, all my work after this was stamped with its image." (He recalled the day as May 9, but may have been in error since his account books show that he was already in Trieste by May.) He felt that this escape from northern darkness into light and sun, into the life of Italy, reshaped all his writing, and even though it took some time for this effect to show itself, from the first his depression over the pettiness of life in Norway was dispelled. In his happiness he rededicated himself to the pursuit of his life's goal in poetry and art.

On his way to Rome he made brief stops at other cities, including Milan. Then on Sunday morning, June 19, he called at the Scandinavian Society in Rome. With a young Norwegian friend, the art historian Lorentz Dietrichson, he toured the city the entire day, finally coming to rest over a bottle of wine at a small inn by the side of the river. Dietrichson saw the change that had come over Ibsen since those bitter and depressed days in Oslo in the winter of 1861. To be sure, Ibsen still condemned Norwegian policy in the Danish war, but he was able to smile over the controversy provoked by *Love's Comedy*. The success of *The Pretenders* still buoyed him up, and Italy promised a rich and rewarding experience.

Two weeks later he moved into the little mountain town of Genzano to escape the summer heat in Rome. Dietrichson had gone ahead and arranged for Ibsen to share a room with the Finnish sculptor Walter Runeberg. (Christopher Bruun's mother also was living there with a son and daughter.) This was a peaceful, contented time for him; the people treated him kindly, calling him Capellone, "big hat," because he wore a wide-brimmed artist's hat. In the afternoons he usually walked in the woods with his friends; in the evenings they made excursions around Lake Nemi. He had not been in such a light-hearted mood for many years, and he came out of his usually withdrawn state so far as to entertain the company with amusing anecdotes and told of a night when he and Runeberg were lodging at the Scandinavian Society in Rome. They were startled out of sleep by the shrieks of the Italian maid and, rushing to her room, found her in her shift, held at bay by a grasshopper. Everytime the grasshopper bounded toward her, she bounded as far in the opposite direction. The two Vikings finally routed the beast and rescued the appreciative maiden.

In September he returned to Rome, where he was joined a few months later by Suzannah and their son and they set up housekeeping in the city. The attraction of ancient monuments and works of art was so strong, however, it was some time before he could settle down to work. As he spent days on the Via Appia or the Via Latina or amid the great ruins of the Baths of Caracalla he was indulging, as he later wrote a friend, in "an idleness that cannot be called wasteful." He absorbed this full panorama of art and nature and folk life, and his imagination was being stored with images on which he would draw in his coming labor. Ibsen began to realize, as do all Northerners who go South, how artistically barren his country was compared with this treasure house of painting, sculpture, churches, castles, palaces, and temples—art from all ages and in all styles.

As this world of art opened to him, his taste became more discriminating. The current vogue was for the classic art of Ancient Greece and Rome, and its later manifestations in neo-classic works. But for him this was a cold art, without the note of personal life he sought. It seemed subservient to rules and conventions that were, in his opinion, more the demand of tradition than a necessary choice by the individual artist. With Dietrichson he argued about the Greek and Roman portrait busts in the Vatican. He preferred the more individualized Roman works, the curl of the lip or the crease of the brow that suddenly revealed the inner life of the man. But he could respond to Greek art as well, as is seen in his comments on the "Tragic Muse" in the Vatican: "The indescribably exalted, yet tranquil joy revealed in the face, the rich, leaf-adorned head, with that almost ethereal yet bacchantic aura about it;

the eyes that look at once inward and through and beyond what stands before them—just so is Greek tragedy." It was inevitable that Melpomene, the tragic muse, would make the deepest impression on him.

After the ancients, his preference was for Michelangelo and the baroque style that flowered in Bernini and his school. This taste was definitely contrary to standard nineteenth-century judgment, which viewed the baroque as a decadent falling off; Bernini was contemptuously referred to as a "theatre artist" by critics. The refinements and order of Rafael did not move him, but Michelangelo was another matter: "In my opinion no one has sinned more than he against conventional notions of beauty; yet everything he created is beautiful, because full of character." This is the baroque—an art rich in life, movement, violent struggle; it strives for powerful contrasts of light against darkness, color against color. In seeking to move and unsettle the observer it is an essentially dramatic art, and in its time modern drama itself was born. The boldly personal quality of the baroque appealed to him, and so he praised Bernini along with Michelangelo: "Those fellows had the courage to commit a folly now and then." He even preferred the bold medieval Gothic to the orderly proportions of the classical Renaissance. There was no sight more overwhelming than the cathedral of Milan: "The man who could conceive the plan for such a structure could have made a moon in his spare time and tossed it into space." Such art fired his imagination; the day was coming when this art would help him find a personal form by which to shape the ferment within.

Various projects competed in his mind. One day in Genzano he spoke to Dietrichson about the Emperor Julian, another great rebel who was ultimately defeated. The play about Magnus Heineson still troubled him; he felt he should write it, but more and more his attention was being drawn to a different kind of play entirely, one born of the memories of home that could not be shaken off. On September 16, 1864, he wrote Bjørnson from Rome: "Here there is peace for writing; I am working on a major poem right now, and thinking of a tragedy, 'Julianus Apostata,' a work which is a great delight and which will be, I am sure, a success. By spring or certainly summer I hope to have both finished."

He was unduly optimistic, and it was impossible to sustain the "great delight," as month after month new financial worries plagued him. The trip for him and his family had been expensive, and by the end of September he had used up both the state funds and the private aid. As he began to borrow, he turned, as all Scandinavians in Rome naturally did, to the German-born Danish consul Johann Bravo. Bjørnson sent him another 100 dollars in the middle of October, and he was able to go on for another two months. When this ran out, he had to wait another six months before getting any more aid from home. A letter he sent Bjørn-son in December was lost; he felt completely forgotten and waited in agony.

In March, 1865, he applied to The Norwegian Scientific Society of Trondheim for a grant of 500 dollars. In the 1860's this venerable insti-tution still gave support to writers; and Ibsen could claim that his drama about the Emperor Julian did in fact fall into the society's field of historical research. Bjørnson wrote a recommendation and asked that, in justice, Ibsen be given the same kind of support both he and Vinje had received. The application was filed too late for that year's grants, but in the fall Bjørnson made another plea, citing Ibsen's strained circumstances and the daily agony he was enduring. The fol-lowing spring the society granted him 100 dollars, but it was too late to be of much help.

Bjørnson had other plans for aiding Ibsen: a benefit at Christiania Theatre, an assistantship with Botten Hansen at the university library, or a job in the customs service, as Ibsen's friends at the "Erudite Hol-land" suggested. Bjørnson's enthusiasm could produce endless schemes: "I'll attack, hammer and tong, if need be! Your money or your lives, you swine, a poet is dying!" His faith in Ibsen was boundless: "You damn well won't die, you're tough, and brave, and lazy—such never die." But this news arrived without money, and Ibsen had to beg for monthly loans while he waited. He thought twice before he spent a penny; he budgeted every expenditure. It was all in all a rather thin atmosphere for great writing.

Bjørnson managed to get him an advance from Councillor Frederik Hegel, director of the Gyldendal publishing house in Copenhagen (then called Gyldendalske Boghandel), on the strength of the unwritten his-torical drama, and in September Ibsen received the money. By now Bjørnson was running out of people to squeeze for money; his friends in Oslo had given all they could. In one of his begging letters to Dis-trict Governor Breder in Drammen, he wrote: "The poet Henrik Ibsen is in dire need in Rome.... I turn to you for immediate aid—you have many friends, a love of literature, and a kind heart toward a gifted man in distress.... God grant that you help me, for I am in despair over this." He got 110 dollars from Drammen, and more money elsewhere. Ibsen's acute distress seems to have been relieved. At New Year's, 1866, things looked brighter than they had the previous year. He was spared until the fall of the year the news that in 1864 a lawyer, hired by his creditors (some from his Bergen days), had just seized his furniture and other things stored in the Norwegian Theatre and had sold them at auction. Even his letters, notes, and manuscripts were scattered. He "screamed" when he learned about it, but for the time being he was spared the news.

In these circumstances, and despite the joy of being in Italy, it was difficult for him to work, particularly since he had not decided on his next project. The play about Magnus Heineson was abandoned for the time being; and even Julian, reluctantly, gave way to new thoughts that occupied him about a poem on a pastor he named Koll, later called Brand. The poem was intended as an indictment of the Norwegian people; despite all his financial trouble he could not ignore the events that were taking place at home, but returned compulsively to them time and time again.

A vivid impression of how concerned he was with the fate of his people is given in Lorentz Dietrichson's account of Ibsen at a party of fellow Northerners held on the outskirts of Rome a few days after his first arrival in the city: "It was the first evening in many days that Ibsen had spent with Scandinavians and he began to tell of the painful, horrifying impressions of the war he had gotten on his journey. Then gradually and quite unnoticed his account became an improvised speech: all his long-repressed resentment, all the indignation at a cause betrayed, all his love of the North now burst forth. His voice took on a strange new resonance; in the growing twilight his eyes flamed. When he ended no one cried Bravo, no one touched his glass, but I think we all felt that the Marseillaise of the North had that evening rung out in the Roman twilight, was heard by the few of us, disappeared then without a trace. I know that I have never been so deeply moved by the power of the living word; nothing ever approached the impression of that evening."

The wife of the Danish painter Frederik Lund must have been speaking of the same evening when she noted that once a speech of Ibsen's so moved her that she remembered it all forty years later. He ended, she said, by rising to his feet, striking his fist so hard on the table the glasses tinkled, and declaring "his son would never step foot on Norwegian soil until the wrong of betraying Denmark had been atoned for!" This tremendous denunciation poured out of him as volcanically as would the poem "Brand."

He had a chance to give many similar speeches that winter in Rome. The Scandinavians generally gathered in an old wine shop in the Via del Tritone, opposite the house Ibsen had rented, close under the Quirinal. Here too he was called "Capellone"; he was the leader of these evening sessions and his tongue had never been so agile in company. The Swedish poet Count Snoilsky recalled these evenings a generation later in a poem he dedicated to Ibsen:

Är sextifyra, Då Dybböls dunder
Ännu gaf eko Bland Söderns lunder,
I silfverskimret Af Romas måne
Hvar kväll vi träffades På Tritone.
Bland vingårdsbönder Kring
    spiselflamman
En flock från Norden Höll troget
    samman.

På härden kocken Vår
    måltid stekte,
Albanerdrufvan I glasen lekte,

Du satt vid midten Af långa bordet
Och bland oss unga Du förde ordet.
Nyss våldet stympat Norrœna-
    stammen;
Vi delte sorgen, Vi delte skammen.

Jag hör dig tala I sena natten,
Det ljungar under Den stora hatten!

In 'sixty-four, when Dybbøl's cannon,
Echoed loudly still in southern groves,
In the silver gleam of the Roman moon
We met each evening at Tritone cafe.
Among vineyard workers around the
    hearth
A troop of Northmen bound close
    together.

On the hearth the cook tended dinner,
In our glass Albanian grapes sparkled.

And you by the long table throned,
The spokesman for all our youth.
The North had late by force been cleft,
We shared the sorrow, we shared
    the shame.

I hear you speak into the night,
And lightning flashes beneath your hat!

One occasion when Snoilsky felt that lightning flash close to home was when he came upon a picture of Count Manderström in the Danish journal *Illustreret Tidende,* with a noose drawn around the prime ministerial neck. As a nephew of the Countess Manderström he felt it his duty to protest to the librarian of the Scandinavian Society, where he had come upon the scandalous art work. Dietrichson, who was librarian, asked the artist to make himself known, and Ibsen rose to his feet. He and Snoilsky settled the matter privately and remained friends, but Ibsen was not to be persuaded to alter his views.

His letters home reflected his obsession with the fate of a nation that could so betray its honor and duty, and as the obsession grew, his views on Norwegian-Swedish foreign policy became more unrealistic. He refused to admit that the Danes might have precipitated the war, and he refused to face the military impotence of Norway and Sweden in relation to the great powers. He saw the whole crisis as purely a moral one; it was ethically necessary for Norway and Sweden to defend Scandinavian national honor against an aggressor, regardless of his size or potential for destruction. The unwillingness of his people to stir themselves was a betrayal which would leave them morally paralyzed forever.

In September, 1864, he wrote to Bjørnson, "Political conditions at home have grieved me and turned many a joy here sour. The whole thing was a tissue of lies and dreams. These events will have an effect on me at least. We may as well write off our ancient history; the Norwegian of today has obviously no more to do with that past than the Greek pirate with the race of men who sailed to Troy and had the help of the gods." The poet Vinje had said much the same in his recent translation of the

Greek poet's lines from Byron's *Don Juan:* the singer who recounts the deeds of his ancestors must blush before his countrymen of today.

If Ibsen was giving his final verdict on all the blatantly romanticized nationalism of past years, he was including himself in the judgment as well. Now he returned again to the poem cycle "In the Picture Gallery," where he described his verses as "bone-dry rustling of paper leaves"; he reshaped the poems into what he would later call "The Gorge" ("Kløften"). His earlier writing seemed to him like a river during a flash flood; when the storm passes the river is gone, with nothing but dead leaves and trash in its bed. He was guilty of keeping this rubbish in view. He had made poems from it:

Det minded fjernt om kildevæld,	At a distance it sounds like rippling
Jeg selv har sværmet der en kveld.	springs.
	I myself have rhapsodized there an
	evening.

He recalls with anguish the times his will served the will of others. Then he was like a performing bear, forced to dance, as he describes in the poem "The Power of Memory" ("Mindets Magt"):

Jeg selv sad engang i kedlen nede,	I too was chained on the iron griddle,
under fuld musik og forsvarlig hede.	with music blaring and burning fire.
Og dengang brændte jeg mer end	Those days burned more than skin;
skindet;	into heart and mind are they burned.
Og det går aldrig mig ud af mindet.	Each time I hear an echo from
Og hvergang genklang fra den tid	that time,
lyder,	I'm bound again on the burning
det er som jeg bandtes i gloende	griddle.
gryder.	
Det kendes som stik under	It smarts like pins under my nails—
neglerødder	and then I dance on feet of verse.
da må jeg danse pa versefødder.	

But he could no longer take part in this dance, this "game of lies with the past" he had used to deceive himself and the people. For the crime in which he was an accomplice the punishment would fall most heavily on the poet:

Thi vi har leflet med en udbrændt	We have pimped for a dead race,
Slægt,	rouged the corpse of a dead past,
og sminket Liget af de stærke Tider,	draped the walls of memory's hall,
og festklaedet alle Mindehallens	swung big swords to please dwarfs.
Sidern,	
till Dverges Fryd, med	
Kæmpevaabens Vægt.	
Om Fortids Dag vi sang i Nuets	We sang of the past in present night;
Natt;	but forgot one thing to note:
men *et*, det store, glemte vi at	Is *he* the one to have the treasured
drøfte:	legacy,

| kan *den* med Rette tage Arvens Skatt, | whose hand lacks strength to lift it? |
| som fattes Haanden, der skal Arven løfte? | |

If the poet's obligation is to be spokesman for his people, then now is the time for confession and remorse:

Se, derfor har jeg vendt mit Syn og Sind	Thus have I turned sight and mind from the vacant saga of the past,
bort fra vor Fortids sjæledræbte Sage,	from the dream-drenched lies of the future,
bort fra vor Løgndrøm om en Fredtids Dage,	I enter the gray world of the now.
og gaar i Nuets Taageverden ind.	

After his first year in Rome he began to feel that his greatest triumph was to have driven the "aesthete" out of his nature. He had never looked at life from a completely "aesthetic" point of view, but the danger had been a real one, and he knew he could have been seduced. He wrote to Bjørnson, "I cannot tell what any number of clever asses might have made of me if they had had me to themselves." He also wrote his mother-in-law, Magdalene Thoresen, "Up there I could never live a coherent inner life; thus I was one thing in my work, another outside it—and my production lacked unity. Now I realize that even though I am all in a state of transition, yet I am passing over firm ground." He placed more value on this integrated soul than on clever perceptions, or artistic sensitivity. And so he began to feel free, as he notes in the same letter: "The decisive and significant thing for me is that I have removed myself far enough away to see the humbug behind all the ready-made lies in what we are pleased to call 'public life,' and the pettiness in all the private sloganeering, which always has words for a 'great cause,' but never has the will, the capacity, or the sense of duty required to make great deeds out of the fine words. Every man-on-the-street in Norway speaks with great self-satisfaction about Norwegian level-headedness—which means nothing more than that lukewarm temperature of the blood that makes it impossible for their decent souls to commit folly in grand style.... Among our nation the impossible commences whenever the demands made exceed those of the everyday routine."

He could never remain lukewarm, and there was always fuel for intense feeling at hand: "Among the Scandinavians here in Rome," he wrote in a letter, "I have found all manner of spiritual corruption. What do you think of the fact that even Danish men and women sat in the Prussian Embassy chapel on Sunday, right along with the Germans, right during the war, and listened devoutly while the Prussian

minister prayed for the success of Prussian arms in their just war! But
you can be sure I thundered and tidied up the situation. Down here I
am not frightened at anything; at home I was afraid when I walked
through the sullen mob and knew their nasty smirks behind my back."
One of his thrusts was a proposal to admit "Danes from Schleswig" to
membership in the Scandinavian Society. This was unanimously approved, but when he tried to exclude Germans he got a single supporting vote, obviously because the only German there to exclude was the
kindly old Consul Bravo. This probably never occurred to Ibsen, so ruthless was he in pursuit of any who fraternized with the hated Germans.

He read in Norwegian papers of the farm boy who had chopped off
his finger to avoid being drafted. In contrast was the story of Italian
mothers taking their teen-age sons out of school and sending them to
fight for national unity with Garibaldi. Other peoples had the will to
sacrifice for great ideals, but not, apparently, Norwegians. This was the
constant theme of his evening harangues at the Tritone cafe, where he
sat at the head of the table and directed the talk. In jesting or in serious
tone the theme remained the same—death to the spirit of compromise!
A standard point of departure was the story of the young English poet
who died of hunger rather than give up his pursuit of poetry. His land-
lord found him with the garret latch-key in his throat—he had embraced
his poverty rather than compromise with the world and take a "steady"
job. Thus the question was asked: Should one swallow the latch-key or
work in an office? When it was suggested that he get an office job, Ibsen
held up the immutable rule that the free man always swallows the
latch-key. To those who found this position unrealistic and immoral,
Ibsen had outrageous paradoxes with which he would twit their bourgeois morality; when they had proved their case as irrefutably as two
and two equals four, he questioned their basic logic — were they sure
the principle held true on Jupiter? And if not on Jupiter, then can it be
universal? Underneath the game, reminiscent of his play with the
"Dutchmen" in Botten Hansen's study, he was seriously at work gathering the ideas that would become *Brand*.

And always there was the over-riding concern that in the hour of
trial the spirit of compromise had triumphed in Norway. "There is in
me a deep anxiety," he wrote Bjørnson, "which says that our nation
has not been granted an eternity, but only a term. When I read of
things up there, when I see all this very proper, very respectable materialism and petty-mindedness, then the same feeling comes over me
as comes upon a madman who stares obsessively at a single, concen-

trated, hopelessly black spot." To Fru Thoresen he wrote: "I often think it dreary to work in an age such as ours. If the spiritual life of a people does not have something of the eternal in it, it makes no difference if it lasts one year or one hundred. This is what I think of Norway and Sweden: we do not have the will to sacrifice when the time demands it. We have nothing to unite us, no great sorrow like Denmark—our people lack the depth of spirit necessary for grief."

No matter how deep his anxiety, he never gave up hope completely; as usual, faith and doubt lived side by side in him. He asked comfort and help from Bjørnson, and added: "Often it seems unthinkable to me that we shall be lost altogether. A state can be annihilated, but not a people. . . . The best in us will live, I know—assuming that the spirit of our nation can be elevated to thrive on suffering; this is the crucial problem. If I could but have faith and confidence!" He felt his duty must be to rouse the slumbering conscience of his people, force it to look honestly at itself, and help it regain a moral basis for its life. In his heart he kept faith that he had the strength for this deed. His writing would accomplish it: "*One* can give light to many—one man's will can move the world."

He had many talks with Christopher Bruun that winter. Bruun had fought at Dybbøl and had risked his life for Denmark; he was the kind of man who could sacrifice himself for duty, and Ibsen respected and loved him. There was something of an Old Testament prophet in Bruun. Bjørnson once wrote of him, "He loves mankind to over-exert itself." There was something more than human in his demand for perfect harmony between deeds and ideals. Ibsen needed this proof that someone else shared his belief. Together they discussed moral and religious problems. Bruun was a theological graduate, but had not applied for a pastorate because he felt his beliefs to be somewhat unorthodox. He regarded the state church as a monstrosity, because in it preaching became an official act where spiritual content was ignored; the church's practice corresponded to its preaching. Kierkegaard had made the same accusation, and now Ibsen's thinking was moving in the same direction.

They spoke about Norway and the Danish question, and now Bruun, in his outspoken way, asked Ibsen why he had not volunteered himself, since he had urged others to do so. Ibsen answered tartly, "We poets have other tasks." Bjørnson had answered the same way; each man had to use his talents where they could do the most good. But Ibsen felt stung at the question; he was, after all, a "partner in guilt" with his countrymen, and the poem "From My Home Life" (Fra mit husliv)

shows how he reacted to the accusation of cowardice. First he shows
us the poet creating his verse, his thoughts dancing:

yr og glad gennem alle de dejlige riger	giddy and glad, through the happy lands,

but if he stops to glance at a mirror:

Derinde stod en adstadig gæst, med blygrå øjne, med lukket vest, og med filtsko, hvis ej jeg fejled.	There stood a stodgy guest, leaden-eyed, waistcoat buttoned, and in slippers, if I'm not mistaken.

The timid bourgeois looks himself in the eye and loses through introspection the courage he so poetically imagined.

Moments of discouragement came, but for the most part the thought
of all he had neglected to do, all he had done wrongly acted as stimulus
and spur to his creativity. Out of his feeling of guilt came the admoni-
tions and challenges to his countrymen, and more and more his poetic
mission became one of waking them to their responsibility. He had never
before felt his mission as poet so strongly. In September he wrote to
Bjørnson: "I am earnest enough now to feel this; I am a severe task-
master to myself." He had hard words for his way of life in Norway:
"filthiness," "imbecility," "swinishness" — words which do not have to
be taken literally. He had rescued himself from his brief time of sloven-
liness in the Oslo cafes. He was talking about the need to purge himself
of the mask of falseness he had assumed when he followed standards
other than his own. Now the great poem he was writing would be a
judgment on the nation and on himself. He was responsible for the
past, but more importantly he felt a responsibility for the future. To his
publisher Hegel he wrote: "Norwegians and Swedes have a fearful
blood guilt to cleanse in their relation to you Danes.... I feel it my life
task to use my God-given talents to arouse my countrymen from their
lethargy and make them understand what direction the great issues of
life are taking." About the same time he wrote to King Carl of "the life
mission which I surely believe and know that God had charged me
with — the life mission that stands for me as the most important, the
most necessary in Norway, to awaken the nation and lead it to think
great thoughts." This would be his purpose in the poem that became
Brand.

CHAPTER EIGHTEEN

BRAND (1865)

"B<small>RAND</small> started to grow within me, like an embryo," Ibsen wrote, referring to the days in Berlin when he watched the triumphal procession of cannon captured at Dybbøl. In Genzano that summer he began to mold it into shape, and he continued to work on it until the next summer.

Even though he associated the poem intimately with the disillusionment of 1864 and the sense of personal defeat he endured then, the theme was one that had lived within him for years. Both the theme and the conflict of the poem are reflected in his 1862 review of Bjørnson's *Sigurd Slembe,* written just after he finished *Love's Comedy.* Ibsen wrote: "The conflict in the play is not so much a matter of the plot as it is of the hero's struggle with himself, and thus the work may be more fittingly called a splendid monologue; the protagonist is consistently shown isolated from the world, in terrible solitude amidst the multitude. Bjørnson has sought to portray a man of great gifts and powerful will, with an unconquerable urge to do great things and the right to act—but rejected and misunderstood by his fellow man."

Ibsen seldom had such praise for a literary work as he showed here, and the emphasis in his choice of the phrase "terrible solitude" is a clue to how deeply the play had touched him. The problem it investigated was his own, and it helped to make the problem clear to him. Two years later the problem was still very real, and he would not be free until he had made poetry of it, poetry that would chastise and warn his nation at the same time as it freed him.

It was difficult for him to find the form for the theme, as deeply felt as it was. In a letter to Bjørnson on September 16, 1864, he does not even mention the work, but speaks of the "irrepressible joy" it was to work on the drama about the Emperor Julian. He felt the need for a new form to embody his concept of a man who strode through life without the least compromise of his will or demands. In tracing this man's career he was no doubt thinking of writing a Norwegian counterpart to the Danish *Adam Homo,* written by Frederik Paludan-Müller in 1849. His poem, like Paludan-Müller's, was to be a narrative in iambic eight-line stanzas, with only the order of the rhymes different. Ibsen could easily adopt the scheme which the other poet announced in his Prologue:

De gamle Tider ere længst forsvundne,	Ancient days are long since gone, when clang of shields accompanied the poet's lyre,
Da Bardens Harpe løf til Skjoldeklang,	when he inspired heroes by his song,
Da han begeistred Helte ved sin Sang	and with it comforted the conquered.
Og trøstede med den de Overvundne.	Old heroes' spirits now lie fettered, cannot be wakened a second time;
De Gamle Kæmpers Aander ligge bundne,	who now speaks of heroes in his song
Og vækkes ikke op for anden Gang;	pours new wine in ancient cups.
Den, som i Sang om Kæmper nu fortæller,	So Today's Muse seeks other paths in poetry's borderless land,
Ny Viin paa gamle Læderflasker helder.	so she reveals her domains to us
Derfor sig andre Baner Musen bryder	in forms that match the present age.
i Poesiens grændseløse Land,	
Derfor i Former, som til Tiden svare,	
Vil nu sin Verden hun os aabenbare.	

The characteristic difference in the hero each of the poets took as the theme of his poem might perhaps be described as a national difference. The Danish poet could create a man who relieved his emotions in cold, underplayed mockery; the Norwegian had to "storm forth with the edged sword of vengeance," and let his fury thunder. Ibsen thus picked as his hero a harsh, unbending martinet who fights ruthlessly, almost insanely, for his ideals, a man quite out of the ordinary. Paludan-Müller, on the contrary, had chosen a man "of everyday cut":

Og Helten, dansk i Sind og Skind og Tale,	And the hero, in mind, heart, and speech Danish,
Skal sig i Hverdagslivet røre frit.	Shall move freely in everyday life.
Han holdes borte fra det Ideale,	He has nothing to do with ideals,
Han uromantisk gaaer i Prosaskridt.	He walks without romance in prosaic steps.

The poet describes his hero in this manner so that:

Skal dog tilsidst et Tankebilled speile	in time the image of an ideal will be reflected by the poem from his life.
Sig i hans Liv, og frem af Digtet gaae.	

Ibsen's poem had the same intention:

Snart stærkt snart lindt er till Sangen mit langspil stemt,	Now strong, now gentle my zither to the song keeps measure,
underspundne Strænge dirrer og farver Klangen,	its sounding base lends color to the harmony,

inderst inde er et Digt i Digtet gjemt,
og fatter du *det,* mig Folk—da fatter du Sangen.

But deep within the poem another hides;
if this you seize, my people—
then you seize my song.

Ibsen proclaimed that the poet should lead his people and "release their yearning with his song"; this idea again put him in harmony with Paludan-Müller's final words in his Prologue:

Og anderledes ei det gaaer en Sanger,
Naar Digtets spire vaagner i hans Bryst:
Han hører forud hver en Fremtidsrøst,
Der gjennem ham at yttre sig forlanger.
Haab, Elskov, Fryd og Veemod, Spot og Anger,
Den bittre Sorg med samt den søde Lyst,
Alt griber ford i hans Hjertes Strænge,
Saa disse tone stærkt og zittre længe.

Not otherwise is it with a singer
when in his heart a poem breeds and buds;
he hears before the voices of the future demanding that he give them form.
Hope, love, joy, grief, scorn, and anger,
bitter sorrow and sweet delight,
each stirs his heart before the rest,
and makes his song, his heartstrings tremble long.

The last lines of this poem Ibsen had echoed more than once in his poetic warnings to Norway; the melody of Paludan-Müller's Prologue had been in his ear for some time. And if his anger was still too keen to allow him to hold up a calm, untroubled mirror to his age, the basic idea of his new poem was the same as that of *Adam Homo:*

Alt Liv er Villen—Villen er det Første
I hver en Sjæl, den mindste som den største

All life is will—will is foremost
in every soul, the least and the greatest

When he sought in *Brand* to create the image of a man whose strength of will knew no compromise, he was still mindful of his weakness and the guilt he shared with his nation. Perhaps he thought his share of guilt to be greater; had he not been the one to insist that words become actions? His guilt was felt so strongly that the prologue to his poem became an anguished cry: "To my fellow culprits" (Till de medskyldige). He recalled how he had helped to "drape the halls of memory," making "all ecstasy, all festivity." He had sung "of the past in present darkness" and had carried on "this frivolous game with the dead." It was just that:

—fælles Skyldvægt rammer ej alle,
med tifold Tyngde truer den dem,
som stilled sig først i Fylkinger frem;
men hundredfold synded dine Skalde!

—on all the common guilt strikes not,
but threatens tenfold those not,
who headed up the phalanx;
a hundredfold your poets' guilt!

It was now the poet's duty, and his honor, to show the road ahead to his people:

han skrifter dets Brøde, talker lydt dets Anger,	he shrives its sins, cries aloud its anguish,
sukker, naar det skakes af Angst; dets dulgte Trang	sighs when it is shaken by distress; its hidden need
Klæder han i Ord, — derfor er han Sanger.	he finds words to reveal—then is he called a poet.

To do this he had turned away from "the soul-killed saga of the past," and had come to grips with the struggles of his own day in this new poem. The man he would create as the spokesman for his ideals must be flesh of his flesh, blood of his own blood: "Brand," he once said, "is myself in my best moments." And the man needed a setting that united him with the people and the environment that could have fostered him. Ibsen now began to recreate his last strong impressions of Norwegian scenery and folk life, the images he had stored from his travels through the mountains and fjords two years ago. These memories mixed with reports by countrymen and other Scandinavians in Rome, and he saw again the steep narrow gorge he had threaded his way through on the way from Gudbrandsdalen to Sogn, and the black-suited pastor who stood beside him on the precipice. Into this memory crept stern young Christopher Bruun, whose image was before him every day in Rome. He remembered the Fanaråk towering over the mountain wilderness, beautiful yet terrifying, wild and severe, a graveyard of wanderers; he recalled the cramped shores of the fjord and the steep mountain slopes where the houses seemed to burrow into the rock screes to find shelter from the huge glaciers that might slash down across their roofs. In the district of Sunnylven he found the right setting for his hero. He was deeply convinced that those who lived with such menace had of necessity to become slaves of the earth, bowed as the "sons of misery" were bowed. On his travels there he learned that the peasants served Mammon first, and hardly ever lifted their thoughts as high as God; even religion was forced to bend for gain. It was easy for him to make this the location for the story he had heard in the parsonage at Lom, the story of the rich farmer's widow who had dug out the money from under her husband's dead body and had clung to it until her dying day.

He also believed there were forces here that could one day burst out and drive these souls to a higher, a freer vision. God spoke on the mountain tops, and when he looked up to the great peaks that scraped against heaven, he knew that no matter how cramped the world below, there was a path that led up to the heights. The man who now stood before him became such a beckoning peak, and from this vision he took the first name he gave him, "Koll," the peak. But this man was more fire than mountain, and so his name became "Brand."

For antagonist he selected an outsider, a pastor who was a government official to the core, one who never tried his wings in higher flight. He felt he had a good model in Pastor Krohg of Vestnes in Romsdalen, and he also had a score to settle with him since those folktale-collecting days. To fill out this portrait he culled many a bourgeois gem from conversation with the Scandinavians in Rome — he always wanted to use more than one model for his characters.

The poem begins with a contrast between Koll-Brand and his former schoolmate, Axel, later renamed Ejnar. The blond Axel has nothing but happy memories of his childhood; the dark Koll is scarred by bitter memories of his harsh, miserly mother (Ibsen based her on the story of the rich widow of Lom, just as he used memories of his friend Ole Schulerud in creating Axel). The two friends meet in summer, high in the mountains. Axel has become engaged to a girl named Agnes, a relationship Ibsen based on the affair between the sculptor Walter Runeberg and Christopher Bruun's sister, the pretty Thea, who had been a favorite of his. However, in the poem her lover is a painter rather than a sculptor. Ibsen's conception of Christopher Bruun's character is made clear in the scene where he has Brand proclaim his calling and go down into the valley with "a crusader's joy" on his face. As he descends, he recalls the incident of the Norwegian boy who mutilates himself to avoid military service, as well as the "multitude-tickling" Constitution Day speech of the "great poet of the people"—undoubtedly a reference to Wergeland. Brand meets the gypsy girl, who cries "to the church!" as she runs away into the mountains. He recalls the ice-covered crevasse in the high mountains, the "ice church" that the image of Fanaråken gave birth to, and in the final scene he stands in his pulpit ready to address his congregation.

This is as far as Ibsen carried his narrative poem, to judge by the draft that has survived. He never finished it, largely because he found it impossible to give the story real unity. What he wrote was a series of episodes which had individual psychological significance, but which impeded the main action and deflected interest from the central character. He labored over the poem without success, so harassed by financial worries that he could not pour his deepest feelings into the work.

In the summer of 1865 he moved to the little mountain town of Ariccia, near Genzano. He worked concentratedly on the poem, and then one hot July day, it suddenly fell into place; he had a complete vision of what the poem should be. He describes it in a letter of September 12 to Bjørnson: "Now all is well; it has been so all along except for those times when I lose my way, not just because of money problems, but because my work stays at a standstill. Things started to come clear one day when I was on an errand in Rome: I went to St. Peter's, and there it suddenly came to me how I could find a clear, strong form for what I had to say.—Now I tossed overboard all that tormented me for a year, uselessly, and in the middle of July I began something new, something which has progressed like nothing else I have ever written. It is new in that I only just began to work it out, but the mood and the material have hounded me like a nightmare ever since the many sickening events home in Norway forced me to look into myself and the way we live there and to think deeply on things that had once passed over me lightly, that I had never been seriously concerned with. It will be a dramatic poem, on a contemporary theme, with serious content, five acts in rhymed verse (no *Love's Comedy*). The fourth act is almost finished, and I feel that I can write the fifth in eight days; I'm working both morning and afternoon, which is something I was never able to do before. It is blessedly peaceful out here, no acquaintances. I read nothing but the Bible — what strength and power!"

It is significant that he mentions St. Peter's as the place where the idea for the new play began to take shape; he felt the connection between that mighty structure and his own work, and in the basilica he saw the spirits of both the baroque and the gothic. Here there was not only the Renaissance style of Bramante, but the boldness of Michelangelo and Bernini; here was that combination of unleashed will and calm harmony that was most dramatic of all because it suggested bondage and freedom, a power that not only lifted the soul but set a firm course for its flight heavenwards. In this setting *Brand* became drama, and in so doing determined Ibsen's future course as a writer; he would never again try to create anything but drama. He had at first planned to narrate Brand's story, but in one vision he saw Brand stand in conflict with his enemy and with himself. The entire play, with its rise to crisis and catastrophe, stood before him, and he suddenly knew what the basis was for his own strength as a writer, the force of his own inner conflict. As he later described the birds of Memnon in *Peer Gynt*, he could say of the ideas that formed his writing:

Zeus, den alvidende,   Zeus all devining
skabte dem stridende.   shaped them warring.

Drama was to be the form in which he would mirror his own conflicting emotions, for drama is shaped by conflict, not torn apart by it; it releases and still controls. The world of Italian art helped him to this inevitable decision, as he summed up his experiences there: "Everything is on a colossal scale, yet an indescribable peace is over all."

Overwhelming force, curbed by organizing will, his own soul felt this need and his writing would create it.

He went about the work with the same driving creativity as he had with *The Pretenders*, but more intensely now. He had never felt his potential so rise within him, had never been so completely himself. It was not just writing, but rather a struggle with life for life, his own and his people's. He was standing on his own Dybbøl: "I was so indescribably happy in all my distress and torment. I felt a crusader's joy; there was nothing I had not courage to face." Day after day from four or five in the morning he wrote, rejoicing in his sense of unlimited capability: "I have such vigor and strength I could kill bears!" He wrote the first four acts in two months, and the fifth, which turned out to be almost a third of the work, was finished in less than a month, by the middle of October, 1865. He immediately began the fair copy, correcting and rewriting frequently, and on October 25 he was able to send the first third of the manuscript to Copenhagen for printing. The remainder followed on November 7 and 15. In all it made a book of 271 pages, nearly twice the size of *Love's Comedy*. To have been completed in such a short period of time was only the first extraordinary thing about it.

It was obvious that the dramatic form of *Brand* had been taking shape for a long time within his unconscious mind before its sudden emergence. He had received influences all the time the idea for the poem was growing. Francis Bull suggests an influence from Bjørnson's new play, *Mary Stuart in Scotland*, which Ibsen read in the spring of 1865. John Knox in this play is a preacher of the Brand type. Ibsen may also have thought of *Sigurd Slembe*. Paludan-Müller's *Ahasverus* (1864) was also very much on his mind at this time, and from it he took the verse form and the tone of bittersweet mockery and deep seriousness. *Brand* is no conscious imitation of *Ahasverus*, but there was always a spiritual affinity between the two poets, which shows in the countless parallels to Paludan-Müller in Ibsen's works from his earliest writings to the great conflict of *Rosmersholm*. It was inevitable that he be impressed by *Ahasverus*, a poem about the last judgment, in which the poet accuses mankind of pettiness and lack of faith, and mocks the familiar talk of majority rights, "humanity," "culture," and the "lukewarm, nauseating, cloying" spirit of tolerance.

He once said: "While I was writing *Brand*, I had a scorpion in an empty beer glass on my desk. Now and then it fell ill, and then I used to toss it a piece of soft fruit, upon which it fell ravenously and poured out its poison. Then it got well again. Isn't it like that with us poets, too?

The laws of nature work in the spiritual world as well." When the poison accumulated in him he would work it out in poetry; thus he settled the score with himself and his people, and still managed to keep aloft the standard of the ideal demands he was making. In a letter to a friend in Rome, written when the play was finished, he expressed the same thing in clearer terms: "Side swipes and floggings for the rascals, and underneath a serious idea."

Throughout *Brand* the same question that had plagued Ibsen for years is encountered: how responsible is the new generation for the sins of the old? Could they ignore their heritage and the possibility of guilt? This is what is at stake between Brand and his mother. Brand thinks he can settle his mother's spiritual debts with his own deeds, pay back the "sum of humanity" she squandered. But to do that repentance is needed, a remorse that will free the heart of all sinful lust. He demands this repentance from the whole people, and his great disappointment comes when he realizes that not a single one can raise himself to this truth. Thus at his death he passes a terrible judgment and sees frightful visions of the future.

When *Brand* first appeared, Georg Brandes noted that the soul of Ibsen's poetry is expressed in Kierkegaard's words: "Let others complain that the times are wicked; I complain because they are trivial; for they are without passion. The thoughts of men are as fragile and thin as lace. The thoughts in their hearts are too petty to be sinful."

This was the cry of all strong men who insisted on the purifying act of the will to redeem the age. In *Die Räuber* Schiller excoriated "this sluggish race of eunuchs, incapable of anything but chewing the cud of the gread deeds of the past; sucking the marrow from old heroes, or trying to blow life into them in rotten tragedies." In his youth, Rousseau lifted his hand against the whole "culture" of the modern world: "I do not accuse the present age of all kinds of vice—the only ones it has are those that go with paltriness: cheating and hypocrisy. The age is incapable of vice that requires courage and strength." But no one made this complaint so fundamental a theme in his whole work as Kierkegaard. He heaped scorn on the man or nation that could not fully "realize itself," and he fought for complete truth in one's conduct in life and outlook, with a merciless emphasis on the individual's responsibility. An honest mocker was worth more than a lukewarm believer, and the worst of all men was the "sneak," the sniveling one.

Brand would proclaim the need for truth in one's personal life, the need for courage and strength in the very accents of Kierkegaard:

Det, some du er, vær fuldt og helt, og ikke stykkevis og delt. ...	Whatever you are, be that entire, not piecemeal or in part.
Kan ej du være, hvad du *skal*, — saa vær alvorlight, hvad du *Kan*.	If you cannot be the man you *should,* then be honestly the one you *can.*

Kierkegaard's "either-or" now becomes "all or nothing":

Hvis alt du gav foruden Livet, saa husk, at du har intet givet. ...	If you gave all but less than life, then know that you have given nought. ...
Inger Prutningsmon i Nøden, ingen Eftergivt i Brøden, — strækker ikke Livet till, maa du villigt gaa i Døden!	No bargaining possible in your need, no indulgence granted for your guilt if life has not sufficed, you must gladly meet your death.

To all who wished to evade his demands he cried: "The spirit of compromise is Satan!" In one's self is where truth must be sought: "Inward, inward! Inward the word!" The will must be marshalled without rest:

Det er *Viljen,* som det gjælder! Viljen frigjør eller fælder.	*Will* alone is all that counts! The will alone frees or condemns.

Echoes of these sharp aphorisms can be found throughout Kierkegaard's works. And a poignant reminder of the philosopher's struggle for the truth amid loneliness and accusations of madness can be heard in the line in *Brand:* "To be mad, to be alone; it is all the same." The man who says this is ironically a cleric who embodies all the official Christian hypocrisy that Kierkegaard loathed — the Christianity that was yoked to the service of the state and turned men of God into civil servants. Kierkegaard could have written Brand's words:

selv den som vil, ej være kan et Menneske og Embedsmand.	Even the man who wishes it cannot be both official and human being.

Brand's other opponent, that "inveterate man of the people," the Sheriff, is also a spokesman for something Kierkegaard hated: the majority. "The multitude is falsehood" is the philosopher's judgment. Thus throughout the play, Ibsen's ideas keep tally with Kierkegaard; he had passed through the "aesthetic" stage and had won his way through to the "ethical." Now was the time for deeds, not talk:

Ikke tusind Ord sig prenter som *en* Gjernings Spor.	A thousand words make not the imprint of a single deed.

The narrative fragment of *Brand* had ended with Brand's return to his home in the valley, when his realization of the spiritual death of his countrymen forces him to mount the pulpit. But in the play he does not preach; rather he leaps into the boat at the risk of his life, thus performing the deed that testifies to his nature and instills trust in his work. Francis Bull has noted the similarity between this scene and the opening of Schiller's *Wilhelm Tell*, a play that made a deep impression on Ibsen in his youth. But the Kierkegaardian overtones unite the scene with the total meaning of the play. Not only this scene, but the entire play seemed to many, especially in Denmark, so much Kierkegaard set to verse that Ibsen was suspected of wanting to dramatize the philosopher's life. Ibsen denied this and it is clear that despite the influence of Kierkegaard on his point of view, he had the theme of the play from his own deepest thoughts and feelings. The demand that a man be true to himself, to the best in himself, is an ethical principle already present in *Catiline*. That hero is defeated because he sins against his own ideal. The same theme appears again in *Saint John's Night, Lady Inger,* and *The Vikings;* and is especially pronounced in *Love's Comedy,* and *The Pretenders.*

The clerical background of the play reinforced for many the similarity with Kierkegaard's life and ideas. But Ibsen repeatedly said that this background was "quite unessential" since "the demand of all or nothing applies to all aspects of life, to love, to art, etc." He makes the same point in a letter to Brandes (alluding to a speech in Holberg): "I would be man enough to make the same syllogism about a sculptor or a politician as about a pastor. I could have achieved the same needed expression of my feelings if instead of Brand I had treated, for example, Galileo (with the change, of course, that he remain defiant and not concede that the earth stands still); indeed, who knows, if I had been born a century later, I might perhaps have treated you yourself and your battle against the philosophy of compromise advocated by Rasmus Nielsen."

But despite all this, there is in the play an echo of the essentially Kierkegaardian position on religion and specifically on Christianity. Brand denies that he is preaching specifically Christian doctrine:

Jeg taler ej som Kirkens Prest;	I speak not as pastor of the church;
knappt ved jeg, om jeg er en Kristen.	I hardly know if I'm a Christian.

Kierkegaard also had said: "I do not call myself a Christian." But for both men the struggle for truth revolved around Christianity. In its deepest significance Brand's demand was not merely ethical, it was religious. He asked not merely that one *be* oneself, but that one *sacrifice* oneself. It is the basic Christian belief: "He that loses his life shall find it." This is Brand's belief:

Sjæl, vær trofast til det sidste!	Soul, be steadfast to the end!
Sejrens Sejr er *alt* at miste,	Victory of victories is losing *all*,
Tabets *alt* din Vinding skabte;—	the loss of *all* is greatest gain;—
evigt ejes kun det tabte!	what is owned forever is what is lost!

This is a creed that goes far beyond humanism, and it must be recognized that despite the play's emphasis on a full and rich life, there is also present in it a spirit that is inimical to the joys of life, a spirit that insists man is nothing unless he is willing to sacrifice his life to his God. Brand must be a servant of God; Ibsen rightly made him a minister.

While Ibsen worked on the play, he inevitably thought again of Pastor Lammers of Skien, the man who had caused the division between him and his family. G. A. Lammers had become minister in Skien in 1848. Ibsen may have heard him preach when he went home for the last time in the spring of 1850. But he certainly knew of Lammers' work in converting his family to his own brand of puritanical Christianity—his sister Hedvig and his brother Ole even left the state church to follow the minister. Lammers felt that his personal religious standards could not be reconciled with his official function in the state church and so in 1856 he finally resigned his ministry and set up a church of his own. Although he returned to the state church four or five years later, the movement he began did not die out. In Lammers, as well as in Christopher Bruun, Ibsen found the characteristics that made up his Brand. It is well to remember that both men were strongly influenced by Kierkegaard.

It is characteristic of Ibsen that political disillusionment should become transformed into a religious-moral problem. Although we hear little or nothing about religion in his life after his youthful break with Christianity, there still remained a good deal of the Christian spirit in him. The ethical demands of religion were deeply fixed in him, and they remained an absolute even when he did not fulfill them himself. The poem that had begun as an attack on the discrepancy between patriotic speeches and actual deeds, had shaken itself free of political polemics. There are still attacks on chauvinistic boasting about the past and on rampant materialism, but aside from these the matter of the play is purely ethical. Brand scourged his people because they lacked an ethical will, and so he became a spokesman for the anger that dwelt in Ibsen; he also became a symbol of the man of pure motivation Ibsen wished to be when he addressed himself to the conscience of his fellow Norwegians.

Brand's struggle is portrayed with masterful suspense; he moves from crisis to crisis, each one a test of his will to endure and not yield. In each test he hardens his heart and affections so they will not betray his greater purpose. He refuses food to his neighbors as long as they refuse to bend their wills to God; he refuses the word of God to his own mother as long as she refuses to throw off all that keeps her bound to the earth. Once he hesitates, when death threatens to deprive him of wife and child, and then the old doctor with kind understanding, gently mocks him:

| Mod Verdens Flok saa ubønhørlig, | To the herd so unrelenting, |
| og mod sig selv saa lett medgjørlig! | and with himself so gently adjustable. |

The doctor holds up the mirror to him:

| Herregud, | Good God, |
| slig ser en Himmelstormer ud! | so this is how a Titan looks! |

And in a short time Brand overcomes the temptation; he would rather see wife and child perish than deny his duty and his call.

A crucial moment comes when the Sheriff reports that the people have joined Brand. Can his demand for personal honesty become a decision for the majority to act upon? Does not such mass acceptance suggest a dilution of the demands of his ideal? Brand flees from this temptation of popular support by escaping from the crowd; he is alone with only the madwoman Gerd as companion. In solitude he finds his end, the only conceivable outcome to his life. A demand as inflexible, which knows no compromise with the realities of the world, must fail. He himself admits it:

| haabløs er en ensom Kriger. | hopeless the lonely warrior. |

And when the avalanche strikes, a voice of thunder cries from heaven: God is "deus caritatis," a God of love. Was Brand wrong, we are forced to ask. Is the voice of thunder a judgment on Brand's life? Was it inhuman, wrong, sinful to make such demands on man? Again and again in the play it is said that Brand was harsh, that God is not so harsh. The symbol of his life's work is fittingly enough the ice chapel.

If this were the whole truth, then Ibsen did not intend Brand as a pillar of fire to shine before the world in its darkness, but rather as a warning against unreasonable hardness. Then Brand's enemies are right. But when we consider the mocking way in which he portrays these opponents — the Sheriff, the Dean, the Teacher, Ejnar — this becomes impossible. These portraits aroused the caricaturist in Ibsen and he cut them out with savage glee. It is unthinkable that at the end he should reverse himself completely, and so it is only in a limited, superficial sense that they are the victors over Brand—it is the everlasting shame of society that they should triumph.

The question remains, however, did Brand sin against the God whose command is "love"? Clearly he needs love himself and can give it; he would spill his own blood for his people if it would win their salvation. It is writhing torture for him to have to hold up the harsh demand of all or nothing to his mother and wife. Gerd may ask him at the end:

Mand, hvi græd du ej før nu?	Fellow, why did you never weep before?

but there have been tears in his eyes before, and he almost unbent in prayer. In the final analysis he made no demand that could not have been fulfilled, for he did not ask for ability to do, but only for an honest will.

The last words of the play remain as the great question mark over the whole work. To interpret them in the Kierkegaardian spirit would be to say that "deus caritatis" was in fact the very God who had shaped Brand's life. By His love God made him lonely and unhappy, gave him the "gift of sorrow," not indeed to create poetry, but to live honestly and teach others to do the same. God took him in love at the end because he had sacrificed all and lost all. By suffering defeat among men he won victory in himself, and communion with God:

Viljens Renhed,	purity of will,
i Troen Flugt, i Sjælen Enhed,—	sublimity of faith, unity of soul,—
hin Offerlydighed, som gav	the will to sacrifice that gave
med Jubel indtil Død og Grav,—	with joy even to death and the grave,—
en Tornekrans om Hvermands Tinding,	on each man's brow a crown of thorns,
se, det skal vorde eders Vinding!	this, this is the profit you take!

This is the marytrdom Kierkegaard demanded of the true Christian; and thus at the end God affirms Brand's struggle and becomes for him a "deus caritatis."

But such a solution to the problem is more convincing as philosophy than as drama—it is an interpretation that we can impose on the play, even while the dramatic impact of the verse creates another impression. Ibsen himself defined the meaning of the last line; when his classicist friends pointed out that the phrase was not correct classical Latin, he replied that he had taken it from church Latin, where it carried the meaning of the heavenly love "that includes the concept of mercy." Thus the very thing that Brand rejected with scorn is restated at the end; the voice from heaven proclaims something that Brand never understood, the one thing he lacked—the gentleness of merciful love. The word "caritas" had been used once before in the play, when the kind and wise doctor said to Brand:

Ja, Mandeviljens quantum satis	True, the *quantum satis* of man's will
staar bogført som din Rigdoms Rad;	is amply entered in your books;
men, Prest, din conto caritatis	but, Pastor, your *caritas* account
er Bogens hvide Jomfrublad.	displays a virgin white page.

It is quite unmistakable that the doctor here speaks for the author himself, at least for that part of the author that represented a quality missing in Brand. Thus the doctor's words come back to the hero in his dying moment; at last he understands, for his work and his suffering have taught him the meaning of the words. Brand has developed during the five acts of the play as his inner stress drives him step by step to a fuller, richer view of life. In the beginning he is only the harsh, cold judge, scarred for life by the bitter childhood memories of his mother's greed. He hates the materialism of the world around him and mercilessly condemns every concession to its spirit. He has dreamt of stirring the world to repentance, but he has forsaken the dream and learns to devote himself to the immediate concerns of his flock. He begins to discover love with Agres, but he neither dares nor can yield to love's demands. Yet the need is there, and each crisis brings it to the fore more strongly. He sins against his mother by refusing to attend her at her death bed, and he sins even more cruelly against his wife. At a tremendous cost Brand stifles love in his heart; he longs to weep and pray but he forces himself not to. His final joy is that, when all is lost, he can do both again. He escapes from the rigidity of law into the warmth of love, and in love he finds God's mercy.

The same process of psychological development took place, on a much smaller scale, in King Haakon in *The Pretenders*. The theme is one of the most basic in Ibsen, this need for love, and he frequently shows it breaking through even in the man who has suppressed it within himself. In Haakon as in Brand, the cry for love is implicit in all his harsh and impatient judgments. Brand's destruction is not just the failure that every man suffers at the hands of a crass society; it is also the consequences of his own fatal flaw. When he sins against the greatest of God's commands, to love, he reveals again the true source of the tragic vision in Ibsen; man bears within him the seeds of his own destruction.

This is not to say that Brand's work is condemned. Ibsen makes him proclaim with sharp clarity that he will sacrifice all, even wife and child, "freely, with open eyes," rather than give up his demand for all or nothing. There is no fault in the demand; it is the man who breaks because he is not able to reconcile it with the command to love. Only in defeat are his eyes opened to the necessity for love, a necessity from which he has fled. If he had embraced love, he could have embraced his ideal as well. Now his victory comes only in understanding at the end. It is as he had once dreamt:

| Med Klarsyn skjønnes skal en Dag, | Clearly will it come out one day: |
| at største Sejr er Nederlag! | victory is greatest in defeat! |

Ibsen does not slacken his demands on the human will; he holds them fast right into the "chasm of death." But he has deepened them, made them warmer with hope:

| Ind i Natten. Gjennem Døden.— | Into the night. Through Death.— |
| Bagom dæmrer Morgenrøden. | Beyond glimmers the dawn. |

Ibsen did not fully identify with Brand, and so was able later to disclaim responsibility for the moral demands the play urges by saying that it was "fully and wholly a work of art and nothing more," not a philosophical tract nor a program for action. On another occasion he said that the play had been meant simply to "portray an energetic personality." Ibsen's attitude here is an excellent example of what the Finnish scholar Yrjö Hirn has called "the miracle of aesthetic transformation," by which no matter how much a work is a product of an inner necessity, once it is realized, it ceases to be a part of the artist and can be looked on by him from a purely aesthetical standpoint.

Brand is built with a firm and steady art that moves the action from tension to tension up to the catastrophe. Despite the intensity of the conflicts, the structure remains harmoniously integrated. That structure is simplicity itself; beginning in the mountains, it logically ends there. These same mountains stand as the great symbol of the playwright's vision. He had used them in a similar manner before, in the poem "On the Heights" and in *Love's Comedy;* now they become the very basis for understanding of the hero. From the valley the mountains are felt to press down on the souls of men so that they cannot follow him up to the heights. Their struggle to reach him is symbolized in their climbing the mountain. In the end he is alone with his mountains, and they finally become his grave. He had dreamed of building a church so high and free that there, one would feel united with God; the church he found was the cold, life-destroying ice. Then he heard the thunder of God.

Thus Ibsen wrote his most powerful drama. Brand was himself, yet a self finally set free. As he wrote the play, he felt he had taken up arms in a sacred crusade; out of the work of art he made a statement that became a life achievement.

CHAPTER NINETEEN

TRIUMPH (1866)

NEVER BEFORE in his life had he felt such anticipation as he experienced while waiting for *Brand* to appear in print. He knew he had never given so much of himself in any work before this, and he was filled with hope—and fear. He believed in the play with "unshakeable confidence," but he expected "all kinds of assaults and attacks." He said that if the book did not raise "howls" then "writing the whole thing was wasted effort." However, the idea of controversy made him tremble.

He wanted to begin the historical play about Magnus Heineson, which he felt was already "full-born" inside him. But months passed and he was unable to work. *Brand* took a long time at the printers, and he waited, "consumed by suspense and unrest." He was furious at the difficulties the publisher was raising, and he hesitated to ask for another advance; as a result his purse was often uncomfortably flat. "My dear Bjørnson," he wrote, "I feel as if I am separated from God and man by a great, endless wasteland." The waiting drained his will and strength.

In the summer of 1865 Bjørnson had gotten his publisher, Frederik Hegel in Copenhagen, to agree to publish Ibsen's projected play on Julian the Apostate. Hegel had been director of the Gyldendalske Boghandel firm for twenty years, during which he had extended its market to Norway and Sweden; from 1860 he had included all Scandinavia in his publishing activities. When Bjørnson signed with him in 1861, his publishing operations accelerated, and in a few years he was backing his aggressive literary and economic Scandinavianism with capital and with initiative.

Now Hegel was to publish *Brand;* the agreement was for 1,250 copies, at a royalty of 30 Danish riksdalers per sheet, and an immediate advance against royalties. Hegel sent the first third of the manuscript to the printer as soon as it arrived in the beginning of November, 1865. Ibsen wanted the book published by Christmas, but there were unforeseen difficulties. Hegel noticed that Ibsen used a highly personal orthography, including many doubled consonants to indicate that the preceding vowel was short; in addition, he used many peculiarly Norwegian words. Hegel was afraid that the Danes would refuse to buy the book and wrote to Ibsen, who immediately gave him permission to normalize the spelling, "in so far as it can be done without loss of time," in printing. And the more Hegel read, the more he discovered that this was not the book Bjørnson had promised him; here was a huge drama in verse with nothing that "the general public" would be interested in. He wrote Ibsen again, saying he could not risk printing more than half the edition, 625 copies; royalties would therefore be only half as much. Again Ibsen agreed; what was more important was to have the book published as quickly as possible.

Due to some mix-up, Ibsen's letter agreeing to the smaller number of copies never reached Hegel, and he delayed printing the book for some time, finally deciding to leave it at the original 1,250 copies. This was in mid-March, 1866.

Hegel's fears proved groundless. In spite of double consonants, Norwegian words and 270 pages, the play sold well in Denmark as well as Norway. Within two months he had sold enough copies to justify a second edition of 500; a third printing was necessary in August, and a fourth in December. This unheard-of demand continued, and larger and still larger printings were necessary within the next few years. When his sister-in-law prophesied to Ibsen that ten printings would be needed, he shook his head incredulously; the tenth printing came in 1885, and it was far from the last.

It was not simply that *Brand* was a great work of art; relatively few readers were interested in its formal perfection. What captured and overwhelmed them was its contents, the burning intensity with which its theme was conveyed. Nearly every review spoke of the play's "powerful impression." Brandes wrote in *Dagbladet:* "This book will leave no reader cold; every impressionable and unjaded spirit will feel, when he is finished, an overpowering, an even shattering impression of having stood face to face with a strong and indignant spirit, before whose piercing look all weakness is forced to cast down its eyes."

The book spoke to the conscience of each reader as he read the words that resounded through the drama: "Choose; you are standing at the crossroads." All or nothing—it became a personal question, one that was taken up by all serious-minded people. Within a month a Copenhagen correspondent wrote to *Morgenbladet:* "Of the new works of literature that have appeared, Henrik Ibsen's *Brand* occupies as distinguished a position as any work of literature ever has. It is read with great interest, its praise is on everyone's lips, and its deep words are in everyone's

mind." *Illustreret Nyhedsblad* confirmed that wherever one went in
Copenhagen, people were talking about *Brand;* a Norwegian had to
beg to be spared more of the same. In Oslo it was the same; *Brand* was
on everyone's lips, and it was even discussed from the pulpit, in one of
W. A. Wexels' last sermons given at Our Savior's Church, on April 15.

Its effect in Norway can be compared with that of Welhaven's sonnet
cycle *The Dawn of Norway (Norges Dæmring)* published a generation
earlier in 1834. Ibsen felt he was, to a certain extent, following Welhaven's lead, and in the poetical fragment had actually parodied a
patriotic speech by Welhaven's opponent, Henrik Wergeland. Like *The
Dawn of Norway, Brand* was a chastisement of Norway, and Ibsen
feared the same kind of bitter personal attack that had been Welhaven's
fate. He was spared this. The storm his play aroused was greater than
anything occasioned by the earlier poems — they had annoyed a few
literary and political cliques; *Brand* roused a whole people.

To understand the full impact and consequences of the play, it must
be recalled that it appeared in the midst of a period of intense individualism in social and cultural life. *Brand* made the individual the focus
of life, and made the individual conscience the battleground where all
issues were to be decided. The doctrine of individual will had never
been enunciated more clearly, and even if *Brand* was vanquished in his
lonely fight with society, he was nonetheless right and society was
wrong. There had been great preparation for this message.

The 1860's throughout Europe was a period of great interest in
liberalism and the freedom of the individual. The emancipation of the
Russian serf and the American Negro forced the issue into political discussion. Socialism and all forms of collectivism were rejected by the
leaders of opinion among the people and among the governments;
older revolutionary leaders like Mazzini and Kossuth rejected socialism
and called for personal freedom as the only program. A policy of laissez-
faire was the goal of statesmen and political thinkers; the agreement
of 1860 between England and France represented a triumph of free
trade policy in Europe. When the Norwegian Storting confirmed a
similar agreement with France in November, 1865, laissez-faire had triumphed in the North as well. On April 14, 1866, the Storting put an
end to the last remnants of the guild system and left crafts in the cities
entirely free. There was a corresponding spirit of liberation in the cultural attitudes of the time, with revolt against traditional authorities,
rejection of the church and its dogmas, and a challenging of old faiths
by a new belief in science. Each man had to rethink his own views on
life. In the natural sciences, as in economic life, there was a new bold-

ness that demanded freedom of action for individual initiative. Above all there was an unquestioning faith in the will and capabilities of the individual. *Brand,* a masterpiece of individualistic philosophy, is deeply rooted in the period from which it springs; it was, moreover, Norway's chief contribution to the period, and it marked the beginning of a new era in Norwegian cultural life.

Not that its teaching was accepted without resistance. The play met less opposition in Denmark because Kierkegaard had prepared the ground; moreover, the national catastrophe of 1864 had created a favorable atmosphere for the inner examination and expiation the play advocated. *Brand* would spur on a trend already begun. In Norway, on the other hand, the attack on national behavior was regarded as unreasonably severe. The first review, by the young critic Johan Vibe, in the newspaper *Norge* April 3, 1866, used the phrase "brilliant madness" in its summary. Ibsen's old friend Vinje wrote in his paper *Dølen* that the play was "too raving mad to be serious," and so he treated it with humor, mocking its "incendiary verse." J. Lieblein, an Egyptologist who reviewed the play in the periodical *Norden,* concluded his pedestrian remarks by calling attention to the end of Brand's career — insanity. Bjørnson himself felt ill after reading the book, and he came to hate it; he believed it put an end to all sincere religion, and that it lacked the spirit of love that alone could have transformed the story into great poetry.

Professor Monrad reviewed the play in four long articles in *Morgenbladet* during September. He pointed out that from a philosophical point of view this play, just as *Love's Comedy,* failed both morally and politically. He suggested that it be read as Juvenalian satire, although warning the reader that it did not fulfill the requirements his aesthetic had established for such satire. He rejected the play's premise, since Brand's "pursuit of extremes" was "a misjudgment of the pure nature of the ideal." True self-sacrifice, he insisted, was precisely in the ability to make compromises. Ibsen's old critic, Pastor Krogh of Vestnes, also took a few swipes at the play, and completely lived up to Ibsen's parody. Krogh warned the reader against the unchristian spirit of the play and insisted that the Sheriff was right all along.

Ibsen felt that the best reply to all these misinterpretations was contained in two articles in *Morgenbladet* for December, possibly written by the young philosopher G. V. Lyng. The articles were directed particularly to Professor Monrad's criticism, and they insisted that Ibsen had not set Brand up as a model human being; on the contrary, he had demonstrated the hero's "tragic guilt," and that could only add to one's sympathy for "this great soul, struggling to find and realize the truth." The writer testified that "the poem has made a powerful and inspiring impression on hundreds of our countrymen."

The opposition obviously came from different quarters and different philosophical stances. There were the petty bourgeois who would naturally be reluctant to champion an ideal that involved risk of life. There were the advocates of realism, sober and unpoetic, whose vision of life did not include anything that seemed to be unnaturally exaggerated or over-excited. There were a great many who could not find any true poetic reconciliation in the play. And finally there were the great majority of critics who simply could not agree on what the poet had done, whether he had "disavowed" his hero at the end, or whether he had shown the hero failing only because the mob was against him.

All this controversy did not hinder the play from making a great impact on its readers, particularly young readers. The book was read and reread, and its lines were quoted so often they became natural idioms in thinking and speaking. Nearly every line from the play quoted in this and the previous chapter is known and used by literate Norwegians; they belong to the general vocabulary of the language, much like the verses of scripture. There is scarcely another literary work, by Ibsen or anyone else, that has given the Norwegian language so many pungent epigrams. The generation of 1866 took it as its gospel, and for twenty years and more it became for them a stimulus to thought and to action and for those who came after.

Brand would be dead in two months, Bjørnson wrote in 1866, but twelve years later when he was going through his most painful period of religious questioning, he wrote to Brandes: "I understand Brand better now. Before I did not appreciate it; one day, mark me, the book will come back. Now at last I am grateful to Ibsen for it; I was not able to be so before." Bjørnson was actually beginning to work on a new theme that was basically the same as Brand's when he wrote this, although it was not until 1883 that he gave it final form as Beyond our Power. The idea here is the problem of harmony between faith and life, between the ideal and the need for action. Bjørnson's solution is not Ibsen's. Brand prays to God, "Teach me to will more than I can do." In Bjørnson one's will must remain within the possibility of human potential if it is to be of any aid; he seeks a human solution. In another major dramatic work, Arne Garborg's The Teacher (Læraren, 1896), the solution is still more humanized; the individual is required to sacrifice, but mercifully everyone is not forced to make the same sacrifice.

These three plays, among the greatest in Norwegian dramatic literature, show the development of a single theme. The setting of the problem is different in each, and the solution differs as well, but in each there is the same intense probing into man's conscience and the statement of the same inescapable commandment: one must be true to himself, one must be sincere in one's relation to life. Wergeland, too, put forth the same injunction, especially in his great epic, the humanist Bible, *Creation, Man, and Messiah*, but Ibsen was the first to successfully create around his characters an atmosphere that itself stated and emphasized the ideal and its frightening alternative. In *Love's Comedy* truth to oneself and sincerity were examined in one sphere, marriage; in *Brand* every man in every condition of life is forced to meet the same decision. For years to come, this theme would be the basic one of his work; for two decades the same theme would be the criterion by which creative writing in Scandinavian countries would be judged. The youth who led the radical naturalism of the 1880's received their sense of dedication primarily from the Ibsen of *Brand*. In Sweden the play was a kind of breviary for the young people gathering around August Strindberg. One member of that generation, Gustaf af Geijerstam, wrote of their fervor: "It would be impossible to try to describe the boundless zeal with which these youths read and discussed the great writer.... Ibsen became the bond between friends and between loving couples; no more sacred gift could be given than *Brand*—it was considered a tribute to one's intelligence and one's character." It is not surprising that the play was first mounted in Sweden, in these same 1880's.

Ibsen had not written the play for performance, and did not send it to any theatre. It was used, however, for a dramatic reading. Laura Gundersen read Act IV before the Oslo Student Society in 1866, and she later repeated the performance at Christiania Theatre. She was particularly fascinated by the poignant struggle between Agnes' love and Brand's sacrificial ideal, and she is said to have been extremely effective as Agnes. But the first complete stage production of *Brand* was not given until March, 1885, at the Swedish director Ludvig Josephson's theatre in Stockholm. Josephson had directed Christiania Theatre for a time in the 1870's, and he frequently mentioned to Ibsen that he would like to direct the play. When he finally did, the opening night performance lasted for nearly seven hours, but despite its length the audience was captivated. In a review in *Aftonbladet* Gustaf af Geijerstam wrote, "*Brand* has become a kind of Bible for the younger generation, and the impression of the first performance on Tuesday at the Nya Teatern was overpowering. It felt as though a strong wind was sweeping through the theatre, driving away every whiff of operetta and farce, opening the ceiling, cleansing the air." Josephson's stage set highlighted the impression of the play by making the viewer feel himself at once confined and elevated among high, steep mountains. Emil Hillberg played Brand and gave the character the stamp of true greatness. On the following evening the playing time was reduced to five and one half hours, but even so the play made great demands on actors and audience alike. It was a tribute to its tremendous power that it was repeated sixteen times.

The next attempt to stage *Brand* was made by Lugné-Poë in Paris in 1895, but his production failed to capture the richness of the poetry or the power of its dramatic theme. When the Swede August Lindberg toured with the play through Scandinavia in 1895 and 1896 there was little to the production but rant and stilted acting. The Schiller Theater in Berlin staged the play in honor of Ibsen's seventieth birthday. (The author of this book was in the theatre, but what he witnessed seemed a parody of a great drama; it must have impressed the Germans as a foreign oddity, instead of the universal play that it is.) In honor of the same occasion, and with Ibsen present, the play was given in Copenhagen, with Martinius Nielsen as Brand. Although Nielsen could be a monotonous declaimer at times, he could still create something of the power of Brand's personality on stage. Fru Oda Nielsen played Agnes with great feeling, and in Act IV Ibsen himself wept the tears his hero refuses to weep.

Brand was the first Ibsen play to be translated into German; P. F. Siebold, a German commercial traveler who spent much time in Denmark and had a love for literature, did a verse translation in 1869, which was printed in Copenhagen and sold in bookstores in 1872. This was followed by a series of German translations: by Julie Ruhkopf in 1874, Alfred von Wolzogen in 1876, and Ludwig Passarge in 1881. None of these conveyed the full power of the original; they were either so free that the meaning of the play was obscured, or so close that they lost its verve and spontaneity. Not until Christian Morgenstern's translation of 1898 did a kindred poetic spirit approach the play. His translation of the play was performed in Munich in 1902, in Dresden in 1905, and later in other German cities. The play could still move an audience, but it was impossible for it to have the same effect as it did on its first hearers; Ibsen's later works had already helped to create an entirely different intellectual atmosphere in Germany.

The uncut version of *Brand* was not performed in Norway until 1904; this production at the National Theatre was so successful that it gave 29 performances in the season of 1904-05. It was revived several times, and ran 34 performances in the autumn of 1922. In the title part Egil Eide created a characterization that surpassed all his earlier achievements; he was firm and authoritative, yet managed to convey an undercurrent of affection in the later acts that brought the complexities of Brand's personality closer to the audience than any reading of the text could have done. The psychology of each character was drawn more clearly than the theme of the play, as was the style in interpretations of other Ibsen roles in the 1920's, and an entirely new aspect of his dramatic art was revealed. The outstanding figure in this production, however, was Fru Johanne Dybwad, in the role of Gerd. She seemed a creature from another world, filled with mystery and madness, a being entirely of fantasy, sweeping like fate about to seize its victim. Her performance was in the authentic spirit of the play and rescued it from the dead-weight of realism that slowed down too many productions and made the symbolism of the work banal.

It was the Russians, however, who finally brought the play to life. When Ibsen began to win a foothold in Russia in the twentieth century, no work of his was more enthusiastically greeted than *Brand*. The Moscow Art Theatre put it into its repertory in January, 1907, and later took it on tour throughout Russia. More than just an artistic success, the play seemed to strike some deep chord in the Russian people, some ideal of liberty. Maria Germanova, the Agnes, commented on the effect of the play: "The ideas of this play complement our times so completely, and so slake the thirst that torments Russia today, that people respond with the same eagerness as when one offers sparkling fresh water in a burning heat. The storm of applause that followed Brand's great speech outside the new church cannot be described; the audience rose as one, and there was not an unmoved face in the whole theatre." Five years later in 1912, when a Russian company with Pavel Orlenjeff played it in a small East Side New York theatre, the success was the same as in Russia. For the Ibsen centennial in 1928, the extraordinary acting couple Georg and Ludmila Pitoëff performed it in their Paris theatre, using the small stage to incredible effect. By limiting the realistic effects they were able to let the passionate theme of the play stand clear. They took the roles of Brand and Agnes and gave to Agnes the final speech: "God is mercy, is love."

The play was revived once again in Norway in 1953, at the new Folketeatret in Oslo, with Per Sunderland in the title role. Sunderland was young and he played Brand young, as the role was written, young in heart and temper, young in faith and idealism. The play was revived in a season when audiences seemed bored with serious drama, yet it filled the theatre night after night. Young people in particular followed the play with intense interest. The last act, however, seemed to have lost some of its power. Perhaps the symbolism of the quest among the heights became too blatant in a realistic setting with realistic acting. The impossibility of Brand's desire rather than his loneliness and isolation was stressed. Yet the man could still speak living, burning truth to all who listened.

Ibsen had never written a play that had such a hold on its readers, nor had he ever given so much of himself. He spoke now with a new voice of authority, a man who knew what he wanted and who felt himself strong and free enough to point the way to others. He won at once a position of leadership in Norwegian cultural life and a secure basis for the rest of his writing career. He would never again be troubled by financial worries.

Bjørnson had been busily at work in his friend's behalf. In the spring of 1865 he spoke with Riddervold, the Minister of Church and Education, and asked him to prepare a proposal to the Storting to give Ibsen the same kind of writer's pension he had been given. Riddervold, however, still remembered Love's Comedy and was just as cold to the proposal as he had been two years earlier. Bjørnson did not despair and kept after Ibsen to apply to the Storting in the fall. They *must* give the money, he wrote. But Ibsen, then in the midst of work on Brand, was not as certain: "I have a notion that my new work will not soften the attitude of the Storting members toward me, but God punish me if I will or can blot a single line for all that, no matter how those vest-pocket souls swallow it. Let me be a beggar all my life. If I cannot be myself in what I write, then the whole thing is lies and humbug — and our country has enough of that without paying pensions to get more." He applied for nothing himself, either from the Cabinet or from the Storting. He did not even ask for another travel grant. "I know too well that it would have been a useless humiliation," he told Bjørnson on March 4, 1866.

Then Brand appeared, and it suddenly dawned on the Norwegians that they had a great poet in this neglected Henrik Ibsen. Bjørnson leaped to the attack once again. He did not like Brand, but he appreciated its artistry; its theme had not yet come completely into realization, but he thought that comfortable financial arrangements would give his friend that "simple love of life which alone makes a poet." He spoke to his friends in the Storting and to Riddervold. The Minister stood fast, but the representatives yielded. Medical Director T. J. Løberg, one of Bjørnson's friends, prepared the proposal to grant a stipend to Ibsen and secured 28 signatures, including those of all the leading Liberal members. The proposal, dated April 17, 1866, concluded with these words: "We cannot as passive observers watch so highly gifted and productive a spirit perish in the struggle for daily bread; and therefore we turn with our request for financial aid sufficient to ease Ibsen's circumstances to that source where in our opinion it should be sought, and will be gladly granted, namely the National Assembly, which by granting Ibsen the means for future subsistence will surely in equal degree honor and benefit itself with him."

No one was certain that the proposal would win a majority in the Storting, particularly since only one or two of the Agrarian members were willing to sign and the conservatives were uncertain. Then Minister Riddervold fell ill, and Minister Frederik Stang, Chairman of the Cabinet, temporarily took charge of the Ministry of Church and Education. Ibsen's "Dutchmen" friends found out through Stang's son-in-law, attorney J. Heffermehl, that Stang was willing to make the proposal a Cabinet resolution. They all went to work: Archivist Birkeland prepared an application to the Ministry and sent it on April 19, with the signatures of O. A. Bachke, Botten Hansen, and Jakob Løkke. Two days later the Ministry had the proposition, the Cabinet approved it, and immediately sent it to the king in Stockholm.

In Rome Ibsen knew nothing of this until one day a telegram from Birkeland advised him to send an application for a writer's stipend to the king. On April 15 he composed a letter to King Carl—twenty years later he characterized it as "pretty lugubrious in style." He ventured to ask for help "in order to live exclusively for my calling as poet." In his struggle to awaken the people to great thoughts, "it rests in Your Majesty's Royal hands to decide whether I shall have to be silent and bow to the bitterest sacrifice that can afflict a human soul, the sacrifice of having to abandon one's mission in life, of having to give ground where I know that I have been granted the spiritual weapons to fight; and this is for me tenfold hard—[and here he repeated a phrase that had once been Brand's] — because to this day I have never yielded."

Perhaps he had begun to think King Carl more than just the "corporal" he had mocked in *Brand,* for he ended the letter by saying that in his life's work he had "assigned himself to do battle under Your Majesty's spiritual banner." But such a flourish was not needed. His letter reached Stockholm on April 25, and "on His Majesty's Most Gracious order" Prime Minister Sibbern sent it to the Ministry of Church and Education in Oslo for "further processing." There it was merely laid aside, for the next day the proposal of the Norwegian Cabinet reached Stockholm and was placed before the King. Both the application and the representatives' proposal were before the Storting on May 12. With only four negative votes a stipend of 400 dollars a year was awarded the poet.

On April 30 the Scientific Society of Trondheim granted him 100 dollars, as has been noted, and on July 28 the government gave him a new travel grant of 350 dollars. Altogether he had 850 dollars for the following year. After years of economic distress he now had so much money that he had no need to collect all the royalties due him from his publisher. He was able to play the lottery; he could indulge his taste for elegant clothes. He was free. And Brandes quickly pointed out the delicious irony in Norway's responding with lavish support to the poet's harsh chastisement, an irony so "delicate that few would have believed" Norwegians capable of it.

Ibsen did not feel he had been granted more than he rightfully deserved. In a speech he gave at the grave of P. A. Munch on June 12, 1865, he said that it was the obligation of the state, in fact it was a precondition of a nation's existence, to give generous support to art and science. He spoke from strong, personal emotion when he said: "That man who performs the spiritual work of a nation has the right to hold his head up proudly." When his case came before the Storting, he had written to Birkeland: "If the grant is not made, my work in Norway is over." He felt that if he was rejected by his nation, he would be cut off from it forever.

He was not cut off, nor could he ever lose touch with his country, for he hated his people like Brand because he loved them so much. They stirred his anger, but they were important enough to save by chastising. This was the basic tenet of his life. None of his previous work had been so deeply rooted in Norwegian life as this play; none was more intensely personal. And as he spoke to them from his deepest heart and became their national poet and spiritual guide, he created the basis for a poetry that would speak beyond Norway's borders, to the world.

CHAPTER TWENTY

IBSEN AND NORWAY

IN A LETTER written in 1870, Ibsen said that when he left Norway in 1864 he went "into exile." He wrote this as he was revising the poem "The Eider Duck," which in the 1851 version had ended on a despairing note as the bird's nest is stripped of its down by robbers:

Da føler sig Fuglen af Haabet forladt,	Then feels the bird bereft of hope,
Da eier den kun et blødende Bryst,	Nothing left it but bleeding breast,
Da sygner den hen paa den øde Kyst.	Pining, pining on a barren coast.

The image is of the man stripped of the dreams that have kept his heart alive, now despairing as darkness falls over his hopes. In revising the poem twenty years later, Ibsen mirrors his own escape in the flight of the bird:

—røves hans tredje, hans sidste skat,—	—but steal his third, his final treasure—
da spiler han vinger en forårs-nat.	he will spread his wings one night in spring;
Da kløver han skodden med blodigt bryst;—	he will cleave the mist with bleeding breast—
mod syd, mod syd til en solskins-kyst!	to the south, to the south, to the sunny coast!

Everything at home seemed to repulse him, to strip him of will and courage. To save himself he had to escape. "I had to get free of the swinishness up there," he wrote from Rome two years after he left home, "to get at least somewhat clean. Up there I could never hold the integrity of my inner life; thus I was one thing in my work, another in my life. My work inevitably lacked integrity." And a year later he wrote to his mother-in-law: "At times I can't see how you bear it up there! It appears to me now that life there is indescribably boring; it bores the spirit out of one's being, bores the energy out of one's will. The curse of petty circumstances is that they make the soul petty."

The pettiness of things back home was both physical and spiritual; no great ideas, no whole and healthy wills—everything was subjugated

215

to the material needs of the day, and these choked off every vital enjoyment, every freedom in art and poetry. Society was so narrow and constricted that everyone rubbed against everyone else, as Ibsen had found
to his distress when small-town gossips confused the art of *Love's
Comedy* with the private life of its author. Perhaps even worse was the
obligation to be always mindful of one's friends' reactions and feelings.
He wrote to Brandes in 1870: "Friends are a costly luxury, and when
one has invested one's capital in a sacred mission, one doesn't have
much left over for friendships. The expense of friends is not in what
one must do for them, but in what one must refrain from doing out of
consideration for them; thus many a spiritual growth is nipped in the
bud. I have experienced this, and now I must look back on several
years in which I wasn't able to be myself." He found it difficult to speak
out freely, especially with his best friends, and was in torment because
he could never be truly and completely himself with them. Instead he
had to assume the coloration of his environment, even though he did
not wish to. "I know well that I am not really myself except when I am
alone with my thoughts."

He had to exile himself and be alone—not simply because Norway
was narrow and constricting, but because it was his home, and he would
have felt limited wherever home was. There were many who wanted
him to return. Three months after he left, Christiania Theatre offered
him the directorship. He refused at once, decisively and curtly, even
though it would have meant financial security, and he refused again
when the offer was repeated in 1870 and 1884. He did not deny that the
idea intrigued him, but he held back for fear of what he knew would
happen: "The thing is," he wrote as late as 1884, "that I would be
quite unable to write freely and frankly up there, which is to say that
I would not be able to write at all."

He left Norway with the idea of staying away a year or two. Nine
months later he could still write with bitterness about his homeland
and swear that he would never return. He was glad when the letter in
which he expressed these uncharitable thoughts was lost, and a few
weeks later he again wrote to Bjørnson: "Actually I must go home after
all." Two years later he said the same thing, but he delayed the return
from year to year. Whenever he thought of home he grew afraid that it
would be the end of his great dreams and hopes; he was like Brand,
when he caught sight of his valley home:

her, ved Nærmelsen af Hjemmet,	Here, as I come towards home,
ser jeg paa mig selv som fremmed,—	I consider myself a stranger,—
vaagner bunden, klippet, tæmmet,	I wake in chains, shorn, tamed,
Samson lig i Skjøgens Skjød.	Samson in the whore's bosom.

During 1866 he thought of settling in Copenhagen, since he felt that this was "the real Scandinavian heartland, least fettered by the prevailing prejudices." But the idea soon passed; Copenhagen was not sufficiently removed from home and he felt that here too he would be torn between friends and enemies. By the 1870's he learned how confining the place was for Brandes, and he feared that the air of Copenhagen might be just as suffocating as that of Norway.

The idea of one day returning came back again and again, particularly when some decision affecting his family life was concerned; for example, when he had to think about an education for his son. But he dreaded making a final break with his new freedom. "How is it possible," he wrote in 1868, "to live anywhere but Italy; above all, how is it possible to lie in Christiania— I can hardly conceive it! I would have to isolate myself there, or otherwise I would make every second person my enemy." A year later he wrote: "It won't do for an author to live there, unless he can coldly reject all sides and take a stand by himself."

From year to year he made plans to visit Norway, but each year he postponed them. The idea of even a winter there frightened him: "Either I would have made everyone an enemy inside a month, or I would begin to wear a mask again and become a lie to myself and to the world." Although he visited Sweden in 1869 and Denmark in 1870, he did not venture home until 1874, and that experience was so unfortunate that the bad taste of it was still with him ten years later. "When I sailed up the Oslo fjord ten years ago, after a decade's absence, my chest literally constricted with a feeling of oppression and nausea. I felt the same during my whole stay up there; I was no longer myself before all those cold, uncomprehending Norwegian eyes that stared at me from windows and on the streets." He was even more firmly convinced then that he could never work or enjoy himself in Norway. After this it was eleven years before he could return.

But he did not cut himself off from all contact with his homeland, although there were times when he thought of doing this, particularly in 1863 and 1866 when he feared that his author's stipend would be rejected by the government. Then he indignantly threatened to renounce his allegiance to his country. Other incidents provoked the same angry reaction. In 1871, H. J. Jensen, the owner of *Illustreret Nyhedsblad* in the 1850's, reprinted *The Viking at Helgeland* and announced that he was going to reprint *Lady Inger of Østråt* as well, naturally without paying the author any royalty. Ibsen was furious at this "assault on my purse" and began legal action; he was doubly angry when his friend Birkeland suggested that the legal issue was not as clear-cut as Ibsen had imagined. "Here I sat," Ibsen wrote, "with my mind happily at peace, working on my new book. From Sweden, from Denmark, and from here I learn nothing but what pleases me; but from Norway it is as if I receive nothing but bad news. What do those people want? Am I not far enough away?" Then he thought of severing all contact. "This is a matter of great importance to me; for if the Jensen plan for plundering me should win sympathetic support at home, it is my intention, come what may, to reject all relationship with Norway and never set foot there again." His anger soon subsided, and two months later he was again writing about going home. He won his case against Jensen in both the local and supreme court and felt that his country was interested in protecting his rights. Such moments of anger only served to keep Norway present in his mind — and both anger and thoughts of home were necessary conditions for his writing.

The break with his parents and family had been possible because he felt spiritually alienated from them, but he was deeply rooted in his country and to cut himself off entirely would have been spiritually destructive. It is of himself he speaks when he has Brand say:

Ens Fædrebyggd for Mandens Fod   One's native soil under foot
er, hvad for Træet er dets Rod;—   is as the root is to the tree;—
er *dei* ej till hans Gjerning Trang,   if there his work fulfills no need,
hans Daad er dømt, og endt hans   his song is ended, his deed is doomed.
    Sang.

Brand must remain home and carry on his struggle; to do otherwise would be treason. Ibsen believed the same thing when he told the actors they must be willing to undergo privation and pain rather than desert their life work. But even in 1862, he recognized that other artists, such as poets and writers, may have to pursue their work in different environments; for them to leave under such circumstances was not to break faith with one's homeland. Ibsen felt he would not be hurt by staying away, even though a Norwegian journalist in 1869 had written a warning to him in a magazine: "It would be well if he returned home for a time; otherwise it might happen that his memories will grow too hazy and his works too obscure." Ibsen was sure that his work would not bear out this prediction.

Abroad he felt more secure against influences that would have made him hesitate in his writing. While he waited for the attacks he felt sure would come upon the publication of *Brand*, he wrote: "Let things take their course—they will not succeed in frightening me." And later, when he thought back on the time he was writing *Peer Gynt*, it seemed to him that he would never have dared to write so "recklessly" if he were closer to home. He knew he was the kind of writer "who by his whole intellectual bent has to risk a great deal," but he also had to feel that he was well defended.

He stayed away, moreover, because he believed he could understand his homeland better at a distance. In 1867 he wrote: "One does have this advantage in living abroad, that one receives impressions of the nation's life purified and in extract; one is spared the daily trivia that take place on highways and byways. That is a great gain." He advised Bjørnson to get away too, "because distance gives greater perspective and you are at the same time out of the good people's sight." In 1870 he wrote: "We humans are farsighted — we see best at a distance; when one is in the middle of the herd, all that is irrelevant, all that is ephemeral acquires an undeserved importance. I've felt it so, at any rate." In his speech to the Norwegian students in 1874 he made the same points and related them specifically to the gift of poetic insight. Both Bjørnson and Jonas Lie agreed with him when he wrote: "I have never seen my home and the pulsating life there so completely, so clearly, and so intimately as at a distance, while I was far from it."

When he was writing *Peer Gynt,* surely his most "Norwegian" play, he looked out over the island of Ischia and suddenly exclaimed "Look! a field of hops!" A Danish friend with him corrected him: "They aren't hops, they're grapevines." Ibsen replied: "Yes, you're right. I have to keep checking myself and remembering that I'm not in Norway." The following summer, in 1868, he made the first of many visits to the Alps, staying in Berchtesgaden. We are told that he enjoyed hiking far up into the mountains, and that he began to paint landscapes again. His guide recalled how enthusiastic he was when he climbed to the high Watzmann peak and looked out over the Königssee. It was so much like a West Norwegian fjord that he could imagine he was back home again. And many years later, in the autumn of 1890, he was on the bridge over the Isar River in Munich, watching the swift and swollen river rush by with logs and trees. The bridge trembled and people fled, but Ibsen remained, remembering the waterfalls of Skien. And when a stranger came and stood beside him, Ibsen was still so far back in his memories that he began to speak to the man in Norwegian. The man was English and so they changed to French for the rest of the conversation, during which Ibsen spoke of the way things appeared and reappeared in life until one's memories take on the quality of dreams.

Everything that he had known in his childhood, even when he seemed most withdrawn from the world, stood deeply etched in his memory and found its way into his work: Skien in *The League of Youth* in 1869, Grimstad in *Pillars of Society* in 1877, and many other instances. He always had a tremendous capacity for absorbing sights and impressions and this is one clue to his greatness as a poet and dramatist. Whenever he spoke about his writing, he always emphasized that it was of major importance for him to have his characters alive before his eyes before he could write about them. He had to know them inside out, so that he not only knew how they thought, but how they spoke, how they walked, and how they dressed, down to the last button. They must be Norwegian, otherwise he could not know them entirely or make them speak naturally. Their temperament, he insisted, had to be genuinely Norwegian. When he published *Rosmersholm* in 1886, a German friend complained that there was something foreign about the book, something a German could never quite fathom. "Yes!" Ibsen cried with more than usual warmth, "you are quite correct. I understand. People up in our country are actually different from you, and anyone who wants to understand me fully must understand Norway first. The mighty but harsh nature that surrounds people in the north, their lonely, secluded lives —farms are often miles apart—compel them to be indifferent to others, and to think only of their own concerns. They thus become pensive and somber; they brood and doubt; they often despair. In my country every other man is a philosopher! Then there are the long dark winters, with the dense fog surrounding the houses...oh, how one yearns for the sun!"

He was describing and trying to explain his own temperament, and if the explanation is neither very original nor striking, it does indicate how deeply he felt himself to be rooted in Norway and its life and scenery. His mind had developed and found its nourishment there, and his writing was an attempt to explain its society, its culture, and its problems. Without this foundation in Norwegian life his work would be other than it is. After six years of travel he could still write: "But I feel more Norwegian at heart than ever before."

He kept up with life in his homeland, and although he associated almost exclusively with Scandinavians abroad, yet he was alone a great deal of the time and it was only a matter of chance when he met some-one who had real news to tell him. He corresponded little with people up there, and months would pass without his receiving a letter. This particularly annoyed him and in 1868 he wrote: "It is intolerable in the long run to be without all communication with my home." He had then been traveling for two months and had had no mail at all. His usual source of information was the newspaper *Morgenbladet*, and occasionally a Danish paper. He read these with a zest that was remarkable, poring over them from beginning to end, absorbing every word, including the advertisements. He devoured his visitors from home in the same way, getting them to tell everything they could think of. Thus he tried to keep track of whatever went on up North. Perhaps he interpreted everything to suit himself; he did not always respond to im-

portant new developments that were reshaping Norwegian life. He saw
things in the light of the memory of his youth and young manhood,
and in the mould of his memory the news of home took the form that
would be of greatest significance for his art.

His life abroad gave him much inspiration for his writing. He said,
"The soil itself has a great influence on the forms in which the imagination creates," and when he looked back on his first works done in Italy,
Brand and *Peer Gynt,* he felt he could say with Christoff in Holberg's
Jakob von Thyboe: "Lo, this was an intoxication of wine." In contrast
is *The League of Youth,* his first play written in Germany. Here he detected something that reminded him of "Knackwurst and beer." German
philosophy and political theory widened his intellectual perspective,
but he was never what the Germans call "eingebürgert," spiritually at
home, in either country. As always, he had to isolate himself in order to
feel free, and it is questionable if he ever had any real familiarity with
the conditions or the trends in the societies where he lived. But he could
at least make comparisons and keep alive his anger at the pettiness of
his homeland.

Ibsen's picture of Norway is certainly not an objective one, but rather
in the nature of a polemic exaggeration. All his writing had arrow and
shaft directed at the homeland, and is at least an unconscious tribute
to it. Norway may not have given him the longed for "gift of sorrow,"
but it did certainly give him the "gift of anger." With Brand he felt
that "one's best love is to hate" one's people, but this hate was really
love too. More than once he pleaded with his countrymen that he did
not hate them: "The blemishes in our social order are what I hate."
He found blemishes enough, and from the anger these provoked grew
his masterpieces.

In 1873 a German reviewer called his poem, "Signals from the North"
(Nordens Signaler) a "mocking attack" on Germany. Ibsen protested
immediately: "There are far too many things I feel I must mock in my
own country for me to take the trouble to mock the Germans." Norwegian folly gave him enough fuel, and so he remained essentially a
Norwegian poet. The idea is basic to the lines he wrote for the millennial
celebration of the Norwegian kingdom in 1872:

Mit folk, som skænkte mig i dybe skåler	My people, who in beakers deep did give me
den sunde bittre styrekedrik, hvoraf	that wholesome bitter steeling drink,
som digter jeg, på randen av min grav,	from which as poet I, beside my waiting grave,
tog kraft til kamp i døgnets brudte stråler,—	drew strength to fight amid the shattered rays of sunset,—

mit folk, som rakte mig den
    landflugts stav,
den sorgens byldt, de angstens rappe
    såler,
det tunge alvors-udstyr til min
    færden,—
dig sender jeg en hilsen hjem fra
    verden!

Jeg sender den med tak for alle
    gaver,
med tak for hver en smærtens
    luttrings-stund.
Hver vækst, som lykkes i mit
    livskalds haver,
har dog sin rod i hine tiders grund;—
at her de spirer fyldigt, rigt og gerne,
det skyldes gråvejrs-brisen fra det
    fjerne;
hvad solbrand løsned, det fik tågen
    fæste;—
mit land, hav tak, —du skænkte mig
    det bedste.

my people, who thrust on me the
    exile's staff,
sorrow's pack, fleet sandals soled with
    terror,
solemn trappings of my journey—
to you I send a greeting from
    the world!

I send it with thanks for all your gifts,
thanks for every hour of cleansing pain.
Each plant that flowers in the garden
    of my life
has roots deep in homeland soil;
if here they thrive, rich, pliant growth,
blown rain from far-off home is cause;
sprung by sun, formed by mist;—
my land, my thanks, —your gift
    was best.

CHAPTER TWENTY-ONE

STRUGGLE AND CRISIS (1866)

WHEN IBSEN RECEIVED *Brand* from the publisher in the middle of March, 1866, long months of painful waiting came to an end. The time had been particularly disturbing, for on March 24 one of his friends in Rome, the promising young Danish sculptor Ludvig David, in a fit of despondency caused by illness took his own life. Ibsen was distracted from his own troubles for the moment as he tried to reconstruct the events around this tragedy. He succeeded in establishing that the young man had most probably been suffering from mental delusions when he plunged to his death.

With the success of his book he felt happier and more secure than he had for years. His good luck even extended to the Danish state lottery, where he tried to follow up his initial good fortune: "I enjoy the excitement of it," he wrote his publisher Hegel. His successful application for state support occasioned a letter of thanks to Prime Minister Sibbern on June 2, in which he wrote, "My future is now secure." This mood of security and happiness is reflected in his letters from these months and in the zest with which he began work again. The only drop of wormwood, as we have seen, was the notice of the sale of his effects in Oslo. He wrote Bjørnson that this was "an indescribably bitter message," especially because, as he noted "my private letters, my drafts, etc. are in the hands of just anybody." He clenched his teeth and never spoke about it again, as was his habit when something beyond remedy had happened.

His success made him feel renewed, and he wrote to Birkeland, "Externally, I have gotten thin," but—more important—"as far as the inner man is concerned, I think I have greatly changed on some points, and yet I think I am more myself now than ever before." Fr. G. Knudtzon, a young Danish student who came to Rome near the end of 1865 and stayed half a year, wrote of Ibsen: "There was a certain precision in his personality as in his dress: a long, buttoned frock coat, a proper neckerchief—the whole thing faultless. The year before, I was told, he

223

went around with holes in his sleeves, as if indifferent to such mundane matters."

Ibsen was healthier, too, than he had been for many years. His walks around Rome became regular hiking expeditions, complete with knapsack on back. Before long he was boasting that he knew every corner of the Papal State. He had by now learned enough Italian to enjoy meeting the people and learning about their lives.

But there was still a restlessness within. He no longer enjoyed the company of the Scandinavians in Rome. His closest friends during the first year had moved on and he found no one new that he particularly enjoyed. "In the Society the men are boring," he wrote to one of his departed friends, "especially some repulsive Swedes." In general, he found that "life is dull . . . I fear, indeed I know that as far as I am concerned the best Roman days are gone for good." He was tired of "shaking these fellows up every day," and he was easily put out of humor. His moods changed from one extreme to another.

The student Knudtzon, whom Ibsen liked and befriended, wrote in his memoirs that at this time "there were so many conflicting minds in him that he could not possibly strike one as a harmonious personality." He summed up the effect of the contrasts in this way: "His high ideals, his great pettiness in everyday matters, his delight in Italy and its art, the vestiges of his bitterness toward Norway, his recent financial difficulties, and his secret need for playing the master—all these and much more that moved within him could cause him to explode in one direction or another, and he stalked around among the Scandinavians like a lion of whom most were really terrified." Knudtzon reported instances of heartless treatment of some poor fellow the poet had come to hate for one reason or another, and instances of great kindliness, especially toward children. He was a man out of balance, struggling for harmony.

He was strangely sensitive about his personal honor. He was on the board of directors of the Scandinavian Society that year, and when someone at a festive occasion proposed a toast for those who had arranged for the food and drinks, Ibsen slammed his glass down on the table and said: "I shall not be toasted as a member of the food committee!" He was furious on another occasion when he and Suzannah were not invited to a society dance. Such touchiness was perhaps natural; he knew his own worth now, and after years of struggle he was justifiably proud of his abilities and resented any real or imagined slights. Recognition was so new and strange that his reactions at times were not very rational. In full seriousness he told Knudtzon that he was going to sit down in Rome and from there "rule them all back home."

He often said that he was not writing just for tomorrow, but for all eternity. When a friend suggested that in a thousand years even the greatest men are forgotten, he turned on him with real anger, shouting as though from the depths of his troubled heart: "Get away from me with your metaphysics! If you rob me of eternity, you rob me of everything." He was in constant fear of anything that might stop his writing —an illness, an accident. He avoided dangerous hills and boat trips, and he was not joking when he wondered what would happen if he were to get a roof tile on the head!

More than once his companions in this period were subjected to his outbursts, particularly if he had had a pint or so. They were afraid of him. They worried how he would behave at the society's Christmas party, for the Norwegian Kristofer Janson was scheduled to read one of his stories, written in Landsmål, or New Norwegian. Ibsen had threatened to leave the party if he did so. At the party Janson decided to read Bjørnson's story, also in Landsmål, called "A Dangerous Court-ship." He was an excellent performer and even sang the lyrics with skill. Everyone breathed a sigh of relief when Ibsen remained. Actually, he was very fond of Janson, and when he heard he was coming to Rome had praised him for "the honorable name he has won with his book in Landsmål." But they often disputed the language question, and in one altercation Ibsen got so angry he flung a chair at the man with the words: "You blasted fishmonger!"* He was even more angered when his wife supported Janson: "Of course! Yes!" he cried. "You're a fishwife yourself!" What he was objecting to was the element of artificiality and exaggerated nationalism he thought he detected in the language change Janson advocated.

Some of his old resentments were still alive. As late as 1867 he could still sputter in annoyance when he recalled how the humorous magazine *Vikingen* had made fun of him more than four years before. He called it being "libeled" in a "muck-raking rag." He could not forget the criticism of *Love's Comedy*, any more than he could lay aside his anger at the political situation. It is said that even in 1867 he was still talking about the behavior of the Germans toward Denmark and the "betrayal" of Denmark by the Norwegians and Swedes. He never spoke of his countrymen except as "the scoundrels." He likewise detested the Swedes for their weak actions, which were particularly ironic in view of their boasting about Gustavus Adolphus or Charles XII. "Keep quiet or you'll

---

*Ibsen used the word *stril*, a derogatory term for the fishermen of the Bergen district. He was alluding to the fact that both Janson and Suzannah were from Bergen, and both were supporting the rural language.

make me ill!" he would shout, then pound the table if anyone praised or excused them. In 1868 he wrote that the worst thing about home was "the bootlicking for the Swedes" that went on.

Some years later he would look back on this year and call it his "Roman Sturm-und-Drang period." Some insight into the deeper causes for the contradictory emotions that buffeted him can be had from the words he wrote Bjørnson near the end of 1867: "You can be sure that in my quiet hours I dig and probe and anatomize quite amusingly in my own entrails;—and just where it hurts the most." He was still implicated in the very things he had criticized in the play and this dissatisfaction with himself made him lash out against others. A few years later in 1870, he wrote that *Brand* had rid him of that which "I had to free myself of through artistic means." After that the book "no longer had any interest" for him. It took time for him to free himself from the moods that had led to the writing of the play, and meanwhile he was in a dangerous temper.

From June to September of 1866 he lived again in the Alban Hills, this time in the town of Frascati, in one of the old villas, Palazzo Grazi-oli, not far from the country house and theatre of Cicero. From his study he had a magnificent view of the Roman Campagna and the surrounding mountains; before him, he said, lay "the field where world history fought its greatest battle." Here certainly was the place to inspire a work about the Emperor Julian: "Now I will soon be getting down to writing," he wrote Botten Hansen in July. "I am still wrestling with the materials, but I know that I'll soon have the beast mastered, and then the rest comes of itself."

But it did not come of itself. At the end of August he began something quite different, a new edition of *Love's Comedy*, that Hegel was prepared to issue. Ibsen spent the month of September "winnowing its language," that is, taking out the Norwegian elements in his Danish, deliberately eliminating all peculiarly Norwegian words that would offend Danish readers. He was also showing his contempt and annoyance with his countrymen, whose nationalistic boasting he found increasingly distasteful. In his preface to the new edition he mocked ironically the "healthy realism" that permitted the Norwegians to sit smugly back in their present state and resist every effort to change. In Frascati the news reached him that the government had given him a travel grant, and when he returned to Rome in October with the revised edition of *Love's Comedy*, he made plans to go to Greece and Paris. He was trying to prepare himself for writing the new play, but on November 2 he wrote to Hegel that he did not know just when he would start. "I have a few other topics in mind; but this very diffusion of interest indicates that none of these ideas is sufficiently matured; I feel confident, however, that this maturing will soon take place, and I hope I shall be able to have a complete manuscript for you sometime in the spring." These words suggest that a new idea was taking shape, and that would be consistent with his thinking during this first year after Brand. He would not let himself be bound by historical drama; he needed once more to plunge into contemporary life. It was no accident that he had returned to *Love's Comedy*. He told Hegel that the play could be "regarded as a precursor" of *Brand;* the mood that produced both plays was still alive in him, and he had to go forward on that road.

Early in 1867 an account of his life and work by A. Falkman appeared in the Danish journal *Illustreret Tidende.* In this first complete presentation to a Danish audience, Ibsen's appeal to the youth of the country was evident. Falkman stressed Ibsen's use of an ethical theme in literature, rather than the boring aesthetical preoccupations of the older Danish writers. Georg Brandes further clarified Ibsen's characteristics in an essay in *Dansk Maanedsskrift* in the fall of the same year. This essay was the first analysis of the psychological basis and impact of Ibsen's writing. Brandes saw that the vital theme in Ibsen was his fierce moral indignation and his hatred of all betrayal and deception. "Greatness and strength of passion, of will, and of will born by passion, these are the ideals of this poet." Brandes now made Ibsen his comrade in his battle against all compromise in life and in thinking (his attack on Rasmus Nielsen's "dualism" had appeared the year before). But Brandes was still so much dependent on traditional judgment that he could not accept Ibsen's literature of anger as authentically poetic. He could appreciate the poetry of *The Pretenders,* but felt that *Brand* represented a deflection from the main course. He ends his essay: ". . . it will be necessary for him to leave the path he has taken in *Love's Comedy* and *Brand.* There is unfortunately no doubt that this will be difficult for him; but . . . he is too much of a poet not to be able to see what after all poetry is, and is not." When Brandes reprinted this essay the next year in his *Aesthetic Studies (Aesthetiske Studier,* 1867), he had to strike out the last sentence: the new work did not live up to his expectation. Ibsen followed his own path, and Brandes would come to realize that this, too, was poetry. The new work was called *Peer Gynt.*

CHAPTER TWENTY-TWO

PEER THE NORWEGIAN (1867)

Aᴼᴛᴇʀ *Brand, Peer Gynt* came, as it were, of itself," Ibsen said in 1870. The writing may not have been as spontaneous as that sounds, but to Ibsen it seemed that way because the new play was so like and yet so unlike *Brand*. Both works originate in the same indignation at compromise and fraud, but *Peer Gynt* sees things in calmer perspective; the angry author is not always present. Ibsen was changing as he wrote the new play, and while his anger subsided rather than vanished, it was seeking new channels and forms within which to express itself. Anger stirred the need for action; as a creative force it broke through old inhibitions and aroused courage.

Brand was a counterpart to the Danish *Adam Homo*, but Ibsen scourged where Paludan-Müller had only satirized. Now Ibsen began to see the comedy in his theme and so decided to create a parallel to Adam in a character who would be at once the type and the caricature of all Norwegians. His mood changed from scolding and anger to mocking humor, a return to the attitude that created *Love's Comedy* and might also be detected in *Brand*, for example, in the portrait of the Dean in the last act. The spirit finds its complete realization in *Peer Gynt*, even though there are still elements of unrestrained bitterness in the play. But what is most in evidence is the bold, frolicking joyousness, born of a feeling of confidence in his strength; the whiplash flickered over man's follies with delight in the performance.

Out of what materials did he create this "hero" who embodies all the empty boasting that he felt characterized the Norwegians? The type had already been sketched in Norwegian folk literature, and as a collector of folktales Ibsen was quite familiar with it and had perhaps heard stories about the character on his tour in Gudbrandsdalen. Peer Gynt had been named and described in P. C. Asbjørnsen's *Norwegian Fairytales and Legends (Norske Huldreeventyr og Folkesagn*, 1847), which had just been reissued in 1866. Asbjørnsen had heard the story from

Anders Ulvsvollen of Sel. "That Peer Gynt was in a class by himself," said Ulvsvollen. "He was a real tale-spinner, and a beautiful liar; he was always good for a laugh, and he always claimed to have played the leading role in every story that ever happened in the old days." Ibsen rather liked the notion that Peer was supposed to have been an actual person who lived two or three generations earlier, although later research has tried to place the real Peer as far back as the seventeenth century. Tradition locates him on the farm Hågå in Nord-Fron, and the surname Gynt can be traced back to the sixteenth century both in Nord-Fron and in Dalecarlia in Sweden. (Ibsen just happened to call his hero's father Jon, but it is actually the name of the first recorded Gynt.) Although no satisfactory explanation of the name Gynt has been found, it is the word which means "boaster" in the region north of the Dovre mountain range. Ibsen probably did not know this when he wrote the play, and in any case he was not particularly interested in the historical antecedents of his character. (The first name Peer is an old spelling of Per, colloquial for Peder or Peter.)

It is not known for certain when he decided to use the legendary Peer Gynt as his hero, although the play might have been one of the "other topics" he mentioned to Hegel in the letter of November 2, 1866. On January 5, 1867 he wrote that he was working on "a major dramatic poem, whose main figure is one of the half-mythical, half-folklorish creatures from Norway's past that survive into the present." He added: "I have had the subject in my head for a long time; now the whole plot is sketched out, and I have begun on the first act."

Using the clue he found in Asbjørnsen, he began to create an enormous imaginative structure. The tales about Peer were the usual fairy-tale type, except for the extraordinary story of the great Boyg in Atnedalen, which would become one of the play's main symbols. Ibsen was actually glad that the sources were so meager. As he wrote to Hegel: "There was not much to build on, but I had so much the more freedom." All that he had learned of the Norwegian folk temperament he attributed to the Gudbrandsdal boaster, and thus made him into the quintessentially Norwegian Peer. The central trait of the true Norwegian was his habit of evading the demands and difficulties of life; this kind of mendacity Ibsen detested from his heart. But the evasions and the boastings that tried to cover the lie both stemmed from an exceedingly fertile imagination, an imagination for which one had to admit a certain fondness, at the same time one mocked it. Thus Ibsen's Peer had to be a totally different creature from Paludan-Müller's Danish Adam. The Dane is all prose, a contemptible bungler and faker; the Norwegian is a wild, unbridled kind of poet, a man who could at least dream great things, but whose ability to act was constantly being sapped by the very seductive charm of those dreams.

The man was Ibsen himself, always dreaming of the great things he would someday do, and always talking about his dreams. He felt he could be a leader, but the years began to slip by and he knew that people were smiling and whispering behind his back; he felt their mockery burn through him. His plans seemed nothing but talk, and he wanted to disappear or take some strong dose to kill the pain of failure. In writing *Brand* he began at last to feel he was acting; but when it was all over, it seemed just another evasion, another instance when the call to action went unheeded. After all, what he had done was merely write a poem. He had tried to resolve the dilemma between the ethical and the aesthetic demands—as Arne Garborg wrote: "*Brand* is ideally what Kierkegaard wanted the man of the age to be in reality. This is the release. The absolute ethical demand is transmuted into aesthetics; in this way its sting is drawn."—But the sting still smarted, and he needed once more to summon himself to judgment. Peer Gynt was to be his next major "self-anatomy."

When in 1874 he spoke of his writing over the last decade, he said that everything in the play had been lived through, was his own spiritual life. In *Peer Gynt* as in *Brand* he recreates that passion for the ideal that characterized him in his best moments. But now he also creates the image of his opposing self, the slag heap of wasted time and false starts. "Yes, gentlemen," he said on this occasion, "no one can write anything for which he does not have a model within, at least to some extent, at least some of the time. And who among us has not at times felt and acknowledged in himself a contradiction between words and action, between the will and the task, between life and ideology? Or who among us has not, at least on occasion, been egotistically sufficient unto himself; who has not half consciously, half in good faith, tried to excuse this fact to himself and to others?" He summed it up in the play:

Blodet er aldrig saa tyndt, en kjender sig altid i Slægt med Peer Gynt.	No matter how diluted the blood, one is always related to Peer Gynt.

Fifteen years earlier, in *Saint John's Night,* he had created in the romantic poet Julian Poulsen a man who ignored the seriousness of life and made it an imaginative play. Ibsen drew a rather external portrait there, without self-involvement, and the tone was one of mockery. In *Peer Gynt* he recognized his own complicity; this is even clearer in the first draft than in the last revision, as such lines as the following indicate:

| Der er noget uhyggeligt, rent uforklarligt i det som en kalder for medansvarligt. | There is something weird, quite inexplicable, in being what is called a fellow culprit. |

The draft makes quite clear that he was still accusing himself of the guilt he had described two years before in the poem "To My Fellow Culprits," the self-deception of romantic nationalism. Thus the banquet scene in the hall of the Dovre King originally began with the singing of the old national anthem, "For Norway, Land of Heroes" (*For Norge, Kjæmpers Fødeland*). He too had championed this anthem, which was one of the few songs he knew by heart. He had also set verses to the tune of the anthem in honor of the hero ancestors. But in *Andhrimner* for 1851 he had denounced the "nationalistic tinsel" of *The Fairy's Home,* which ends with the singing of the same boasting song. By making the anthem a symbol of narrow-minded nationalism, he was castigating his own sins as well as those of his countrymen.

He also accused himself of not having taken life seriously, of having "gone around" his problems. The illegitimate child in Grimstad, an affair that left him feeling "foul and despoiled," was an example. He had been a coward, and even more he felt guilty of a kind of sacrilege which would haunt him so that he would always "come attended with all those demons in his train."* What Brand had said was true:

| Gaar en det *største* udenom, al Resten mildner ej hans Dom. | If one evades the *most* important, the little things won't soften the judgment. |

Now he makes Peer's worst fault his evasion of responsibility when he follows the Boyg's command: "Take the way *around.*"

Peer Gynt took shape as Ibsen subjected himself to critical examination. Now memories arose and added new characteristics to the portrait. "This poem contains a great deal that originates in my life as a young man," he wrote in 1870. He thought of his father, who had given him his first insight into the disastrous effect of the imagination on thinking and on one's respect for the truth; first the wild spending while the money lasted, then the daydreams about getting back what had been lost. Old Knud Ibsen appears in a more elaborated manner in "the rich Jon Gynt," but the basis for the portrait was his own memories. The same is true with regard to his mother. "With necessary exaggerations," he portrayed her as Åse, Peer Gynt's mother. Although the only similarity between the two women is their unfaltering love, Ibsen may

*The weakling character in the play, Mads Moen, may have been named from a sheriff who worked in Berkenes in the 1840's; such a sheriff came to Ibsen to collect the first allowance Ibsen was obliged to make for his illegitimate son.

have drawn on actual experience when he describes Åse by her son's bed, making up fairy-tales and singing ballads.

He also remembered the great dreamer and restless projector, the violinist Ole Bull, who had once engaged him in the cause of nationalism. Bull no sooner founded the Norwegian Theatre in Bergen than he hurried on to new enterprises. In the spring of 1852 he went to America to start a Norwegian utopia at Oleana in the woods of northern Pennsylvania. The memory of this scheme is perpetuated in the "Ballad of Oleana," a satiric portrait of Bull's Eldorado written by the journalist Ditmar Meidell. The ending of the project was sad; Bull lost all his money and the ideal society fell apart. Ibsen obviously had this ill-starred venture in mind when Peer dreams of his empire of Gyntiana; there is more than a little of Bull's nationalistic fantasies in Peer Gynt.

Another of the fantasts Ibsen pressed into service in creating Peer was the attorney F. G. Lerche, Storting member, patriotic radical, not a dreamer like Bull, but a man who unconsciously took his own fantasies for sober truth. Lerche had been a byword in the *Andhrimner* circle in 1851, and A. O. Vinje particularly used to mock him for making the expression "factual information" synonymous with "lying." It was Lerche's unfortunate talent to tell the truth in "an artistically free translation," so that the result was more than just the simple truth.

And of course Ibsen thought of Vinje himself — not the brooding, troubled doubter, but the spirited madcap who could race from one mood to another, the untiring protean mind forever returning with new hope. Ibsen's "Dutchmen" friends immediately recognized Vinje's traits in Peer, particularly his delight in quoting himself. Ibsen also had a little score to settle with Vinje for having suggested that *Brand* was all a great joke—Ibsen resented any attempt to poke fun at his work, although he was rather liberal with his mockery of the work of others. He took particular delight in the figure of Huhu in Act IV of the play, where he laughs at Vinje's efforts in the national language movement.*

Many memories, many ideas, and many men were fused into the portrait of Peer Gynt, but his life comes from the background of Norwegian folklore. Ibsen steeped himself in this world while writing the play, and he filled it with themes and creatures not taken from any single tale, but suggested by a number of stories and reshaped by his imagination. Peer was thus deeply and intimately Norwegian, and the poem is filled with a glory of fresh, playful verse unequaled in Ibsen's writing.

He was unusually light-hearted while working on the play. The theme

---

*The reference is to the Madhouse scene where Huhu advocates returning to the primitive language of the orangutans— Ibsen's satirical thrust at the supporters of Ivar Aasen's *landsmål*.

had crystallized for him around New Year's, 1867, and he began to shape the material immediately, hoping to have it completed by early summer. "It's growing under my hands," he wrote optimistically; actually he was barely able to get the first two acts into shape during the next four or five months. In May he left Rome for the island of Ischia, off Naples, where he remained for three months in the little town of Casamicciola, right below the old volcano Epomeo, on the northern slope of the island. Here the first three acts were put into final form, and work on the last two begun.

The summer was extremely hot, but Ibsen managed to work, again noting that the summer was his best working period. When others went limp and were worn out by the heat, he was stimulated—like the viper that basks in the sun, storing up its venom for attack. He told the young Danish writer Vilhelm Bergsøe: "Now I'm going to work; I feel like a rearing stallion ready for a race." He worked mornings and after-noons, even when an awful July sirocco arose with dry, stifling air and a heat close to 100 degrees Fahrenheit day after day. He was in good humor and told Bergsøe: "Ah! It's going to be a jolly comedy," then added a quote from Holberg's barber, Gert Westphaler, "There is, i'faith, no loose talk nor unbecoming speech in it." He was especially ready with quotes from Holberg this summer, feeling probably that he was now ready to take over his office as Norwegian "state satirist."

Then a minor earth tremor shook the island and he abruptly left. (The natives discounted it at the time, but in 1883, the entire town of Casamicciola was devastated by an earthquake.) He settled in Sor-rento and there completed the last two acts. Except for the scare of a cholera epidemic in Naples and a momentary fear that Suzannah had been infected, his work and his spirits continued full of joyful energy and vitality.

Peer Gynt bears clear evidence of the ebullient spirit with which it was written; it is the least organized and structured of his plays. He began, as he always did, with the ending definitely in mind, but though he knew the nature of the judgment Peer would have to face, he had not clearly outlined the path that would take him there. He said that he had no idea when he began, that he would be going to Africa with Peer. The fourth and fifth acts are particularly marked by this free play of the imagination. He felt the need to experiment with an open and flexible form, and, as he said, he "slapped down" minor and major things, just as "caprices."

Perhaps he was filled with the idea that would come so often to him later, that this might be his last work. He had to express fully all that lived in his imagination, even stray themes that he had not yet utilized.

Thus it is that the story of the boy who mutilated himself to avoid military service appears in the play. He had used it first in the rejected draft of the poem on the Brand theme; now it is used in a final form, but for a new purpose. In the Brand poem it was a sign of Norwegian cravenness, now it stands as contrast to Peer Gynt's inaction.

The play is full of echoes of his reading, sometimes openly, sometimes in disguised and concealed form. There are allusions to books he read as a boy, for example, the world history of the German K. F. Becker and the Latin fables of Phaedrus. Other references are from his first year in Oslo when he studied Hegel. He again makes use of the Egyptian fable of the statue of Memnon, which he had once employed in a play prologue in Bergen in 1855 (he may have picked this up in J. L. Heiberg's translation of Ovid). The scene in the Cairo madhouse is apparently derived from a vivid description that appeared in *Skilling-Magasinet* in 1848, and this may in fact have given him the idea to send Peer to Africa. There are passages that suggest *Adam Homo* and other poems of Paludan-Müller. And there are reminiscences of Oehlenschläger's *Aladdin*, of poems by the Finnish-Swedish Runeberg, and of the farces of Wergeland. There are an amazing number of literary allusions in the play; more amazing is how they are all fused into a new and wholly personal idiom.

Like *Brand,* the work was called a "dramatic poem," but he never wrote anything less strictly dramatic. The work is a chronicle of the hero's entire life, from youth to old age, rather than a single dramatic conflict. The first three acts are, of course, closely knit into a single plot with an inner psychological conflict. Peer still has the possibility of choice and the hope of success in life. Even if he dreams constantly and lies his way out of any demanding situation, we see that he has the potential for a life of willed action and moral responsibility. He can love, that is, think of others besides himself and be willing to sacrifice himself for others—as in *Brand* "to be oneself is to slay oneself." Peer can be saved from both the King of the Dovre Mountains and from the Boyg: in the first instance, by thinking of his mother; in the latter, by thinking of Solveig. But each time he wins he is weakened rather than strengthened. In the King's hall he learns the slogan, "Be sufficient unto yourself!" and from the Boyg, "Take the way *around.*" When faced with decision, he fails. He flees his responsibility when he refuses to face the struggle of life with Solveig, and when he jests to avoid his mother's fear of death and damnation. Thus he tears out his own heart and has nothing to give anyone; his life is nothing but self-love now, a life of lies and illusions.

The inner conflict of the play is completed in the first three acts. When we see Peer again in Act IV, he has already lived much of his life on the basis of his decision. Thirty years have passed between the third and fourth acts; Peer was twenty, now he is fifty. But the gap in time, always a danger because the essential change in character seems to take place during the intermission, is particularly noticeable here because the last two acts lack the unity of the first three. Ibsen, of course, means to indicate that Peer has remained the same during the time lapse; his spiritual fate was already settled. All that has taken place in the intervening years is a series of external events. The last two acts lead him to judgment and the catastrophe.

Ibsen fills these last acts with all manner of "caprice": mockery of Norwegian-language nationalism, Swedish cultivation of the heroic past, Anglo-American materialism, and German historical philosophy, and there are even digs at the Egyptologist who had not properly appreciated *Brand*. He hacked away freely, since he was far from home and thus safe.

These episodes help to reveal the seamy half of the "Gyntian self" and make judgment more inevitable. They also serve to lift Peer out of the limited reference of a Norwegian type and to universalize him into a symbol of all human self-limitation and self-deception. He is "born Norwegian, but world citizen by temperament." Ibsen gradually came to realize that the petty nationalism he attacked in his Norwegians was not at all true nationalism; on the contrary it put an end to all nationalism since it killed the soul. In the same manner "being sufficient unto oneself" destroyed a man's true self. The judgment on Peer's life was more severe now; he had sinned against a universal law of life.

And so he meets the Button Moulder, his judge. The scene has certain superficial similarities to Heiberg's "apocalyptic comedy" *A Soul After Death (En Sjæl efter Døden, 1840)*. The themes are alike in that Heiberg's soul is not condemned for great sins, but for ordinary bourgeois pettiness. It simply never had any understanding of spiritual or ideal reality, but had been content to live for tangible things, without striving for an authentic, personal existence. There is a line of development that leads from *A Soul After Death* through *Adam Homo* to *Peer Gynt*, with the philosophical implications of the works becoming more serious as one reaches *Peer Gynt*. In Heiberg the test to which the soul is put is still largely aesthetic; in Paludan-Müller it is moral; in Ibsen this moral demand is so intensified that it becomes a matter of life and death. The man who does not follow his call loses the very right to live—he is worth less than the chaff that is tossed into the fire. Ibsen has learned from Kierkegaard's intensity, and so can dramatize moral decision as an either-or case. The Button Moulder is his vehicle for this heightened moral awareness, and that figure is far more terrifying than either Heiberg's Mephistopheles or Paludan-Müller's Advocatus Diaboli. The genesis of the character is found in Ibsen's boyhood when he himself did button-moulding. Now the image of the tin being melted down came to stand as a symbol of a wasted life being erased from the books. That is all Peer Gynt comes to be worth.

Then in a sudden turn-about he is exonerated and saved, in as surprising a reversal as that final condemnation of Peer's obverse, the severely idealistic Brand. All Brand's will had been devoted to the great ideal of self-realization through self-sacrifice. Yet, he was not acceptable. Peer spends his life dodging every responsibility, rejecting the content of the ideal while mouthing its slogans with great bravado, and he is forgiven—because a woman made her love for him the meaning of her life. It is understandable that one reviewer reacted to this apparent illogic by saying that the play was "equally absurd in a Christian or in a general psychological sense." It seemed as though Ibsen wanted to restore the very idea he allows Brand to mock, that love can atone for the worst self-indulgence and weakness of will:

saa en sit Maal, og dog ej stred,   if one saw the goal, but didn't struggle,
han sejre kan—i Kjærlighed!   one still could win—by love alone!

This is Peer's attitude, and now Ibsen was giving him the victory.

Paludan-Müller's conclusion to Adam Homo suggests itself here; the hero is saved because a woman could say on Judgment Day:

I Live og Død var denne Sjæl min   In life and death this soul was my joy!
Lyst!

The idea that woman's love has the power to save man is a frequently repeated theme in all romantic writing. "Das ewig Weibliche," which Goethe praised and Peer Gynt caricatured, is the divine idea in man's soul, the natural innocence which lifts him up to heaven. The theme appears in Ibsen's early writing when the gentle Aurelia takes her own murderer, Catiline, with her "to the place of light and peace." That play ends with these words to her:

Du har Mørkets Magt beseiret ved   With your love you have overwhelmed
din Kærlighed!   the power of darkness!

The same idea appears in other plays, among them Saint John's Night, Olaf Liljekrans, and Brand. But it is not likely that Ibsen intended Peer's salvation to come exclusively as a gift from a loving woman; that would be too easy. Peer's life holds the clue to his salvation, just as the judgment on Brand had been prepared for throughout the course of the play.

The two previous occasions when Peer had been rescued from destruction were explained in the following manner:

Han var for stærk. Der stod Kvinder bag ham.	He was too strong. There were women behind him.

His strength came not only from these two women, his mother and Solveig, but from the sincere love, if only a small grain, that he felt for them. Hardly a trace of this love appears when we meet him in Africa; self-love seems to dominate him completely. Yet even here is a suggestion of love. In the middle of the act, when Peer has his misbegotten love affair with Anitra and has shrugged off women with: "They're a sorry lot," Ibsen introduces the simple, yet hopeful song of Solveig:

—engang vil du komme, det ved jeg visst; og jeg skal nok vente, for det lovte jeg sidst.	—some day you'll come, I know that well; and I shall wait, I gave you that promise.

The thought that Solveig waits for him comes to Peer at his loneliest moment in the desert.* When Ibsen prepared the script for dramatic presentation in 1874, he made the song part of a vision that comes to Peer. This clarifies the meaning of the song and it can be seen that the memory of Solveig still remains in some part of his heart. The vision is a preparation for Peer's speech in the madhouse at Cairo, where again the cry for Solveig rises in him as he remembers that:

Jeg var i en Kvindes Eje en sølvspændt Bog.	I was a silver-bound book in a woman's hand.

Regret and longing, or at least the possibility of these feelings begin to grow within him. In the last act these feelings grow stronger. The Strange Passenger who appears before him in his hour of shipwreck is the first sign of that "Angst" that begins to trouble his soul. The idea for this scene may have come from Paludan-Müller's "The Balloonist and the Atheist" (*Luftskipperen og Atheisten*, 1852), but Ibsen uses the scene to probe Peer's conscience more deeply. Terror takes hold of him. He cries out in despair as he dreams he is auctioning off his goods back on the home farm: "A dream about a silver-bound book!" And when he really hears Solveig singing in the cottage, Peer grows "deathly pale." He hears the lament within for all he has not done:

Vie er Tanker! du skulle tænkt os!	We are thoughts! You should have thought us!
Vi er et Løsen; du skulle stillet os!	We are a watchword; you should have posed us!

*For a possible source for Solveig's song see the notes on references for this chapter.

. . .
Vi er Sange;
du skulle sunget os!

. . .
We are songs;
You should have sung us!

. . .
Vi er Taarer,
der ej blev fældte.

. . .
We are tears
that were never shed.

. . .
Vi er Værker;
du skulde øvet os!

. . .
We are deeds;
you should have done us!

Then he meets the Button Moulder, and Ibsen gives Peer some of the most moving lines ever written about the feeling of remorse for a life largely wasted. Peer sees himself completely without recourse now, although throughout his life he has never burned all his bridges, never used the word "completely," always left enough room to be "master of the situation." Now he suddenly realizes that this is exactly how he has wasted every opportunity. He has erased himself from the book of life, and the chasm waits for him:

Saa usigelig fattig kan en Sjæl
    da gaa,
tilbage til intet i det taagede graa.
Du dejlige Jord, vær ikke vred,
at jeg tramped dit Græs til ingen
    Nytte.
Du dejlige Sol, due har sløset med
dine lysende Stænk i en folketom
    Hytte.

So unspeakably poor can a soul return
to nothing again in the gray mist.
Oh lovely earth, be not angry,
that I bent your grass to no end.
Oh lovely sun, your generous light
was wasted on an empty home.

Now he faces for the first time the possibility of "the victory that terror brings," and as he stands for the third time outside Solveig's cottage, he no longer takes the way around:

Nej; denne Gang
tvers igjennem, var Vejen aldrig
    saa trang!

No. This time
straight through, no matter how
    narrow the way!

In Solveig he finds himself, but only because he accepts life and the responsibilities it brings. He had saved a remnant of his soul all through, and it saves him now.

Or was it all a dream? The last words sung over Peer are:

sov og drøm, du Gutten min!   sleep and dream, O my lad!

Ibsen would hold to the dream. He had given too much of himself to destroy him, and he was too much a part of the Norwegian people to leave them without hope, even if only the hope of a dream. Thus he was, truly with Peer Gynt, to the end "a notorious dreamer."

CHAPTER TWENTY-THREE

THE AFTERMATH (1867-68)

THE FIRST THREE ACTS of *Peer Gynt* were sent to the printer from Ischia early in August, 1867, even though Ibsen was still working full speed on the outline for the last two acts. The poet was sufficiently confident in his plans so that he could take the rather risky chance of letting the first part out of his hands. When he sent the fourth act from Sorrento in mid-September, he asked that the cast of characters not be printed yet, "as I might possibly add more minor figures." He was obviously quite willing to introduce more of his "caprices" if need be.

After completing the fifth act the following month, he was ready to take a rest, and to celebrate his success he took a sight-seeing tour of Pompeii and Naples in late October. He then continued on to Rome— this part of the trip proving much more exciting, as he was caught in the midst of the turmoil that followed Garibaldi's unsuccessful attack on the Papal State and had a good deal of difficulty in getting to the capital. With Napoleon III's support of the Papal cause, the situation returned to normal and by the middle of November Ibsen had found a place to live.

A flood of happy news followed him to Rome: a copy of Brandes' brilliant essay written for *Dansk Maanedsskrift;* his publisher's report that the first large printing was almost sold out and a new printing of 2,000 copies was being considered; a deeply felt and encouraging letter from Bjørnson, then in Copenhagen: "My dearest Ibsen! I am so thankful for *Peer Gynt* that in all the years of my literary career I can't think of any other book that has more made me want to take the author by the hand and thank him for what he has given me." Bjørnson spoke warmly: "I don't speak of anything these days but your poem; you're always in my thoughts—so I must tell you myself what I feel. The loyalty I see in you (and how loyal this book is!) has captivated me, heart and soul. I love your loyalty to our great aims, from the Danish cause to those less tangible, high ideals. I love your anger, and the way it has fortified courage. I love your strength, I love your recklessness—Ah!

239

wasn't it the taste of seaspray after the stuffiness of a sickroom! My thoughts turned joyous, ripe for action, recklessly honest. I saw trivial things as trivial; greatness gleamed, enflamed my longing. I felt as if I had been too long speaking French in a salon, and now yearned for Norwegian, even the release of swearing."

Bjørnson also wrote that he had immediately sent a review of the play to his newspaper, *Norsk Folkeblad.* This review, written the day after the book appeared, extolled *Peer Gynt* as a literary masterpiece and a glorious achievement that had a meaning for every Norwegian. "*Peer Gynt* is a satire on Norwegian selfishness, narrowmindedness, smugness. It is so well done that I did not just guffaw, even roar with laughter time and again: it made me feel that I had to personally thank (as I am doing publicly) the man who wrote it." Bjørnson had some reservations about the play's recklessness of imagery, versification, and phrasing; at times he found this so disturbing that he wondered "if one could allow everyone to read the book." Nevertheless: "In its details as well as in its totality it embodies a message greater and more courageous than any that has ever come through to us in our bewilderment." Bjørnson also clearly understood the poetic structure of the work. He was the only one in his day, and in fact the only one for many years, who saw how Peer's right to salvation had been made inevitable throughout the play.

Such perceptive appreciation delighted Ibsen. Now he was certain he had achieved his intention. The answer he began to write to Bjørnson was full of gratitude, for "it makes one inexpressibly grateful to be understood." But before he sent the letter, he came upon a copy of the Copenhagen newspaper *Fædrelandet* with Clemens Petersen's review of the play. The rage into which this review threw him was enough to drive out of his mind any idea that he was finally being understood. He tore up the letter.

Petersen's importance as a critic should be explained. For ten years he had been a reviewer for *Fædrelandet* and had come to be regarded as the leading Scandinavian literary critic. *Fædrelandet* was the chief organ of the liberal "intelligentsia" in Denmark and exercised considerable influence. It was, moreover, virtually the only Danish newspaper read in Norway and Sweden. Petersen's reviews were considered quite liberal at the time, although read today they impress one as strangely dogmatic and pedantic, without any real sensitivity for poetry. They are significant, however, because they broke away from the formal aesthetics of J. L. Heiberg and placed as the first consideration such questions as: Is the writing sincere? Is it born of a deep inner need?

Ibsen felt that criticism of this nature had helped him to turn from

treating poetry as a mere literary exercise. It had shown him the way
to writing poetry as a necessary act of creation. Petersen had shown
little understanding of Ibsen's poetry, as is evident in his critique of such
personal works as *Love's Comedy* and *The Pretenders*. He tended to
look at Ibsen through the spectacles of Bjørnson, with whom he had
had a close friendship since his youth and from whom he expected a
new literary spirit to emerge. Even though *Brand* moved him, he
thought, as Bjørnson had, that the work was unrealized, that it had
"more idea than image," and "thus broke the contact with reality in its
development." Ibsen had nevertheless been pleased with the considerate
tone of the review of *Brand,* just as he had been delighted that the
critic had bothered to write so extensively about *Love's Comedy.* He
knew how important reviews by such an influential critic could be,
and he had ever written to ask him to look favorably on *Brand.* When
at work on *Peer Gynt,* he wrote again, in part to thank him and in part
to prepare him for the new play: "I hope that in my new work you will
find that I have taken a substantial step forward."

Petersen agreed that *Peer Gynt* showed certain advances. "There is
more humor, more true spiritual freedom, less vehemence, less strain-
ing than in *Brand.* It fits more naturally the poet's spirit, and thus
makes a saner, more balanced, and thereby more poetic impression."
After this, however, Petersen's aesthetic theories took over: "Neither *Brand*
nor *Peer Gynt* is really poetry." Why not? Because "the ideal is missing."
What this means is not too clear, but in any case Ibsen felt it a gross
injustice. Even worse were Petersen's comments on "the lack of strict
consistency in the development of the plot, and the lack of complete
honesty in its execution." Ibsen's artistic integrity was being questioned
in this last statement. *Peer Gynt* was simply a clever allegory; the characters in the play were not fully realized, living human beings; the
allegory itself was a failure, often nothing more than intellectualized
humbug. In conclusion, the book was no better than *Corsaren,* the
Danish humor magazine, in a Norwegian, less witty and less elegant,
version.

After Bjørnson's enthusiasm, Petersen's review fell on Ibsen like a
thunderbolt. The effect of the adverse criticism was particularly stunning since he had almost convinced himself that he was above worrying
about people's reactions to the play. He had felt himself safe from
critics' barbs, even Petersen's as the following anecdote shows. In Ischia
the Danish poet Vilhelm Bergsøe read to Ibsen Petersen's scathing
review of his own first collection of poems. The two men were on an
excursion to the top of the volcano Epomeo, and as Bergsøe read they
emptied pint after pint of wine. Ibsen was in high spirits and he toasted

the poet at every salvo the review made. Then he summed up Petersen: "I don't think he can write himself, but so help me he can tell others how." The two men started down the mountain, almost coming to grief in a rockslide their unsteady feet had set in motion, and finally arrived safely in Casamicciola. Ibsen brushed himself off, then rolled the copy of *Fædrelandet* into a megaphone, through which he tooted his greeting to the critics: "Critics go hang!" No critic, and certainly not Clemens Petersen, was worth much respect.

But when he read the review of *Peer Gynt*, he fell into a rage and fired off a new letter to Bjørnson in place of the thankful note he had first begun. "What kind of damned nonsense is this that keeps cropping up and coming between us? It's as if the devil himself threw his shadow between us." He felt that Bjørnson was equally responsible for the review. "If I were in Copenhagen and knew someone as closely as you know Petersen, I would have beaten him senseless before I let him perpetrate such a deliberate crime against truth and justice." There was falsehood in Petersen's manner of reviewing the play, falsehood in what was left unsaid as much as in what was said, and he was certain that "this article will one day burn and char his soul." He put his entire will in the protest against Petersen's judgment: "My book is poetry. If it is not now, it shall be. The idea we have in our country, in Norway, about what poetry is shall change and adapt itself to my book." Petersen would not recognize this, and that was his greatest treason against the sacred commandment the poet's conscience must obey. Ibsen was not cowed: "I am glad just the same for the injustice done me; a god's help and providence is in it, for anger will make my powers grow. If it is to be war, let it be! For if I am not a poet, I have nothing to lose. I'll take a turn as photographer. One after the other I'll hold my contemporaries up before me, the same as I did with the language reformers. I'll not spare the very child in the womb, nor the thought behind the word of any soul who merits inclusion in my gallery." And he ends by saying: "What I have written is probably quite incoherent; but the sum and substance of it is: I refuse to be an antiquarian or a geographer. I will no longer sharpen my wits for Monrad's philosophy. I short, I refuse to follow good advice." He would be only himself.

This was December 9. He slept on the letter, and the next day wrote the postscript "in cold blood." He was not much calmer, although he was not so angry at Bjørnson. He felt that everyone at home would say that Bjørnson was trying to attack him indirectly through Petersen, and thus their friends would take opposing sides in the argument. He wanted to remain on friendly terms with Bjørnson himself, but he kept on the offensive: "I won't yield willingly, and Mr. Clemens Petersen cannot beat me off. It's too late for that. He might force me out of Denmark; but then I'll be giving up more than a publisher. Do not underestimate my friends and supporters in Norway. The party whose newspaper permits such an injustice will find out that I am not alone. Past a certain point I have no scruples, and if I'm careful, as I can be, to match the fire of my anger with a deliberate choice of means, my enemies will learn that if I can't be constructive, I am capable of tearing things down around me."

After he sent the letter, his anger began to ebb. He wondered if he had not done Bjørnson an injustice and the thought plagued his days. He had announced a war to the end, and he dreaded that he would have to launch it. His mood was bitter and despondent. But Bjørnson took the accusations quite differently than might have been expected. He felt completely innocent. Far from being a collaborator, he had quarreled many times with Petersen, not only about such general questions as the nature of poetry, but specifically about *Peer Gynt*. Bjørnson had told him directly that he thought the review unjust. So much he wrote to Ibsen, and with genuine feeling said that in the struggle over *Peer Gynt* they would stand shoulder to shoulder. But he was frightened, nonetheless, at the sudden fury that could make Ibsen so lose control of himself as to threaten to change his ultimate aims in life and in literature, and all because of an article in a newspaper. With his quiet strength and his balance, Bjørnson felt there was something sickly in such vacillation. "If this is anything physical," he wrote, "you must leave Rome and the South immediately: two or three such attacks would be enough to mark you as though by the devil's own claw. If it is anything psychological as well, pray to your Lord and Savior, you strong, truth-seeking soul! Pray with all the intensity God has given you, pray as to break through the cloud of your own understanding, pray as a child —then you will be just to us and confident in yourself." Above all he urged Ibsen to hold fast to himself and not let himself be enticed into deeds of spiteful anger.

Bjørnson's letter arrived on Christmas Day, and Ibsen was overjoyed: "A more blessed greeting I could never in the world have had." The fears that had so blackened his mood were gone. He told Bjørnson that he need not worry about these fits of anger: "They are in no wise sickly, either in one way or the other." He thanked him for his friendliness, and promised a long letter before long. But ten years were to pass before he wrote another word to Bjørnson. He could not free himself from suspicion that this friend, despite all he said, wanted to guide him on another path than the one he had chosen. He noticed that Bjørnson's praise contained many reservations, reservations that were very much like Petersen's criticism. Other factors contributed to Ibsen's suspicion and fear of Bjørnson. To begin with, Ibsen was sensitive and suspicious, a heritage from the long years of struggle and suffering. He was quick to think he was surrounded by enemies. Even in the midst of their friendship, he worried whether Bjørnson would make "counter-maneuvers" to block his plans for a new edition of *Love's Comedy*. He thought it would take a great deal of pressure to get Jonas Lie to give up the rights to the play. He also felt that Bjørnson could have prevented the auction of his property in Oslo and wrote him an angry letter (now lost) about this. Although he later apologized for the letter, the incident reveals a basic insecurity in their relationship. Ibsen was perhaps put off by the somewhat paternal tone of Bjørnson's letters; he instinctively rebelled against any guardian.

More fundamental differences could have arisen because of the divergent attitudes each took on religious and philosophical questions. Ibsen must have felt strange at Bjørnson's last appeal that he pray to his "Lord and Savior" to be freed of his violence, pray, moreover, as a child. In this same letter (December 16, 1867) Bjørnson hailed the Danish philosophers Rasmus Nielsen and Rudolf Schmidt as the battling geniuses of the new thinking that would triumph in their era. Ibsen, however, has just read Brandes' little pamphlet "On the Dualism in Our Recent Philosophy," and he must have approved of Brandes' criticism of the "half-measures" in the philosophy that wished to hold on to both scientific thinking and Christian faith in miracles and dogma. Shortly after, Ibsen himself wrote with scorn of "Rasmus Nielsen's philosophy of compromise." He must have felt it ludicrous when Bjørnson warned him against Brandes on the score that that "there is something misleading in every person who does not center his life on faith in God."

There were lesser points of disagreement as well. In the same letter Bjørnson urged Ibsen to join him in rejecting royal decorations. Ibsen felt that he could not honestly say that he disliked decorations and other insignia of honor, and Bjørnson's disappointment with his answer must have been reported to Ibsen by mutual friends. Thus major and minor differences of opinion fed his distrust, and when in the next year he wrote about his mood in the early part of 1868, he said: "I was feeling like a beast of prey, and I had reasons enough."

To counterbalance the severe criticism of *Peer Gynt* in Denmark were the much more favorable reviews in Norway. In both *Morgenbladet* and *Aftenbladet* there were exhaustive articles, running through two issues, which gave strong praise to the wealth of poetry and ideas in the play. F. Baetzmann, the reviewer in *Aftenbladet,* protested against the Danish critics' attempt "to lock up an author in a particular stall." He did, however, prophesy that readers would eventually tire of polemics and look for "something less polemic-nihilistic, something more straightforwardly beautiful and aesthetically satisfying." Such a reaction had already taken place in Denmark, and this accounts in part for the tone of Brandes' review in *Dagbladet*. *Peer Gynt* is here classified with "those literary products, even more common now, whose purpose is to give us man from his moral underside, and on whose scapegoat-hero all human viciousness is heaped." The particular viciousness that Ibsen chastises, "cowardly egotism in the form of self-deception and lies," is traced back to Goethe and Kierkegaard. Ibsen now condemns as sin the failing which H. E. Schack had described as illness in *The Fantasts (Phantasterne*, 1857). Brandes was tired of this kind of theme: "If the old epigram of the French romantics, 'the ugly is the beautiful,' were true, then *Peer Gynt* would be a work of beauty; but if this rule is somewhat dubious, then Ibsen's new work is a total failure." He admitted that the book "contained great beauties . . . and some great truths," but "beauties and truths are far less valuable than beauty and truth in the singular, and Ibsen's poem is neither beautiful nor true; the misanthropy and self-hate on which it is built make a poor basis for poetry." Brandes caps his argument with the cry: "What wormwood joy can he take in thus sullying humanity! This endeavor must now surely have run its course. Surely this must be enough and will come to an end."

Belittlement of this kind was certainly more annoying to Ibsen than the angry cries from some of the Norwegian nationalists, particularly the language reformers. He had deliberately taken aim at all forms of nationalistically inspired isolationism—particularly in the scene in the hall of the Mountain King, where the slogan is, "Be sufficient unto yourself!" The figure of Huhu in the Cairo madhouse is meant as a satire on the language movement. Ibsen was perhaps not quite fair in his evaluation of the language reform movement as it existed when he was writing the play. Bjørnson was right in saying that the true isolationists were the reactionaries who were then taking over *Morgenbladet*. There was, moreover, little truth in the accusation that leaders of the national movement like Johan Sverdrup, J. E. Sars, and A. O. Vinje were trying to cut the country off from foreign influences. One of the leading voices in the new language movement, Kristofer Janson, wrote two angry articles for *Aftenbladet* on the subject, and concluded with the wish that Ibsen would "soon tire of spitting and scolding off in his own chimney corner." Janson correctly pointed out that Ibsen's ideas of the aims of the language reformers were quite out of date; they were not trying to restore the dead language of ancient Norway, but rather to elevate the living speech of the people to its just position in literature. Ibsen's attitude had been influenced by the language reformers he had known in Bergen who had made efforts to go as far back as possible toward Old Norwegian. Huhu was, therefore, an unfair caricature; nevertheless, it did reflect one aspect of the language controversy of the day, and as proof there were the outcries of protest. Ibsen was prepared. The cries stirred his spirit for battle, and as he felt that spirit grow, he took delight in the strength of his attack.

The controversy over *Peer Gynt* was as lively as Ibsen could have wished. And from the first the play took such deep root in the emotional life of Norway that its phrases have become, as with *Love's Comedy* and *Brand*, the ordinary way to express oneself in hundreds of situations. For the Norwegian people the play has beome just what it was for Ibsen, at once a pet, nicely domesticated, and at the same time an incorrigible brat. The play's genuine poetry has proven Ibsen right. From *Peer Gynt* on the "idea we have in our country, in Norway, about what poetry is" changed from what it had once been.

CHAPTER TWENTY-FOUR

POLITICS:

THE LEAGUE OF YOUTH (1868-69)

In his review of *Peer Gynt,* Bjørnson had written: "It has proven what we already knew, that the closer Henrik Ibsen gets to satiric comedy (or is it farce?), the closer he gets to his true talent." To Ibsen he wrote the same: "If you need to relax, you should let yourself go in a satiric comedy; that's your true bent, and you need only crook your finger, and it will write itself for you." Ibsen replied: "I think I will follow your suggestion to write a comedy for the stage; I have been thinking of the same thing myself." Perhaps this thought was in his mind when he threatened to turn "photographer" and make caricatures of his fellow Norwegians. How far the idea had gotten, or even if it had taken clear outline in his mind is not known. It would be safe to say, however, that at this time it had not occurred to him to fashion his comic hero in the image of Bjørnson himself.

In February, 1868, he wrote to his publisher Hegel: "My next work will probably be a stage play. It will, I hope, not be long before I get down to serious work." At the time, however, he was working on something quite different—the old idea about Emperor Julian. Family problems, however, kept intruding; for example, should he return to Norway for his son's schooling? In mid-May he left for the North, first stopping at Florence and then going on to the Alps where he would spend the summer. By mid-June, probably with the help of Consul Bravo in Rome, he settled in Berchtesgaden, in the southeast corner of the Bavarian Alps. He missed Italy, especially the climate that he had gotten quite adjusted to in four years, but he found the mountain scenery delightful and made many hiking expeditions during his three-month stay. His plans now were to spend the winter either in Munich or Dresden, then return to Norway. After a few weeks in Munich he took an apartment in Dresden at the beginning of October. This would be his home for the next six or seven years; nothing came of his plan to return to Norway.

The outline for the new comedy took shape in Berchtesgaden, and in Dresden he began writing what was to become *The League of Youth*. So complete was his concept of the play that he first thought he could complete the actual writing in three months. Actually it took six, a delay that might have been occasioned by his reluctance to brave a German winter in his study. A more certain explanation is that he was trying to make the play as technically perfect as possible; he was working for the stage, and he wanted the play to be as right for performance as he could make it—and his standards were higher than ever before.

He was determined, as he wrote from Berchtesgaden, that the new play be "completely realistic"—and he added, with a sly twist, as "the heavy Germanic atmosphere dictates." It was not just that he had crossed the border from Italy to Germany; more importantly he had passed his fortieth birthday. Now his self-discipline was greater than ever, the inevitable stamp on his character placed there by years of testing soul and conscience. His experiences would be shaped into works of art; these would be instruments of his ethical will. The inner revolt he felt took form naturally as poetry, yet at his most self-critical moments he felt this poetry to be merely "aesthetics," dreams and self-deceptions, all evasions of the ethical demand. He came to realize more fully that creativity was in fact to be his life work, and that this creativity was valid living and doing. So he threw his whole soul into the act of writing; it was in response to an ethical demand that he hammer out each line with the greatest skill he could master. No more "caprices" now; only a severe discipline in things great or small.

About his new comedy he wrote to Brandes: "I have treated the form with care, and among other things I have performed the trick of getting by without a single monologue, nay, without a single aside." The remark shows the influence of Brandes' *Aesthetic Studies*, which he had read that winter. There he had also read Brandes' essay on himself and in this and other essays he saw more clearly than he ever had the importance to the playwright of self-concealment. The playwright must not be seduced into displays of his own virtuosity, he must let his characters come fully and freely alive and speak according to their own nature. He was trying to break free from old theatrical forms and to achieve dramatic truth—the artist's pursuit of technique was an ethical struggle as well.

The realism of the new play, which Ibsen continued to emphasize, was in marked contrast to the bright imaginativeness of his earlier plays. Not that he intended to limit himself to the photographer's view, as he had threatened in his first anger over *Peer Gynt*. He was obviously using the word satirically, as he had ten years earlier in a theatrical review in *Illustreret Nyhedsblad,* when he spoke disdainfully of those who wanted art "to stand in a photographic relation to reality." On the contrary, everything he had written about the theater from as far back as the *Andhrimner* days insisted that truth in art was not a question of reproducing exact copies of everyday people and everyday events. The play created its own truth, which the playwright and the actor had to make credible to the audience, but that truth was more than specific circumstances, it was life transformed into symbol.

As he worked on the play, anger and indignation stimulated his imagination. The result was a piece of polemic that many were to judge uncomfortably close to photographic realism, even though he kept assuring everyone that it would be "a peaceful play." The new play was a child of the previous one, for its theme was really Peer Gynt, politician. The new hero is a hero of words, a great orator who deceives everyone including himself, with beautiful, fiery phrases and always has his own interests at the back of his mind. He is fantast and egoist at once.

Ibsen wrote that his intention was "to picture a divided, affected individual, a split personality in general." In another letter he said that many of the traits of Attorney Stensgård had been produced, as were those of Peer Gynt, by "self-anatomy." He was quite aware these basic traits were his, especially the "divided personality" with which Stensgård is charged. There had never been peace and harmony in his own soul; there had always been a struggle between desire and ability, and for too long he had served wills and goals not his own. He dreamed and cut himself off from real life. And as he made his reckoning in *The League of Youth,* it was inevitable that this Peer Gynt be a politician, for in politics had come his greatest disillusionment. Dishonesty and irresponsibility were most vividly represented there. The platitudes, the empty hullaballoo of politics had been scorned in the narrative version of *Brand,* but these attacks had not been incorporated into the play. Now they would appear.

Other old themes and feelings found a place in the new work. In 1851 he had used *Andhrimner* (and possibly *Arbeider-Foreningernes Blad* as well) to lash out at speechifying politicians who prattled of democracy and the common man, but never failed to turn tail when action was needed. He had even written a short political comedy, *Norma, or, A Politician's Love,* an opera parody directed mainly at the Liberal leader A. B. Stabell, whom he rewarded with a cabinet post. Another target was the Agrarian leader O. G. Ueland; his peasant

slyness is incorporated into the figure of Old Lundestad in the new play
(Ueland came from the parish of Lund). The description Ibsen wrote
of Stabell in 1851 certainly fitted his concept of the political hero for the
new play. He was "one of those true dramatic characters," mentioned
by Heiberg, who was in fact not a character at all, but a man without
character, one of those "whom one must divine rather than conceive
and who winds up at the end of the play at a place you'd least expect
him to from the way he began."

Further external evidence of the influence of the *Andhrimner* period
on the new play is the use of the paper's printer, N. F. Axelsen, as the
model for Printer Aslaksen. The play echoes the picture of their paper's
future Ibsen and his friends had drawn for Axelsen: "Now things are
going to be stirred up; an end is going to be put to all this . . . all the
big shots are going to be made laughing stocks." And Printer Aslaksen's
forlorn reply, based on his experiences, is also an echo from twenty
years past: "I can't make a living on a good newspaper."

Ibsen went even further back in memory, back to his first impressions
of political activity. In the last year he had lived at home, there had
been considerable conflict over one Herman Bagger, a Danish editor
who had moved to Gjerpen in the 1830's, and had founded the newspaper *Correspondenten* in Skien in 1843. Bagger was obviously using
the paper to get himself elected to the Storting, and he went after the
leading officials of the city and its environs with dispatch. During this
campaign it was revealed that he had transferred an old mortgage to
his name and established his franchise by buying a farm in Gjerpen.
In addition, he had secured his position in Skien by taking out a merchant's license. After a ruthless campaign he succeeded in becoming an
elector in 1844, but won a mere three of the country's 38 elector votes.
In later years he did win a seat as the representative for Skien, the last
time in 1868-69. As early as 1844 he was accused of trimming his sails
to the prevailing wind, and after the labor conflict of 1851 turned more
and more conservative. So many of the details of this old controversy
are suggested by Ibsen's play that it seems certain he had it in mind
when he drew the outline of Attorney Stensgård. Ibsen must have received a clear impression of Bagger during his boyhood at Venstøp, for
the politician and his father were friends then and only fell out in the
year Ibsen left Skien.

There are other Skien reminiscences. The name "Bratsberg," used for
the chamberlain, comes from an old estate near the town where Ibsen
had been inspired to write "At Akershus" in 1850. Making the chamberlain owner of an ironworks was probably suggested by the ironworks

at Fossum. The model for Daniel Hejre was, according to old Skien residents, a bankrupt old merchant named Vibe, noted for his sharp tongue. According to Ibsen's habit of reshaping names, there is a logical substitution of one bird name, Hejre (heron), for another, Vibe (lapwing). From his father he also took details—the ruined speculator who kept up his courage by making sarcastic remarks, a kind of self-deceiver, although a different type from Attorney Stensgård.

But the political windbag who bore the ironic name Stensgård (rock farm) could not have come to life without inspiration from the politicians Ibsen had observed at first hand. The leaders of the Liberal cause had to be the model, for they were most open to the temptations of demagogy. The Conservatives did not feel the need to woo the masses; they had power in their hands and were satisfied. The kind of politician Ibsen needed was to be found among such men as Johan Svedrup, Bjørnstjerne Bjørnson, and Ole Richter, to all of whom he owed a great debt of gratitude. To Bjørnson he was most in debt, but the others had helped him during his first lean years abroad, and had signed the proposal requesting he receive a poet's stipend. But he was not thinking of gratitude when the play took possession of him; he was too delighted with the way his characters took on their own independent life as he worked. If anyone had suggested that he was making Bjørnson, Richter, and Sverdrup look like conniving Stensgårds all, he would have been amazed, and he would have protested as violently as he did a few months after the play appeared. He wrote to Hegel after hearing that Bjørnson had been hurt by the play: "Can this really be true? Surely he can see that it is not he, but his pernicious and 'vacuous' party circle that has served as my models." He was convinced that he had found enough affectation and dishonesty in that circle to more than justify his severe judgment. He was, however, judging and chastising himself, and that he felt more than excused him. He admitted that he had modeled his characters from life—a writer of comedy could no more avoid doing so than any other kind of writer—but, as he said in a letter of February, 1870, "there is a great difference between a model and the finished portrait." He helped himself to what he thought would be useful. He used Attorney Richter's avid pursuit of a wealthy marriage (to which Professor Schweigaard had indelicately alluded in the Storting in 1866), as well as his purchase of a farm in the country to make himself (by his own admission) eligible for election. From Johan Sverdrup he took the flowing oratory and the courting of the farm population.

The outward shape of the comedy is drawn, perhaps unconsciously, from none other than Bjørnson, and Bjørnson recognized this, as his letter to Hegel written the next year, makes clear: "He is an ingrate, and an ingrate is capable of anything. So, watch out!" It is clear that by this time Ibsen felt no responsibility to take Bjørnson's feelings into consideration; he was even ill-disposed toward him, as is shown by his refusal to be associated with the magazine *For Idé og Virkelighed*, once he learned that Bjørnson would be one of the editors. Three months earlier he had spoken favorably about the magazine, but when he wrote in January, 1869, to one of the Danish editors, Rudolf Schmidt, refusing to cooperate in the venture, he said: "I cannot bring myself to work with men who, I know from personal experience, will use the first available opportunity to turn their newspaper and their pens against me." When Brandes told him that Bjørnson had asked him to join the magazine, Ibsen wrote on July 15, 1869, "This has not surprised me; for him there exist only two kinds of people: those he can make use of, and those who can be an embarrassment to him."

There is no complete explanation of this purely personal dislike of Bjørnson, although a possible clue to a source of the animosity can be found in a letter of May, 1870, where he wrote that on a visit to Stockholm in the summer of 1869 he felt he had received "complete certainty" concerning "the dishonorable hypocrisy" that Bjørnson had shown. Ibsen's companion then had been Jakob Løkke, the headmaster and fellow "Dutchman." A member of the "Dutchman" circle may have been the source of the charge made in a letter to Rudolf Schmidt in December, 1869, that Bjørnson had "most infamously abused" him "publicly, before many," and did this "at the same time, perhaps the very day," that he wrote "a long letter full of the most ardent assurances of friendship, . . . all of which can be documented and proved by witnesses." The reference here seems to be to an event that happened in December, 1867, at the time of Bjørnson's last letter, and before *The League of Youth* was begun. What Bjørnson said or what Ibsen actually accused him of having said is not known, but the break seems to have taken place before the visit to Stockholm.

Suspicion and ill temper took the place of friendship, and now Ibsen felt no compunction over borrowing traits for his political windbag from his former friend. In a somewhat obvious bit of sarcasm he even has Stensgård repeat the line that his "Dutchman" friend told him Bjørnson had said: "Have you ever had the capacity to appreciate me?" The question is asked of Dr. Fjeldbo who represents the dry, critical temper of the "Dutchman" circle. A more general point is Stensgård's tendency to invoke the deity on every occasion, and while this was not a habit unique with Bjørnson, few did it with such childish persistence as he. The mélange of the religious and the secular in one man is under-lined even more in the first version, which bore the title, *The League of Youth, or, The Lord and Co.* Stensgård concludes his patriotic speech at the end of Act I with the words: "It is up to us if we wish to rule our little world—Hurrah for the Lord and Co." After the League of Youth is founded, Dr. Fjeldbo greets Stensgård with, "Well, if it isn't the Lord, Jr." Ibsen removed this broad comedy after Hegel objected to the suggestion of blasphemy, and so the play is less patently directed against Bjørnson than first intended. But the whole tone of Stensgård's speech is unmistakably of Bjørnsonian parentage.

Ibsen dated each act when he began and ended, and thus it is pos-sible to follow the work on the play rather closely. He began on Octo-ber 21, 1868, and finished the first draft on February 28, 1869. As he made a clean copy, he decided to make so many corrections and changes that he had to do it over and did not finish until the second of May. Each time he went over the play, it took on more of the flavor of real life; he filled it with memories of the struggles of his day, saturated its language with the slogans and idioms of contemporary politics, some-times taken fresh from newspaper reports or Storting debates. From *Aftenbladet* he borrowed the phrase about "our local circumstances," which the conservatives used to block all demands for reform, and which Richter justly held up to scorn in articles in 1857 and 1859. When old Ueland gave a speech in the Storting on March 12, 1869, which he called his "political testament to the Norwegian people," Ibsen im-mediately put his words into Lundestad's mouth.

There is the feeling of Aristophanes in the recklessness with which Ibsen here, as in *Love's Comedy*, exploits people and events; at the same time he insisted that he had welded all together into a higher, "symbolic" form which would live beyond the present moment. This is why he thought the play so "peaceful," and this is why he insisted to his publisher that it would be as suitable in Denmark or Sweden as in Norway. He went so far as to write, "I doubt that one would find in it any particularly Norwegian expression that will not be acceptable on the Copenhagen stage." Despite this belief in the universality of the play, Ibsen did not object when the Danish actor Vilhelm Wiehe used "the Norwegian accent" in playing Stensgård at the première at the Royal Theatre in Copenhagen in 1870. (The actor who played Bastian Monsen did the same.) Ibsen saw the production in the autumn and thanked Wiehe for his "masterful performance." "Everything was splen-did," he wrote, "and I do not know of any detail that I would want done differently. You have grasped my intention completely, and you

have recreated my idea with the truth of genius." It became a kind
of tradition at this theatre to play Stensgård in Norwegian, and Johannes
Poulsen did so in 1923. Some Norwegians were irritated, but it did not
violate the spirit of the play.

Although politicians of Stensgård's stripe can be found the world
over, it is true to say that he is an authentic Norwegian type, as surely
as Tartarin de Tarascon is Gascon. But what gives *The League of Youth*
its universality is that each character is so vividly and independently
alive that he exists in his own right. Ibsen had never before created a
play with such an assemblage of distinctive individuals—old Lundestad,
Chamberlain Bratsberg, Daniel Hejre, Printer Aslaksen, Monsen, Bastian, Madame Rundholmen — everyone is fully known, but especially
Attorney Stensgård, the hero of words who intoxicates others and himself with his phrases, but never takes them seriously. Ibsen strips him
to the soul, and only fails at the end when he allows the comedy to
degenerate into farce.

Ibsen's contemporaries emphasized the relevance of the play to the
struggles of the day, and it was received as if it were a party pamphlet.
Ten days before it appeared, Bjørnson wrote a friendly letter to Ibsen,
telling him he was looking forward to reading the new comedy, which
he had urged Ibsen to write. But after the play was out, he felt it was
a treacherous attack on all the progressive elements in the country. His
protest took the form of a paean to Johan Sverdrup, hailed as the mighty
leader of progress. The allusion to *The League of Youth* is clear:

Skal Poesiens Offerlund	If the grove of poetry shall not be
for Snigmord ikke fredlyst være,	inviolate from assassination,
er *det* det Ny, som er i Gjære,	if *this* is the new in our time,
da viger jeg i samme Stund.	then I withdraw that very moment.

Many years later he explained what he meant by "assassination":
"*The League of Youth* tried to show our young party of freedom to be
a herd of ambitious speculators, whose patriotism consisted of mere
phrases; more important, prominent men were first made recognizable
and then had false hearts and mean minds and sham societies pasted
on to them."

At the first performance at Christiania Theatre on October 18, 1869,
a few student adherents of the Liberal Party and the language reform
movement whistled. Since this was the signal for a controversy, it
seemed like a joke for the theatre to give Bjørnson's *Between the Battles*
on the evening between the first and second performance. On October
20, a benefit performance for Ibsen, there was a great "whistling con-

cert" in the theatre. At the third performance on October 25 a regular battle between the "whistlers" and the clappers took place. *Morgenbladet*, the conservative newspaper, was delighted to announce that "the Stensgård family" was out demonstrating. Ibsen was equally delighted: "I was prepared for resistance, and I would have been disappointed if it had failed to come." Off in what seemed like another world, he got news of the demonstration; it kept alive in him the memory of his own state of war:

Giftfluen stak,	The noxious insects stung,
det gav mindelser vamle,	bringing sickening memories back,—
Stjerne, hav tak,	Star, have thanks,—
mit hjem er det gamle!	my home is still unchanged!

CHAPTER TWENTY-FIVE

IN FINE COMPANY (1869-70)

I<small>N SPITE OF</small> the controversy stirred up by *The League of Youth* and *Peer Gynt*, they continued the success that had begun for Ibsen with *Brand*. Now there was no Scandinavian writer more in the public eye than he; if Bjørnson had taken the lead earlier, Ibsen was now outstripping him.

Whether he had intended it or not, the last two plays clearly defined the differences between the two intellectual circles in which he had once participated, the progressive Norwegian Society and the conservative "Dutchmen" group. It was with the latter that he was now identified. After *Peer Gynt* and *The League of Youth*, Michael Birkeland himself had no doubt that Ibsen was the greatest of Norwegian writers, even though he was still giving that honor to Bjørnson as late as 1867, after the publication of *Brand*. Ibsen had not intended to make any final choice between the two groups, as is evident from his frequent hints that he was anxious for a reconciliation with Bjørnson, one of the most vigorous supporters of the Liberal *(Venstre)* Party. Bjørnson, too, would have welcomed a reconciliation, but his politics got in the way. An instance of this is the angry resentment he caused when he opposed the erection of a monument to Professor Schweigaard, the leading conservative. No monument to Schweigaard, he said, until one is raised to Wergeland, the liberal.

In the years around 1870, party conflict in Norway reached its first climax in a firm cleavage between Right and Left, Conservatives and Liberals, not only in politics, but also in art, literature, religion, and science. Neutrality was impossible, and Ibsen was judged a Conservative, one of those who had kept his good bourgeois reputation intact. An indication that he was now "acceptable" was his admission to the stage of the Royal Theatres in Copenhagen and Stockholm. In 1869 he sent a play to Dramatiska Teatern in Stockholm for the first time. The arrangements were made by his friend, the recently appointed professor of art history, Lorentz Dietrichson, and on December 11, 1869, *The League of Youth* was played with great success. The première of the play in Copenhagen was delayed for a time by one of the theatre's readers, old Carsten Hauch, who did not like Ibsen's contemporary plays any better than he had the historical ones. Hauch betrayed his lack of understanding of living theatre by accusing Ibsen of having "accustomed himself to an unfortunate fragmentary mannerism, which at every moment seems to chop the speeches into pieces." He rather naively found the play obscure: "One has to be privy to all the methods of deceiving through forged letters of credit and to the secrets of swindling if one wishes to follow the plot and really understand it." He doubted if the Danish audience could manage and concluded that the play "is not at all suitable for the theatre." The director of the theatre was not satisfied with this critique and asked Hauch to think it over. Hauch then replied that if the director thought "the play has a significance as political satire which it lacks aesthetically," he would not oppose the performance, but he made clear that he washed his hands of the whole thing. The play was approved and Madame Heiberg directed it. The first performance on February 16, 1870, was a success.

Ibsen had managed to transfer *The Pretenders* to the publisher Gyldendal and a new edition appeared in the fall of 1870. Once more he sent the play to the Royal Theatre in Copenhagen; Hauch was not consulted and the play was accepted without further ado. The Dane Peter Heise composed music for it and it reached the stage on January 11, 1871. Ibsen was now enjoying the novel experience of having time to think about the actual production of his plays and ways of promoting their success. *The League of Youth* had been submitted to the theatre even before publication; doors flew open for it in an unheard of way. There was a new joyous mood in his letters as he wrote from Dresden on May 28, 1869: "I live a pleasant, carefree life." In another letter three weeks later he said the same thing.

He was beginning to stand on firm financial footing. Each year at New Year's he and his publisher settled accounts like any other businessmen; he was able to put money in the bank, and he had enough to gamble on the lottery. He could afford to live well, to send his wife and child on a vacation, and to travel when the mood seized him. This wellbeing is reflected in a letter to Dietrichson in the spring of 1869 in which he asks his friend to write a short biographical sketch of him for a German periodical: "Don't make me into a poverty-stricken poet any longer, that won't do. Tell them instead that the government and the parliament have put me on salary, that I travel, that I live 'in dem

grossen Vaterlande,' etc." Dietrichson later wrote that when he received
this letter, he did not recognize the handwriting. Ibsen's writing was no
longer in his free and easy style; now he used a firm, strong hand with
strokes that leaned slightly back. It was a handwriting with a will, one
that did not let itself go but worked thoughtfully and steadily. When
Ibsen's portrait arrived three weeks later, it was just as unrecognizable.
He had shaved his beard, leaving only the sideburns; now one saw a
pair of firmly compressed lips and an equally firm and strong chin.
Gone was the careless fellow. He had become elegant, with an expensive
velvet jacket edged in silk. There was nothing of the former Bohemian
here; a stylish gentleman of means had taken his place.

A month later he came to Stockholm. He had planned to move to Oslo
after the winter, but he postponed this move and decided to spend some
time in Stockholm first. When he had finished (except for a clean copy)
The League of Youth, he applied to the Norwegian government for a
grant to spend a year in Sweden studying art, literature, and general
culture. On July 3, 1869, he was given 300 dollars and was in Stockholm
within three weeks.

The first thing he did was take part in the inter-Scandinavian conference on orthography, held the last week in July, where members from
the various university towns met to try to coordinate some rules of
Danish, Norwegian, and Swedish orthography. The Norwegian delegation consisted of Professor Ludvig K. Daa, an old supporter of spelling
reform, the headmasters Knud Knudsen and Jakob Løkke, and Ibsen,
invited as a substitute for Hartvig Lassen. Now that he had become a
Scandinavian writer, Ibsen was eager to join the movement to eliminate
needless differences in spelling for the three languages.

The conference was able to propose successfully the elimination of a
certain amount of orthographic redundancy. The proposals probably
had most effect in Norway, where Ibsen had already initiated a good
deal of reform in his own writing; for example, eliminating double
vowels and silents e's (*ris* for *riis; tro* for *troe*). The conference proposals were intended to bring the written languages closer together,
as in its suggestion that lower case letters be used for nouns, and that
ej and *øj* instead of *ei* and *øi*, *g* and *k* instead of *gj* and *kj* before palatal
vowels. Ibsen readily accepted all these changes and even gave up his
own use of double consonants (*foss* for *fos*). This particular Norwegian
idiosyncrasy could be sacrificed for the greater goal of Scandinavian harmony. Three years earlier he had tried to eliminate all Norwegian
peculiarities from *Love's Comedy;* in writing *The League of Youth* he
had been on guard against them. Common rules of orthography, he felt,

would help him win his desired place in all Scandinavian countries. But as it turned out, he became practically the only writer in Norway and Denmark to use this new orthography which although intended to be generally Nordic became virtually Ibsenite, a testimony to his pan-Scandinavian thinking.

His old dislike for the Swedes was now gone completely. When he again met Count Snoilsky in Stockholm, he told him that his attitude toward Count Manderström's policies was different now than when they had clashed in Rome. Unfortunately Snoilsky had also changed his mind, so they still disagreed, although this did not affect their friendship. Ibsen looked at Sweden and everything Swedish with a friendly eye; nothing troubled his Scandinavian sympathies here. Nevertheless, he did not stay out the year as he had planned; in the summer he sent his wife and son back to Germany for their vacation and then to settle in Dresden again. The trip to Stockholm had lasted ten weeks.

It had been a glorious time. After two months he wrote Hegel: "My stay in Sweden continues to be one great festival; on all sides I find a graciousness and a good will that is indescribable." The reasons were clear. He was portrayed by Dietrichson in *Ny Illustrerad Tidning* as "one of the greatest, if not absolutely the greatest writer of our time." He was introduced to the best society in the capital, artists and book-lovers, the upper class and the nobility, and even royalty. For the first time the elegant world opened to him, and he was grateful and happy as a child. To one who had been at the bottom of the social ladder, it seemed like a kind of restitution to be thus acclaimed by the best of society. He was animated and charming and took everyone by storm. All his life he had yearned for elegance and beauty; to have it now was balm to his soul.

The day before his departure at the end of September, his new friends held their last party in his honor. The greatest triumph came when King Carl XV summoned him to the royal palace and made him a Knight of the Order of Vasa, his first order. He was not at all averse to getting more such honors. After leaving Stockholm he made a brief stopover at Dresden. His ultimate destination, however, was the Suez Canal, since King Carl had appointed him one of the two Norwegian delegates to the elaborate dedication ceremonies by Ismail Pasha, the free-spending Egyptian khedive. The other delegate was the Egyptologist J. Lieblein, the same man who had damned *Brand* as a piece of insanity. In spite of his blindness to poetry, Lieblein was a pleasant and liberal-minded person with whom Ibsen quickly made friends. Ibsen associated mostly with the Danish contingent, particularly the literary historian Peter Hansen. He was honored to be included in the delegation and fascinated by the opportunity the trip gave him.

At the beginning of October, the khedive's guests assembled in Paris. From that point the khedive was to pay for the festivities even though he had had to borrow money. They took the steamer directly from Marseilles to Egypt, where the stay was, as Ibsen wrote home, "one grand royal festivity," graced by "a hospitality with the opulence of a fairytale." He was with the first fleet that sailed through the new canal to the Red Sea in the middle of November. He also sailed up the Nile as far as the first cataract, seeing mighty temples, obelisks, and pyramids. He finally made the personal acquaintance with the Sphinx he had not had when he wrote *Peer Gynt*. He saw a dead culture, its mighty past buried in the sands, and at the same time he saw the power of new life, not only in the canal itself, but in the warships of powers great and small. The opening festivities at Ismailia were "like a tale from the Arabian Nights." To his brother-in-law J. H. Thoresen he wrote, "You might be interested to hear that in Ismailia I was presented to and spoke with Abdel-Kader, and in Luxor, the Empress of France."

In the beginning of December he was back in Paris, where he stayed a fortnight at his own expense in order to see the art treasures; he returned to Dresden in mid-December. A year later he wrote, "The stay in Egypt was the most interesting and instructive period in my life." He had kept a diary on the entire trip, as he planned to write a series of descriptions of the journey. Nothing came of this, but the fragment he did write indicates that he was mainly interested in contemporary conditions, particularly the contrast between the past and the present.

The only shadow these happy events cast was the possibility that he would not get the order that had been promised to all the delegates to the ceremonies. After a year he wrote to King Carl's influential master of ceremonies to remind him: "This honor," he wrote, underlining the word, "would be most flattering to me, and at the same time it would be of the greatest value to my literary position in Norway." The order was Turkish, and thus the khedive had to get the certificate from Constantinople, which caused the delay. It finally arrived in May, 1871, "the star of a Commander of the Medjidie Order, a splendid object," as Ibsen wrote to Hegel.

For the first half of 1870 he remained in Dresden, trying to get down to work after five whole months. It was not easy, for his mind was crowded with many thoughts. On March 8 he wrote to J. H. Thoresen, "As for me, I am fully occupied with literary work, revising my travel notes from Egypt; a collection of poems and a new edition of *The*

Pretenders will also appear. Besides, my trip has brought down on me a disturbingly extensive correspondence." He also had promised articles to *Morgenbladet* and *Dansk Tidsskrift,* but nothing came of them.

A letter written to Hegel on December 14, 1869, right after his return, shows that he was thinking deeply about "the plan for a new serious drama of contemporary life," no doubt the same plan he told Thoresen was complete in a letter on July 6. He thought he would do the writing during the coming winter, but as late as April, 1870, he admitted that he had "not yet gotten any farther than the outline." In the brief "Notes" written at this time, the serious drama had become a comedy, with a conflict between a man and a woman. There are some hints of the theme that was to become *Pillars of Society* or even *An Enemy of the People.* Then it all came to a standstill.

His first task was to finish the revisions for the new edition of *The Pretenders,* most of which consisted of changing to the new Scandinavian orthography. He also took heed of Brandes' criticism that certain speeches sounded more like platitudes than psychological character analysis; for example, "To love, sacrifice all, and be forgotten, that is woman's saga." Such speeches were now made more personal. On the whole, he felt he could say, "I found the dialogue so solid, the speeches so consistently built on one another, that I could not improve it or tighten it up further." Choral passages had to be written for the performance at the Royal Theatre and some cuts made. To produce anything original, however, seemed impossible. "It looks as if it will take a long time to arrange my travel notes," he wrote in April.

He had been thinking of another trip north in the summer, particularly to Copenhagen, no doubt in connection with the production of his plays at the theatre there. He did not get started until July 19, the day war broke out between France and Germany, and stayed in Copenhagen until the latter part of September. Again he thought of going to Norway and again nothing came of it. The reception in Copenhagen may not have been as overwhelming as that in Stockholm the year before, but here, too, he was received as the great writer. His special patron was publisher Hegel, foremost in the Danish book trade, with the title of Chancery Councillor. He was invited to all the best homes, including that of Mme. Heiberg. Again he was deeply appreciative of all the kindness and friendliness he met. He decided then that Denmark should do him the same honor as Sweden; he wanted the Danish order, the Dannebrog. Before leaving he wrote to the lawyer Anton Klubien, whom he knew from Rome, asking him to help. Both Andreas Munch and Welhaven had been made Knights of Dannebrog;

Ibsen thought he deserved it more. "I must tell you," he wrote, "that I am downright greedy for any recognition I can get from Denmark. You can't imagine the effect in Norway." He joked a bit about his "honette ambition," but he was serious.

He thought more of it when he was home in Dresden; he grew afraid that he would be "regarded as simply an ordinary vain person." He was troubled with the feeling "as though I had gone out into the street unwashed. I can't bear this; I must get back my self-respect." On January 8, 1871, he wrote to Klubien and asked him to drop the whole thing. But by that time the mills had started grinding. Klubien had spoken to Mme. Heiberg, who had spoken to Minister of Justice Krieger, who in turn had taken up the matter with Minister of Culture Hall. On February 13, Ibsen received by mail "an exceedingly beautiful document." He was a Knight of Dannebrog. "I can never," he wrote Hegel, "be grateful enough to the men who have arranged this! Now my countrymen will think my collection of poems twice as good as before!"

It is important to notice that when Ibsen spoke about his orders he always had in mind their effect on the Norwegians. At home they should know that he had arrived; they could scorn him no longer. And in his triumph they also shared. It was not just a question of snobbery that made him want as many decorations as possible; a decoration was a kind of weapon to serve his people and to protect his spiritual freedom. With an order on his breast he could enter bourgeois society on equal terms; he was one of them, or better. With this freedom he could wage his battle against society with more security. Even a Turkish decoration could be useful. One of his friends from Rome, the art historian Fr. G. Knudtzon, wrote forty years later in his memoirs of Ibsen's need for recognition: "Ever since his youth in Bergen and Christiania he had felt it an evil fate that had deprived him of entrée to fine society; until this misfortune was remedied during his visit to Copenhagen in 1870, it was painful to him to feel so deeply about being excluded from the elegant upper classes. The visit to Mme. Heiberg's and his 'Balloon Letter' to her express his delight in and gratitude for some of his most exalted moments." Knudtzon was in many ways a skillful psychologist, and although there may be a touch of malice in this description of the "outsider" by one who had been on the inside from his youth, he hit on an essential point. It is undeniable that Ibsen's social ascent during these years, along with his triumphs as a writer, freed him from the inferiority complex that had ridden him from his youth. A decoration was an outward sign of this victory.

The consequences for his writing—whether a gain or loss is a matter of opinion—were greater calm, greater confidence. The inner struggle quieted, yet without bringing any evident change in his view of life or society. On the contrary, in the following years, his opinions would be more revolutionary than ever. Still he was not sure of himself. In March of 1870, he warned Brandes against "friends," because of all the things one did not do out of consideration for them. He had thought that he had behind him the years of suffering on this account. Even so, he did not dare return home; he could write with freedom only in "exile."

CHAPTER TWENTY-SIX

THE CALL FOR FREEDOM (1870-71)

THE LAST PLAYS had been nurtured on his own inner conflict; now Ibsen felt a profound need to gather his strength, to come to terms with himself, to put his vision of the great problems of life in sharp focus. It would take further inner conflict to bring him to that peace of mind for which he longed.

When he returned to Dresden in September, 1870, signs of the war were all around him: "The city is full of the sick and wounded; at any hour one is certain to meet military funerals or new transports bound for the military hospitals. There are also some thousands of French prisoners.... The country suffers dreadfully; all activity has virtually come to a halt; boys half-grown and middle-aged fathers are called up and sent to France; nearly every family is in mourning.... It is frightful to live here." This first impression did not improve with time. He was terrified to see Prussian "state machinery" and repression turn men into numbers and subject the world to tyranny. His son Sigurd was attacked in school when he refused to take Germany's side; his schoolmates tried to beat him into compliance. As those principles he hated seemed to take power, it was only natural as he wrote to Brandes, that "the world events occupy a great part of my thoughts." Inevitably, his writing suffered.

"In these turbulent times I cannot collect my thoughts," he wrote to Hegel. He struggled to shape the play on a contemporary theme that he had planned the year before. As soon as he returned from Copenhagen, he wrote Hegel that it "has now shaped itself sufficiently in my head so that one of these days I can start to lay hands on it in writing." Nothing happened and in December he was writing to Brandes: "One morning some time ago my new play dawned on me clearly and force-fully," and filled him with "exuberant joy." But "the mood did not last," and nothing was written. He tried to pass the time by writing an opera about Sigurd the Crusader, one of Norway's medieval kings. He wrote to Hegel for the volume of P. A. Munch's history that dealt with Sigurd, or else for Snorri Sturluson's *Heimskringla* from Norway. (Oddly enough, Bjørnson had thought of the same theme at this time.) Ibsen had already spoken of the idea with the Danish composer Heise that summer in Copenhagen. He worked out a plan for a five-act opera, but nothing came of it and he never mentioned the outline again.

In the midst of these efforts to start work again came certain events that forced him to turn his thoughts inward, to think of himself and the ideas he lived by. His new friend, Peter Hansen, wrote and asked him to contribute an account of his spiritual development to an anthology of Nordic poems. After three weeks Ibsen wrote, on October 28, 1870, a survey of all his work, adding the very important evaluation that they had all grown out of experiences that were internal and spiritual. Another occasion for this kind of self-analysis was the result of a plan to publish a collection of his lyric poems. Jakob Løkke had spoken about this in the summer of 1869 and had later offered to get copies of all the poems printed in various newspapers as far back as 1849. Early in 1870 Hegel proposed the same idea (he was then publishing a collection of Bjørnson's poems), and Ibsen agreed. Since his collection could not appear at the same time as Bjørnson's, he had to postpone the idea until the following fall, and it was actually not until early in 1871 that he got started.

In the meantime world affairs brought his views on life in general to a new testing ground. The most crucial event was the victory of military power in the Franco-Prussian War, at the same time the revolutionaries in Italy had seized Rome from the Pope. To Ibsen this meant that politicians had control of the city and had taken it away from "us human beings." What made the whole affair so intolerable was that until this time Rome had been the only city in Europe free from "the political tyranny of freedom." "All that is delightful—the spontaneity, the disorder, the filth—will now disappear; for every statesman born down there an artist will be lost." At the same time he heard that Johan Sverdrup, the leader of the Norwegian Liberals, had joined forces in that year's election with Søren Jaabæk, the Agrarian leader and his "farmer friends." This meant that the rabble, the "plebs," were taking over; here, too, was the hand of the politician.

Such things made him fear that modern civilization was on the way to destruction. He thought about what he had seen in Egypt and concluded that he stood "on the ruins of a broken dream." In Dresden he felt as captive and hemmed in as the Frenchmen in Paris; one had to go up in a balloon to think freely. Thus at Christmastime 1870, he sent out his "Balloon Letter to a Swedish Lady" (Ballonbrev til en svensk dame), calling to account the forces that were gaining the upper hand. Although the piece takes the form of a jocular account of his Egyptian travels, it carries his serious reflection on the fearful parallel with modern society those ancient ruins had suggested. He asks himself why the civilization of Egypt is stilled forever, while that of Greece is alive in our own day. His answer is that:

Hvor personligheden mangler,	Where personality is lacking,
hvor ej formen i sig bær	where the form does not bear in itself
hadet, harmen, jublen, glæden,	hate, anger, ecstasy, joy,
pulsens slag og blodets skær,	the pulse's beat, the blood's throb,
der er hele herligheden	*there* the whole truck's
kun en benrads tørre rangler.	but a skeleton's dry bones.

And now? Now we are again standing:

lodret over Faraonen.	right above the Pharaoh.
Atter er kong Gud på tronen,	Again King God is on his throne,
atter flyder bort personen . . .	Again personality fades . . .
Atter rejses pyramiden	Again the pyramid is built
Som produkt af hele tiden . . .	the product of the era . . .
Hvor egyptisk hver og en	Egyptian-like one and all
fuger ind sin lille sten	fits his own little stone
på dens plads i helheds-formen!	into its place in the whole!

Just so was the German advance on Paris. Who was victor there? No great personal hero, no ideal, only "the regiment, the squadron, the staff." The free individual had vanished.

Ibsen would not share in the process that took this course; he revolted against the repression of the spiritual in both peace and war. He refused to believe that this was true progress:

Tvivlen kommer lindt til orde:	Doubt will lightly lift its head:
er det rigtig stort, det store?	are the great things really great?
Ja, hvad gør vel stort et værk?	Well, what makes for true greatness?
ikke værkets store følger,	Not the consequences of an act,
men personen klar og stærk,	rather the person, sharp and strong,
som i værkets ånd sig dølger.	who lives within the spirit of the deed.

No poetry, nothing spiritual could grow from the victory of the machine; thus he could assert his own hope in the face of German armed power. He had, after all, seen a far more significant victory in the celebration at the Suez Canal, "the spirit's hope of life."

under skjønheds-lampers brand	mid flames from beauty's lamps
styre frem til morgenrøde	advancing to the rose dawn,
på sejlads mod løftets land.	sailing to the land of promise.
Thi mod skønhed hungrer tiden.	For beauty our age is thirsting.
Men det véd ej Bismarcks viden.	But Bismarck's vision sees it not.

In a letter to Brandes on December 20 he said the same: "The old fairytale France has been torn apart; when the new factual Prussia has also been torn apart, we will in one leap be in the age of the future. How ideas will come tumbling down around us! And it's about time.

Everything we've been living on up to now is merely crumbs from the
revolutionary banquet of the last century, and that fare has been chewed
and chewed long enough. We need a new content, and a new insight
into our ideas. Liberty, equality, and fraternity are not the same things
they used to be in the days of the late guillotine. The politicians don't
understand this, and so I hate them. These people want nothing but
particular revolutions, revolutions in external things, in politics, etc.
That's all just piddling. What really matters is the revolution of the
human spirit."

In Stockholm in 1869 he had discussed these ideas with the young
Swedish politician Adolf Hedin, whose dreams were as big as Ibsen's,
but who wanted to create freedom through the workings of practical
politics. Hedin called Ibsen a reactionary when he refused to join in
the day-to-day activity of the politicians. In reply Ibsen wrote the poem
"To My Friend the Revolutionary Orator" (Til min ven revolution-
staleren"):

Jeg går ikke med på at flytte brikker.	I won't play at moving chessmen.
Slå spillet overende; da har De mig sikker.	Knock over the board; then I'm with you.
. . .	. . .
I sørger for vandflom til verdensmarken.	You furnish the deluge for the world.
Jeg lægger med lyst torpedo under arken.	I'll gladly torpedo the Ark.

He demanded a radical reshaping of intellectual life, the creation of a
race of independent human beings through the restoration of full
spiritual freedom. Every man has within himself a calling which he
is duty-bound to fulfill. In 1870 he had written to the young Norwegian
lady who had ventured to write a kind of sequel to *Brand:* "The important thing is to remain true and faithful to yourself. It is not a question
of willing this or that, but of willing what you must do because you
are yourself and cannot do otherwise. Anything else leads to falsehood."
This will to self-realization gave life its importance to him; thus he
mourned the loss of what he called "true freedom" in Rome — "the
splendid craving for freedom itself." "For myself I must say that the
only thing I love about freedom is the struggle for it; I do not care for
the possession of it."

The constant struggle for freedom, the endless effort to reveal the
true self, these were the sources of spiritual exaltation, in art and in
poetry, in all true culture. The future would depend on the creation of
poetry out of action, on recasting into art the conflicts of the day in such
a way that art became a meaningful force in the life of the people. This
was Ibsen's true religion; he believed it because he believed in him-

self. The same theme is expressed in the poem "Without Name" ("Uden navn"), written to King Carl in Stockholm in 1869:

Mer end livet, mine herrer,	More than life, gentlemen,
er en drøm, som ej fik liv.	is a dream never brought to life.
Den er lig det digt, jeg spærrer	It is like the poem I lock
ind i sjælens staengte kærrer;	within the barred cell of my heart;
løve-vildt det hugger, snærrer,	with lion's rage it slashes, snarls,
kræver nat og dag mit: bliv!	demanding night and day to be!

His own life work consisted of turning "dreams" into poetry, and he measured his life in terms of his poetic ideal. In *Love's Comedy* he had indicted the morality of his contemporaries as "lies"; in the poem "The Death of Abraham Lincoln" he had condemned the whole rotten fabric of society. All his recent work held up his ideal demands against petty, everyday human cravings.

Brandes demanded a fuller explanation of the revolutionary ideas Ibsen had expressed in a letter in December, 1870. Ibsen was somewhat reluctant to debate with one as trained in philosophy as Brandes, but he began to clarify his views in the draft of a letter written on February 17, 1871. Feeling, rather than strict logic, took the upper hand. He was extremely irritated by the tinkering of political reformers; all that he wanted was freedom for the individual. He had learned by heart the teaching of Goethe:

Nur der erwirbt sich Freiheit wie das Leben	Only he gains life and freedom
der täglich sie erobern muss.	who daily must conquer it anew.

In speaking of the opposition between particular "freedoms" and true "freedom" he was taking as his slogan words that had been used by both Voltaire and Karl Marx, although he did not know it. His interpretation was his own, in that he rejected all the "freedoms," all work for civil rights in the state. "The state is the curse of the individual. — — The state must go! That revolution I will join. Undermine the idea of the state, set up free consent and spiritual kinship as the only important basis for union,—that is the beginning of a freedom worth something. —Yes, my dear friend, it is simply a question of not letting yourself be frightened by the venerability of tradition. The state has its roots in time; it will reach its climax in time. Greater things will fall; all religion will fall. Neither moral concepts nor art forms have any eternity in store for them. How much must we really hang on to? Who can guarantee to me that 2 and 2 are not 5 up on Jupiter?" Some of these ideas were in his mind when he wrote *Brand,* and he had issued the same threat to religion: "All that is created has an end in store." His revolutionary thinking seemed to have grown ever more emphatic.

But when one turns to what he wrote during this year about people who had actually revolted against tyranny, the effect is rather puzzling. He criticized the French as "a revolutionary nation without self-control or discipline." He advised "restraining the rebels" among the actors at Christiania Theatre. "Vae victis," he wrote, "was the motto of the ancients; it should be said today as well." He spoke about the "internal dissolution" toward which Sverdrup and Jaabæk were leading the Norwegian people, and came out in support of the conservative government: "I support it with my pen and all my talent." His only reservation was that the government was not severe enough: "People who let Jaabæk and Bjørnson run around loose are fit for jail themselves." The respect for the state and the demand for strong government cannot be reconciled easily with that hatred for the state he proclaimed elsewhere. It would not be useful to try to systematize these casually spoken paradoxes into a political theory. He had no system at all. What lived within him were the contradictions that had made such an impression on the people in Stockholm. They had expected the author of *Brand* to look like a grim, unworldly ascetic; instead they met an elegant, gay man of the world. In actuality, Ibsen was the most bourgeois individual imaginable, a born conservative. The revolution was entirely internal in his thoughts. He bowed to the mighty while lighting a bomb under them. The conflict in his soul made him hate and worship the same thing. He was anchored firmly to ordinary life, but his ideals and dreams reached far beyond that. This contradiction within him made him the great enigma of his age, an explosive force in intellectual life, a conscience for society. He could be all these things because he was above all a poet, a dreamer, and a visionary.

CHAPTER TWENTY-SEVEN

A GATHERING OF POEMS (1871)

As HE LOOKED BACK on his work, Ibsen recognized that it all represented the visible sign of the struggle to release his inner life; it was this understanding that guided him as he selected and polished his earlier poems for the new collection.

He had thought of such a collection from time to time. In 1850 he considered publishing his Grimstad poems under the title "Miscellaneous Poems," a title which aptly characterized their lack of unity. He eventually rejected every one of the poems. Further plans for a collection were made in 1857-59 and again in 1863, but nothing came of these either. But now the time had come, and when the copies made by Løkke arrived he threw himself into the task with zest. For nearly two months he worked day and night, selecting, rejecting, and reworking the old verses. By February 25 he felt the work finished, but since there was still some editing to be done, the collection would not appear before the end of April.

To Brandes he wrote: "It has been an accursed job to work my way through this thicket of attitudes I finished with long ago. All the same, taken together they do make a unity." When he sent the book to Minister of Justice Krieger, with thanks for the good will shown him, he wrote: "The book contains poems from the most varied periods of my writing career. There are many contradictory things in it, and a great deal that I can no longer accept; but it is all part of a continuing development."

He did not give the reader much help in tracing the course of that development. The poems were not arranged chronologically but according to a completely arbitrary scheme; moreover, some of them were rewritten to yield a different meaning. The first poems from Grimstad were missing, since the manuscripts had been lost in the 1864 auction —he would probably have made little sense of them now. In their place he resurrected from his papers a dozen later, unpublished poems and wrote two or three new ones. It is remarkable how few poems he found

good enough for the collection; of the 55 garnered, forty had been previously published. The collection of 1871 is a slim volume and although
he was fastidious in his choice, a few of the poems are of minor
importance.

As he was completing the collection in April, 1871, he wrote:

Prosa stil er for ideer,
         vers for syner.
Sindets lyst og sindets veer,
sorg, som på mit hoved sneer,
         harm, som lyner,
fyldigst liv jeg friest skænker
just i versets lænker.
	Prose style is for ideas,
	         verse for visions.
	Heart's joy or heart's woe,
	sorrow that snows upon my head,
	         anger that flashes,
	to these I give fullest life freely,
	precisely in the fetters of verse.

It is somewhat difficult to reconcile this statement with the fact that he
wrote so few spontaneous lyrics in his life. By far the greater number
of his poems were written to order, for festivals or special occasions,
and not to satisfy any inner compulsion. It is true that into some of
these occasional poems he had poured so much of his deepest feelings
that he felt they could be included in a collection tracing his inner
development. But the greater part of these verses was left in oblivion.
The early plays had exhibited a rich vein of lyricism and contained
many songs, but by 1871 this period was over, and the lyrics he wrote
after this do not materially add to the collection. At only two or three
periods in his life had he felt the need to express his feelings in lyric
poetry. In his first year in Oslo (1850-51), before he had clearly understood that the drama would be his medium, he wrote the first, and perhaps the best, of his lyric poems of ideas. He certainly did not think
that prose was the only "style for ideas" then. During some of the
Bergen years (1853-56), he created a more emotional lyric, at the same
time as he was writing *The Feast at Solhaug* and *Olaf Liljekrans*. Perhaps this "lyric seizure" (to use Holberg's phrase) can be traced to his
love affair with Rikke Holst. During the next Oslo period he wrote two
major poems, "On the Heights" (1859) and "Terje Vigen" (1861), besides writing *Love's Comedy,* but there were no shorter lyrics until his
first years in Rome (1864-65), and these were followed closely by *Brand*
and *Peer Gynt.*

The short lyric was obviously not a form that fitted his needs or his
genius, but the poems he did compose in this form are extremely important, since they give us a more intimate glimpse of his inner life
than many of his plays. A number of them have, moreover, an intensity
that make them enduring masterpieces.

Five poems from 1850 were included, and one of them, "Fiddlers"
(Spillemænd) was placed at the beginning of the collection as a kind

of thematic argument. He made virtually a new poem of this, and one can measure the growth and transformation of his inner life in the twenty years between the first and final version. The poem was taken from a longer romantic-patriotic piece, "A Saturday Night in Hardanger," and compressed from nine to four stanzas. Ibsen's mastery of the art of concentration and formal modeling is evident here; more significant revisions are seen in the handling of the theme. The original romantic image of the water-sprite is now charged with symbolic value, and everything is used to emphasize the suffering that has made the fiddler an artist, i.e. that made Ibsen a poet:

fossen gru og sange veg aldrig fra mit sind.	the terrifying music of the waterfall has never left my soul.

(Can this be an echo from his childhood in Skien, "the city of the waterfalls," whose screaming sawblades he was to recall in his memoirs?)

The third poem in the collection "Building Plans" (Byggeplaner), shows a similar reworking of the theme to emphasize the poet's sacrifice of happiness in love. In the 1850 version Ibsen had humorously suggested that poetic visions would occupy only a small wing of the poet's dream palace, while love would be installed in the main hall. Now the palace itself is too small for the poet's visions, and love has fled. Being a poet and only a poet is both a joy and a sorrow; life has become what he described, albeit ironically, in the poem "Storm Swallow" ("Stormsvalen") from the 1850's:

Det er en færd mellem flyven og
    svømmen,
som midt mellem himmel og afgrund
    drømmen.
For tung for luften, for let for
    bølgerne—;
digterfugl, digterfugl,—*der* har vi
    følgerne!
	It is a course midway twixt flying and
	    swimming,
	hovering like a dream twixt heaven
	    and abyss.
	Too heavy for air, too light for wave—;
	poet-bird, poet-bird,—*such* are the
	    consequences!

Only two or three of the poems take us back to the thoughts and feelings of the youthful poet. One of these, "Bird and Bird Catcher" (Fugl og fuglefænger), is reprinted with minor interesting changes in structure. The theme here is the terror of being enclosed in a cage from which there is no escape. "Afraid of the Dark" (Lysræd) suggests that the poet can be brave and overcome his fear only if he is alone in the dark. There is, perhaps, a slightly ironic and therefore unusual note in the last stanza, added to the poem in revision:

Men fattes mig nattens foerværk, jeg ved ej mit arme råd;— ja, øver jeg engang et storværk, så blir det en mørkets dåd.	But if I lack the sheath of night, I know not what to do;— If I ever perform a deed, it will be a deed of darkness.

Other poems from 1850 were reshaped in a manner suggesting the liberation of his genius he had experienced: "The Eider Duck" (Ederfuglen), had been a picture of the cruel exploitation of the bird, leading to its death, but now ends with the bird's escape, "To the south, to the south, to a sunny shore." "The Miner" (Bergmanden) had been revised in 1863, and its spirit of resignation had been changed to one of defiance. Defiance and escape had been Ibsen's own saga, and when he finally reached his sunlit land, he wrote poems that described how he had once slaved under the will of others. In Rome he composed "The Power of Memory" (Mindets Magt), on the theme of the bear who is tortured into dancing to his master's merry tune. In "The Gorge" (Kløften), originally a part of the cycle "In the Picture Gallery" from the 1850's, he pictures himself daydreaming, only to have the rainbow drops turn into the rustling of dry leaves and brush.

The most striking quality of these and other poems in the collection is their sparse, epigrammatic form. They are not preoccupied with emotions, but rather with events: the miner is busy hacking ore out of his mountain; images of the past rise over the fortress of Akershus; the swan sings its dying song; young people tour in the mountains; King Oscar is dying; the elderly lady tells about her faith. The moment of action is then clinched with a sharply edged epigram. The dramatic author is revealed in even the shortest poem.

It is more than a matter of form; the poems are actually dramatizations of conflict. Their purpose is not to touch or move the heart, and they do not rely on sentiment, although the poet can concentrate a powerful mood in a few compact lines of simple words that cling to the memory. It is our wills that the poem strives to touch, stimulate, and strengthen to action. Filled with faith in an ideal, a dream he wants to realize, the poet believes in poetry as the truest, greatest force in life. For this he will do battle, although between his dream and the reality of life there is a powerful tension. Dreams must be turned into deeds. The theme is constant in poems and in plays, "More than life, gentlemen, is a dream never brought to life." The poet's deeds are poems, and thus he gives mankind what makes life worth living, the spirit that rules all free men and gives their actions beauty.

Ibsen's creative impulse was a profound ethical imperative. He had to use his best talents to make his poems as formally perfect as possible. The result was a truly sculptured classicism. It may be surprising that there was so little color in the poems; after all, the poet was also a painter and he placed great emphasis on the value of color in stage sets. He had, however, a deep aversion to any kind of ornamentation for its own sake; he preferred to have each noun speak for itself and create the complete image. The only poem he wrote with a broad palette is the narrative "Terje Vigen," and there are similar effects in the poem "Distress at Sea" (I Havsnød), which was a kind of preliminary study for "Terje Vigen." These poems may have been influenced by the more colorful style of his Grimstad days. All his later poetry was essentially poetry of ideas, where images were symbols of ideas and needed little ornamentation. But even when he does not use color words, he sometimes achieves the same effect through the use of terms from nature that suggest them, as in the vivid descriptions of "Mountain Life" (Høifjeldsliv):

I dalen er der sommernat	In the valley there is summer night,
med lange skyggers slør.	a veil of lengthening shadows.

Or in the poem "At Port Said" ("Ved Port Said"):

Østerlands dag	The orient dawn
over havnen glittred.	glittered over the harbor.

When he reshaped "At Akershus" in 1863, he supplied more color by making the fortress "white," by giving the king a "red glow to his eye," and by letting blood flow through the story.

Ibsen worked meticulously and consciously to find the most effective word. In revising his poem he did not seek to obliterate the original inspiration, but rather to intensify it; for example, in "A Birdsong" ("En fuglevise") he altered "she stared quietly before her" ("hun stirred stille for sig hen") to simply "two brown eyes shone" ("to brune øjne lyste").

Two of the new poems were expressions of gratitude. One of them, "Letter in Rhyme" ("Rimbrev"), written in the first week of April, 1871, was a note of thanks to the Danish actress Johanne Luise Heiberg for what she had just done for him and his plays in Copenhagen and, more importantly, for all the "beauty-filled" memories of the times he saw her in 1852. He envisions her "mystically bound to Denmark" by all she had created in the theatre, and his poem, with its glimmering image, has kept her memory alive. In his imagination he describes her in roles that he has never seen her play. The source of his greatest joy is that in this "beauty-starved" age there still persists so much that is beautiful, that an art is being created that is so rich it will be a glorious legend, a myth for the future. In Fru Heiberg he also saw the embodiment of an ideal for which he was fighting more vehemently than ever before, the achievement of harmony between poetry and personal freedom.

The other tribute went to his wife, Suzannah, in a poem called quite simply "Thanks" (Tak). Her image had not appeared in his writing since *The Vikings at Helgeland* and *Love's Comedy,* and none of the poems he had written to her during their engagement were included in the collection. Nonetheless, he felt she was the solid support on which he leaned in work and in controversy. Thus he could say:

Hendes slægt er de skiftende skikkelsers rad, som skrider med viftende flag i mit kvad.	Her race is the motley pageant of figures who stream through my song with banners triumphant.

And just as he gave thanks to his wife, so he came to acknowledge his debt to his homeland; the very publication of his poems indicated that he considered himself a Norwegian poet. He seemed to underscore the point by including his polemic verses of 1859, written in defense of Norwegian theatre art and poetry, his "open letter" to H. Ø Blom. Moreover, in revising the old poems he made extensive use of colorful, expressive words of Norwegian origin. And at the end of the entire collection he placed the poem "Burned Ships" (Brændte Skibe), written on the theme of his own exile. He had had to escape from the cold land of snow to sun and summer, but although his country had wounded him deep within his soul, at the same time its chastisement had strengthened him. It could still raise "loathsome memories," but it still held him too fast for him ever to escape. His longing for home is given shape in words that are perhaps the most moving of the entire collection:

Mod snelandets hytter fra solstrandens krat rider en rytter hver eneste nat.	To the homes of the snowland from the shores of the sun there rides a horseman each single night.

CHAPTER TWENTY-EIGHT

THE THIRD EMPIRE:

EMPEROR AND GALILEAN (1871-73)

Once the collection of poems was finished, Ibsen could get down to work on the drama about Julian the Apostate which he had planned for so long. Although this represented in one way a return to history after the bold depiction of contemporary life in his last plays, yet, as he explained to his new friend, the English critic Edmund Gosse, "the historical theme I have chosen has a closer connection with the movements of our time than one could have foreseen." He added, "I consider this an absolute necessity for any modern treatment of so remote a theme, if it is to hold our literary interest." He could say with complete truth that "I infuse into this book part of my own spiritual life; what I portray I have lived through myself, in other ways." The work was a necessary labor for him now.

The idea had come to him one summer day in Genzano in 1864, when he heard the Roman historian Ammianus Marcellinus' account of Emperor Julian. There is no record of his first conception of the drama, although Julian probably appealed to him as another of those great but defeated rebels — Catiline, Skule, Magnus Heineson. Moreover, Julian had revolted against the Christian church, the most powerful spiritual force in his day as well as in Ibsen's. He saw his life and his struggles mirrored in the story of the man who had been Christian, but who had lost his faith and turned to pagan philosophical mysticism to find expression for his spiritual needs. The same kind of struggle, to find a faith to live by, constantly engaged Ibsen in his first years in Rome. One result of this conflict had been *Brand*. Now his own problem appeared to him in broad historic perspective in the revolt raised by Julian; through Julian he could dramatize the essential forces that shaped man's life and thought on the stage of world history. It was a drama that was repeated from generation to generation.

He realized that it was a theme of vast dimension, and it grew as he thought more deeply about it. "Why can't one write a drama in ten acts?" he asked Lorentz Dietrichson, who had read *Ammianus* to him,

"I simply don't have enough room in five." As he worked with what he called "uncontrollable joy," he borrowed books from the German library on the Capitoline hill, and made excerpts from old and new historical accounts. He had the theme so completely in hand that he thought he would be finished by the summer of 1865.

Then Brand forced Julian aside, and it was not until the spring of 1866 that he could return to the historical drama. At that point the newspapers reported that the Dane, Carsten Hauch, had just published a long tragedy entitled *Julian the Apostate*. Ibsen assured Hegel that this would not make any difference to him: "I am convinced that my conception will be fundamentally different in every respect from his." To avoid confusing his ideas, he made up his mind not to read Hauch's book, but he could hardly have done himself any damage; Hauch's play was a feeble work of the man's old age, which failed to dramatize any of the conflicts in Julian's personality and settled for proclaiming the virtues of religious tolerance. It is more likely that whatever influence Hauch had on Ibsen came from his play on Emperor Tiberius, written in 1828. Hauch analyzed the causes for paganism's failure and depicted some of the psychological factors in the emperor's behavior. Ibsen did, however, profit greatly from a number of articles about Julian written by the Danish church historian A. Listov for *Fædrelandet* in May, 1866.

He spent the summer in Frascati, where he felt he could see all the history of civilization spread out on the Roman plain below. But the "beast" Julian would not stir, and soon *Peer Gynt* drove everything else out of his mind. Again, in the first months of 1868 he returned to Julian, and again the research and planning came to nothing. "Why can't one write a tragedy in nine acts," he asked his Danish friend Vilhelm Bergsøe. "Why not nineteen?" Bergsøe replied with a laugh. Ibsen turned indignant eyes on him: "No nonsense! I want to write it in nine acts." Bergsøe suggested that it would be rather too long to play in the theatre, " unless you divided it." "Yes . . . I could divide it," Ibsen said, and fell silent.

When he left Rome later that spring, supposedly for a brief time, he left all his drafts behind. In the years that lapsed before his return all his old notes had vanished. He did not pick up the old theme immediately. In March, 1869, he wrote to a young Dane who also wanted to write about the emperor: "I am not thinking about Julian at the moment and do not intend to tackle him in the near future; I rather dread the man and the idea." But later that spring he changed his mind. In June he told Hegel he had begun and asked for copies of the

Fædrelandet articles on Julian. "I feel that [the theme] has developed sufficient clarity, and once I begin I will rush on." In a letter a few days later he wrote, "It occupies all my thoughts . . . I think something great can be shaped from this material." Again nothing came of it. He went to Stockholm and to Copenhagen and made various other plans; it was another two years before he could bring himself to think about Julian again. In these years he went through such a process of self-examination and evaluation that the resulting maturity of outlook enabled him to come to terms with the "beast" Julian.

Many years later Ibsen recalled that living in Germany had had "a transforming power" over him. He had, in fact, lived in Germany during a period of tremendous intellectual and spiritual ferment. Although the old Hegelian philosophy was still dominant in Norway, in Germany its rule had been broken by new, radical thought. Schopenhauer had begun with his proclamation of the power of blind will in life; Haeckel and Carl Vogt were challenging the established systems of psychology; Lotze's philosophy of idealism sought an understanding of man's spirit on an entirely different basis than the old system of thought; Fechner's "psycho-physics" was turning psychology into a natural science; Marx was redirecting the labor movement on the basis of a materialistic and deterministic theory of history; Büchner's pamphlet *Kraft und Stoff* lay down an entire program for the transformation of society. It seemed as if all traditional belief would collapse as philosophical materialism, the spawn of the new scientific movement, gained more and more adherents.

How much of these new writings Ibsen read, if he read any, is not known. When Brandes chided him for not having "mastered the present state of science," Ibsen defended himself by saying that "what we laymen do not have as knowledge, I think we have in some degree as intuition or instinct." If he did not have first-hand acquaintance with the seminal works of the day, he did have an uncanny ability to sniff out the vital, challenging ideas in circulation. As a diligent newspaper reader he kept abreast of latest developments. In Dresden he usually attended the Literarische Gesellschaft, where he spoke with well-informed people and heard lectures and discussions on contemporary issues. He must certainly have taken part in the heated controversy aroused in 1869 by Eduard von Hartmann's *Philosophie des Unbewussten*. Hartmann's attempt to unite Schopenhauerian pessimism with the theory of evolution, to combine the idea of blind will with faith in a chain of causality, aroused violent antagonism and provoked discussion which the many reprintings of the book kept alive. Ibsen would be particularly interested in Hartmann because in his analysis of essential problems of the human condition he emphasized new psychological interpretations. Ibsen himself was deeply concerned with the need for greater psychological orientation in literature in general and particularly in the drama.

It was Hegel's belief that he had successfully wedded Christianity to philosophy. When the problem presented itself to the Danish philosopher Rasmus Nielsen, he tried to solve it by letting them live apart, independent but with equal validity. This solution of the conflict proved impossible for Ibsen, and he saw his attitude vindicated when natural science and the higher criticism turned their weapons on traditional Christian beliefs. As the struggle raged on all sides, it seemed as if the religion that had dominated Europe for a millennium and a half would be finally overthrown. In this setting, the theme of Julian's revolt took on a contemporary interest; the conflict between the old and the new faith broke out again. For Ibsen the conflict was a personal one as well, a conflict he had experienced and not yet resolved.

The correspondence with Georg Brandes during these years helped to keep alive Ibsen's dramatic plans for *Julian* and the problems associated with them. His relation with Brandes dated back to the time when he had first heard of the young critic from his friend Ludvig David in Rome, and had read his polemic against Rasmus Nielsen. Brandes' articles on *Brand* and his artistic development convinced Ibsen that here was a man who understood the nature of his personal struggle, a man with whom he could discuss his problems as a spiritual kinsman. He created for himself an image of what the critic looked like, so that even though they had not met, he could confide in this image. Brandes' battles were similar to his own; he wrote that he could very well have used Brandes' controversy with Rasmus Nielsen as the subject of *Brand*. When Brandes had recovered from an illness in the spring of 1871, Ibsen wrote (May 18) that he never really felt his friend was in danger: "One doesn't die in the first act; the great World Dramatist needs you for a leading role in the 'Haupt-und-Staatsaktion' he is no doubt readying for a very esteemed audience." (A "Haupt-und-Staatsaktion" was a German spectacular of the seventeenth and eighteenth centuries; Ibsen's allusion to the contemporary scene involves a play on the German words.)

Ibsen's own "Haupt-und-Staatsaktion" was in preparation. He had written to Brandes about the coming "revolution of the human spirit" where Brandes "will be one of those who leads the way." The tribute moved Brandes deeply, and in January, 1871, he answered in a poem

that describes his past lonely struggle and his happiness now that he
has found a comrade in arms:

Broder! jeg fandt dig. Hvad gør det mig vel	Brother! I have found you. What does it matter
at du en Høvidsmand er uden Lige	that you are a chieftain unsurpassed,
mens jeg ble skabt til som Væbner at krige,	while I was born to fight as your squire;
sammen vi høre med hele vor Sjæl.	we belong together with all our hearts.
Ja, vi til Oprør vil Aanderne kalde!	Yes, we will summon the souls to revolt!

In mid-summer 1871, they met. Brandes stopped in Dresden on his
way back to Copenhagen and immediately called on Ibsen. "He pressed
me to his breast so that I almost lost my breath," Brandes later wrote.
Morning and evening they were together, talking about the literary and
cultural controversies in their homelands. They enjoyed one another's
company tremendously. Brandes reported that Ibsen "was full of plans
and hopes, besides being highly belligerent. 'You annoy the Danes and
I'll annoy the Norwegians,' he called smilingly to me as we parted."

It was about this time that Ibsen began to work seriously on *Julian*.
Brandes, meanwhile, was preparing the lectures that made up the first
volume of *Main Currents in European Literature of the Nineteenth
Century*. He wrote to Ibsen and urged him to "raise up the standard,"
and on September 24 Ibsen replied that his new play, whose first act he
had just finished, "will be a kind of standard," on which is blazoned a
philosophy that will be "the final verdict on all that is now winning
through to victory."

Brandes' lectures, given during the fall term at the University of
Copenhagen, aroused great controversy, which persisted when they
appeared in book form early in 1872. In analyzing the psychological
temper of European cultural life in the first half of the nineteenth
century, Brandes had created a fully dramatized portrait. The lectures
urged a new literature whose program would be to "take up problems
for discussion," in a new freedom both intellectual and political. *Brand*
is used as an example of a literary work that made an ethical demand
in an era that was dull and without will.

Ibsen was working on the second part of the play (which he later
combined with the first), when he began to read Brandes' book. As a
rule he read little while working on a play, but now he devoured
Brandes' words. The book took possession of his thoughts and left him
sleepless. "A more dangerous book could not have fallen into the hands
of a pregnant poet. It is one of those books that create a bottomless
gulf between yesterday and today." Thus he wrote to Brandes. This
was revolution, and he was a part of it.

Brandes returned to Dresden and spent the month of September in almost daily talks with Ibsen, who tossed off all his wildest paradoxes about the kind of freedom people ought and ought not to have. He even delivered a panegyric on the cat o' nine tails, which "frees people of unhealthy fat." But about the play nearing completion he was less talkative. "I never write a line," he said, "without asking myself: what do you suppose Georg Brandes will say about that?" But it was too late to change anything in the play except minor details, and it would have to stand as it was, regardless of Brandes.

Ibsen's many notes on the play testify to the number of sources he investigated in order to enter fully into the life of Julian and his era. Since he could not read Greek (he had failed to pass it in his university entrance examination), he had to read those sources in translation. He could struggle through Latin, but in order to avoid mistakes read his chief source, Ammianus, in German translation. He read David Strauss' famous 1847 lecture, "Der Romantiker auf dem Throne der Cäsaren," but commented to Hegel, "the book has nothing but reasoned madness, and that I can make up myself. Facts are what I need." These he found in a brief study by August Neander, *Ueber den Kayser Julianus und sein Zeitalter* (1812, reprinted 1867), and in J. E. Auer's *Kaiser Julian der Abtrünnige im Kampfe mit den Kirchenvätern seiner Zeit* (1855). As late as July he was still writing to Hegel for more histories, particularly the articles by Listov in *Fædrelandet*. And about this time he discovered excerpts from Albert de Broglie's great work, *L'Eglise et l'empire romain au IVe siècle* (1859), partially reprinted in the Danish *Nyt Tidsskrift for udenlandsk theologisk Litteratur* (1861-62).

When he began writing on July 24, 1871, he thought of opening the play with a prologue, an idea no doubt suggested by the prologue in Goethe's *Faust*. Faust was certainly on his mind as he wrote of Julian, for both were great seekers and doubters, struggling for faith. He may also have been influenced by Paludan-Müller's dramatic poem *Kalanus* of 1854, which although more discussion piece than drama, does present a struggle between two religions, one earthly and the other spiritual. A prologue would be useful in making the meaning of the conflict clear. It would be set on "the firmament of the bottomless chasm" which the gospels fixed between the rich man and Lazarus. On one side is light, darkness on the other. And on this battleground where spirits struggle, Julian took his stand. Ibsen discarded the prologue, but an echo of it remains when Julian describes himself at the final moment of choice as hanging "over the firmament of the bottomless chasm, — midway between light and darkness."

From the time of *Brand*, Ibsen too, had been poised here; through

Julian he would try to find a resolution to the conflict. The hero of his
new play would be carried into the center of the battle when, shaken
by anguished doubts, he would feel himself rejected by God, a prey
to the evil growing within him. The young prince lives in jeopardy from
both Emperor and Christ; both would exclude him from life, both
would stifle his yearning for life. But life is what he longs for, life and
the self-won truth that can reconcile it with dogma and faith. The
imperial court and the world around him offers the prince a revolting
contrast between faith and deeds. When he turns from the Christians
to Libanios, the pagan philosopher, he finds the same brutal contrast.
He cries out for a new revelation.

At this point Julian is led from inner turmoil to religious ecstasy
through the mystic, Maximos. The new revelation given him is in reality
the theme of Schopenhauer's philosophy. The will to live is the eternal,
unceasing force that drives all existence, blindly, uncontrollably, unless
curbed by a self-denial that will finally achieve Nirvana. Thus Julian
dreams of being absorbed in the Eternal, of dying away from life. His
resolution is the paradox expounded by Schopenhauer: "What is, is not,
what is not, is." The dichotomy between thought and action is healed,
at the same time that the two antithetical forces in existence, the enjoyment of life and the negation of self, are harmonized.

In his ecstasy Julian goes far beyond Schopenhauerian formulations;
he wants to unite in himself all the forces of life, to bring forth himself
a new race that would never know the struggle between them. The
first draft of the play, more than the final version, suggests the mysterious relationship between religious and erotic ecstasy. In a similar manner, the first draft defines more clearly the nature of the opposites that
are to be harmonized; the opposition of "spirit" and "matter," corresponding to the "spirit" and "flesh" of Saint-Simonean thinking, are to
"leaven," to permeate one another, and become ultimately one. Heine
had called the contrasting elements "Hellene" and "Nazarene"; in Ibsen
"the empire of matter" was "founded by the serpent in the tree of knowledge," while "the empire of the spirit was founded by the great prophet
of Nazareth." What he did was to personify the elements as his dramatic instincts bid him: the Emperor, Lord of this world; the Galilean,
Lord of the other world. Thus the story of Emperor Julian became the
drama of *Emperor and Galilean,* and its theme became the harmoniza-
tion of opposites in "the third empire . . . the empire of the great mystery,
the empire to be founded on the tree of knowledge and the cross,
founded on both because it hates and loves them both."

The concept of the third empire, the new world that would arise from the conflict between the opposing forces of life, had its roots in the same neo-Platonism which Libanios and Maximos cultivated and which played such a great role in all the medieval Christian mystical writings that describe man's yearning for something beyond his ability to comprehend. At the beginning of the nineteenth century the idea was again taken up by philosophers; it entered quite naturally into Hegelian dialectics, which seeks to reconcile opposites in a higher unity. It even found a place in the positivism of Comte. Ibsen's theme was, therefore, one that many of his contemporaries had meditated on. He had already expressed his longing for a harmony between the joy of life and the majesty of God in *Brand*, when the hero shuts down his church and in his great speech tries to lead his people into a conflict with life itself.

Brand had failed to create this harmony, and thus Ibsen was forced to have Julian ask: how does man reach the third empire? This brought him up against the mystery of will: was it man's will, or a will over man that ruled? Did man have a choice, after all? The new science forced this question on man more urgently than it had ever been asked before; hitherto it had been primarily a religious issue, concerned with man's relation to God, now it applied to every facet of life. The battle was being joined between the philosophy of determinism and the impulse of the human spirit to believe in its ultimate freedom. While working on the poetry for his collection, Ibsen wrote a short poem that seems to have the same inspiration as the play on Julian. The poem is about Judas, who also stood between heaven and hell and who served both. "But what if Judas had not willed to act?" is the question with which the poem ends.

The answer Julian receives is that he must walk "the way of freedom," which is the same as "the way of necessity." When he sees the hand write on the wall, "You shall and you must," he rebels: "I defy necessity! I will not serve. I am free, free, free!" But the question remains: can he will anything but what must be willed? Although Maximos, who proclaims the third empire, announces his belief in the unity that harmonizes freedom and compulsion, Ibsen admitted that he himself became "something of a fatalist" while working on the play. Julian's tragedy is that by his struggle he advanced his enemy's cause; against his will he becomes an agent of a greater force (as von Hartmann has said all men are). But though an agent of external forces, he must bear responsibility for all he does.

The intellectual content of *Emperor and Galilean,* its psychological investigation of the problem of freedom and compulsion, is concentrated in the first three acts, the section of the play Ibsen intended as an independent unit with the title "Julian and the Friends of Wisdom." This was to be followed by a section called "Julian's Apostasy," in which he deserts first emperor and then Christ. A third section, "Julian on the Throne," was to depict his fruitless battle against Christianity.

This plan for the drama was not adhered to. At the end of September, 1871, he wrote to Hegel that *"Emperor Julian* is moving ahead rapidly," although he had only one act ready and it would take three more months to finish the next two. He worked feverishly, gripped by an inspiration that made him experience at a profound level the doubts as well as the ecstasy of Julian. The power of these acts is undeniable and despite the over-elaboration of some scenes and the occasional weakness of diction, it is unquestionably authentic drama, filled with passion and vitality, with an overwhelming psychological crisis. But he had said all he wanted to about the decisive questions in Julian's life; the rest of the play would be largely a work of duty, with the further inhibition of having to follow his historical sources. The second section, also in three acts, was written in the spring and summer of 1872. (It was a warm summer, but as he wrote to Hegel while working on *Peer Gynt,* "the warm season is my best working time.") He spent six months on the play, with an interruption in mid-July for a vacation, during which he toured Bohemia for a few days before settling down in Berchtesgaden in the Bavarian Alps, as he had done in 1868. He remained here until the end of August and in this period wrote a final copy of the second section.

He had been obviously fatigued when working on this section, but when he started on the third section in Dresden in September, his energies returned. Now he reviewed the completed second section and realized that he had not created a unified drama. With renewed inspiration he threw himself into the task of revising it, particularly the first two acts that described Julian's battles against his Germanic enemies and the treachery of the Emperor—in no fewer than seven separate scenes. Losing nothing of significance, he compressed all this into one act and one scene, with a resulting increase in dramatic intensity that stemmed largely from substituting psychological development for external influences on the characters and the action. The revision is a remarkable example of how a series of events could become honed to intense drama in Ibsen's mind.

With this section now reduced, it could be joined to the first in a single five-act play, *Caesar's Apostasy.* A rich inner tension and vivid character portrayal are evident in the play, particularly in Julian himself, who stands forth in all his dynamic inner contradictions. The theme of the last two acts is not as profound or as compelling as in the first three. Julian is no longer driven to find an answer to the enigma of life; it has become simply a question of whether he will summon the courage to fight for his vision of life. The play ends with his revolt, it is true, but that irrepressible yearning we once saw in Julian is gone. Doubt has plagued him for so long that he has lost "his full-blooded will." The goal of Julian's ambition has narrowed; he does not raise his standard for "the third empire," for a harmony between emperor and Galilean. He is now for emperor against Galilean, a lesser man in will and in vision.

The play that now became the second part of the whole drama reveals this weakening even further, not only in Julian's character, but in psychological content and artistic development. The section was written in a bare three months, from November 21, 1872, to February 13, 1873, according to the plan previously worked out. Unfortunately, Ibsen never revised this section, but built a five-act play along the same lines as the play he had just rejected as without unity. Every act is broken into three or four separate scenes, with the result that we never see Julian in intensified conflict, concentrated into great moments. Instead we watch a slow, agonizing struggle from scene to scene, particularly unsatisfying in the first three acts. Julian himself suffers such loss of stature that he fails to win our sympathy as he had at the beginning.

In writing the first section of his drama, Ibsen had been rather free in his handling of historical sources, using his critical judgment to develop a sympathetic portrait of Julian. In the last section he appears to have accepted every derogatory statement made against Julian by his enemies; at times he seems to credit Julian with even more evil practices than his Christian contemporaries did. The Julian of the first part is a greater man than objective history will credit; the Julian of the second part is not only less of a man than history allows, but his inner life is shallower and less interesting. He begins to worry more about himself than the cause he is advocating; he seems to be playing a role in which the thing he pretends to be is more important than what he truly is; he wants to be flattered and made much of. The Julian who had developed a hatred for all books and "learning," now speaks constantly about transforming the world with his own books. He speaks a good deal about wisdom, but we are given very few insights into the nature of this wisdom.

While there is an actual historical basis for this reversal, Ibsen did not utilize it in the play. He seemed to be trying to mock himself in this portrait of Julian. In his moments of ecstacy, he too felt his books would set the world on fire, only to admit later that it was all "aesthetics" and no action. Julian's growing misanthropy may also have a personal basis. Brandes' conversations with Ibsen in the fall of 1872 convinced him that "his contempt for people was limitless," that he was "an aristocrat in the extreme," and that he had welling up in him "forty years of bitterness and hate." Because the misanthropy is diffused throughout the play it does not strike the reader forcefully, but its presence must be acknowledged.

In the end Julian breaks free of the quibblings of the learned and sets off to conquer the world anew. The pace of the drama gains momentum from this point, reaching a climax in the struggle in which Julian falls. To explain this fall is, in effect, the reason why Ibsen wrote the second half of the drama. As with all the other rebels he had portrayed, he wanted to show that Julian's defeat had already taken place within. Although he becomes emperor in full control of his domain, doubt rules him. His words echo from Ibsen's own heart when he says of Christ: "Anyone who has ever been under His sway—he will never break entirely free." Ibsen shows Julian's gradual realization that he could not win, that he must acknowledge within himself the mighty spirit that possessed these Christians, these Galileans, and made them willingly embrace death. Above all he wanted to show how Julian still tried to shut his eyes to the truth, only to be torn apart by the struggle to believe and deny at once. He gives up, too mean a man to carry on the struggle he had begun; Nemesis overtakes him.

When he began serious work on the play, Ibsen had written to his publisher: "The affirmative philosophy the critics have demanded from me, they can find here." While working on the play and after completing it, he insisted that it was his central drama, the embodiment of his philosophy of life. Years later in 1887, in a speech given in Stockholm, he spoke of his program for the future, which was concentrated in one phrase, in *Emperor and Galilean,* "the third empire." He believed, he said, "that an age will soon dawn when the political and the social will cease to exist in their present form, but out of both concepts will grow a unity which will, at least for now, contain all the prerequisites for mankind's happiness." In the same manner he believed "that poetry, philosophy, and religion will fuse into a new category and a new vital force, about which we who are now living can have no clear conception." All he had said about the third empire is underscored here; it is impossible to derive any clear conception of it. And he himself was perhaps the one who understood it least. Viktor Rydberg, the Swedish poet whose own battle against Christianity began about this time, reported that one of his friends had asked Ibsen to explain the basic theme of *Emperor and Galilean*. The friend was forced to admit: "I never heard Ibsen talk nonsense except this once."

Ibsen was never a philosophical thinker, and despite all the philosophical speculations he had tried to absorb while writing the play, and despite all the ideas that crowd the play, he wanted to let the "philosophy of history" make itself evident in the only way a drama could, through the plot and the characterization. In the letter to Brandes in which he defended himself for not keeping up with the latest scientific thinking, he wrote: "A poet's task is primarily to *see*, not to reflect; that would be especially dangerous for me." He believed that his play gave "the historical truth"; the reader would have to find the "philosophy" for himself. *Emperor and Galilean* does not depict a contest between philosophical systems or an intellectual dispute over doctrines and concepts; rather, it dramatizes a conflict between opposing attitudes toward life and the world, one secular, one religious. Such a conflict must end with a question, or at best a riddle and a hope. Ibsen, himself the battleground where both attitudes joined, would remain the great questioner, asking, asking, but leaving each to find his own answer.

When *Emperor and Galilean* appeared in October, 1873, it did not arouse the same controversy as had *Brand*, *Peer Gynt*, and *The League of Youth*. But if it lacked the vehemence necessary to stir partisans, it could stimulate discussion and interpretation. In lectures and discussions, newspapers and articles, many solutions were offered to its riddles. Most people were inclined to give the play a Christian meaning and regarded the Third Empire as a prophecy of the ultimate victory of Christ on earth. While it is true that the spiritual force of Christianity is pictured with more profound understanding and empathy than is paganism — Ibsen could use himself as a model for the Christians' strength of mind and even for their arrogance—yet the spirit that informs the work is not Christian. The inflexible, merciless world will that makes instruments of Julian and all others is certainly akin to the Hebraic and Calvinistic God, but it bears the impress of the inexorable laws of nature that the new science had made master of the universe. Ibsen bowed before this power, and even if the power was not a transcendent one, there is still something of religious awe in his acknowledgement of its omnipotence. And as he humbled himself, he revolted. He could not blot out the vision of a kingdom where the human spirit would find freedom in the midst of compulsion, a future, close enough at hand for him to feel kinship with, where the human and the super-human would come together and be one. His vision was not clear; all that was clear was the conflict. "What will come of this death-struggle between two epochs I do not know," he wrote to Brandes, "but any-thing rather than what is now: this is all that counts for me." The struggle had begun, and he was happy. But his dream and his longing reached beyond the struggle and beyond the present. It was not a yearning that led one past human existence, placing its hopes in another world; he wanted, on the contrary, to bring the all-mighty, the all-beautiful to men on earth. It was not Christianity, but it was sacred.

CHAPTER TWENTY-NINE

POWER AND GLORY (1873-77)

A YEAR AFTER *Emperor and Galilean* was published, Ibsen spoke to a group of Norwegian students who had come to greet him with a torchlight procession: "At the end of his career, when Emperor Julian watches everything fall to ruin about him, no thought brings more despair than the realization that his only victory is the respectful acknowledgement of cool, logical thinkers; his opponent, on the other hand, is rich in the love of responsive, living hearts." His words echo those of Ernest Renan, who says in his life of Jesus that the Messiah's greatest accomplishment was to win a love that has never died. Ibsen was deeply moved by this passage, and in speaking to the students about Julian's sense of being deprived of love he said that this aspect of the play "grew out of something experienced: its origin is in a question I have asked myself at times down there in my loneliness."

When, in the summer of 1873, he again considered making a trip home, a Norwegian visitor to Dresden told him: "When you return to your homeland, you will be met with an effusive welcome from every class of Norwegian." The sincerity with which this was said moved him and made him believe it might be so, despite the public and the private disappointments; despite the scorn which often greeted his best efforts, he felt the worst was past and his work was being accepted and appreciated. Ibsen's actual reputation in Norway in 1873 was evaluated by Arne Garborg: "He is read with interest, almost with extreme eagerness; his books are sold out with a speed unheard of in our literary world; as soon as it is merely rumored that a new work of his is expected, the public is seized with an excited anticipation that at times comes close to fever, and when the book is out and read, nothing else is spoken of for a long time in any circle that has the least interest in such things."

But Garborg's words, written in a special study of *Emperor and Galilean,* were qualified by the admission that Ibsen was not yet beloved, not truly popular. He was too "negative" for that; he did not charm people with works of beauty. He was a poet of problems. Garborg believed it was a mark of intellectual impoverishment to reject Ibsen on this basis, yet he could not urge people to become partisans of the great writer: "For with all his wealth of ideas, he really has nothing to give; he is himself merely a seeker." Ibsen was a doubter, his works without tranquility or inner harmony; this was the way in which he reflected his era, and it was the very reason why he could not win over the people of his era. One of the riddles of the play is then turned wryly against its author: "What he is, he is not; what he is not, he is." Ibsen was against his age because he was at one with it. But the objections Garborg raised were in fact directed against the very quality that made Ibsen great. He did not make people happy; he shocked them and troubled their conscience, he put society into turmoil by forcing people to test themselves and the truths they lived by. Quite possibly one may come to love his chastiser, if only in retrospect, but winning such affection is not the point. Ibsen turned all the great issues of life into personal dilemmas for each individual; he brought the issues home to each one by embodying them in living characters who fought their battles before our eyes, fought in such a manner that they seemed to be part of oneself. This genius made him a force in his age; what cause had he to demand more of himself than that?

Many events told him of the change in his position over the past decade. When the collection of poems appeared in 1871, the publisher was sufficiently confident to print an edition of 4,000 copies and new editions were soon needed. The large and costly *Emperor and Galilean* was also printed in a 4,000 copy edition that sold out before the end of 1873, requiring a second edition of 2,000 copies within the year. At the same time requests began to come in for works written before *Brand;* a third and fourth edition of *Love's Comedy* appeared in the 1870's, and the play was finally produced at Christiania Theatre near the end of 1873. The new Swedish director, Ludvig Josephson, had more talent for creating a colorful, imaginative production than his predecessors had and scored a great triumph with the play. *The Pretenders* appeared in a new, slightly revised version in 1870 and ran through five editions in the 1870's. Josephson opened the 1873-74 season with a new production of it. It was even performed at the Royal Theatre in Copenhagen in 1871. The second edition of *The Vikings at Helgeland* appeared in December, 1873, more than fifteen years after the first; now a mere three weeks elapsed before a third edition was called for and a fourth and fifth came out before 1880. The play was accepted at the Royal Theatre in Copenhagen by the new reader, the poet Chr. K. F. Molbech, who reversed the decision made by his predecessor J. L. Heiberg in 1858. The performance in February, 1875, was so successful that the frugal director voluntarily doubled the honorarium from 1,000 to 2,000 kroner. In Stockholm it was performed at Stjernström's Nya Teatern in 1875; at the Dramatic Theatre a year later. *Lady Inger of Østråt* was reissued in a new edition at Christmas time, 1874. Ibsen had rewritten it completely, making it more solid in structure and more penetrating in psychology. He also modified its nationalistic aspects by excising all the angry anti-Danish references—thus the battle cry "Out with the Danes!" becomes "Out with the foreign lords! Out with the governor's henchmen!" When his friend, the Norwegian historian Ludvig Daae, still protested about the degree of unhistoric nationalism left in the play, Ibsen placated him by striking the word "historical" from the play's sub-title. Even so, the Danes would have none of it. When it was proposed for the Royal Theatre, Molbech pronounced it so full of bleak pessimism that it would depress the audience and drive all faith in life out of their hearts. Although it never played on that stage, Josephson gave it as a festival play for the author's birthday, March 20, 1875, which was also the twenty-fifth anniversary of the publication of Ibsen's first book. The play also appeared at Dramatiska Teatern in Stockholm in the fall of 1877.

Thus the works of his youth returned to life. In 1874 he made an acting version of *Peer Gynt* and persuaded Edvard Grieg to compose the incidental music. Josephson staged it at Christiania Theatre in 1876, in a tremendously successful production whose brilliant stage design surpassed anything ever done at the theatre. The following year *The Vikings* was also given a magnificent production by Josephson; in October, 1876, the same play opened the new Norwegian theatre in Bergen. It had become profitable to stage Ibsen.

When in 1872 old Riddervold made the refusal of a new travel grant to Ibsen, one of his last gestures before leaving the cabinet, the playwright could say with complete sincerity: "I do not feel my honor in the least affected; the Norwegian Ministry of Church and Education can in no way affect my honor." His position in public esteem was already secure; in a short time he would receive more than enough recognition. In 1873 he served as Norwegian and Danish judge at the art exhibition at the Vienna world exposition. The two summer months he spent there were strenuous but instructive; he worked conscientiously and became aware of the cultural and artistic life of Eastern Europe, especially Russia. While in Vienna, his old desire for a Norwegian order was quite unexpectedly fulfilled; on King Oscar II's coronation day he became a Knight of St. Olaf "for literary services." Two years later the king sent him the "Oscar Medallion" with a letter personally congratulating him on his festival anniversary. In 1877 the University of Uppsala made him honorary doctor at its quadricentennial celebration; he insisted on being addressed as "Doctor Ibsen" after this. He was now more dignified than ever before; the elegant velvet jacket gave way to a long black frock coat that made the girls of Tyrol, where he visited, mistake him for a Catholic priest, kissing his hand and asking for a blessing. Such things amused him, but he was plainly determined to become, or seem to be, as respectable a citizen as possible. Contemplating his hard-won position seems to have given him pleasure; he relaxed from the work on the second part of *Emperor and Galilean* in the fall of 1872 by doodling sketches of his medallions.

He also began to win a following in countries where he could not be read in the original, particularly in Germany. He and the German temperament came to a rapprochement, each on his own terms. Since the war with Denmark over South Jutland, he had felt a deep aversion to Germany, and he detested the reckless power politics played by Bismarck. He did not conceal his opinions, and when his poems appeared in 1871, a German periodical took him to task for his "scornful and mocking words against Germany." Ibsen defended himself by saying that he hated only "ideas, principles, systems," not the German people. His attitude was still that of a pan-Scandinavian nationalist, and when Bjørnson demanded a "change of signals" in relation to Germany, Ibsen attacked him angrily in a poem that called him "the weather-vane" for advocating a policy of "pan-Germanism." It is wellknown that Ibsen did not care for the atmosphere in Germany in those years and that he felt himself a stranger there. But while working on *Emperor and Galilean,* he began to realize how much he owed to the vitality of German cultural life. He had found his way from a "nationalistic" to an "ethnic" point of view, he felt, and was now able to include the Germans in his patriotic sentiments. The production of *Emperor and Galilean* gave him a sense of facing Germany's cultural problems directly. "More contemporary" than he had dreamt it, the play took its place in the new German "Kulturkampf," where the antagonists were church and state, Christianity and culture. He was writing for Germans as well now, not only for Scandinavians and countrymen, and as Germans began to accept his work, his old enmity gradually softened.

In February, 1872, the first German translation appeared, a version of *Brand* by a businessman named P. F. Siebold. But most of the spirit of the play had vanished in translation, as did most of the playwright's personality in a biographical study published by Siebold in *Illustrierte Zeitung*. The first important contribution to Ibsen's German reputation was made by the critic Adolf Strodtmann from Flensburg who, in addition to publishing translations of *The Pretenders* and *The League of Youth* in 1872, wrote enthusiastic and perceptive comments on him in a series of articles on Danish cultural life in *Hamburger Fremdenblatt*. These appreciative essays with some of Ibsen's poetry appeared in book form in 1873 as *Das geistige Leben in Dänemark*. In 1874 and 1876 new translations of *Brand* appeared, the latter version by a man with some claim to being a poet, Alfred von Wolzogen, theatre director in Schwerin. There was now the chance that Ibsen's greatness as a poet would begin to be appreciated in Germany. Von Wolzogen's introduction, which Ibsen thought both honest and well-expressed, compared *Brand* to *Faust* and called it the greatest, most thought-provoking drama since Goëthe's masterpiece.

German interest in the plays raised an economic problem; would translators and foreign theatre directors pocket all the profits, leaving him with nothing but the prestige? Now he began to learn that authorship could be a profitable business as well, and laid the ground for that boast he would make years later that he had been a "good businessman." Since neither Denmark nor Norway had any treaties covering the foreign rights of authors, Ibsen's books had no protection against foreign exploitation. At first he thought that the Norwegian government ought to pay him and other Norwegian writers for what they lost in this way. In 1874 the government agreed to ask the Storting to increase authors' annual stipends from 1,600 to 2,400 kroner, but the agrarian leader Jaabæk, who controlled such matters, succeeded in having the proposal defeated by 53 to 24 votes. This was on May 1, 1875, and Ibsen found it a rather niggardly greeting so soon after his twenty-fifth anniversary celebration. The controversy that had erupted between the government and the Storting convinced him that it was useless to use the government to present his case. Therefore, he turned to the leaders of the Liberal majority in the Storting, first to Johan Sverdrup in 1877, then to H. E. Berner in 1881 and 1882. He succeeded in getting them to introduce resolutions to increase the stipends, but the measures failed. By this time, however, Ibsen had taken other measures to proect himself from loss, and they proved to be much more profitable than any meagre supplement to his stipend. In 1876 he began to issue "original editions" of his works in German, with the aid of Emma Klingenfeld of Munich. First to appear were *The Vikings at Helgeland* (German *Nordische Heerfahrt*) and *Lady Inger*. Since German theatres were beginning to produce his plays and would pay him well when he offered the plays himself, he regretted that Strodtmann had "taken away from him" *The Pretenders* and *The League of Youth*.

Before Ibsen, Bjørnson had been the first Norwegian playwright to win a place on the German stage. Although his stories had appeared in many German editions since the end of the 1850's, and the plays since 1866, including a production of *Between the Battles* by the famous Meiningen players in 1867, he did not win a definitive triumph until 1875 with *A Bankruptcy*, which played at theatre after theatre all over Germany. Coming at a time of economic crisis after a period of brisk speculation, the play became a manifesto for a new realism, a fighting drama that stirred enthusiasm in the young. None of Ibsen's plays that could be performed in German at this time had such fiery appeal; his moment had not yet come, even though both *The Vikings* and *The Pretenders* would be recognized by the Germans after the country's union in 1871 as dramas that spoke directly to their feelings of nationalism.

The Vikings was first, at the Court Theatre, Munich, on April 10, 1876. Ibsen described the momentous day: "The house was virtually packed, and the play was received with thunderous applause. I watched from backstage, and was called out five times. After the performance the literary men of Munich gave an impromptu party for me that lasted far into the night." In another letter he adds: "The next day the same enthusiasm and curtain calls in a full house. . . . The King of Bavaria has sent me a letter of congratulations through his cabinet secretary." In October the play was performed at the Burg Theatre in Vienna and at the Court Theatre in Dresden. In Vienna Charlotte Wolter played Hjørdis, and although she was a great tragedienne in the same style as Laura Gundersen, she felt somewhat insecure in this Norwegian Viking world. She wanted to make clear to herself the nature of Hjørdis's feelings, but she could not understand what Ibsen had meant about the relationship between Hjørdis and Sigurd, or, more precisely, what had happened on their supposed wedding night. She had the director write to Ibsen, who answered that no matter how hard Sigurd had "pressed Hjørdis to his breast" that night, it had not "zum Aussersten gekommen," and that was precisely why she doubted his love. With this hint Frau Wolter was able to create a powerful characterization of the role.

The Pretenders was first played by the Meiningen group, who brought

it to Berlin in 1876 and performed it for nine days beginning on June
6. The Duke of Saxe-Meiningen invited Ibsen to attend the première
and he accepted with alacrity. He was impressed by the "brilliant
splendor" of the production and reported home to Norway that "the
play was received with great applause, and I was called out several
times." The press reception did not please him as much, and being
somewhat suspicious in such cases, he believed that the Berlin critics
envied him his success because so many of them were playwrights themselves. But his annoyance was offset by the Duke's invitation to accompany him back to his palace, Liebenstein, near Meiningen. He remained
four or five days, and on his departure was decorated with the knight's
cross of the first class of the Sächsisch-Ernestinsche house order. The
Norwegian draft of his letter of thanks is extant: "In truth, Your Highness has made me most happy, not only by the symbol of your Highness'
grace and favor given me on my departure, but also by fulfilling a dream
I have long and longingly nourished, and finally not least by the impressions of beauty and truly noble humanity that I received at Liebenstein, a treasure that will enrich me in days to come." The stay at the
Duke's had been "like a beautiful idyll," and the charm of it so intoxi-
cated him that he imagined himself one of the old Icelandic skalds in
springtime longing for the royal courts of the south and living on
memories of them for long after. To him this was a "momentous episode"
in his life, one that would surely be recreated in "a poem," or at least
"permeate" his poetry.

The Pretenders was performed at the end of the year by the Court
Theatre in Schwerin and in Wismar, where von Wolzogen was director.
Thus the play won a place on the German stage, and if the name of
Ibsen had not yet been crowned with glory, the way was prepared.

During this time Ibsen began to attract some attention in England,
largely through the efforts of the critic Edmund Gosse. When Gosse
was on a North Cape cruise in Norway in the summer of 1871, a zealous
bookdealer in Trondheim, H. L. Brækstad, literally forced Brand and
the poetry collection on him. He later said that it was a "happy day"
when he first struggled through these books, and from that time he was
a faithful advocate of Ibsen in England. He wrote about the poems in
the Spectator for April, 1872, and about The Pretenders and Peer Gynt
later that year, and about the other plays the following year. He contributed an entire article on "Ibsen, the Norwegian Satirist," to John
Morley's Fortnightly Review for January, 1873, and proclaimed that
Ibsen had the potential to become a "world poet," whose works would
soon win the "homage of Europe." Gosse translated some of the poetry

and passages from the plays, but the first complete English translation was, strangely enough, of *Emperor and Galilean,* by Catherine Ray in 1876. Two years later the first act of *Catiline* was translated by A. Johnstone, but only in a private edition. With these two unusual choices, one could not say that the best of Ibsen was available to English readers; few paid any attention to him, and it would be years before he made a fitting entrance.

Some tentative steps had been made in the direction of the non-Germanic world. While Mlle. Leo Quesnel's short piece in a French periodical in 1874 was insignificant, there was a good omen in the sympathetic essay on *Brand* which appeared in *Revue bleue* in 1877; the author, Mme. Charles Vincens, better known under her pen name of Arvède Barine, was keenly aware of world literature and would later help to make Ibsen known in France. More remarkable was the appearance of a little book about Ibsen in Warsaw in 1875. Written by Count Lars von Engeström, a Polish critic of Swedish ancestry and a translator of Tegnér, this was the first full-length book about Ibsen published anywhere in the world.

As his reputation grew, Ibsen's happiness and self-confidence kept pace. He now had courage to return home, and in spite of last-minute doubts started out for Norway in July of 1874. Whether this would be a summer visit or the beginning of a permanent stay he could not tell. No matter how much he had heard, he still could not be certain how his own people would receive him.

For two and a half months he stayed in downtown Oslo, leaving for only eight days in August to attend the international archaeological congress in Stockholm with Oluf Rygh—where he no doubt spent more time at the banquets than at the congress. In Oslo he associated for the most part with his "Dutchmen" friends, and was invited to the home of the editor of *Morgenbladet,* Christian Friele. He described his cordial reception in a letter of September 16: "I have been received with extraordinary good-will by everyone here. All the old ill-will is gone now." He refused all public appearances, however, except for the Student Society's procession in his honor on September 10, the same evening he was given such an enthusiastic welcome at the curtain call for *The League of Youth* at Christiania Theatre. Another testimony to the change in attitude was the performance, a few days later, of *Love's Comedy,* which the theatre had once rejected.

During the torchlight procession, the students sang a song written by F. Gjertsen, which had words of thanks for Ibsen and a thrice-shouted "Welcome home!" Ibsen's answering speech was both "an explanation" and "a confession." It was obvious that he felt the need to explain why he had to write as he did; and at the same time to express his deep desire to meet his countrymen on terms of the most intimate understanding. The friendliness he had encountered released emotions long held in check. He had the same feeling of unburdening himself a half-year later when he wrote the preface to the new edition of *Catiline*, the forgotten play of his youth, which he now selected to mark his twenty-fifth anniversary as a writer. Memories of old controversies were awakened by working again on this play, as they had a short while back by work on *Lady Inger*, but now his mood was tranquil and conciliatory. He was at "the conclusion of an epoch" in his life; he may also have felt for a moment that the days of struggle were over.

CHAPTER THIRTY

A CORPSE ON BOARD:

PILLARS OF SOCIETY (1875-77)

T HE FIERY SPIRIT had not been quenched; there was still the same tempest within, driving him on, forcing him to question unceasingly, to probe the surface, to seek a harmony between life and ideal. Ibsen's was a conscience that could never be satisfied with anything less than absolute personal truth.

The visit to Norway was outwardly peaceful, but it sowed seeds of discord. Now he was witness to the growing conflicts, primarily social and political, but also intellectual, that were dividing his homeland. The king's government was arrayed against the Storting, the Right against the Left. In 1872 the Storting voted lack of confidence in the government; the election the following year divided the people into warring parties. Bjørnson had plunged into battle as a leader of the Left; when Ibsen returned home, he was hailed as the poet of the Right. His "Dutchmen" friends were in the vanguard of the conservatives, as were those who had gathered to honor him on his birthday in 1875. The predominantly rightist tone of that gathering was merely emphasized by the presence of Dr. D. C. Danielssen, a Bergen friend who was a member of the Left in the Storting. In addition, Professor Monrad, who eulogized the poet before the Student Society, was placed in the Conservative camp through his connection with *Morgenbladet*. Although the Liberal Erik Vullum spoke of Ibsen before the Artists' Society, the Conservatives still counted him as one of their own. Ibsen, of course, had given them good reason, both in the tenor of his recent writings and in the decidedly conservative stamp of his utterances during the visit. As Jonas Lie wrote in a letter, he seemed to have become a man "who favored completely the stringent social philosophy of Bismarck."

He was, nonetheless, disturbed at being pigeonholed in any party; whatever he was, he was certainly not a party man—that kind of restraint on his freedom he would never accept. He was well aware of the growing Conservative hostility to intellectual freedom, whether in religious or in scientific questions. During the summer there had been a bitter controversy over the appointment of the Liberal J. E. Sars as professor of history. On September 2, Professor Lochmann railed against the contamination of the new philosophy of positivism and materialism at the university; *Morgenbladet* kept its readers on guard against the "freethinker" Sars. Ibsen was alarmed by these friends who seemed to be opposing the very kind of freedom he wanted for himself; he may even have begun to feel that in the agitation of the Socialists lay a promise for a renewal of society.

Conflicts of this nature kept him from feeling entirely at home in Norway in spite of the friendship and adulation he met. Even if he had been able to relax, he knew that he would ultimately have to leave in order to escape the inevitable encirclement and constraint. In the long run there was no place for him in the Conservative opposition; he would have to return to the fight. His position shifted in the next several years. In 1874 he tried to deal directly with the government in obtaining an increase in his stipend, but by February of 1877 he decided to work through the Liberal party leader Johan Sverdrup. In this application he did not hesitate to say that he had no illusions about getting the increase without the aid of the Liberal majority in the Storting. He was not simply time-serving; more and more he felt himself driven to the Liberal cause. He canceled his subscription to *Morgenbladet* and began to take the Liberal *Dagbladet;* there was too much rebellion in him to suffer classification as a "Conservative poet."

And now after almost seven years in Dresden, he decided he had had enough of the city where he still remained a stranger, knowing few Germans and receiving few Scandinavian visitors. He used the opportunity furnished by his son's changing school to move to Munich in the spring of 1875. He enjoyed himself much more here; as he later wrote, "I feel as if I am in my spiritual home." He felt closer to life here, where there were many Scandinavian visitors, especially a group of painters who were shaking off the old romantic tradition and were groping toward new techniques and goals. The literary figures he met here were of a totally different spirit than the men who dominated German political life. With such friends as the writer Paul Heyse he met for "pre-luncheon beer" at Hotel Achatz near Maximilianplatz. Once a week there was a gathering of a small literary group that called itself "The Crocodile"; here Ibsen met the theatrical figure Franz Grandaur, who would do a great deal to get his plays staged at the

Hoftheater. Munich, in sum, offered the kind of people who were interested in the ideas that filled his mind; these same people could, in turn, interest him even more intently in the problems and struggles of the day. The German "Kulturkampf" was reaching a fever pitch at the time when Ibsen moved to Munich, and the spiritual civil war would rage on throughout the '70's. A deeply troubled society was riven still further by the struggle that accompanied the formation of the Socialist party in 1875. Ibsen could not live in the midst of this turmoil without experiencing a reawakening of his social and moral sense.

The stimulus he needed came from Georg Brandes, who thus paid Ibsen back in kind. Ibsen had fed Brandes' thinking and had taught him that contemporary writing had to deal with contemporary problems and take sides in the struggle of the day. Brandes had at first rejected *Brand* and *Peer Gynt*, but after a time he realized that he had actually been frightened by the very pertinence of the works. His incisive exposition of Ibsen's poetic ideals turned those ideals into new stimulants for the poet. Ibsen, in turn reshaped Brandes' slogan about "taking up problems for debate" into: "In our time the function of all literature is to move boundaries." They both felt that in the coming struggle they had to stand together.

In 1874 Brandes invited Ibsen to contribute to a journal he and his brother were planning as a platform for their views on literature and criticism. Ibsen urged him to give the journal as wide a frame of interest as possible and to examine the problems of all Scandinavia rather than just those of Denmark or even Copenhagen. He wanted to participate, but he also wanted to make sure that the work would be as cosmopolitan as possible. The periodical was called *The Nineteenth Century* and by the spring of 1875, when it had been appearing for half a year, Ibsen proposed to "treat the intellectual movements of the age" in a series of rhymed letters to the editor. No more than two of these letters were actually written, but they indicate the direction Ibsen was now taking.

His old pan-Scandinavian feelings revived when he was invited to attend a student meeting at Uppsala, and with much emotion he addressed a poem to them, entitled "To Sweden" ("Til Sverige"). The poem's appeal for unity and its demand that one look forward rather than to the past were not new; what was different was the note of hopefulness, a suggestion that the poet sees signs of the coming new era in which he longs to take part:

Nystemt vår-sang er at høre   New-tuned spring songs can be heard
gennem tiden gå;   sweeping through our times;

Lydhørt er en sangers øre;	sensitive the singer's ear;
nyn må han forstå.	a grace note he must grasp.
Sanger-skaren er de unge,	The singer's chorus are the young,
og i folkets sind	and the singer's task
sanger-hvervet er at sjunge	is to chant a new age
nye tider ind.	into the people's heart.

Shortly after writing this poem he composed the first rhymed letter to Brandes, "Far Away" ("Langt borte"), in which he excuses his Uppsala poem on the grounds that it sprung from "a second's faith between doubts." He actually had no more faith now in the will to action of the youth of his homeland than before; in the festive procession he felt he saw "ghosts of defunct ages and men," and in the vapor of words and incense he saw rising a "mirage of world history." For great deeds there was nothing but a dream. And his will to shake his people out of their trance, to call them to action, burned stronger. The question with which the letter ends is also an appeal:

Når kommer og rusker os op	When will the genius of our
af døsen	epoch come with the word
århundredets ånd med	that will rouse us from our slumber?
århundredets løsen?	

His secret hope was that his "singer's task" would be to serve as the great awakener, and so the next rhymed letter turns from question to outcry. "Why does man make progress so slowly," the young Henrik Wergeland had cried impatiently nearly a half century earlier. Now Ibsen, more anxiously, less courageously asked "Why does our generation seem so strangely melancholy?" His will to remove the obstacles to man's progress was as strong as Wergeland's had been, but he saw that those obstacles lay much deeper in man's psyche than Wergeland had imagined. There was "progress" enough now. "Europe's packet steamship" was streaming full speed ahead, but the inner life did not keep step with this outward advance, and he cried out his chilling warning, "I fear we sail with a corpse on board!" This cryptic statement becomes explicable in terms of Ibsen's other writings. Ever since *Brand* he had been obsessed by the image of the dead past that his age was carrying on its back and was attempting to restore to life. Now, ten years later, the metaphor had taken on deeper significance; it was no longer just the nationalistic daydreams of past glory that hobbled the present, it was the whole burden of traditions, defunct concepts of religion and morality that had no place in modern society, ideas that had no basis in the present. All this was a lie, a force threatening destruction.

As this notion took shape in his mind, he formed it into a new kind of writing, a series of dramas that have been called "social plays," but which should rather be called "social-morality plays." They are not attacks on society or the social order; rather they intend to show how social morality has become perverted to such an extent that it now actually frustrates those moral imperatives that independent, free men must assert. In the dramatist's imagination, moral "ghosts" of all kinds were seen engaged in a mortal struggle with genuine moral truth. As Ibsen's ethical fervor burst forth once again, its range was a far greater area of life than it had been at the time of *Brand.* The poem about the "corpse on board" strongly suggests the theme of *Pillars of Society,* which must have been taking shape in his mind; although the symbol and the dramatic technique were new, the essential theme was a familiar one with an unmistakable connection with his earlier writing.

First plans for the new play go back to 1869 and 1870, right after *The League of Youth* was finished. At the end of 1872 he returned to them, as he was completing *Emperor and Galilean.* He wrote to Hegel that "if all went according to plan" he would write next year "a full-length comedy, whose plan is already quite developed." When he finally began writing in 1875, he told his publisher directly that the play could "in a way be regarded as a counterpart" to *The League of Youth:* that is, while the latter had been filled with negative mockery of those who claimed to be fighting for freedom, *Pillars of Society* would be a positive contribution to the struggle. His notes from 1870 indicate that the basic theme would be "liberation from all narrow conventions, a free and beautiful new life." The "conventions" were the trammels the past laid on man, the very ones he had attacked in *Love's Comedy.* His return to this theme in 1869-70 could be related to his trip to Egypt, where he had seen the past as a dead weight oppressing the soul and hindering free development. (The image of "Europe's packet steamer" may itself be a memory of the voyage.) There is, in any case, a vital connection between his thinking in 1869-70 and the ideas that were shaped into this and later plays.

In the first plan, the play's protagonist had been a naval officer who returns after long service abroad and turns society on its ear. Part of the conflict centers on a young woman who struggles to win her freedom. The spokesman for respectable bourgeois morality is the naval officer's brother, a ship owner surrounded by local officials, whom "small town life has dulled." The revolt against convention is symbolized by a "great riding excursion with all the young ladies of the town," followed by a sailboat trip, both of which "give offence." (There are other sailing motifs, perhaps reminiscences from Grimstad.) It took Ibsen five years to mature his plan, and by 1875 little was left of the original.

This five year process can be seen as a parallel to the spiritual development of Bjørnson, whose first social play, *A Bankruptcy*, was also slowly
evolving during this same period. In 1868 Bjørnson imagined he would
be able to finish his play in a few months; it was not written before 1874.

This parallel development between two writers, otherwise so unlike,
was no mere coincidence. The two plays were rooted in similar personal
and social circumstances. The powerful demand for social morality in
Brand had undoubtedly stimulated Bjørnson, precisely because he
had found the play at first so unrelenting, so inhuman. The need for
truth in life and in writing was as much a part of Bjørnson's temperament as Ibsen's; both men had experimented for years with value
systems that at times proved false, and both felt the collapse of hope.
Their personal crisis was reflected in the outer world. The prosperity
in Norway and in Germany in the 1870's after the Franco-Prussian
War gave way to the financial crisis of 1873. Demands for moral as
well as economic stock-taking were heard in both countries.

Bjørnson led the way. *A Bankruptcy* appeared in March, 1875, and
could not have been more contemporary. Ibsen wrote immediately
to Hegel for a copy of the book, and in June saw it performed at the
theatre in Munich. He received the impetus he needed to return to his
old plan, which he was able to do when he settled at Kitzbühel in the
Austrian Tyrol in August. For the better part of the month, he worked
on a complete scheme for the play, already called *Pillars of Society*.
He began the actual writing in his new Munich home in October.
He acknowledged Bjørnson as both stimulator and mentor of the play,
and when he finished it in 1877 sent him a copy with a friendly note,
although they had had little contact for more than eight years, and
their relationship had, to say the least, been lacking in warmth. But
Ibsen's new tranquility of mind seemed to dispel the antagonism he
felt toward Bjørnson, and he readily acknowledged his genius. The
prose plays *The Editor* and *A Bankruptcy* had helped him find a form
for his new vision and in 1877 he discovered the remarkable drama
The King. As he read and re-read this play, he was more and more
moved by it; for a time he could hardly speak of anything else but the
profundity of its theme and the harmoniousness of its composition. He
had already finished writing *Pillars of Society*, so there is no question of
influence here; what it gave him was a greater feeling of being comrades-
in-arms with Bjørnson.

At this time he gave up writing in verse. With the exception of *The
League of Youth*, all his previous work on contemporary themes had
been in verse, because it seemed to give him the freedom he needed to

express his anger. Now he began to feel a dislike for verse, and he summed up his changed attitude in a letter to an actor, written eight years later: "Verse has been extraordinarily detrimental to dramatic art. . . . It does not seem likely that verse will be used to any extent in the drama of the near future; the poetry the future will aim for will certainly not be compatible with verse forms. The day of verse is over . . . I myself have written scarcely a single line in the last seven or eight years, but have concentrated on the far more difficult art of composing in simple, honest everyday language." It was more difficult for him to write prose; rhythm and rhyme were his natural medium of expression, and he felt awkward without them. In the past he had used prose successfully only when imitating some obsolete style, the old sagas, for example. In verse, on the other hand, he had freed himself from imitating such former models as Oehlenschläger, Welhaven, and Wergeland; the style he had created was a personal one.

This facility with verse can be partially attributed to the growing familiarity Ibsen and his generation had with Danish, the written language of Norway. In 1853 P. A. Munch, who was only 17 years older than Ibsen, said that Norwegians wrote the language with less ease than Danes because they did not think in it and had to channel their thoughts into "words and idioms different from those of speech." By about 1830 a spoken Dano-Norwegian had evolved in educated circles, with so many Norwegian features of pronunciation that, as the philologist Sophus Bugge would later point out, it seemed like a mother tongue. Ibsen's generation no longer needed to translate their thoughts as they wrote; thinking and writing were in the same idiom. Ibsen thus had the great advantage over the preceding generation of writers of being able to work in his own spoken language. Nevertheless, it cost him strenuous effort to achieve complete freedom in writing, particularly in prose where the demands for a natural style are so much greater than in verse. As usual, the appearance of naturalness was achieved with the greatest expenditure of art.

Bjørnson led the way in this struggle for a written language; his goal was to write what he called "bryst-norsk," Norwegian from the heart. The first significant victories for a natural, spoken language in contemporary dramas were won by *The Editor* and *A Bankruptcy*. Ibsen learned from his example and then surpassed him, perhaps because Bjørnson was always being distracted from the strictly artistic aims of his work by the many "errands" he ran at the same time, in this case, nothing less than the total reformation of the whole language. The only task Ibsen set for himself was to write as honestly and as naturally as possible. To this end he pared away everything that was irrelevant or did not contribute to the dramatic development; he concentrated and stylized his idiom so that even casual words were filled with new dramatic intensity. Thus the dialogue in these plays, from *Pillars of Society* on, with growing mastery in later works, echoed living contemporary speech as never before on the stage.

The conflicts of his age gave the theme for *Pillars of Society*. The "corpse on board," the corrupt moral center of the old order, found its living symbol in the rotten vessel that Consul Bernick would send to sea with a slapdash repair job. More than just a symbol, Bernick's act was founded on reality; in 1868 the issue of shipowners' sending rotten ships to sink in order to collect their insurance was raised in the English Parliament by Samuel Plimsoll. Plimsoll finally succeeded, in 1873, in getting a law passed establishing standards of seaworthiness. When these standards proved inadequate, he launched a new campaign, only to meet even stiffer opposition than before—the first law had been passed as a sop to guilty consciences and was deemed enough. In the House of Commons on July 22, 1875, he indicted the shipowners as "murderers" and their political agents as "scoundrels." The law was passed. Plimsoll's campaign was carried throughout the world by the press, and received particular attention in such seafaring countries as Norway. The parliament debate was reported in detail by the Norwegian newspapers, including *Morgenbladet*, to which Ibsen subscribed. The Liberal press supported Plimsoll, and as it happened, *Dagbladet* printed a letter from England on the issue on July 18, 1874, the same day the paper welcomed Ibsen home to Oslo. Another letter appeared on September 1, while Ibsen was still in Oslo. The next day the relevance of the issue for Norway was made clear when the insurance company *Norske Veritas* debated the case of a vessel that had been declared seaworthy, but had sprung a leak at sea and was discovered to be completely rotten. Two similar cases from the summer and fall of 1874 were considered the following September. The report *Veritas* filed spoke of "dishonest working methods," "inadequate caulking," "false bolting." The repairs had simply hidden the conditions, not remedied them. The era of the sailing ship was coming to an end, and in southern Norway a number of shipowners were living comfortably off old ships that foundered all too easily. Ibsen's attack on social morality would, therefore, be rooted in native facts.

If the drama were to have life, it would have to be based on the society he knew from his years at home; while *The League of Youth* grew out of memories of Skien, *Pillars of Society* would be set naturally in Grimstad, the little coastal town where he had spent so many years of his youth. Many things in the play recall Grimstad: names like Vigeland, Holt, Tønnesen, or the vessel *The Palm Tree;* sailing trips and picnics; the theatrical troupe in sailmaker Møller's hall; the actor's wife who stays behind and makes a living sewing and washing while the town gossips; the damaged vessels being repaired at the shipyard; the foreign sailors creating havoc—all these details that give color and life to the play. The first conversation in the play is based on an event in his last autumn there, when the labor agitator Marcus Thrane had come to town and organized a workers' society. The theme of an audacious businessman forging to the top through risky ventures is also a Grimstad remembrance. While he was there Morten Smith-Petersen had returned from abroad; at first he managed his mother's business, but soon was forced to sell out, barely breaking even. He then started his own shipping firm and yard, established a bank and a marine insurance firm, finally founding the *Norske Veritas* company. (He died in 1872, but his sister, Margrete Petersen, a talented woman who taught writing and other subjects, was still living while Ibsen was writing the play.)

These memories were combined with others from later years, among them the railroad projects that were being debated in the 1870's. All these realistic details were used to illuminate the moral conflict that was his major concern. As he dramatized this conflict, he began to charge more and more "lies" to those "pillars of society" he was portraying. At first he planned to let the big businessman work to get a railroad for the town; he would finally cause the man to give approval to the railroad plan only because he has bought up all the right-of-way along the proposed route. This was the commercial "morality" which could be covered up by a distinguished family name. As the character of Consul Bernick developed, Ibsen began to make it appear that the clever businessman had laid the basis for his wealth by a rich marriage, while betraying the woman he loved. Ibsen's next idea was to show how this initial lie leaves a disease in Bernick's soul that spreads and drives him from lie to lie. He lets his oldest friend take the blame for the financial difficulties of his own firm, and in the end is prepared to send a ship to the bottom of the sea to rid himself of this friend and the danger of "scandal." His only concern is to save appearances, even if it means the loss of all inner integrity.

Ibsen was terrified enough of scandal himself to appreciate such fear, but he knew the evil of both the cowardice and the deceit, and his works pass harsh judgment on them. Bernick undergoes such a crisis of conscience that he tears out the lie and confesses it openly just when he is about to, as Ibsen had recently been, receive the honor of a procession. Bernick's inner struggle is the main theme of the play; it climaxes in his battle-cry for the new morality: "The spirit of truth and freedom—these are the pillars of society." It was, however, not to save society that Ibsen proclaimed this ideal; he was thinking more of the individual than of society, and he believed that true happiness consisted in being "true and faithful to one's self." The play is thus resolved on a note of positive idealism, an idealism, it should be noted, that triumphs. The man who has sunk deeper and deeper into falsehood and deceit rises suddenly and makes himself free and honest at once, just as the businessman does in *A Bankruptcy*. The atmosphere of youthful hope and trust that gives this play its bright tone is further strengthened by the fact that the light that searches out the truth comes from America, the image of hope and freedom, where all dream (as the play states) that there is "a loftier sky . . . a freer air."

The dénouement of the play gives it a popular quality that can also be noticed in the appeal it makes to one's emotions. *Pillars of Society* is the only one of Ibsen's plays that can provoke tears. The other plays may upset one's conscience, strengthen one's will, brace one's mind, one may be angered or shocked, contradict or agree; this play speaks directly to one's heart, the others do not. Perhaps he was confident that his words would be able to destroy at one blow all the lies in "this shabby society" or (as one of his drafts reads) "this faithless generation." Lona Hessel proclaims his program in the first act: "I want to let in the air." He thought he could drive out the odor of death from close rooms.

His intention was to put on stage a segment of real life that would have a powerful influence on the present; therefore the form of the play had to be as realistic as possible. Bjørnson's example was some help here, but more important was the work of the German dramatist Friedrich Hebbel. As far back as 1852 Hettner had recommended Hebbel to him, but not until Ibsen began writing realistic plays on contemporary themes would Hebbel be of any use. Hebbel's special qualities, as Julian Schmidt, the German literary critic, pointed out, were these: "He draws his characters and develops his plots with a consistency that knows no compromise; every detail of the action is closely tied to the basic theme." It would cost Ibsen a good deal of hard work to construct his play in this fashion. The difference can be seen in the time it would now take to complete a play. In the past a new idea would force itself to completion in two, three, or four months. *Peer Gynt* took a mere nine months; the dual drama *Emperor and Gali-*

lean was completed in a year and a half. *Pillars of Society* would occupy him for nearly two years; it would not be sent to the printer until July, 1877. During these two years he was, of course, distracted by the need to protect his copyright in Germany, and similar economic problems; nonetheless, the very planning of this play proved more difficult than was usual for him. He thought the worst part was over with the completion of the first act in October, 1875: "This is always the most difficult part of a play," he wrote. He hoped he would be finished in a few months, but then he found he had to rewrite the first act—there are actually five different drafts for this act, and it seems certain he made many more. He was working with these ends in mind: to link every detail firmly with the main action; to cut away all extraneous detail, dialogue, and character; to tighten the dramatic structure from beginning to end; and to create an undeviating inner unity for each character. These goals become clearer as we follow from draft to draft his efforts to realize them.

The dramatic technique he developed in *Pillars of Society* remained his own throughout the rest of his career. In effect it was a recreation of the form of ancient Greek tragedy; the essence of the play becomes one great catastrophe. The one dramatic masterpiece of his youth, *The Vikings at Helgeland,* had been written in this form, and now it would become his standard technique, the exposition of an action in which old sins are suddenly revealed and bring down on the actors Nemesis, an inescapable judgment. The first act must thus plunge headlong into the crisis, pitting the truth and the buried sin against each other. The playwright's task was to make this seem perfectly natural, simply artless. Ibsen's struggle to give the action of the first act naturalness and inevitability can be seen in his early drafts, and although he did not succeed in his aim in the final version, the basic pattern for future success is indicated. Through ordinary words and casual talk there emerges those clearly defined opposites that will erupt into a life or death struggle. The ability his plays have to capture an audience is the result of his remarkable ability to embody moral opposites in ordinary life, so that we are always convinced these are flesh and blood people engaged in a breathless struggle over the greatest issues of life. The themes and the indignation were not his alone; what he could do better than anyone was to project his ideas through people we recognize as kin, or in fact our own selves wrestling with our consciences. Great themes and living human beings are the hallmark of the drama he created.

During these years Ibsen and Bjørnson seemed to be engaged in a kind of competition to create drama that exposed the corruption of social morals. Bjørnson had led the way, not only in the three plays already mentioned, but also with *Leonarda* (1879), and *The New System* (1879), both in the same year as *A Doll's House.* He produced no new plays while Ibsen was publishing *Ghosts* and *An Enemy of the People*, then in 1883 he brought out *Beyond Human Power, Part I*, a play that probes so deeply into the psychology of the religious experience that it must be considered a masterpiece of world drama. By this time Ibsen had created an intellectual ferment beyond anything occasioned by the earlier works of either dramatist. Ibsen's success was a result of the consistency with which he adhered to his dramatic goals, and it is precisely this consistency which distinguishes the work of one from the other. Bjørnson's characters are often more richly developed than Ibsen's; with more suggestivity about them, they seem to have a wider choice of courses of action and are not so relentlessly bound to a single path. They are simply more human, and at the same time less dramatic. Ibsen's fearful strength lies in the way he constructs the whole drama and every character in it so that we are forced to acquiesce in every fated event. He takes hold of us at once and does not let go until he has brought us to the inevitable. It is no wonder that he found it incomprehensible that Bjørnson could sit down and write a new last act for a play he had already completed. Every play, he believed, must aim for a determined goal; the problem was to find the way that led there. Once the goal was reached, the play was complete, its form unalterable.

There is, perhaps, a somewhat dated atmosphere about *Pillars of Society*, due in part to the traces of popular drama in it, and also because the play loses stature when compared with the masterpieces that were to follow. Yet with this play, Ibsen won his first popular success. The publisher issued an edition of 6,000 copies and had to ready 4,000 more within seven weeks. There were, at the same time, performances on all the stages of Scandinavia, first in Odense and Copenhagen, then throughout the other countries. In Germany success was almost as great. Besides the authorized translation by Emma Klingenfeld, two others appeared in 1878. Theatres competed for a chance to produce the play. In February, 1878, it was in the repertory of five different theatres in Berlin alone, an unheard-of event in the city's theatrical history. Before the year was out, twenty-seven theatres in Germany and Austria had staged it, and during the next few years it was played wherever German was spoken. In 1879 it was translated into Czech, and in 1880 it received one performance in English in London.

A Bankruptcy cleared a path for Ibsen's plays in Germany, although in German opinion, *Pillars of Society* did not measure up to Bjørnson's play and for a time Ibsen was overshadowed by his countryman. But *Pillars of Society* laid the foundation for Ibsen's future fame in Germany. The influential theatre manager Otto Brahm recalled the effect the play had on young people in his day. He was a twenty-two-year-old student when he saw it in one of the small Berlin theatres and it was "the first powerful theatrical impression" of his life, "the first conception of a new world of literature." He felt he had been dedicated to the cause of a new realistic art. The feeling was shared by his companion, Paul Schlenther, who would become a great theatre director. The performance was a decisive event in his life as well, opening up a new world and a new concept of art. Many others were to feel the power of the revolution that Ibsen was fomenting.

CHAPTER THIRTY-ONE

WOMEN AND SOCIETY:

A DOLL'S HOUSE (1878-79)

W E DON'T NOTICE WOMEN," says Consul Bernick in one of the early drafts of *Pillars of Society*. Lona Hessel, the rebel of the play, is given the line in the final version, and the words are turned against the men: "You don't notice women." Now woman herself was rising in revolt against society and demanding her rights.

Women's rights had become a burning issue. John Stuart Mill's *The Subjection of Women* (1869), which raised the problem, was translated by Brandes into Danish in the same year. In 1871 Norwegian Mathilde Schjøtt published the anonymous pamphlet *A Conversation among Friends about the Subjection of Women* and her aunt, Aasta Hansteen fought for "emancipation" in her own name. Camilla Collett's volumes, *Last Pages (Sidste Blade)*, published in 1872 and 1873, made a deep impression with their picture of the mental suffering endured by enslaved women and their analysis of how men become brutal and crude through contempt for women. The same theme had been basic in all of Mme. Collett's work since *The Governor's Daughters* in 1855. Now was the time to work for practical measures. Women began to organize clubs such as The Women's Reading Society of Oslo, founded in 1874, to expand their intellectual opportunities. They began to win places for themselves in the civil service and the school system. The issues were kept alive by Collett's *From the Camp of the Silent (Fra de Stummes Leir,* 1874), and by the sensational case of a Swedish noblewoman who came to Norway to announce in a series of lectures and in pamphlets that she had suffered a great injustice at the hands of a Norwegian student who had seduced her and then refused to marry her. Aasta Hansteen took up the cudgel on the noblewoman's behalf and the case was turned into a general debate on women's rights. Such "unfeminine" and uninhibited polemics antagonized all "good society,"and by 1880 things had become so difficult for Aasta Hansteen, that she left for the greater freedom of America, not returning until 1889.

Aasta Hansteen was the model for Ibsen's Lona Hessel (at first named, even more suggestively, Lona Hassel). He had noticed the indignation her activities had aroused while he was in Norway in 1874, and he longed to put down her narrow-minded detractors. A robust and warm-hearted woman like this was just the kind of person he needed to break through the hypocritical family and social life of the Bernicks. Thus the first drafts of the play suggested it would be more on the woman's rights issue than it actually turned out to be. In the early drafts Ibsen ridiculed the "domesticity" of the old-fashioned housewives and contrasted them with the emancipated woman, bold in speech and even bolder in action. The new woman could win a victory for truth because she made use of that truly feminine gift of giving men "a glimpse of that non-logical, intuitive mode of thinking" that "has an inspiring and cleansing effect." Ibsen knew this gift from close observation of the "illogical" but strong-willed woman he had married. As long ago as 1870 he had described her consuming hatred of all convention.

The theme of his play was that man should not make it his goal in life to become a "pillar of society," but should rather become himself. The theme is basic to Ibsen's life as well as his writing. In everything it was a question of "realizing oneself" as a free agent. In the summer of 1879 he wrote to Bjørnson that his mission as a writer was "to inspire individuals, as many as possible, to freedom and independence." He reiterated his stand in reply to Bjørnson's request for support in his agitation for a "pure flag" (Norwegian red-white-and-blue without the foreign colors that marked the union with Sweden). "There are not in all Norway twenty-five free and independent souls. Let the mark of union stay; but erase the signs of monkhood from minds; take away the mark of prejudice and narrow-mindedness and subjection and baseless faith in authority, so that the individual can sail under his own flag. What they sail under now is neither pure nor their own."

This applied no less to women than to men. In *The Pretenders* a quiet, pathetic complaint sighs from the lips of the king's mother: "To love, to sacrifice all, and to be forgotten, that is a woman's story." In *Pillars of Society* the young Dina Dorf has the courage to defy society and refuse to bow to "all these intimidating considerations . . . all this killing respectability." In the first draft Ibsen shows her as willing to enter into an unconsecrated union with the man she loves; she would throw off all external bonds, even this hated thing of "betrothal," in order to be free, herself alone. She is a version of Svanhild in *Love's Comedy*, a new version that will not let "the world take her," but rather meets its challenge proudly. She is a woman of the same mettle as Hjørdis of *The Vikings at Helgeland.* Ibsen, it seems, believed that a woman could raise the standard of revolt against the conventions that trammeled the free mind more readily than man.

Ideas like this had been latent in him since youth; now they broke out in revolutionary form, particularly after his association with Camilla Collett in Dresden in 1871. At that time she had been amazed and angry with his old-fashioned attitudes toward women; when she came to Munich in the spring of 1877 and discussed marriage and the position of women with him again, she was still further provoked by the opinions he defended. He was probably in jest part of the time; he was completing *Pillars of Society* and contradicting Camilla was one way by which he could penetrate deeper into the thinking of this rebellious woman. The first impulse to write a play with emphasis on women may have come from these conversations; the idea for a new drama dealing precisely with woman's rebellion could have led him to eliminate from *Pillars of Society* a good deal of the material relating to women and their cause and to keep his attack concentrated on social morals, as the inclusiveness of the title indicates.

An old theme was about to take on new form. When *The League of Youth* appeared, Brandes had pointed out that the story of Selma, the youthful Mrs. Bratsberg, might well have been developed into a drama in its own right. This was the idea to which he now returned. Selma, "the fairytale princess," longing for the true fairytale, always kept on the outside and never permitted to make her contribution or to participate in the struggles of real life. She must always be protected from all that is ugly. Finally she cries out in anger: "You dressed me like a doll; you played with me, as one plays with a child. I would have rejoiced to bear a burden; I longed with all my heart for everything that storms, that lifts up, exalts." In *The League of Youth* it was no more than an outburst, it was not drama. Now, a decade later, the outcry became rebellion. The theme had strong roots in his past thinking, and even in *Pillars of Society,* but he did not immediately discover the right form. *Pillars* came out in October, 1877; then an entire year passed before he made serious plans for the new play. He said that when he was through with a play he felt completely exhausted, emptied as though everything in his head had already been said.

In the meantime his hands were full of business matters. With the great success of his play in Germany, it became more important than ever to protect his rights to the income from his work. It was necessary that he appear as a German author, not simply a Norwegian or Danish one. Even in the Scandinavian countries he had to make contracts with the regular theatres and the traveling troupes and became involved in quarrels and lawsuits over various production problems.

When the theatre in Bergen was reorganized in 1876, he personally drew up the contract he wanted with it. As the money came in, he had the added problem of investing it to secure his future. His publisher Hegel took care of the royalties from theatres in Denmark and Sweden; he handled the rest himself and began to invest in various Norwegian enterprises—the new streetcars in Oslo, a new bank in Bergen, a new steamship company in Kristiansand. He was not always lucky, but things generally went well and he accumulated a fortune that grew from year to year.

In August, 1878, he left Munich with the intention of returning to live in Rome; his son Sigurd had finished the Munich *gymnasium* and wished to study at the University of Rome. Ibsen himself longed for the warmth of the South. After a pleasant summer in Gossensass in the Alps, the town he had enjoyed so much in 1876, he arrived in Rome at the end of September.

Before he left Munich, he had gotten a letter from Victor Kieler, a teacher in Hillerød, Denmark, informing him briefly that he had been compelled to commit his wife to an insane asylum. The letter was to have a major effect on his thinking about the new play, and would in fact suggest its central conflict. In 1870 Kieler's wife, Laura, had sent Ibsen a "continuation" of *Brand,* which she called *Brand's Daughters.* She was Laura Petersen at that time, a twenty-year-old girl living in Trøndelag, and her book was a kind of edifying Christian tract, intended as an answer to the inhuman moral demands of Ibsen's play. Ibsen took an interest in the young girl and advised her to try her hand at writing *belles lettres.* When he met her the next year in Copenhagen, he was still more interested, for she was hardly what he had expected, but young, pretty, and vivacious. He invited her to Dresden and she came the following summer. For two months she was in the Ibsen home virtually every day; he liked her very much and gave her the name "the lark." Two or three years later she married in Denmark and began to write short stories. The young couple was poor, her husband's earnings as a teacher were low, and he fell ill as their financial troubles began to press down on him. According to their son, Kieler's temperament was "explosive," and he would fly into rages over household expenses. The doctor advised a long vacation in a warmer climate, and Laura secretly borrowed money in Norway to finance the trip. In 1876 they set off for Switzerland and Italy, and on their way home stopped in Munich for a few days. Laura confided in Mrs. Ibsen and told her of her difficulties with the debt she owed for the trip, which she had not dared to tell her husband about. She had hoped to pay off the loan with money earned by her writing, but she had not been able to get anything published. In March, 1878, she sent Ibsen the manuscript of a book she wanted him to try to place with Gyldendal. Ibsen answered that the book was so hastily written that it was not in condition to be published—she herself had mentioned in her letter that she rushed the writing of the book. He sensed something behind this haste and wrote that "there must be something you are concealing in your letter." The only advice he could give her was to urge her to tell her husband about the debt so that he could help her. This was the last thing she dared to do, trying instead to get the debt postponed. When this failed, she wrote a forged note. The forgery was detected immediately, she got no money, and her husband learned of the whole thing. In a fury he demanded a divorce, and when she suffered a nervous breakdown she was committed to an asylum. In this catastrophe the marriage was dissolved.

As late as October 7, 1878, Ibsen was writing to Hegel for detailed information about the Kielers, and did not learn the full story for some time. The whole incident moved him deeply; he saw before him the vivacious young woman, secretly assuming burdens for the sake of her husband, even forging notes on his account, looking forward to the pride he would feel in her when the truth was known—and in the end driven to mental collapse and divorce. Ibsen knew well the power such frustration had to kill love; he had depicted it in *Brand,* when Agnes leaves Ejnar after discovering that he lacks the courage and strength to risk his life for another's salvation. He must have recalled what he had read in Kierkegaard's *Seducer's Diary.* The seducer describes the anticipation he has created in the young girl; she has something "eager, almost foolhardy in the way of expectation" in her eyes, "as if they demanded and were prepared to see the extraordinary every second." Kierkegaard called this "extraordinary" thing the "miracle" (det "Vidunderlige"), and he used the word again in *Repetition,* in referring to the love that reached "the threshold of the miracle." Did not every woman in fact live in expectation of the "miracle"? The problem for Ibsen was: what consequences when the "miracle" failed to happen? In placing the issue in the context of a violation of social customs and legal limitation he visualized the whole revolt that would follow upon the clash between a woman's unlimited demand and social regulations and accepted morality.

On October 19, 1878, three weeks after his return to Rome, he made the first "Notations for a modern tragedy." A point to be emphasized is that the gist of these "Notations" did not concern women's rights. When he wrote *Pillars of Society,* he was concerned with the falseness of society in general; now he wanted to dramatize the universal tragedy of the conflict between convention and truth, the conflict, as he said in his notes, between "natural feeling on one hand and faith in authority on the other." For him the true spokesman for the "natural" was woman, as he revealed in the chance remark in *Pillars of Society:* "Your society is a society of bachelor souls." He elaborated on this in "Notations" and wrote that modern society "is exclusively a male society, with laws written by men and with prosecutors and judges who judge female actions from a male point of view." Conflict was the inevitable result, for "there are two kinds of spiritual law, two kinds of conscience, one in man and a different one entirely in woman. They do not understand each other." A woman's natural point of view, her defense in every action, is the phrase: "But I did it for love." Laws that hinder acts of love or punish them are inconceivable to her. The result is that "the wife in the play finally does not know where to turn to find the right or the wrong." She loses her footing in society, and she must flee a husband who cannot free himself from social conventions and burst forth to what would be for her the "miracle."

This was the foundation for the drama that would be called *A Doll's House.* Ibsen had to reverse the tragedy of the Kieler household. There the husband wanted to leave; he would have it the other way around. At his own side was a woman who never bowed to conventions that offended common justice; he identified his own spirit of rebellion with hers.

It was a while before he could get down to steady work on the play. During the winter of 1878-79 the theme matured within him, but it took time for the moral dichotomy he pondered to take shape as recognizable human beings. Later, he told his wife that at first he saw the whole thing as in a world of mists, but out of this, little by little, human beings stood forth in stronger and stronger light. That winter he kept to himself, feeling the need to be alone: "Now and then, you know, one has to steal away even from one's own family," he once said. At the Scandinavian Society he would read newspapers from home, and sometimes fall into conversation or attend meetings and dinners, but it was evident that he was in a belligerent frame of mind. One evening after a meeting he stayed and drank Swedish punch, and then launched into an attack on several Danish theologians who were present, denouncing Christianity and all the superficial dogmas the clergy used to bulwark the old social order. He grew more and more fierce and when he went home in the early hours of the morning supported on each side by a young friend, he saw the world running completely downhill, with people growing more paltry by the minute, and their goals less and less worthy. Gunnar Heiberg, one of the young supports and eventually a distinguished Norwegian playwright, tried to comfort him by saying that at least he had written great and true things. But when he began to quote from the "Balloon Letter" Ibsen cried contemptuously, "Verse! Verse! Nothing but verse!"

Plans for the drama turned his thoughts more and more to the problems of women. There is a story that at this time he tried to persuade a Danish woman to start a magazine exclusively for women. In January, 1879, he proposed to the Scandinavian Society that a woman librarian be hired. As a second measure he recommended that women be given the right to vote in the society. This notion met with stronger opposition than he had anticipated, and at the decisive meeting on February 27 he had his comments for the debate carefully written out. He insisted that the present situation was a "humiliation" to women who, he insisted, possessed along with young people and the true artist, "the instinct of genius that unconsciously hits upon the truth." This view of women derives from the romantic tradition; it had given birth to such characters as Agnes in *Brand* and Solveig in *Peer Gynt*. What was different now was that the view became the basis for social demands on whose behalf Ibsen would take action. As he spoke before the society, he became so emotional that he abandoned his notes and spoke from his heart, fluent and powerful. Nonetheless, the cause was lost. He was furious and at his table in his usual haunt he would have none near him but those who had voted in favor of his proposal. He would not speak to any of his old friends who had voted against him; he would not even greet them in the street.

When he turned up at the society's spring banquet, in full regalia and with all his orders, everyone was delighted. He sat down somewhat apart, then suddenly he moved up to the table and began to speak, quietly at first, saying that he had recently wanted to introduce the society to new trends of the times, for no one could escape the force of great ideas, not even here. And how had they received his gift? As though he were a footpad, an assassin! Even women had conspired and agitated against him. By this time he was in such a furor of indignation that he could scarcely control his words. With flashing eyes and trembling lips, with his great mane of hair shaking, he upbraided the women with harsh, almost crude words. At last a Danish countess swooned and he quieted down, but he went on talking about the generally miserable state of most people, especially women, and their unnatural resistance to new ideas that would make them better, richer, more important. When he finished, he took his coat and walked out. He had had his release.

The account of this episode is derived from Gunnar Heiberg's recollections, written thirty years later and inevitably colored somewhat by his imagination. The effect must have been an impressive one, nevertheless, and the account gives an unquestionably accurate account of Ibsen's temperament in those days. His nerves were always keyed up while the creative process was going on.

By summer the play had taken shape enough for him to begin writing. Because of the city's heat he moved in the beginning of July to Amalfi, the old coastal town on the south side of the Sorrento peninsula. He did not live in the town proper, but in an old monastery that had been converted into a hotel, situated on a cliff that fell sharply into the sea. There was a view, the ocean for a refreshing swim, and the air was fresh.

He rewrote the play three times in the course of the summer, and each time the characters became more believable, the plot and speeches firmer and more natural. The first drafts spoke of the "woman problem," but this was forgotten as the play began to reflect life, not a theory. The young lady who would be the central character he called Nora. Many years later when he was asked why he had chosen this name, he answered quickly, "Well, you see, her name wasn't really Nora. She was christened 'Eleonora.' But at home they called her 'Nora' because she was such a little pet." Both names were taken from Ole Schulerud's sister, in fact, but the reply to the question indicates how thoroughly he had entered into the life of his heroine. One day while working on the play he said to his wife: "I've just seen Nora. She came right over to me and put her hand on my shoulder." "What was she wearing," his wife asked. "A simple blue woolen dress," Ibsen answered in all seriousness.

Ibsen used Laura Kieler for his model, at least in part. She herself was certain that Ibsen based Nora on her and maintained that he had first used the phrase "a doll's house" in referring to her home. There is no evidence, however, that Ibsen ever visited the Kielers in Hillerød, and Mrs. Kieler had a tendency to color facts with imagination. It was this very quality that made her so valuable to Ibsen. She had a warm heart and a desire to help all who suffered. And although she had an appreciation of the beautiful and a genuine sense of justice, she had no comprehension of the letter of the law and no consideration for simple facts. In copies of Ibsen's letters that she sent to the author of this book there appeared statements that did not correspond to the given dates. When he inquired about this, she answered in all innocence that she had simply exchanged something in one letter with a passage in another letter that she thought was better expressed. She did not understand that it could make any difference. Such an attitude easily explains how she could have begun telling little lies to her husband about the money she suddenly had in hand. The personality trait would be useful to Ibsen in creating his Nora. But Mrs. Kieler was not his model for Nora's decisive act of leaving her husband at the end of the play. For this he drew on his wife's character in part, and in greater degree from himself as well. A few of Nora's traits may have been taken from little Rikke Holst, who was so fond of pastries. In any case, his thoughts had gone back to Bergen, for he found there models for both Dr. Rank and lawyer Krogstad.

There was certainly no connection between Laura Kieler's husband and the Helmer of the play; the one evening they had spent together in 1876 was hardly enough to give Ibsen any knowledge about him. A more probable model was a Norwegian acquaintance in Munich, a pleasant, sociable person, who was said to rule his German-born wife with an iron hand. Helmer was first called "Stenbo," the same name first given to Stensgard in the drafts of *The League of Youth*. The name's obvious allusion to "stone" was considered too blatant a parody for the political whirligig of that play; here too the reference to the domineering husband was too obvious and the name gave way to the neutral middle-class Helmer, an echo from the Grimstad days. As happened with Consul Bernick, Helmer became less interesting the more Ibsen worked on him. In the first draft he was a man with a passion for science and art; a self-made man whose ignorance was an excuse for his coarse behavior. Ibsen gradually let him dwindle to an ordinary husband, neither better nor worse than most, except that he is an egotist of such dimensions that we can hardly take him seriously. There is an undeniable touch of caricature in having him say in the last act "Nora, I'm saved!" instead of the originally intended "Nora, you're saved!" The psychological gulf between Helmer and Nora is thus widened to a chasm.

The sharp outlines of the play's structure greatly add to its effectiveness. Every character has a function in terms of the main action, and every one helps to exert pressure on Nora until the final inescapable crisis which will either give her the "miracle" or else the death blow to her love. The action of the play is undeniably hurried. The wicked lawyer Krogstad is converted during one short conversation, and it takes little more than a day to transform Nora from a "lark" to an independent woman. But this is not psychologically implausible if one considers the long preparation for the change in her attitude. In the hands of a great actress the final conversation between Nora and her husband grows naturally out of the "lark" and her past; a greater challenge is to make the audience perceive that Nora is already beginning to throw off the "lark"-disguise in Act One, that she is merely acting the part her husband requires. (Among the many actresses the author of this book has seen in the part, only Tore Segelcke was able to do this, when she played it at the National Theatre in Oslo in 1936.)

The play was finished toward the end of September, 1879, and published three weeks before Christmas in an 8,000 copy edition. A month later, and again three months later, new editions were required. A German translation entitled *Nora* appeared in Reclam's *Universal-Bibliothek* before the end of 1879 and sold in the thousands. Translations followed one upon the other: Finland 1880, England 1882, Poland 1882, Russia 1883, Italy 1884, etc. In a few years it had a world audience accorded to few books.

But this success was nothing in comparison with its triumphs in theatres around the world. Before Christmas 1879, the Royal Theatre in Copenhagen gave the première with Betty Hennings in the leading role. Next to stage it were the Dramatic Theatre in Stockholm, with Elise Hwasser, and Christiania Theatre in Oslo, with Johanne Juell, both in January, 1880. Various companies toured smaller Scandinavian towns. In February Ida Aalberg performed it in Finnish in Helsinki and it was given in German in Flensborg at the same time. Residenz-Theater in Munich was the first regular German theatre to stage the play on March 3, 1880, with Maria Ramlo; Ibsen himself was present to receive the tribute of the audience. Hedwig Niemann-Raabe played Nora in Hamburg, Dresden, Hannover, and Berlin soon after this. The next year it was given in Vienna and in Leningrad (in Polish); and in 1882 in Warsaw. Toward the end of the 1880's, the play became a standard feature in most theatre repertories and was played in every conceivable tongue in every conceivable location. Ibsen had become a world writer.

A Doll's House had an explosive impact on its time. The happy ending of *Pillars of Society* made it acceptable to all social circles and to people of divergent opinion. *A Doll's House* was relentless, carrying its moral conflict forward to an irreconcilable break with society's ordinary moral precepts, arousing opposition and dividing men's minds.

Never before the subject of so much controversy, Ibsen was the topic of debate in newspapers, periodicals, and books throughout Scandinavia and Germany. Ministers delivered sermons on the new play; people argued privately and publicly about it. The legal question of whether Nora could actually be condemned for forgery by the letter of the law was discussed at length. Some questioned the plausibility of Nora's sudden rejection of that almost-inherited and well-drilled morality and her rebirth as a rebel. This was, in fact, the most meaningful question, but it was overshadowed by the problem that concerned the play's contemporaries most: was it morally right for Nora to abandon her husband and children for the sake of her own intellectual freedom? She was being judged as an actual person, not as a character in a play. In one way this was Ibsen's greatest triumph. People did not ask whether Nora *had* to do what she did; they asked if she *ought* to have done it. Here was the crux of the problem, and it served to focus attention on the whole issue of women's rights. The play was interpreted as a plea for the emancipation of women, and Ibsen was hailed as the special poet of women, not simply as a rebel fighting for spiritual freedom in the abstract. He thus became the most dangerous enemy in the eyes of those who opposed rebellion, whether in society or in moral issues, and those who opposed women's rights.

He had, along with Bjørnson, so indoctrinated his Scandinavian readers that they had the courage to face the real issue he raised and reply affirmatively to his call for freedom. Ibsen had led the way in the movement which, by the end of the 1870's, saw a general victory in Norway for concepts of freedom and honesty, whether in history or natural science, in social or religious matters, in painting or in art. The voice of authority with which he now spoke lent strength to his work as a playwright.

Opposition to the play was much stronger outside Scandinavia. The German reaction was typical. Leading directors in Hamburg and Vienna told Ibsen that it would be impossible—or dangerous—to do the play with the original, unreconciled ending. When played this way at Munich, there was a clash between those who applauded and those who hissed their disapproval of the harsh, "immoral" outcome. The actress Frau Niemann-Raabe flatly refused to do the ending as written: "I would never leave my children," she explained. Ibsen was warned that some enterprising translator would rewrite the ending, and so he decided to do the "barbaric act of violence" himself. In the altered version Helmer forces Nora to look in on her children in the bedroom; she cannot leave them and so agrees to stay with her husband. The true Ibsenian spirit was missing, and in 1880 when Frau Raabe played it, she could not capture the audience. In Berlin they laughed at the most moving passages, and Brandes, who saw the performance, shook his head: "Germany will never understand Ibsen." It soon became clear, however, that the original version would find its audience. Frau Ramlo's Munich performance was a triumph in spite of all opposition. Within a few years it was impossible to imagine the play in any other version than the original. When Frau Niemann-Raabe performed it this way, she secured the success that eluded her in 1880. Hedwig Wangel, a young German actress who played Nora in 1892 and then went on to a whole series of Ibsen roles, declared that *A Doll's House* had "opened the door to a whole new world for German women." In Germany, as elsewhere, the play fostered spiritual freedom.

The role of Nora was the first of a long series of parts that would prove so attractive to performers. After Nora came Mrs. Alving, Dr. Stockmann, Hjalmar Ekdal, Rebecca West, Hedda Gabler. . . . Frequently performers, particularly actresses, thought they would please Ibsen by thanking him for the magnificent parts he had written. He reacted with annoyance and cut them short: "I have never written parts; I have created human beings and human destinies." And it was precisely by creating true, three-dimensional human beings that he also created good acting parts. He cut away much that was mere theatricality, externals, and probed deep into the souls of his characters, exposing every secret yearning, and so he forced the actor to do the same, to exercise his talent to the utmost in order to reveal the full psychological truth in each character. The plays of Ibsen revitalized and renewed the integrity of the art of acting: they demanded greater empathy, greater honesty, a more complete giving of one's self than any dramatic art since Shakespeare.

One actress after another made the role of Nora her entry into success—from Johanne Juell in Norway to Miss Mori and Miss Mizutani in Japan. The Ibsen roles were moreover so rich that they kept pace with the emotional maturity of the performer. When Betty Hennings returned to the role of Nora after twelve years, she changed her interpretation completely; she was able to penetrate more deeply into the soul of the woman who was at once so childishly unaware of life and yet so brave before the unknown—weak and strong, rich and impoverished. The Nora of Johanne Dybwad changed in the same way. In 1890 at Christiania Theatre she was young herself, and her Nora was little more than a child, the happy "lark" girl who could not quite fathom the new reality; sixteen years later at the National Theatre she was a woman who hid a secret fear of life and whose sudden insight into terrors forced her thoughts into strange paths. New truths awoke in her almost compulsively, involuntarily. Dybwad's interpretation may have been influenced by Johanne Juell, her mother; she in turn passed the tradition on to Tore Segelcke, who was able to suggest an even deeper understanding of the change Nora undergoes.

The play itself seemed to change with time. More than once Ibsen said that he had not intended to write a play about women's rights, but only about human beings. And he never allowed the "women's rights ladies" to make him one of them, even though his moral indignation at subjugation never diminished. Twenty years later he told the

Norwegian Society for Women's Rights that he actually did not know what women's rights were; he wanted to secure freedom for all mankind. Gradually both actors and spectators learned to see more of the humanity and less of the ideas of the play. In the beginning, Nora's lines in the last act were spoken as though part of a public debate; the great interpreters of the role made them a moment of private reckoning. Interpretation and audience reaction, however, did not always keep pace: the author of this book recalls an occasion when there was an obvious conflict between what was being played and what the audience wanted to hear. In 1908 the great Nazimova played the role in New York, with a passionate intensity that made Nora's transformation at the end completely an inner reality, conveyed in low-pitched, emotion-laden words. The audience, on the other hand, applauded every line as though it were a political harangue, a collection of ideas that were still felt to be startling and revolutionary. Little by little the topical controversy died away; what remained was the work of art, with its demand for truth in every human relation. The artist could achieve no greater triumph.

CHAPTER THIRTY-TWO

PHANTOMS FROM THE PAST:

GHOSTS (1880-81)

A DOLL'S HOUSE grew naturally out of *Pillars of Society; Ghosts* grew just as inevitably out of *A Doll's House*. Themes and problems, character traits and human destinies carried from one play into the next. The seeds of the new play were those thoughts on heredity that he had removed from the drafts of *A Doll's House;* in a similar manner *A Doll's House* had developed out of those rejected elements in *Pillars of Society* that concerned the woman question. No outer stimulus was needed this time; the new play came to him as naturally as anything he had ever written. And it turned out, in some way, to be more rebellious than anything he had done before. Tranquil and alone, he gathered courage for a step that was bolder and more provocative than even he knew.

As in the past, the theme would not take shape at once. His plans for work after *A Doll's House* seemed to indicate something totally different. The new play he mentioned in September, 1879, can hardly have been *Ghosts,* rather it points further ahead. By the spring of 1880 the idea of a new play was so remote that he could think of nothing better to do than to write his memoirs, a plan that came to little. In the fall of 1879 he returned to Munich for his last winter there for a long time to come. In the summer of 1880, wearing a Tyrolean hat, like a regular German tourist, he headed for the Alps, settling for the third summer in Berchtesgaden. In the quiet, secluded little mountain village Ibsen lived peacefully, and if he no longer climbed the peaks, he still took long walks along the valley roads. He spent every Saturday evening with the Norwegian novelist, Jonas Lie, and his wife. Mrs. Ibsen and his son Sigurd were traveling in Norway, and his regular companion was John Paulsen, the young Norwegian writer who would be his future Boswell. The more than usually rainy and foggy summer suited Ibsen's mood. When Paulsen asked him what he was working on, he replied, "A family story, sad and gray like this rainy day." *Ghosts* does in fact take place on a rainy day, and Ibsen places it in the worst Norwegian rain-country he knew, the region around Bergen.

In Berchtesgaden he wrote nothing for the play, and when he returned to Munich there was a further interruption. The Norwegian Ministry of Church and Education informed him that Sigurd could not take a Norwegian law degree without first taking a lower degree (the so-called "second examination"). Ibsen was incensed by this "genuinely Norwegian" obstinacy, and swore that he would "one day erect a suitable literary monument to the black theological gang that presently rules the Norwegian Ministry of Church and Education." Reverend Manders, portrayed with such fiendish glee in *Ghosts*, may well have been inspired by his wrath over this incident. He had to leave Munich to accompany his son to Rome, where the boy planned to continue his studies, and in the fall he rented an apartment in the Via Capo le Case, the same street where he had lived in the old days, but in a building a little closer to the Villa Borghese. (The upper end of this street was later renamed Via Crispi; on the house where Ibsen lived after 1880 a memorial plaque was placed in 1910. It stated that here he "wrote *Brand* and planned *Peer Gynt*"!) That winter he made the first few notes on the new play.

It has been reported that his mood this winter was as bellicose as it had been when he was struggling with *A Doll's House*. He went every day to read the newspapers at the Scandinavian Society, and sometimes chatted amiably with an old friend, the Danish composer Ravnkilde, then president of the society. He could not, however, refrain from criticizing the directors, even for such petty things as using too many stamps on one of the newspapers. It relieved his nerves to carry on in this fashion, but in blowing up minor things into matters of great principle he contradicted his own behavior two years before when he had fought for genuine principles. When some of the younger members tried to honor him by asking him to stand for president of the society, he answered partly in jest, "I must tell you that I will be obliged to side with the opposition." He visited just as regularly a little tavern in Via due Macelli, and although he would be charming to anyone who came with him, his bad temper broke out when he got drunk and had to be helped home. Then his young support became a "frightful puppy" and an older one an "awful person." It took very little to put him on edge, and he did not restrain his abusive tongue in those angry moods.

When he celebrated Norwegian Constitution Day, May 17, at his home, however, he made it a festive, pleasant occasion. On the same day Bjørnson was unveiling a statue of Henrik Wergeland in Oslo; Ibsen's guest of honor was Camilla Collett, Wergeland's sister. In his speech honoring the day, he mentioned that he had gone to the Swedish-

Norwegian Embassy residence, but, of course, found no flag flying. Then he spoke of Norway and how sadly lacking it was in freedom: "Norway has a hundred and one freedoms, but no freedom." That was the decisive thing in his opinion, and when the new play appeared, he would discover how right he had been.

With the approach of summer he was at last ready to begin. On June 18, 1881, he wrote to Hegel that he had given up the idea of writing his memoirs and had instead "begun on one of the first days of this month to tackle the material for the play that has filled my mind for a long time and has now forced itself on me so strongly that I could not possibly let it lie dormant any longer." He would not reveal the title or the theme of the play, other than to say that it would be "a family drama in three acts," and would probably be ready in four months. Then he added: "That this play has nothing whatever to do with *A Doll's House* should not need saying." His remark was not precisely true, if one considers the deepest implications of both plays. A few years later he wrote that *A Doll's House* "forms a kind of introduction or preparation" for *Ghosts*. The themes of the two plays are different, of course, and Ibsen probably felt the new play would not arouse the kind of controversy *A Doll's House* had. He would be greatly mistaken.

Now he needed quiet for writing, and at the end of June he moved to Sorrento, where he stayed until the beginning of November. He kept to himself even more than he had in Berchtesgaden, and although he lived in the same hotel as Ernest Renan, did not even make his acquaintance. He worked intensely on the play, living with it constantly.

Would it be possible to rid man of all the phantoms from the past that rode him like nightmares? That was the question he set himself to answer as he struggled with his feeling that "all mankind is a failure," and had "gone astray." Although he felt the need to revolt against fate and to try to turn evolution into other paths, it seemed a hopeless task. The past was so potent that it alone seemed to determine man's life. He brooded over the relationship between past and future, between family and society on one hand, and the individual human being on the other, just as he had done in *Brand:*

| Där begynder ansvarsvaegten af ens arvelod fra slaegten? | Where does the burden of responsibility for one's heritage begin? |

In that play the formulation had been religious and moral: the new generation had to suffer for the sins of the fathers. The image was of the Old Testament Jehovah, the stern God who would not let the guilty go unpunished, but carried His vengeance to the children and the children's children. In *Brand* Ibsen had created a man strong enough to

assume the burden of guilt and undertake the penance necessary to
save man from this heritage of sin. In *Peer Gynt* he had created a
mocking portrait of a weak, cowardly man who finds this sharing of
responsibility too "spooky." But Ibsen's own attitude toward inherited
guilt was uncertain. In 1871 he wrote to Brandes, "If only one had the
courage to ignore it completely, then perhaps one could shake off the
ballast that is the heaviest weight on one's own personality."

But now the problem took another form, without changing in significance. One after another of the characters of *The League of Youth*
had been explained in terms of heritage and social environment. In
Emperor and Galilean, the idea was stated as a general philosophical
problem: could the individual tear himself loose from the totality of
the world? Ibsen steadfastly insisted on the right every man had to
be himself, to "realize himself" fully; at the same time it was evident
that the individual as well as society carried a "corpse on board," and
the question was whether it could be shaken off. A moral and a dramatic
conflict lay behind the question. The old concept of responsibility was
given a new basis by the new laws of heredity that the natural sciences
were proposing in the 1870's. Darwin's *Origin of Species* in 1859 had
already suggested the existence of such laws, but it was not until 1871
when he applied them to man in *The Descent of Man* that they became
known to the general public. (J. P. Jacobsen translated both books into
Danish in 1872 and 1875.) In the widespread discussion of these new
theories the very basis of Christian morality seemed to be called
into question.

Ibsen was inevitably affected by this controversy since it hit on the
moral dilemma involved in the question of personal freedom. The drafts
of *A Doll's House* reveal how the new ideas intrigued him, particularly
in his first sketches for Dr. Rank (modeled on J. A. Holmboe, a young
doctor he had known in Bergen.) In the early drafts the doctor delivers
full-length lectures on the influence of living conditions and family
inheritance on human personality: "Get acquainted with the natural
sciences, ladies, and you will see how there is a law in everything."
The laws, of course, are the Darwinian and Spencerian doctrines of
"natural selection" and "the survival of the fittest." Only slight traces
of these ideas are left in the final version of the play, although they
are enough to indicate their importance to Ibsen. We learn that Rank
is suffering the effects of his father's youthful excesses, and from this
he has deduced a general moral law: "In every family there is in some
way or other just such an inexorable retribution."

Such ideas are not simply fashionable intellectual talk; they are
germane to the basic theme of the play. Helmer's speech about the

heritage of lies that passes from mother to children and destroys their lives is one of the strongest motivations for Nora's leaving home. (In one of the early drafts Mrs. Linde says the same thing to her.) The conflict that gives rise to the tragic catastrophe stems from the fact that Nora has not fulfilled the scientist's law that she adapt herself to her environment. Or put another way, she had adapted herself in a purely external way, laughing and playing as her father and husband wish her to; however, she had not created a proper relationship between her outer and her inner life. At last she must break out of her doll's house and try to find herself in a society she has not previously understood.

The old problem of man's relationship to society had been placed in a new context, and like Nora, Ibsen has to think it through again. In *Ghosts* he wanted to show how Nora's attempt to solve the problem turned out; in reality Mrs. Alving is a Nora who has tested life and her inherited doctrines and has formed opinions on these matters.

When *Ghosts* was published, attention was directed primarily to Oswald and his sickness, and for a long time the play was performed as if he were the central character. The play could thus be called a piece of "hospital literature" by Paul Heyse, and doctors would debate whether the disease was correctly diagnosed, as though the play stood or fell on Ibsen's handling of the medical problem. Oswald is obviously a new version of Dr. Rank, and this time the motif of the son suffering for the father's sins becomes a major one in the play. But the real tragedy is not the insanity of Oswald; his pathological condition is a symbol of the sinful heritage that gnaws away at the strength of living men. The true tragedy is the struggle Mrs. Alving wages against the past and its spiritual as well as physical heritage. The original title of the play had in fact been "Mrs. Alving."

The awful question of how her dishonest life would affect her children had brought Nora face to face with tragedy. In one of the early drafts for *Ghosts* Ibsen asked what kind of children would come from "these women of today, mistreated as daughters, as sisters, as wives, deprived of their heritage, embittered in heart." Nora was now to be analyzed as mother. After the play was finished, he said to the English critic William Archer that "his idea had been to show in Mrs. Alving how a badly-brought up, badly-educated woman had to react in excess when resisting people whose minds operated like that of Pastor Manders."

Mrs. Alving had been able to break with old beliefs. "This is a central point," Ibsen had written in one of his first notes, "she has been a believer and a romantic." But the struggle was not over, even if she thought she was finished with it, for old ideas "are not erased com-

pletely by the attitudes one comes to later . . . Ghosts in everything."
Again he wanted to concentrate every struggle into one play: "The
play will be an allegory of life. Faith undermined. But one can't say
so . . . Ghosts in everything." An entry for another day reads: "The
basic mood will be set by the rapidly expanding cultural life around us
in literature, art, etc., and in contrast: all mankind gone astray." That
is: the contrast between the new ideas of the era and the generation of
men who cannot live by them.

For her one unforgivable sin Mrs. Alving was to be tried; she had
married for "extraneous reasons." Ibsen's original idea was that she
married Alving in order to "save" him, a notion fully consonant with
traditional Christian morality. But such a deed must, in Ibsen's opinion,
"bring Nemesis on the offspring." The same theme can be seen in
The Vikings when the son of Hjørdis and Gunnar proves of little worth
because the mother did not marry for love. The same is true in the
case of Mrs. Alving. Oswald is diseased not because his father was a
rake, but because his mother obeyed an immoral code of social morality.
As always in his work, Ibsen's starting point was a purely moral concept; he was concerned not with medical history but with the original
sin that brings vengeance on the woman.

Two fateful problems bring the consequences home to Mrs. Alving.
One is Oswald's half-sister, the illegitimate child of Chamberlain
Alving. The original statement of this problem was different from the
final version. The proposal of marriage between the two Alving children
was intended to save the girl from moral depravity, not to rescue
Oswald. Mrs. Alving would thus suffer the consequences of her love-
less marriage. The second problem she faced was whether to take the
life of her son when he was reduced to a sub-human level of existence.
In a draft for *A Doll's House* Dr. Rank says that such creatures ought
to be done away with; of course, he adds, "we have not reached that
point in our development yet." As Mrs. Alving stands over her ruined
son with the bottle of poison in her hand, does she have the courage
to defy all accepted standards of morality? Ibsen does not answer this
question any more than he does the previous one; he lets the curtain
fall and the decision is hidden from us.

Shortly after the play appeared, William Archer asked him bluntly
how he himself imagined the outcome: does Mrs. Alving give him the
poison or not? Ibsen laughed and replied thoughtfully: "I don't know.
Everyone will have to find out for himself. I would never dream of
deciding so difficult a question. What do you think?" Archer answered
that if she did not give him the "helping hand," it would be because
of "ghosts," phantoms from the past still alive within her—assuming,

of course, that the disease was in fact incurable. Ibsen thought that this might be the solution; the mother would keep waiting before she gave her son the "helping hand," excusing her delay on the basis that as long as he lived, there was still hope.

In that summer of 1880, Ibsen is said to have probed people's response to the play's question by asking their opinion on a story by the Danish writer Holger Drachmann, "Two Shots" ("To Skud"), which had appeared a few years earlier. The dilemma of conscience that the story poses is whether it is right to kill, out of love, someone who is hopelessly ill. The woman in the story who has the strength to dare this has grown up outside an ordered, conventional society. Mrs. Alving's courage, on the other hand, has been destroyed by the moral code of the society in which she has lived; therefore she stands hesitant, uncertain, at the moment of decision.

There is no evidence to suggest that any particular incident was the occasion for the conflict of the play as Ibsen conceived it. Francis Bull has pointed out a certain similarity to one of Mauritz Hansen's short stories, "The Daughter" ("Datteren"), where a highly placed officer marries off his housemaid, whom he has made pregnant, to an invalid caretaker. When the daughter later comes into the officer's household, she is repelled by the peg-legged caretaker who is supposedly her father. Nothing certain can be said about the influence of this story on Ibsen's thinking, although there are elements of similarity between story and play.

There do not seem to be particular models for Mrs. Alving and for Oswald, although at this time Ibsen said he regularly based his characters on models; he had to have actual human beings in mind or else he had trouble bringing his characters to life. He had to see them and hear them—how they walked and stood, how they dressed, how they behaved, how they spoke. Once he had gotten this down, they could begin to take on a life of their own. The only known model used for *Ghosts* is for Regine, who is based on a German maid he had in Munich, a very pretty girl who liked to play the lady and often showed off her few scraps of French. Some of Oswald's remarks reflect the artistic milieu Ibsen had known in Munich. Most of the elements in the play, however, go back to characters in earlier works, especially to *A Doll's House:* Mrs. Alving is an older Nora, as noted before, and Oswald a younger Dr. Rank. That defender of conventional morality, Pastor Manders, is actually schoolmaster Rørlund of *Pillars of Society,* turned minister as Lona Hessel had prophesied. Manders fully agrees with Rørlund's belief that it is one's duty "to stand before the eyes of society in as immaculate a light as possible." The strong inner relation-

ship between these plays suggests that Ibsen's imagination may have
worked out the psychology of the characters of *Ghosts* without other
models. In addition, it is clear that if some of his own rebelliousness
went into the character of Nora, even more so is evident in Mrs. Alving.

All three plays deal with the same problem: how is one to escape
the heritage of the past? Must one always contend with it? This was
the external drama of human life, as Ibsen understood it, and it was
his own drama as well, an idea that had tormented and challenged
him since his youth. In one drama after another it created the tragic
catastrophe. The past avenges itself on Catiline, on Lady Inger, on
Hjørdis, and on Sigurd. The vision had now widened to include all
mankind; the past was the dead weight that dragged men down, hindering them from reaching freedom and happiness. "What right do we
human beings have to happiness?" asks Pastor Manders, and although
the question could well have been Ibsen's own, he had begun to rebel
against the external duties imposed on man by ancient, exploded principles of morality. True morality must be found within the individual,
within his own duty to himself; in this way every individual had a
chance to find that life that would mean happiness for him.

In taking this as a life goal, Ibsen was not far from the attitude of
John Stuart Mill, whose philosophy he had once ridiculed. In 1861
Mill had tried, with his doctrine of utilitarianism, to counter the pessimism of Schopenhauer and Eduard von Hartmann, who maintained
that no man could attain happiness in life. Schopenhauer had rejected
all happiness except self-denial, leading to annihilation in Nirvana;
Hartmann found the goal of life in a negative feeling of happiness which
was identical with personal resignation. Mill, on the other hand, said
that man's need for happiness was a struggle for something positive,
something that gave him a sense of gain and to the greatest possible
number the greatest possible happiness.

When Brandes translated Mill's *Utilitarianism* (1861) under the title
of *Morality Founded on the Principle of Utility or Happiness* (1872),
Ibsen ridiculed him for bothering with a "work which seems to rival
Cicero or Seneca in Philistine pretentiousness" (Cicero was a *bête noir*
from his youth). He did not believe at the time there would be "any
progress or any future in the Stuart Mill movement," but less than
ten years later he was adopting Mill's ideas. There he found the vexing
question, "What right do you have to be happy?" And now he answered
with Mill: "That is just what I do have a right to be." From *Ghosts*
onward this becomes an insistent note in his writing; man shall demand
and shall have life and happiness. When Mill wrote: "The present
miserable education and miserable organization of society are the only

real obstacles to everyone's attaining such a life," Ibsen agreed. In the summer of 1879 he wrote to Bjørnson that the only cause he found worth fighting for in Norway was "the introduction of a modern school system," especially a new religious training that would put an end to all "medieval nonsense" and develop human beings who could think for themselves. As he insisted in A Doll's House, all the old precepts had to go into the melting pot. To Mill, the idea of happiness was a social demand to be realized in politics; for Ibsen it was to be found in the liberation of the individual.

When the characters in his plays speak of happiness and the joy of life, they usually do not give a precise notion of what they mean. But if we look for the concept that is contrasted with happiness, we almost invariably find the word "duty." This suggests the content of the happiness Ibsen spoke of: freedom from all external demands, the right to be oneself, to develop one's capabilities in complete freedom. Antagonism to such personal freedom comes from all the traditional social forces that live around—and within—one. It was necessary to do battle with the past; that is the prison where man is shackled and is angrily striking at the bars. But will he ever escape?

CHAPTER THIRTY-THREE

A PUBLIC ENEMY (1882)

P. O. SCHJOTT, professor of Greek at the University of Oslo, wrote in a review: "Of all the modern dramatic literature we have read, *Ghosts* comes closest to the drama of antiquity.... Classical drama is called a drama of family and fate because of the tragic destiny inherited by the family. Here we also have a family tragedy, but a social drama as well—classical tragedy, reborn on modern soil." The Greek quality in Ibsen's play is apparent not only in the powerful theme of Nemesis on which it is constructed, but also in the severity of its form; we are led directly to the catastrophe, which is ignited by the sins of the past. Firm, incisive strokes define the plot and characters; everything irrelevant or trivial is cut away. As in *A Doll's House*, there are five characters, and every one of them has a crucial part in the main plot. This time Ibsen managed without even a housemaid or a butler. The result is a quality of impressive stylization about the whole play.

Most of Ibsen's contemporaries, however, did not think so, and to many it appeared as the epitome of the worst kind of naturalism. Ibsen was compared to Zola, whose series of novels about the Rougon-Macquart family had been published over the last ten years. Zola's graphic descriptions of the gross immorality and coarseness of bourgeois society had been capped by *Nana* (1880), a study in unbridled animalism. To be coupled with such a writer was naturally a great irritation to Ibsen. Of course he wanted to write realistic, uncompromising descriptions of life as it was, but he was by temperament closer to Flaubert, a romantic turned realist, who wrote in a realistic mode yet kept an emotional commitment to romanticism. He was not interested in analyzing the consequences of sexual vice in society; the individual was his concern, and social values and norms were judged according to whether they helped or hindered a man in being himself. He was a social critic because he set an ideal goal for society, and by setting such a goal, the realism he evoked had a significance beyond itself and was in fact symbolic.

Whether Ibsen had ever read anything by Zola is not certain; half a year later when a Swedish painter asked what he thought of the French author, he answered shortly: "I don't read books, I leave that to my wife and Sigurd." Sigurd was in fact devoted to Zola, and Mrs. Ibsen was a great reader of novels. If Ibsen had read Zola, he would probably have caught the note of romantic idealism that was in him as well, but he was very anxious to emphasize the differences between them. When the same Swede praised the novelist and *Nana* in particular, Ibsen cut him short: "Zola is a democrat; I am an aristocrat." On another occasion he gave a more exact summary of his literary method: "Zola goes down into the sewer to bathe, I to clean it out."

But to his contemporaries there were more similarities than differences, and *Ghosts* repelled them. It was highly improper for Ibsen to bring that "nasty disease" onto the stage; still worse, he seemed to be defending incest and euthanasia. Nice society reacted as though struck by lightning when *Ghosts* appeared at Christmastime, 1881.

While working on the play in the spring of the year, Ibsen wrote with confidence to his publisher: "I feel certain that the book will be received with interest by the general public." By the time he finished, he realized there would probably be controversy: "*Ghosts* will perhaps cause alarm in some circles; but that will have to be. If it did not do so, it would not have had to be written." He expected that the Conservatives, those he called "stagnation men," would scream protests, but he was not disturbed by the prospect. His other plays had blackened his name with them and now he neither wished nor expected approval from that quarter. In 1878 he told Gunnar Heiberg: "You've been abused in *Morgenbladet*. You must have talent." With *Ghosts*, Conservative indignation toward the apostate leaped to fever pitch and their newspapers hastily blessed themselves to ward off the "nihilistic" immorality of the new play.

The reaction of the "fanatics" was even worse than Ibsen had anticipated. The situation is probably echoed later in *Rosmersholm*, when Rector Kroll cautions Rosmer on proclaiming his loss of religious faith: "You are a naive soul, Rosmer. You cannot imagine the flattening storm that will descend on you." The unexpected revelation, however, was the timidity that seized most of the so-called liberals of the Left. Although they were radical in their political opinions, they were still authentic conservatives in religious and moral issues, or at any rate did not dare expose their free-thinking. When Bjørnson opened the attack against orthodox theology in 1879, they were unhappy. They were not much pleased by Alexander Kielland's "Christmas Story"

Elsie, published just a fortnight before *Ghosts.* The play was the last straw; the Liberal party disclaimed all responsibility.

It was reviewed by *Oplandenes Avis,* one of the leading Liberal newspapers, edited by O. Arvesen at Hamar: "As a work by our cele-brated countryman it must, of course, be reviewed, although in our opinion total silence would be the best review." In the reviewer's judgment: "This is, to put it briefly, one of the most dismal books we have read in a long time.... It is a motley assortment of immoral, criminal, and emasculated individuals, living in the midst of corrupting circumstances and decaying institutions." Such a picture, the reviewer was happy to point out, had no relation to conditions in Norway, and he felt obliged to defend his country from this native-born author who had lived abroad for so many years. In conclusion he wrote: "The only comfort one can get from reading the book is that it is, at least in our humble opinion, much more poorly written than the author's previous works."

This was the general tone of the Liberal papers around the country, following the lead set by the most influential, *Dagbladet* in Oslo. On the day the book came out, Mrs. Margrete Vullum, daughter of the Danish Liberal Orla Lehmann, asked for the opportunity to review it in *Dagbladet.* Although she had been reviewing for the past two years and thought she would be assigned the new book as a matter of course, Nicolay Grevstad, the editor, who had already gotten some idea of Ibsen's play, felt he could not entrust it to her. He insisted that her review be ready for the afternoon edition the same day, and when she naturally objected, denied her the book. That was the end of her writing for *Dagbladet* as long as Grevstad was in charge. One of the regular staff members wrote the review, and his judgment was as follows: "The total impression left by the book is decidedly unpleasant. As one reads it, one finds oneself unconsciously thinking how fine the old poetry was: one could at least read that without putting his nerves in peril.... It seems as if Ibsen took great delight in saying all the worst things he knew, and in saying them in as extreme a way as possible." Ibsen has turned his radicalism against the age, the re-viewer explained: "Again the victim is marriage. And never has there been a more ruthless, more vehement assault against that institution on which our society is founded."

Ironically enough, these were almost the same words with which *Love's Comedy* was attacked by *Aftenbladet,* the leading Liberal paper, twenty years earlier. *Ghosts* was the target now, and the reviewer who felt such alarm at the attack on marriage was none other than Arne

Garborg, the radical and liberal who had even published a book called *A Freethinker*. Such a review from such a man is the best indication of the kind of moral revolt embodied in *Ghosts*.

There were, of course, those who dared to admit the greatness they recognized in the play. Bjørnson replied to Garborg's moral qualms in an article in *Dagbladet*, and although the editors quickly squelched any further discussion, Ibsen was deeply grateful to Bjørnson: "In truth he has a magnificent and princely spirit, and I shall never forget it." Oslo's other Liberal paper, *Verdens Gang*, did not condemn the play but called it "a plea for repentance in a powerful and graphic form." The first issue of *Nyt tidsskrift*, edited by J. E. Sars and Olaf Skavlan, contained the perceptive review by P. O. Schjøtt, quoted above, which ended: "When the dust stirred up by purblind criticism settles, hopefully in a short time, Ibsen's drama will remain in all its bold and flawless contour, not only his most honorable deed, but also the mightiest work of art yet produced by him or our entire dramatic literature."

In Denmark the outcry of the Conservatives was just as violent as in Norway, but there was more of a "literary Left" to counterattack. Brandes' review in *Morgenbladet* had warm praise for the play's courageous message. But the usual judgment here, too, was that the book was godless, immoral, and a danger to society. People had no business reading it. The same voices were heard from Sweden, but Ibsen felt that the level of criticism was higher there: "A Swedish literary attack never offends, for it is always conceived and carried out in an aristocratic manner; in Denmark the manner is bourgeois; in Norway, plebeian." In the same letter, written to Sophie Adlersparre (who used the pseudonym "Esselde"), who had lectured and written in defense of the play, he developed this idea, suggesting a kind of program of Scandinavian literary cooperation: "We three countries have all the qualifications for forming an intellectual union, in which Sweden will furnish the intellectual nobility, Denmark the bourgeoisie, and Norway the proletariat." He may have been influenced by the fact that he was writing to a Swedish noblewoman, but he did believe in an intellectual aristocracy, and he hoped that one might develop in Norway as well.

Calculating from past sales, the publisher had printed a first edition of 10,000 copies, much of which had been pre-ordered by Scandinavian booksellers. But Hegel had been too optimistic, and he had to take back many copies that were ordered in advance, including some from dealers who had bought on account. This Christmas he sold fewer books by Ibsen than usual; people had obviously been frightened off.

The "unanimous aversion" and "loathing" gave Christiania Theatre a good excuse to reject the play, and for the first time since *Love's Comedy*, theatres did not dare perform an Ibsen play. When the theatre in Bergen followed suit, *Dagbladet* had the courage to protest against "this brutal suppression." But popular opinion was unquestionably on the side of the theatres, not only in Norway, but in Denmark and Sweden as well. Frans Hedberg, director of the Göteborg Theatre, is said to have planned a production, only to be deterred by hostile public reaction. The new reader for the Copenhagen Royal Theatre, the musical-comedy writer Erik Bøgh, gave his considered opinion. In most cases he would have "exempted" such a master of the drama from any kind of criticism, but "when he writes a drama whose central theme is a repulsive, pathological morbidity, and which at the same time undermines the morality on which our social order is based, then I think I am not justified in giving any 'exemptions,' since neither law nor morality is any respecter of persons, and the magnitude of the themes examined only increases the magnitude of danger in such an attack." His final judgment was: "In my opinion the detrimental tendencies are so pronounced that I find it my inescapable duty, without considering the masterful composition and development of the play, to unconditionally recommend its rejection." In Germany things were as bad or worse, and no one even dared translate the play. It was not until 1884 that Frau Maria von Borch's German version appeared, and it was another two years before it was produced in Germany; even then it had to contend with police censorship.

The first performance of the play was, strangely enough, in America. A small Dano-Norwegian theatre group in Chicago performed it in the original language in May, 1882. Although the production was repeated in Minneapolis and other midwestern cities, it did not reach the general public. In spite of the pioneer efforts of Sir Edmund Gosse, Ibsen was still almost completely unknown in the English-speaking world. The single performance, in abbreviated form, of *Pillars of Society*, given at London's Gaiety Theatre on December 15, 1880, made no more impression than the first English performance of *A Doll's House*, (under the title of *The Child Wife*) in Milwaukee, Wisconsin, on June 2 and 3, 1882. *A Doll's House* was first performed in London in 1884, under the title of *Breaking a Butterfly*, but it was not given an adequate production until 1889. *Ghosts* was not produced until 1891.

The first European performance of *Ghosts* was the result of the initiative of August Lindberg, a Swedish actor-director whose troupe performed it at Helsingborg, Sweden, in 1883, and then toured all the Scandinavian capitals. At the same time two Danish companies toured the minor cities of Denmark and Norway with it. When the Dramatic Theatre in Stockholm followed with a production shortly after this, the ice was broken. But the controversy did not die down, and the play became a rallying point for radical-minded, independent young people everywhere.

Only a short time before Ibsen had seen the world open for him, with the promise of victory. Now he was the outsider again. Within a week after *Ghosts* appeared, a flood of letters and newspapers brought ample testimony of the storm he had raised. At first he was not concerned; it would surely pass quickly. But he soon realized that he had stirred up deeper social antagonism than he first imagined. The Danish reaction he attributed to ill will, the Norwegian to "feebleness of judgment." But he could not hide his real disappointment with the behavior of the "liberals": "Those leaders who carry on about freedom and liberalism, and at the same time enslave themselves to the imagined opinions of their subscribers! I get more and more confirmation of my belief that there is something demoralizing about politics and parties. I could never, under any circumstance, join a party that had a majority on its side. Bjørnson says, 'The majority is always right.' I suppose he has to say so as a practical politician. I, however, must say: the minority is always right. Naturally, I'm not thinking of that minority of stagnant men who have been outstripped by the great center grouping that we call 'liberal'; I mean the minority that is out in front, where the majority has not yet reached. The one who is most closely in tune with the future is the one who is right." (It should be noted that this letter, dated January 3, 1882, was in all probability written before Ibsen had seen Bjørnson's defense of *Ghosts*, which began to appear in *Dagbladet* on December 22, 1881. Ibsen was in Rome at the time, and his letter about Bjørnson's "princely spirit" was written on January 24.)

In letter after letter from now on words such as these, written to Brandes right after New Year's, 1882, occur. His eyes had been suddenly opened to how "utterly alone" both he and Bjørnson were in their homeland; back home there was still no true freedom. He had felt this all along, and now he put aside all dreams that it might be different. Now he wanted to stand alone. On January 24 he wrote to Olaf Skavlan: "I want to stand as an isolated sniper on the outpost, working on my own." In this mood he moved forward to *An Enemy of the People;* now he was himself a public enemy.

Ideas for the play had been in his mind even before *Ghosts*, first stirring during the controversy over *A Doll's House,* then being pushed aside by work on the former play. Now the theme crystallized and by the middle of March, only three months after *Ghosts* was published, he was hard at work. The ideas for the play had been with him ever since his first contact with Kierkegaard, who had declared: "The multitude is falsehood." The phrase sums up many different kinds of nineteenth century individualism—from Tocqueville's phrase "the tyranny of the majority," and Mill's philosophy of the individual demand for freedom against the majority—to Bismarck's call for men who would not yield to the masses. (In a speech in November, 1881, the chancellor had poured scorn on "the courtiers of the majority, the registrars of the majority.")

In the *Andhrimner* period Ibsen had been at odds with the "liberal" majority as well as the reactionary minority. In creating the character of Dr. Stockmann Ibsen seems to have been thinking of those days, particularly a speech his friend Abildgaard gave at the Workers' Congress in 1850. Abildgaard noted how the king's veto could block a law through three successive Stortings: "And who can assure us that a law passed after so many years still corresponds to the needs of the time?" He was not ready to grant truth a life of even twenty years. The truth was short-lived then, and those who professed it were in isolation against the herd. When he wrote *Brand*, Ibsen emphasized the same points. Brand says that it is "dreadful to stand alone...hopeless to be a lonely warrior." But the point of the whole play is that no matter how dreadful, it is the only thing worth doing. The sheriff and the dean, who cultivate the majority, are ridiculed, as is Peer Gynt who boasts that "when the majority swears that one is the real thing, it would be sheer stupidity to contradict."

Fearing the effects of such subservience to popular opinion, to ties that would restrict his freedom, Ibsen had left his native country. Even friendly ties could be dangerous; in 1872 he warned Brandes about building his hopes on societies and organizations: "It seems to me...that the lonely man is the strongest."

Ibsen's deep-rooted antagonism to politics and politicians of all colors can be seen in *The League of Youth* and in his letters to Brandes throughout the 1870's. The new edition of *Catiline* in 1875, for example, carried a slurring reference to Cicero, "the indefatigable advocate of the majority." He even used the case of the French eviction of the monks from their monasteries as an example of the corruption by majority rule. In a conversation with Kristofer Janson on New Year's Eve, 1880, he said, "Haven't I always maintained that you republicans are the worst tyrants of all? You don't respect the freedom of the individual. A republic is that form of government where the freedom of the individual is least respected." Janson defended the actions of the French by saying that the majority of the people approved. Ibsen then lost his temper: "The majority? What is the majority? Ignorant masses. Intelligence is always a minority. How many of the majority do you think are entitled to an opinion? Most of them are dolts." He was sincere, but he was quoting almost verbatim from Schiller, who gives the lines to the solitary dissenter in the Polish Parliament:

Was ist die Mehrheit? Mehrheit ist der Unsinn;	What is the majority? Majority is stupidity.
Verstand ist stets bie Wenigen nur gewesen.	Intelligence has always belonged to the few.

Ibsen thought the same about the people back home. Once he said to Janson, quite seriously: "Norway has passed one good law since 1814, the one that protects quacks; now we can hope that more thousands of idiots will be killed off each year than otherwise." On another occasion he said: "If only there would soon be a revolution back there! One of my greatest pleasures then will be to stand on the barricades and gun down Norwegian farmers." No one bothered to think or to put great ideas into action; everything was trivia. "The only ones who have my sympathies are the nihilists and the socialists; at least they are consistent and thorough-going in what they want." Shorty after the controversy over *Ghosts* had broken out, he wrote in a letter: "As usual, the Norwegians proved the most cowardly of all, and the most cowardly among these cowards were of course the so-called Liberals." In another letter he called them "poor fellows to man a barricade with."

He stood on the barricades symbolically by giving so much of himself to the "enemy of the people" he created, the man whose life teaches him that the strongest man is indeed the one who stands alone—Dr. Stockmann. The title for the new play may have been suggested by Shakespeare's *Coriolanus;* it too is about a lonely man, contemptuous of the mob. But Shakespeare wrote a tragedy, while Ibsen's play developed into a comedy. His other plays were chaste and stylized in form, profound and penetrating in theme; they were not designed to rouse sentiment. Now his love of satire led him to write a comedy that does appeal to sentiment, where the characters and especially the hero, are developed for their own sake, not merely as a means of driving the play forward.

The hero's name is taken from the house in Skien where Ibsen was born, but "Stockmann" also was a name he could symbolically give himself. The "badger" Morten Kiil is also a Skien memory. And if the town could hardly be called a resort for invalids, it could with some justice be the home for "all the truck from· Mølledalen, all this vile smelling business," for Mølledalen ("Mill Valley") is a paraphrase of Skien's Kverndalen (also "Mill Valley") where the brook known locally as Lortebekk ("Dirty Brook") ran. The preceding winter Ibsen had been working on his memoirs, looking back on his childhood in Skien, and while the memoirs were never completed, the self-portrait in the play was. When he finished, he wrote to his publisher: "Dr. Stockmann and I get along famously; we agree on so many things, only the doctor's head is somewhat more befuddled than mine, and moreover, he has a number of traits that will make people more willing to listen to ideas that they might not accept so readily from me."

Years later, after seeing a performance of the play in Berlin, Ibsen said to a German friend: "Stockmann is in part a grotesque fellow and a blockhead." In spite of the elements of Ibsen's personality that are in Stockmann, there are many details drawn from other sources, enough to give him a reality independent from his creator. A Munich friend of his, the young German poet Alfred Meissner, had told him about an experience his physician-father had in the famous Bohemian resort of Teplitz in the 1830's. When an epidemic of cholera broke out, he had felt it his duty to make the fact known. Because the guests were frightened away, the town's citizens were furious with him; they stoned his house and he was forced to move away. If this story suggested the plot, the ideas for the main character were found closer to home. Since 1872 a struggle had been going on in Norway between the directors of the Christiania Dampkjøkken (Steam Kitchens) a popular, low-priced restaurant, and the apothecary Harald Thaulow. One of the most famous episodes in this controversy (still very much alive in February, 1881) was a meeting held in October, 1874, three weeks after Ibsen's last visit to Norway, at which Thaulow read what he called his "speech of truth." He justified his exposure of some very unpleasant facts about the operation of the restaurant by saying, "I would have to deny my nature if I do not now, as before, tell the truth for its own sake." In a still more Ibsenian tone he issued a pamphlet against the restaurant directors in 1880, and called it *Pillars of Society in Prose*. In February, 1881, he addressed a meeting of the directors and read a pamphlet which tried to prove that Christiania Dampkjøkken was the greatest fraud in the city. The meeting turned into a stampede and Thaulow could not get the floor. He left, crying out: "One cannot resist the crude herd. I will have nothing more to do with you; I will not throw pearls in the dirt. This is an evil abuse of a free people in a free society. I am leaving now. Kindly go sit in the dunce's corner and be ashamed of yourselves!" Fourteen days later he was dead.

The report of this meeting, accentuated by the death notice which followed immediately after, no doubt lent much to the mood and tempo of the scene in the play where Dr. Stockmann tries to tell the truth to the townspeople. The personality of the apothecary may have influenced Ibsen as he drew the doctor's character; Thaulow was independent and audacious, with many unusual notions. (In 1881 Jonas Lie had pointed out the similarity between Thaulow and his cousin, the poet Wergeland.) But Ibsen himself indicated two sources for his portrait of Stockmann: Jonas Lie and Bjørnstjerne Bjørnson.

Jonas Lie was one of his oldest friends and although they had fallen out once, they had since made it up. In 1862 Lie had published *Love's Comedy*. In the summer of 1880 they were neighbors in Berchtesgaden, which Ibsen had recommended to him. Lie was an extraordinary person, with a liberal and tolerant understanding that is quite evident in his letters to Ibsen during the controversy over *Ghosts*. But it was often difficult to follow his thinking; in writing or in conversation he tended to express himself in brilliant insights, each forceful and incisive in itself, but frequently lacking any obviously coherent pattern as a whole. Ibsen found him fascinating and spent many summer evenings studying him. Much of Stockmann's abruptness as well as his kindness can be attributed to Lie.

The doctor's inflexible will and forcefulness, however, comes from Bjørnson, whose "free, bold, and brave" stance in the *Ghosts* controversy had done much to heal the breach between the two men. Bjørnson's nine-month tour of America kept him in Ibsen's mind during the winter of 1880-81, when he was shaping the theme of *An Enemy of the People*. Ibsen thought it courageous and even a bit foolhardy for him to undertake such a potentially dangerous trip, and he worried at every mention of storms at sea or illness. On March 8, 1882, eight days before the first letter that mentions the new play, he wrote to Bjørnson: "Then it was suddenly clear how infinitely much more you mean to me than all the rest. I felt that if any accident should befall you, if so great a misfortune should strike our country, all creative joy would leave me." When Bjørnson celebrated the twenty-fifth year of his writing career a few months later, Ibsen gave him the highest praise he could bestow on any man: "His life is his best poem." He felt that Bjørnson had attained the greatest goal man can reach: "To realize himself in his every act."

The impressive thing about Bjørnson was that he had never been afraid to risk everything. In the flag controversy in 1879 he had presided at a stormy meeting where the whole city became one mob against him; after the meeting the house of one of his companions, H. E. Berner, was stoned. Ibsen had had no sympathy with this cause, and as a result

Bjørnson refused to call on him when he passed through Munich the following autumn. Nevertheless, Ibsen was deeply concerned over the way Bjørnson was being persecuted for agitating for a separate Norwegian flag. He kept asking for news of the affair: "It interests me," he said, "because it is so sickening." When the Oslo upper classes boycotted Bjørnson's speech at the unveiling of the Wergeland statue in the spring of 1881, Ibsen had more than enough material for the portrait of an enemy of the people. The reckless but exhilarating spirit with which Bjørnson fought this battle stirred Ibsen's admiration and respect, and gave him the imaginative substance out of which to carve his crusading doctor.

Ibsen caught some of this crusading fervor himself, especially after his first anger subsided and he could laugh at the affair. He linked his new play to his previous comedy, *The League of Youth*, by bringing back printer Aslaksen, not as a rather down-at-the-heels, rootless fellow, but as a householder and petty bourgeois. Old radicals were now good conservatives and attorney Stensgaard had become a district judge. How could one expect such people to show a spirit of true freedom? The new play is also linked with *Pillars of Society* by having Dr. Stockmann placed in somewhat the same position as Consul Bernick, working for new ideas in a community of purblind men. Morten Kiil had almost appeared in *Pillars*, and schoolmaster Rørlund stalks menacingly across the background of the new play. Tying together old and new in this manner is typical of Ibsen; he sought a solid, inner unity to his entire writing.

He enjoyed writing the new play and it came easily to him; nine months after *Ghosts* it was finished. He was in good humor and wrote, as he had done with *The League of Youth*, that it would be a "peaceful play," one "that can be read by cabinet members and merchants and their lady wives; one from which the theatres need not recoil." The play was, in fact, more universal in its appeal than *The League of Youth*, and could succeed on any stage. In structure, characters, and language it was as fresh and lively as anything he had ever written.

He could not prevent people from taking sides on the opinions expressed in the play. Conservatives enjoyed the mockery of politicians of the democratic majority; anarchists welcomed it as a plea for their social ideals. The strength of the play, however, was not in its opinions but in the life that surged through it, in the boldly conceived characters that animated it, all children of a genuinely poetic imagination.

CHAPTER THIRTY-FOUR

PITY AND CONTEMPT:

THE WILD DUCK (1882-84)

U NDER the largely comic tone of *An Enemy of the People* there
is a current of biting contempt for the mob, whether cultured or vulgar,
Liberals or Conservatives, whom the enemy of the people must throw
off. Ibsen had for many years nurtured a similar contempt as a psychological defense throughout his years of depression and frustration.
But now, when his belief in himself no longer needed this defense,
he could release his scorn in laughter. New problems, however, quickly
arose. What about these people he scorned; did they ever have a
chance to be different? Did they not also have the right to live, and
were they not justified in that right? Had he the right to heap contempt
on them? His attitudes toward man and human existence had to be
re-examined. The result would be a new interpretation of the psychological motivation of human behavior and morality.

His own psychological state during these years is very hard to
determine; he no longer poured his feelings out in verse, and his letters
became more and more reticent. He deliberately forbade access to
his inner world, even laying aside the memoirs he had begun in 1880-81.
After the *Ghosts* controversy he was always on guard lest anyone take
the opinions of his characters as his own. He refused all responsibility
and kept his own counsel like the sphinx.

Since leaving Norway in 1864 he had cultivated what he once called
"a really full-blown egotism," that is, a disciplined self-centeredness
that enabled him to ignore any consideration except the demand that
he do his work as perfectly as was in his power. By 1886 this single-
minded sense of purpose would be expressed in this way: "More and
more I have fallen into the habit of occupying myself with one thing
at a time, putting everything else to one side as I mull over and over
again a single line of thought." Regular working habits developed
gradually. In Rome during the 1860's he invaded the inns and taverns
with his friends and took an active part in discussions and conversations.
When he returned in the 1880's, he still frequented the cafés, but now
he was usually alone. Every afternoon he watched the traffic on the
Corso from his regular chair in front of the Caffé Nazionale, but he did

not usually like being approached. He preferred to ignore people on his regular walks about town and would rather have his friends not greet him. He was, however, a gracious host and often entertained in the evening, but he never spoke of personal matters.

He lived in Rome every winter from 1880 to 1885, always in the same house in Via Capo le Case. He spent the summer of 1881 in Sorrento, and the three following summers in the Tyrol, in the village of Gossensass in the Brenner Pass. Always more at ease among German-speaking people than among Italians, he found the friendly Tyroleans particularly delightful. His favorite place in the Tyrol became Gossensass, situated beautifully and also conveniently amid high mountains that blocked off the north, but opened to the south. In a letter of 1889 he wrote that he found "magnificent nature and splendid air" there. As he walked the fine paths through the spruce forest along the Eisach river and the Pflersch brook, he could imagine himself back in Norway; the foaming waters of the brook so intrigued him that the villagers named him "das Bachmandl," the brook gnome. From a hill above the village he could look down into the sunny valley, behind him marshes and wilderness. In 1889, his last summer there, the village dedicated an "Ibsen-platz" to him on this hill; in gratitude he would make a complimentary allusion to the village in *Hedda Gabler*.

He once said that he remembered Gossensass with such gratitude because he felt a spiritual kinship with the good friends he found there. Actually he did not have much company and spent most of his time alone, except in the evenings when he would gather together a small group of friends. He also said that he was grateful to the village because he had made the first sketches for many of his plays there— perhaps a reference to *A Doll's House, The Wild Duck*, and *Hedda Gabler*—and had completed two of them there—*An Enemy of the People* and *The Wild Duck*. The latter play is particularly associated with Gossensass, as it grew out of the intellectual reorientation he underwent in these years.

As early as January, 1883, a mere six weeks after *An Enemy of the People*, he wrote to his publisher: "I am already working out plans for a new play on contemporary life. It will be in four acts, and I hope I will be able to get down to work within a few months at the latest." It was to take longer, and one indication that he was progressing slowly was his offer, made in February, to prepare a new edition of *The Feast at Solhaug*. This would not "noticeably delay my new work." And so he set to work on the old play.

At one time he had not even wanted to acknowledge *The Feast at Solhaug* as his; it did not meet the standards he now demanded of his work, and he had not been enthusiastic about Hegel's earlier offer to republish it along with other works of his youth. But in 1879 the young Finnish literary scholar Valfrid Vasenius had written his doctoral dissertation on Ibsen's earlier works—the first scholarly work ever written on Ibsen—and had analyzed the play in the perspective of Ibsen's development. Vasenius' full-length study, published in 1882, gave what Ibsen himself called "a correct and exhaustive interpretation of the play." (Ibsen supplied him with much useful information for the study in the spring of 1880.) Ibsen had been annoyed by Brandes' long essay, also published in 1882, which repeated the old charge that *The Feast at Solhaug* was patterned after, or at least influenced by *Svend Dyrings Huus,* and he determined to use the spring of 1883 to revise his old ballad-play.

The only changes he actually made were a few minor details in the language of the play, but he did write a long preface in which he made a vigorous effort to prove that it was a completely independent work. What is psychologically revealing about the preface is not only the strong self-assertiveness, but the intense indignation he still felt toward a newspaper critique more than 27 years old. In addition there was the scorn he could still feel for the Norwegian critics of the 1850's. The implacable contempt that can be read in the preface is in the same spirit as that seen in *An Enemy of the People.*

There is still a certain ambiguity about Ibsen's decision to publish a new edition of *The Feast.* It is, after all, largely written in verse, and Ibsen had for many years renounced verse as a medium of expression. Right after completing work on the new edition he wrote a letter severely denouncing verse drama as harmful and moribund. He is said to have made the same statement to the young Norwegian poet Theodor Caspari the following winter. There seems to have been a contradiction between his actions and his professed aversion to poetic drama; one may ask how clear his attitude toward the debilitating effects of verse actually was. By the following spring of 1884 he retreated from his dogmatic position and wrote to Caspari: "I recall that I once expressed myself somewhat disrespectfully about the art of poetry; but this was due only to my own relationship to this art form at the time. I have long since stopped setting up universal norms, for I no longer believe that they can be maintained with any inner justification. I believe that all of us have nothing else and nothing better to do than to realize our own selves in truth and spirit. In my opinion this is the only true liberalism, and for this reason the so-called liberals are so repellent to me in so many respects."

A change was taking place in him, and it became clearer to him during 1883 and 1884. The change has a direct bearing on that contemptuous attitude toward humanity that found expression in *An Enemy of the People*. Now the theme of the new play that he kept turning over in his mind was the question: Are not men in fact too weak to have "universal norms" set up for them? He thought back on the ideals of truth and freedom he had urged in his writing for two decades, and he felt a profound disgust with himself and his followers. What to him had been an ideal based on inner rebellion and liberation had been degraded by others into crude formulas with superficial, external significance. Different groups argued over passages in his works that could be twisted to support their own party line or dogmas. But the individual soul was all he was ever concerned with, and there began to grow in him a burning desire to escape from this blunt-minded herd, who saw everything in terms of deceptively simple "absolutes." He could agree with Bjørnson, who developed the idea that men overreach themselves in struggling for the great Christian ideals, the main theme in his powerful psychological drama, *Beyond Human Power, Part I*, published in November, 1883. As early as his preliminary notes to *Ghosts*, he had expressed the same idea: "All mankind, and especially Christians, suffer from megalomania." And as a result, ideals became lies on which their lives foundered.

There was bitter contempt in this idea of human destiny, but there was also pity, an emotion that expressed not only "wretched creature," but also "poor man!" The emotion would lead him on to a still deeper understanding of these wretched, pitiable human beings.

Among Ibsen's literary remains was found a page of notes of the same kind that had usually been written for the plays. The notes are not attached to the drafts of any one play, and they are not dated. Although they cannot be dated by any external evidence, they were clearly written after the fall of 1882, since there is a reference to a vote in the lower house of the Storting which had asked the town councils for their opinion on the question of separate estates for married women. There is another sentence alluding to an article by Brandes which states that Holger Drachmann was becoming a conservative. The author of this book dated these notes 1883 when he published them in Ibsen's *Efterladte skrifter* (1909). Subsequently, a German writer who signed himself A. K. (Alfred Klaar?) reported that Ibsen showed him the notes in December, 1882. If we can accept this testimony, we can connect the notes with Ibsen's letter to Hegel in January, 1883, where he speaks of his plans for a new play. They would seem to be, therefore, the first notes on the drama that he called *The Wild Duck*.

The transition in Ibsen's thinking during these years can be clearly seen in these notes (now published in the Oxford Ibsen, Volume VI, pp. 429-31). They reflect only in vague outline the play that became *The Wild Duck,* and a number of ideas suggested here would not be utilized until *Rosmersholm.* He did put one of the notations to use in *The Wild Duck,* however, the description of the "photographer, the unsuccessful poet," "an idle dreamer," and his marriage, which "in one way has become a 'true marriage' in that during his married life he has sunk down or in any case has not grown." There is also a reference to the school friend who visits him in his poverty, but here the friend is a "sybarite," who "enjoys an aesthetic indignation at poverty and misery." (He suggests an inverted Ulrik Brendel, who also calls himself "a bit of a sybarite.") The shipwrecked photographer dreams of a revolution in social and intellectual life; he is a socialist, but one who does not dare to realize his dreams—in effect, an undeveloped Rosmer. There is no hint of how the dramatic conflict between the photographer and the friend was conceived; the only suggestion of a catastrophe is the note that the photographer "like printer A [slaksen] ...has had a glimpse of a higher world: that is his misfortune." The dramatic conflict appears to be between his yearning for new ideas and the failure of his will to action, making him a new kind of Peer Gynt, set in the conflicts of modern society.

Echoes of earlier plays can be detected in the notations. "Modern society is not a society of people; it is merely a society of males" *(A Doll's House).* The photographer-hero "has come to the conclusion that no improvement is possible by emancipation; the work of creation has been a failure from the start" *(Ghosts).* In one of the drafts of *Ghosts* he had written: "When man demands the right to live and develop in a human way, this is megalomania." Now, three years later: "Liberation consists in securing the individual's right to liberate himself, each according to his own need." More and more convinced of the relativity of values, of the right of every individual soul to its own life, he had to give up all "universal norms." The last notations read: "Conscience is not a stable thing. It varies in different individuals and in changing times." This idea of the conflict between "the antiquated and the coming consciences" would be the dramatic theme of *Rosmersholm.* But for now the influence of the idea would lead him to suspend all legalistic, precedent-bound judgment on the myriad variety of human beings.

One unique feature of the early notes for *The Wild Duck* is that Ibsen identifies the models for his main characters. "The photographer, the unsuccessful poet," is referred to as "E. L." and "the sybarite" as "A. K." In a separate note on "models" he lists the full names: Edvard Larssen and Alexander Kielland.

Larssen was a young man who came to Oslo in 1860 to prepare for his university entrance examination, but he never got that far. He became a photographer, and it was he who took in 1861 or 1862 the first photograph we have of Ibsen. He also tried his hand at poetry and published a little collection of *Poems* in 1862. When Botten Hansen reviewed them in *Illustreret Nyhedsblad,* he could find nothing kinder to say than that people ought to buy them to help a poor fellow out. Larssen went to Bergen, where he worked in business and journalism, finally emigrating to America. His career in Norway had certainly been "unsuccessful," but nothing is known of Larssen that would justify the traits Ibsen gives his photographer. The painter Magnus Bagge (who signed himself "von Bagge" in Germany) has also been suggested as a model for Hjalmar Ekdal, but his name is not on Ibsen's list. The painter C. M. Ross, whom he had known in Rome, is, however, and he may have taken traits from both these men. Ekdal's "heart-winning" quality of voice is taken from the writer Kristofer Janson, whom he had known and argued with in Rome in the winter of 1880-81. In 1884 he wrote that Janson "can sound downright lovely even when he's twaddling at his worst." There was much to recommend him as a model for the poseur Hjalmar Ekdal.

Alexander Kielland's name is surprising in this context, for Ibsen knew him only through his books, which he followed closely. In December, 1881, he discussed *Working People* and *Elsie* with William Archer. He objected to Kielland's habit of describing all vice as something forced on the poor by the rich, without taking account of the vice that sprang up among the poor themselves; such an attitude was simply fabricating a "ghost" in place of reality. He probably had heard that Kielland was a bon vivant, and so imagined that his indignation at the condition of the poor was purely "aesthetic." Ibsen ultimately decided, however, not to use "the sybarite" in the play, and Kielland was never actually pressed into service as a model. He would work out an entirely new concept for the school friend whom he called Gregers Werle.

In comparing the character of the photographer as suggested in the notations with the final version of Hjalmar Ekdal, we can see how different the finished play is from Ibsen's first thoughts. Ekdal is no longer the socialistic dreamer whose "delicate nature" prevents him from yielding to his radicalism. He no longer says witty or profound things about social or intellectual problems, and we hear no more about his hobby-horses, "magnetic influences" and "the sixth sense." The suggestion for changing the character may quite possibly have come from the character's profession. In the play he is a photographer in a sym-

bolic sense as well, a man who does nothing but reproduce ("regurgi-
tate," in Dr. Relling's phrase) all kinds of stock responses and clichés.
His skill in "retouching" can be observed in his account of old Werle's
elegant dinner party. The profession of photography becomes a symbol of his entire existence.

Probably no play was more thoroughly reshaped in his imagination
while it was still in the formative stages. The composition of the play
can be followed in some detail. In June, 1883, with the new edition of
The Feast at Solhaug finished, he wrote to Brandes: "Now I am
grappling with the draft of a new dramatic work in four acts. From time
to time various follies accumulate in one, and a person naturally likes
to find an outlet for them. But since the play will not deal with impeachment of the cabinet or the absolute veto or even the pure flag, it
can scarcely count on getting any attention from the Norwegians." This
is a clear indication that the play would not deal with the kind of
controversies he had previously been interested in. In the same letter
he wrote: "Your books contain a new element, an element of the future,
that very often absorbs my thinking; something has entered into the
writing of history that I do not think was there before. Thus your work
on Disraeli seems to represent a great and profound literary achievement." Ibsen was attuned to this new "element" because he was about
to create something of the same order himself. He felt in harmony with
Brandes, and as he read "with the most vivid interest" the volume of
Main Currents that dealt with French romanticism, he began once
more to work toward a new orientation to the romantic impulse in his
own spirit.

A few weeks after this letter, he left for Gossensass to work on the
new play. There was no word from him all that summer or the rest
of the year, with the exception of a letter to Hegel on September 5:
"My new play will not be finished by the end of this coming winter;
but I hope that this slow progress will not be detrimental to it." In
January, 1884, he wrote that he had experienced "one of those periods
when I sit down at the writing desk with only the greatest of distaste."
In April he gave an explanation for the slow pace: "The political complications in Norway have prevented me all winter from seriously
getting to work on my new drama with undivided peace of mind." It
is surprising that he should have been so engrossed by Norwegian
politics, but an event demonstrated that the liberal leaders were not
just phrasemongers like attorney Stensgaard, but could fight for their
ideals. The election campaign in the fall of 1882 had arrayed the con-
tending elements in battle formation. In April, 1883, the Liberal majority
in the Storting impeached the Conservative cabinet. The case was

fought throughout the year until February, 1884, when a Supreme
Court impeachment of the cabinet confirmed the Liberal position that
the cabinet could not defy the will of a Storting majority. A new form
of government was thereby introduced, resembling the English system
in which the will of the elected parliament is greater than royal power.
The Liberals then overthrew the Conservative government, and in June,
1884, Johan Sverdrup became prime minister of a Liberal government.

There was much to ponder over and much to be concerned with in
these developments, and Ibsen could not help following the conflict
with sympathy. His changing attitude is evidenced by the letter of
sympathy he sent to Sverdrup on the death of his wife. In January,
1883, he wrote on behalf of all Scandinavians in Rome, "Be assured
that all our thoughts are with you in your sorrow." By the spring of 1884
his political thinking was even more unusual. He agreed "with great
pleasure" to join Bjørnson in petitioning the Storting on behalf of
separate estates for married women, even though he did not think
much would come of it. On March 28 he sent Bjørnson a letter full of
his political "tinkerings." He proposed that "all the underprivileged"
should join in a "strong, resolute, and aggressive party," whose program should be "reforms!" He insisted that he was speaking about
"practical and productive reforms," not ordinary politics; among the
reforms he suggested were "a very liberal extension of the suffrage,"
certainly a venture into ordinary politics, "regulation of the position
of women, liberation of grammar school instruction from all kinds of
medievalism, etc." Two weeks later, in a letter thanking the student
society Fram for a birthday greeting, he expressed a heart-felt wish for
progress in "every up-to-date reform in the intellectual and social area."
He was again, as he had been a dozen years before, a friend, not an
enemy of reform. He still emphasized that these had to be social and
intellectual reforms, and he still doubted if the Liberals would concern
themselves with such things, but his temper had changed nonetheless.

He also began to re-evaluate his attitude toward Norway. "Patriotism
and such things are but passing phases," he had written in the first
notes for *The Wild Duck;* in a letter of 1888 he similarly said, "The
old concept of one's fatherland is not enough for a reasonably cultivated
person today. . . . I believe that national consciousness is about to die
out, to be replaced by racial consciousness. I, at any rate, have gone
through this evolution." His actions, however, contradicted his words.
Although he had sworn that his son would never be a Norwegian and
had educated him abroad, he tried to have him enter the University
of Oslo in 1880, and it was only when this plan fell through that he
decided to let the boy become an Italian citizen. Sigurd took his doctor

of laws degree at Rome in 1882 and prepared to take the examination that would lead into the Italian diplomatic service. But when the time came for him to become an Italian citizen, both father and son drew back. (Mrs. Ibsen had most likely helped to keep her son's patriotism alive, particularly on their visits home to Norway.) In November, 1883, Ibsen wrote: "Here we stand at a point from which we find it so difficult to continue. To cut all ties to one's fatherland— that is a serious matter." He turned to his old "Dutchman" friend, O. A. Bachke, then Minister of Justice, asking if Sigurd might get a post in the Norwegian-Swedish foreign service, and thus retain his Norwegian citizenship. The effort met with success, and the following year Sigurd was given a post in the Norwegian civil service and later in the foreign service, so beginning twenty years of service in Norwegian politics. Sigurd may have insisted himself on returning home, but Ibsen too was feeling a renewed attachment to his homeland, encouraged by his pondering the events of 1883 and 1884.

Another indication of this changed attitude toward Norway can be seen in his response to a poem Theodor Caspari had written in honor of their meeting in Rome. Ibsen wrote in June, 1884, that the poem "moves and affects me each time I read it." The only remarkable thing about this otherwise dull performance is the impassioned cry with which it ends: "Turn homeward"—

Kom hjem til din Arne, til Gaard	Come home to your hearth, to farm
og til Graend,	and to folk,
lad Hjemmet faa varme dit Sind!	let your homestead warm your heart!

There is no indication that he made any progress on *The Wild Duck* from June, 1883, to April, 1884. The most important evidence that the play was still very much with him is a list of "dramatis personae," not yet named but briefly characterized. The two central characters from the first notes are here, along with their parents. First there is "the old dismissed official" (another note indicates that he was imagined to be a judge, convicted of embezzlement), now "whitehaired, broken in spirit by his imprisonment: earns a little by clerical work." His wife is "half-crazy because of the family misfortune" and comforts herself by "stupid adulation of the son." The son's self-adulation is derived from her. He is described as: "The son with the great wasted talents. Feeling of piety towards his parents holds him, the family shame oppresses him." His wife is somewhat older, "prosaic, from a lower-class home." In contrast to these there are "the rich old ship owner and merchant— an old roué in secret," and his son, "the rich social writer, advocate of the rights of the poor, regards it as a sport."

There is still no mention of the conflict of the drama or, even more strangely, of Hedvig, the photographer's daughter. Hedvig first appears on a subsequent list of characters as the name of the wife; this is crossed out and Gina, possibly an echo of Regine in *Ghosts,* is substituted. Hedvig is given again, this time as a 14-or 15-year-old, the oldest daughter in the house, with three younger children after her. And with this list, which is certainly as late as the spring of 1884, comes the first word: "Comparisons with wild ducks: when they are wounded—, they go to the bottom, the stubborn devils, and bite on fast—...— Hedvig like the wild duck."

Ibsen had reached an unusually advanced stage in his meditating on the play before he discovered the symbol which would be the central focus of the drama, relating first and above all to Hedvig, and then standing as a symbol for all the slain hopes the play would chronicle. The image is derived from Welhaven's well-known early nineteenth century poem "The Seabird" (Søfuglen), which tells of a wild duck who is struck by the bullet of a thoughtless hunter and dives in silence to the bottom of the sea. This symbol out of the romanticism of the past came to represent for Ibsen the romanticism of life itself; the wounded duck in the Ekdal garret gathers to itself all the defeated dreams of the household.

Memories from his past found their way into the play; during this time his thoughts turned again and again to Norway and the Venstøp farm of his childhood. He recalled his father, a great huntsman whose love of the sport was passed on to his sons Johan and Nicolai. Old Ekdal has much in common with Knud Ibsen, not only in this but also in his vivid imagination and in his love of tippling. Ibsen was also familiar with guns from his childhood. Hedvig's name is, of course, that of his beloved sister. Perhaps he remembered her most clearly as she was at their last meeting in Skien, seventeen, full of excitement and hope, yet precociously serious. She had been a part of his life in the days when he leafed through the old picture books at Venstøp, books like the great *History of London* from 1775, filled with castles and churches and ships that carried his thoughts far off. Together they may have looked over the old volume with the hour-glass and Death and the maiden in the engraving, the picture she found so "awful." The mystical quality these books kept in his memory he now distilled into his portrait of Hedvig, but hers would be a mysticism that would have to succumb to the harsh realities of life.

It took time to make a drama of all this; he wrote two complete drafts, the first in Rome from April 20 to June 13, the second, largely in Gossensass until August 30. The revised drafts of his plays were always complete revampings, designed to give "the subtler shaping of language and the more energetic individualization of characters and speeches," but the revisions in *The Wild Duck* were even more fundamental. Only at this point was old Ekdal transformed from judge to lieutenant, owner of forests and mills—still closer to Knud Ibsen. Hedvig's character also did not fully emerge until this point, due in part to a young German girl whom Ibsen met in Gossensass. And not until now was all the dross of the dishonest social reformer refined out of Gregers Werle, so that he could stand forth as the totally sincere, totally blind proclaimer of truth, unfortunately suffering from "rectitudinal fever." And finally, only now did the wild duck become so central an element in the play that it served not only as a symbol for Hedvig, but for almost all the others.

When he finished, he wrote to his publisher: "In certain ways this new play is in a unique position among my dramatic works; my method of procedure is in various respects different from my usual one. . . . The critics will discover these things, I trust; in any case they will find a good deal to disagree about, a good deal to interpret. In addition, I think that *The Wild Duck* may possibly lure some of our dramatists down new paths, which I would consider desirable."

The change in dramatic technique was primarily in the emphasis on symbolism as a structural device. There had been frequent incidental use of symbols in earlier works, but they served simply as points of reference; for example, the new church in *Brand,* the rotten vessel in *Pillars of Society,* or inherited syphilis in *Ghosts.* They were used to underscore the central theme, or to expand it through allegory, as in the case of the "corpse on board." But the symbol of the wild duck is both a living reality and a force in the conscience of every character; the play is aptly named. The action of the play is so natural, so realistically everyday, that one might easily take it for the same kind of "family drama" as Ibsen had described *Ghosts,* but the wild duck, in spite of the careful, plausible explanation for its presence in the garret, is so potent a symbol that it forces the action into another dimension. Without this, it would be easy to criticize the irrational nature of so much of the behavior in the play. As a symbol of the secret, subterranean movements of the soul that it both represents and illuminates, the wild duck gives the play its final and new truth. Ibsen had shown a different path to dramatists.

The wild duck has a special meaning for each of the three main figures, as well as for old Ekdal. He is the first to be compared to the wild duck, which becomes a symbol of the illusion he uses to try to rescue a fragment of his life. Hedvig, herself a wild duck, not only bears the tragedy within her, but becomes the victim of the interplay of tragic forces in the others. In Hjalmar and Gregers we can see Ibsen settling accounts with himself. Here are Peer Gynt and Brand opposing each other in bitter parody. Regardless of the models he used, it is himself he drew upon, more completely for the portrait of Gregers. Perhaps the stress of this self-portraiture brought thoughts of his homeland vividly back to him as he walked through Gossensass, the place that could seem at times so like Norway.

When Hjalmar cries out that he is living on a great sorrow, or when he swears he will die as soon as he has achieved his life goal, or when he speaks of having begun his memoirs—all of this is sheer self-parody. And can one imagine Hjalmar Ekdal without the velvet jacket that Ibsen himself affected? Hjalmar lived on borrowed "spiritual" goods, as Ibsen once thought he himself did. With Peer Gynt, Hjalmar deludes himself with poetry and make-believe; the illusions are protection against anything unpleasant or painful. But Hjalmar is so artificial a person that the intention cannot be anything but parody; he is a compendium of all the traits Ibsen wished himself rid of. When the protecting shell of the life-lie shatters and catastrophe stalks him, the result is not true tragedy, only tragi-comedy.

Gregers is the one whom tragedy strikes. With his emotions atrophied because of the antagonism between his father and mother, he wanders with diseased conscience, plagued with the knowledge that he did not speak out when his father committed wrong. Now the only conviction he has is the crucial necessity to bring truth into personal relations as Ibsen had urged in play after play. But Gregers does not realize that he too bears a "wild duck" within, the illusion that the truth will save everyone, anyone. He imagines that the death of the wild duck will create a new, honest love between Hjalmar and Hedvig; his tragic defeat is that catastrophe results. The ideal of truth is defeated; his time is over.

Or is it? Like *Ghosts, The Wild Duck* ends in a question, or rather two. We can accept Dr. Relling's cynical remark that within nine months "little Hedvig will be nothing for (Hjalmar) but a pretty theme for declamation." But we are not sure about his judgment on Gregers. When Gregers says, in the last scene, that it is his fate in life to be thirteenth at table, he obviously means that he intends to take his own life: he had already said that he would soon be through with life. Relling's reply, the last words of the play, is: "The Devil you say!" The question thus remains: Does Gregers kill himself? There is no answer; perhaps life failed to turn into authentic tragedy for him, too. Ibsen could have heaped no greater scorn on his own ideal of the truth.

The play was both tragedy and liberation for Ibsen. He had lost his faith in man's ability to endure the full truth, and he was angered at such miserable creatures. But he pitied them too, and his anger turned on those who presented men with such inhuman demands. His deepest pity was for the innocent child who had to suffer for the lie and the truth. As in *Brand*, his need for love was most fully expressed in terms of the child, and the stunning impact of this play derives largely from its child-victim. The poignancy of the tragedy is made even more emphatic by the use of comedy throughout. This sharp contrast between casual humor and great distress adds to the pathos of the climax; it is an inexorable judgment on the life-lie and a tender defense of it. Dr. Relling, cynic that he is, can thus become a spokesman for Ibsen himself.

His own struggle with himself gave fire to the play; by mocking the idealistic pursuit of truth he was, perversely enough, being truest to himself. This was a kind of dualistic attitude which, in the words of Vinje, saw the right side and the wrong side at once, a psychological insight that was both merciless and loving. It is clear why he wrote, after he had completed the play, "The people in this work have, in spite of their many weaknesses, become dear to me through the long, day-by-day living with them." They were judged and censured, but in the end they were absolved, simply because they were weak and human.

The richness of *The Wild Duck* is perhaps best measured by the many different interpretations it can support. When it was first played at Christiania Theatre with Arnoldus Reimers as Hjalmar, he was the irresistible central figure around whom the others revolved, charmingly false in his declamation, pitiable and ridiculous in the moment of reckoning. When Johanne Dybwad played Hedvig, she filled the stage, and the tragedy of the play became her desperate struggle to win back her father's love. Her performance was strengthened by the contrast offered by the plain, solid interpretation of Gina by Ragna Wettergreen. When Ingolf Schanche played Gregers at the National Theatre, that character had a chance to stand forth with tragic power—up to then Gregers had seemed like a supporting role with no value of its own. Schanche gave the role a dynamic center that made apparent what Ibsen had intended.

Penetrating in its psychological insights, profoundly human in its compassion, fully realized in dramatic terms *The Wild Duck* is Ibsen's greatest play.

CHAPTER THIRTY-FIVE

AT ODDS WITH NORWAY (1884-86)

Norway was drawn more emphatically to Ibsen's attention while he wrote *The Wild Duck* than it had been even by *An Enemy of the People*. The very language of the play evokes the homeland; never had his style been so vigorous and authentically native. Two weeks after finishing the play, the epitome of everything Norwegian came to him in the person of Bjørnson, who wrote from Schwaz in the Tyrol, where he had gone to finish his novel *The Flags Are Flying*, asking if they might meet when they both had completed their work. Ibsen had looked forward to such a meeting ever since Bjørnson had failed to visit him in Munich five years earlier; now that Bjørnson was eager to see him he went from Gossensass to Schwaz in the middle of September and spent three days there.

It was more than twenty years since they had met, and both men were deeply moved, although conscious of the differences as well as the similarities between them. Bjørnson later wrote to Jonas Lie that Ibsen was "purified and well-meaning," but much aged. In a letter to Hegel he called him "a good, well-meaning old gentleman, with whom I did not agree on many things, particularly in outlook and methods, but with whom it is extremely interesting to exchange opinions." Ibsen wrote to his wife that they spoke "about political and literary and many other topics"; he said nothing else about Bjørnson except that "B. was often quite impressed by my statements and frequently came back to them." Bjørnson thought his own interests were wider and his perceptions much richer, but he was aware of Ibsen's greater strength, and his ability to exploit to the fullest what he knew: "The capacity of his mind for calculation, consideration, cleverness is extraordinarily great . . . that yields a greater percentage in the long run."

By thus meeting the two men publicly declared that they stood united in their efforts on behalf of the Norwegian people. *Verdens Gang* in-

357

terpreted it in this manner and hailed the intellectual progress that
would be the result; moreover, Ibsen had clearly shown that he was
not a "Conservative poet."

Bjørnson attempted to coax Ibsen home by suggesting that he take
over the management of Christiania Theatre. The idea filled Ibsen with
"restlessness and longing"; he had no plans for another play yet, and
in such periods he felt more strongly than ever "the lack of a regular,
ordering activity." Bjørnson, reacting with the zest he felt for any idea
that stirred him, believed at once that Ibsen "had the most burning
desire to go home and take over the theatre"; he stressed the point
that Ibsen "had no other absorbing interest than that of setting up a
good theatre in a new building in Norway." Nothing but "the scruples
of an old man," he felt, made Ibsen hesitate, and even after they
parted, he flooded him with letters urging him to take over the theatre.

There was more to Ibsen's hesitation than "scruples." He had a vivid
memory of how work in the theatre had interfered with his writing
in years past, and he remembered even more clearly how living at
home had prevented him from writing as "freely and forthrightly"
as he must in order to be true to himself. The visit with Bjørnson may
very well have made him nostalgic for his homeland, but all he
actually wanted was to return to a solitary life in the country. He
would not, in any case, make a decision about the theatre for at least
a year, perhaps two; he used as an excuse the almost certain opposition
that would arise from those in power at home. A month later he read in
Dagbladet a report of his having expressed willingness to assume the
direction of the theatre. He issued a statement immediately: "In the
inconceivable event that the present board of directors should invite me
to be director of the theatre, I would reject the offer unconditionally."

Bjørnson was making plans for himself as well, and Ibsen's objection
to them is indicated in some cryptic words in a letter to his wife: "I
have been able, in one respect, to avert by this visit a true misfortune
for our country. But I will not commit anything of this matter to paper."
It is impossible to know for sure what the reference is, although a
possible interpretation is that he may have persuaded Bjørnson not to
launch an attack against the new Liberal government in Norway. In
any case, Ibsen's remarks indicate that he was following developments
at home, and that he wished his homeland to be at peace with itself.

That summer Mrs. Ibsen and Sigurd visited Norway on a trip to the
distant North Cape: they brought some flavor of the old country back
with them when they returned to Gossensass in October. A new tie with
Norway was about to be formed; Sigurd was to enter the government
diplomatic service. But to counterbalance this was Mrs. Ibsen's report

that her husband had fallen more into disfavor with the Conservatives than he had suspected. None of his old friends could be depended on now.

The criticism that greeted *The Wild Duck* when it came out in November, 1884, totally confounded him. Norwegians had always had conflicting and vehement opinions about his plays, an indication of how closely they were rooted in the life of the country. But it was not so much strife as bewilderment this time. "It is a queer book," wrote *Fedraheimen*, and this was undoubtedly the general feeling, confirmed by Henrik Jaeger's article in *Christiania Intelligentssedler:* "The public does not know which way to turn, and they will not be much wiser after reading the criticism that has appeared: one paper says this and the other that." The reviewer in *Aftenposten* wrote, "One can puzzle and puzzle over what Ibsen means and still not find it out." Margrete Vullum, one of the few to appreciate some of the profundity of the play, analyzed its difficulty: "There is a mockery here that has depths upon depths. Statement is opposed to statement, so that each time one thinks one has caught 'the intention of the play,' a new statement comes to erase one's impression."

Morgenbladet did not understand the play at all, and explained why everyone was so confused: they had gotten used to Ibsen and so were anticipating something quite different. "Since people had expected some truth or other that the author wanted to impress on his age, or some kind of problem that was to be discussed, their expectation will hardly be satisfied." The action of the play was thus "just as peculiar as it is tenuous . . . it would be hard to string together a stranger set of details . . . and the total impression is hardly anything more than a strong feeling of emptiness and uneasiness."

Olav Lofthus' review in *Bergens Tidende* is a clear indication of the disappointment the Liberals felt. He admitted that it was "a brilliant book," but added: "We may admire Ibsen, all of us may, without regard to party, admire him; we admire his handling of dialogue, his sweep as a dramatist, his precision and sureness of portraiture; he is a great philosopher, but he cannot stir our hearts as does Bjørnson. . . . He does not appeal to the individual with the same force; he has no faith that his writings can ennoble men: he poses the problems splendidly, understands them, but makes no attempt to show one the path ahead; he chastises with authority, but makes no demand for improvement."

This says in effect that if Ibsen is no Conservative poet, neither is he a Liberal. But attempts were made, notably by Irgens Hansen in *Dagbladet,* to fit the play to a Liberal pattern. Noting a new element in it, "the evolution to a new stage of an important development," he wrote: "What Ibsen had not done before, he has done in this book; from a basis of humanity he advocates the cause of humanity, even a very tattered humanity. He has become a realist in the full sense of the word." Since the late 1870's Hansen had been the foremost exponent of realism in Norwegian literary criticism; he was still so committed to this point of view that he could not perceive the different form that Ibsen had here adopted. Elsewhere there was praise for the play for quite other reasons: Erik Bøgh, the reader for the Royal Theatre in Copenhagen, advised its acceptance not only because it "is constructed in all respects with his extraordinary mastery," but also because it "has an easily demonstrable and healthy moral which is lacking in many of the plays that suffer from its same failings—unrelenting painfulness and a dreary ending."

Ibsen could well feel somewhat of a wayfarer in Norway after this kind of criticism, and he did not feel much more at home in the rest of Scandinavia. Consolation came, however, through the great success the play won on the stage after New Year's, 1885. Arnoldus Reimers' exuberant interpretation of Hjalmar Ekdal in Christiania Theatre set the style for the role for many years. The triumph helped Ibsen to forget the "cold, uncomprehending eyes" that frightened him when he thought of Norway.

He was now almost sixty; living abroad had begun to lose its attraction for him, and his desire to return home was accentuated by the somewhat poor health he was experiencing for the first time. In the spring of 1885 he thought seriously of buying a small house by the fjord outside Oslo, "where I could live quite isolated, exclusively occupied with my work." He had had the same idea the year before when he met Bjørnson, but now it was more than a passing fancy; later in the spring he left Rome for the North, and in passing through Copenhagen again, said that he intended to live the rest of his life in Norway. It was his final departure from Italy; of the twenty-one years of his "exile," ten were spent in Italy, and although there are no apparent influences of Italian culture on his work, there is no doubt that he found peace in Italy and enjoyed living with its friendly people. He would always remember his years there with gratitude.

When he arrived in Oslo in early June, he was in time to hear the first great Storting debate on the issue of religious and moral freedom (on June 10): the question of a stipend for Alexander Kielland had initiated the first open conflict between the "moderate" and the "radical" Liberals. The resulting defeat for the kind of free thinking that Kielland stood for made him indignant, and this feeling was intensified by the failure of the Sverdrup ministry to be present in the Storting during the discussions. Although he did not say much about the case, he did express his regret that the first Liberal government the country ever had could yield to "the opinions of the victims of pastoral stupefaction." The next day, when he took the train for Trondheim, he told Bjørnson's son, the young Bjørn: "Greet all that is young in Norway; beg them to keep faith, and tell them that I will join them as pivotman on the left side, the left pivotman! What looks like the madness of youth will be victorious at last—be sure of that!" He had expressed much the same to the student society Fram the year before: "Support on the part of young people is dearer to me than any other. I sincerely hope that the years will never bring me to the point where I feel a stranger among the spiritually young."

When the Trondheim Workers' Society honored him with a procession on June 14, he spoke about the disappointment he had suffered in his homeland: "I have seen that the most indispensable rights of the individual are not yet as secure as I had dared to hope they might be under the new government. A majority of the ruling party will not permit the individual either freedom of belief or freedom of expression beyond an arbitrarily established limit." He urged those who were still excluded from all power, workers and women, to work for a new society based on the freedoms that had now become the most important considerations for him. Those who had been excluded, he felt, might well be the ones to bring to democracy the quality of nobility it sorely lacked: "I am certainly not thinking of nobility of birth or of wealth, nor even the nobility of knowledge or that of talents and gifts. I am thinking rather of the nobility of character, the nobility of will and intellect. That alone can liberate us." He wanted to call freed minds to arms and to leadership in society, and he promised to work unceasingly for a transformation of society that would raise new classes to power.

He and his wife waited almost a month in Trondheim for their son to get a vacation from his duties in Stockholm and join them. These weeks passed peacefully, as did the following two months in Molde, a little town by the Romsdals fjord which was just then becoming known for its splendid scenery. Ibsen may have decided on the place because his wife and son heard of it on their trip the previous summer, or he may have been influenced by Bjørnson's beautiful poem about it. When they met in 1884, Bjørnson had just received the setting Christian Sinding composed for his poem and must have told Ibsen about it. He began to think of settling down in Molde, and when back in Copenhagen spoke with Hegel about buying a house there.

At this point he probably did not plan on spending more than a summer in Norway. He was shocked by the crass party squabbling he found in both Oslo and Trondheim, where the maneuvering for political power made it virtually impossible for Liberals and Conservatives to associate with one another. The impeachment issue enflamed passions still further and after it came to a head in 1884 it was a good while before the defeated Conservatives could endure the sight of the victors. Ibsen sought out the radical Liberals both in Oslo and in Trondheim, openly taking sides with the radical Left. The Conservatives naturally shunned him, and he was so conscious of the hate being directed at him that years later he recalled he had been afraid people on the street might use their canes on his back or even spit at him.

The hostility could be felt even in quiet, remote Molde. Three or four days after his arrival there, on July 11, he wrote that it "is one of the most beautiful places on earth as far as the panorama is concerned. There is a delightful fjord, encircled by an infinity of colossal, snow-decked mountain peaks, in addition to a luxuriant, almost southern vegetation. But I would not care to live here for any length of time; the property purchase I contemplated will not take place." They kept mostly to themselves and he would go for long walks or stand on the dock and gaze into the water for long periods of time. Two weeks after his arrival the local people gave a party in his honor at one of the hotels. Only the Liberals took part; however, the Conservatives, who were conspicuously absent, later showed their opinion of Ibsen by failing to invite him to their receptions for such celebrities as Gladstone and the Prince of Wales. Ibsen's old friend Professor Lorentz Dietrichson was also in Molde, but he soon noticed that Dietrichson was avoiding him, a concession to the Conservatives in the town, as Ibsen found out. Dietrichson denied this, but Ibsen found enough supporting proof. Later he described his encounters with Dietrichson: "During our daily association, there appeared more and more meanness of heart and mind in him, a debilitation of his character, a pitiable concern about the judgments and opinions of others which could only impress me as detestable." Despite the outer serenity of his life, there were enough disturbing factors beneath the surface to annoy and disgust him.

Not all his companions had such a distressing effect; the arrival of Count Snoilsky, the Swedish poet, made the fresh sea breezes and the brilliant scenery even more delightful. Although Snoilsky was an old friend of both Ibsen and Dietrichson, he spent his four days (August 11 to August 15) in Molde almost entirely in Ibsen's company. There was much to draw the two together; both were, in fact, in similar situations. Six years earlier Snoilsky had broken with his haughty and conservative family and had gone abroad, now he was returning to his Swedish homeland for a visit. He was not welcomed as he thought he might be, and with this feeling of isolation it was only natural that he and Ibsen should turn to one another. In revealing talks they discussed their writings, their old memories, their plans for the future and themselves. They spun dreams but also laughed together. Four years later Snoilsky evoked an image of Ibsen amid mountain peaks and wild flowers in a poem about Molde:

Jag glömmer ej en Augustikvall
Med Ibsen i Blomsternes By—
Han står för min tanke liksom
    ett fjäll,
Hvars hjässa höljs i en sky.
Jag ser den mäktiga pannans form,
Som mulnar allt mer och mer,
Som känner komma en dunkel
    storm,
Då seklets sol skall gå ner.
Men snart mot en gammal vän
    och kund
Hans drag kunde ljusa opp
Och öfver hans fasta, slutna mund
Det vackraste leende lopp.
Den gåtfulle grubblaren minnes
    jag nog
Bland fjäll med ovädersky,
Men glömmer ej heller hur godt
    han log
Bland rosor i Blomsternes By.

I will never forget an August night
with Ibsen in the city of flowers—
he stands in my memory like a peak,
its crown hidden in a cloud.

I see the forehead's powerful form,
darkening still more and more,
shadowing forth a fearful storm
when our century's sun will set.

But then to an old companion, friend,
his face would lighten,
and over his lips, firmly pressed,
the winning smile would play.

This enigmatic brooder I still recall
with stormclouded peaks above,
but how he smiled I will not forget,
midst roses in the city of flowers.

In February, 1886, Ibsen wrote and thanked Snoilsky for the pleasant time they passed at Molde: "This meeting, seeing you again and becoming acquainted with your wonderful wife's noble spirit was a refreshing and enriching experience. It is without question the best memory we brought back from Norway." More than this, the experience would have a profound effect on the theme for a new drama that filled his mind at this time.

When the Molde Chorus and Band serenaded him outside his hotel window on September 4, the day he left town, he cautioned them that the "ideas which were vitally necessary for him to bring into the world would not win the sympathy of all." The allusion was to the idea for a new play, one that he felt might occasion more strife. His only hope to avoid it was if "those elements in society that might be offended would respect his opinions as he respected theirs." He went on to say that his visit to Molde "with its charming natural setting and quiet, peaceful townspeople" might possibly "soften in some way what he felt compelled to say." He had no desire to instigate another controversy.

There seem to have been fewer sources of friction in Bergen, his next stop. It was now twenty-two years since he had been in this city where he had endured so many of the struggles of his youth, and he could not help feeling somewhat embarrassed when old friends who were not quite of the best society greeted him from the docks with a hearty cry of "Hello, Henrik!" These calls were drowned out by cheers, and for the next eight days or so he had a chance to revive old memories, including those of his one-time sweetheart, Rikke Holst, who now as Fru Tresselt came to call on him. The directors of the theatre, under whom he had once toiled, now invited him to a festive performance of *Lady Inger of Østråt*. Under his personal direction, and with Laura Gundersen in the lead role, the defeat of thirty years ago turned into a great triumph. The audience gave a triple shout of "Long live Henrik Ibsen," which was ovation enough for him; he successfully eluded the Craftsman's Society's plan to honor him with songs and a torch-light procession.

He was back in Oslo in the last week of September, only to have his visit to Norway end on a sharp note of dissonance. He had politely declined the offer of the Workers' Society and the Student Society to organize a procession in his honor; to his radical friends who had forced the proposal through the Student Society in the first place, he said that he did not care for the reactionary tone of the organization. Lorentz Dietrichson was president of the society, and Ibsen let it be known that he would be most delighted if the radical wing in the group could gather enough strength to oust Dietrichson from the presidency.

The next day, September 29, he took the steamer to Copenhagen, where he stayed for only eight days. His fighting mood was still evident according to an account by the American Minister in Copenhagen, Rasmus B. Anderson, of meeting with Ibsen. Anderson, who was of Norwegian ancestry, introduced himself to Ibsen one evening outside the Hotel d'Angleterre and was invited in. Ibsen produced two bottles of champagne, most of which he drank himself, and chatted into the night about the aggressive quality his books would more and more take on in the future; he had only made a beginning, and now would not stop until he had turned society on its ear, because it was rotten to the core and needed a thorough purging. On he went until three in the morning, when Mrs. Ibsen appeared in her nightgown and carried him off.

At a dinner party given by his publisher Hegel, Georg Brandes made a speech thanking him for having laid bare the failings of society, but this time Ibsen refused to be drawn in. When pressed to say something, he replied that all he had ever written was based on self-examination, so that it was his own self he had bared to his readers. Anderson was also at the party, and wrote that "what Ibsen meant by this was a riddle to all who heard him." The statement should not be mysterious to those who know Ibsen's life work; Ibsen himself was probably made even more aware of its truth because of the performance of *The Wild Duck* he had just seen at the Royal Theatre.

On October 3 he appeared at a festival held by a new radical student society, Studentersamfundet, organized three years earlier in opposition to the non-political, conservative Studenterforeningen. Speeches in his honor were made by philosophy Professor Harald Høffding and Brandes, who said that if Ibsen did not feel any kinship with Norwegian students, it was because "there are no students in Norway." At first Ibsen would not rise to this bait either, but at last he said that if his work had had "any significance" it was because there was a kinship between him and his age. He thanked the students for the fellowship he felt in their company.

And now suddenly the remarks he had made to the students in Oslo ignited a whole storm of conflict; when his statement about Dietrichson was reported to the Student Society, the lightning began to flash. Dietrichson telegraphed him in Copenhagen and demanded to know what he had actually said; on October 5, his last day in Copenhagen, Ibsen sent back a reply explaining his refusal of the procession: "Among other things I said I did not wish a student celebration on the occasion of my departure. What I really meant was that I do not feel any kinship with a student society under your leadership." At the next meeting of the society Dietrichson gave a lengthy account of the entire affair, trying to demonstrate that "the great poet has on this occasion proved himself to be of small dimension"; he accused Ibsen of "one-sidedness and narrow-mindedness," and even elevated his complaints into verse, which he had the society sing the same evening. In the song he accused Ibsen of "failing to live up to his own principle" because he tried to force on the students a view other than their own: in retaliation, therefore, he would "shrug him off in a chorus of laughter" and describe for all how:

Den norske Student føler Harme og Sorg, for hver Gang en Stjerne mon segne.	The Norwegian student feels anger and sorrow, each time a star doth fall.

At meeting after meeting the affair came up for discussion, during which the majority of the students rallied to the side of their president. Some Conservatives went so far as to insist that what they were doing was simply resisting the devil himself. The Radicals, on the other hand, held a protest meeting to proclaim that youth was on the side of Ibsen. As late as October, Ibsen's anger and indignation over the episode was still so strong that he wrote a long, biting letter to the Student

Society, stating his position clearly and protesting that "Lorentz Diet-richson's attempted assassination" of his character would leave an ugly memory with him for the rest of his life.

In retrospect the entire affair acquires a rather comic flavor, and within a few years Ibsen himself preferred not to hear anything more about "the stupid story." But since it had happened at a time when the entire cultural and social life of the country was in a convulsive up-heaval, it sparked a desperate struggle between the Conservative and the Liberal press; no event in those days could be kept separate from party controversy. Camilla Collett's discussion of "the great event" in *Nyt tidsskrift* underlined the broader significance given to it: "It came like a sudden whirlwind, unsettling, exhilarating—more profound, more portentous than any of us imagined. For myself, I must admit, it was delightful. It was a truly refreshing experience to follow the special pleas, the confessions and explanations on the part of the 'offended' party; the thoroughness of self-exposure here has done more than any-one could wish, to compromise their position. At last! I said. At last a clear split has appeared in that husk of phrases that wraps around everything in our city. It will widen more and more and show us the abyss. But it took Ibsen to strike the first blow."

The ultimate consequences of the clash were, in fact, not very impor-tant, except in the student world where the split in parties grew wider until the Liberal Student Society was formed in November, 1885, and im-mediately elected Ibsen to honorary membership, along with the other "great" authors—Bjørnson, Lie, Kielland, and Camilla Collett. But the founding of the society was followed almost immediately by the so-called "Bohemian" controversy over sexual morality and the limits of free expression in writing, in which the society broke up after exhibiting a radicalism that went beyond Ibsen's, even though his example had made it possible.

The revolt among the students pleased him. When he wrote a letter thanking the Liberal Student Society for their protest meeting against Dietrichson's group, he told them that they had strengthened a hope he had never been able to abandon, "the hope that the great majority of young students in Norway, as in the rest of Europe, will finally reveal itself as at one with the struggling, illuminating, and forward-marching forces of life in the fields of science, art, and literature." When he thanked them warmly for the honor they had given him, he was taking a more open, more personal stand for radicalism then he had ever done before.

He was, nonetheless, repelled by much of the crudity that came to the surface during the "Bohemian" controversy in Norway. The Liberal

Student Society asked Brandes to come to lecture in Oslo in the spring of 1886, but when he spoke about the suppression of freedom in Poland, some of the "Bohemians" attacked him for not speaking instead of the same thing taking place in Norway, where the police had just banned Hans Jaeger's book *From the Christiania-Boheme*. When they called Brandes "unprincipled" and "mean," he retorted by suggesting that there might be more important issues in the world than the squabble over this particular book. For Ibsen the episode provided a "valuable addition to the character-portrait of our progressives." He wrote to Brandes: "Never have I felt myself more of a stranger to the *Thun und Treiben* of my fellow Norwegians than after the lessons of this past year. Never more repulsed. Never affected more unpleasantly. But I still will not give up hope that this crude, temporary behavior will some day be refined into a true cultural content, in a true cultural form. This possibility, however, does not interest anyone at the moment up there. Nor do I believe that the forces active among us now will be able to carry through any more profound or more deeply affecting programs than they have at the present time. And perhaps not even these."

He was incensed to find that Sverdrup's Liberal government was turning its weapons against the very freedom that its politicians had announced as their goal. But the way in which individual Liberals attacked Sverdrup angered him even more; he thought the attacks mean, ungrateful, and thoughtless, betraying an ignorance of what he himself had no difficulty in understanding—that there had to be a difference between the behavior of a party in opposition and in power. It was the immaturity of Norwegian political and cultural life that struck him now and crystallized his feelings into the first poem he had written in many years, "Stars in a Nebula" ("Stjerner i lyståge"). He felt himself looking into a chaos when he contemplated the nation's cultural life, "with scattered wills and deviating paths . . . with no yearning toward a central point." But he believed still that out of this confusion of a shapeless "nebula" would one day coalesce "a star brightly shining," a unified will. There was still a long way to this crystallization and this union, for the new spirit of the people was only "in its first making."

In the beginning of October, 1885, he returned to live in Munich. He had actually never left the city completely, having stored his paintings and some other effects in an attic during the five years he had spent in Italy. He liked the climate here better than anywhere else except Rome, and because of the city's close ties with the cultural life of Germany, it was perhaps his favorite place. Since his son's schooling no longer kept him in Rome, and since he could be closer to all the business activity his books demanded, he rented a suite of stately, high-ceilinged, but rather chilly rooms in the important business street Maximilianstrasse. He lived here for nearly six years, becoming more firmly established in this apartment than he had been anywhere for many years, since he stayed on through each summer as well as winter.

His life became as regular as it had been before, if not more so. In the afternoons he walked through the streets, dressed always in long frock coat and high hat, stopping wherever people gathered in order to observe very carefully what went on. Every evening at the same hour he went to the Café Maximilian, located in his street, and sat at his regular table for nearly an hour, drinking beer or brandy, or beer and brandy, reading or pretending to read the newspapers, watching carefully the people around him. Now and then he attended meetings of the Authors' Association. He liked to entertain at home, but his real life was lived within, and never again would he give himself to such a controversy as he had in the fall of 1885.

CHAPTER THIRTY-SIX

A CONFLICT OF CONSCIENCE:

ROSMERSHOLM (1885-86)

THE ENCOUNTER with Norway gave impetus to a new drama which would embody many of the ideas growing within him since he made the first notes for *The Wild Duck*. He would now go back to his initial conception of the character of Hjalmal Ekdal, the one that did not materialize in the final version of the play. For Hjalmar had not become the kind of noble dreamer Ibsen had envisioned at first, a man prevented only by cowardice from announcing his revolutionary new ideas. The Hjalmar he created never had the spark of greatness in him; he was instead a born bungler, a more outrageous self-deceiver than even Peer Gynt. Ibsen still had not created the image of a man whose "refined nature" prevented him from coming to grips with life and putting his great ideas to work, a man suffering the dichotomy between "wishing and willing." He knew he could draw this likeness from the contrast in his own divided nature between courage and fear, eagerness to do battle and anxiety about his own person, his silk hat, his fine gloves. But he had gradually come to learn that the price he had to pay for striking out at others was to become a target himself. (A revealing instance of his one-sided attitude is in a comment he made about retaining corporal punishment in schools: he was asked if he would like it if his son got a thrashing: "No," he answered with a smile, "but I'd like to give him one.") On the visit to Norway he had taken more of a public stand on issues than he had for years, and as a result had become entangled in a bothersome, unsettling conflict. Seeing Norwegian party fanaticism at close quarters angered him, and underscored the psychological dualism in his own nature, still unresolved and still gnawing at his conscience.

And in Norway he had encountered the man who became for him the embodiment of all these inner conflicts, Count Snoilsky. The Count's destiny as a poet had been as extraordinary as that of his personal life. When Ibsen first knew him, from his twentieth to his thirtieth year, he had been a facile and vigorous writer of verses that breathed optimism and certitude. Then suddenly he fell silent. He entered government service in Stockholm, married, and for an entire decade did not write a single poem. "I have thrown my life away," he wrote in 1874, "and I haven't the courage to change." But at last he did find the courage to break free: he was almost forty when he resigned his post, went abroad, was divorced and later remarried. He found his voice as a poet again, and suddenly volume after volume of his poems came out. This transformation, which took place in the early 1880's, involved more than the reawakening of creativity after years of stagnation. Now this refined nobleman and discriminating art lover was drawn into the class struggle and democratic movement of the era, he longed to make contact with the people, to find friends among the workers, "the serving brother." But his past, his social and intellectual background, held him back and prevented him from making this approach. In 1883 he wrote to a friend who had urged him to use his poetry in the struggle for social improvement: "Literature undoubtedly has a great influence when it concerns itself with social themes, as Ibsen has shown. ... Nonetheless, my own strength is not enough for so arduous a task or so high a flight. My ambitions are not that grand. Moreover, I know my major weakness—not having lived the life of the *people* from my youth: my upbringing and narrow classical education have made me, like the vast majority of our literary men, unfit for speaking to the classes on which society is built in a language they can understand. But unlike my colleagues, I often find this barrier a painful one, a limitation I am trying to overcome."

At the time of his visit to Norway, Ibsen had spoken about the kind of nobility of spirit he longed to encounter, and in this man he saw an unquenchable yearning and a sense of helplessness, the true spirit of nobility—but it was a nobility deeply scarred, too tender to grapple with life in all its crudity. Snoilsky became the model for the Rosmer of *Rosmersholm,* and helped Ibsen to discover the vital form to dramatize the psychological problem that absorbed his attention.

The following February, in a letter thanking Snoilsky for his companionship, he wrote: "For myself, I am fully occupied with a new play that I have had in mind for a long time, and for which I made careful studies during my trip to Norway this summer." As early as April, 1885, he had told his publisher about a new play that he thought might be ready by fall. When it was finished, not that fall, but the next, he again indicated that it "may be regarded as the fruit of study and observation I had a chance to make last summer during my stay in Norway." At the same time he wrote to Brandes: "The impressions, experiences, and observations of last summer's trip to Norway had a disquieting effect on me for a long time. Only after I had become thoroughly clear as to what I had experienced and had drawn my conclusions from it, could I think of turning it all to profit in a play." Month after month he pondered on the nature of the psychological drama whose outlines he had traced in Snoilsky. Not until late in May, 1886, did he understand with sufficient clarity the form the conflict would assume to enable him to begin work. Now a letter from Snoilsky, dated April 4, brought the figure of Rosmer even more vividly to life. Snoilsky wrote that he was "sung dry," and that it was Ibsen who had taught him the "untenability of an exclusively aesthetic conception of life." He had come to regard "as something superfluous any literature that fails to deal with the great concerns of our life and times." Thus he himself had become a superfluous thing, and there was nothing for him but to "retire." In these words Ibsen could hear both Rosmer and Ulrik Brendel speaking.

Reminiscences of Molde, with the figures of both Snoilsky and Lorentz Dietrichson, play such a large part in the new drama that it is natural to assume that Ibsen chose that town as the setting, particularly the old estate of Moldegaard. The stage directions indicate that the action takes place "in the environs of a small fjord town in western Norway." But since the landscape he describes around the estate does not correspond with that around Moldegaard, it has been suggested by the English critic John Northam that Ibsen may actually have had in mind the Fossum estate outside Skien. Ibsen knew this from childhood, and moreover, it had a river with a waterfall, although somewhat further upstream than the play has it. Professor Otto Mohr subsequently located an old estate with precisely the kind of scenery described in the play: Kalvell in Vestre Moland, between Grimstad and Lillesand, has a millrace and foot bridge right outside the main building. Quite likely Ibsen passed this way in his Grimstad days and his tenacious memory kept the image all these years.

But the Moldegaard estate gave the impetus to his imagination and enabled him to create the setting the theme demanded. The place, moreover, presented a stimulating contrast between inherited nobility and modern radicalism (old Thiis Møller, the owner, was a vigorous member of the opposition who never backed off from a fight.) For the master of the old, lonely estate Ibsen used Count Snoilsky, who had, despite his Swedish nationality, the Norwegian tendency to brood over the meaning of life and the responsibilities of being human. The man became at once rebel and prisoner, yearning like all Norwegians for sun and warmth, for freedom. He wanted to "create the genuine rule of the people in our country ... to make all people aristocrats ... to liberate their souls and chasten their wills." At first Ibsen intended to give him the name of a noble family, trying such old Norwegian names as Bolt and Rømer (even hyphenated as Bolt-Rømer), and then making up originals such as Sejerhjelm and Rosenhjelm. Finally, Rosenhjelm and Rømer were combined to give Rosmer, which also suggests the Danish ballad about Rosmer the merman, who entices an earthly maiden into the sea, but loses her in a struggle with her brothers. Thus a mystical element entered into the man he was creating; his Rosmer would not be entirely of this world, and he would therefore have to suffer defeat.

The nobleman Rosmer dreams of awakening the people, but to be tied as he is to the old traditions can be fatal for one who yearns to break free. These forces of the past are symbolized by the ghosts that haunt the estate, the "white horses" that appear before misfortune or death. Ibsen may have heard of such a legend at Moldegaard; he first named the play *White Horses*, but although they were symbols he could use, they never assumed the kind of importance in the dramatic action that the wild duck had in the previous play. They are used only as an underlying motif in the unconscious of Rosmer and his housemates, messengers from mysterious powers, living "ghosts" that were both frightening and compelling. There are other symbols in the play: the millrace, the white shawl that Rebecca crochets and that becomes her shroud, and above all, the old estate of Rosmersholm itself, summing up all the power of the heritage from the past. It is fitting that this is the name he finally gave to the play.

Rosmer's conflict is once more the story of Mrs. Alving, the basic theme that Ibsen repeated from his youth: the past, living in the present, capable of avenging itself at any moment. In Mrs. Alving the struggle is against the past as it appears in the ideas ingrained by education and social custom; in Rosmer the struggle is against the legacy of the past in his own temperament. The problem is unresolved in *Ghosts*; now Ibsen probes to a far deeper psychological level and follows Rosmer's struggle through to the end—an end which must come in death, since the "white horses" prove to be invincible.

In placing Rosmer between two women, one dead and one living, he may have been influenced by Snoilsky's marital experiences, although he had made use of the same theme in his work from *Catiline* to as recently as *Pillars of Society*. There is a variation on the theme in that Rosmer's first wife is never physically present, although she is always alive in the memory of those who survive, a part of the past that belongs to the "white horses." Her self-sacrifice to release her husband may have been suggested by a story Ibsen heard from Ludwig Passarge, his first

German biographer, who visited him in Gossensass in the summer of 1884 while he was working on *The Wild Duck*. Heinrich Stieglitz, one of the poets of the "Young Germany" movement, had published a few books in the early 1830's but had been unable to do anything more after that. His wife, Charlotte, got the idea that a "great and genuine sorrow" would so affect him that his poetic genius would be re-awakened, and so she committed suicide. Unfortunately, the husband was not inspired to great heights, and her sacrifice was in vain. The story impressed Ibsen, particularly since he had once entertained the idea that a great sorrow would help him become a poet. He was at the time writing the last act of *The Wild Duck*, where Hedvig sacrifices her life for her father, and it was natural enough that the story fix itself in his mind, there to become the seed of a new theme and a new work. There was a good deal in the Stieglitz affair to invite psychological speculation, particularly since some people thought that Charlotte might have had other, less altruistic, reasons for taking her life. When he sent Mrs. Rosmer to her death, Ibsen did it against a backdrop of suggestion and mystery that threw dark shadows over the relationships of those who survived her.

The woman who lives, Rebecca West, may in part have been suggested by the poised, lofty-minded Countess Snoilsky, the Count's second wife. But Ibsen also drew on his recollection of Laura Gundersen's interpretation of the role of Lady Inger at a recent performance in Bergen. Her brilliant, tempestuous acting taught him much about feminine psychology and the way a transition between conflicting impulses is made by imperceptible degrees. (Laura Gundersen was greatly disappointed that Ibsen thought she was too old to play Rebecca and gave the role to another actress. She was confident that she could have created the role, and described Rebecca in a single image: "She should be like a black night, with glittering stars.")

At first Ibsen was not entirely certain of the nature of the relationship between Rosmer and Rebecca; in one of the drafts she is Rosmer's second wife and their marriage is poisoned by his discovery of her past. It seems to have been an ordinary love story, with her involvement rather superficial. Ibsen's first notes, dated December, 1885, where she is still nameless, describe her as "emancipated, warm-blooded, quite ruthless but in a refined way." A later notation reads: "She is a scheming woman and she loves him." Gradually she acquired an inner life that demanded new and deeper psychological exploration; in the end she was as much the focus of the play as Rosmer himself.

Ibsen had to invent a history for her; unless her past could account for the power she held over Rosmer, that power might seem almost magical. He deliberately set out, in fact, to give the impression of some mystical, secret element in the relationship. Rebecca West was born and raised in Finnmark, in northern Norway, which legends old and new called the home of witches and witchcraft. From there too had come Hjørdis, the first sorceress he wrote about. Rebecca tries to conceal her origin by changing her name—her real father bore the genuine Finnmark name of Gamvik—just as she tries to conceal other things in her past. Was it not possible that she had been her own father's mistress? A wild "lust," some of the same soul fire that burned in Hjørdis, sweeps over her like a storm from the sea, such a storm as those that break in winter in the distant north, making vain all resistance. And when the storm calms and rest falls over the soul, it is like the stillness on a birdcliff under the midnight sun. The pulse of the sea thus beats in Rebecca, and when Ulrik Brendel calls her "mermaid," he speaks more truly than he can know. In the end even she compares herself to those sea demons who cling to ships and prevent their sailing free.

Ibsen had never seen the far north, but his wife and son had been there recently and must have spoken of it to him. In Trondheim he had met his mother-in-law, Magdalene Thoresen, who was on her way to Finnmark; perhaps he borrowed traits for Rebecca from her sensual nature. He did not, however, think this quality of mysteriousness peculiar to just the north of Norway, as he mentioned to his new German friend, the young writer Felix Philippi, right after the play appeared (see Chapter 20). It was simply that the conditions he described, lonely dwellings, long dark winters, seashore fog, all that makes the Norwegians brooders and yearners—all this he believed was most strongly felt in Finnmark and north Norway. Since his own temperament was reflected in this somber mood, he understood the place and the kind of people it produced.

The northland had made Rebecca West a woman of great strength and great longing, and because her witchcraft is the exact opposite of all that the white horses represent, conflict between them is inevitable. In the beginning she must seem the stronger, gaining the upper hand; thus she is able to drive Rosmer's sickly wife into the millrace. But the hidden sense of guilt that is a mark of her vulnerability is apparent in her need to conceal so much. Ibsen strikes this note at once in Act One when she says that she loves the fragrance of flowers because it "makes one forget so beautifully." This guilt is the weakness in her armor, and through this the forces she meets at Rosmersholm, the traditional Rosmer view of life, make their attack and gain ascendancy over her; she is "ennobled" and finally "broken."

The transformation undergone by Rebecca is actually the main theme of the play, one that has great consequences for Rosmer. Rebecca has helped him in his struggle to free himself from the influence of the past, but when he finally understands her, her guilty heart as well as her rebellious will, then it becomes clear to him that it is not simply a question of ridding oneself of the past; one must carry the past forward into the future. It was the old culture, as Ibsen now saw clearly, that alone could give Rosmer that "nobility of character" on which his new freedom is to be founded. He must be chastened and free of guilt, and gradually Rebecca realizes that she must become no less than this herself. And so she attains true nobility.

As Ibsen worked on the play, reshaping it and refining its theme again and again, he realized that the ending had to receive an entirely different emphasis than he had first intended. It was not enough to have the "demon spirit" awaken in Rosmer when he discovers what Rebecca has been, so that in his "pain and bitterness" he wants to die with her. Now it must be Rebecca who sees no recourse but in death, since she cannot go on living and taking part in the struggle for freedom unless she is innocent herself. Thus Ibsen's original idea of the conflict (to judge from the notes to *The Wild Duck*) as a struggle between the "obsolete and the coming conscience," became a struggle within the single, individual conscience. And it was no longer a question of victory for one or the other kind of conscience; each could be justified, and the future had to be a harmony between the new freedom and the old ideal of duty. He had dramatized the same struggle and the same goal in *Emperor and Galilean,* and so it was quite natural for him to refer to the "third empire" in which he still believed, in a speech he gave in 1887, shortly after *Rosmersholm* was published.

Ibsen intensifies Rosmer's dramatic conflict by placing him in the midst of the Norwegian political scene with all the party hatred and the passionate strife that showed no respect for the individual. He had seen it all just recently, and the most vivid impression it left was that only a strong, rather coarse-grained nature could bear up under such treatment. Rosmer's very concept of a free personal life precluded his being a successful fighter in that struggle. The freedom Ibsen longed for went deeper than any political program, and in making Rosmer, like Brand, a clergyman, he once again translates politics into morality and religion.

When Rosmer tries to free himself from the shackles of traditional religion, he comes inevitably into head-on collision with the prejudices of Norwegian society. Ibsen had no difficulty finding models for his representatives of the usual intellectual repression of his day; he had had more than enough experience with it by now. One type is represented by headmaster Kroll, well-informed and astute, and thus much more dangerous in his intellectual poverty and his fanatical contempt for the common people. His cross-examination of Rebecca is a more ruthless version of what Nora endured at Helmer's hands. Ibsen once indicated that he had a particular individual in mind when he created this character, but there are a number of traits from various "Dutchmen" friends and a liberal sprinkling of phrases from *Morgenbladet*. Another type is the democratic editor Peder Mortensgaard, a Liberal himself, who cynically calculates just how much freedom his readers and his party can be trusted with. In the phrase applied at the time to right-wing Liberals, he was an authentic "rabbit," burrowing his way underground in order to snare captive souls. Ibsen knew the type well, and in Mortensgaard has given a word that has become proverbial for a conniving journalistic spirit.

Among the other figures used to define the relationship between the main characters, the only ones given definite characterization in the first drafts were Rosmer's two daughters; the older a "richly endowed" woman about to "succumb to inactivity and loneliness," the younger still only "an observer," but with "incipient passions." Both of them were dangerously imprisoned by the rigid Norwegian sense of propriety and by the covert struggle in the Rosmer home. Ibsen dispensed with force most of these characters, however, perhaps because they would have given too much life to Rosmersholm, and he was intent upon letting the forces of death take the upper hand. He did make use of the one called "the journalist" in the first notes, the "genius" and "vagabond" who becomes Ulrik Brendel. The name Ibsen recalled from Skien; the mannerisms and phraseology he borrowed from Joachim Welhaven, a brother of the poet, who had tried to become an actor in Oslo in the 1850's but left the theatre because major parts did not always come his way. There may also be suggestions from Lorents Brandt, the old down-and-out academician in Camilla Collett's novel, *The Governor's Daughters*. Both Brandt and Brendel are melancholy caricatures of those romantic liberals who had proved to be intellectually barren and elegantly verbose, even though in the midst of all their prattle they could occasionally make a telling observation. Ibsen once told Otto Brahm that he had also taken as a model an acquaintance from Italy who used to create masterpieces in his imagination, although he disdained to write them down. (Ibsen as well might have felt himself guilty on this score.) Brendel serves as a tragi-comic parody of Rosmer at the same time that he clarifies the relationship between Rosmer and Rebecca.

The first impulse to write the play had come from the political feuds in Norway, but these were not to be the theme of the play, except insofar as he could seek out the roots of the conflicts within the hearts of his characters. He was certainly not indifferent to political issues. One day while making plans for the play, he said to Felix Philippi: "Every one of us must strive to improve the present state of the world; I do so to the best of my ability." But where his interests truly lay was in the drama that resulted when moral forces clashed in the human soul. A year later he said in a speech that his "polemic interests were decreasing," and that he felt that his writing "was about to assume new forms." Both *The Wild Duck* and *Rosmersholm* were steps in this direction; they indicate that he was no longer interested in "moving boundaries," but rather in penetrating into the inner recesses of human psychology and creating new characters inspired by his imagination.

Shortly after the play was published, a society of young students in Oslo wrote to him (the school's president was a nephew of Bjørnson's, which may explain their boldness in approaching Ibsen directly) and asked him to explain his intention in the play; their own conclusion was that he must have wanted to emphasize "the necessity of work." Ibsen answered that this theme was certainly present, but more importantly the play dealt with "the struggle that every serious person has to engage in with himself in order to bring his life conduct into harmony with his understanding"; this struggle results from the fact that "our moral consciousness, our conscience" has such "deep roots in tradition and generally in the past," that it does not keep pace with purely intellectual advances. But "first and foremost the play is, of course, a literary work about human beings and human destinies."

His contemporaries were not easily reconciled to the image of an Ibsen no longer actively participating in the conflicts of the day. When *Rosmersholm* appeared before Christmas, 1886, it was perhaps even less understood than *The Wild Duck*. The difficulty of finding actresses who could interpret the complex character of Rebecca West further delayed appreciation of the play. It seemed, in fact, to require a whole new generation of actresses to create the roles Ibsen was now writing.

He was approaching sixty and although his pugnacity was inevitably decreasing, his determination to follow his own way was not. Outwardly his life grew quieter, but as the Danish writer Herman Bang had said, while the rest of us "just go on living," great spirits like Ibsen's "go even deeper into life." As his experience and wisdom grew, Ibsen would probe more deeply into man's nature than ever before.

CHAPTER THIRTY-SEVEN

THE SHACKLED WILL:

THE LADY FROM THE SEA (1887-88)

Rebecca west was the first Ibsen character to be deeply influenced by the country in which she had grown up; the others had usually felt lonely and abandoned when in the woods or the mountains. Although Ibsen had responded to "the voice of nature" in Grimstad, since those days he had almost always been more interested in individuals and their relations with one another than in their relationship with nature. His only attempt to portray a "natural" creature, the "grouse of Joste-dalen," was a failure despite the three efforts he made to bring her to life. The relation of many of his characters to nature was brief and inconclusive. Eline in *Lady Inger* strolls along the fjord and longs for a happier place; in *The Vikings* Hjørdis endures the winters of the north as so many endless nights, and every night an endless winter, and thus her only desire is for escape; Gregers Werle had lived alone in the dark Højdal forests, meditating and brooding and creating a sick conscience for himself. Only Brand came close to identifying with his birthplace; the mountains became the great, overpowering symbol of the forces he was struggling with. (Mountains played an even more significant part in the poem "On the Heights"; here the man who wanted to protect himself from mankind by hiding among them ceases to be human as his heart turns to stone.) Nature had, of course, no place in the social plays, for here man stood against man. It was not until *The Wild Duck* that nature returned as a living symbol, even though it was nature locked up in an attic. With Rebecca West nature would become a psychological force.

The summer in Molde had reawakened in Ibsen those memories of the sea that had lain dormant since Grimstad. The sea had never made any special impression on him after those days, even when he encountered its open, majestic form along the Norwegian coast, or saw it spread out wide and blue off Italy. It was only when he began to understand all the secret passions that stirred beneath the surface in man that he saw the sea as a potential symbol. The sea in Grimstad and in Molde had been disguised by islands and mountains; it did not offer its full expanse to him. Now he longed to see it free and unfettered in all its strength, just as he had conceived it as part of Rebecca's character. As soon as he finished the play, he decided he would go the following summer to Skagen, the northernmost tip of Denmark, to see the ocean there.

When he left Norway after his summer trip in 1885, he vowed he would return every summer, but as he gathered his memories and impressions, he realized how impossible that would be. Almost everything in Norwegian politics and religion repelled him, and he would not submit to such distressing experiences again. He remained in Munich the entire summer of 1886, working on *Rosmersholm,* but the next year he left at the beginning of July, going first to Fredrikshavn, a small town in Jutland. The plan to go on to Skagen was changed because the many artists and summer guests there would interfere with the "peace and solitude" he desired. He actually preferred it in Fredrikshavn where he could be by himself, or just walk down to the harbor and chat with the sailors. But when Mrs. Ibsen found the place too urbanized, they decided to move to the out-of-the-way village of Sæby on the east coast, a little farther south of Fredrikshavn.

It was an unusually fine summer, for which he was especially grateful since it had been a cold spring in Munich, but he would rather have been on the west coast, where he could see the ocean in storm. In Munich he had written, "Even if the bad weather should pursue us up there, the sea would be all the more magnificent." If he did not actually see any great storms, he did have the unconfined, open sea before him. Deeply impressed, he would remain a long while each day simply gazing out to sea. He had a kind of seat that he could attach to a stick, and sitting on this, he could look at the sea comfortably for long periods of time.

It was, however, always the human aspect of nature that he saw; in describing the Danish landscape he compared it with "a soulful face, constantly changing expression as its mood changes." Now he saw the sea in the same way. "There is something endlessly enthralling about the sea," he told Henrik Jæger at the end of the summer. "When you stand staring down into the water, it is as if you see the life that moves on earth, only in another form. There is continuity and correspondences everywhere. The sea will play a part in my next work."

At the seashore he often enjoyed the company of young ladies who were living in Sæby or at the Hotel Harmonien where he was staying. He liked to chat with them, and when one of them left, he thanked her in a little farewell note for "the ray of sunlight you with your refreshing

youth cast over an old man walking toward death." He probably did
not feel particularly aged at the time, but he no doubt wished himself
much younger when in the company of such youth. One day he told
a sixteen-year-old girl he used to meet on the shore: "I need a little
person to talk to. I am writing down your 'other self' in my new play.
You have no idea how much significance a little person like you will
have." The young girl came to believe that he had described her in
Hilde Wangel, and he may very well have drawn on her, as well as
the other young girls he met. He observed them all carefully, that is
certain, even if he did not use any one exclusively for a main character
in a play.

He stayed in Jutland for two full months, mostly in Sæby, with the
exception of a week or so at the beginning and end of his visit passed
in Fredrikshavn. He had planned at first to go directly from there to
Munich, but the climate of the coast had so refreshed him that he
decided instead to visit friends and acquaintances elsewhere. It was
apparently at this time that he began to realize he was not as ignored
in the North as he had once thought. When Hegel had suggested that
a biographical study be published on his sixtieth birthday, Ibsen tried
to persuade him to give up the idea. Before leaving for Jutland he
had written: "For me it would be most pleasant if this memorable day
in my life . . . could pass soundlessly and without a trace in the Scandinavian countries." He reminded Hegel of "the position in which my
controversial activity has for the time being placed me at home." But
when Henrik Jæger, the future biographer, visited him in Fredrikshavn,
he got the impression that if neither the Conservatives nor the Liberals
in Norway could call him their own, he was still of major importance
to the people of the Nordic countries.

In the beginning of September he went to Göteborg, where the
literary society Gnistan ("The Spark") held an impromptu celebration
in his honor. From there he went to Stockholm, where another celebration was held. After a fortnight he went on to Copenhagen, where
Hegel feted him, and finally by mid-October he was back in Munich.
On this festive circuit he gave a series of little speeches that reveal a
great deal about his thinking and his literary plans. Although he confided to Jæger that it was a horror for him to make speeches before a
large audience, and that he could never really learn how, he could
speak about himself with remarkable frankness when required to do
so. He had become more self-confident and open than he had been in
his earlier years, and of course it was good for him to be met with
understanding and good will.

It became something of a formula for him to tell his well-wishers, as he told the German artists and writers who honored him early that year in Berlin, that the hearty friendliness he encountered filled him with a joy that could not but leave its mark on his writing. Even if it were a formula, the phrase does reflect his eagerness to accept whatever would contribute to his peace of mind. In Copenhagen on October 5, he spoke about what the summer in Jutland had meant to him. He had "discovered the sea" there; "the smooth, smiling Danish sea that one could approach without mountains blocking the way" had given his soul "respite and peace." And now "he bore memories from the sea that would be significant in his life and writing." His mood was the same, although his words more general, when he spoke in Sweden. On September 12 in Göteborg he said that his writing was "on its way to discovering new forms"; it was a help to find such understanding and appreciation. In Stockholm on September 24 he gave a well-prepared speech about the new age he felt the world was entering: he suggested that the scientific theory of evolution applied to intellectual life as well and that the old political and social concepts would now come together into "a unity that includes within it all the prerequisites of human happiness." He could call himself an optimist "to the extent that I fully and confidently believe in the capacity of ideas to reproduce themselves and to evolve." He reaffirmed his belief in the coming of the "third empire," and he would be perfectly satisfied if his daily labor could prepare their minds for the holiday that was to come. "But above all," he added, "I will be satisfied if my labor can help to steel spirits, for that working week which must infallibly come after."

This was a kind of program, even if one could hardly call it a very clear program. A week later a journalist asked him to interpret his words more exactly, and he explained that he believed so firmly in the splendid future of socialism that he could very well call himself a socialist. A short time later he announced that "of all classes of society in our country the working class is closest to my heart." He added that his psychological investigations had led him to "the same conclusions as the social democratic philosophers had arrived at through their scientific research." He continued to emphasize, however, that it was not possible for him "to work in any direct way for the benefit of the laboring class." No more than earlier could he join any party: "It has become a necessity for me to work entirely on my own."

In Copenhagen he did not visit the radical student society (Studentersamfundet) as he had done two years earlier; instead he accepted an invitation on October 1 from the older group (Studenterforeningen), after he had been assured that the occasion was non-political. Brandes was displeased at this defection and wrote to Countess Snoilsky: "Ibsen was here and this time fraternized for a change with the reactionary student society. I was able to speak a few words to him, but I did not get much out of the conversation." The change in Ibsen's outlook was becoming evident; he was withdrawing from the arena. His own mission now had become to "portray human character and human destiny." He wanted to be nothing but a writer. The great moral problem for him was how man could achieve the intellectual freedom and the courage needed to enter the future, the central theme in all his plays of moral criticism from *Pillars of Society* to *Rosmersholm*. It could be summed up in the words "truth and freedom." The drama of life was the conflict in man's mind between the demand for freedom and the forces that hindered its realization, and he went on ceaselessly experimenting with new ways to analyze this conflict in dramatic terms.

As early as January, 1887, only a few months after he had sent *Rosmersholm* off, he was writing about "various new dramatic fancies" that were "tumbling about" in his head, and he thought that by spring he would be able "to get some coherence out of them." He had many other things to occupy him, however, including performances and translations of older works. Although he rested well during the two months in Jutland, how much progress he made on the new idea is not certain. When William Archer visited him in Sæby, Ibsen said nothing but that he hoped he would have "some folly ready for next year." The only thing already decided was that the sea would be a factor in the new play, and he must have settled this even before he went to Jutland. The idea was a natural continuation of the thoughts that had occupied him during *Rosmersholm,* when he created the "mermaid" Rebecca. But the image of the storm-driven ocean as the great force in men's minds would be replaced by the sea lying quiet, almost without will, concealing below its surface dangerous, compelling forces.

During these years he returned to his youthful interest in hypnotism, telepathy, compulsive ideas, and similar problems. He could get quite indignant about people who experimented with hypnotism for the fun of it. In the notes for *The Wild Duck* he had indicated that "the sixth sense" and "magnetic influence" were favorite ideas of the "dreamer" character. In the first notes to the new play he wrote: "The sea possesses a power over one's moods that has the effect of a conscious will. The sea can hypnotize. So can nature in general. The great mystery is the dependence of the human will on 'the will-less.'" He became intrigued by the influence one person could wield over another; for example, Gregers' success in persuading Hedvig to make her sacrifice, or Rebecca's triumph over both Rosmer and his wife. Ibsen had had to struggle to free himself from dependence on others, as he had indicated long ago in "On the Heights." *Catiline* and other early plays show that this struggle for inner freedom was a continuing concern both in his life and in his writing. Now the sea became the symbol of all that drew human beings with the power of the unconscious. The sea could come to life, staring at one with eyes almost human; it was a symbol of all that lay beyond conscious will.

He did not set to work immediately after returning to Munich in October, 1887. All, winter he complained of being "loaded down with correspondence," most of it business matters. Then there came the distraction of the tributes that poured in on him from all directions for his sixtieth birthday in March, 1888. He was his own secretary and so most of the work fell to him, although he did unload some of it on Hegel in Copenhagen or Hegel's agent in Oslo.

It was, however, more than external circumstances that prevented him from working; his own will was at fault. He deliberately let the theme grow in his mind for a long time, thus making conscious art out of what had begun so often in the past as a compulsive need to come to terms with the ideas that pressed in on him. Time and time again in the past, the ideas he had rushed to shape into finished works proved to have needed a longer period of germination. No matter how he struggled with the material, no matter how often he felt he had brought it to completion, the effort was largely wasted and the expectation frustrated. The long and painful struggles with *Love's Comedy, Brand, Emperor and Galilean,* and *Pillars of Society* are examples of those occasions when he knew what he wanted to create, and yet could not make his conception live. Gradually he had learned that he could not coerce the dimly perceived dramatic images to emerge from the distance. Impatience did not help; he had to wait and let the visions grow clear and strong of their own accord, so that on one day they would suddenly stand forth in full light, fully alive. Experience had taught him what scientific psychology would come to understand, that the hidden creative process went on below the level of conscious thought. Ibsen no longer tried to hurry the process, but rather let the silent growth follow its own laws. With the years had come patience.

He had also learned a great deal about the psychology of the unconscious, and now his insights were more profound, more penetrating than ever before. If his characters were no longer sparked into life by the fire of his wrath, they reveal a more sharply defined awareness of the hidden impulses in man's soul. Or to put it more accurately— women's souls. It is interesting to observe how often he made a woman his leading figure, or at least his most psychologically interesting one.

In his plays of social criticism women were depicted as rebels because he felt that social pressures and schooling had not yet inhibited their naturally independent emotional and intellectual life. Although Herman Bang remarked that Ibsen idealized women because he did not know them, many actresses have testified that through Ibsen's role they have come to understand the deepest levels of the feminine psyche. Ibsen had, in fact, explored the secret, unconscious life of his feminine characters, and he came to see that the very lack of education and emotional discipline that made them ripe for rebellion also left them receptive to hypnotic influence and compelling forces that sapped their wills. It was to be a woman, therefore, who in his new play would feel the hypnotic power latent in the sea and struggle against it.

He did not begin to put his plans on paper until June 5, 1888, when he made some rough notes on the play's contents. But within five days he was working steadily, and by the end of July had completed the fifth and last act. He revised the whole play thoroughly, rewriting practically everything, and the clean copy he began at the end of August turned into something of a revision itself. By September 25, after three-and-a-half months of work, he was able to send the play to the printer.

He had called it *The Mermaid (Havfruen)* at first, but changed this to *The Lady from the Sea (Fruen fra havet)*, because the image of a creature drawing a man down to her in the sea is not accurate for a play about a woman who is herself drawn to the sea. The sea stands for the attraction of the unknown and perhaps even for the mystery of man's ultimate origin Ibsen knew of Haeckel's theory (propounded in his *Natürliche Schöpfungegeschichte,* 1868)that the fish was probably the first link in the evolutionary chain that led to man. And he asked himself: "Are vestiges of this origin. to be found even now in the human psyche? Or in the minds of some?"

Inspiration for the play's main character came in part from his own mother-in-law, Magdalene Thoresen, a woman closely bound to the sea. She had spent her childhood by the peaceful Little Belt on the Jutland coast; when she came to Norway at twenty-three to marry a minister in Sunnmøre, she found a counterpart to her own tempestuous nature in the landscape of her adopted country. But only when she discovered the sea did she find herself; she could not stand to live far from it, and even in old age she had to swim out to the waves each day. Ibsen drew many external traits from her for his "mermaid," whom he first called Thora. Later he changed this to Ellida, from the romantic saga of Fridtjof the Bold, where Ellidi is the (masculine) name of the hero's ship, which is almost a living creature, a child of storm and magic. Mrs. Thoresen had had a stormy love affair in her youth, and although she broke free by fleeing to Norway, she was tormented throughout her life by the conflicting demands of the old and the new love. The longing for the sea that Ibsen had seen so strongly marked in her and which he felt in himself as well, became a symbol of the longing all men have for the hidden and the mysterious.

Another inspiration was the result of a story he had been deeply moved by that summer in Sæby. A young girl had longed to become a writer and escape to a fuller, freer life, but shot herself at the age of twenty-one. This had happened four years ago, but Ibsen inquired closely about her, visited her home, looked at pictures of her, went to her grave, and even read the books she had owned. It was the sea, he felt, that had inspired her longing for the unattainable.

Ibsen believed that there was something peculiarly Norwegian in this reaction to the sea, although it was primarily Danish-born women who gave him his living examples—Mrs. Thoresen, however, considered herself Norwegian, since she had been "born anew" in Norwegian nature. While working on the play, he told a German friend: "People in Norway are spiritually under the domination of the sea. I don't think other people can really understand this." However little a man of nature himself, he felt he reacted in a Norwegian manner on this score, and so he knew that the action of his play could take place nowhere else but Norway, in Romsdalen around Molde.

The "magnetic" force of nature, just beginning to be called "hypnotism" in the 1880's, was personified by the Stranger with eyes like a fish, to whom Ellida had once been engaged. The relationship between these two characters is in part derived from a story Ibsen had heard in Molde from a Nordland woman. She had spent an evening recounting strange tales and legends, including one about a Finn who used the magic power of his eyes to entice a clergyman's wife away from husband, children, and home. This story combined in his imagination with another about a sailor who had been gone for so many years that he was given up for dead. When he returned, he found his wife remarried. Ibsen thus gave the Finn—whom popular lore had always regarded as possessing magical powers—a power from the past over the soul of the woman he wants to take with him. He was also thinking of the way he and Rikke Holst had consecrated their union by fastening their rings together and tossing them into the fjord, so letting the sea wed them.

The "magnetism" exercised by the man with the fish eyes was transformed into a force in the soul of the one attracted by them, the Ibsen theme of the heritage and the reminiscence of the past. In the beginning he had even let Ellida break her engagement with the sailor because of the prejudices instilled in her by education, prejudices with which she was still struggling. But as he worked on the play, he gradually eliminated this aspect; the kind of liberation he was concerned with now was different, it was a contest for full mastery of the unconscious forces in the soul.

Ellida is married to a man with grown children, as was Magdalene Thoresen. Ibsen had intended to use these stepchildren for the two daughters in *Rosmersholm,* another indication of the close ties between these two plays about "mermaids." He had first named the younger, the one with "incipient passions," Frida, sufficiently German to suggest the young girl he met in Gossensass in 1884 and whom he used for Hedvig in *The Wild Duck.* The suitor of the older daughter also recalls this play; in its lists of characters he was called "Institute Instructor Nanne" and now he is called "Schoolmaster Arnholm." The tubercular sculptor, for whom a young German painter was to be "used as a model," also appears first in the notes to *The Wild Duck.* These interrelationships are only external evidence of the essential inner connection between *Rosmersholm, The Wild Duck,* and *The Lady from the Sea,* which stand as a distinct group in Ibsen's plays, more strongly marked than any of his other work by symbols from nature.

He had told William Archer that obviously there was a great deal of symbolism in his plays, since life was full of it. And he was convinced that any work of literature that aimed at deeper significance must be symbolic in itself. Previously symbols were not given great emphasis, but in his last group of plays they would have a vital role in the dramatic action.

The two stepdaughters are used to help drive Ellida into that dream life where she is trapped. Between themselves and their father they have a host of memories about their mother, his first wife; they exclude Ellida from these and she is isolated and alone. At the end of the play, however, the sisters (or at least the younger one) can offer her a challenging task that becomes a recompense for the lost dream-world where she has been living secretly and involuntarily with the runaway, and perhaps even dead, sailor to whom she was once engaged. Ellida scarcely dares to admit her dreams to herself; the secret world both terrifies and thrills her. And as she lives in that undefined place between the well-lighted and the darkened areas of her conscious, a sickness preys on her will. Her ability to control herself seeps away bit by bit until the great crisis. Chance events have brought to vivid life the image of the man to whom she was once bound by such an unfathomable power, and her anticipation is unbounded. When he returns, this mysterious man with eyes like a fish, she is saved from him and her own delusion only because her husband sets her free to choose on her own responsibility. With the marriage bond no longer binding her will, the attraction of her former engagement loses its power over her. She becomes free and whole again at the moment when the compulsive idea of her old love releases its hold on her mind.

When Ibsen finished the play, he wrote to his publisher: "I feel confident that this play will win the attention of the public. In many respects I have entered upon a new path here." His contemporaries were, however, not aware of any "new paths." What struck them was that this play, in contrast to *The Wild Duck*, was "free from the oppressive nightmare of pessimism," so that its effect could be "entertaining and pleasant," not "painful and depressing" like that of the two previous plays; in other words, the play "has a happy ending." People were gratified that husband and wife found one another at the end, and did not separate as they had in *A Doll's House*. "The great questioner this time really gives us an answer," this particular reviewer concludes, adding, however, that the answer "is not a very tangible one."

Some of this is obviously true, but it ignores the essential psychological and artistic connection that exists between this play and the previous ones, even though the polemic element of the latter plays is missing here. The symbolic meaning is more pronounced and the theme is more directly psychological; there is nothing like the mockery of *The Wild Duck* or the hostility to certain modes of thinking in *Rosmersholm*. There is no conflict over moral viewpoints; there is nothing, in fact, but a soul struggling with itself. Psychological conflict had always been the life-giving basis of Ibsen's art, but in this play the conflict was one individual's effort to gain mastery over his own soul. That was the new element, the new path this play took.

The aphorism, in the old Ibsenian style, with which the play ends— "Freedom with responsibility"—was added in the very last revision. It could be omitted, and ought to have been. The play speaks so clearly that a platitude like this comes as a heavy-handed pointer, especially poorly motivated in stage production. The phrase, moreover, misled readers into discussing the work as though it offered a moral program, when in fact Ibsen was concentrating primarily on psychological liberation.

When Camilla Collett read the play, she thought she recognized her own struggle, and she wrote to Ibsen telling him she knew he had been thinking of her when he drew Ellida's portrait. She had never spoken to Ibsen about her youthful, but never conquered, passion for Welhaven, but she had told Mrs. Ibsen; now she wrote saying that this

was how she imagined the story reached him. When he finally answered
her after two months, he thanked her for her appreciation of the play,
and then went on to the sensitive issue of her personal story: "Yes, there
are points of resemblance. Many of them, in fact. And you have seen
them and been affected by them. I mean points that I could only have
known intuitively." The words are equivocal, although they have generally been taken as a confirmation of Mrs. Collett's belief. It is clear
that Ibsen did not wish to offend her by denying the story outright,
but he also seems to indicate that he did not know in advance that
Ellida's struggle was reminiscent of Mrs. Collett's experience. In any
case, he had succeeded in so depicting a woman's struggle that as
sensitive a person as Mrs. Collett could recognize its truthfulness to life,
even her own life.

To judge from the reviews, people reacted to the play according to
their preconceived notions of what to expect from Ibsen. The play was
obviously another marriage drama, like *A Doll's House*, only this time
it showed what a "real marriage" ought to be. But the play could teach
them little, since it was concerned with only a "peculiar psychiatric
case." Thus they ignored its deepest psychological import, calling the
play unclear and full of irrelevant mysticism, and suggesting that Ibsen
enjoyed "making vaporous pronouncements in a philosophical tone."
The Radicals tried to keep him in their camp; Irgens Hansen wrote in
Dagbladet that Ibsen had proved himself again a "realist" and even a
"naturalist," despite all the mysticism. He admitted bluntly that he
did not understand all the business about the sea in the woman's personality. Nor did many others, for that matter, and the play generally
aroused more bewilderment than perception, failing in theatre after
theatre wherever it was performed.

But this first judgment proved false when the play was revived by
Agnes Mowinckel at the little theatre Balkongen in Oslo for the centennial celebration of Ibsen's birth in 1928. What struck one after so
many years was the play's modernity and its close relation to recent
psychological theories, particularly those of Pierre Janet, developed in
the 1890's, and of Sigmund Freud, from the same period—although
given general circulation in the early years of the twentieth century.
The play took on new meaning and new life, because psychologists
had turned their attention to the pathology of mental life and had
begun to illuminate various kinds of border conditions between the
conscious and the unconscious life, trying to track the effects of suppressed unconscious drives and to analyze the conflicts between primary, repressed desires and acquired, consciously organized intentions.
Ibsen's poetic intuition had perceived this beforehand in the image of

a woman who felt herself bound and shackled because she had married not for love but merely for security; the repressed desires that smoldered within gradually took possession of her. Ibsen quite naturally gave her the physician she desperately needed in her husband (he had been imagined a lawyer at first). And the cure he proposed for her, to dig out the roots of sickness by giving her back her full consciousness of freedom, was again a reiteration of his constant demand for personal liberation, now being used as an agent for psychological healing.

Long ago Kierkegaard had shown how the diseased soul could be saved by being faced with the necessity for choice. The basic idea of *Either/Or* was to force man to the "crossroads" where he would have to choose—and then he would choose correctly. When man emerged from the prison of the unconscious to the clear light of consciousness, he secured his freedom in the "leap" that Kierkegaard made the goal of every human life. No matter how many years had passed since Ibsen first read the philosopher, he retained the memory of Kierkegaard's ethical demands.

Seen in this light, *The Lady from the Sea* loses its bewildering quality and reveals in clean focus the profound psychology on which it is built. The roots of Ibsen's thinking in the play are still the demands for psychological truth and freedom that can be read as far back as *Love's Comedy,* where war is declared on all marriages founded on anything less than total freedom. Now he pictured a marriage that is transformed from a financial "transaction" into a voluntary giving of oneself. Ellida would experience the "miracle" denied to Nora. Ibsen's choice of marriage as the testing ground for the ideal of freedom was dictated by his conviction that although marriage was not the only condition where issues of psychological compulsion and free choice arose, it was the one that produced the greatest dramatic conflicts and was the crucial testing ground of the will's capacity to free itself and become fully realized.

The optimistic tone of *The Lady from the Sea* derives from the victory that is won over the forces of compulsion. The same kind of optimism was evident in *Pillars of Society,* the play which was the first to state in unmistakable terms the demands of truth against the morality of society. He had believed at that time that simply to announce the ideal of truth was to insure its victory. Then had come disappointment and uncertainty, until now, when he found a new battleground and new weapons. Once more his faith in the ultimate outcome of this psychological struggle was affirmed. This confidence would in turn founder, and in the next struggle for psychological freedom there would be tragic failure.

CHAPTER THIRTY-EIGHT

REPRESSED DESIRES:

HEDDA GABLER (1889-90)

Ibsen had spent the summer of 1886 in Munich working on *Ros-mersholm;* two of the other summers since his departure from Rome were taken up with his visits to the North, and in the summer of 1888 he again remained in Munich to work on *The Lady from the Sea.* The following year he was finally free to return to his beloved Gossensass after an absence of five years. On this, his last visit, he stayed for a full three months, from July to September. His regular routine was a bit upset because he could not have his usual hotel room, but he was received as an old friend and enjoyed himself thoroughly. This was the summer the town dedicated the "Ibsenplatz," his old lookout on the hilltop. He could no longer make his way up the steep mountain road with his former ease, but nonetheless he dutifully led the festive procession right to the summit and graciously accepted all the homage of the townspeople.

He preferred to be by himself both at meals and on his daily walks, making an exception only to chat with the ladies, especially the young ones. He had always been attracted by feminine charm and liked the opportunity these women offered him for psychological speculation. When Mrs. Ibsen would advise him to "keep all those hysterical females at arm's length!" he would reply, "Don't worry . . . I want to have a closer look at them." He was actually at work in these moments, and it could at times be arduous work, as he indicated in a letter written after his return to Munich: "It was no time of rest, this summer in Gossensass. I have been very busy and have had more than ample opportunity to study and make observations among the many guests. It was most interesting, and in some respects profoundly disturbing. I must above all try to find some rest now, and then sum up and put what I have experienced to use."

The "disturbing" aspect was undoubtedly a reference to a young woman who had piqued his curiosity more than any of the others. He came to feel a special bond with a lovely, wistful, patrician young lady from Vienna, Emilie Bardach. Ibsen first noticed this eighteen-year-old girl in the hotel dining room, and when he met her in the forest on the evening of the celebration in his honor, he spoke to her. She thought he was "shy," but he was soon eagerly cross-examining her about her life. He urged her to speak freely, and in conversation after conversation he probed this young mind where ambiguities and contradictions were constantly disguised and exposed. It was an intriguing and thoroughly delightful game.

Was he infatuated with her? In one sense, at least for the summer. When they parted late in September, he called her "the May sun" in the "September" of his life. The profound need he had always felt for a woman's affection now threatened to burst forth in a passionate love. He told her that only suffering and self-denial could make a poet, but now the closer he drew to her the more insistent became the urge she inspired in him to break all restraints. At first she was terrified, but more and more "this volcano, so fearfully handsome" began to move her; when she returned his love, he was ecstatic. Some time later he told a young man who spoke of the joy of loving: "Oh, anyone can love! but I am happier than the happiest, for I am loved!" He dreamt of their going away together, of her working with him, and at the same time he knew that this was an impossibility. And she knew it as well.

An open declaration of their feelings seems to have taken place on September 19, as the summer drew to an end, for that is the date in *The Master Builder* of the encounter that Hilde reminds Solness of: "You seized me in your arms and held me back and kissed me . . . many times." Whether this actually happened in Gossensass cannot be certain, but Emilie's diary clearly indicates they had experienced some great upheaval. The next day Ibsen wrote in German in her commonplace book: "Exalted, agonized happiness—to struggle for the unattainable." She may not have read this yet by the 21st, when a young woman from Munich who knew them both wrote in her diary: "Die B. mit I. ganz toll" ("Miss B. is totally mad for Mr. I."), for this entry is followed on the next day by "Die B. geknickt" ("Miss B. grief-stricken"). Emilie must have realized by now just how "unattainable" was that relationship which Ibsen had described to her.

She left a few days later. Up to her last evening he was still speaking of wanting to "have" her and to travel around the world with her. He had already asked her to write to him—long letters that would help them recall their beautiful days together. For four months they corresponded. His letters are strangely ambivalent, yearning for her and rejecting her at the same time. He speaks of the benches by the

Pflersch Brook or windowseats in the hotel lobby, now empty, lonely; he just barely hints that it was her presence that gave these places such sweet life. He recalls how they once spoke of the difference between "Dummheit" (stupidity) and "Tollheit" (madness), and asks which one they were guilty of; then he answers his own question by saying it was neither, it was a necessity of fate. He repeats over and over that she will have to ponder on this herself, find out for herself what it means—he leaves his thoughts unfinished. He imagines her as many different things: she is a mysterious princess whose riddle he cannot solve except to say that it holds all that is beautiful; she stands before him adorned with pearls, and he puzzles over the secret hidden in this vision. (It is not certain how this would be interpreted by Freud or other psychologists—whether Ibsen imagined her as seductive or the opposite, a cold mermaid—since pearls are not mentioned among the dream symbols in Freud's *Traumdeutung*.) She is always present in his fantasies, and he stimulates dreams and fantasies in her as well. His letters often seem to be written as experiments in psychology, a possibility made even more likely since at times he wrote drafts of the letters first. But aware of the danger of the correspondence, he finally broke it off, announcing: "It is a matter of conscience for me." A bit late for the arrival of conscience, one might say, but he must be given credit for wanting to free her from a kind of half-life that could never become real. The relationship had become a burden for him.

She felt the blow deeply, and it seems evident that her emotional involvement had been greater than his and came to have more and more power over her. Soon after they first met, she told him that she could not imagine marrying some nice young man; she did not really want to marry, but was fascinated by the idea of taking a man from his wife. Ibsen understood both the naiveté and the demonic impulse revealed by this statement and was wary. More affectionate than he, she proved less able to accept the reality. The letter she wrote the day after receiving his (February 7, 1890) is full of despair. She almost begs him for at least an occasional sign from him, reminding him that she had returned his affections when she realized how he felt. She could never forget, nor would she ever be ashamed to admit, how happy she had been all those months. The meeting with Ibsen was without question the single event that shaped the rest of her life.

To Ibsen it was an interlude, although one with enduring results. He had looked deep into the emotions and fantasies of a young woman; some day these insights would quicken in his imagination, but first he would have to keep the whole episode at arm's length. Almost exactly a year after their break, he told a German friend, Dr.

Elias, that he was now ready to use Emilie as the model for a new play. By this time he could smile at the memory of their relationship, but with a shudder as he thought of how much like a little vulture she was and how close his escape. "She didn't get me," he said, "but I got her for my writing." He even reached such a state of real (or pretended) indifference that he asked his wife to burn her photograph—the one Emilie had signed "Prinzessin von Apfelsinien" (Princess of Orangia) because he had called her "princess." But something continued to live in his heart, and when she sent him a greeting on his seventieth birthday he wrote to her: "The summer in Gossensass was the happiest and most beautiful of my whole life. Scarcely dare think of it. And yet I must always do so. Always!"

During that summer a new dramatic theme began to take shape; the first mention of it is in a letter of September 7, where he says that he is "now going around with new plans for a dramatic work." The idea was still so vague that he realized it would take all of the following summer to clarify it. His first letter to Emilie the following month indicates that he intended to work on the new idea during the winter, but he adds: "I will try to imbue it with the gay mood of this summer. But it will end in sadness. That I can feel in my bones." A month later he wrote: "I am now busily occupied with the preliminary work on a new play; I sit for almost the whole day at my desk,—just go out a little in the evening,—dream and remember, and go on writing." The letter of October 15, however, emphasizes that it is impossible for him to make anything out of his recent experiences, at least not now. And even though there would be some reminiscences of the summer in the new play, an inkling here and there of what he had seen in a woman's most secret heart, the theme of the play developed out of earlier experiences.

While he worked on the play, he spent much time in the company of another young lady he had met in Gossensass, Helene Raff. She had already known a number of Ibsen's Munich friends, among them Dr. Elias and Paul Heyse, and was studying to be a painter. She too seems to have been infatuated with Ibsen that summer, for it was she who wrote in her diary, perhaps with a touch of jealousy, "Die B. mit I. ganz toll." She was twenty-four, somewhat older than Emilie, and undoubtedly more of an intellectual. As soon as she came back to Munich, she began reading Ibsen's plays in German, but before long she was trying to learn Danish.

She was eager to see Ibsen again, and he may even have suggested that they meet in Munich. She would walk in the afternoon in Maximilianstrasse, where he lived, and "finally," after two weeks, as she states in her diary, they met. At first it was just a pleasant chat. A few days later the conversation was "extremely interesting, but somewhat disturbing," and the stroll an hour long; when they parted, his emotions were stirred up. He was still writing to Emilie, and the peculiar feeling of psychological experiments that those letters convey was most probably due to the conflict he experienced as he grew closer to Helene. They met again, and again there was an affectionate leave taking. Finally he visited her at her studio, with a gift copy of Henrik Jaeger's biography in German translation. But the forwardness of this visit disturbed him, and he was anxious to place their relationship on a different footing. She called on the Ibsens on September 30, and that same evening he wrote her that he had been thinking how wonderful it would be to have "such a dear and lovable daughter" as she.

Helene probably felt as deep and as sincere a love for him as Emilie had, but she was a wiser woman and was satisfied with the pleasures of friendly conversation. He began to call her "child," as he had Emilie, using the more endearing German term "kind" instead of the Norwegian "barn." He liked to talk with her, and she satisfied his need to have someone to confide in, something he always found easier with a young woman who respected him and was full of attention. For a year and a half, until the spring of 1891 when she went to Paris to continue her studies, they met regularly on the street and sometimes in his home. "You are youth, my child," he once said to her, "youth personified, and I need it for my writing." At one time she objected to his speaking to her in words she had heard him say to Emilie Bardach, but he shrugged it off with, "Ah, that was in the country; in the city one is much more serious."

She began to keep an "Ibsen-Tagebuch," in which she wrote down the more interesting things he said in their talks (she published excerpts from this after his death). In one passage he explains to her how difficult it was for him to speak the whole truth: "I for one always have to keep something back for myself." What one kept back was in reality the most precious part of all. What lived within was one's real life, and that was not so much a question of what one had experienced but of what one made of experience. He often spoke about the inner life and the unconscious forces in the soul that worked on it—about compulsive ideas and hypnosis and the tremendous power of the will. He thought that women too often let themselves drift into a sick emotional life where they dreamed and longed and waited for the unknown that would give their life meaning. When the unknown never materialized they broke under the disappointment. He considered philosophy worthless unless it had a practical application, and of specialists who knew nothing but their specialty he said, "I have grave doubts about them."

Many of these random thoughts can be seen in the play he was working on at the time, *Hedda Gabler,* and perhaps even more in the next, *The Master Builder.* His thoughts moved between Emilie and Helene all the time he was working on the two plays, and when he sent Helene a copy of *The Master Builder* on New Year's Eve, 1892, he inscribed it: "A voice within me cries out for you." He still wished that their relationship had been something more.

An attack of influenza in early 1890 and minor tasks interfered with his plans for working on *Hedda Gabler,* and although he had started making notes in the fall in 1889, he was not able to begin shaping the play until July, 1890. He seems to have had especial difficulty penetrating to the vital center of the woman he wished to depict. From the beginning his image was of a woman with no goal or purpose in life; the problem was to determine what her imagination would be filled with in these circumstances. The theme may have begun to intrigue Ibsen when he created Ellida and the two daughters in *The Lady from the Sea.* When the play ends there are still so many things possible in their lives.

The German scholar Roman Woerner has suggested that Ibsen's thinking goes back to Rebecca West in *Rosmersholm,* the strong, courageous woman who is nonetheless broken by the influence of the Rosmer view of life. A bit of purely external proof of the relation between themes in the two plays is that Hedda Gabler was first called Hedda Rømer, the family name first given to the Rosmers. But a more substantial link between the two is that both women share a like desire to meddle in the fate of another person. This quality was what Ibsen labelled "demonic" in Emilie Bardach, and among the many notes for *Hedda Gabler* there is one direct reference to Emilie: "To take something away from someone, that I think would be lovely." The line was not used in the play, but the thought belongs unquestionably to Hedda.

The very first notes for the play, however, indicate nothing of this theme. They rather speak of "the married woman's growing delusion that she is an important character, and as a consequence her need to create sensational news. If an interesting female appears in a novel or a play, she assumes she is being portrayed." Camilla Collett's reaction to the portrait of Ellida in *The Lady from the Sea* comes immediately to mind. Mrs. Collett, in spite of her restless traveling about, most certainly had a goal in life, and could not have been considered as a model for Hedda Gabler. If anything, she was probably the influence behind another note that is diametrically opposed to the first one: "Women have no influence on public affairs of state. Therefore they want to have influence over the minds. And then so many of them have no goal in life (their lack of one is a heritage)." One of the primary ideas in shaping the psychology of the character is contained in the note: "Hedda's despair is the conception that there no doubt exist many possibilities for happiness in the world, but that she cannot catch sight of them. The lack of a purpose in life torments her." Then he defines the "major points" in the psychology of women like Hedda: "1) Not all of them are made to be mothers. 2) There is a sensual quality to them, but they are fearful of scandal. 3) They realize that there are life-tasks in their age, but they cannot become engaged with any of them." Hedda compensates by sniffing around life; she satisfies her sensual nature by furtive conversations about coarse eroticism, so that the man she lures into teasing her with this talk calls her, as one note has it, "a bitch . . . cold . . . marble-cold bitch." She does not "have the courage to indulge in such things" herself, since her intellectual and emotional life is repressed by "the conventions." Not daring to thrust herself into life, she flees from all responsibility, but most of all she flees the thought of scandal. She has never passed beyond the aesthetic stage of life, and all she desires is to be rid of everything that is ugly. Thus she is closed off from life; with all her lusts locked up within her, she in turn is locked in a marriage that exists solely as a compensation for her lost paternal home. Ibsen called his play *Hedda Gabler,* even though she is technically Mrs. Tesman: "In this way I have wished to suggest that as a personality she is more to be considered her father's daughter than her husband's wife." She had desired to be free, to have no one rule over her soul and her life; what she encounters instead are outside forces whose demands would bend her to their will.

Thoroughly disgusted with this half-life she leads, utterly bored with everything, she falls prey to the "demonic" that rises within. She thirsts for power over a human destiny, and urged on by envy and jealousy makes the experiment that will lead to the play's catastrophe. Ibsen places her between two men, her husband and the man she gives herself to in fantasies. Both are scholars—one the kind of specialist Ibsen had "grave doubts about," the other gifted with great ideas and visions. (An episode much discussed when Ibsen was in Norway in 1885 is similar to this arrangement of characters: two young scholars had competed for a university fellowship, which went to the one many thought the least gifted; the winner then married a beautiful society girl who seemed to expect a great deal from life. Since he did not know the parties personally, it seems unlikely that Ibsen used them as models.)

The actual models for the two scholars were two friends Ibsen knew in Germany. Jørgen Tesman was drawn from the young literary scholar Julius Elias, whom he had come to know in Munich. (Ibsen was at the party given for Elias when he received his doctor's degree and had such a lively time he had to be carried home.) Elias was among Ibsen's foremost spokesmen in Germany, a man with a deep appreciation of art and a zest for life. There was nothing of Tesman's pedantry in him, with the exception of that zeal for "bringing order into other people's papers," which the two had in common; Ibsen himself made frequent use of Elias' eagerness to be of service in all kinds of practical matters. Elias could be as delighted and satisfied with himself as a child.

The melancholy genius Ejlert Løvborg was based on Julius Hoffory, a Danish-born professor who lived in Berlin and was one of Ibsen's most active disciples. Hoffory was extremely talented but so emotionally unbalanced that he eventually became insane. (In a letter of 1890 Ibsen pictured him on the verge of insanity.) It was general knowledge that Hoffory associated with the generous lady Ibsen pictured as "the red-headed Mlle. Diana" (one of Hoffory's lady-friends was actually named Rotbart), and he once even lost the manuscript of a book on one of his sprees. The name "Løvborg" is probably a result of association with the "vineleaves in his hair" (Norwegian *løv*, leaves); the leaves themselves being suggested by the fall festivals held by the Scandinavians in Rome. The vineleaves of the bacchanalias became for Hedda the symbol of all that should make life—and death—beautiful. The symbol means more to her than life itself and forces everything to yield to the demand that nothing ugly even stain it.

There is much of Ibsen in the portrait of this woman—both the fear of risks and of responsibilities and the urge to experiment with human souls. And there is much of him in the two different spiritual worlds he pits against each other. On one hand there is the decent, everyday bourgeois world. The house of Tesman epitomizes the virtues of solid citizens, where the diligent workhorse Jørgen does not stretch his sights above the work at hand, where Aunt Julle makes her kindly sacrifices, and where the guardian spirit, the proper Berte, supervises all. Against this is pictured the world of the spiritually restless, freed from moral prejudices and restrictions, without moral sightings of any kind but preoccupied with the riddle of life, longing for a "bohemianism" that could lead to a great and extraordinary experience. The least significant of these people is the gourmet and sybarite Judge Brack. The one who dares the most is Løvborg, who writes about "the cultural wave of the future" and "the cultural movement of the future," and who harbors a dangerous fire that would dart out and consume everything that strangles desire.

The two worlds contend against each other within Hedda herself, but she is both a part and no part of the struggle. She experiments with Tesman and also with Løvborg, but she wants to do it in such a manner that she will bear no responsibility for the results. In the first drafts of the play she utilizes Tesman for her operation on Løvborg, but in the final version she alone lures him down those uncharted paths where she seems to lurk like a fatal beast of prey. How malevolent is she? There is no question of her vicious behavior in burning Løvborg's manuscript. (This incident derives from two stories Ibsen had been told: one about the wife of a Norwegian musician in Copenhagen who burned the manuscript of his symphony out of jealousy; the other about a woman in Norway who drove her husband to bouts of drinking to prove her control over him, and thus destroyed his rich talents.) Ibsen wrote that most of Hedda's character is based on a woman he had known in Munich, who had ended her life by poison. The name Gabler is even supposed to be an anagram of her name, Alberg. The details of her life that gave him inspiration for the play are not known, and can only be conjectured from the action of the play.

Hedda ends by shooting herself, but first she succeeds in persuading Løvborg to kill himself. As he proves he has the daring to perform what is in her eyes a splendid, beautiful act, she has a vicarious sense of participating in life at last. But for the first time she is forced to accept the responsibilities that life forces on one; her action proves to be the chain that binds her to the will of another. Her only escape is to flee from the life that has finally caught up with her. As in *Rosmersholm*, death is the only possible solution for the conflict. The play is thus another statement of Ibsen's perception of the contrast between man's desire and his achievement. All the pessimism of *The Wild Duck* is here, with an even more searching analysis of the human soul's hidden depths.

Only those who stand to one side, with souls too shallow for conflict, escape with their lives—Jørgen Tesman and Thea Elvsted. Ibsen seems to have had some difficulty defining Mrs. Elvsted (Mrs. Rising in the first draft). One of the early drafts reads: "Tesman is propriety. Hedda is the sophisticate. Mrs. R is the nervous-hysterical modern person." She can "only dimly glimpse, not understand" Løvborg's thoughts. In a conversation with Dr. Elias early in 1891, Ibsen hinted that he originally intended to model her on Emilie Bardach, but in the end he made the character stronger and healthier, with something of Norwegian solidity about her, as he seems to suggest by recalling in her name, Rising, the farm where his father's mother had lived. Mrs. Elvsted is a woman after his own heart, one who directly and without hysterics or concern for the "scandal" does the brave thing she feels is right and necessary for the man she loves.

So at least three of the important figures in *Hedda Gabler* were derived from non-Norwegian models. (Aunt Julle is the only one known to be based on a Norwegian, an old Bergen lady, Elise Holck, whom Ibsen had known in his Dresden years and whom he had seen sacrifice herself patiently for a sick sister.) It was not surprising that when the play appeared at Christmas, 1890, it was regarded as less Norwegian in feeling than any of his other works. There are, nevertheless, unmistakable Norwegian elements. The setting is obviously Oslo, when it was still a small town, and Norwegian enough is the petty bourgeois thinking that dominates the characters, the snobbery that attaches such importance to being the daughter of a general, the concern about what "people" will say. He had transformed his foreign models in terms of those feelings and thoughts of his homeland that still lived within him.

Caught in a struggle between dreams and action, Ejlert Løvborg is brother to Hjalmar Ekdal and Rosmer as well as to Ibsen, for he too occasionally felt the same urge to throw all restraint to the winds. Løvborg was enough of an authentic Scandinavian for August Strindberg to see himself as the model. Hedda seemed less Norwegian, but the writer of this book recalls an incident about a year or two after the play came out when he met a woman whose lover had just shot himself because all his hopes had been crushed. "Wasn't it magnificent!" she cried with blazing eyes. She too seemed to have been experimenting with life and longing for the extraordinary. Still it is true that such women are obviously not the product of any particular national culture, but of modern upper-class society in any country where there are women without goals or missions in life, trapped by the laws society lays down for them. Hedda was a perfect example of the kind of problem which twentieth-century psychoanalysts would examine. She had forcibly repressed the desires that were ready to overwhelm her senses and her whole intellect, and so these desires avenged themselves by forcing her to toy with all that attracted and enticed her. Bit by bit she drove herself into a trap from which she lacked the psychological strength to free herself.

Ibsen had to search out the explanation of this tragedy, and he tried various approaches. In one of the drafts Hedda says: "Remember that I am the child of an old man—a spent old man at that—maybe even decrepit. This could have left its mark." He struck this out and tried another motivation: Hedda is pregnant, and this condition can upset an already-disturbed woman. Moreover, this brings home to her what she is most reluctant to accept, responsibilities, the demands of life. But not even this is necessary to explain her behavior; for the catastrophe would have happened even without this. In trying to discover the roots of this inevitability, Ibsen succeeded in capturing the elusive, hidden movements of the human soul more fully than any modern playwright had ever done. What Dostoevsky had achieved in the novel he had done in drama. He stood in the first rank of world literature.

CHAPTER THIRTY-NINE

CONTROVERSY AND FAME (1886-91)

For more than a quarter of a century Ibsen had lived in the midst of controversy, gradually moving to the foreground in the intellectual struggle that he hoped would herald a new era of freedom, with new ideals of morality. Ibsen would never be a leader, Bjørnson had once commented—"a tiny gnome of a fellow, without rump and without chest." But it was of no significance that Ibsen the man lacked these attributes of a born leader; his writings were his weapons.

When the struggle began in 1863 with *Love's Comedy*, it was a purely Norwegian affair; three years later, *Brand* aroused controversy in all the Scandinavian countries, and from that moment Ibsen became a force in Nordic cultural life, despite widespread opposition. His new works were eagerly awaited, and usually pitted party against party and divided public opinion. *Ghosts* had aroused the most violent antagonism, and until Ibsen's seventieth birthday in 1898, no regular theatre in either Oslo or Copenhagen dared perform it. The Bergen theatre was particularly venturesome when it staged the play in 1890. The first performances in Norway were given by traveling companies led by the Swede August Lindberg and the Dane Olaus Olsen. When Lindberg gave the play for the Kristiania Arbeidersamfund (Workers' Society) in September, 1889, a special bond was established between Ibsen and the working class. Ultimately the play became a battle-cry for all young radicals, who demonstrated against the authorities by shouting, "Long live *Ghosts!*"

The clearest indication of the dissension over his work was on the occasion of his sixtieth birthday in 1888, when only the Liberal press honored him. Although *Verdens Gang* of Oslo called him "a man of the dawn," the Conservative *Morgenbladet* did not even mention his name. In the more moderate *Aftenposten* there appeared a front-page article on "our greatest living writer." There were "many dubious" elements in Ibsen's writing, the article declared, but still Ibsen must

be appreciated for his provocative spirit and his voice that "is refreshing in the midst of the fatuousness and compromise of everyday life."
When Ibsen sent his thanks to the writer of the article, the distinguished jurist Professor Bredo Morgenstierne, and to the paper's editor,
Amandus Schibsted, he told them how distressed he was at being identified with either of the rival political parties. Understanding was what
he longed for, he wrote, and he deeply appreciated the gesture they
had made.

When he finally began to turn from controversial themes to analyses
of the buried mysteries of the human psyche, another, and this time
international, controversy erupted over his works. On their own strength,
his books were waging war.

From 1878 to 1880 there had been enough discussion in Germany
over *Pillars of Society* and *A Doll's House* to make his name widely
known. In 1880 and 1881 the critic Ludwig Passarge published translations of *Peer Gynt, Brand,* and Ibsen's poems, and in 1883 he did a
full-length study of Ibsen, the first to attempt a thorough investigation
since Strodtmann's ten years earlier. Ibsen was not, however, particularly pleased by the book, especially not by the dedication to Lorentz
Dietrichson and Hartvig Lassen, "the two men," he wrote some years
later, "who of all my Norwegian literary friends and acquaintances
have perhaps least been able to penetrate to what I regard as the core
of my life work as a poet." He thought he had found evidence that the
book reflected the opinions of the two men; in any case he felt it was
totally lacking in any appeal to German youth. The book was poorly
timed and made virtually no impression. A deeper impression was made
by Brandes' study, translated about the same time in the periodical
Nord und Süd, but even this could not revive Ibsen's reputation. It
would be three years before *Ghosts* or *The Wild Duck* was translated,
since both were believed too eccentric for German tastes, and neither
translators, publishers, nor theatre directors dared become involved
with works that made such a sharp break with the petty bourgeois
romanticism that still dominated German theatre and literature. Ibsen
would not regain his standing in German cultural life without a vigorous
struggle, but in this struggle he would become the standard bearer for
a host of enthusiastic pro-Ibsen rebels.

Ghosts was translated in 1884 by Mrs. Maria von Borch, who had felt
impelled to do the play because of the similarity between it and her
own experiences. The translation received little attention until the
spring of 1886 when Felix Philippi read it in Munich and asked Ibsen
for permission to have it produced. Philippi persuaded August Grosse,
the director of the Stadttheater in Augsburg, to stage it, but the police

forbade public performances of so immoral a work, and Grosse could realize no profit from the venture. He did, however, have it performed for a specially invited audience on the afternoon of Good Friday, April 14, 1886. Circumstances did not permit an ideal production, but the young performers managed to convey their growing appreciation of the play to the audience, who responded enthusiastically and gave the author, who was present, an ovation. The police ban naturally aroused curiosity, and people rushed to buy the book that had been branded so unspeakably immoral. More important support came from the critic Ludwig Fulda who launched a full-scale attack on German drama in *Die Nation* by contrasting Ibsen with the conventional spirit rampant in German theatre. With Ibsen would come a revolution, he announced: *Ghosts* is a concentrated attack on the ruling powers of society that calls into question their entire moral basis. Otto Brahm emphasized the same link between the artistic and the social conflict in his article in *Deutsche Rundschau*.

One theatre director in Germany did not have to trouble himself about police censorship—Duke Georg of Saxe-Meiningen. *Ghosts* was performed at his theatre on December 21, 1886, in an excellent production with Maria Berg as Mrs. Alving and Alexander Barthel as Oswald. "Unübertrefflich" (unsurpassable) was Ibsen's one-word comment on the performance. He was the duke's guest now, as he had been ten years earlier when *The Pretenders* was given, and he wrote to his wife boasting that his accommodations were finer than those of any other guest: "Four colossal salons with all possible conveniences." Moreover, "the duke and his wife surpass each other in showering attentions on" him and he was thoroughly happy. He was so childishly delighted when the duke elevated him to the honor of commander of the Sächsisch-Ernestinische house order that he wore both the knight's cross and the commander's star. The German critic Paul Lindau tried to explain that this was not proper, but Ibsen brushed it aside with, "I don't understand that," and defended himself: "This knight's cross was the first decoration I got in Germany; to me it is a precious memory, and I will not part with it." He stood a bit more on his dignity than absolutely necessary. When Lindau used some rather casual words at dinner table about the lively Regine in *Ghosts,* and all the rest laughed, Ibsen's face set and he replied, "I thought that truth had beauty in itself." After the meal Lindau tried to excuse himself, but Ibsen was not to be placated: "Certain things should not be the subject of jest, and among these I consider intellectual work." Lindau finally managed to thaw him out, and Ibsen said: "Well, let it go. I have often been sorry that I don't understand joking."

The duke's authority was limited to Saxe-Meiningen, and when he tried to send the production to other cities, the police interfered. But the crucial battle over the play was fought in Berlin a few weeks later when Arno Anno, the director of the Residenz-Theater, produced the play at the insistence of an actor who wanted to play Oswald. Professor Julius Hoffory lent his support to the venture and kept spirits up when the police arrived with their prohibition. Otto Brahm and Paul Schlenther assisted the director, and the play was given a private showing on Saturday, January 8, 1887. The public had sensed a scandal in the wind—the book was already sold out and the publisher had shipped 5,000 more copies to Berlin. Now, fourteen thousand people tried to get invitations to the performance. Emanuel Reicher played his first Ibsen role, that of Pastor Manders; Charlotte Frohn was Mrs. Alving; and the other parts were also in competent hands. The air was tense as the play unfolded and gradually captured the audience. In the intermissions Hoffory rushed around proclaiming to all who cared to listen that: "A new age in German literature is opening." After each act the audience seemed to catch its breath for a moment, then break out in a storm of applause that called actors and author out for repeated bows. At the end there were ringing bravos for Ibsen, as well as a few catcalls that were quickly drowned in the general applause. It was a festive as well as perturbing occasion.

Two days later, all of literary Berlin turned out for a great celebration in Ibsen's honor at the Hotel Kaiserhof. In the main address, Otto Brahm declared that Ibsen was the great pioneer and trailblazer of modern drama, the courageous advocate of truth, the poet-realist who would rescue German theatre from the insipid techniques of the French and give it authentic life. Ibsen expressed his gratitude by saying that it seemed like a fairytale for him, the stranger, to be so warmly received; he hoped the time would come when he would no longer be as a stranger in the great German homeland.

Newspapers and magazines were full of the controversy that had been sparked by the Berlin performance. On one side was the old guard, crying out against this attack on all idealism, this repulsive coarseness, offensive to the modesty of all decent folk, this socialistic spirit of rebellion. To induce this into literature was to subvert all ideals of beauty. On the other side were the young, demanding that literature concern itself with contemporary problems and describe life with uncompromising honesty. Brahm was a leader of this party; he published his article from *Deutsche Rundschau* in book form, and wrote in *Die Nation*. When the opposition mocked the "Ibsen-congregation" that was trying to force a foreign prophet on Germany, Ludwig Fulda replied in *Die Nation* that the "congregation" actually regarded Ibsen as a chosen advocate for the true German spirit, because the ideas of the times spoke more vigorously in him than in any other writer. The argument was continued in 1888 when Leo Berg published his essay on *Henrik Ibsen und das Germanenthum in der modernen Literatur* to demonstrate how truly Germanic Ibsen was.

When people expressed displeasure with the police ban that forced private performances of *Ghosts,* Ibsen answered in that deliberate, thoughtful manner he had acquired: "The time has not yet come. But I know that the time will come. And I can wait. I can wait." And gradually he began to win. In 1887 there were two separate translations of both *The Wild Duck* and *Rosmersholm,* one of them by Mrs. von Borch. *An Enemy of the People,* that "dangerous play," was produced at the Ostend-Theater in Berlin on March 5, 1887, and ran for fourteen successive days. When Felix Philippi and August Grosse decided to produce *Rosmersholm* in Augsburg on April 6, 1887, even before it appeared in Oslo, Ibsen came from Munich to take part in the final rehearsal. He watched the performance in dismay, however, starting at every word from the stage, digging all ten fingers into the plush of the seat, and groaning half-aloud "My god, my god!" Then he shrugged it all off, saying decisively, "I'll just forget whatever I had intended to say, and then it will work out all right." He realized that the actors would not be able to fulfill the new kind of demands his plays made on them, and he bowed to the inevitable restrictions on a dramatist. He watched the performance the next day in quiet, accepted the curtain calls, and thanked the actors with praise.

A month later *Rosmersholm* was given at the Residenz-Theater in Berlin, with Emanuel Reicher and Charlotte Frohn again in leading roles. In the resulting controversy some insisted that the whole thing was sheer nonsense, others rated it more offensive than *Ghosts.* But the "Ibsen-congregation" had gained the upper hand by now, and final victory came in 1888. The police ban on *Ghosts* was removed; in October it was played in Berne and Basel in Switzerland; and the Meiningen players began touring with it throughout Germany and Austria. In March, 1888, *The Wild Duck* was a great success in its debut at the Residenz-Theater, directed by Sigmund Lautenberg; "a masterful performance" according to Ibsen who saw it the following year. For Ibsen's sixtieth birthday the great Friederike Gossmann came out of retirement in Vienna to score a brilliant success as Nora.

There would have been many celebrations in honor of his birthday in theatres throughout Germany if Kaiser Wilhelm had not died a few days before. But virtually every German newspaper of importance observed the day, March 20, 1888, with articles about him. To celebrate the occasion, translations of *The Feast at Solhaug*, with a foreword by Julius Elias, and *Emperor and Galilean,* with a foreword by Otto Brahm, appeared. To Ibsen the tributes were totally unexpected. As letters, telegrams, and flowers poured in, he walked around his room in a daze, repeating over and over, "This is too much, this is too much!" German literary and artistic figures brought him greetings, and Bjørnson summed it all up in his telegram: "Today the world comes to the solitary one."

Ibsen had triumphed in Germany and for the next twenty years, at least, would be master in the German theatre. Henrik Jæger's Norwegian biography appeared in translation the following year, and early in March there was an "Ibsen Week" in Berlin, where he received the acclaim of audiences watching *The Lady from the Sea* at the Royal Theater, *The Wild Duck* at the Residenz-Theater, and *A Doll's House* ("Nora") at the Lessing-Theatre. Then he went on to Weimar to be feted like a conquering hero by duke and commoner. Later he wrote to Hoffory: "I regard my visit to Berlin and everything connected with it a truly great happiness to me. It has had a wonderfully refreshing and rejuvenating effect on my soul and will certainly leave its mark on my future writing."

But if he had triumphed it was as the leader in a battle for progress, surrounded by hostility. When Freie Bühne opened in Berlin on September 29, 1889, it was a foregone conclusion that the opening play be *Ghosts.* Ibsen became the rallying point as the new theatre took up the fight against censorship and "approved" taste, uniting radical art with radical social theories, naturalism with socialism. Ibsen would be followed by such young German writers as Gerhart Hauptmann, whose entire outlook was changed after seeing a performance of *Ghosts* in 1887, Hermann Sudermann, and others. But Ibsen was always recognized as the central figure in the radical revolt, still much in evidence as late as 1906, when the Minister of Ecclesiastical Affairs in Prussia banned the purchase of Ibsen's works by the teachers' colleges. Despite such lingering resistance, the decisive battle was won between 1887 and 1889; from then on the Germans acknowledged Ibsen as their own, as a German writer in fact. To some extent he recognized the kinship himself. When numerous letters from Hungarians and Poles living in Vienna arrived after the "Ibsen Week" festival in 1887, he told Hoffory that there must be some connection between the diverse nationalities they represented and the "universality of the Germanic spirit, which predestines it to a commanding position in the world." He added: "I feel clearly and certainly that I owe the possibility of my taking part in these currents to my entry into contemporary German life." Germany also implied Austria and German-speaking Switzerland, as well as the Netherlands. His spokesmen in the last-named were J. O. H. Rössing, the liberal editor of the paper *De Lantaarn*, and his brother, publisher A. Rössing (Mrs. Rössing helped by triumphing in his plays on the Dutch stage).

In the same years controversy erupted in England. Earlier critical work had had little impact. Edmund Gosse expanded and republished his old essay in *Studies in the Literature of Northern Europe* in 1879, but his comments were still restricted to the historical and poetical works. Success would come here, as it came elsewhere, with the social dramas. Their realistic technique tempted Henrietta Frances Lord to translate *A Doll's House* (1882) and *Ghosts* (1885), the latter for a socialistic journal, but the translations were not successful and they did not win new readers for Ibsen. It was not until 1888 that the first modest success in arousing interest in Ibsen was won by the critic William Archer. A Scotsman with Norwegian relatives, Archer had learned the language as a child. He sought out Ibsen in Rome in the winter of 1881-82 and again in Jutland in 1887, and was soon the acknowledged leader of the Ibsen movement in England.

Archer had been able to have his translation of *Pillars of Society* privately performed on December 15, 1880, but was unable to find a publisher for it until 1888. A performance of *A Doll's House* on March 3, 1884, made no impression. But as the 1880's neared their end, signs of new ferment in social and intellectual life began to appear, and Ibsen's time had come. In 1888 Walter Scott of London published a collection of three plays, *Pillars of Society, Ghosts,* and *An Enemy of the People,* the first two translated by Archer, the last by Mrs. Eleanor Marx-Aveling, a daughter of Karl Marx. The collection sold well, and thus a circle of Ibsen admirers developed and struck the first blow with a performance of Archer's translation of *A Doll's House* at the opening of the Novelty Theatre on June 7, 1889, The great Shakespearean actress Janet Achurch played Nora with such success that several performances were given. Opposition was, of course, inevitable, since dramatic realism was a novelty on the English stage and the moral standards of the play too revolutionary for the bourgeois English. The newspapers were full of the same kind of moralistic platitudes that had greeted the play at first in Scandinavia and Germany. The same happened when *Pillars of Society* was given a single performance in July, 1889. The first conflict between Ibsen and England did not secure a triumph for his dramatic art. When Miss Achurch took *A Doll's House* to Australia and America, the reaction was the same; there were catcalls in some places, and harshly contemptuous reviews in the newspapers.

The name of Ibsen, however, had entered into general discussion in England, and Walter Scott found it advantageous to issue a collected edition of the prose plays, from *The Vikings at Helgeland* to *Hedda Gabler,* in 1890-91. William Archer supervised the translating, with the aid of his brother Charles and his sister-in-law Frances. This was the first English edition that had Ibsen's approval and the first collection of his works issued anywhere in the world. *The Lady from the Sea* was, oddly enough, published in two more translations in 1890, one of them by Mrs. Marx-Aveling, with an introduction by Edmund Gosse. At the same time Henrik Jæger's biography was translated into English, and Gosse included a new section on Ibsen's later plays in a reissue of his *Studies.* With all this activity, the Ibsenites were encouraged to make new forays. Gosse and Archer were interested primarily in Ibsen's dramatic art; others took greater interest in his revolutionary spirit. In July, 1890, George Bernard Shaw lectured the Fabian Society on "Socialism in Ibsen." In the resulting newspaper discussion, Ibsen was asked his opinion on socialism; he replied that he was in some respects happy that his conclusions were the same as those of "the social democratic moral philosophers." The statement could be interpreted as his authorization to the radicals to continue the struggle on his behalf.

The conflict reached its peak in 1891. When *Rosmersholm* was given at the Vaudeville Theatre in February, the London press responded with angry disapproval. For the production of *Ghosts,* an Independent Theatre, patterned on those of Germany and France and directed by the Dutch-born J. T. Grein, made its debut. The censor banned *Ghosts,* and there was talk of an interpellation in Parliament to protect public morality. The play could only be given once for members and guests on March 13, 1891, but this was enough to whip the press to a fury. A collection of terms of abuse heaped on the unspeakable drama would fill pages. It was called "disgusting," "unutterably offensive," "an open drain," "gross, almost putrid indecorum," and so on in the same vein. Ibsen's admirers were "lovers of prurience and dabblers in impropriety who are eager to gratify their illicit tastes under the pretence of art." (A much larger sampling of abuse can be found in Shaw's *Quintessence of Ibsenism,* which draws upon an 1891 article by Archer in the *Pall Mall Gazette.—Translators' Note.*) William Archer came to Ibsen's defense in the press, and Shaw's expanded lecture antagonized the opposition still further by its hearty disquisition on Ibsen's battle against all forms of dated bourgeois "idealism." One of Shaw's biographers has, however, suggested that *The Quintessence of Ibsenism* was really intended to present Ibsen's ideas in a form that would agree with Shaw's.

Shaw did put Ibsen to work in his running battle with Shakespeare. Some years later in *The Philanderer,* Shaw would mock all the cranks and crackpots who gathered under the banner of Ibsen.

Through the lively acrimony of the 1890's, Ibsen's name came to be so well known that revue theatres could put on satirical skits based on *Ghosts.* More important was the success the plays themselves gradually won. In April, 1891, the American actress Elizabeth Robins scored a personal triumph as the lead in *Hedda Gabler* in a production that she had also staged. Gosse later called this the best Ibsen performance ever given in England. Two years later in January, the abominable *Ghosts* reappeared at Grein's Independent Theatre, and *The Wild Duck* scored an even greater success there in May, 1894. The battle was won and "Ibsenism" no longer looked upon as an aberration. The plays had been one of the weapons used against the old "Victorian" ideals in literature and social life, and the final, almost symbolic capitulation came when Queen Victoria attended a performance of *Ghosts* in 1897. But despite these successes, Ibsen's influence on the English theatre was never as pervasive as it was in Germany, and he never won as firm a position in the English repertory. The English theatre-going public, as a whole, was not accustomed to having the stage used as a platform for serious revolutionary ideas, and although at times certain plays drew large audiences by virtue of the controversy surrounding them, by and large, Ibsen's plays were for the few. Actors and actresses might fall in love with Ibsen roles and playwrights might be stimulated to greater seriousness, but he had no permanent place in England.

As might be expected, Ibsen entered America by way of England, with some preparatory work done by Norwegian, Danish, and German immigrants. In 1882 Professor Rasmus B. Anderson of the University of Wisconsin, a son of Norwegian immigrants, wrote at length about Ibsen in a literary journal called *The American.* In May of the same year, a Dano-Norwegian amateur group performed *Ghosts* in Chicago and other cities of the midwest. The first performance in English, however, was a garbled version of *A Doll's House* given in Milwaukee, Wisconsin, on June 2 and 3, 1882. (This production owed its inception to the enthusiasm of a local school-master who had read it in German translation and could not rest until he had seen it on the stage.) There was a single performance in Louisville, Kentucky, on December 7, 1883, with Helene Modjeska in the lead, but it drew little comment. The same held true when the great German actor Friedrich Mitterwurzer of Vienna played *Ghosts* in a number of cities in 1887. Clemens Petersen saw it in Chicago and wrote to Bjørnson that it was excellently played, but "the theatre was dismally empty." It was given a mere six performances, and "the German newspapers here greeted it with the most frightful abuse I have ever read."

Success in America did not begin to come until 1889, when the English actress Beatrice Cameron played Nora in Boston, New York, and other major cities. Still more attention was paid to Janet Achurch and her English company when they toured in 1889-90 after their return from Australia. New controversy began to agitate audiences and critics, further increased by the spectacular triumphs scored by Mrs. Minnie Maddern Fiske, first as Nora, then in a number of Ibsen roles that she added to her repertory. It was she who put Ibsen's play over on the American stage. Mrs. Fiske was asked in 1928 how she happened to begin playing Ibsen. She laughed and replied, "I was eighteen years old and newly married to Mr. Fiske, my director. He had great faith in me and wanted to have something new. Then he got *A Doll's House* from a friend in London, the play everyone was talking about. But it was no success in the beginning; our cultural life was on a low level, and the theatrical critics were hopelessly stupid and ignorant." Asked what aspect of Ibsen she found most fascinating, she countered: "What fascinates us most in a sea in storm?" What seems to have appealed to her more than anything was the depths of his work; she never felt she had exhausted the possibilities in a role.

The debate over Ibsen was taken up in France too during these years, led mainly by non-Frenchmen, just as in England the Scots, the Irish, and the Dutch had been the first to fight on his side. In the spring of 1887, Jacques Saint Cère reported in *Revue d'art dramatique* the violent controversy over Ibsen he had witnessed in Germany. At the same time a Russian diplomat in Switzerland, German-speaking Count Moritz Prozor, was doing the first French translation of Ibsen. Count Prozor had served in Stockholm and married a cousin of Count Snoilsky. When he saw *Ghosts* in 1883, he was so moved that he became a passionate Ibsenite. He saw the play again in Switzerland, where the police had banned it, and decided then to give Ibsen an entry into France. He translated *Ghosts* and *A Doll's House*, and got the Swiss writer Edouard Rod to help him find a Paris publisher. He wrote an enthusiastic preface to the volume which appeared in 1889.

It aroused as little excitement as the English version the previous year, except for an occasional notice. Jules Lemaître, the critic of *Journal des Débats*, wrote favorably of it, and Emile Zola, who glimpsed in Ibsen a comrade-in-arms, brought the plays to the attention of André Antoine. Antoine's recently established Théâtre-Libre was dedicated to presenting a more realistic art than that which dominated the French stage. He decided to stage *Ghosts,* but since he was dissatisfied with Prozor's version, made a new translation with the help of a French businessman who knew some Norwegian. When the play was given on May 29, 1900, Antoine's performance as Oswald revealed a depth of quiet suffering that the audience found most compelling. Although the rest of the cast was not up to his level, the play was effective. Ibsen had come alive in France and the struggle began. The kindly old "Uncle" Francisque Sarcey made himself the spokesman for traditional bourgeois taste. He would have none of these explosive themes and in the name of "common sense" and "French joie de vivre" rejected the foreigner's solemnity and rebelliousness. The general opinion from the beginning was that Ibsen was unclear and ambiguous. *Ghosts* ends in uncertainty; such a complete disregard for French logic indicated that Ibsen was "un-French" and thus unacceptable. He was alien in spirit, as well as in nationality. Jules Lemaître defended him at first against this accusation of obscurity, but as Lemaître became more nationalistic and more conservative, he also began to think that Ibsen did not suit the French spirit. By the mid-nineties Sarcey was certain that he had pronounced Ibsen dead in France.

He was mistaken. The seed had been sown and it would continue to grow. A small book on Ibsen written with youthful enthusiasm by the Belgian Charles Sarolea appeared in 1891. More comprehensive and serious was Auguste Ehrhard's *Henrik Ibsen et le théâtre contemporain,* in 1892. The Swiss Ernest Tissot published his *Le drame norvégien* in 1893, dealing with both Bjørnson and Ibsen; less sympathetic to Ibsen, he has a high regard for his art. Such books helped make Ibsen comprehensible to the French, but they were in greater need of direct experience with the works themselves. Prozor and others continued to translate the plays, and the Paris publisher Albert Savine, issued six more volumes of *Théâtre d'Henrik Ibsen* between 1892 and 1893, with ten plays translated by Prozor and others. These were reprinted from time to time. Antoine gave close to two hundred performances of *Ghosts* in various parts of the country and produced *The Wild Duck* at his theatre in April, 1891. *Hedda Gabler* was done that same year at the Vaudeville Theatre, and in December, 1892, the theatre society Les Escholiers performed *The Lady from the Sea.* From 1893 on Ibsen became a regular part of the repertory of Lugné-Poë's independent theatre, L'Oeuvre, starting with *Rosmersholm* and *An Enemy of the People* and continuing through a whole series of other plays.

There were certain disadvantages to this development, for just as Prozor became the "authorized" French translator, Lugné-Poë held a monopoly on performances. Unfortunately, Lugné-Poë's acting talents did not correspond to his good intentions; he could not adapt to the roles, and the results on stage became somewhat monotonous and unimaginative. However, his fidelity to the task he had set himself kept Ibsen a living force in France, and he did not block the way of others. The greatest triumph came with Gabrielle Réjane's interpretation of Nora at the Vaudeville in April, 1894; no one interested in contemporary theatre could afford to ignore this great actress in a commanding performance.

Ibsen never became a playwright for the ordinary theatre-goer in France. Edouard Rod had pointed out in 1889 that it took effort and acclimation to enter the Ibsen world, and Frenchmen were in general too accustomed to their own theatrical style to make the effort. The Prozor translations were in part an obstacle to acceptance. Since he was not French, he could not be expected to write the vivid, precise language Ibsen would have demanded, but the playwright was so delighted to be available in French that he gave Prozor both approval and exclusive rights. Asked what he thought of the translations, he answered evasively that all translation was equally good and equally bad—that it was impossible to carry the poetic idea whole and unaltered into a foreign language. The efforts of one German translator after another to improve and refine the German versions indicated what efforts could be made to find an adequate form for the original. No such effort was made in England or in France. Archer tried to render the original faithfully, but he was not a creative writer, and Prozor even less so. Performances were the most important influence in France and England, and on the stage good actors were able to give life even to mediocre translations.

The controversy that had first greeted the plays now gradually subsided; never again would there be such bitterness as in the German, English, and French receptions in the early 1890's. There might be flare-ups of hostility toward a play at its initial appearance, but in country after country Ibsen became a playwright whom everyone knew and many loved. Friends who could speak on behalf of his art were now everywhere.

In the 1890's the plays were translated into one language after another and were performed wherever there were theatres. Great performers from England, America, Germany, and France toured the world in his roles. Possibly the greatest of all was Eleonora Duse. From the early 1890's, her creative collaboration with Ibsen resulted in victory throughout Europe and America, first with Nora, then Rebecca West and Hedda Gabler. Her tragic intensity and brilliant intuition made the plays seem forever new; Ibsen had found the perfect interpreter of all his most profound thoughts.

It is characteristic of all great literature that it assumes new meaning for new generations, and so Ibsen's plays seemed to adjust themselves to the passing years. They had come initially out of his personal development; now as the problems they had raised were resolved, their spirit of rebelliousness seemed to die away. Of course, for those peoples still struggling for freedom and the right to exist, the works still awakened courage and hope—as they did with those who lived under the oppression of the Russian czars, where translations were secretly printed and distributed only at great risk. But where people had won some perceptible degree of that spiritual freedom which was Ibsen's ideal, other aspects of the plays began to be appreciated. In this transformation the new focus became the profound study of character and psychological conflict discoverable in the works. A play like *Pillars of Society* could fade because it had not searched deeply into struggling, suffering human souls, but *A Doll's House, Ghosts,* and the plays that followed had the enduring strength and significance to move generation after generation.

The whole complex story of Ibsen's international reputation does not fall within the scope of this book, but a part of the story of his life is the controversy his works aroused and the way his triumph in that controversy came to change the significance of his work.

He was always vitally interested in the success of his writing around the world and always deeply grateful to all who helped make it known and understood. When Edmund Gosse had first written about him in 1872, Ibsen wrote to him, thanking him for taking the first step "toward the realization of one of my dearest literary dreams." Although he had never had any special fondness for England—he had thought of it mainly as a country filled with materialism and coal smoke—now the English became "a nation of aristocrats—in the best sense of the word," and he saw their practical genius "combined in so strange a way with a pure and noble emotional life." The English stood very close to "us Scandinavians." When the Scotsman William Archer became his best defender in England, he even had "a conviction that my Scot descent has left very deep traces in me."

He was as enthusiastic in thanking Rasmus B. Anderson in 1882, August Lindberg in 1883, and Valfrid Vasenius in 1884. To Vasenius he wrote that it was a "special joy" for him "when any of my literary works gain a foothold in Finland, to whose people I feel so strongly attracted and where I have so many dear friends." He was most grateful to Julius Hoffory, and when Prozor began his translations in 1889, he wrote that it had been "a fond dream" for him to succeed in France, but until then he had thought it "something completely insuperable and unattainable."

He eagerly gave necessary information and directions to all his supporters. He told Anderson that in America one should not begin with *Ghosts,* but rather let *Pillars of Society* and *A Doll's House* come first "as an introduction or preparation" for the former, which was "the most extreme of the three works." He wrote in the same letter: "I lay great stress on having the language of the translation kept as close to ordinary everyday language as possible; all purely literary turns of phrases must be assiduously avoided in dramatic works, especially in ones like mine, which make a point of evoking in the reader or spectator the feeling that he is witnessing a segment of reality." What he was saying was quite revolutionary for the time, and he said the same in 1883 when he wrote to August Lindberg about the Swedish translation: "The language must sound natural, and the mode of expression must be in character for each person in the play; one human being does not express himself like any other." He requested that these instructions be carefully followed at rehearsals "until the speeches become completely believable and realistic," because, he continued, "the effect of the play depends to a great extent on the spectators' feeling that they are hearing and seeing something that is taking place in real life." He again repeated the idea in a letter to a Frenchman who wanted to translate *The Wild Duck* in 1891.

His knowledge of languages enabled him to check only the Swedish and German translations, but he was always willing to explain and clarify any aspect of his writing. The most remarkable instance of his patience with questioners is the interview he gave to a Norwegian-American newspaperman while he was in the midst of work on *Hedda Gabler.* The questions were a peculiar mixture of the significant and the trivial, political, literary, and personal, and although he refused to answer everything, he did reply to many questions that one would not have expected him to answer. His publisher and his friends in Norway were always kept informed of his successes abroad: he usually spoke of the "joy" the success had given him. He personally handled all his correspondence with foreign publishers and translators and much of the correspondence with theatrical directors, and although he often complained about the burden this was, he could not bring himself to turn it over to a secretary. He made himself, as he said, a "businessman." This activity became a part of his life, his line of communication with the world outside.

CHAPTER FORTY

FAREWELL TO GERMANY (1891)

I<small>N THE SUMMER</small> of 1891 Ibsen left Germany, never to return. There had been much conflict in his last year there, but success as well. And despite the controversy or the acclaim, his primary concern was for his works to be understood. He waited calmly for this to come, and if anyone complained that it was slow, he replied simply that he allowed ten years for each play to be fully comprehended. But what if the "Ibsenites" themselves failed to comprehend?

With the appearance of *Hedda Gabler* at Christmastime, 1890, there was renewed argument over his intention and meaning, just as there had been with *The Lady from the Sea*. The latter play had at least a kind of moral in the concluding statement about "freedom with responsibility," but there was no such guide in *Hedda*, and the phrase about "dying in beauty" was not much help. So German opinion relegated Hedda to the domain of the "incomprehensible" Ibsen females, despite the fact that the play was the least Norwegian that he had ever written, and one that had many ties with Germany. But the German radicals had adopted him as their standard bearer and expected him to continue on the same controversial path. He was, in fact, being trapped by his own reputation; the controversial plays were now winning world-wide name. Eleonora Duse played *A Doll's House* in Milan on February 9, 1891, the first performance in Italy, and the reputation of this play and *Ghosts* spread his fame. No matter how much he insisted that he was concerned primarily with the psychological examination of human beings, most people and many critics refused to accept his word. He was for them the "controversial" playwright.

In Munich a "Gesellschaft für modernes Leben" was organized and held its first meeting on January 29, 1891. The theatre director M. G. Conrad, a friend of Ibsen's, was the leading spirit behind this. He announced that there was some hope of founding a *Freie Bühne* in the city, one which could open with productions of *Ghosts* and *The Wild*

Duck. The world première of *Hedda Gabler* took place two days later, Saturday, January 31, at the Court Theatre. But the victory was, in the words of the press, only pyrrhic. Ibsen was present and was disappointed in the leading actress, who did not speak simply and naturally, but declaimed her lines in a way that indicated she did not understand the role. Many in the audience hissed and whistled. Ibsen was silent at his curtain call; he shrugged his shoulders and said, "The audience prefers to laugh."

When he attended the play's opening at the Lessing-Theatre in Berlin on February 10, the results were much better, for the theatre had Anna Haverland for the leading role. But even the friendly critics found the play irrational, and the liberal journalist Theodor Wolff wrote a parody in *Berliner Tagblatt* called "How Little Rosa Müller Died in Beauty." The Berlin Freie Bühne felt it had a kind of proprietary right to Ibsen but had to be content with his presence at a performance of Sudermann's *Ehre*. The success of *Hedda* was so limited that the Lessing-Theatre had to fill in the gaps between performances with a revival of *An Enemy of the People*.

Two months later Ibsen went to Vienna at the invitation of the Burgtheater, which was going to give the first performance of *The Pretenders* in Austria on April 11. There would be no controversy here, only, as the papers pointed out, a severe test of the audience's patience, since the play lasted until well after eleven o'clock. However, he was cheered at the end of each act and after the performance was honored at a party arranged by the theatre and the literary circles of Vienna, primarily young men of the "naturalistic school," who paid him homage in verse and prose. Well past midnight he made a speech thanking them in words that had almost become his formula for expressing gratitude. He told them that whenever he was touched or made happy, the experience found expression in his writing; now he saw something bright, beautiful, and joyous in his imagination, and "I think it will become a poem." The guests cheered, and he went calmly back to his dinner.

Later in the evening a radical member of the Reichstag spoke about the "political" Ibsen, the man with the revolutionary principles. But, he concluded, "it cannot but puzzle us that you nevertheless sit here with a great order on your breast. Why is that?" Ibsen was somewhat taken aback at first, then he replied: "This order, given to me by my sovereign, I am pleased to wear in the company of younger friends who can be expected to celebrate far into the wee hours; it will remind me that I must keep within certain bounds." The hints of irony in both question and answer suggest a certain distance between Ibsen and the Ibsenites.

While Ibsen was in Vienna, various women's organizations sent delegates to thank him for his championing of women's rights, and he was even elected an honorary member of Verein für erweiterte Frauenbildung. His stay prompted the formation of a Freie Bühne and a society for Moderne Literatur, that is, for naturalistic theatre and literature for a cause. An Ibsen play was to inaugurate the proceedings and he was elected an honorary member. When the Deutsches Volkstheater gave *The Wild Duck* on April 16 with Friedrich Mitterwurzer as guest artist, there was a great deal of controversy. At first there was so much applause that Ibsen had to take a curtain call after the second act and thank the audience; as the play progressed, a regular contest developed between hissers and well-wishers. The conflict did not end until Ibsen tipped his hat to his friends and left the theatre. The opening performance had been sold out, but the play drew so little after this that is was taken off after three days. The theatre's director later said that he had considered it his duty to open his stage to Ibsen, but the duty was not a rewarding one, and he lost money on the production. Ibsen had not yet secured a popular footing here. There was another party in his honor on April 18, with many speeches from journalists and other literary men. His own response was short enough: "I am no speaker whatever." He did, however, express his gratitude not only for the "ardent understanding," but for the "honest opposition" as well.

From Vienna he went to Budapest, where the National Theatre gave a performance of *A Doll's House* in his honor on April 20. The play had been in the theatre's repertory long enough for all controversy to have subsided. He listened intently to his lines being spoken in an unfamiliar language, and when the applause of the audience called him to the stage, he thanked the leading actress, Mrs. Emilie Markus-Pulszky, in a carefully prepared speech. Then, according to the newspaper report, "he opened his eyes wide behind his even wider glasses" at the storm of applause that rained down on him. He confirms this in a letter from Budapest: "Applause here is very different from what one hears in other theatres; regular torrents break like waterfalls through the air, making the house tremble and people reel." Thus the Hungarians greeted Ibsen who was for them primarily the revolutionary writer; the jubilation pursued him into the street, and he finally had to flee into a carriage to escape the students who crowded around him. Two banquets were given: the first and more official for members of Parliament, the Academy of Science, and the press. Count Apponyi, the nationalist leader, spoke with brilliance and passion. Ibsen thanked them by saying that the experience was a fairytale he would never forget. The second banquet was given by the younger people, some of whom could even greet him in Norwegian. Ibsen recalled his youthful poems in praise

of the Hungarian independence movement. In effect, the entire visit
to Budapest was one long triumph. The Hungarian journalists questioned him on everything, and the German journalists were amused at
how much their "enthusiastic colleagues could ask and how little Ibsen
cared to answer." He was pleased and touched, and he asked the press
to publish his note of thanks saying that the lively and vital movement
for progress he had found there had made an impression on him that
he would cherish as one of the most deeply moving of his life.

After these festive excursions he must have returned to Munich with
rather mixed emotions. One of the Viennese orators proclaimed that
Ibsen had won a home there, and in some ways he could feel at home
anywhere in Germany as well, especially since he had already emphasized how important his understanding of German culture and
thought had been to him. His plays, both old and new, were constantly
being played in both countries. *The Pretenders* was a great success at
the Berlin Hoftheater at the end of May, and he attended the revival of
The Vikings at the Residenz-Theater in Munich late in June. He had
become so fashionable that some thought it was a bit overdone. In May,
1891, Berlin's *Der Zeitgeist* printed a long comic poem called "The
Song of Ibsen":

Ibsen, Ibsen überall!	Ibsen, Ibsen everywhere!
Da geht nichts mehr drüber!	Nothing else will do!
Auf dem ganzen Erdenball	Right around the earth's sphere
Herrscht das Ibsen-Fieber!	the Ibsen fever rages!
Alle Welt wird Ibsen-toll,	All the world's Ibsen-mad,
Wenn auch wider Willen,	though against its will,
Denn die ganze Luft ist voll	for the air is swarming
Ibsen-Ruhm-Bacillen!	with the Ibsen-fame-bacilli!
Keine Rettung! Ueberall	No escape! Everywhere
Kunden Ibsens Namen,	Ibsen's name proclaimed,
Preisend mit Posaunenschall,	trumpeting the praises
Moden und Reklamen.	of fashions and novelties.
Auf Cigaren, Damenschmuck,	On cigars and ladies' baubles,
Torten, Miedern, Schlipsen,	Pastries, bodices, cravats,
Prangt das Wort in gold'nem Druck:	Gleams the word in gilded letters:
Ibsen! A la Ibsen!	*Ibsen! A la Ibsen!*

The five long stanzas of the poem attest to Ibsen's notoriety, but it was
not necessarily an indication that he was understood as he wished to be
understood. He had to admit to himself that the Ibsen who was so
much in fashion was the reckless rebel, champion of sensational causes.
He had reached a peak of fame in Germany, but whether he could
any longer feel at home there was another matter.

In the same spring of 1891, he attended a banquet given by the
journalists and literati of Munich in honor of the Prince Regent's
seventieth birthday, March 12. When the evening was well advanced
and the wine well tasted, the poet and dramatist Martin Grief, known

for his ardent nationalism, proceeded to launch an attack on those foreign playwrights who crowded out native talent. Naturally there were a few sharp stabs at Ibsen. After a while Ibsen tapped his glass and asked for the floor; this was unusual for him and everyone waited in suspense. With a quiet smile, but a truculent glint in his eye, he praised Munich, the city which had a welcome for every artist, foreign or native-born, and all to its credit for so had it gained its world-wide renown. Why Greif had singled out foreign dramatists he found hard to grasp; everyone knew that Greif was a lyrical and not a dramatic writer. For himself, however, he could not take the attack personally, for he did not think of himself as a foreigner in Munich; he was performed as often, with at least as much praise as Greif himself. Ibsen sat down and the whole company went into an uproar; some laughed, but all realized that Ibsen had been angered. Dr. Conrad, the chairman, persuaded Ibsen and Greif to shake hands, but despite his efforts to smooth things over, Ibsen still muttered angrily.

He was a bit unsure of his footing when he left the dinner, hanging heavily on Dr. Conrad's arm all the way home. But his mind was still alert enough to continue jabbing at Greif. "What did he want, really, this Martin Greif? I don't understand. What kind of plays does he write? Plays about people who have been dead a long time, people he never knew! Can you write plays about people you never knew? Why should Martin Greif be concerned with the dead? He should let them rest in peace and dramatize the living all he wants to. Now he's rifling the graves of the dead princes of Bavaria. When he's through with them, I suppose he'll start on the Hohenzollerns. Well, there are enough dead princes; history is broad. But this is not what dramatic writing is about today." Conrad reminded him that he had started by writing about Catiline. Ibsen retorted that "in the first place Catiline was not a king, but an anarchist, and in the second place I was not then a dramatist, but a druggist. *Catiline* was a druggist's first attempt at drama. Has Martin Greif ever been a druggist? Well, now what?" There was obviously no answer to this, and in any case they had arrived home. But was this his home, or was he a stranger in Munich too? The question ached and the resentment would not die.

About a week after he saw *The Vikings* at the Hoftheater he left Munich. He was going home to Norway.

CHAPTER FORTY-ONE

HOME AGAIN (1891)

Ibsen never fully explained why he decided to return to Norway. He once told Georg Brandes that it was easiest to manage the income from his plays there, but since this income was derived mostly from Germany and Denmark, this could not have been the reason. Mrs. Ibsen believed that he returned because he wanted to die in his homeland, and this may have been the underlying, if unexpressed and unacknowledged, explanation. On his last visit home, when he had first brought up the idea of returning to live there, he had been ill; another reminder of his age came in the severe attack of influenza he had suffered, right after New Year's, 1890.

That the thought of death was with him is suggested by a story Herman Bang told about Ibsen's behavior during a lecture he gave on Maupassant on November 10, some months after Ibsen had returned to Norway. For the entire lecture Ibsen sat in a front row, staring down into his tall hat and apparently ignoring the lecture, but when Bang began to speak of the idea of death in Maupassant, symbolized by the intolerable bluebottle fly buzzing and buzzing around the imprisoned man, suddenly he felt Ibsen's eyes fixed on him. The intense fixity of the look reminded him of a caged lion staring into the night with unspeakable sorrow. In that second he realized that Ibsen had looked at death.

With the thought of death must have come a longing for home and the sea, the limitless, eternally shifting sea that seemed to evoke some response in his own restless heart. When he left Munich at the beginning of July, his first plans were to spend a fortnight by the sea at Øresund, and then continue to Norway. He decided, however, to go straight to Oslo, arriving there on July 16. The first thing he did was to realize a twenty-year-old dream to visit the North Cape. He did not climb the cape but stayed rather on ship, since it was the sea he had come for. On August 7 he returned to Oslo where he would remain for the rest of his life.

At first he thought he would return to Munich before winter; the idea of settling in Norway came to him only gradually. While on the trip to the North Cape he decided to spend the winter in Oslo, and once established there it seemed natural to remain. He had no conscious plan in any of this, but once he was home he seemed bound by it. He may have been influenced by consideration of his son. In 1889 Sigurd resigned from the Swedo-Norwegian foreign service where he had served since 1885, because the Swedish authorities limited the opportunities for his advancement. The whole problem of the joint foreign service was causing great conflict between the two countries, and when Sigurd returned home he became such a champion of extreme nationalistic demands and wrote with such force and logic on the issue that the Norwegian Liberals greeted him with joyous expectation. By 1891 he saw that he had a future as a leader in Norwegian politics; he made personal alliances and contacts with the leaders of the national cause, and was soon being spoken of as the first probable Norwegian foreign minister. His mother followed his campaign with enthusiasm, prompted as much by her own intensely patriotic spirit as by her close attachment to her son. Ibsen himself did not care too much for his son's politics, but he was gratified by the respect and the influence Sigurd was winning. He felt he too was being drawn closer to Norwegian society again.

Ibsen later said that he found conditions at home so greatly changed that what had once been impossible for him—to live in Norway—was now easy and perfectly natural. He was, however, still the center of controversy. Here, as in Germany, he was considered the first and foremost of radical writers; now as Sigurd Ibsen's father this label was fixed even more firmly on him. The day he arrived in Oslo from Copenhagen, he was met on the dock by journalists from the liberal newspapers *Verdens Gang* and *Dagbladet*. The latter had hailed him in the name of "all liberal-minded Norwegian men and women" and carried daily notices about his activities.

Many of the Conservatives also wanted to lay claim to him; he was, after all, the most famous of all Norwegians, with only Edvard Grieg as a rival, and all his countrymen shared some of the glory. His official record was still clean, since he had never taken part in the struggles of either party, and his closest friends were Conservatives. Thus it came about that the Conservative *Aftenposten* was the one to urge him publicly to remain in Norway. The article, which appeared on July 17, 1891, praised the poet, but it also declared its disagreement with his views and betrayed its ulterior motive: to use him as a counterweight to Bjørnson:

"Our great, celebrated poet is visiting his native land now after several years' absence.

"This time also his stay will be quite short; but we would like to express the wish that it may be long enough for the poet to learn that his countrymen also know how to appreciate the fame he has won for himself by his distinguished works and the glory he has thereby helped to shed on his homeland.

"We do not share, as our readers are aware, Ibsen's views of human life or social conditions; but we are capable of seeing and admiring the mighty creative force which his country has fostered in him,— and we would wish that Mr. Ibsen could free himself from the bitter feelings that have long caused him to prefer other countries to his fatherland; for when all is said and done, it is from the spiritual soil of his homeland that Henrik Ibsen has drawn his best strength, and if he could decide to live among his countrymen, his incisive pen and his keen critical intelligence would soon find enough to attack, here where vulgarity is so rife in the intellectual sphere, and where superficiality and dilettantism call the tune under Bjørnson's aegis."

As both sides engaged in virtual competition for his approval, the ambivalence of his temperament was again strongly marked by his inability to feel at home with either.

Brandes was in Norway this summer and stayed for a time at Ibsen's hotel in Oslo. They were again on completely friendly terms, and on August 16, a week after Ibsen returned from North Cape, Brandes gathered a group of Liberals from the journalistic, literary, and artistic fields to honor Ibsen. Ibsen was reluctant to come, however, and Brandes could only persuade him by saying that just a few of his friends would be present. He was quite annoyed when he learned how many were actually there; he practically had to be carried in and was more than usually taciturn. Brandes spoke and went out of his way to pay him witty and humorous compliments, but Ibsen kept fretting and complaining so that even he lost his composure. At the end of the speech Ibsen said: "That was a speech against which many objections could be taken; I, however, prefer not to make them." Brandes urged him to be frank, but Ibsen refused: "I prefer not to do so." In the same manner he cut short an actress, who had just played Hedda Gabler at Christiania Theatre and was thanking him for the many brilliant roles he had given to women. But finally, in spite of the bad humor that all could notice, he thanked Brandes heartily when he left, adding: "It was a very successful celebration." Even though he had disappointed the company, he had had a pleasant time—it was always pleasant for him to receive homage.

A fortnight later, on August 28, he attended the performance of *Hedda Gabler* that opened the season at Christiania Theatre; he had not been there since *The League of Youth* and *Love's Comedy* were played in 1874. Now he took the seat of honor in the front box before a packed house; his presence moved the actors to a more vivid, fiery performance than usual. Thunderous applause greeted him at his arrival and at the end of each act; at the final curtain "all Christiania" hailed him with a veritable storm of hurrahs.

On September 14 there was another festive occasion at the theatre, this time to mark the hundredth performance of *The League of Youth,* the largest number for any Ibsen play so far. Resplendent with decorations Ibsen sat in the middle of the orchestra among the most fashionable people of the city. The applause was as enthusiastic as before and he rose and bowed his thanks, but refused repeated cries to come to the stage. After the performance there was a party at Tivoli Restaurant, and a speech by the theatre director Schrøder. In his reply, Ibsen urged the building of a new theatre because now the cultural interests of the city seemed to him strong enough to make such an enterprise possible.

If the tone of this evening seemed to suggest that the "conservative" Ibsen was being honored, a few days later, on September 17, the "revolutionary" came into his own when August Lindberg and his Swedish company played *Ghosts* at Tivoli Theatre—Christiania Theatre had rejected that play. Young people and radicals all turned out, and their shouts for Ibsen had the sound of a battle cry. This time he did come to the stage to give his thanks, which was taken as tacit acknowledgment of his true sympathies. He was still the radical.

Party antagonisms continued so strong that many old Conservatives refused to recognize him. His contacts with his "Dutchmen" friends were broken; some time later he would say with something between a smile and a sigh, "Good heavens, there was a time when even Ludvig Ludvigsen Daae would speak to me!" Professor Daae was generally thought to have been the model for Kroll in *Rosmersholm,* although this was not so. Daae was enough of a fanatic, but he was not as arid a pedant as that. Daae had heard the rumor, however, and he made no secret of his conviction that Ibsen was a kind of vermin let loose in society, whom one had to avoid at all cost. Not all Conservatives shared this view. Kristofer Randers dedicated a collection of his polemic verses to "Henrik Ibsen, poet of individualism, in profound gratitude for what he has taught me: to write poetry and scorn the masses." Ibsen expressed his own idea of a writer's function in lines he wrote early in September in the autograph book of the Swedish singer Sigrid Arnoldson: "I think we two agree when I say that our goal is not to celebrate victories, but to ennoble human hearts through images of beauty and the interpretation of truth." As always, he wanted to stand outside party factions and more than ever remain nothing but a poet.

Early in October the young writer Knut Hamsun sent him tickets to a series of lectures on Norwegian literature he was giving. The year before, Hamsun had published *Hunger,* a remarkable book that can be said to have begun a new era in Norwegian literature and to have inspired a new generation of writers to abandon realism and polemic writing for psychological investigation of the profound, wordless realm of the unconscious. In the fall of 1891 he had lectured on his new literary program in various Norwegian cities, among them Bergen and Stavanger, and now as he prepared to come to Oslo, word of his bold and sarcastic attacks on older writers preceded him. Chief among these were those who were termed the "four greats," Kielland, Lie, Bjørnson, and Ibsen.

The growing suspense increased in intensity when Ibsen came to the first lecture and took seat number one in the front row. Hamsun was not a man to be intimidated: "I am going to apply forceful strictures this evening—so forceful that some will probably be both astonished and outraged." He forged ahead, condemning all the "great" Norwegian writers for lack of psychological depth. Norwegian literature was based on crude, easy portrayal of types and was interested only in practical application, as befitting a democratic peasant population. He cited various examples, from Ibsen and the others, trying to show how large areas of man's inner life were left unexplored, unilluminated.

Ibsen's face was expressionless as he listened; his intense blue eyes never left the speaker. For the next lecture two days later, the hall was packed, many attending out of curiosity to see this encounter between the old and the new writer. Ibsen came and listened with seriousness as Hamsun once more did away with him and the others. He did not say what he thought of it all, but there was a twinkle in his eye and he obviously found Hamsun's cockiness amusing; he was certainly not afraid of the new movement. On his last visit to Norway he had sworn that he would always be on the side of youth; then the cry was for controversial writing. Now young writers were taking a new path away from controversy and toward the inner world of man. Ibsen was with them here too, and here too he had helped to break new ground. The conflicts in which he had been engaged helped him to find his way down to the "heart chamber of the hidden," which he had longed to penetrate since his youth. More than anyone else, he had prepared the way for the new psychological school, and now he felt sympathy rather than antagonism for the young man who called for psychological

insight by striking out at Ibsen. If the new program took root, he would
not be a stranger in Norway.

Before the end of September he had made up his mind to stay, and
a few days after the lectures, he moved into his new home, an apartment in the fashionable new complex at Victoria Terrasse, number 7B
(later 13B), facing the open square on the southwest corner. Mrs.
Ibsen was spending the summer in Valdres and so he could amuse
himself by arranging the furnishings. Six months later he wrote to
his publisher: "I have furnished a study for myself which is, according
to my taste, very handsome, convenient, and practical, where I can be
quite undisturbed. I could not be so in Munich, and so I often felt
hampered in working down there." That he missed Munich during
these first few years in Oslo is apparent in a letter he wrote to Helene
Raff in March, 1892: "I do after all belong so very much down there."
He made some plans to visit Munich and Copenhagen, but soon became
tied to Oslo; the advance of age is reflected in his dread of the effort
needed for travel and moving. For six and a half years, from the fall
of 1891 to the spring of 1898, he did not leave the city. He liked the
climate and found it easy to work, and there was the feeling of being
welcomed by his countrymen. In the freer and more energetic cultural
atmosphere the country had developed, he felt that his work would
have a wider field in which to prosper.

Now he could answer the question he had asked twenty years earlier
in the nostalgic poem "Burned Ships." In January, 1892, a bookseller
donated a set of his works to a raffle at an artists' festival, and on the
flyleaf of *Catiline* he wrote two stanzas:

Mod snelandets hytter	To the homes of the snowland
fra solstrandens krat	from the shores of light
red hjemløs en rytter	there rode a horseman
hver eneste nat—	homeless each night—
Nys steg han af hesten,	Just now he dismounted,
fandt åben hver dør—	found open each door—
Kunde hjemløse gæsten	Could the homeless guest
kanske kommet lidt før?	have come back before?

There was, of course, a good deal of wishful thinking in his belief that
society and culture in Norway had freer rein now than six years before.
There was, it is true, a more liberal, intellectual atmosphere than when
he had last lived at home, thirty years earlier. The struggle for freedom
that he and so many other writers, journalists, and scholars had engaged
in for so long had finally made headway with the Norwegian people.
But it was equally certain that new ideas were met with stiff resistance
when they were first proclaimed here as elsewhere; there was still
enough wrong with society to stimulate the "sharp critical sense"

that *Aftenposten* had asked him to use. If his work now would contain less criticism of society, less controversy, it was not because social conditions had improved so remarkably; it was because he had become a different person. It was no longer a matter of utmost urgency for him to uncover the lie in social morality, but rather to test himself and to explore the human psyche. He could be happy living at home.

In the summer of 1892, when a political crisis threatened to topple the government and shatter the union with Sweden, he wrote in a letter: "I did not become personally involved in the conflict; this would be against my nature. And they respect this here as far as I am concerned. Since my return last year, I am in the fortunate position of knowing personally and from daily experience that I have both the Conservative and the Liberal party on my side. I can thus work with undisturbed peace of mind." Proof of his statement can be seen in his attending a celebration in honor of the well-known Liberal historian, Professor J. E. Sars, where Bjørnson was the main speaker, and in the same spring appearing at meetings of Andvake, the predominantly Conservative literary society founded by Lorentz Dietrichson. There he associated with men like Professors Monrad and Morgenstierne, and confessed that "although he had once thought his life interests better served by the Liberal party, now he had moved further and further away from it." He became reconciled with Dietrichson and even said of their 1885 controversy: "You were right and I was wrong then; but I did not know the conditions at home."

One of his strongest links with the Liberals was his son Sigurd, who bound himself still closer to the party in 1892 by marrying Bjørnson's daughter, Bergliot. Bjørnson now was a constant caller, and although Ibsen would speak warmly about their old friendship, he was removed from the ideas and interests that preoccupied his fellow-writer. His telegram congratulating Bjørnson on his sixtieth birthday in December was quite cold and brusque in comparison to the warm greeting he sent Jonas Lie the next year.

Sigurd Ibsen had been led by the Liberal government to expect a position that would allow him to organize a Norwegian consular service and an independent foreign office. With the fall of the government in the spring of 1893, the plan had to be postponed until the Liberals returned to power in 1898. Meanwhile, an effort was made to establish a professorship in sociology for him. Ibsen was so concerned that he spoke of the matter with Jakob Sverdrup, Minister of Church and Education, and with some of the leading newspaper editors in Oslo. When the plan failed, he was so disappointed that he actually thought of giving up his Norwegian citizenship and returning to Germany. This event, in 1897, confirmed his long-standing belief that Norwegian politics consisted mostly of squabbles and empty flourishes. He wrote to Dr. Elias that he would much rather be among his friends in Berlin than sitting amid the "dreariness" at home. He told Brandes that he missed "the great liberal and liberating cultural milieu" of the outside world: "Here all channels are closed in every sense of the word, and all the routes of understanding are choked up." But nothing came of such desires and he remained in Oslo.

His life at home had all the precise regularity he had accustomed himself to abroad. In the mornings and afternoons he worked at his desk, if not on some new idea, then on the correspondence with directors, translators, and publishers of his plays. Every afternoon at the same hour he walked with short, careful steps down Carl Johan Street in full dress and took his regular chair in the café of the Grand Hotel. There he had his afternoon apéritif, read the newspapers, and then returned home at his regular time. He became a part of the life of the street and everyone took care to leave him to himself.

Mrs. Ibsen did not like the apartment at Victoria Terrasse, and on her insistence Ibsen rented a new place in the fall of 1895, in a newly constructed apartment house in Drammensveien, at the corner of Arbiensgate. There were more rooms and larger ones and a view of the palace park, but not as much sun as before. Ibsen's study faced north, a large and handsome room which they called the "library" since he had covered the walls from floor to ceiling with books. It became the only actually cozy room in the entire apartment. To compensate for the lost sun, King Oscar gave him a key to the private section of the palace grounds, the "Queen's Park," and he was able to enter this freely.

Above his desk in the new study he hung a portrait of August Strindberg, which he had bought at a spring exhibition that year. Sigurd had persuaded his father to buy the portrait, which was by Christian Krohg. The son called it "The Revolutionary," but the father called it "Incipient Insanity" and said he enjoyed looking at it because of its "satanic eyes." "He is my mortal enemy, and he shall hang there and watch over what I write," he said of Strindberg. On the desk he had some gutta-percha devils with red tongues—"there must be trolls in what I write," he explained. When he was wrestling with a particularly difficult problem in his writing, he closed the door and took out his "arch-devil," a fiddle-playing bear that beat time with its foot; it probably reminded him of the time when he too had danced "on feet of verse."

In the first few years he saw a fair number of people, going out and receiving callers. Hans Heyerdahl painted his portrait in the winter of 1893-94, and in the spring of 1895 he was painted by Eilif Peterssen and Erik Werenskiold. He was working on a new play while Heyerdahl was doing the portrait, and the artist reported that he "was so peevish and cross that it was quite unbearable." The other two, whom he had known before, got to him when he was free, and he was a gracious and obliging model. Werenskiold painted him in sitting and standing positions, and had nothing but kind words about how "terribly winning, magnificently friendly, and full of jest" he was. And strong too: "He stood like a statue, usually for a couple of hours at a time. He was incredibly strong. Even the last time I saw him, he was as firm and solid as a rolling pin." Before the painting sessions they would usually sit and chat about current events; Ibsen "was inquisitive, he kept asking all kinds of questions. He was particularly interested in women. When I could tell him something about unusual women, he was as watchful as a beast of prey and would not rest until I had told him all I knew." That same spring he stood for the sculptor Stephan Sinding, who was making a statue of him for the front of the proposed new theatre. His patience here was also remarkable.

At parties he did not enjoy himself unless he had a pleasant woman as table partner; otherwise he might remain stand-offish throughout the evening. He actually preferred the company of friends at small gatherings. After he was elected to the Oslo Academy of Science, he usually attended meetings, but when Sigurd did not get the expected professorship he stopped coming out of resentment against the secretary-general of the academy, Professor Gustav Storm, who Ibsen believed was most to blame.

When the formation of a Norwegian Authors' Society was suggested late in 1893, Ibsen at once entered his membership. He had always been interested in the legal and economic conditions of authorship, and he signed his name to the invitation (sent out on April 29, 1894) to an organization meeting on May 7. He attended the meeting with Dietrichson, but would not appear again. The evening was a total disaster. There had been an ominous warning of trouble three days before when a young author, Gabriel Finne, attacked the whole idea of the society in an article in *Dagbladet*. He wrote that the old members, who were filled with hatred for all that was young, vital, and new, would snatch all the power for themselves. He managed to cite Ibsen in support of this attack—Ibsen "whose entire production is a burning defense of the nobility of the isolated individual and an indictment of the baseness of people who cling together in societies." At the meeting itself, the business of organization and establishing rules was followed by a social evening. Some drank more than they should have and suddenly Nils Kjær, the essayist, leaped to his feet and began to speak. He started out on the topic of women, but his words became more and more hysterical and he finally delivered a screaming attack on the old writers who had never been able to depict women and who always stood in the way of youth. He did not mention Ibsen by name, but he spat out his words in the direction of Ibsen's table. He ended by crying: "We hate you! But your time is past! If you want to see Norway's future poet, he is sitting here!" The young man whose shoulder he tapped was Gabriel Finne, unfortunately fast asleep with his head on the table. A painful silence fell, and Ibsen whispered to Dietrichson: "Shall we leave?" Dietrichson thought they should remain and ignore what had happened. Then Vilhelm Krag got up and made a pleasant little speech about Ibsen, and J. B. Bull more emphatically called the young people to task for boasting of what they had not done, when the master who had done so much was present. Throughout, Ibsen sat without moving, looking straight ahead. When he left, he told Dietrichson: "That was the most unpleasant gathering I have ever attended; I will never again set foot in that society." Nils Kjær is said to have come to Ibsen the next day, full of contrition and begging forgiveness. Ibsen's parting words were said to have been: "The secret of drinking, young man, consists in not drinking less on one occasion than on another." He kept his word that he would not attend future meetings of the Authors' Society, and a year later on a visiting card, confirmed his decision in writing.

More and more he was coming to live by himself. Mrs. Ibsen was ill a good deal now and on several occasions had to take long trips to bathings resorts in Italy. At such times his daughter-in-law Bergliot, of whom he was very fond, visited him regularly and helped him in many ways. Otherwise, he often sat alone reading during the long evening hours. He had become no more talkative than in the years before his return and he did not open up to his friends. He kept his dignity and insisted on the formalities being observed, not only toward himself, but even in his relations with others. But his kindness of heart could break through formality whenever he had to show his sympathy for a friend touched by sorrow or illness.

His ease with children was remarkable; here he felt he had nothing to fear and could be free and open. He often remembered his friends' children with gifts and all kinds of little things that delighted them. Children in turn were quite relaxed with him. Once at Grefsen Bath, while he sat in the living room of a doctor who was a grandson of Mrs. Sontum in Bergen, a little daughter of the house brought him her doll to play with. He knitted his bushy brows at first, but took part in the doll's play with all seriousness. He often spoke with the children at the Ruseløkka grammar school nea• his home and amused himself by tossing them coins to catch. Every Saturday a small group of boys came to his house and were rewarded with a 25-øre coin each. The old housekeeper complained that they tracked up her freshly washed floors. "And besides," she said, "I want to let the Doctor know that they go right down to the bazaar and buy two-shilling cakes with the money." Ibsen replied, "Why shouldn't boys like these enjoy two-shilling cakes?" With children he could find an outlet for his need to love. But more than ever before, his life centered on his writing, and the question became more insistent: was this the kind of life that would bring fulfillment?

CHAPTER FORTY-TWO

THE CRISIS OF AGE:

THE MASTER BUILDER (1891-92)

AFTER HIS RETURN to Norway in 1891 there were more and more indications that he was now an old man, a relic of a past era. He had, in turn, to examine himself to see what traces of age appeared in his thinking and in his attitudes. He was still physically strong, although naturally not as vigorous as he had once been; during his last summer in Gossensass in 1889 it was obvious that he could not keep up the same walking pace as before. He began to walk with short, slow steps, and he did not dare climb North Cape on his trip there in 1891. He noticed the changes in his outlook that age was bringing; even in the fall of 1887, before he was sixty, he said that his "polemic interests were diminishing." He still kept his old delight in provocative statements. When he was in Vienna in the spring of 1891 and heard about Austrian party strife, he suggested they shoot the people who stirred up such internal dissension. When he was told that one simply could not do that, he replied, "naively" as we are told, "Why not?" He sometimes sounded as deliberately bloodthirsty after he returned home, and he certainly had no mercy for trouble-makers and agitators. But he would no longer be a party to any controversy; he was content in his old poetic habit of "seeing" rather than doing.

His relationship with Emilie Bardach and other young ladies in Gossensass must have given him a feeling of new life; at the same time he could not help measuring his age against their youth and admitting disparity. Out of this sense of closeness and separation grew the theme of a new conflict. In the following years he would say time and again to Helene Raff: "I need youth!" As age drew on, he wanted them near, keeping him young in mind and spirit.

It was his good fortune that no sooner had he settled in Oslo than he met the young woman who for many years would be as he described in a letter of 1899, "a good, wise, and faithful friend." Hildur Andersen, a gifted pianist, first roused his affections by evoking fond memories of

431

his own youth. She was a daughter of his childhood friend O. M. Andersen, now city engineer in Oslo, and a granddaughter of that Mrs. Sontum who had watched over him when he first went to Bergen. Hildur's ardent and courageous artistic temperament, and her deep understanding of his work sealed their friendship: "She is personally very close to me," he wrote, also in 1899. He addressed her with the informal *du* and always used her first name, something quite extraordinary for him to do with a woman. In 1895, when he read Brandes' article on Goethe and Marianne von Willemer he felt he could recognize something of his own life. He realized that "the rebirth of youth" in the aged Goethe's writing was the result of his being "favored with the grace of something as lovely" as his meeting with the youthful Marianne. "Fate, destiny, chance," he wrote to Brandes, "can really be quite gracious and obliging now and then."

It can be said with certainty that he was not referring to the erotic bond between Goethe and Marianne when he spoke of the similarity between their relationship and his with Hildur. What he valued in their relationship was the joy of opening his heart to a young, richly gifted feminine soul. Hildur came with faith in him and in the future; her inviolate, noble strength could give new stimulus to his creative powers.

The idea for a new drama had occurred to him before he left Germany. When he saw *Hedda Gabler* in Berlin in February, 1891, he told Julius Elias about the "deviltry" he was going to write next. He was thinking of Emilie Bardach, who had set him struggling to probe the psychological life of a woman who had something, perhaps a great deal, of the beast of prey in her. He said that it would make an "interesting, a very interesting" play. In the last years in Munich he frequently would lead conversation into the question of how one person could maintain psychic control over another, as well as the problem of hypnotism and compulsive ideas. At this time a married couple, complete strangers, came to him for his advice. The wife thought that another woman had hypnotized her husband. He was intrigued by the mysterious aura such cases had, and he kept asking his friends if they had ever experienced anything like this. It was too serious a matter for fun, and he did not appreciate hypnotic experiments conducted as parlor games. As he turned the theme over in his mind and worked out the idea of his female beast of prey, his attention was caught by the image of the man who was being stalked. As he looked more deeply into his own problems that had just begun to emerge, the drama of *The Master Builder* took shape.

One day in April, 1890, while he was walking with Helene Raff, she mentioned the story of the architect who had built the church of St. Michael in Munich. He had been so terrified by the thought that the great arch of the church might collapse that he had thrown himself off the tower. Ibsen listened carefully and said: "That tale must have come from the North; at least we have one, or even more, similar stories." Helene replied that every famous cathedral in Germany has such a builder's legend. "Do you know why?" he asked her, and when she said no, he remained silent for a moment, then answered: "People are right to feel that no one can build so high and go unpunished."

The theme of Nemesis had always been a compelling one for him. He knew that vengeance strikes him who walks in pride seeking nothing but his own will. The parallel between his own work and the story of the cathedral builder became clear to him at once. Later in Oslo Erik Werenskiold met him on the street, scrutinizing some new buildings. "So, you're interested in architecture?" he asked Ibsen, who replied: "Yes, it's my profession too." In Master Builder Solness, he once said, he created a character "who was in some manner related to me." And on another occasion he admitted that the play contained more of his own self than any other. By "anatomizing" himself he gave to the builder the same infirmity he suffered more and more with age, his fear of looking down from great heights or into deep chasms. This fear was a symbol of the terror that gripped him when he peered down into the depths of his own soul, for in those depths he saw the drama of a tragic conflict between the youthful dream an old man clings to and the mounting doubts of his own strength.

The traveling and moving in 1891 prevented him from getting to work on the play, but right after his arrival in Oslo he wrote to Hegel that he was about to start. In the spring of 1892 he wrote the stanzas that he called a "mood introduction" to the play. The poem tells of two old people who have lost their joy in life:

> De sad der, de to, i så lunt et hus
> ved høst og i vinterdage.
> Så brændte huset. Alt ligger i grus.
> De to får i asken rage.

> They sat there, those two, in so
> snug a house
> in fall and in winter days.
> The house burned down. All lies in
> ruins.
> Those two must rake the ashes.

No matter what the ashes yield, they cannot find anything on which to rebuild their lives:

> aldrig *hun* finder sin brændte tro,
> *han* aldrig sin brændte lykke.

> never will she find the ardent faith,
> never will he his vanished joy.

Solness bears within him a diseased conscience, just as Rosmer did. He has built his career on the fire that destroyed his wife's childhood home and her children, and he cannot rid himself of the knowledge that he wanted it to happen. The "demons" in his mind have taken control, and he will never again feel free of guilt or happy. The problem in his life becomes the question of whether he will ever again find courage to dare "the impossible," as he did successfully when he had his youthful faith. The inner struggle is between his repressed longing to live his life freely and manfully, and the consciousness of guilt that represses him. Like Johannes Rosmer, he too carries a "corpse" on his back: what the dead Beate was for Rosmer, the living Aline is for Solness. But Aline is also dead, for Solness has "drained all the life blood out of her" and has sacrificed her for his happiness so that now she only seems to be alive. And thus his past, his sins, keep him bound eternally to her.

Ibsen modeled Aline on his own mother, whom he had seen wither away in an arid and joyless marriage while striving merely to do her "duty." From her he took the sad image of Aline clinging to her childhood dolls and playing with them even when grown up and married, a symbol of the dead past within which she still lives. Part of this situation may also have come from Ibsen's feeling that he had deprived his own wife of something by having lived so intensely and self-centeredly for his art. Solness seems to speak out of Ibsen's own heart when he tells of what he had to pay for his position as artist: "Not in money. But in human happiness. And not only in my own happiness. But in others' as well. . . . And every single day I have to come here and see the price being paid for me again." The lines are so intensely felt that they suggest a personal experience behind them. If Ibsen felt that his wife had failed to satisfy him in their marriage, he seems to indicate here that for her, too, the union had not brought fulfilment.

Now youth comes with the demand that Solness yield his place. The young people want room, they want to get ahead by pushing him to one side, as Knut Hamsun had said they would do to Ibsen himself. To Solness this is Nemesis, "retribution" for having pushed others aside. He clings to his position and fights against the intruders, until youth in another guise comes to strengthen and encourage him. The Hilde who comes to the master builder derives many traits from Ibsen's relationship with Emilie Bardach; she is the "princess" in Solness' dreams, and her kingdom is called "Orangia." He likens her to an untamed beast of prey in the forest wanting to capture him. He yields to her saying, as Ibsen had said to both Emilie and Helene, that he needs and longs for her youth.

But the young woman in *The Master Builder* has been transformed into something different from her models. Miss Bardach of Vienna became a girl from the Norwegian mountains, the same girl, in effect, as the youngest daughter in *The Lady from the Sea*. Thus Ibsen emphasizes that her origin is in thoughts that go back beyond Emilie, back to the theme of the awakening to life he had in mind even when making plans for *Rosmersholm*. Before this there was the brave young Dina Dorf in *Pillars of Society*, who wants to win her beloved freely, without consideration of social conventions. Hilde is thoroughly Norwegian, an untamed, strong Viking woman of the Hjørdis type, with all the drive of a contemporary Oslo skier. When Emilie saw *The Master Builder* in Munich in 1908 she said quite rightly: "I did not see myself, but I did see Ibsen. There is something of me in Hilde; but in Solness there is little that is not Ibsen."

The Norwegian tone of this play, the first since his return home, distinguished it clearly from his last "German" play, *Hedda Gabler*. The names of the characters are particularly native ones: Halvard Solness, Hilde, Knut and Ragnar Brovik, Dr. Herdal, Miss Fosli. The ardent patriotism of his new friend, Hildur Andersen, is most probably reflected here. From her he also learned the free and casual style of speaking that young Norwegian women were using now. Although Hildur was abroad studying music throughout the spring of 1892, Ibsen was in constant correspondence with her about his work, even by telegraph. His first clean copy of fall, 1892, he later gave to her.

Many of the problems that had filled his mind in the last few years are concentrated in *The Master Builder*. There is much talk of mysterious forces, of a variety of "demons" within, of unexpressed wishes translating themselves into action, of unconscious thoughts that have a life of their own, of the power of one spirit over another—Hilde has power over Solness, he over Kaja Fosli. Ibsen was undoubtedly thinking of hypnotism, as is evidenced by his approval of Johan Fahlstrøm using the gestures of a hypnotist when he played Solness at Christiania Theatre. But hypnotism is not the central theme of this play. What gives it its tragic meaning is the conflict within the master builder, which reaches a crisis when Hilde tries to tear him loose from his past and his feelings of guilt. She wants to give him back his "robust" conscience, and for a time he actually believes that he can recapture his dream of happiness, build "a castle in the air on a firm foundation." The task is impossible, and even Hilde comes to feel how painful it is to rise up against one's past. The rebel is literally dashed down to earth.

When the play appeared just before Christmas, 1892, everyone realized that Ibsen had turned to symbolic drama. Looked at from a purely realistic point of view, the action is absurd from beginning to end. But the symbolic intention did not prevent a good deal of controversy. Many found the words about "robust conscience" particularly irritating since they sounded like a declaration of war against all orthodox moral standards. Was Ibsen seriously proclaiming that every man had the right to place himself before any consideration of others? The play appeared just as Nietzsche and his *Uebermensch* morality were being discussed. Brandes had written a series of articles in *Tilskueren* in 1889 about "Aristocratic Radicalism" in Nietzsche, and the resulting argument between Brandes and the philosopher Harald Høffding was given much attention. The question that was now debated was whether Ibsen had joined sides with Nietzsche.

When Nietzsche died in 1900, Ibsen said that he "did not know much about him." It can be assumed that he had read at least what Brandes had written. In any case he felt a certain sympathy with Nietzsche, as his further comments on his death indicate: "He was a strangely gifted person. But on account of his philosophy he could not become popular in our democratic age." Ibsen's dislike of democracy was evident as far back as 1872, when he and Brandes spoke of the matter in Dresden. At that time Brandes had to conclude: "He was an aristocrat in the extreme and took the consequences of his view." Brandes had eventually come around to the same aristocratic position, but Ibsen would never equate his aristocratic view with the emphasis on the superman's exclusive rights that Nietzsche advocated.

In *The Master Builder* as in almost all his other works Ibsen urged revolt against those social conventions that restricted the freedom of the spirit. By pointing out the evil one could do by following his own desires, he sought to restrain the harmful exercise of the will. His basic concern was with the will to freedom, not the will to power. Those characters in his earlier works who were motivated by the will to power — Bishop Nicholas and Emperor Julian — were judged sinful, suffering from a dangerous flaw in their characters. Nemesis overtakes them as it does Solness. But Ibsen was not preaching morality; he was interested in the interplay of conflicting impulses within men and the consequences in thought and action.

The dramatic strength and intensity of *The Master Builder* derive from the great explosive force of Solness, the powerful and talented man who battles for his right to live, inspired by a new love. The part was a challenge to the most talented actors both in Scandinavia and in Germany, and none was able to make this man as magnificent or as vital as he had to be. The most successful interpretation was, oddly enough, that of Lugné-Poë. Although his theatre in Paris, created primarily to play Ibsen, had not won over the French public, and although his own talents as an actor were minor, he managed to give the role of Solness the inner force that it needed. In the fall of 1894 he came to Norway and played the part before Ibsen himself. Ibsen sat quiet and motionless through the first act. In the second, as the relationship between Solness and Hilde built in intensity until their passion swept like a fire through the audience, Ibsen rose involuntarily, his eyes so fixed on the actors that they could sense their blaze and responded with eagerness. By the third act he was leaning over the edge of the box. *The Master Builder* had triumphed: "This was the resurrection of my play," Ibsen said. Once more he had lived over all its torment in his own heart.

CHAPTER FORTY-THREE

ASSESSING LIFE: *LITTLE EYOLF* AND

JOHN GABRIEL BORKMAN (1893-96)

AFTER HE WROTE what would be his last play in 1899, Ibsen said that *The Master Builder* had been the first of a new series of closely related dramas. But at the time he did not appear to have been conscious of this new development; he rather felt that he had written himself out on this particular theme. Well into 1893, he busied himself with other plans, particularly the idea of writing an opera, which he had toyed with twenty years before. Now he wanted to use *The Vikings at Helgeland* as the basis for a libretto, and he still wanted Edvard Grieg to write the music. Grieg was now fifty years old and because of poor health was at the Grefsen Baths. When Ibsen approached him with the idea for the opera, he was not enthusiastic, even though Ibsen said he had the first act almost finished. The draft of the libretto reveals that he had simply turned the lines of the play into rhymed verses that did not have the youthful vigor necessary for a good opera text. It is not known if Grieg rejected the first act, but in any case Ibsen went no further with the scheme.

Ibsen may have returned to this old idea of writing an opera as part of his general tendency then to look back over his youth. The trait is common enough in age, and the same evidence of the years now gaining on him can be seen in *The Master Builder*. A speech he gave in 1898 clarifies somewhat his attitude toward growing old. He noted that he and Solness were closely related, but he added with emphasis that he had never been afraid of youth nor would he ever be. He might still feel the need to protect himself against the force of youth—Solness was, after all, what he could have been—but he had an inner certainty that he had so outstripped his contemporaries that he stood side by side with youth. It was in this sense that he "needed youth." There is, nonetheless, an unexpressed admission of his age in the words, and the suggestion of a longing to recapture his youth once again.

The idea found expression in the verse about the man and woman who raked the ashes to find the faith and happiness they had lost. These lines had been the starting point of *The Master Builder;* they now became the germ of the new play he began to shape. He even thought of using the lines in the play, in a speech by the main character, where they would clearly define the intent of the action.

His thoughts traveled back as far as his childhood in Skien as he sought material for the play. At this time he received letters and even a visit from his sister Hedvig Stousland, who still lived in Skien. He thought of taking a trip there himself, but he may have been so afraid of destroying the image he still kept, that he never went back. He tried to remember what the place had meant to him in his childhood, and he puzzled over the talk he and Hedvig had had on the hill overlooking the town the last time he was there—about the perfection he wished to reach before he died. There are reflections of all these things in the play.

In a letter to Hegel in September, 1893, he makes the first reference to the play: "I have now begun planning a new dramatic work which I intend to complete in the course of the coming summer." In the long-established rhythm of his creative life, the plans that rose in one year did not take firm shape until the following summer. He anticipated the same now and calmly let the drama grow in his imagination through the winter and spring. In January, 1894, he writes that he is just "turning over" his plans. He is described as "in his brilliant mood" in February. Elise Aubert reports that "he sparkled and glittered with sallies and thrusts" in conversation. He had met Mrs. Aubert, now married to a professor in Oslo, in Lom in 1862; now he told her that he was busy with some "deviltry again" about marriage. He was clearly disturbed about his own marriage and spoke to Mrs. Aubert about it. He had many conflicts with his wife at this time, and on occasion his anger was so extreme that he threatened to leave her. These outbursts were only momentary, and he knew that they would never separate. Both the hostility and the sense of attachment would be part of the new play.

His plans were not definite enough to let him proceed until June; by October he was finished with the play he called *Little Eyolf.* The play's indebtedness to other works, particularly *The Lady from the Sea,* has been demonstrated by Didrik Arup Seip. The similarity is to a certain extent a question of mood; both plays end with more hope and faith in the future than most of the plays since *Pillars of Society*. *Little Eyolf* even runs up a flag for the new working day to come (Bjørnson thought it was "touching"). But before that day could come, both the husband, Alfred Allmers, and his wife, Rita, had to go through the same kind of "transformation" as Ellida Wangel had. The change involves a process of psychoanalysis, and the psychologists were quick to point out the similarity between Ibsen and Freud. Ibsen saw the connection between the two plays; he even has Allmers virtually quote from the other work when he protests against the idea that we are only "men of earth"—"We are a little akin to sea and sky as well," he says.

In *Little Eyolf* the main character is again a man placed between two women. On the one hand there is Rita, who has her man but would much rather have taken him from another woman, in the style of Emilie Bardach. Opposed to her is Asta, whom Allmers believes to be his sister, warm-hearted and wise, thinking more of someone else's happiness than her own—she may perhaps have something of Hildur Andersen in her makeup. Allmers stands between them with the same kind of guilty feelings toward each that had hounded Catiline, Consul Bernick, and many others. He has wronged both women; he has married Rita out of physical infatuation and desire for her money, and he unconsciously feels he has betrayed Asta, who is his rightful "traveling companion." This becomes clear when he discovers that she is not his sister after all.

Allmers' sense of guilt is epitomized in his son, Little Eyolf, whose name derives from his pet name for Asta. The secret wish Eyolf's parents have to be rid of him comes back to haunt them in his deformed body, the symbolic punishment they must endure. Ibsen was recalling his brother Nicolai, whose back was damaged in childhood when the maid dropped him; he, too, failed, like Eyolf, in the struggle of life. Vengeance comes through another Skien memory; "Ratwife" who goes back to an "Aunt Ploug" of Skien who had borne this nickname and had left a terrifying impression on Ibsen as a child. At first he had called her "Miss Varg" ("Wolf") or "Aunt Ellen." She enters the play almost like Ulrik Brendel in *Rosmersholm*, and her mysterious words about the things that gnaw and stir in souls set the action in motion.

The solitary wayfaring on the mountain heights from which Allmers returns in the play is for Ibsen a symbol of the process of self-examination which leads to transformation of the soul. The same symbol occurred in the poem "On the Heights," where the man learns to steel his heart and regard life as a mere play. Allmers' experience yields the opposite. As he wanders in the endless wasteland of glaciers and mountain peaks with only the frozen stars overhead, life itself seems to vanish, and he realizes that he had no claims on life, but rather that life has a claim on him. For ten years he has struggled to write his great book on "human responsibility," but now he realizes that it is useless to write books. It would be better for him to give up his dream of writing and instead sacrifice himself to life itself, working for progress and the future generations of men. Mathilde Prager is most probably correct in stating that the symbol of the mountain journey is more than merely a sign of Allmers' psychological growth; the desolate mountain lake he must make his way around is an image of all the metaphysical speculations that men must rid themselves of to achieve an authentically human existence.

In the spring of 1894 there was much discussion in Norway of the relation between literature and life. One opinion, held by Christen Collin, insisted that literature should strive to build man's courage to live his life; this was at odds with those artists and critics who held that literature should be concerned with nothing except its own inner demands. Ibsen followed the controversy with keen interest, for the problems were his own. Collin made his own coinage "livskunst," the "art of living," the slogan of his program, and Ibsen felt the word had long been a part of his own vocabulary. When he had made the first reckoning between the demands of art and life in *Brand*, he had Brand say to Ejnar: "Remember—living is an art." In *Little Eyolf* he tried to make the art of living the great goal of all human education. He may have even adopted Collin's word in reply to his accusation that the last plays had weakened the younger generation's moral commitment to life. Collin was mistaken; Ibsen was eager to serve life, and so he lets Alfred and Rita succeed in what had not been possible for Solness and Aline—to rake out of the ashes peace of soul and tranquility. A new goal makes their life and their union bearable and fruitful, ennobling, and perhaps finally happy.

Ibsen was not absolutely certain that the "transformation" would take place, and the play ends as so many of the others did, with a question. When he saw *Little Eyolf* played for the first time, he asked a close friend, Mrs. Caroline Sontum: "Do you think Rita will start up with those rascals? Don't you think it is just a holiday fancy?"

What answer he himself would give is not known, but the question is meant sincerely in the play, as it was in his own life. His own hope and faith had been worn down by living, and now he felt himself under "the law of transformation," the same hope of transformation and the same promise of new life that casts such an atmosphere of autumn and fallen leaves over the whole play. There is perhaps more of resignation than of will here, but there is still a part for the will. Ibsen still wanted to believe in the ennoblement of souls, for which Rosmer had died and the very thing he himself had proclaimed to the workers of Trondheim.

A play that ends on a note of resignation must inevitably be less dramatic than was usual with him. The old secret that is unearthed, Allmers' semi-incestuous relation to Asta that underlies the dualism of his nature, does not have the explosive force of the secrets in other plays. When it is revealed, its only effect is to help the characters look more honestly at themselves, much the same as the accident with which the play opens. The relationships between characters do change in the course of the play, but the change is an inward one.

There is much more explicit dramatic action in the next play in which Ibsen continued his assessment of life. In *John Gabriel Borkman* the tone is harsher, even savage. As in *The Master Builder,* there is an old man who must make a reckoning of his life, and Ibsen is again engaged on a very personal level with the theme of the play. It was not until some time after he had finished *Little Eyolf* that this play began to take shape within him, not until the spring of 1896 as far as can be determined. In the summer of 1894 he told the German critic Paul Lindau that every play he wrote now seemed surely to be the last he could write; he had already said everything he wanted to say. But, he added, material would accumulate in him quite unconsciously and would become a new drama. He knew that a new play would develop this time too, but external circumstances kept intruding.

The most annoying event was the necessity to move. Mrs. Ibsen had not liked the apartment he rented in her absence. At the end of 1894 she left for the baths in Italy and remained away until the following fall, but in the meantime she wrote that when she got home he would have to have another place for her. Sigurd and Bergliot helped him to find and furnish the new apartment in Arbiensgate. Even with their aid, the move was a great expenditure of time and energy for him, and he worried that his wife would not approve (fortunately, she did). He was being painted and sculpted during this period and this too kept him away from his desk, even though sitting for his portraits could become a process of self-examination such as his most recent works had undertaken.

In the summer of 1895 he seems to have been absorbed by this process. When he made the half-joking comment about his great-grandmother's Scottish blood leaving "deep traces" in him, he went on to say: "I have been thinking over many things lately." What he was searching for was an explanation of himself, and where it might lie in his past. When Hildur Andersen was touring in Telemark he wrote to her about Skien and how he had been marked in his youth by the noise of its waterfalls.

John Gabriel Borkman, written in the summer and fall of 1896 and published before Christmas that year, was a product of just such soul-searching. The main character is a counterpart to Solness and like him drawn from the Ibsen who might have been, not as he was. He had had enough time to assimilate some of Nietzsche's philosophy, and so there is more of that philosophy in this play than in *The Master Builder.* In Borkman he created a superman who believes he has the right to exploit everyone on behalf of the great things he wants to accomplish. Ibsen had felt such a call, more important to him than anything else in the world. But as *Brand* makes clear, it is dangerous for a man to push everything and everyone out of his path to follow his own calling; he might end as a cold-blooded egoist. Thus the judgment on Borkman, a judgment much more severe than the sentence for embezzlement.

The events of the play were based on old memories and on recent happenings. In the 1880's there had been much discussion of a great scandal in Arendal, where an influential bank president had been sentenced to prison for various criminal acts involving the credit of his bank and certain powerful enterprises. The boom of the 1890's led to many improvements in Oslo, but it also tempted many to speculation and excessive profiteering. It was natural then for Ibsen to make his main character a big businessman, and as a sign of his place in the world to give him an English-sounding name. He still had the *Brand* image of England as a country under the coal-smog of materialism, even though he had recently come to appreciate the greatness of the English spirit. "Gabriel," the name of the archangel, was added to suggest Borkman's exalted plans.

For the greater part of Borkman's character, Ibsen returned to the memories of his youth. In 1851 a high officer had been accused of misconduct in office; he at first rejected the charge with disdain, then attempted suicide. He was tried, convicted, and sentenced to four years in prison. His release came just about the time that Ibsen made his second visit to Oslo. There was much talk about how the man had locked himself into his own home and passed the rest of his life in lonely brooding. It was said that he never again spoke to his wife. (Ibsen once referred to the affair in an article in *Andhrimner*.)

Although Borkman keeps going over his case, bringing himself to trial and exonerating himself, he bears a guilt for which Ibsen knew no forgiveness; he has betrayed the most precious thing in his possession. In order to secure another man's help in getting the post of bank president, he yielded to the man's desire for the woman he also loved. To ensure the success of his great plans, he gives up his love and marries her sister. The situation is the familiar one; like Sigurd or Consul Bernick, Borkman sacrifices love for "higher" considerations. (There is a difference here in that the two women are sisters, even twin sisters.) The betrayal avenges itself in the usual way; the heart hardens and the springs of life dry up. Bernick can rescue the best in himself, but Borkman is finished with life, a living corpse, the miner sealed in his mine.

Like that other ex-convict, Lieutenant Ekdal, Borkman has his life-lie to sustain him; he keeps expecting that he will some day be called back to his life's work. To underline this lie, even in caricature, Ibsen places beside him the old copyist Vilhelm Foldal with the tragic drama that he is eternally revising and which he is certain will one day bring him fame. Foldal is said to have been modeled on an acquaintance from Ibsen's youth, the old copyist Wilhelm Foss, who once published a small collection of poems, but nothing else. Before he used him as Borkman's companion, Ibsen had had Foss in his mind as far back as *Pillars of Society* and *The Lady from the Sea*, for in both plays he had thought of a part for him.

Borkman's life is a dream. When the wounded wolf, prowling his cage, ventures out into the real world, he meets death. In the play Ibsen draws what Edward Munch has called "the most powerful snowscape in all Scandinavian art." Winter and snow dominate the whole play, and especially its ending, where the symbolic meaning emerges out of a vividly real scene.

The action takes place at Grefsen near Oslo; in these days when Ibsen came to visit Dr. Sontum he would climb, albeit with some effort, to the top of Grefsen Ridge to view the Oslo valley below. It was the natural location to place his caged eagle, longing to fly away.

Music plays an important part in Borkman's life, an unexpected trait in an Ibsen play, since he himself was not at all musical and hated to attend concerts. He knew of course of the conflict between Wagner and Nietzsche, and this may have suggested the use of music to him. It was in all probability Hildur Andersen who made music come alive for him at this time. He had heard her play the Saint-Saëns "Danse Macabre" that Borkman so loved to hear. He may even had told her what Borkman tells little Frida: "Never be so foolish as to doubt yourself."

Borkman deceives himself into thinking that restitution will some day come for him. How sincerely he believes this is difficult to say; he is always shoring up his faith with mighty protestations, and he seeks support for his belief from poor old Foldal. But Ibsen has no hope for him, and he drives the old man's tragedy through to the end. In *John Gabriel Borkman* Ibsen lived through what might have been his own fate if his vision had not been great and his heart not full of love; there is a deeper tragic meaning in this play than in any other of his works.

AT SEVENTY (1898)

WHEN IBSEN'S WORKS are analyzed as expressions of his psychological needs, testifying primarily to the drama of his own mind, the reason why his contemporaries found them so hard to interpret becomes clear. Not realizing how deeply personal his work was, they were puzzled and mystified by things that can be explained naturally by reference to his inner life. Readers and critics searched for the meaning in each new work, only to become more and more confused as the poetic symbols received more emphasis and the themes derived more fully from the hidden life of his soul. The plays of Ibsen's old age were strangely misinterpreted as a result. Solness was taken to be a portrait of Bjørnson, of Bismarck, even of Gladstone, and Hilde became the morality of the future appearing as a flesh and blood young lady. Mathilde Prager, the Austrian who wrote under the name of Erich Holm, imagined the final series of drama to contain a sociopolitical program, analyzing, chastising, and reforming all bourgeois society. The game of tracking down clues to the meaning behind character and dialogue in these plays became an absorbing pastime. By the early 1890's Ibsen was commonly referred to as "the great sphinx" or "the sphinx of the North." In the fall of 1891 the humorous magazine *Krydseren* published a series of epitaphs for famous people. Ibsen's read:

Nu ligger jeg truffen af Dødens Pil.	Here I lie struck by the shaft of death.
Mon Gaaden nu løses?—	Is the riddle solved now?—
Jeg har mine Tvivl!	I have my doubts!

The unresolved enigmas annoyed many; some thought he was simply affecting an air of mystery. Everyone caught the reference when in 1895 Garborg has the "Magician Whitebeard" in his poem "Haugtussa" speak the following lines:

Eg talar Taake med Vismannsgjerd,	Vapor I utter in sage's style,
so alle med Tyding tevlar;	so all may compete in solving;
die Meining finner, der inga er,	Meaning they find where none is
og gjeng der dumme som Djevlar.	meant,
	and stay as stupid as devils.

Des meir dei lovar den vise Mann,	Still more they praise the pundit
som tala det ingen visste;	who speaks what no one knew;
snart hev eg trolla det heile Land	Soon I'll have charmed the entire land
um til ei Daarekiste.	and turned it into a madhouse.

At times Ibsen was annoyed to see his plays interpreted in ways he never dreamt, and although he occasionally explained his plays to friends, he had little interest in doing the same in public. He may even have enjoyed the spectacle of all the fumbling and guessing that went on. His sense of the comic had not died, as is evident even in as late a play as *John Gabriel Borkman,* and his teasing spirit was not entirely averse to leading good people astray.

This side of Ibsen's character is illustrated in a story Georg Brandes tells. Brandes' daughter Edith was twelve years old when *The Master Builder* appeared, and when he visited Ibsen in Oslo, he was asked: "Well, what does Edith say about my play?" Brandes replied: "She says what is appropriate to her age, that the play has only one honorable person in it, Mrs. Solness, and moreover, she regards Hilde as detestable because she runs after a married man." A few years later Edith called on Ibsen: "But there's my Hilde," he greeted her with a smile, "coming to me exactly as I had imagined her!" "I am not at all like Hilde!" Edith replied with spirit. But Ibsen insisted: "But of course you are." He gave her a photograph of himself and wrote on the back: "What is Edith like?" But when she asked, "Well, what am I like?" he could only reply: "I don't know. You go to the country and stay for a month and then come back. I'll be thinking it over." When Edith returned to have the question answered, he wrote: "Edith is not like anyone in the world, she is only like herself. Therefore Edith is so...." And again he left the statement in suspense. "But what am I?" she insisted. "I don't know yet," he answered. "Go home to Copenhagen and come back in a year. Then I'll have thought it over and will add the ending." Brandes comments on this incident: "This bagatelle points up Ibsen's love of suspense, his desire to create uncertainty, to pose questions and riddles, his inclination to break off just at the most interesting moment, and finally the dramatist's technique of postponing the solution of the riddle until some time in the future."

Ibsen was well aware that the riddles and ambiguities in his plays increased interest in them and added to their sales. In fact, he began to spin great webs of mystery and suspense around his plays, first by announcing in advance when a new one would appear, but keeping the title and the theme a secret until copies were in the bookstores. Then journalists raced to get copies and the newsmills started to grind away. When someone managed to get hold of a few pages of

Little Eyolf from the printer in 1894 and told a newspaper man, who immediately published the information, Ibsen was furious and threatened to have the culprits punished or fined. Of course the little tempest helped to boost sales enormously, serving as a nice fanfare in advance of the book. Although 10,000 had been the normal edition for his plays since *Pillars of Society, Little Eyolf* immediately went into two additional printings of 10,000 each; *John Gabriel Borkman* appeared in an edition of 15,000, unheard of at that time.

Ibsen kept careful watch on all the economic aspects of his writing —the size of editions, sales, translations, productions, and performances. A portion of each day was set aside for correspondence on these matters, and he kept a close account of the income due him from both publications and performances. Since Denmark did not become a signatory to the Berne convention on international copyright until 1903, his books were usually unprotected, except when he provided for simultaneous editions in other countries. He did this as a general rule, and although it involved more work, it brought in enough money for him to become a well-to-do man. As his income increased, it took more time and work to manage, but he continued to handle it all personally, with great care and efficiency.

In addition to keeping an eye on the economic state of his works, he was also concerned with the way they were produced around the world. In Oslo he was able to pick the actors and actresses for the plays and to give instructions on performances. For the rest, he had to be satisfied with giving advice to translators and directors. His name and reputation were valuable to him as an economic and a spiritual reality, and he had to protect them. Some things he could not prevent; for example, if some actor in the American Wild West stepped on stage and accepted the crowd's ovation as "Mr. Ibsen," or if directors in remote areas began to rewrite the plays to suit local circumstances or steal his titles for their own plays. These things became more or less common, at least on the outer fringes of the cultural world. In most places, however, there was such respect for his name by now that few dared to violate his rights.

Some people ridiculed his manner of doing business with his name and the iron grip he kept on his plays, but for him it was entirely natural to feel a certain responsibility for the fame he had won throughout the world, and with that fame had come the duty to protect it. His passion for order is evident here; he bent all his genius to making his plays as perfect as possible, and so it became necessary to see them into the world with as much diligence. In great things as well as small he was a circumspect, orderly man, a patient and painstaking worker.

He no longer lost his temper when his works were misunderstood or deliberately misconstrued. This was part of the fate of such world-wide renown and he could accept it with composure. At sixty his name just begun to be heard outside Scandinavia; at seventy he was known throughout the world. Only Zola and Tolstoy among his con-temporaries could compare with him in this respect. There were already some seventy books about him, from Norway and Denmark, Sweden, Germany, England, France, the Netherlands, Italy, Spain, Poland, Russia, and Hungary. In 1895 a journal in Rio de Janeiro wrote: "At this moment Ibsen is the name that preoccupies the critic and the interpreter of literature in all civilized countries." If he came to look at himself and his career as a part of history, it was perhaps inevitable.

Right after *John Gabriel Borkman* was published, Ibsen's German friends, particularly Julius Elias and Paul Schlenther, began making plans for a collected edition of his works that would include even the newspaper articles, all the rejected poems and the unpublished plays of his youth. Ibsen hesitated at first, since he did not want to print material he thought inadequate, but he yielded to Elias' insistence and eventually was delighted by the whole enterprise. The German col-lected works, with critical introductions to each volume by Schlenther and Brandes, could begin to appear on his seventieth birthday, in March, 1898.

This project stimulated the publishing firm of Gyldendalske Bog-handel in Copenhagen to undertake a collection in the original language, but without the previously unpublished works (these eventually ap-peared in a supplementary volume in 1902). Ibsen wrote a preface to this edition, in which he urged the reader to study his works in their chronological order. He believed that "the strange, inadequate, and misleading interpretations" given his later plays happened because the younger generation had not seen them in connection with his earlier work: "Only by comprehending my entire production as an interconnected, continuous whole will one receive the precise effect intended by the individual parts." He now decided that he would carry out the plan to write the book that he had first thought of in 1880-81, "a book that ties together in an illuminating whole my life and my work." Nothing came of the idea this time, either, but it again indicates his attitude toward his life's work.

When his seventieth birthday came on March 20, 1898, he threw himself with spirit into the festivities and the celebrations that surged around him. In earlier years he had not looked forward with pleasure to his birthday, "that dreadful day," as he once wrote to his wife. When his publisher asked him where he would be on that day, he

wrote in reply: "If it were entirely up to me, I would flee to the mountains, to a place where it would be delightfully lonely." In another
letter he said that he would not accept "festivities," even if they were
offered; he dreaded wearing a mask of cheerfulness and gratitude
for the benefit of people he hardly knew. At length he came to feel
that it was a duty he owed history to accept this homage, and of course
his vanity was tickled since the homage testified to his position at
the summit of society.

No Norwegian before or since has ever received such homage. Letters,
telegrams, and flowers from all parts of the world poured in. Well-
wishers streamed to his home, everyone of any importance in Norwegian cultural, social, and political life, deputations from the authors'
and artists' societies, from the theatres and women's organizations, and
at the head the presidents of the Storting with speeches of thanks on
behalf of the entire Norwegian people. Forty English literary and
artistic figures sent an elegant scroll with an even more elegant silver
bowl. *Festschriften* were issued in his honor and festive articles appeared in every newspaper. The article in *Dagbladet*, probably written
by Erik Vullum, epitomized his life's work in one phrase from his
Stockholm speech of 1887: "to steel our thoughts." But what Ibsen meant
for the world was most clearly seen in the many performances of his
plays given in his honor that day: at two theatres in both Oslo and
Copenhagen, at three in Stockholm, six in Berlin, four in Vienna, and
wherever there were theatres throughout Scandinavia and Germany
and all of Europe, even as far as Japan. The festivities continued into
the following days, and he had to attend dinners and performances,
listen to speeches and think of something to say in return, something
always hard for him and now even more taxing.

On the day itself Christiania Theatre gave scenes from *Peer Gynt*
and all of *The Feast at Solhaug*, and Centralteatret gave a production
of *Ghosts*. When Christiania Theatre gave *The Master Builder* the
next day, Ibsen was present and had to come forward time and again
to accept the acclaim of the audience. On the following day the students
staged a torchlight procession to his home in Arbiensgate; there were
songs and speeches and Ibsen came out on the balcony to thank them.
He had no speech prepared, but he did make some comments on the
relation between *The Master Builder* and his own life. He ended by
telling them that when youth came and knocked on his door, he greeted
them with joy.

At the major official event on Wednesday, March 23, Wexelsen,
Minister of Church and Education, emphasized, in a speech made up
largely of generalities, that "there is hardly any aspect of our people's

cultural life on which Ibsen has not left deep and enduring imprints."
Ibsen had a prepared speech with him, but he tried to make it sound
impromptu by beginning: "When I called for your attention just now,
a sudden silence fell around me." He mentioned that he was planning
to write a book about his life and his work, and also noted that he
still had "various follies in store" for new dramatic works. He went
on to comment on the great changes in conditions in the country,
how much richer cultural life now, and how much more understanding
for the writer. He wanted to correct the false impression "that absolute
happiness must be a companion to the rare, fairytale fate that has
been mine: to win fame and reputation in many countries abroad."
On the contrary, it could happen "that one who has won a home in
many countries, may not in his innermost heart feel truly at home
anywhere, scarcely even in his native country." In the greater cultural
harmony that existed at home he thought he would be spared "the
painful sense of being regarded as the poet of a party." Thus this
festive evening might be the beginning of a sense of being finally at
home in his country, and for this he must thank them. The speech is
a vital document in the story of his life because it indicates the
newly won peace he felt in his soul.

After Oslo came Copenhagen. He had been invited in January and
at that time promised he would come at the end of March. He left
by rail on March 29, and since he was getting unsteady on his feet,
he had the young journalist Nils Vogt accompany him. When they
passed Göteborg in the morning, he received a telegram informing
him that King Christian wished to confer on him the Grand Cross of
the Order of Dannebrog. He was delighted because he believed no
other Norwegian had ever received so high a Danish decoration. As
soon as he arrived in Copenhagen, he wired the great news to his wife
in Oslo. The new Grand Cross was an even greater honor than the Grand
Cross of the Norwegian St. Olav order, which he had received five
years earlier. That was the first, and for a long time the only, occasion
on which the order was given to an author. But the Order of Dannebrog
was to be given him without precedent, since he had never received
the commander's order. "How beautiful!" he said. "It is indeed a great
honor; since Oehlenschläger, no Scandinavian author has been granted
so high a Danish tribute."

Hegel had made arrangements for him to stay in the "royal suite"
at the Hotel d'Angleterre, and on March 31, the festivities began with
a performance of *The Wild Duck* at the Royal Theatre, followed by
a torchlight procession. His speech of thanks said little more than just
that and was scarcely audible except to those who stood close to him.

At the major official event on April 1, things did not go very smoothly. It was an unfortunate time for the celebrations since a parliamentary election was scheduled for April 5, and Easter was only a short time off. Thus the newspapers and people were preoccupied with other interests. Many prominent people were missing from the dinner, including a goodly number of actors, some of whom were ill, and others busy at the Royal Theatre, which had decided at the last moment to change its scheduled performance. Ibsen was supposed to have Betty Hennings for his dinner partner, but since she could not come, he had to be satisfied with Mrs. Eckardt. She was attractive enough, but close to sixty and not at all comparable to Mrs. Hennings.

Even more upsetting was the difficulty with the speakers for the occasion. The main speaker had been art historian Professor Kroman, but he sent his regrets a few hours before the dinner began. When another refused to take his place, Peter Hansen, the theatre director, had to step in. He was a literary historian and an old friend of Ibsen's, but he was unprepared and preoccupied with the theatre and arrangements for the celebration. As last resort, he decided to deliver a casual, bantering talk. He began by reminding Ibsen of the old days and contrasting his own bald head with Ibsen's white mane. Then he pointed out the similarity between Shakespeare and Ibsen, which he decided consisted in both having published one small collection of poems, and then sticking to writing plays. He commended on the amount of work Ibsen had given the theatre by writing so many plays, and concluded with: "There is thus every good reason to say that Ibsen has been a force of the first rank." He proposed a toast, saying that surely no one in the company would object or refuse to join in.

Ibsen was not used to being treated in a bantering way, and responded by saying that the remarks had so "confused him" that he could not use the speech he had prepared. He would have to improvise, although he did repeat a number of ideas he had noted beforehand. He cited an incident that had taken place on the rail journey to Copenhagen. When he and Nils Vogt came out of Norway and saw the sound before them, Ibsen had said he felt as if he had just come out of a tunnel into the sunshine. "But don't tell them I said so back home, at least not until I'm dead!" he told Vogt. Now he compared his reaction to the Danish Sound to the feeling he had in 1864 when he came through the Alps and saw Italy before him. He expressed his thanks to Denmark for giving him this vision of freedom.

Peter Hansen's speech had embarrassed a number of people and many took the floor afterwards, among them the literary historian and critic Vilhelm Andersen. He said that he thought it better to speak of the soles of Ibsen's shoes, rather than the hair on his head; at least in this way one could think of the firm ground on which the playwright stood. His speech, along with Poul Levin's, made the audience cheer Ibsen. But the evening had been spoiled and he did not enjoy himself.

On the following day, a Saturday, he stood first in audience before King Christian. He was somewhat embarrassed, in spite of the king's friendly, natural manner. What made the deepest impression on him, because it gave such a vivid image of his world-wide position, was the king's remark: "My two daughters, the Empress of Russia and the Princess of Wales, would like to meet you." After this there were celebrations in the Women's Reading Society and in the Student Society, with speeches and a few brief remarks on his part. The official dinner had introduced him to authorities and important people; in the Student Society he met part of "radical" Denmark. Vogt said that the best speeches of the entire celebration were given here, by Professor Høffding and Valdemar Vedel. But Ibsen was still in bad humor, which did not improve when young Vedel turned to him and addressed him with, "Master, thou who—" using the intimate form of address. Afterwards Ibsen remarked drily that he had not realized they were on such intimate terms. His good spirits did not return until he saw *Brand* at the Dagmar Theatre on Sunday evening, April 3; he was deeply touched, and discovered that he had forgotten much of it. He was lively and talkative afterwards during the party at the home of Martinius Nielsen, the theatre's director. On the ride back to his hotel in the early hours of the morning, he insisted on having two pretty, young actresses with him in the carriage, and he laughed and jested with them.

On April 6, Ash Wednesday, he left for Stockholm, and on his arrival was met by the governor of the city himself. He stayed at the "ministerial suite" of the Hotel Rydberg, and spent the rest of Holy Week resting, or driving around looking at the city. On Saturday he had an audience with King Oscar, and although their conversation lasted only five minutes, it was a thrilling moment for him. The king had written some words of praise in one of the Norwegian birthday *festschriften;* now he addressed Ibsen with "we two kings" and presented him with the Grand Cross of the North Star Order. "This was the greatest honor that could have been conferred on me," Ibsen said later. That evening the king gave a dinner for him at the palace.

The festivities continued on the day after Easter, April 11, with a dinner given by the Swedish Authors' Society at Hasselbacken. Count Snoilsky, the society's president, had said it would be just a "family party," with only members present and no speeches, but Gastaf af

Geijerstam made an impromptu speech and Ibsen whispered some words of thanks, apologizing that he was used to expressing his thoughts in books, not in speeches. Later on, however, he livened up, and when Oscar Levertin made a little farewell speech, his tongue loosened. Now he made the remark about never having been a member of any society. He belonged to the Norwegian Authors' Society, he said, merely "for the sake of appearances." He agreed that such societies could do a great deal of useful work, particularly toward getting Scandinavian books read in the original languages in all three countries. He concluded by saying that he was particularly fond of Sweden because there he found an old culture with strong traditions.

On the next day he attended a festive performance of *The Pretenders* at the Vasa Theatre and on the thirteenth the official banquet at Grand Hotel. Count Snoilsky was the speaker, and he discussed the most profound of all of Ibsen's themes: his struggle with the demons "in the hidden recesses of heart and mind," and his efforts to probe his own "heart chamber" as well as the characters he had created. Ibsen's prepared speech of thanks was brief but sincere; his reception in Stockholm, first by the king and now at this dinner, seemed like a dream. "My life was like a long, long Passion Week; now, in a real Passion Week, my life has been transformed into a fairytale play, indeed into a midsummer night's dream—thank you, thank you for the transformation!"

On the following day a deputation of students from Uppsala visited him and he invited them to lunch. In the evening there was a performance of *Lady Inger of Østråt* at the Dramatic Theatre; the king attended and Ibsen was acclaimed by an elegantly dressed audience.

The Swedish festivities had been more successful than the Danish, but one section of the population was dissatisfied: the women. There had been only men at both dinner parties; now two women's organizations in Stockholm, the Fredrika Bremer League and Nya Idun, joined forces and persuaded Ibsen to extend his stay and come to their celebration. He quickly regretted his decision and was not put in better spirits at the dinner when he was forced to sit between the presidents of the two societies, old Lady Anckarsvärd on one side and Ellen Key on the other. Professor Montelius gave the first speech, in which he hailed Ibsen as both a fighter and an author. Then Ellen Key gave a long speech which offended Ibsen from the start—she began with: "Henrik Ibsen! Du..." using the intimate form merely for rhetorical purposes. What she said about his struggle for "the liberation of personality," especially for women, was true and well-intentioned, but Ibsen objected to being portrayed as more of a doubter than a believer in a new world. His response was short. He merely thanked them for the understanding he had met in Sweden and promised that it would bear fruit in his subsequent writing. It was obvious that he was tired now, but he livened up considerably when the "Friends of Folk-dancing" brought on a group of pretty young ladies who danced Swedish folk-dances. He chatted animatedly with the girls and remembered the occasion long afterwards.

On the following day, Sunday, April 17, he took the train back to Oslo, where there were still more celebrations. On May 26 the Norwegian Society for Women's Rights invited the Ibsens to a dinner. In his rather long speech of thanks he insisted that he had been "more poet, less social philosopher" than people had tried to make of him; he had not worked for "causes," but had tried to portray human beings. He sounded almost critical of the group when he emphasized that only as mothers could they help to bring progress to the people. The program he urged in them was to create "culture and discipline" in mankind.

The festivities he had gone through were above all a warning and a reminder to him to re-examine his life and consider what he had done in terms of what he had hoped to do. Now the conflicts and struggles that had animated the work of his youth and manhood seemed rather remote; he was coming to understand clearer than ever before that what was strongest in him was the poet.

CHAPTER FORTY-FIVE

EPILOGUE:

WHEN WE DEAD AWAKEN (1899)

Ibsen had now reached that dangerous age when, as the old saying has it, "a man begins to regret the sins he never had a chance to commit." He returned from the festivities in triumph with two grand crosses and much tribute, but he did not feel any happier than before he set out. Now at home, without peace or contentment, he kept returning to that reckoning with his own life that had occupied him for the past years. A decade earlier he had said that when a play was finished it no longer interested him; now he did little else but ponder his old works. Even if he tried to avoid this, the demands for the collected editions of his works, and the countless performances he had to attend, kept forcing him to re-examine and to interpret what he had written.

What he had to ask himself was whether his writing had itself been life, or if he had sold his life for his art and a poet's fame. At one time he could agree with Henrik Wergeland's proud deathbed words: "I was nothing else but a poet." For Wergeland, poets were "spiritual leaders and teachers of the people"; poet and champion were one and the same. But now Ibsen began to think: I have been only a poet, and the word "only" made it all sound so contemptible. It was not enough for a man to be a poet, and so he had been a kind of "half man," such as Bishop Nicholas, one who only made plans and let others do the fighting. In Ibsen's character courage lived side by side with fear; he had always wished to stand foremost in the struggle, and none judged him more harshly than himself when he turned away.

Time after time he had depicted men who betrayed love for power or honor, and who were then consumed and led to the abyss by their feelings of guilt. He had returned to this theme so frequently, most recently in *John Gabriel Borkman*, that it formed an indelible part of his own inner dilemma; the theme reflected longings and needs which were deeply rooted in his own heart. In this play there is also a note of sadness and regret in the cry for life that young Erhart Borkman utters, just as Oswald and Hedvig and Johannes Rosmer had once done.

As Erhart rebels against his father, mother, and foster-mother, each of whom would use him for his own ends, he insists on having his own life: "I am young! I want to live life once, too! I want to live my own life!...I want happiness! I want to live, live, live!" Life is still unknown to him; all he knows is the yearning to experience the happiness that beckons him in love. In these impassioned speeches Ibsen seems to pour all his sad realization that perhaps his own life would have been more fulfilled if he had followed the promptings of his heart and simply thrown himself with all his vigor into living.

One encounter during the festivities in Stockholm threw a brilliant light on the whole question of what was true happiness in life. At the women's rights dinner he so unwillingly attended, he met Rosa Fitinghoff, one of the young folk-dancers. She was almost 26, but Ibsen thought her much younger, recalling Emilie Bardach and that summer in Gossensass. He asked Rosa to come to the station the next day to see him off, and when he received a postcard from her after his return, he called it "a warm spring message." He seemed to be looking forward to another summer idyll.

They corresponded for several years. His letters to her are in some ways reminiscent of those he had written to Emilie ten years earlier; they are full of phrases broken off, allusive words that suggest many things but say little directly. He called her by her first name but always used the formal pronoun. When she sent her photograph, he wrote that he could now sit and look into her eyes every day. He asked for long letters, even though his own were brief: "What I do not write I will say to your photograph." He told her he kept her letters in a special place in his writing desk, "and when I start my work in the morning, I always look there and greet Rosa." When she sent him a sofa pillow for Christmas he wrote: "Every day I lay my head against it and imagine that the little fairy has come to me." He compares her with "a young princess from the land of fairytales," just as he had done with Emilie.

Although this relation did not have the same intensity as the one with Emilie, it left clear traces in the last play Ibsen was to write, forming a link between it and the inner drama he was experiencing. In the spring of 1897 he had begun "planning something new in the way of drama," but he did not then see clearly what it would be. "I feel the basic mood already," he wrote to his wife, "but I see only one of the characters yet. Well, the other will appear, too." A few weeks later he wrote that he was "meditating" on the new play: "In this connection I have lengthened my walks, going first out to Skillebaek and back, and then downtown; I thrive on this." But other work intervened, particularly the German collected edition of his works, and on the day before his seventieth birthday he told an interviewer: "I have made some notes and jottings.That is, nothing yet that I will use, but the kind of thing that may be of value later, to stimulate my thinking and produce the right thing. I haven't been able to do more." Another reason for the delay was that he still had thoughts of writing the story of his life and works.

In the late summer he had added several characters to the original one. He told William Archer, "I've put them out to pasture, and I hope they fatten." In February, 1899, he began actual writing, and from then on worked at it feverishly to the end, although further interruptions prevented him from completing it until late in November. He called this final reckoning with himself, *When We Dead Awaken; A Dramatic Epilogue,* which was immediately interpreted to mean an epilogue to his entire life's work. Ibsen's meaning was somewhat different. He said at first that it was intended as an epilogue to the series of plays that had begun with *A Doll's House;* then he said it could also be called an epilogue to the plays beginning with *The Master Builder.* Its relation to these last three plays is obvious enough; all are stamped with the same process of self-analysis, further emphasized by the use of "we" in the final version of the title and by the use of an artist as the central character who settles accounts with his own art.

Ibsen seems to be deliberately pointing up the identity between himself and the sculptor Rubek. The opening conversation between him and his wife could have been taken directly from life: "Are you happy that you returned home from abroad?" And the answer: "No... to tell you the truth...not really very happy....Perhaps I've been away too long." Despite his world-wide renown, Rubek is not happy; he has created one monumental work of art, and then spent the rest of his life doing portrait busts (which he made to resemble all kinds of animals, as Ibsen had done in his youth). The deeply felt personal note in this whole conversation bears directly on Ibsen's relation to his realistic art and his final parting with it.

In making the main character of his play an artist, Ibsen indicates that he is coming to terms with himself. He had done the same with the poet in *Love's Comedy,* the only other play to have an artist in the central role. But this time the personal point of reference is given almost completely without disguise. "I am an artist, Irene," Professor Rubek says, in extenuation of having used the young woman he loved merely as the raw material for his work of art. Irene's harsh response is simply: "Poet!" And when he asks why she calls him that, she says: "Because you are flabby and insipid and ready to excuse every act of your life and every thought." But she adds, less severely: "There is something apologetic about the word, my friend. Something forgiving, that spreads a cloak over all your weaknesses." He has exploited her soul for the sake of his art, and left her life empty and desolate, a shadow of her self. And the same thing has happened to him; he has pushed life aside, and in so doing has killed his genuine artistic genius. He has longed for something different: "All this business about the artist's calling and the artist's task—everything like that—all began to strike me as empty and hollow and meaningless." For all this he would substitute life itself; but the longing is in vain. Art is, in fact, his life: "I am born to be an artist, you see...and will never be anything but an artist in any case." It is impossible to restore what has been laid waste: "When we dead awaken...what do we really see? We see that we have never lived." Nor ever will. In the struggle between the demands of art and the demands of life there is no solution but death. Only death brings peace.

It appears that Ibsen had not at first intended the play to end in catastrophe. He may have thought of letting Rubek find life on the mountain heights, thus granting him the same grace as that other "poet," Peer Gynt. But his judgment is more severe now; nothing but death for him who has committed what is called "the great mortal sin" in *John Gabriel Borkman*, "the crime for which there is no forgiveness... the sin of murdering the love life of a human being." Rubek is placed between two women, but they meet for the first time during the action of the play, and the struggle that develops is not something out of the past. The struggle is very tenuous, in any case, since Rubek's wife is thoroughly bored with him and runs off with the first virile man who can offer her what she wants of life.

The conflict develops within Rubek himself when Irene, the model for his great sculpture, whom he had not dared to touch, comes and wakens the past to new life. When he rejects her love as useless to him, she lets her life disintegrate until she finally loses her sanity. Now a Sister of Mercy must watch over her at all times. She imagines herself already dead, but the meeting with Rubek brings her back to life. Here Ibsen remembered the words he had written to Brandes about Goethe's having been "favored with the grace" of a new love, and he lets Rubek call Irene "my bride of grace." (The original is "min benådelses brud," which Archer translates as "my grace-given bride.") The noun "benådelse" is an unusual derivative of the adjective "benådet," the word Ibsen used in the letter to Brandes. In both cases the allusion is to the angel's greeting to Mary at the annunciation (Luke 1, 28), in Norwegian "Hil vaere dig, du Benådede!" in the King James version, "Hail, thou who art highly favoured" (but cf. the Latin "gratia plena." *Translators' Note*) But it is too late for love to be realized Ibsen has given her the name Irene, that is, peace, because she is to give Rubek the peace of death. The idea is rather unnecessarily underlined by the Sister of Mercy's cry of "Pax vobiscum" after the two have vanished in the avalanche. The similarity to the end of *Brand* is obvious, but there is less profound significance here, and perhaps even a sense of bathos.

The question of a particular model for Irene is difficult to answer. Laura Kieler was certain that Ibsen had her in mind. She visited him in Oslo and in a long conversation told him the entire tragedy that had led her to an insane asylum. *A Doll's House* had made it even harder for her to bear, she insisted. Later she reported that Ibsen was moved to tears by her story—but her lively imagination must be taken into account. When she asked him to announce publicly that she had not committed the forgery that Nora had to suffer for, he refused. Now *When We Dead Awaken* appeared, she discovered herself in many details, from Irene's dress to lines she speaks. It is not improbable that Ibsen took some characteristics from Mrs. Kieler, but she does not otherwise appear to bear any relation to the essential meaning of Irene or to the charge she makes against the artist. Other women may have influenced the portrait, but in the main Irene is a creature of Ibsen's imagination; one might even call her a dream-woman fabricated by Rubek's poetic imagination. She was necessary to personify the artist's sense of regret over his wasted life, and so she came into being.

This epilogue written for his life's work seemed irreconcilably tragic to Ibsen, and in creating it he brought to perfection the art form he had been evolving in the last few years. He who had once seemed to be the great master of realism in the theatre had now become the foremost poet of symbolism. Of course, his writings had always been symbolic at heart, but in this last creative phase, the symbolism became more and more dominant, particularly so when he turned inward for his material. Then the words of the play had less and less to do with the strife in the outer world; they took on the reverberation of things hidden, things far removed. Everyday words were colored with a vibrant undertone so that one had to ask: Is this life? Is this a dream?

He had turned away from the world outside and now his gaze was directed within. The drama he created was the conflict still raging in his own heart. It was now, as it had always been, "dangerous, dangerous to dream," and to look within. But it was there he found the judgment on his life.

CHAPTER FORTY-SIX

THE LAST YEARS (1900-06)

WHEN WE DEAD AWAKEN represented such a final coming to terms with Ibsen's life and work that it would seem to preclude anything further. But still he wanted to go on writing, although he realized that now he would have to make a radically new departure. In March, 1900, he wrote to Count Prozor: "I do not know if I will write any new plays; but if I can retain the mental and physical strength I now enjoy, I imagine that I will not be able in the long run to keep away from my old battlefields. But then I would appear in new armor, with new weapons."

It is significant that he uses the imagery of warfare in referring to the new work he contemplated; at the same time he made clear that he had given up for good the idea of doing a biography and a study of his earlier work. Whatever the new project would be, he wanted to take the year of rest with which he usually followed the completion of a play. At the end of 1900 he told a reporter that he was at work on "some preparatory studies and works," but a year later he told the same reporter that he had made no further progress: "The work on my next production has so far been only preparatory, and even this has had to be interrupted until my health improves." This is the last time he would speak about his "next production," nor would he ever indicate what it was to have been. He did continue to think about playwriting. At New Year's, 1900, he wrote to Jonas Lie that he thought his new novel could be adapted quite successfully into a popular play, and he worked out an outline for a five-act play based on the novel. But illness put an end to all his plans, and *When We Dead Awaken* remained his last work.

In the spring of 1900 he fell ill, "for the first time in my life," as he wrote to Rosa Fitinghoff. This was not exactly true, although he probably meant that he had never been seriously ill before. He was not confined to bed, but his physician, Dr. Sontum of Grefsen, forbade him "association with pen and ink." He went to Sandefjord Bath in the summer and after three months there felt greatly improved. He called Dr.

461

Sontum his "rescuer." But in spite of the improvement, he had to give up his walks down Carl Johan Street to the Grand Hotel: "I now walk mostly in my neighborhood, the handsome sidewalks out here by Drammensveien," as he characterized them to an interviewer later that year.

In 1901 he suffered his first stroke. In the summer the Oslo newspapers prepared their obituaries, expecting the "catastrophe" momentarily. He recovered, only to experience a second stroke in the spring of 1903 that led to a new crisis. Now his health was so broken that it was only a question of time; he was so weakened that he could not leave the house except in carriage or sleigh. His intellectual faculties had also been impaired, and he suffered from verbal amnesia that made it difficult for him to speak. The writer of this book had a conversation with him in the fall of 1904 after he had assisted in the publication of his letters, during which he involuntarily kept using the wrong words, saying, for example, "lexicon" when he meant "letter." It was obvious that this pained him greatly. His eyes seemed dull, but they did flash into life on two occasions during the conversation, first when I gave him greetings from old German friends of his I had visited recently, and when I mentioned that I knew his sister Hedvig well. Then his eyes suddenly turned a steely blue and shot a lightning glance at me.

One day his son came into his room and found him struggling to print letters on a piece of paper: "Look," said the old man, "look at what I'm doing: I'm learning to write letters—letters—and I was once an author." In February he managed with great difficulty to scratch the single word "Thanks" on a calling card to Dr. Edvard Bull, whom he was then seeing. This is the last word he ever wrote.

In the first years after *When We Dead Awaken* he managed, through interviews, to let his voice be heard on current topics, and his views were clear and firmly stated. While he was working on the play, Bjørnson had launched a vigorous attack on the New Norwegian language movement, and Ibsen gave him his full support. He wanted to protect the works he had so labored to create in the Dano-Norwegian language. "I will not be my own executioner. I will not be that," he said, and even recalled his own attack on the movement as far back as *Peer Gynt*.

His concern for the fate of his works persisted, as did his involvement in the practical aspects of his writing; he continued to manage his own business affairs until 1903. On one of the major international crises, the Boer War, he reiterated his former opinion that the English had as much right to conquer the land of the Boers as the Boers had had to take it from the natives; the lower form of culture had to yield to the higher. Although he was not averse to harsh penalties for crimes and rebellion, he was opposed to all "interference with personal freedom." He still felt that Norwegians were willing to "let themselves be pushed around and treated like under-age children." The idea of a stronger political, economic, and cultural union between the three Scandinavian kingdoms was of vital interest to him, as he asserted in an interview February, 1903, his last public statement.

As death approached he became bedridden, watched over night and day by his wife. One morning he woke from a restful sleep, fully conscious and with clear eyes. "You see," said his wife to the nurse, "the doctor will be well again." Then his body jerked forward, his eyes fixed on some invisible thing in the far distance, and with a vigor that made the others start, cried out one word "Tvertimot!"—on the contrary. The word with which he called on death had in fact summed up his whole life. A few days later, on May 23, 1906, he was dead. He had completed his seventy-eighth year.

His funeral was arranged by the Norwegian state, and in it appeared the same kind of contrasts that had run through his life. The eulogy was spoken by Pastor Christopher Bruun, the man who had once helped to give form to Brand, but the rest of the ceremony was an official tribute to an outstanding member of society, with king, government, parliament, officers, clergy, and even a high functionary who carried Ibsen's decorations on a cushion. Wreaths and condolences from home and abroad came in an endless procession, all under the strict direction of a government master of ceremonies. It was a magnificent occasion.

Alfred Kerr, the German critic, wrote home about the funeral: "The rulers of Norway had a demon in their midst, and they wound up burying a man of position." Ibsen had been and had wanted to be both, but the man of position was the mask. His soul, the true Ibsen, was the demon, the eternally restless, questioning searcher of man's heart, the chastiser and visionary, the poet who could not submit until he had cut a path through to the deepest level of human existence.

In his old age he had asked himself if his writing had in fact the same value as life itself. The answer he found in a greeting sent on his seventieth birthday, more valued than a hundred others because it came from a man who lived in action. Fridtjof Nansen, scientist, explorer, statesman, sent his thanks "to the man who put his stamp on my youth, determined the course of my development, the man who proclaimed the necessity of obeying one's calling and the nobility of the will." Nansen was not the only one who owed that debt of gratitude to Ibsen; generation after generation would say the same. For Ibsen had helped to create a new spirit in the world; he had taken hold of many and had led them toward the new frontier he had discovered in man's search for truth.

Much of his own yearning for happiness was perhaps sacrificed to the demands of the calling that took all his genius and all his life. But he knew it *was* his calling, the only thing that could give meaning to his life. In his creativity he felt, with pain and ecstasy, that life and great deeds grew out of the struggle within; thus his life was transformed into enduring works of art, and in these works his life was made eternal. He was nothing but a poet, and because of this was able to create works that rise in strong, chaste, virile forms, alive with the pulse of his own heart. He gave every moment of his life to his art, and so to every new generation his art reveals a meaning that becomes an integral part of its life. The works testify to what he was, a poet and a man.

REFERENCES

In these notes only those works are mentioned that have served as sources for the contents of the several chapters. The references to all books and periodical articles have been abbreviated to the last name (or in the case of several with the same last name, to the first and last name) of the authors and the dates. In the bibliography that follows these references, all authors are listed alphabetically and contributions by the same author are listed chronologically. Newspaper articles have not been accessible to the translators and have not been reviewed for accuracy of reference, as have books and other articles, and they are therefore not included in the bibliography. All such newspaper articles are, however, to be found in the references where Koht has noted them.

Chapter 1
THE DRAMATIC POET
Translators' Note: On the Pronunciation of Norwegian Names.

Readers who might wish to pronounce Norwegian names with some semblance of authenticity should keep in mind (1) that words of more than one syllable are stressed on the first, unless they are of non-Scandinavian origin, (2) that in stressed syllables the vowels are long before one consonant or none, short before two consonants or more, and (3) that in unstressed syllables the vowels are short, but clearly enunciated (not slurred as in English). The vowels have "continental" values (a = ah, e = eh, i = ee) except that o sounds like oo and u like French u, while y, æ, ø, and å (or aa) stand for sounds roughly like those of German ü; ä, ö, and o, respectively. Consonants also have continental values (r trilled as in Italian, j like English y, w like v) except that k, sk, and g are "soft" (i.e. like ch, sh, and y) before j, i, and y (hence Skien is "shayn" or "sheen"). There are many silent letters, among them h before j and v, d after l and n (hence Brand is "brunn"). For details and further assistance see the introduction to Einar Haugen, Norwegian-English Dictionary (University of Wisconsin Press, 1965).

Chapter 2
FAMILY HERITAGE

On Ibsen's ancestors see Bergwitz 1916 (incomplete and unfortunately not entirely reliable); Plesner 1917; Finne-Grønn 1943; Flood 1933. Cf. also Hauch-Fausbøll, "Henrik Ibsen's Forfædre i Stege," Politiken (Copenhagen), Feb. 8, 1926.

On Knud Ibsen see Mosfjeld 1949, pp. 18-26, 60-92; Schneider 1924, pp. 240-49. There are notes by Rudolf Sokolowski in *Berliner Tageblatt* 1902, March 27 (No. 157, 1. Beiblatt) and by Paulus Hoell in *Varden* (Skien) 1905, No. 111. The letter from Knud Ibsen that is mentioned in the text is printed (not quite exactly) in Bergliot Ibsen 1948, pp. 73-74.

Chapter 3
BOYHOOD IN SKIEN (1828-43)

The chief study is Mosfjeld 1949; see comments by Bull, Koht, and Winsnes in *Edda,* vol. 51 (1951), pp. 81-120.

Individual reminiscences: Henrik Ibsen, *Samlede verker, hundreårsutgave* (Oslo 1930), vol. 15, pp. 365-71 (written in 1881, first printed by Jæger 1888, pp. 6-16); letter from his sister Hedvig Stousland is quoted in the same book by Jæger, p. 5 and 19-22; Hedvig Stousland, in *Varden* (Skien) May 16, 1903; Thalie Ording, b. Cudrio, in *Varden* (Skien) October 16, 1920 (again in *Nationen* (Oslo) November 10, 1921); Daniel Grini in *Nationen* Aug. 4, 1920; Boye Ording in *Fædrelandet* (Oslo) May 22 and June 8, 1878; Karl Haugholt (on Venstøp), in *Politiken* (Copenhagen), September 20, 1924; Gerhard Jynge (on the "flying Dutchman") in *Tidens Tegn,* (Oslo) March 17, 1928. Besides, I have made various notes from conversations with Hedvig Stousland.

Not everything that is told about Ibsen's childhood is equally reliable, e.g. it is very doubtful that he gave pennies to farm boys so they would not accompany him on his way from Venstøp to school in town, as reported by John Paulsen 1913, p. 46.

On the dating of his residence at Snipetorp just before his departure for Grimstad see Koht 1954.

On paintings and drawings by Ibsen see Mohr 1953. Cf. also *Varden* for 1900, No. 264. Reports have appeared in the press in 1932, 1944, and in 1949 that he painted on a trip to Sweden in his youth, but it has always proved to be a different Ibsen.

Nothing has been included in this chapter about the story that first appeared after his death, to the effect that his true father was someone other than Knud Ibsen; the story is in conflict with known facts, see Mosfjeld 1949. Nor is there any factual basis for the supposition that Henrik Ibsen himself or anyone in his day had suspicions of this kind. Anything that has been written about the influence of this on his thinking is therefore entirely baseless.

Translators' Note: The Struggle for Norwegian Intellectual and Cultural Independence in the 1840's.

Norway had been politically united with Denmark, under a common (Danish) king, from 1387 to 1814, when the countries were forcibly separated by the great powers after the Napoleonic wars. By the treaty of Kiel (1813), Norway was given to Sweden as a compensation for the loss of Finland. The Norwegians refused to accept this settlement, to which they were not even parties, and declared their independence on May 17, 1814, when a free constitution was adopted. Under pressure of the great powers, Norwegians accepted a union with Sweden later in the same year, on condition that the constitution be respected and that only external affairs be handled by the Swedish royal authority. This uneasy arrangement persisted until 1905, when the Norwegians achieved full independence.

The first generation after 1814 saw the building up of free institutions and the gradual growth of national spirit. Norwegians were seeking an identity of their own, distinct from that of either Denmark or Sweden, and found it to a great extent in their ancient native traditions and in the country folk. Sagas, folktales, ballads, and folk music were discovered and exploited in the spirit of romanticism. Even so, Norwegian cultural life continued for a long time to be largely dependent on that of the former capital, Copenhagen, where literary, musical, and theatrical activity was highly developed. One reason for this dependence was that the two countries had a common literary language developed during their centuries of union.

Chapter 4
GRIMSTAD (1844-50)

On the dating of Ibsen's departure for Grimstad see Koht 1953. Ibsen's own story of his Grimstad years is printed in the preface to the second edition of *Catiline* (1875), reprinted in *Samlede verker, hundreårsutgave*, vol. 1, pp. 119-24 and vol. 15, pp. 355-60. Cf. the letter he wrote to O. Schulerud's widow June 9, 1870, printed in Sigurd Høst 1927, pp. 288-92.

One of his friends from Grimstad, Chr. Due, published a volume of memoirs in 1909 (based on articles originally published in *Aftenposten* 1904, nos. 560, 574, 588, 602); cf. also his article in *Verdens Gang* 1906, No. 216. Other reminiscences from this period have been printed by H. Terland in *Eidsvold* (Oslo, 1900, no. 233, 235, 238, and in *Medlemsskrift no. 10* of Selskabet for Grimstad Bys Vel (Grimstad, 1930), pp. 17-41; by D. Grønvold in *Grimstad-Posten* October 11, 1909; and by Bendix Ebbell in *Morgenbladet* March 15, 1928. There is less source value in G. Peter Bakke, "Henrik Ibsen i Grimstad," *Oslo Illustrerte* 1928, No. 11, pp. 18-19. Reminiscences by Fru Sophie Tofte, b. Holst, to whom Ibsen wrote his last Grimstad poem, are reported in *Aftenposten* 1906, no. 461.

Eitrem 1940 is built on independent collection of data as well as older writings; see also his 1910 and 1915 articles.

On *Catiline* see Eiliv Skard 1924 and Haugholt 1952.

Chapter 5
LEAVING HOME (April 1850)

On the dating of Ibsen's last stay in Skien see Koht, 1954. See also the letter from Hedvig Stousland to Hanna Stenersen in *A-Magasinet* (Oslo) August 9, 1928 (No. 32, p. 6).

In the paper *Fremskridt* (Skien) March 17, 1928, editor J. Brunsvig published a story he had heard, that in 1859 Ibsen returned to Skien to ask the Paus family for financial aid. This story was later expanded to include a second visit for the same purpose in 1860. These stories are in complete conflict with Ibsen's own statements and those of his nearest kin and cannot be considered historical. In part they are based on a confusion with his visit in 1850. On this point see Koht 1951 and 1954.

Chapter 6
APPRENTICE YEARS IN OSLO (1850-51)

Ibsen has told about his first years in Oslo in the previously mentioned preface to *Catiline* (1875). Some information is available in J. Schulerud, *Verdens Gang* 1910, no. 167 and 168, and in P. Botten Hansen's biography of Ibsen in *Illustreret Nyhedsblad* 1863, no. 29.

On the Literary Society of Studentersamfunnet see Fr. Ording in *Morgenbladet* June 18, 1905 (no. 311). On his journalistic work see Koht 1928 and his article, "Henrik Ibsen i 'Arbeider Foreningernes Blad'", *Arbeiderbladet* (Oslo), March 17, 1928 (no. 77); also Sigmund Skard 1933. On the first edition of *Catiline* see Arthur Thuesen in *Morgenbladet*, April 12, 1950.

On Ibsen's relation to Kierkegaard and J. L. Heiberg see Kihlman 1921. A special investigation of Ibsen and Kierkegaard is la Chesnais 1934; see also Beyer 1924, pp. 114-19, and Erichsen 1923, esp. pp. 252-69 and 323-55.

Chapter 7
AT THE THEATRE IN BERGEN (1851-57)

On Ibsen in Copenhagen see Robert Neiiendam, "Henrik Ibsens første Besøg i Kjøbenhavn 1852," in *Politiken*, Feb. 29, 1928, and *Aftenposten*, June 8, 1929 (No. 282); reprinted with additions in his 1931, pp. 113-32 and with some new additions in his 1950, pp. 87-102.

On Ibsen's life in Bergen, Herman Bang has written in his 1889 article, based on "reminiscences of a woman friend," i.e. told by Henrikke Tresselt, b. Holst ("This article is unreliable from first to last," wrote Ibsen in a letter dated March 13, 1895). A correct retelling by Fru Tresselt is given by Victor Smith in *Lørdagsvelden* (*Abeidsbladets Underholdningsblad*), December 22, 1923 (no. 51). Fru Tresselt told both Herman Bang and John Paulsen (1906, p. 121) that Ibsen appeared at a May 17 celebration in the theatre dressed as a miner and delivered a patriotic speech to the audience. I have not found anything about this in the reports on May 17 celebrations in Bergen during the years Ibsen lived there. I suspect it may be a confusion with the May 17 celebration of 1855 when Fru Louise Brun declaimed a prologue by Ibsen at the theatre, which was followed by a tableau with people in all occupations, each with his own dress.

On Ibsen's theatrical work see Platou 1906, pp. 25-34: Wiesener 1928; John Paulsen, "Ibsens læreaar i Bergen," *Tidens Tegn* August 22, 24, 31, 1918; cf. Paulsen 1906, pp. 54-56, 99-106, 199-205; Bøgh 1949.

Personal reminiscences of Ibsen from his theatre days are found in Blytt 1907; Wolf 1897; H. Wiers-Jensen, "Assisterende forfatter," *Aftenposten* December 24, 1912 (no. 695), based on a story by Marie Bull, b. Midling, Fredrikke Nielsen, b. Jensen, and Peter Blytt; Sophie Monsen, b. Bränberg, "Fra den nationale scenes første dage," *Bergens Tidende*, Jan. 13, 1913.

See also Harald Beyer, "Henrik Ibsen og Bergen," *Bergens Tidende*, March 24, 1928.

Translators' Note: Norwegian and Danish Speech.

Although, as indicated in the Translator's Note to chapter three, Denmark and Norway had a common literary language, pronunciation of this language differed widely in the two countries. Norwegian pronunciation was the more conservative, closer to that of Swedish; Danish, with its extensive changes from Old Scandinavian, could at times be difficult for Norwegians to understand. Nevertheless, Danish actors, using Danish pronunciation, were traditionally preferred on the stage until well after the middle of the nineteenth century. In Ibsen's generation a change occurred, thanks to the agitation of Bjørnson and others, and cultivated Norwegian pronunciation was introduced on the stage to replace the characteristically Danish sounds. The difference was comparable in degree to that between an extreme Oxford pronunciation and a general American pronunciation.

Chapter 8
FROM *SAINT JOHN'S NIGHT* TO *LADY INGER* (1852-54)

On Ibsen and Henrikke Holst, later Fru Tresselt, see Paulsen 1906, pp. 107-27; anonymous (Victor Smith?), in *Aftenposten* March 17, 1928 (no. 142). On *Saint John's Night* see Jæger 1896, vol. 2, pp. 569-70. On "Vandresang" see Alexander Rasmussen in *Aftenposten* July 4, 1911 (no. 436). On *Lady Inger* see Dalgard 1930.

On influence from Shakespeare see Koht 1945.

On the discovery of Ibsen's authorship of *Lady Inger* see Wiers-Jensen's 1912 article cited in the preceding chapter; he must have had it from Peter Blytt, though he appears to have dramatized it somewhat. Paulsen (1900, p. 197) says that the authorship appeared when he was called out after the first performance; but I have found nothing about any such call. Wiers-Jensen's story is supported by a reminiscence of an old actor, O. A. Olsen, who played in *Lady Inger* at Christiania Norwegian Theatre in 1859. He had heard from Bergen how Ibsen had taken Nils Lykke's role from Prom with the words, "You are quite mistaken," and then had read it himself (*Aftenposten*, April 10, 1922, no. 185).

The historical works referred to in connection with *Lady Inger at Østråt* are Carl Ferdinand Allen, ed., *Breve og Aktstykker til Oplysning af Christiern den Andens og Frederik den Førstes Historie* (Copenhagen, vol. 1, 1854); Johan Nikolas Høst, *Danmarks, Norges og Sverrigs Konge* Christian II (Copenhagen, 1854); Frederik Hammerich, *Danmark under Adelsvælden*, vol. 1 (Copenhagen, 1854).

Chapter 9
BALLAD DRAMA (1855-56)

On *The Feast at Solhaug* and *Olaf Liljekrans* it is worth reading what Valfrid Vasenius wrote about these plays in his 1882 book on Ibsen, pp. 71-102. Ibsen himself referred to this book when he recounted the story of the origin of *The Feast at Solhaug* in the 1883 preface to that play (*Samlede verker, hundreårsutgave*, vol.

3, pp. 27-34, and vol. 15, pp. 371-379). See also Paasche 1908.

On The Society of December 22 see Bull 1918.

On the performance of *Olaf Liljekrans* the painter Marcus Grønvold (1925, p. 140) reported that the play was highly successful and that Ibsen was called out; Grønvold claims he was present. But this must be a confusion with *The Feast at Solhaug*.

Chapter 10
SUZANNAH THORESEN. *THE VIKINGS* (1857)

On Fru Ibsen see Dietrichson 1917, vol. 4, pp. 388-99; some of my information comes from oral reports by Fru Dorothea Falsen, b. Thoresen.

On *The Vikings* see Lynner 1909.

Chapter 11
THE NATIONAL MOVEMENT (1857-59)
See Lund 1925; Seip 1914.

Translators' Note: Language Reform.

In 1853 the linguist and poet Ivar Aasen (1813-1896) had published the first specimens of a new Norwegian language which he proposed as a replacement for the Dano-Norwegian literary language then in use (*riksmål*, "Official Language," now called *bokmål*, "Book Language"). He based this language on his researches in Norwegian rural dialects, which he considered to be the proper heirs of the Old Norwegian of the Middle Ages. The new literary language, which came to be known as *landsmål*, "National Language," was a kind of common denominator of the dialects, constructed on the principles of comparative grammar; it was, in effect, a modern version of what Norwegian would have been if Norway had not been united with Denmark. Of the Norwegian writers referred to by Koht, only Arne Garborg, Kristofer Janson, Olav Duun, and A. O. Vinje accepted this language as their medium. Ibsen rejected the language and wrote in *riksmål*, although he was not uninfluenced by *landsmål*. (In Ibsen's time, *bokmål* was spelled almost exactly like Danish, but was given a native pronunciation which has since been adopted as the norm for its spelling.) The problem of acceptance or rejection of *landsmål* (now usually called *nynorsk* or "New Norwegian") became one of the great issues of Norwegian education and politics and is still not resolved. For a detailed account see: Einar Haugen, *Language Conflict and Language Planning: The Case of Modern Norwegian* (Harvard University Press, 1966).

Chapter 12
A MIND DIVIDED (1858-62)

On Ibsen's "Dutchmen" friends see Ording 1927; Daae 1888.

The statement made by Fru Ibsen after the birth of her son Sigurd was told me by Fru Karoline Bjørnson, who heard her say it; she was living in the same building at the time.

The date of "Terje Vigen" given to J. B. Halvorsen by Ibsen is "near the end of 1860"; but this must be a slip of memory. There can be little doubt that the poem is later than "I Havsnød," which was printed in May 1861, with a special notation to the effect that it was written in March of that year. It contains numerous expressions which clearly point forward to "Terje Vigen."

On the illness which at one time in his Oslo years nearly drove Ibsen to suicide, both Suzannah Ibsen and L. Dietrichson spoke to Julius Elias in 1906 after Ibsen's death (see Elias 1906). Ibsen himself said once that he had never been ill, so one may at least suppose that it was very seldom. For this reason I have assumed that it would be correct to attribute this story to the only instance of illness that is documented in this period. I refer to a notice in *Aftenbladet* for December 5, 1861, which reports "many illnesses" at the Norwegian Theatre in Oslo and adds that "the artistic director is also ill and cannot take care of the affairs of the theatre."

On the historical basis for the poem "Terje Vigen" there was a great controversy in the newspapers in 1906 when a monument was to be raised for Terje on his grave in Fjære churchyard. A whole series of testimonials was then presented, by Sigurd Ibsen, L. Dietrichson, Chr. Due, and Thv. Dannevig, to the effect that Ibsen had clearly stated that no single person or event was the model for his poem.

Translators' Note: Knud Knudsen.

Knud Knudsen (1812-1895) was an educator who agitated tirelessly for the "Norwegianization" of the common Dano-Norwegian literary language as an alternative solution to the proposed all-Norwegian *landsmål* of Ivar Aasen. He wished to change the essentially Danish spelling of the language to one that corresponded to Norwegian pronunciation and at the same time he tried to introduce native replacements for the more Germanized vocabulary of Danish. His principles were to a great extent adopted in the successive spelling reforms of Dano-Norwegian of 1907, 1917, and 1938. Ibsen did not adopt Knudsen's spelling nor his neologisms, but he did favor a very gradual Norwegianization of the language; Bjørnson held more radical views in these respects.

Chapter 13
IN SEARCH OF FOLKLORE (1862)

See K. Visted, "Da Henrik Ibsen samlet folkesagn," *Aftenposten* January 31, 1931 (no. 55 and 57). Reminiscences of his trip in Sunnmøre are told in *Aalesunds Avis,* August 29, 1924; by Barman 1904, pp. 49-50; and by his son in the paper *Glommen* (Sarpsborg), September 20, 1924.

Chapter 14
THE ANGRY POET: *LOVE'S COMEDY* (1862)

See Bull 1931, pp. 211-42; also his introduction to *Kærlighedens komedie* in Ibsen's *Samlede verker, hundreårsutgave,* vol. 4 (1930). Other references are Møller 1888; Bing 1907; Else Høst 1941.

Chapter 15
FAITH AND DOUBT: *THE PRETENDERS* (1863)

See Freihow 1951; W. Vogt 1924; Koht 1950; Jonas Jansen, "Historie og dikt-ning," *Morgenbladet* November 12 and 19, 1938. Carsten Hauch's opinions about *Lady Inger* and *The Pretenders* were printed in *Gads Danske Magasin*, 1910-11, pp. 276-77.

Chapter 16
THE GREAT DISILLUSIONMENT (1863-64)

[No references]

Chapter 17
THE FIRST YEAR IN ROME (1864-65)

On Ibsen in Rome see especially L. Dietrichson 1896, volume I, pp. 317-46; cf. volume III (1901), p. 126. Dietrichson read the pertinent section of volume I aloud to Ibsen before printing it and corrected a few things on the basis of Ibsen's comments. See also Bull 1931, pp. 280-87, and Faaland 1943, pp. 126-48.

On Ibsen in the Scandinavian Society see Øyvind Anker in *Morgenbladet,* August 6, 1953.

Edmund Gosse 1911, pp. 174-75, reports a conversation with Professor Molbech, in which the latter said that in 1865 Ibsen and Bjørnson were constantly engaged in quarrels in Rome. Since the two of them were never in Rome together, the whole story is pure fantasy.

Chapter 18
BRAND (1865)

Brand has probably received more extensive comment than any other Ibsen play; only publications specially devoted to the play will be listed here: G. Schneider 1908; van Dijk 1913; Klein 1914; Bing 1919; la Chesnais 1933; Freihow 1936 (comments by Berggrav and Bull, 1937). See also Eitrem 1908, Kinck 1930, Sigurd Høst 1931, Haakonsen 1941, Else Høst 1941, Janzén 1954.

Ibsen himself approved A. von Wolzogen's interpretation in the introduction to his German translation: "In der . . . Vorrede finde ich über 'Brand' alles ausgesprochen, was überhaupt zum richtigen Verständnis der Dichtung notwendig ist... Die Tendenz des Gedichtes habe ich nie vorher so durchsichtig dargestellt gesehen (*Samlede verker, hundreårsutgave,* vol. 19, p. 249).

On the influence of Paludan-Müller see Eitrem 1912-13. Svensson's 1930 attempt to demonstrate influence by Tegnér was quite properly rejected by Marcus 1930. On *Brand's* influence in Sweden see Böök 1929.

Problems connected with the 1907 Larsen edition of the epic *Brand* were the subject of a polemic between Brix 1908, Eitrem (*Morgenbladet,* Oslo, 1908, no. 63 and 69; *Verdens Gang* 1908, no. 44, 46, 47), Drachmann 1908, Koht 1908. The ms. had come to the Royal Library in Copenhagen in 1903 from the late Danish collector Andreas Pontoppidan; his story of the manner of its acquisition cannot have been correct, as was shown by statements made in the press after its appearance. Ibsen had deposited it with other papers in the archives of the Scandinavian Society in Rome in 1868 and could not find it when he returned in 1878. Much later, when the archives were cleared out, Pontoppidan must have come across it and taken it with him.

A French translation of the narrative *Brand* by P. G. la Chesnais, with a literary introduction, appeared in the *Mercure de France* in 1909.

Chapter 19
TRIUMPH (1866)

[No references]

Chapter 20
IBSEN AND NORWAY

[No references]

Chapter 21
STRUGGLE AND CRISIS (1866)

On Ibsen's life in Rome during this year see especially Knudtzon 1927 and Janson 1913, pp. 71-77.

Chapter 22
PEER THE NORWEGIAN (1867)

For reminiscences of Ibsen during his work on *Peer Gynt* see Bergsøe 1907.

Books on the play are Logeman 1917, Beyer 1928, Bull 1947, Nilsen 1948. Other essays: Christian Collin, introduction to the 17th edition of the play (Copenhagen, 1917, pp. vii-xliv); Collin 1906; Bergsgård 1915; Eitrem 1906, 1912-13, 1920; Stavnem 1908; Anstensen 1930; Andrews 1914, 1916, 1917; Lidén 1940; Svendsen 1922; Zucker 1942; A. Ljono, "Omkring dårekistescenen i 'Peer Gynt,'" *Morgenbladet,* August 9, 1948.

For information on the historical Peer Gynt, aside from Asbjørnsen's version, see Aasmundstad 1903; Kleiven 1930, pp. 320-27; Kluften 1930, also in *Arbeider-Magasinet* 1937, no. 46-49; cf. Egil Hartmann in *Morgenbladet* 1901, June 1 (no. 340), Hallvard Sand Bakken, "Var Peer Gynt i virkeligheten en adelig tysker?", *Aftenposten* July 5, 1930 (no. 338), and Pål Kluften, *ibid.,* July 19 (no. 364). On a Swedish Peder Gynt, farm owner and miner in Klingsbo, Dalecarlia, named in a series of documents 1476-1491, see *Diplomatarium Dalecarlicum,* I-III. On the name "Gynt" see Ross 1895, s.v. On the Boyg see Liestøl 1927.

[The following paragraph appears in the text in the 1954 edition. Translators' Note.]

A poem by Jonas Lie entitled "Solveig is Watching" appeared in *Illustreret Nyhedsblad* August 3, 1862, immediately after Ibsen's return from collecting folklore. Solveig sings the song while waiting for her lover, a sailor who actually has been shipwrecked and drowned:

Den Solveig har kaaren,	Whom Solveig has chosen,
Han kommer i Sommer	he'll be coming this summer,
Med guldstævnet Hærskib i Vik.	with gold-prowed warships in the bay.

The poem is a poor one, which Ibsen no doubt quickly forgot; but a name and an idea may have stuck in his memory long enough to come to the surface four or five years later.

Chapter 23
THE AFTERMATH (1867-68)

[No references]

Chapter 24
POLITICS: *THE LEAGUE OF YOUTH* (1868-69)

On Herman Bagger as the model of Stensgaard see the Henrik Ibsen issue published by *Fremskridt* (Skien), 1928, p. 12 [by J. Brunsvig] and the pamphlet by J. Brunsvig (1952), pp. 14-33. On printer N. F. Axelsen as the model of Aslaksen see H. Koht in *Glommen* (Sarpsborg), September 19, 1928 (No. 220), p. 4, and Bjarne Nygård 1943. See also Henrik Ibsen, *Efterladte skrifter* (1909) I, p. LXXIII ff.

Chapter 25
IN FINE COMPANY (1869-70)

The judgments of Carsten Hauch on *The League of Youth* are printed in *Gads Danske Magasin*, 1910-11, p. 278.

Chapter 26
THE CALL FOR FREEDOM (1870-71)

[No references]

Chapter 27
A GATHERING OF POEMS (1871)

On Ibsen's revision of his older poems see Koht 1908. See also Haakonsen 1950; Iversen 1937.

Chapter 28
THE THIRD EMPIRE: *EMPEROR AND GALILEAN* (1871-73)

On the historical sources of this play see Paulus Svendsen 1933 and 1937 (in the last an assumption of la Chesnais 1928 is disproved); la Chesnais 1937 and in his translation of Ibsen, volume 10, pp. 593-640. See also E. Strömberg 1902, pp. 63-66.

The comparison between Julian in history and literature is made by William Archer in Ibsen, *Collected Works,* volume 5 (1907), pp. XXVII-XXXI. On the historical philosophy of the play see Koppang 1943, pp. 177-97 and Möhring 1928; also Koht 1916.

Chapter 29
POWER AND GLORY (1873-77)

On the doctor's degree at Uppsala: Annie Wall 1926, p. 52, tells a story she says she heard from Bjørnson in 1903 to the effect that the University of Uppsala had intended to confer the degree both on Bjørnson and Ibsen, but that Ibsen refused to accept if Bjørnson were also to receive it. I have found no confirmation of this story.

Chapter 30
A CORPSE ON BOARD: *PILLARS OF SOCIETY* (1875-77)

On Ibsen in Dresden see *Dresdner Anzeiger* 1906, June 1. In *Edda,* vol. 43 (1943), pp. 56-57 it is said (by John Paulsen) that Ibsen left Dresden because he was excluded from Literarische Gesellschaft. This could only have occurred in 1871, and since Ibsen did not leave until 1875, the story is obviously false.

On Ibsen in Munich in 1875 see Dietrichson 1899, vol. 1, pp. 357-59 and Marcus Grønvold 1925, pp. 137-45; cf. John Paulsen 1906, pp. 151-53 and 166-67.

On *Pillars of Society* see Gunnar Høst 1946. It is worth mentioning that Ibsen regarded the play as best interpreted by Nordahl Rolfsen in *Bergensposten* 1877, Nos. 246, 248, 250, 256.

Chapter 31
WOMEN AND SOCIETY: *A DOLL'S HOUSE* (1878-79)

On *A Doll's House* see Else Høst 1946. On Ibsen and Laura Kieler see B. M. Kinck 1935; cf. John Paulsen 1913, pp. 141-43 (which is not correct in detail) and 1901, pp. 130-33. On Ibsen in Rome 1879 see Gunnar Heiberg in *Aftenposten* 1911, Nos. 217, 237, and 250.

Chapter 32
PHANTOMS FROM THE PAST: *GHOSTS* (1880-81)

On Ibsen in Berchtesgaden 1880 see John Paulsen 1913. See also Erik Lie 1928, pp. 43-69. On Ibsen in Rome 1880-81 see Georg Pauli 1924, pp. 108-19; cf. letter from William Archer in *Edda,* vol. 31 (1931), pp. 460-64.

Chapter 33
A PUBLIC ENEMY (1882)

See Pauli 1924 and Archer 1931; also Janson 1913, pp. 77-80; Dietrichson 1899, vol. 1, pp. 361-65; Erik Lie 1908, pp. 254-56. A report on the meeting with Harald Thaulow is in Ibsen, *Efterladte skrifter*, vol. 1, pp. xcvii-xcix.

Chapter 34
PITY AND CONTEMPT: *THE WILD DUCK* (1882-84)

See Tennant 1934 and Wyller 1936. The only contemporary, as far as this writer can see, who realized Ibsen's self-reckoning in the two characters Gregers Werle and Hjalmar Ekdal in *The Wild Duck* was the Danish author Herman Bang. See his lecture given in Göteborg on 21 February, 1885, cited in *Göteborgs Handels- och Sjöfarts-Tidning* for that year, No. 44 (reprinted in *Bergens Tidende,* same year, no. 52).

Chapter 35
AT ODDS WITH NORWAY (1884-86)

On Ibsen's stay at Molde 1885 see Per Andersen 1952 and Tveterås 1933. On the conflict with L. Dietrichson and The Norwegian Student Society see Wallem 1916, pp. 840-65; cf. Bredo Morgenstierne in *Aftenposten* Nov. 12, 1916 (No. 587) and L. Dietrichson vol. 4 (1917), pp. 287-94. On Ibsen in Copenhagen, October 1885, see R. B. Anderson 1915, pp. 484-86. On Ibsen in Munich after 1885 see Felix Philippi in *Neue Freie Presse* Oct. 27, 1902 (No. 13713); *Aftonbladet* 1887, No. 8 and 9; M. G. Conrad in *Lothar* 1902, pp. 121-30; Irgens Hansen in *Dagbladet* 1888, No. 86; Gerhard Schjelderup in *Morgenbladet* 1906, No. 91.

Chapter 36
A CONFLICT OF CONSCIENCE: *ROSMERSHOLM* (1885-86)

Felix Philippi has quoted remarks made by Ibsen to him in the year 1886 in "Mein Verkehr mit Henrik Ibsen," in *Neue Freie Presse* (Vienna), October 27, 1902 (No. 13713). The letter from Snoilsky to Ibsen April 4, 1886, is printed by Francis Bull in *Göteborgs Handels- och Sjöfarts-Tidning,* September 22, 1949.

Chapter 37
THE SHACKLED WILL: *THE LADY FROM THE SEA* (1887-88)

On Ibsen in Sæby in the summer of 1887 see Fr. Ording in *Verdens Gang* 1909, No. 165 and 172; Aage Barthold Vaslev in *Aftenposten* June 1, 1940 (No. 263); *Aftenposten* September 9, 1906 (No. 529); *Magasinet Politiken,* March 11, 1928. "*The Lady from the Sea,*" says Ragnar Vogt 1930, p. 75, "is an excellent demonstration of a psychoanalytic cure." Ibsen regarded a series of articles in *Aftenposten* in December 1888, by A. Sinding-Larsen, as having analyzed the characters very well, and they were therefore published separately in 1889.

Chapter 38
REPRESSED DESIRES: *HEDDA GABLER* (1889-90)

On Emilie Bardach see her article, "Meine Freundschaft mit Ibsen," in *Neue Freie Presse*, March 31, 1907 (No. 15304), tr. in *Verdens Gang*, April 3, 1907. Her letters to Ibsen are printed in Ibsen's *Samlede verker*, vol. 19, pp. 531-33; they are in the papers of Dr. Julius Elias at Universitetsbiblioteket, Oslo. Excerpts from her diary in Gossensass are printed by Basil King in *The Century Magazine* 1923.

On *Hedda Gabler* see among others Ingjald Nissen 1931, pp. 142-83. Ragnar Vogt 1930, p. 76, says "*Hedda Gabler* describes what the Freudians call narcissism with frigidity and sadism."

When Helene Raff died at the age of 77 in Munich in 1942, she left behind a diary which is now in Bayerische Staatsbibliothek, Munich, from which I have borrowed. This diary contains only jottings for each day. The separate *Ibsen-Tagebuch* for 1889-91 she probably burned before her death. She printed undated excerpts from it in *Tägliche Rundschau* (Berlin, 1906); a few dated excerpts are in Dr. Elias's papers in Oslo, and there are also some letters from her about Ibsen. The letter from Ibsen which is mentioned in the text on page 394 is dated "Freitag Abend spät." She told Dr. Elias in 1904 that this was September 30, 1889, but since this was not a Friday and since Ibsen was still in Gossensass on that day, I changed the date to October 4 and it was so printed in the centennial edition of Ibsen, vol. 18, p. 221. But her diaries prove that the correct date was really November 29, 1889 and so the letter has an entirely different background and a new meaning.

Chapter 39
CONTROVERSY AND FAME (1886-91)

On Ibsen in Meiningen 1886 see Paul Lindau 1917, vol. 2, pp. 373-75 and 376-77. On *Ghosts* in Berlin see Hoffory 1888. Other references on Ibsen in Germany are Irgens Hansen, *Dagbladet* 1888, Nos. 86, 88, 92, 95; Otto Brahm, *Neue Freie Presse* May 10, 1904 (No. 14263); Stein 1901; [for a survey see Eller 1918]. The rehearsal of *Rosmersholm* in Augsburg, April 6, 1887 is here described according to Dr. Julius Elias in *Der Tag*, June 22, 1906 (No. 311); a little differently by Gerhard Schjelderup in *Morgenbladet* 1906, No. 91.

On Ibsen in England and America see Ibsen, *Speeches and New Letters* (1910), pp. 121-202; Quamme 1942; Decker 1952, pp. 115-30; Haugen 1935; Carl Norman in *Verdens Gang*, March 14, 1953; [for surveys and bibliography see Franc 1919 and Annette Andersen 1937].

Chapter 40
FAREWELL TO GERMANY (1891)

On the conflict with Martin Greif on March 12, 1891 see M. G. Conrad in *Lothar* 1902, pp. 129-30, reprinted in Norwegian translation from *Dagbladet* May 28, 1906, in Ibsen, *Samlede verker*, vol. 19, pp. 187-89. In *Samlede verker*, vol. 20, p. 231, is reproduced (from *Der Bücherfreund*, March 1928) a portrait of Ibsen drawn by Emil Orli, dated in the caption Marienbad 25. VI. 1891. But Ibsen was never in Marienbad, and in fact it says on the drawing: "Maximstr. [i.e. Maximilianstrasse] München."

Chapter 41
HOME AGAIN (1891)

Herman Bang's account of Ibsen at his lecture in 1891 is told in Bang 1906, pp. 239-40. On the celebration at Grand Hotel on August 16, 1891, see Georg Brandes 1906, pp. 219-21. On Ibsen in Andvake etc. see Bredo Morgenstierne in *Aftenposten*, Nov. 12 (No. 587); excerpts in Dietrichson 1917 (vol. 4), pp. 289ff. On Ibsen as a model see Erik Werenskiold in *Dagbladet*, March 20, 1928. On Ibsen and the Norwegian Authors' Society see Dietrichson 1917 (vol. 4), pp. 416-17; and Brochmann 1952, pp. 27-33. On Ibsen's daily outdoor life in Oslo see *Lørdagsavisen*, March 18 and 25, 1933, with drawings by Gustav Lærum.

Chapter 42
THE CRISIS OF AGE: *THE MASTER BUILDER* (1891-92)

See Didrik Arup Seip, introduction to *Bygmester Solness* in *Samlede verker*, vol. 12 (1935); Neumann 1923. On Ibsen and Nietzsche see Aall 1906; Winsnes 1946; Pavel Fraenkl in *Aftenposten*, June 18, 1947. On the morality of self-assertion see Høffding 1899, vol. 1, 191-93.

Chapter 43
ASSESSING LIFE: *LITTLE EYOLF* AND
JOHN GABRIEL BORKMAN (1893-96)

[No references]

Chapter 44
AT SEVENTY (1898)

On the celebration in Copenhagen see Nils Vogt 1906 and Peter Nansen in *Aftenposten* 1917, Nos. 114, 119, and 127. Lange 1900 is a parodic description; cf. Thomas P. Krag in *Politiken*, Nov. 23, 1900. Høffding's speech in The Student Society is printed in Høffding 1905, pp. 213-16. On the celebration in Stockholm see Wall 1926, pp. 144-48.

Chapter 45
EPILOGUE: *WHEN WE DEAD AWAKEN* (1899)
[No references]

Chapter 46
THE LAST YEARS (1900-06)

On Ibsen's last years see *Aftenposten*, March 14, 1928 (No. 135), p. 8; *Morgenbladet*, May 23, 1931 (No. 158). Newspaper interviews from this period are collected in *Samlede verker*, vol. 19.

AALL, ANATHON. "Ibsen og Nietzsche." *Samtiden,* vol. 17 (1906), pp. 146-63, 279-300.

AASMUNDSTAD, PER. "Segn og historie om Peer Gynt, omfram Asbjørnsens Huldre-eventyr." *Syn og Segn,* vol. 9 (1903), pp. 119-30.

AGERHOLM, EDVARD. "Henrik Ibsen og det kgl. teater, blade af censurens historie." *Gads Danske Magasin,* 1910-1911, pp. 276-80.

ANDERSEN, ANNETTE. "Ibsen in America." *Scandinavian Studies and Notes,* vol. 14 (1937), pp. 65-109, 115-55.

ANDERSEN, PER. "Ibsen og Molde." *Edda,* vol. 52 (1952), pp. 261-72.

ANDERSON, RASMUS BJØRN. *Life Story.* Madison, Wisconsin, 1915.

ANDREWS, ALBERT LEROY. "Ibsen's Peer Gynt and Goethe's Faust." *The Journal of English and Germanic Philology,* vol. 13 (1914), pp. 238-46.

——————. "Further influences upon Ibsen's Peer Gynt." *The Journal of English and Germanic Philology,* vol. 15 (1916), pp. 51-55, and vol. 16 (1917), pp. 67-69.

ANSTENSEN, ANSTEN. "Notes on the text of Ibsen's 'Peer Gynt.'" *The Journal of English and Germanic Philology,* vol. 29 (1930), pp. 53-73.

ARCHER, WILLIAM. "Ibseniana." *Edda,* vol. 31 (1931), pp. 455-64.

BANG, HERMAN. "Lidt om Henrik Ibsen som Ung (En Venindes Erindringer)." *Af Dagens Krønike,* vol. 1 (1889), pp. 340-44.

——————. "Personlige Erindringer om Henrik Ibsen." *Det ny Aarhundrede,* vol. 3, part 2 (1906), pp. 237-42, 325-30.

BARMAN, OLE O. *Erindringer fra 1861 til 1867.* Trondhjem, 1904.

BERGGRAV, EIVIND, AND BULL, FRANCIS. *Ibsens sjelelige krise. Brand. Bruun. Innlegg ved doktordisputas.* Oslo: Gyldendal, 1937.

BERGSGARD, ARNE. "Kring Solvejg og Peer Gynt." *Syn og Segn,* vol. 21 (1915), pp. 49-65.

BERGSØE, VILHELM. *Henrik Ibsen paa Ischia og "Fra Piazza del Popolo": Erindringer fra Aarene 1863-69.* Copenhagen: Gyldendal, 1907.

BERGWITZ, JOHAN KIELLAND. *Henrik Ibsen i sin afstamning. Norsk eller fremmed?* Kristiania: Gyldendal, 1916.

BEYER, HARALD. *Søren Kierkegaard i Norge.* Kristiania, 1924.

——————. *Henrik Ibsens Peer Gynt.* Oslo, 1928 (Det Norske studentersamfunds folkeskrifter, 14).

BING, JUST. "Henrik Ibsens Ungdomsudvikling." *Tilskueren,* 1907, pp. 934-43. (Repr. in *Festskrift til William Nygaard,* Kristiania 1913, pp. 106-19.)

——————. *Henrik Ibsens Brand, en kritisk studie.* Kristiania: Steenske Forlag, [1919].

BLYTT, PETER. *Minder fra den første norske Scene i Bergen i 1850-Aarene. Et kulturhistorisk Forsøg.* Bergen, 1907.

BØGH, GRAN. *Henrik Ibsen på Ole Bulls teater. Tekst til to tegninger.* Bergen, 1949.

Böök, Fredrik. *Svenska litteraturens historia,* ed. by Otto Sylwan. Vol. III. Stockholm: P. A. Norstedt och Söner, 1929.

Brandes, Georg. "Henrik Ibsen." *Det ny Aarhundrede,* vol. 3, part 2 (1906), pp. 208-26.

Brix, Hans. "Henrik Ibsens episke Brand og Prof. Karl Larsen." *Det ny Aarhundrede,* vol. 5 (1908), pp. 308-14.

——————. "Om Grundformen af 'Brand.'" *Det ny Aarhundrede,* vol. 5 (1908), pp. 396-404.

Brochmann, Georg. *Den Norske Forfatterforening gjennom 50 år. Et bidrag til norsk åndslivs historie.* Oslo: De Norske forlegger-forening, 1952.

Brunsvig, Joseph. *Henrik Ibsens barndom og ungdom og fødebyen i hans diktning.* Skien, 1952.

Bull, Francis. "Fra Ibsens og Bjørnsons ungdomsaar i Bergen—'Foreningen af 22. December.'" *Edda,* vol. 10 (1918), pp. 159-64.

——————. *Studier og streiftog i norsk litteratur.* Oslo: Gyldendal, 1931.

——————. *Henrik Ibsens Peer Gynt, diktningens tilblivelse og grunntanker.* Oslo: Gyldendal, 1947.

——————. "Henrik Ibsen og Skien." *Edda,* vol. 51 (1951), pp. 81-105.

Collin, Christen. "Henrik Ibsens fremtidstdrøm." *Samtiden,* 1906, pp. 385-96, 481-96.

——————. "Dengang Ibsen skrev Peer Gynt." (Introduction to) Henrik Ibsen: *Peer Gynt, jubilæumsutgave.* Copenhagen: Gyldendal, 1917.

Daae, Ludvig. "Paul Botten Hansen." *Vidar,* 1888, pp. 307-357.

Dalgard, Olav. "Studiar over Fru Inger til Østerraad." *Edda,* vol. 30 (1930), pp. 1-47.

Decker, Clarence R. *The Victorian Conscience.* New York: Twayne, 1952.

Dietrichson, Lorentz. *Svundne Tider.* 4 vols. Christiania: Cappelen, 1899-1917.

Diplomatarium Dalecarlicum, ed. Carl Gustaf Krøningssväard and Johan Lidén. 3 vols. Stockholm, 1842-46.

Drachmann, Anders Bjørn. "Til Ibsens episke Brand." *Nordisk Tidskrift,* 1908, pp. 274-86.

Due, Christopher. *Erindringer fra Henrik Ibsens Ungdomsaar.* Copenhagen, 1909.

Eitrem, Hans. "Mystifikationer i Peer Gynt." *Samtiden,* vol. 17 (1906) pp. 591-98.

——————. "Ibsens Gjennembrud." *Samtiden,* vol. 19 (1908), pp. 569-80, 617-38.

——————. "Henrik Ibsen—Henrik Wergeland." *Maal og Minne,* 1910, pp. 37-48.

——————. "Nogen av de danske forudsætninger for Brand og Peer Gynt: Paludan-Müller og Henrik Ibsen." *Gads Danske Magasin,* 1912-13, pp. 455-62.

——————. "Henrik Ibsen Stellanea." *Edda,* vol. 3 (1915), pp. 68-92.

——————. "Den fremmede passager i 'Peer Gynt.'" *Edda,* vol. 14 (1920), pp. 272-75.

——————. *Ibsen og Grimstad.* Oslo: Aschehoug, 1940.

Elias, Julius. "Christiania-Fahrt." *Die Neue Rundschau,* vol. 17 (1906), pp. 1455-67.

Eller, William Henri. *Ibsen in Germany, 1870-1900.* Boston, 1918.

Erichsen, Valborg. "Søren Kierkegaards betydning for norsk aandsliv." *Edda,* vol. 19 (1923), pp. 209-429.

Faaland, Josef. *Henrik Ibsen og antikken.* Oslo: Tanum, 1943.

FINNE-GRØNN, STIAN HERLOFSEN. *Slekten Paus, dens oprinnelse og 4 første generasjoner*. Oslo: Cammermeyer, 1943.

FLOOD, INGEBORG. "Rådmann Knud Pedersen Hind, Henrik Ibsens tipp-tipp-oldefar." *Ibsen-årbok*, 1953, pp. 82-94.

FRANC, MIRIAM ALICE. *Ibsen in England*. Boston, 1919.

FREIHOW, HALVDAN WEXELSEN. "Henrik Ibsens 'Brand,' litterær-psykologisk studie." *Skrifter utgitt av Det Norske Videnskaps-Akademi i Oslo*, II. Hist.-Filos. Klasse, 1936, No. 2. Oslo, 1936.

————————. *Ibsen-studium um Kongsemnerne*. Oslo: Gyldendal, 1951.

GOSSE, EDMUND. *Ibsen*. London: Hodder and Stoughton, 1907.

————————. *Two Visits to Denmark: 1872, 1874*. London: Smith, Elder and Co., 1911.

GRØNVOLD, MARCUS. *Fra Ulrikken til Alperne. En malers erindringer*. Oslo: Gyldendal, 1925.

HAAKONSEN, DANIEL. "Henrik Ibsens 'Brand.'" *Edda*, vol. 41 (1941), pp. 350-78.

————————. "Henrik Ibsens lyrikk." *Edda*, vol. 50 (1950), pp. 135-53.

HAUGEN, EINAR. "Ibsen i Amerika, en ukjent førsteopførelse og et Ibsenbrev." *Edda*, vol. 35 (1935), pp. 553-59 (also in English in *Journal of English and Germanic Philology*, vol. 33 (1934), pp. 396-420.)

HAUGHOLT, KARL. "Samtidens kritikk av Ibsens 'Catilina'." *Edda*, vol. 52 (1952), pp. 74-94.

HØFFDING, HARALD. *Mindre Arbeider*. Copenhagen: Det nordiske forlag, 1899.

————————. *Mindre Arbeider. Anden Række*. Copenhagen: Gyldendal, 1905.

HØST, ELSE. "Ibsens lyriske dramaer." *Edda*, vol. 41 (1941), pp. 379-406.

————————. "Nora." *Edda*, vol. 46 (1946), pp. 13-28.

HØST, GUNNAR. "Ibsens samfundsstøtter." *Edda*, vol. 46 (1946), pp. 1-12.

HØST, SIGURD. *Ibsens diktning og Ibsen selv*. Oslo: Gyldendal, 1927.

————————. "Mere Brand." *Edda*, vol. 31 (1931), pp. 102-5.

HOFFORY, JULIUS. "Henrik Ibsen i Berlin." *Tilskueren*, vol. 5 (1888), pp. 61-70.

IBSEN, BERGLIOT. *De tre. Erindringer om Henrik Ibsen, Suzannah Ibsen, Sigurd Ibsen*. Oslo: Gyldendal, 1948.

IBSEN, HENRIK. *Brand*, tr. by Alfred von Wolzogen. Wismar, 1877.

————————. *Collected Works*, ed. by William Archer. 12 vols. London: Heineman, 1906-1911.

————————. *Episke Brand*, ed. by Karl Larsen. Copenhagen and Kristiania: Gyldendal, 1907.

————————. *Efterladte skrifter*, ed. by Halvdan Koht and Julius Elias. 3 vols. Kristiania and Copenhagen: Gyldendal, 1909.

————————. *Speeches and New Letters*, tr. by Arne Kildal. Boston: Richard G. Badger, 1910.

————————. *OEuvres complètes*, tr. by Pierre Georget la Chesnais. 16 vols. Paris: Librairie Plon, 1918-45.

————————. *Samlede verker, hundreårsutgave*, ed. by Francis Bull, Halvdan Koht, and Didrik Arup Seip. Oslo: Gyldendal, 1928-58.

IVERSEN, RAGNVALD. "De viktigste metaforene i Henrik Ibsens 'Digte' (1875)." *Edda*, vol. 37 (1937), pp. 508-524.

JAEGER, HENRIK. *Henrik Ibsen 1828-1888, et literært livsbillede*. Copenhagen: Gyldendal, 1888.

——————. *Illustreret norsk literaturhistorie.* 3 vols. Kristiania: Hjalmar Biglers forlag, 1896.

JANSON, KRISTOFER. *Hvad jeg har oplevet, livserindringer.* Kristiania: Gyldendal, 1913.

JANZEN, ASSAR. "Ibsens Brand—en självuppgörelse." *Göteborgsstudier i litteraturhistoria tillägnade Sverker Ek.* (Göteborg, 1954), pp. 105-24.

KIHLMAN, ERIK. *Ur Ibsen-dramatikens idéhistoria, en studie i dansk-norsk litteratur.* Helsingfors: Söderström och Co., 1921.

KINCK, B. M. "Dramaet 'Brand', opfatninger og tolkninger." *Edda,* vol. 30 (1930), pp. 81-95.

——————. "Henrik Ibsen og Laura Kieler." *Edda,* vol. 35 (1935), pp. 498-543. (also in English in *London Mercury,* Nov. 1937, pp. 12-15.)

KING, BASIL. "Ibsen and Emilie Bardach." *The Century Magazine,* vol. 106 (1923), pp. 803-815; vol. 107 (1923), pp. 83-92.

KLEIN, PAUL. *Ibsens Brand. Die Tragödie eines christlichen Idealisten.* Mannheim: Haas, 1914.

KLEIVEN, IVAR. *Fronsbygdin.* Oslo: Aschehoug, 1930.

KLUFTEN, PAL. "Per Gynt." *Edda,* vol. 30 (1930), pp. 120-128.

KNUDTZON, FREDERIK GOTSCHALK. *Ungdomsdage,* ed. by Julius Clausen. Copenhagen: Gyldendal, 1927.

KOHT, HALVDAN. "Henrik Ibsens digt 'Till de medskyldige.'" *Nordisk Tidskrift,* 1908, pp. 422-32.

——————. "Skapinga, menneska og det tredje rike." *Festskrift til Gerhard Gran, 1916.* (Repr. in Koht, Halvdan, *På leit etter liner i historia; utvalde avhandlingar utg. til åtti-års-dagen hans.* Oslo: Aschehoug, 1953. pp. 124-35.)

——————. "Henrik Ibsen i 'Manden.'" *Avhandlinger utg. av Det Norske Videnskaps-Akademi i Oslo,* II. Hist.-Filos. Klasse, 1928, No. 1. Oslo, 1928.

——————. "Shakespeare and Ibsen." *The Journal of English and Germanic Philology,* vol. 44 (1945), pp. 79-86.

——————. "Kong Håkon og hertog Skule." *Syn og Segn,* vol. 56 (1950), pp. 261-65.

—— ——————. "Henrik Ibsen og Skien." *Edda,* vol. 51 (1951), pp. 118-20.

——————. "Når reiste Henrik Ibsen frå Skien?" *Ibsen-årbok,* 1953, pp. 56-62.

——————. "Data om Henrik Ibsen i Skien." *Ibsen-årbok,* 1954, pp. 58-66.

KOPPANG, OLE. *Hegelianismen i Norge: en idéhistorisk undersøkelse.* Oslo: Aschehoug, 1943.

LA CHESNAIS, PIERRE GEORGET. "Le 'Brand' épique d'Ibsen." *Mercure de France,* vol. 80 (1909), pp. 212-31, 417-37, 612-34.

——————. "Ibsen traducteur de français." *Edda,* vol. 28 (1928), pp. 96-114.

——————. *Brand d'Ibsen; étude et analyse.* Paris: Mellottée, 1933.

——————. "Ibsen disciple de Kierkegaard?" *Edda,* vol. 34 (1934), pp. 355-410.

——————. "Les sources historiques de 'Empereur et Galileen.'" *Edda,* vol. 37 (1937), pp. 533-64.

LANGE, SVEN. *Hjærtets Gærninger; roman.* Copenhagen: Gyldendal, 1900. (Chapter 1 printed as "En Spøgelsesfest" in *Tilskueren,* 1900, pp. 435-58).

LIDEN, ARNE. "Peer Gynt i Egypten." *Edda,* vol. 40 (1940), pp. 237-65.

LIE, ERIK. *Jonas Lie, oplevelser.* Kristiania: Gyldendal, 1908.

——————. *Erindringer fra et dikterhjem.* Oslo: Aschehoug, 1928.

LIESTØL, KNUT. "Den store bøygen." *Festskrift til Hjalmar Falk, 30. desember 1927, fra elever, venner og kolleger.* (Oslo: Aschehoug, 1927), pp. 20-26.

LINDAU, PAUL. *Nur Erinnerungen,* 2 vols. Stuttgart/Berlin: Cotta, 1915, 1917.

LOGEMAN, HENRI. *A commentary, critical and explanatory, on the Norwegian text of Henrik Ibsen's Peer Gynt: its language, literary associations and folklore.* The Hague: M. Nijhoff, 1917.

LOTHAR, RUDOLPH. *Henrik Ibsen.* Leipzig, 1902.

LUND, AUDHILD. *Henrik Ibsen og det Norske Teater 1857-1863.* Oslo, 1925 (Småskrifter fra det litt.-hist. seminar XIX).

LYNNER, FERD. G. *Hærmændene paa Helgeland, Henrik Ibsens forhold til kilderne i den norrøne litteratur.* Kristiania, 1909 (Smaaskrifter fra det litt.-hist. seminar VI).

MARCUS, CARL DAVID. "Ibsen och göticism, en replik." *Edda,* vol. 31 (1931), pp. 81-97.

MÖHRING, WERNER. "Ibsens Abkehr von Kierkegaard." *Edda,* vol. 28 (1928), pp. 43-71.

MØLLER, CHRISTEN. "Elskovskravet. En sammenligning mellem Søren Kierkegaards 'Gentagelsen' og Henrik Ibsens 'Kærlighedens komedie.'" *Nordisk Tidskrift,* Ny följd, vol. 1 (1888), pp. 293-314.

MOHR, OTTO LOUS. *Henrik Ibsen som maler.* Oslo: Gyldendal, 1953.

MOSFJELD, OSKAR. *Henrik Ibsen og Skien.* Oslo: Gyldendal, 1949.

NEIIENDAM, ROBERT. *Mennesker bag Masker. Fra Arkiv og Teater.* Copenhagen: Jespersen og Pio, 1931.

————. *Gennem mange Aar. Afhandlinger og Kranikker.* Copenhagen: Branner og Korch, 1950.

NEUMANN, FRITZ. "Baumeister Solness, Skizze zu einer Wesenerkenntnis Henrik Ibsens." *Edda,* vol. 20 (1923), pp. 1-56.

NILSEN, HANS JACOB. *Peer Gynt, eit anti-romantisk verk.* Oslo: Aschehoug, 1948.

NISSEN, INGJALD. *Sjelelige kriser i menneskets liv: Henrik Ibsen og den moderne psykologi.* Oslo: Aschehoug, 1931.

NYGARD, BJARNE. *En miskjent Ibsen-modell: Boktrykker Nils Fredrik Axelsen.* Oslo: Damm, 1943 (Småskrifter for bokvenner, No. 33).

ORDING, FREDRIK. *Henrik Ibsens vennekreds, det Lærde Holland; et kapitel av norsk kulturliv.* Oslo, 1927 (*Historisk Tidsskrift* 3.-4. levering 1927).

PAASCHE, FREDRIK. *Gildet på Solhaug, Ibsens nationalromantiske digtning.* Kristiania, 1908 (Smaaskrifter fra det litteratur-historiske seminar V).

PAULI, GEORG. *Mina romerska år.* Stockholm: Bonnier, 1924.

PAULSEN, JOHN. *Mine erindringer.* Copenhagen, 1900.

————. *Nye erindringer.* Copenhagen, 1901.

————. *Samliv med Ibsen, nye erindringer og skitser.* Copenhagen: Gyldendal, 1906.

————. *Samliv med Ibsen, 2. samling.* Copenhagen and Kristiania: Gyldendal, 1913.

————. "Aftnerne i Arbinsgade." (Ed. Harald Beyer.) *Edda,* vol. 43 (1943), pp. 34-60.

PLATOU, VALBORG. "Henrik Ibsen og Bergens Teater." *Lidt om bergensk scenekunst.* Bergen, 1906.

PLESNER, TELEPH. *Skiens-slegterne: Plesner-Myhre, Stub, Ibsen, Munk.* Kristiania, 1917.

QUAMME, BØRRE. "Ibsen og det engelske teater." *Edda,* vol. 42 (1942), pp. 113-121.

ROSS, HANS. *Norsk Ordbog.* Christiania: Cammermeyer, 1895.

SCHNEIDER, GEORG. *Das religiöse Problem in Ibsen's "Brand"; zwei literarische Predigten.* Mannheim: H. Haas, 1908.

SCHNEIDER, JOHAN ANDREAS. *Fra det gamle Skien.* 3 vols. Skien, [1924].

SEIP, DIDRIK ARUP. "Henrik Ibsen og K. Knudsen, det sproglige gjennembrud hos Ibsen." *Edda,* vol. 1 (1914), pp. 145-63.

SKARD, EILIV. "Kjeldone til Ibsens Catilina." *Edda,* vol. 21 (1924), pp. 70-90.

SKARD, SIGMUND. "Forfattarskapet til 'Andhrimmer', ein bibliografisk etterrøknad." *Festskrift til Halvdan Koht på sekstiårsdagen 7 de juli 1933* (Oslo: Aschehoug, 1933), pp. 295-310.

STAVNEM, P. L. "Overnaturlige væsener og symbolik i Henrik Ibsens 'Peer Gynt'." *Sproglige og historiske afhandlinger viede Sophus Bugges minde,* (Kristiania, 1908), pp. 97-111.

STEIN, PHILIPP. *Henrik Ibsen: zur Bühnengeschichte seiner Dichtungen.* Berlin: Otto Elsner, 1901.

STRÖMBERG, ELVER VILHELM. *Studia in panegyricos ueteres latinos.* Upsala, 1902.

SVENDSEN, MARTIN. "Den fremmede passager i Peer Gynt." *Edda,* vol. 18 (1922), pp. 165-68.

SVENDSEN, PAULUS. "Om Ibsens kilder til 'Kejser og Galilæer.'" *Edda,* vol. 33 (1933), pp. 198-256.

————————. "Noen bemerkninger om Ibsens 'Kejser og Galilæer.'" *Edda,* vol. 37 (1937), pp. 525-32.

SVENSSON, SV. "Brand och den svenska göticismen." *Edda,* vol. 30 (1930), pp. 316-99.

————————. "Svar på 'Replik'." *Edda,* vol. 31 (1931), pp. 98-101.

TENNANT, P. F. D. "A Critical Study of the Composition of Ibsen's 'Vildanden.'" *Edda, vol.* 34 (1934), pp. 327-54.

TVETERAS, HARALD L. "Ibsen og Snoilsky." *Norvegica,* 1933, pp. 119-71.

VAN DIJK, ISAAK. *Ibsen's Brand. Met nabetrachting.* Groningen, 1913.

VASENIUS, VALFRID. *Henrik Ibsen; ett skaldeporträtt.* Stockholm: Seligmann, 1882.

VOGT, NILS. "Paa reise med Henrik Ibsen." *Samtiden,* vol. 17 (1906), pp. 329-34.

VOGT, RAGNAR. *Den Freudske psykoanalyse: dens historiske bakgrunn.* Oslo: Gyldendal, 1930.

VOGT, WALTHER HEINRICH. "Hákonar saga—Kongsemnerne." *Edda,* vol. 22 (1924), pp. 113-54, 300-25.

WALL, ANNIE. *Människor jag mötte.* Oslo, 1926.

WALLEM, FREDRIK BARBE. *Det norske Studentersamfund gjennem hundrede år, 2 Oktober 1813-1913.* Kristiania: Aschehoug, 1916.

WIESENER, ANTON MOHR. *Henrik Ibsen og 'Det Norske Theater' i Bergen.* (Bergens Historiske Forenings Skrifter, 1928, No. 34.)

WINSNES, ANDREAS HOFGAARD. "Ibsen kontra Nietzsche." *Samtiden*, vol. 55 (1946), pp. 502-519.
————————. "Henrik Ibsen og Skien." *Edda*, vol. 51 (1951), pp. 106-118.
[WOLF, LUCIE]. *Skuespillerinden fru Lucie Wolfs livserindringer.* Kristiania, n. d. [1897].
WYLLER, ANDERS. "Villanden, en innledning og en kritikk." *Edda*, vol. 36 (1936), pp. 269-305.
ZUCKER, A. E. "Goethe and Ibsen's button-moulder." *Publications of the Modern Language Association of America*, vol. 57 (1942), pp. 1101-7.

489

Printed in U.S.A. by
NOBLE OFFSET PRINTERS, INC.
NEW YORK 3, N. Y.